The Tempest

SHAKESPEARE CRITICISM
PHILIP C. KOLIN, *General Editor*

ROMEO AND JULIET
Critical Essays
edited by John F. Andrews

CORIOLANUS
Critical Essays
edited by David Wheeler

TITUS ANDRONICUS
Critical Essays
edited by Philip C. Kolin

LOVE'S LABOUR'S LOST
Critical Essays
edited by Felicia Hardison
Londré

THE WINTER'S TALE
Critical Essays
edited by Maurice Hunt

TWO GENTLEMEN OF
VERONA
Critical Essays
edited by June Schlueter

VENUS AND ADONIS
Critical Essays
edited by Philip C. Kolin

AS YOU LIKE IT
FROM 1600 TO THE PRESENT
Critical Essays
edited by Edward Tomarken

THE COMEDY OF ERRORS
Critical Essays
edited by Robert S. Miola

A MIDSUMMER NIGHT'S DREAM
Critical Essays
edited by Dorothea Kehler

SHAKESPEARE'S SONNETS
Critical Essays
edited by James Schiffer

PERICLES
Critical Essays
edited by David Skeele

THE TEMPEST
Critical Essays
edited by Patrick M. Murphy

THE TEMPEST
CRITICAL ESSAYS

EDITED BY PATRICK M. MURPHY

ROUTLEDGE
NEW YORK AND LONDON

Published in 2001 by
Routledge
29 West 35th Street
New York, NY 10001

Published in Great Britain by
Routledge
11 New Fetter Lane
London EC4P 4EE

Routledge is an imprint of the Taylor & Francis Group.

Copyright © 2001 by Routledge

10 9 8 7 6 5 4 3 2 1

Cover photo: Alec McCowen (Prospero) and Sarah Woodward (Miranda) in a scene from the Royal Shakespeare Theatre 1993 production of *The Tempest,* directed by Sam Mendes. Photograph by Malcolm Davies, The Shakespeare Birthplace Trust, Stratford-upon-Avon; used by permission of The Shakespeare Birthplace Trust.

Library of Congress Cataloging-in-Publication Data

The tempest: critical essays / edited by Patrick M. Murphy.
    p. cm.—(Garland reference Library of the humanities ;
  2014. Shakespeare criticism; 22)
    Includes bibliographical references and index.
    ISBN 0–8153–2471–5 (alk. paper)
    1. Shakespeare, William 1564–1616. Tempest. I. Murphy, Patrick M., 1955–
  II. Garland reference library of the humanities; vol. 2014. III. Garland reference
  library of the humanities. Shakespeare criticism ; v. 22.
    PR2833 .T465 2000
    822.3'3—dc21   00–056149

Printed on acid-free, 250-year-life paper
Manufactured in the United States of America

FOR MY MOTHER
MARY MARGARET ROSSI MURPHY
AND
IN MEMORY OF MY FATHER
JOHN C. MURPHY

Brad Haines (Stephano), Kevin Molesworth (Trinculo), and Benjamin Derby (Caliban) in *The Tempest*, October 16–26, 1997, by the theatre department at the State University of New York at Oswego, directed by Mark Cole. Original photograph by Jon Vermilye; used by permission of Mark Cole.

Contents

General Editor's Introduction

The continuing goal of the Shakespeare Criticism series is to provide the most influential historical criticism, the most significant contemporary interpretations, and reviews of the most influential productions. Each volume in the series, devoted to a Shakespearean play or poem (e.g., the sonnets, *Venus and Adonis*, the *Rape of Lucrece*), includes the most essential criticism and reviews of Shakespeare's work from the seventeenth century to the present. The series thus provides, through individual volumes, a representative gathering of critical opinion of how a play or poem has been interpreted over the centuries.

A major feature of each volume in the series is the editor's introduction. Each volume editor provides a substantial essay identifying the main critical issues and problems the play (or poem) has raised, charting the critical trends in looking at the work over the centuries, and assessing the critical discourses that have linked the play or poem to various ideological concerns. In addition to examining the critical commentary in light of important historical and theatrical events, each introduction functions as a discursive bibliographic essay that cites and evaluates significant critical works—essays, journal articles, dissertations, books, theatre documents—and gives readers a guide to the research on a particular play or poem.

After the introduction, each volume is organzied chronologically, by date of publication of selections, usually into two sections: critical essays and theatre reviews/documents. The first section includes previously published journal articles and book chapters as well as original essays written for the collection. In selecting essays, editors include earlier as well as contemporary criticism. Their goal is to include the widest possible range of critical approaches to the play or poem, demonstrating the multiplicity and complexity of critical response. In most instances, essays have been reprinted in their entirety, not butchered into snippets. The editors have also commissioned original essays (sometimes as many as five to ten) by leading Shakespeare scholars, thus offering the most contemporary, theoretically attentive analyses. Reflecting some recent critical approaches in Shakespearean studies, these new essays approach the play or poem from many perspectives, including feminist, Marxist, new historical, semiotic, mythic, performance/staging, cultural, and/or a combination of these and other methodologies. Some volumes in the series even include bibliographic analyses that have significant implications for criticism.

The second section of each volume in the series is devoted to the play in performance and, again, is organized chronologically, beginning with some of the earliest and most significant productions and proceeding to the most recent. This section, which ultimately provides a theatre history of the play, should not be regarded as different from or rigidly isolated from the critical essays in the first section. Shakespearean criticism has often been informed by or has significantly influenced productions. Shakespearean criticism over the last twenty years or so has usefully been labeled the "Age of Performance." Readers will find information in this section on major foreign productions of Shakespeare's plays as well as landmark productions in English. Consisting of more than reviews of specific productions, this section also contains a variety of theatre documents, including interpretations written for the particular volume by notable directors whose comments might be titled "The Director's Choice," histories of seminal productions (e.g. Peter Brook's *Titus Andronicus* in 1955), and even interviews with directors and/or actors. Editors have also included photographs from productions around the world to help readers see and further appreciate the way a Shakespearen play has taken shape in the theatre.

Each volume in the Shakespeare Criticism series strives to give readers a balanced, representative collection of the best that has been thought and said about a Shakespearean text. In essence, each volume supplies a careful survey of essential materials in the history of criticism for a Shakespearean text. In offering readers complete, fulfilling, and in some instances very hard to locate materials, volume editors have made conveniently accessible the literary and theatrical criticism of Shakespeare's greatest legacy, his work.

Philip C. Kolin
University of Southern Mississippi

Acknowledgments

Many people have helped to bring this book into print. First, I thank the contributors who have written specifically for my volume—Robert Hapgood, Geraldo U. de Sousa, Barbara Ann Sebek, Christopher D. Felker, Alan de Gooyer, James Stephens (who introduced me to Shakespeare studies), Edward O'Shea, and Claudia Harris. Philip Kolin also deserves special thanks for entrusting me with this project and for his ongoing support. I am also grateful to all the authors, journals and presses, as well as the photographers and theatre companies, that gave me permission to reprint the items collected here.

I thank the staff of Penfield Library at the State University of New York in Oswego for their diligence in tracking down *Tempest* materials—especially Shirley Omundson and her team in the Interlibrary Loan office and Inez Parker, who not only found but also delivered a copy of Schlegel's lectures to me on a particularly difficult day. Edward O'Shea and my colleague in the History department, Mark Kulikowski, also helped in gathering *Tempest* materials. Georgianna Ziegler and Lori Johnson at the Folger Shakespeare Library and John Powell at the Newberry Library also deserve many thanks for locating and preparing some of the illustrations used here.

Geraldo U. de Sousa and Edward O'Shea also deserve special thanks for reading various drafts of my introduction and for making suggestions about where to cut and to add materials. Edward O'Shea has been the mentor behind this effort—my first attempt at a critical anthology. He always listened as I talked my way through difficulties, and he often advised me about how to proceed. Any errors are, of course, mine.

In the early stage of gathering *Tempest* criticism, Laura Halferty diligently attended, with accuracy and ease, to innumerable bibliographic citations and photocopying. Christopher D'Innocenzo then took over for her while he also scanned essays and illustrations for reproduction. His youthful enthusiasm for this project often compensated for my fatigue when the nature of the task seemed overwhelming. Christina Gruber, a graduate assistant

xiii

(funded by my department's graduate program and Jack Narayan, the Dean of the Graduate School and Office of Research), helped to proofread copy in the final stages. To Joan Wallace and Rosalie Battles, my department's secretaries, go many thanks for the thousands of things they do to make the day run smoothly so that essential tasks get done. This volume was also supported by two grants—first, from the State of New York and the United Union of Professions in the form of a Professional Development and Quality of Working Life grant, and, second, from the Scholarly and Creative Activities Committee of the State University of New York at Oswego. Byron Smith and Emily Crane helped to disburse the funds from the first grant; both grants contributed significantly to covering the costs for copyright permissions.

In the early stages letters and phone conversations or brief encounters with Stephen Orgel, R. A. Foakes, Linda Woodbridge, David Bergeron, Gail Kern Paster, Jean Howard, Terence Hawkes, Douglas Bruster, Frances Dolan, and Richard P. Wheeler, whose insights into Shakespeare's own individual historicity and *The Tempest* may most strongly influence future readings of this play, helped me to shape and design this book. Good friends, who have tolerated my various absences, also deserve special thanks: Jack Schoppman (and Beth, Mary Ann, Colleen, and J. P.), Briankle Chang; John Duvall; Steven Brown (and Katya and Gabe); Dave Schrodt (and Stephanie); and Christopher Felker (and Aimee and William). And thanks to my students, especially: Adam Hall, Sara De Groat Cole, Salvatore Labaro and Erin McCarthy (and the whole gang in the Rainbow Alliance), Jonathan Style, John Clark, Paul Hilliker, Teresa Willmore, and Terry Mason. In Mark Cole's fine, local production of *The Tempest,* staged while I was writing this book, Kevin Molesworth's Trinculo drew upon the comedy of Martin and Lewis, as well as Laurel and Hardy, in a good college performance. Several colleagues also listened as I worked through vague and stubborn problems, especially: David Vampola, Jean Chambers, George Baloglou, Bennet Schaber, Ed Keen, and Matthew Friday (who also helped prepare the illustrations in electronic format). Among family members Beth (whose kindness and genealogical skills amaze me), and Meg (whose generosity knows no limit), and Tom (who taught me, among other things, how to read) deserve extra special thanks. Thanks as well to: John, Kathy & Sara; Mary Therese and John (and theirs, Tracy and Tony, Rebecca and Tim, Clare and Matt); Pete & Donna (and theirs, Tim, Greg and Karen); Charlie; Mike & Mary Jeanne (and theirs, Josh and Robin); and Kay and Eric (and theirs, Korie and Taylor)—and not to forget the next generation: Tony, Delaney, and Brennon. From John and Mary Margaret, to whom this book is dedicated, we (their children, grandchildren, and great grandchildren) can learn how to take on large responsibilites and to persevere.

Patrick M. Murphy
State University of New York at Oswego
March 2000

PART I.
The Tempest
and the Critical Legacy

Interpreting *The Tempest*
A History of Its Readings

PATRICK M. MURPHY

"and next to truth, a confirmed errour does well"
(JONSON, BARTHOLOMEW FAIR 16)

The Tempest has a complex history of performances, editions, adaptations, parodies, rewritings, allusions, and critical interpretations. Its first recorded performance was on Hallowmas in 1611 at Whitehall. However, as Stephen Orgel warns, "A record of performance at court implies neither a play written specifically for the court nor a first performance there" (Introduction 1). The court appropriated the play again in 1613 when it was used (as one of fourteen works) to celebrate the wedding of Princess Elizabeth to the Elector Palatine. Performances at the Globe were also probable. In 1669 Dryden suggested *The Tempest* was performed at Blackfriars (*Tempest* 3). Recently Andrew Gurr proposed that "*The Tempest* was the first play Shakespeare unquestionably wrote for the Blackfriars rather than the Globe" because it "is uniquely a musical play" (92) and shows "unequivocal evidence that it was conceived with act breaks in mind" (93). Moreover, for Gurr, "The whole play depends on the initial realism of the shipwreck scene. It is the verification of Prospero's magic and the declaration that it is all only a stage play" (96). However, as a published text, *The Tempest* always seems to frustrate attempts to limit its significance to any specific theatrical context, to determine its meaning, or to appropriate its repetitions. Initially printed as the inaugural work in the First Folio of 1623, *The Tempest* became a subversive monument. "Whether it was placed [first] by its editors or its publishers, and whatever their reasons," writes Stephen Orgel, "the decision has profoundly affected the play's critical history" (Introduction 1).

Shakespeare unquestionably wrote *The Tempest*; however, Greg's sense of the text as "unassisted" must be qualified (418). Ralph Crane, the scrivener for the King's Men who prepared several other plays by Shakespeare for the

3

printer, may have added some detail to the stage-directions. In descriptions like "a tempestuous noise of thunder and lightning heard," Crane may have described aspects of early performances. Jeanne Addison Roberts noted that the stage directions "are the most elaborate and detailed in the Folio" (214). Roberts speculated (along with Greg) that: "It is certainly not impossible that [Crane] was close enough to the King's Men to be familiar with their plays and that he could have seen an unrecorded performance of *The Tempest*" (218). Although the idea is discredited now—Fleay, Robertson and Law suggested that the masque was written by either Beaumont or Chapman. And W. J. Lawrence, Dover Wilson, Greg, and others have all contributed to the "formidable" opinion that the betrothal masque Prospero conjures for Ferdinand and Miranda was perhaps Shakespeare's addition in 1613 to the first recorded version of 1611 (Kermode xxii). However, Glynne Wickham's argument about the topical ambiguity of Ferdinand deserves consideration in any discussion about the relevance of the masque in 1611.

The relations among the dramatic work, its sources, performances, reviews, printed editions, and criticism continue to perplex the priorities and values of *Tempest* interpretations. Different expectations, customs, rules, and conventions of reading come into play among these various uses of the text. Stephen Orgel surveyed the theatrical history to find that all performances of the play's powerfully subversive energies are partial (Introduction 64–87). Trevor Griffiths in 1983 and Virginia and Alden Vaughan, in an ambitious survey of *Shakespeare's Caliban*, published in 1991, discuss the political and colonial contexts that shape Caliban's history on the stage. In two essays reprinted in this volume Mary M. Nilan discusses the contrast between critical readings of the play and Kean's production in 1857, and she surveys performances and reviews of the play at the start of the twentieth century, particularly Herbert Beerbohm Tree's 1904 production which ended with Caliban, played by Tree himself, left alone on the island. Each period's appropriation of the play seems to destablize alternative preconceptions about the work, bringing about seemingly endless crises of purpose, agency, form and materiality.

The Folio *Tempest* granted Shakespeare's play a relative stability and coherence in relation to the more ephemeral nature of theatrical productions. *The Tempest*'s adherence to the unities of time and place, a highly unusual practice for Shakespeare, also reinforced this sense of its coherence. However, Ernest Schanzer suggested *The Tempest* is "Shakespeare's most extended mockery of the critics' demand for unity of time" (60). For the critical Schanzer, Shakespeare refutes the rules of commentators: "It was Shakespeare's last thrust in his scattered skirmishes against that bloated, tyrannical upstart, the doctrine of the unity of time" (61). Whether or not the focus is upon text or performance, there is always a remainder, a supplement—something futural that anticipation cannot discern. When Schanzer discovers the dramatic character of Prospero ironically controlled by the neoclassical principles of the critics, performance is folded into (and momentarily dominated by) criticism, while criticism is mocked by a performance seemingly authorized by the writer's irony—expressed and realized in critical commentary. Neither text, nor performance, nor criticism can have the last word—although the rhetorical posture of each often contains a pretense of finality.

I. INITIAL USES: ALLUSIONS, COMMENTARY, AND ADAPTATION

One of the first recorded allusions to *The Tempest* occurred in the Induction to Ben Jonson's *Bartholomew Fair* (1614). Jonson's reference is brief. When the comment is set in context, however, its consequences may substantially alter our understanding of Shakespeare's presence in the play as the "mighty workman" who drowns his book, pronounces a valediction to his most potent art, and petitions the audience to set him free by their indulgence.

Jonson's Induction satirically represents a scene of nascent (performance) criticism while perhaps allegorizing the history of London's emerging institution of the theater. After apologizing for a delay, the Stage-keeper (or handyman) warns the audience that the play is "like to be a very conceited scuruy one, in plaine English" (13). This Stage-keeper, who "kept the stage in Master Tarlton's time," attacks the "master-poet" for his omissions of realistic detail about the fair and for his aggression (14). Jeffrey Masten has suggested that this Stage-keeper is the "spokesman for the improvisatory and collaborative mode of theatrical production of an ostensibly prior era" (109) which was being displaced by a patriarchal idea of authorship that effaced the homoerotic, collaborative processes of theatrical production. This displacement is enacted when the Book-holder (or prompter) and the Scrivener enter and question the Stage-keeper who defends his "rare discourse" saying that "the understanding Gentlemen o' the ground here, ask'd my iudgement." The Stage-keeper is banished when the Book-holder commands: "Away Rogue, it's come to a fine degree in these *spectacles* when such a youth as you pretend to a iudgement" (14). The Book-holder then announces his purpose: "I am sent out to you here, with a *Scrivener* and certain Articles drawne out in hast betweene our *Author* and you; which if you please to heare, and as they appeare reasonable, to approve of; the *Play* will follow presently" (14–15). The judgment of the audience is potentially subversive, and the contract becomes a protocol of instruction with an aim towards containment.

There are five conditions stipulated in the contract. First, audience members (and readers) must be patient; second, they must know the place that was purchased for them and not exceed their wit; third, their judgment must be consistent, unchanging, and independent of the responses of others; fourth, their expectations must be realistic; and, finally, the reader must avoid searching out topical references but may enjoy them when noticed—as if to say, critical inquiry should not become "solemnly ridiculous" nor out of step with the propriety of entertainment and pleasure. No person, according to the fourth condition, should expect "more then hee knowes, or better ware then a *Fayre* will affoord":

> If there bee neuer a *Seruant-monster* i' the *Fayr*; who can help it? he [the Author] sayes; nor a nest of *Antiques*? Hee is loth to make Nature afraid in his *Playes*, like those that beget *Tales*, *Tempests*, and such like *Drolleries*, to mix his head with other mens heeles . . . (16)

Curiously, Jonson echoed Stephano's (and Trinculo's) description of Caliban in this carefully contrived allusion (3.2.4–17). The scrivener also referred to the competition among playwrights and acting companies while gesturing to the philosophical debate about Nature and Art (which Kermode found at the center of *The Tempest*'s structure and meaning). The same debate also rests at the core of Montaigne's "Of Cannibals," a significant source for Shakespeare's play. Some readers think the scrivener's remark signals Jonson's disapproval of Caliban (Vaughan 89). However, since this comment is usually used as evidence for the date of the play's composition, its potential significance is sometimes lost, for example, when Morton Luce called it "little more than good natured banter" (xxiii).

In 1969 Harry Levin thought the scrivener's comment was an overt attack on *The Winter's Tale* and *The Tempest* and similar in content to ideas in Jonson's preface to the quarto of *The Alchemist*, first performed in 1610 and published in 1612. "The paradox is that Jonson, for once, was criticizing Shakespeare from the standpoint of nature rather than art" (49). Levin speculated that since *The Alchemist* and *The Tempest* were introduced in the successive seasons of 1610 and 1611, perhaps the same actor (maybe Burbage) played the parts of Subtle and Prospero. Shakespeare is attracted to an exotic location; Jonson's scene is London. Jonson provides a "character-sketch that accompanies the entrance of each personage" so character is static; Shakespeare lets his characters speak for themselves. Shakespeare's plots are parallel and symmetrical, in Jonson "Human contrivance is bound to be outdone sooner or later by chance, and his contrivers are alert in adapting themselves to the main chance" (53). For Levin the two plays have closely related themes; yet, they are antithetically designed: Prospero becomes a response to Subtle, Miranda to Dol Common, the hoax staged for Dapper is the closest parallel to the masque staged for Ferdinand and Miranda. In *The Tempest* everyone is changed for the better by their island experience; yet, in Jonson attempted transmutations leave the subjects "basically unchanged" (57). Levin concluded, "That *The Tempest* came after *The Alchemist* means, of course, that Shakespeare had the opportunity to reflect and reply, as he is said to have done in the so-called War of the Theatres" (57–58).

In 1983 Thomas Cartelli, following Harry Levin's lead and using Harold Bloom's theory of influence, read *Bartholomew Fair* as Jonson's somewhat anxious response to Shakespeare. However, Cartelli also agreed with Anne Barton that Jonson managed in *Bartholomew Fair* to achieve an inclusiveness previously unachieved, perhaps because Shakespeare had recently retired from the stage (165). Unlike Levin who perceived confrontation, Cartelli relied upon C. L. Barber's work to argue that Jonson used Shakespeare's saturnalian breakthroughs in *A Midsummer Night's Dream*, *As You Like It*, and especially *The Tempest* to come to terms with Shakespearean influence and inheritance (155). The Induction is evidence that Jonson had grudgingly conceded to give his audience what it wanted, and he intended to do this by presenting a " 'naturalized' version of the Shakespearean romances to which he alludes" (161). According to Cartelli, this project continues in *Bartholomew Fair* when Leather and Joan Trash discuss the merits of Joan's gingerbread wares by mentioning "what stuff they are made on" as "Nothing but what's wholesome." This passage compels the audience "to compare Shakespeare's inflation of 'airy nothings' with Jonson's own leveling of material reality" to a "stand of gingerbread" which includes a " 'gingerwork' of 'Ceres selling her daughter's picture' " (163). More recently Douglas Bruster has suggested that *Bartholomew Fair* is propelled by fetishistic desire from the beginning (*Drama* 91). In an essay reprinted in this volume that argues for the primacy of a "local *Tempest*" which uses metaphors of colonialism to represent the business of the stage, Bruster suggests that "none of the playwrights who commented on, borrowed from, revised, or otherwise paid homage to *The Tempest* before the closing of the theaters seems to have been any more interested in colonialism than Shakespeare—or for that matter, showed that he believed Shakespeare, in *The Tempest*, was talking about the New World" (36). Instead, for Bruster, "*The Tempest* is a play about art, but it is deeply about the work that art requires" (53).

There are several important consequences to these observations: if Levin, Cartelli, Masten, and Bruster's readings of *The Alchemist* and *Bartholomew Fair* are right, then Jonson's early critical response to Shakespeare's *Tempest* does not distinguish among play writing, critical commentary, and performance—unlike our current conventional distinctions among these different kinds of response. If *The Tempest* sublimates *The Alchemist* (as Levin suggests), it is as critical of Jonson as the Induction to *Bartholomew Fair* is of Shakespeare. One dramatic work becomes the pretext for another. And the criticism in *Bartholomew Fair* therefore begins as citation, repetition, mockery, and as a varied (somewhat anxious) imitation of the phrases (*lexia* or fragments) of Shakespeare's anterior text. Moreover, Jonson's phrasing in the Induction uses the language of the legal contract to sketch out the roles of author and audience, redescribing the reactions of a heterogeneous audience as a rule-governed behavior that applies to everyone, depending upon the cost of admission.

In *Comus*, first performed in 1634 and printed in 1637, John Milton used *The Tempest* to experiment not only in dramatic form but to question the very idea and function of *form* itself. Noting the irreconcilable differences among readers who insisted that Milton's work was either some kind of comedy, or a masque that had broken free of the drama, or perhaps a pastoral drama, in 1959 John Major thought there was agreement that *The Tempest* and *Comus* worked out the same theme: "that upon the spiritual strength of the righteous depends the preservation, in this life, of truth, order and justice" (179).

While trying to think about Milton's work as a dramatic comedy in the festive tradition, C. L. Barber decided instead that "Milton's masque is a masque!" Believing that Milton succeeded "in making a happy work which centers, seemingly, on the denial of impulse, when typically in the Renaissance such works involve, in some fashion or other, release from restraint," Barber explained his difficulty by discovering that questions about the conflicting expectations about the form of Milton's work "provide a means for understanding how it orders and satisfies feeling" ("Mask" 188). In a feminist and Lacanian reading of *The Tempest*'s relation to *Comus*, Mary Loeffelholz began with Barber's insight that Milton's work is not so much about dramatic events but about "the *creation* of the situation" which enabled Milton "to present a trial of chastity" (197, 198): "For preserving chastity involves keeping a relation with what is not present: the chaste person is internally related to what is to be loved, even in its absence" (Barber, "Mask" 198). Curiously, Loeffelholz wanted to "open a feminist inquiry into Shakespeare's presence in Milton's *Comus* by considering the relation of Prospero's interrupted betrothal masque of Ceres in *The Tempest* to Milton's masque" (25). And she thinks this happens through a series of "defensive substitutions" (39). Concentrating upon how Prospero offers Miranda a myth which substitutes for her absent memory of her mother and which displaces Miranda's actual memories of the "four or five women" who once attended her, Loeffelholz finds that the success of the masque of Ceres "is precisely that Miranda as produced and brought into circulation among men does not need the maternal body" (30). If Barber and Loeffelholz are right, then about thirty years before Davenant and Dryden found in *The Tempest* a nascent and undeveloped "Design" concerning (in contemporary terms) sexual difference and homosocial exchange, Milton had discovered in the masque an alternative form embedded within *The Tempest* that cast the debate about virtue (the rarer action) in terms of femininity.

Ben Jonson's use of *The Tempest* as a pretext gave way to the dramatic experiments of John Suckling in the *Goblins*, to the work of John Fletcher and Philip Massinger in the *Sea-Voyage*, and to Davenant and Dryden's highly popular adaptation, *The Tempest or the Enchanted Island*. According to Dryden, Davenant "found that somewhat might be added to the Design of

Shakespear, of which neither *Fletcher* nor *Suckling* had ever thought" (*Tempest* 4). That is, Davenant's and Dryden's *The Enchanted Island* needs to be read in terms of Fletcher's romance as well as in light of Shakespeare's use of the form. Recently Michael Dobson suggested that Fletcherian romance was used after the Interregnum to both accept and deny historical realities: "Ideally, the theatres could be used not only to provide. . . the temporary, escapist illusion that the Civil Wars had never happened, but to supply harmlessly replayed versions of the Interregnum itself, plays depicting tyrannous usurpations reassuringly concluded by the providential restorations of legitimate heirs" (*Making* 20–21).

The Sea-Voyage was probably first performed shortly after it was licensed on June 2, 1622. The editors of the California edition of Dryden's works noted that Fletcher's play "was revived by the King's Company on 25 September 1667, less than two weeks before the first performance of the Dryden-Davenant *Tempest*, and it continued running as a rival attraction. Perhaps knowing that their rivals [Davenant's Duke's Men] were intending to stage an elaborate production of *The Tempest*, the King's Company had decided to gain the initiative" (Dryden, *Tempest* 345). If we accept Dryden's account, then within eleven years after its first recorded performance Shakespeare's *Tempest* may have become a source (rather than merely a pretext) for writers who attempted to use Shakespeare's work for their own purposes, before *The Tempest*'s publication in the First Folio and before the reopening of theaters after the restoration of Charles II. Significantly, Dryden's Preface introduced the ideas of the "Original" and the "Copy" into *Tempest* criticism. These concepts were not at work in Jonson's use of the text in *Bartholomew Fair*. Dryden's and Fletcher's imitations differed from Jonson's playfully contentious, somewhat anxious, redescription of Shakespearean romance.

If Shakespeare's play is not a source for Fletcher, *The Sea-Voyage* clearly wrestles with some of the same perplexities by introducing reasonable variations into a recognizable scenario. It appears retrospectively to be a transitional work, the step between the dramatic commentary of *Bartholomew Fair*, on one hand, and the Davenant-Dryden adaptation, on the other. *Tempest* criticism begins, even before the Restoration, with these kinds of gestures: as the repetition of phrases or allusions and as the varied imitation of a design in a context of a theatrical rivalry informed by emergent political affiliations. Readings of *The Tempest* that stress its themes of paternity, patriarchy, and relevance for the court are sometimes unaware of how Davenant's royalist affiliations shaped the play's reception and use through the nineteenth century, while he exposed faultlines within the text as possible points of exploration or amplification in both performance and criticism.

Samuel Pepys, who responded to Dryden's play as "the most innocent" he had seen, saw the adaptation five times in four months (Orgel, Introduction 65). Having been transformed perhaps by Shadwell into an opera, Dryden's

Enchanted Island was "more often revived than any other play between 1600 and 1700; innumerable contemporary allusions indicate that virtually everyone was familiar with it" (Maus 189). So familiar, in fact, that in 1675 Thomas Duffett wrote a parody of it, *The Mock-Tempest*. The influence of the Davenant-Dryden and Shadwell adaptations was long-lasting: Stephen Orgel believes that the adapted version of the *Tempest* held the stage, in one form or another, until William Charles Macready produced Shakespeare's version (with some additions) at Covent Garden in 1838 (68–69).

Dobson thinks that Davenant's and Dryden's adaptation "owes its lasting appeal to its representation not only of patriarchal monarchy but of the patriarchal family which both provided its basis and served (as it arguably still does) as the last refuge of its ideology" (*Making* 43). Dobson argues Dryden strategically implied both Shakespeare and Charles I were deceased kings, that Shakespeare, like Prospero, was a magician who is "being kicked upstairs" to make room for the next generation of writers. Davenant and Dryden "supplement and qualify Shakespeare's fatherhood of *The Tempest* by extending Prospero's family. In their version, the Duke of Milan acquires two entirely new dependants, a dangerously naive younger daughter, Dorinda, and an equally troublesome ward, Hippolito" (*Making* 41). However, in 1991 Matthew Wikander noticed "The superabundance of dukes in this *Tempest*, like its absence of kings, sets the adaptation apart from its model, and suggests that some political ideas in Shakespeare's *Tempest* might have been too embarrassing (or subversive) for the adaptors to touch" (91–92).

Dryden's comments about Caliban (written for an argument about the "grounds of criticism in tragedy" in his preface to an adaptation of *Troilus and Cressida* in 1679) anticipated and shaped the discussion of *The Tempest* in the eighteenth century. Dryden's comments were a touchstone for Addison and Steele, Joseph Warton, and Samuel Johnson. It is also possible that Charles Gildon's remarks about the relations between *fable* and *conduct* in Shakespeare's *Tempest* were intended to qualify Dryden's discussion of *plot* and *manners*. Alden and Virginia Vaughan have suggested that Dryden apparently described "his own Caliban more than Shakespeare's, a Caliban without imagination, without love of beauty, without any redeeming qualities—a 'hobgoblin' who epitomizes humankind's worst traits" (94). The Vaughans think that Dryden agreed with Thomas Rymer's comment in 1677 that Caliban was human despite his monstrous and grotesque body: " 'tis not necessary for a man to have a nose on his face, not to have two legs: he may be a *true* man, though awkward and unsightly, as the *Monster* in *The Tempest*" (qtd. in Vaughan 95). Interestingly, Rymer may have been alluding to Davenant, implying that Caliban is an apt image for *The Tempest*'s first adapter. "Davenant's amorous exploits," according to Schoenbaum, were more dangerous than his royalist affiliations, "he contracted syphilis, and the resulting disfigurement after mercury treatment—he lost his nose—provided wits with matter for amiable jests" (98). Clearly, for Dryden, Caliban is a hybrid, congenitally malformed by a mixture of elements compounded from an Incubus and a Sorceress, and for this reason "distinguished from other mortals." And so it seems is Caliban's language. Significantly, Dryden did not describe Caliban (or his language) as either "natural" or "unnatural," but only says that he *seems* to be a person "not in Nature," and (naturally) "a Species of himself," whose person, language, and character "suit him" ("Preface" 239, 240). Caliban becomes his own criterion, measured by (and against) the attributes of his mother and father: discontented, sinful, dejected, (and because abandoned) ignorant. Recently Barry Gaines provided substantive confirmation for Dryden's insight into Caliban. "Between 1561 and 1609, twenty-two ballads dealing with monstrous births were recorded in the Stationers' Register" (54). Gaines believes that one such pamphlet, published on July 25, 1609, matches Prospero's initial descriptions of Caliban.

In 1712 Addison thought, "It shews a greater Genius in *Shakespear* to have drawn his *Calyban*, than his *Hotspur* or *Julius Caesar*: The one was to be supplied out of his own Imagination, whereas the other might have been formed upon Tradition, History, and Observation" (2: 586–87). Yet, a concern stayed with Addison: "There is a kind of Writing, wherein the Poet quite loses sight of Nature, and entertains his Reader's Imagination with the Characters and Actions of such Persons as have many of them no Existence, but what he bestows upon them" (3: 570). When in the same essay Addison applies this principle to Shakespeare's "noble Extravagance of Fancy," he concludes: "we have no Rule by which to judge of them, and must confess, if there are such Beings in the World, it looks highly probable they should talk and act as he has represented them" (572, 573). Gradually Dryden's comment is elided as Caliban's categorical difference (as a construct of imaginative artifice) is subsumed within a redescription of *nature* and *the natural* as what is probable given "the essential quality or character *of* something" (Williams, *Keywords* 219). Perhaps this distinction is already blurred in Shakespeare's play. Joseph Warton admitted "I always lament that our author has not preserved this fierce and implacable spirit in CALYBAN, to the end of the play"; instead, Shakespeare has "injudiciously put into his mouth, words that imply repentance and understanding" (160). Certainly Samuel Johnson found that the discussion of Caliban's language had strayed from probability:

> Whence these critics derived the notion of a new language appropriated to Caliban I cannot find: They certainly mistook brutality of sentiment for uncouthness of words. Caliban had learned to speak of Prospero and his daughter, he had no names for the sun and moon before their arrival, and could not have invented a language of his own without more understanding than Shakespeare has thought it proper to bestow upon him. (123)

Although readers were preoccupied with Caliban, Miranda also attracted some attention. William Richardson thought in her "simplicity is intended to be the most striking circumstance" (64). He also felt that Miranda "never supposes that they [the shipwrecked strangers] may be suffering from punishment for heinous guilt" (64). For Richardson's rival, Maurice Morgann, Prospero "departs a little from his Integrity, and in order to appease *Miranda*, substitutes *Probablity* for *Truth*" (298).

During the eighteenth century, response to *The Tempest* found several forms of expression: in the supplementary notes and commentary attached to the critical editions of Rowe, Pope, Theobald, Hanmer, Warburton, Johnson and Steevens; in the periodical essays of Joseph Warton in *The Adventurer*, Addison and Steele in *The Spectator*, in the emerging literary essays of William Richardson, and in the engravings collected in John Boydell's "Shakespeare Gallery" and the painting of William Hogarth. Although Maurice Morgann's "A Commentary on *The Tempest*" was not published until 1972, it provides a sense of the eighteenth-century debates surrounding the play. As adaptations of *The Tempest* were also published (sometimes including prefatory commentary as well), both the textuality and the theatricality of the play were used to make Shakespeare's work into an unchanging monument *and* into a dynamic critical force possessed by no singular authority. That is, the history of the book worked counter to the history of the theater, while each tradition contributed to (and often undermined) the other.

Charles Gildon's contribution to Rowe's edition concerning the "Argument of *The Tempest*" may be one of the most telling instances of the struggle between the editorial and performance traditions of *The Tempest* in the eighteenth century. Gildon's inquiry seems to respond not only to the performances of the adaptation but also to Dryden's earlier publication of the text of *The Tempest or The Enchanted Island* as well as to statements in his Preface to the play. The tension seems generated by the threat of a rival textual monument which Dryden's published work created for the Folio text of 1623 and its various eighteenth-century editions, including Rowe's. Since Dryden drew upon a Platonist discourse of perfection to justify his alteration of Shakespeare's work, it made sense for Gildon to reply with an Aristotelian formalism that also made it possible for him to assess the strengths and weaknesses of Shakespeare's "fable and conduct."

Hogarth's painting, "Scene from *The Tempest*" (c. 1735–40), may also be evidence for some tension between the editorial and performance traditions. Robin Simon argued that Hogarth's scene represented the painter's direct approach to Shakespeare's text (rather than a rendering of a performance, as in Hogarth's treatment of the revolutionary quality of Garrick's acting in Cibber's *Richard III*). Noticing that the only performances of the play which Hogarth could have seen would be the Shadwell opera based upon the Davenant/Dryden adaptation, Simon writes: "It is Hogarth's triumph to have ignored such contemporary enticements and to have interpreted in paint the complex moral distinctions of Shakespeare's play" (217). Ronald Paulson extends Simon's observations saying that Hogarth deliberately avoided painting a scene from the operatic *Tempest* because he wished "to replace foreign operatic entertainments, including decorative history painting by the Italians, by a true English product. Since there was no native stage tradition that served for this play, Hogarth was forced back on the literary text itself" (48).

The failure of Garrick's operatic adaptation of *The Tempest* in 1756 may reveal the growing tensions between the emergent editorial tradition (established by Rowe and Gildon, Pope, Theobald, Hanmer, and Warburton) and the established performance traditions of the eighteenth century. This is not the usual understanding, however, since evidence for this view seems to be lacking. The more conventional view is that the theatrical and the editorial or textual traditions did not significantly engage one another. Finding that "The stage history of *The Tempest* from the Restoration to the beginning of Victoria's reign exhibits a remarkable coherence" (Introduction 69), Orgel traces a few significant developments in the treatment of Ariel, Caliban, and Prospero's magic during this period, but he thinks that for the most part the play as adapted by Davenant, Dryden, and Shadwell and produced by Garrick, Cibber, and Kean remained a matter of spectacle, "a machine-play *par excellence*" (72). Orgel thinks, "What is especially notable in this history is the separateness of the performing and the editorial traditions, which intersect only rarely and relatively briefly" (Introduction 69). Perhaps the growing availability of Shakespeare's writing in reliable editions began in part to create different expectations that challenged the popular theatrical adaptations of the work, or perhaps audiences were simply growing too familiar with the spectacle.

In an essay reprinted in this volume, Michael Dobson surveys the complicated uses of *The Tempest* in eighteenth-century England. According to Dobson, *The Tempest* was first adapted as a "fiction of gender relations" to support Stuart patriarchy; as such, Caliban played a rather insignificant role in performances based on the Dryden adaptation. However, after conditions made it possible to return to Shakespeare's original text, uses of the play shifted toward race-oriented readings which centered upon Caliban (99). Dobson finds evidence for this shift in Garrick's 1756 operatic abbreviation, performed during the Seven Years War, "as Britain vied with France for control over vast colonized territories in India, the Far East, and the Americas" (104–5) and in the frontispiece to Bell's acting edition of 1774 which depicts the drunken Caliban as a Negro swearing his allegiance to Trinculo and Stephano ("Remember" 105). Before the end of the century however, there was a "relapse" to the Davenant/Dryden adaptation in the anonymous puppet play *The Shipwreck* (1780) and in J. P. Kemble's standard acting text employed at the Theatres Royal in 1789. Stephen Orgel's observations agree with this view, noticing that in 1777 Sheridan, during his first year at Drury

Lane, after Garrick's retirement, "retained Garrick's text but reintroduced both the masque of Neptune and Amphitrite and the 'Grand Dance of Fantastic Spirits' which inaugurates Shadwell's disappearing banquet scene" (Introduction 67). Dobson speculates that this return to the Restoration *Tempest*, with its preoccupation concerning gender relations, was informed by the pressures of the French Revolution, including Rousseau's *Emile*. The play was mobilized in a counter-revolutionary manner "to discipline susceptible English womanhood and to warn the youth of Albion against the temptations of French libertinism" ("Remember" 106).

Michael Dobson also qualifies some commonly held views about the identification of Shakespeare with Prospero. Following the lead of Horace Howard Furness, Quiller-Couch, and Samuel Schoenbaum, many readers have believed that Thomas Campbell first identified Shakespeare with Prospero in 1838. However, Dobson makes it clear that this association was already well established by 1741 when a statue of Shakespeare that contained an inscription from Prospero's revels speech was erected in Westminister Abbey. "The explicit adoption of Prospero as an unmediated Shakespearian self-presentation" Dobson suggests "is initiated by Gildon just a year before [*Robinson*] *Crusoe*'s publication [in 1719]." Gildon had quoted Prospero's revels speech as Shakespeare's definitive statement on human nature in his "Shakespeariana: or Select Moral Reflections, Topicks, Similies and Descriptions from SHAKESPEAR" (103). In his conclusion about *The Tempest* in the eighteenth century Dobson writes: "From sustaining Stuart patriarchy, it had come to certify the enchantedness of Stratford and the cultural superiority of the English bourgeoisie, eventually being invoked to defend family life and property against the threat of Revolution" ("Remember" 107).

II. NINETEENTH-CENTURY CRITICISM AND PERFORMANCE: TOWARD TOTALITY

Nineteenth century writers, critics, actors, and directors obviously repeated some of the uses of *The Tempest* inherited from the eighteenth century; yet, they also found ways to link the play (and its *lexia*) to the century's changing material conditions and its emerging attitudes toward reason, feeling, knowledge, description, inquiry, classification, and human nature. Critical and theatrical use of *The Tempest* changed with almost every significant development in the period. Writers of the Romantic and Victorian periods repeated many of the phrases already formed about *The Tempest*, at times borrowing terms from Ben Jonson's Induction, Dryden's Prefaces, Addison's essays, or Samuel Johnson's notes. However, nineteenth century writers also developed many of the concepts implied by these phrases while finding ways of submitting ideas from different regimens to a single finality. By the end of the nineteenth century a rhetoric of totality and purpose dominated discussions of *The Tempest*.

A. Romantic Appropriations of The Tempest

Jonathan Bate's *Shakespeare and the English Romantic Imagination* provides ample evidence that *The Tempest* was central for early nineteenth century thought about the creative imagination. Bate demonstrates that Blake, Wordsworth, Coleridge, Hazlitt, Keats, Shelley, and Byron (when they were not directly lecturing, reviewing, or writing about *The Tempest*) alluded to the play in their poems and correspondence, often measuring themselves by means of Shakespeare's achievement while assessing their projects in terms of Prospero's magic, Ariel's servitude and liberty, and Caliban's intractability. Bate finds that the masque section of the play "held peculiar sway over the Romantics because it was so intimately bound up with the imagination, the supernatural, and human transience" (89).

Among Coleridge's prose remarks on *The Tempest* two texts are particularly significant: "The Transcript of Lecture 9" from 1811 and his "Notes on *The Tempest*," published in *Literary Remains* by Henry Nelson Coleridge in 1836. Our knowledge of Lecture 9 depends upon John Payne Collier's transcript since, as R. A. Foakes observes, "No notes by C[oleridge] for this lecture have been found" (*Collected* 344).

In Lecture 9 Coleridge indirectly gestured to some of Dryden's concerns, particularly in discussing the unities of Time and Place to show how Shakespeare surpassed the Greeks. Seeking to justify Shakespeare's genius by using a notion of analogy with the ancients, Coleridge disclosed Shakespeare's organic difference from them. His effort also resulted in a close study of the text itself. "It is rather humiliating," Coleridge said, "to find that since Shakespeare's time none of our Critics seems to enter into his peculiarities" ("Transcript" 102). By ridiculing commentary, Coleridge defined and contained it. "Schlegel's lectures rarely descended to particulars" says Jonathan Bate; however, Coleridge "analysed opening scenes in detail, as no one had before, because it was in openings that the germ of the whole could be discerned . . ." (*Romantic* 13–14).

In his "Notes on *The Tempest*" Coleridge kept his distance from Samuel Johnson's assertion in 1773 that the success of the work was a matter of Shakespeare's skill with a regular (and rule-governed) plot rather than his wild, natural, or serene genius. Coleridge thought Johnson incapable of conceptualizing illusion—as an intermediate state between "delusion" and "full reflective knowledge" (92). Coleridge also made in these notes one of the first turns toward genre criticism: "*The Tempest* is a specimen of the purely romantic drama" (94). He altered the notion of a rule—by insisting *The Tempest* followed a pattern associated with the illusory, improbable, dream-like nature of the romance as a genre: "It is a species of drama which owes no allegiance to time or space, and in which, therefore, errors of chronology and geography—no mortal sins in any species—are venial faults, and count for nothing" ("Notes" 94–95).

While Coleridge directly challenged Johnson, he may also have indirectly refuted the Johnsonian elements within Schlegel's reading of *The Tempest*. Schlegel's idea of the play turned against Coleridge's perception in Lecture 9 that each moment organically *prepares* for the interactions that it anticipates: for instance, with Ariel's arrival as Miranda sleeps, or with Caliban's carefully designed entrance. Instead, Schlegel opposed Coleridge's sense of motion with an image of stasis.

> *The Tempest* has little action or progressive movement; the union of Ferdinand and Miranda is settled at their first interview, and Prospero merely throws apparent obstacles in their way; the shipwrecked band go leisurely about the island; the attempts of Sebastian and Antonio on the life of the King of Naples, and the plot of Caliban and the drunken sailors against Prospero, are nothing but a feint, for we foresee that they will be completely frustrated by the magical skill of the latter; nothing remains therefore but the punishment of the guilty by dreadful sights which harrow up their consciences, and then the discovery and final reconciliation. Yet this want of movement is so admirably concealed by the most varied display of the fascinations of poetry, ... that the *dénouement* is, in some degree, anticipated in the exposition. (394)

When Ferdinand and Miranda first "change eyes," Coleridge retrospectively found progression by asserting that the first encounter between Ferdinand and Miranda prepares for the courtship scene in the beginning of the third act ("Notes" 98). Coleridge also diverged from Schlegel concerning the conspiracy plots of Antonio and Sebastian, on one hand, and of Caliban, Stephano, and Trinculo, on the other. In both scenes of conspiratorial seduction "the imagination and fancy are first bribed to contemplate the suggested act, and at length to become acquainted with it" (100–101). Furthermore, "The scene of the intended assassination of Alonzo and Gonzalo is an exact counterpart of the scene between Macbeth and his lady," Coleridge writes (100). That is, in his "Notes on *The Tempest*" Coleridge answered Schlegel's positions with an uncanny exactitude, even though he did not explicitly dramatize their differences.

Hazlitt reformulated Coleridge's phrases about the real and the ideal: "His ideal beings are as true and natural as his real characters; that is, as consistent with themselves, or if we suppose such beings to exist at all, they could not act, speak, or feel otherwise than as he makes them" (238). Hazlitt used chiasmus to describe the play: "As the preternatural part has the air of reality, and almost haunts the imagination with a sense of truth, the real characters and events partake of the wildness of a dream" (238). He sensed that there was some force which determined the relationships among the setting and the characters and the subject of the play. Prospero, Miranda, Ferdinand, Ariel, and Caliban, and "the drunken ship's crew," Hazlitt thought, "are all connected parts of the story, and can hardly be spared from the place they fill" (238). The determining force was Shakespeare who had an "absolute command" over his audience and "the most unbounded range of fanciful invention, whether terrible or playful, the same insight into the world of the imagination that he has into the world of reality; and over all presides the same truth of character and nature, and the same spirit of humanity" (238). Looking at this statement from the perspective of narrative theory, we might be tempted to say that Hazlitt found the play is determined by a semiotic logic that he displaced onto the author as an agency of meaning: chiasmus yields to totality. For Hazlitt the play's parts "cannot be spared from the place they fill" (238). Yet, elements can be polarized: "Shakespeare has, as it were by design, drawn off from Caliban the elements of whatever is ethereal and refined, to compound them in the unearthly mould of Ariel" (241).

The interactive and mutually defining tensions among Johnson, Coleridge, Schlegel, and Hazlitt's discussion of *The Tempest* produced rhetorical patterns, images, figures, phrases, and propositions which became the critical basis (or the interpretive repertoire) for the thesis-bound writing of the early twentieth century, as the mode of expression in literary criticism moved from the editorial comment, the periodical essay, and the aesthetic lecture toward the critical and scholarly monograph. Interpretations of Shakespeare's play (rather than observations, notes, or statements) begin to emerge when various chains of binary oppositions were linked to (and separated from) each other in an effort to grasp *The Tempest* as a coherent whole. Whether or not Shakespeare's play actually constitutes a unified totality is, however, still debated today in both theory and practice.

B. Developing Patterns: Victorian Optimism and Pessimism

In 1848, while trying to prove Shakespeare an atheist, W. J. Birch thought Caliban's decision to be wise and seek for grace was "done in ridicule of religion" (533). The romantic emphasis upon *The Tempest*'s supernatural idealism was replaced in part by a Victorian pessimism stressing the naturalistic elements of the play.

> What a thrice-double ass
> Was I, to take this drunkard for a god?
> And worship this dull fool?
> (5. 1. 294–97, punctuation in Birch)

Birch found satire in Caliban's words, namely, that religion is an invention of man—"according to what he is, so will he construct his divinity. An ass will have a fool for his god" (533). Edward Dowden appears to have been slightly unsettled by Birch: "The spirit of his [Shakespeare's] faith is not to be ascertained by bringing together little sentences from the utterances of this one of his *dramatis personae* and of that. By such a method he might be proved (as Birch tried to prove Shakspere) an atheist" (33). Yet, Birch apparently agreed with Dowden on method: "Shakspere taken piecemeal will ever share the common fate of versatile delineators of character—be quoted by the most opposite parties in favour of the most opposite views. The diversity of opinion among modern critics, respecting his philosophy and religious sentiments, is only to be harmonized by studying him as a whole" (Birch 17). Both Birch and Dowden appealed to the "totality" of Shakespeare to stabilize their own (conflicting) judgments and to secure authority for their claims. It would take more than a century for Shakespeare criticism to understand the discursive pressures that created the need for this kind of totality, to appreciate the semiotic conditions that continually frustrate that demand, and to find more adequate concepts for establishing the connections between a writer's intentions and the formal design of an art work.

Birch redescribed characters other than Caliban as well. He contrasted the Boatswain's wise actions to save the ship with the impractical prayers of the court party. Even though Miranda is an "unsophisticated child of nature," according to Birch, she "passes judgment on the want of mercy in the higher powers, who permit shipwrecks and other mundane calamities," when she tells Prospero: "Had I been a God of power, I would have sunk the sea within the earth" (524). Disagreeing with Charles Knight who read Prospero's revels speech from the perspective of Bishop Berkeley's idealism, Birch asserted that Prospero proclaims the perpetual change of matter: "perpetual loss of identity, which is the case with ourselves: as those spirits vanished, so shall we disappear" (527). In his elaborate note on the word *rack* (or *wreck*) Furness documents the nineteenth-century preoccupation with the problem, touched off by Malone's suggestion that *wrack* refers to the final destruction of the world— of towers, palaces, temples, and the globe—rather than to the insubstantial pageant (Furness 212–217). Birch defends his version of atheism (and Shakespeare's) from the charge of immorality by citing Ariel's comment that Prospero's affections would become tender upon seeing the charmed Alonzo, Gonzalo, Antonio, and Sebastian: "The sight of evil . . . in a natural condition of humanity," he believed, "is and would be a sufficient guarantee against the commission of injuries" (531).

Written in 1859–60 and published in 1864, Robert Browning's "Caliban Upon Setebos; Or, Natural Theology in the Island" repeated nineteenth-century disputes about divinity by satirizing anthropomorphic foolishness in an undecidable manner. Recently Ortwin de Graef has argued (by taking issue with readings by the Vaughans, John Howard, and Michael Timko) that Browning's poem invites yet frustrates all hermeneutic readings. In 1972 Arnold Shapiro noticed that a series of questions complicate the satirical nature of the poem. How primitive is Caliban; is he a brutish half-man or a shrewd spokesman for a developed intellectual view; or is he a savage with the introspective power of Hamlet? Some readers believe the poem attacks Darwinian ideas; others think it censures Calvinism or religious thought in general. Shapiro used Shakespeare's play and Browning's epigraph, taken from Psalm 50 (where God says, "Thou thoughtest that I was altogether such a one as thyself"), as his clues for reading the dramatic monologue. Caliban mistakes Setebos as a projection of his own thoughts, behaviour, and feelings while he imagines that Setebos also answers to a higher force called the "Quiet." Relying upon D. A. Traversi's reading of the play, Shapiro argued that Browning's Caliban "cannot escape the prison of self. The world he creates in his mind, his view of existence, is simply his reflection in a mirror" (62). In 1986 Joseph Dupras, using the theoretical work of Paul de Man and Harold Bloom, read Browning's "Caliban" as an allegory: "The process of reading the poem, like the process of writing it, involves boldly resisting dominance and anxiously daring authority to assert itself in order to compose a text that is never fully composed" (75). Dupras's Browning upstages Shakespeare: "Despite the antecedence of *The Tempest* and Shakespeare's poetic reputation, Caliban's soliloquy about life's tyrannies and insurrections transforms *The Tempest* into a dramatic sequel that Browning might have written" (81–82). Perhaps Oscar Wilde had some of the undecidability of Browning's poem in mind when he wrote in the 1891 Preface to *Dorian Gray*: "The nineteenth century dislike of Realism is the rage of Caliban seeing his own face in a glass. The nineteenth century dislike of Romanticism is the rage of Caliban not seeing his own face in a glass" (3). Both positions have become untenable: the first destroys idealism, but the second indicates the wish for encounter with a transcendental order remained.

Signaling Victorian affiliations with the idea that evolution might be given a moral and religious interpretation, Daniel Wilson appropriately began his chapter on "The Monster Caliban" with an epigraph from Tennyson's "In Memoriam" (Section CXVIII, 25–28). Tennyson used scientific materials in his elegy for Arthur Hallam to enrich poetic language, and in "Lucretius," which alludes to Prospero's revels speech, he undermined, through the stoic's "chemic" dissolution (1.20), Epicurean pretensions toward self-knowledge. Daniel Wilson inverted Tennyson's poetic project and found that Shakespeare's art was a precursor of science, specifically of Darwin's theory about an early progenitor of all vertebrates. Citing Schlegel's and Hazlitt's views that Caliban is "half brute, half demon," Wilson states: "Shakespeare assuredly aimed at the depiction of no such foul ideal" (80–81).

Gesturing to the eighteenth-century debate about the originality of Caliban's language, Wilson contrasted Caliban's poetic thought and expression with the coarse talk of the ship's crew and the debased and besotted discourse of Stephano and Trinculo. Prospero becomes the brute, since he exacts and compels service by relying "only on the agency of enslaved power" (81). "According to the ideas of an age which still believed in magic, he has usurped the lordship of nature, and subdued to his will the spirits of the elements, by presumptuous, if not altogether sinful arts" (81–82). Wilson's evolutionary theory retrieves Caliban from the misunderstanding and abuse heaped upon him by magical force that masquerades as knowledge. "Shakespeare has purposely placed the true anthropomorphoid alongside of these types of degraded humanity, to shew the contrast between them" (88). Wilson necessarily disagreed with the idea that Caliban was the offspring of Syrorax and the devil: "Caliban is in perfect harmony with the rhythm of the breezes and the tides" (90). Instead, Caliban is, according to Wilson, a "pre-Darwinian realisation of the intermediate link between brute and man" (78).

Wilson was one of the first critics to see through Prospero's masque of morality and virtuous restraint *and* to propose an alternative morality in its place: "It may be, as modern science would teach us, that our most human characteristics are but developed instincts of the brute" (84). Moreover, this use of the discourse of nineteenth-century evolutionary theory challenged traditional, sentimental readings of the play (and the morality that grounds them). "Man, by reason of his higher nature which invites him to aspire, and his moral sense which clearly presents to him the choice between good and evil, is capable of a degradation beyond reach of the brute" (88).

Edward Dowden acknowledged Wilson's reading, but he contained its subversive force by restricting his interpretation to Caliban, overlooking his comments about Prospero and morality, and by displacing his use of Darwinian theory by citing an alternative "scientific reading" that suggested Prospero "is the founder of Inductive Philosophy" (377). Avoiding the extreme atheism of Birch and the excessive (Manichaean) theism of Edward Russell—who thought Prospero almost occupies "the place of the Deity" (qtd. in Furness 368), Dowden built upon (and modified) Coleridge's binary of the real (hidden in the ideal) and Hazlitt's chiasmus (between preternatural reality and a realistic dream realm), while he redefined the nature of the relations among force, vengeance, virtue, and freedom. "A thought which seems to run through the whole of *The Tempest*, appearing here and there like a colored thread in some web, is the thought that the true freedom of man consists in service" (Dowden 373). Using this thread, Dowden contrasted Ferdinand and Miranda with Caliban and Ariel: "while Ariel and Caliban, each in his own way, is impatient of service, the human actors, in whom we are chiefly interested, are entering into bonds—bonds of affection, bonds of duty, in which they find their truest freedom" (374). Gonzalo's utopian vision, because of its idealistic absurdity and self-contradiction, allows us to believe more fully in Miranda's and in Ferdinand's use of the language of bondage to express "with sacred candor" their mutual affection and duty (375). We associate Prospero with Shakespeare, according to Dowden, because of his "harmonious and fully developed *will*": "Prospero has entered into complete possession of himself" (371). Dowden thought Shakespeare showed Prospero's flaws ("his quick sense of injury, his intellectual impatience, his occasional moment of keen irritability") to strengthen the reader's awareness of how "his abiding strength and self-possession" are grafted "upon a temperament not impassive or unexcitable" (371, 372).

III. TWENTIETH-CENTURY APPROPRIATIONS OF *THE TEMPEST*

In 1972 Howard Felperin suggested that twentieth-century criticism of *The Tempest* began with Henry James's apparent rebuttal of Lytton Strachey. Strachey had dismissed romance as worth "little or nothing" in relation to life and simultaneously attacked Edward Dowden's Victorian understanding that Shakespeare had finally achieved a serene self-possession. Felperin identified in James's Preface to *The Tempest* (1907) an interpretive dynamic recently associated with cultural materialism and the new historicism—namely, that art both mirrors and intervenes in human culture. "The tension James discerns in the mind of the artist between 'human curiosity' and 'aesthetic passion' corresponds to the tension in the finished play between *mimesis* and *poesis*, the equal and opposite impulses to represent life as it is and to give life a form it does not have, which in successful fiction are resolved to the satisfaction of the audience" (*Shakespearean* 310). Felperin's last clause demonstrates that in 1972 an aesthetics of pleasure and artistic autonomy often predominated over a theory of cultural intervention. However, by 1995 another way of phrasing takes hold of Felperin's writing. Fredric Jameson replaces Henry James: the politics of hegemony and the utopian impulse redescribes the genre of romance, and *The Tempest* becomes "Shakespeare's greatest *history play*" ("Political" 59).

While trying to understand the permutations within interpretive practice during the twentieth century, in 1976 Hayden White distinguished among the normative, the reductive, the inflationary, the generalized, and the absurdist (or poststructuralist) modes of literary criticism. In each mode the relationship between a work, the world, the writer, and the audience is configured according to different expectations and values, which draw upon concepts and anterior phrases from previous historical periods. While twentieth-century interpretations of *The Tempest* loosely conform to the patterns that White identified, I will add another, the materialist mode, to account for developments since 1976. However, *The Tempest*'s interpretive history seriously qualifies one claim within White's essay—namely, that "In literary criticism anything goes." Believing that "This science of rules has no rules" (261), White overlooked how the structures of *inquiry* and *interpretation* interact to determine the expectations and criteria used to assess a reading. Two preliminary examples, taken from different phases of *Tempest* criticism, will show both the reason criticism may appear to be arbitrary and why this view is mistaken.

In *The Heart's Forest*, published in 1972, David Young asked about the structure, style, and themes of pastoral to restore Shakespeare to the present (ix-x), and he studied *The Tempest* in light of the Italian *commedia scenari* to argue that Shakespeare deliberately drew attention to cumbersome dramatic artifice to retrieve the serious purposes of pastoral from "slightly shabby and popularized materials" (159). Building upon the work of Kermode and Empson, Young concluded that almost every element within *The Tempest* relates to "the characteristics and concerns of the pastoral." Prospero's magic represents the pastoral ideal of harmony between man and nature, and the play's dream-like atmosphere repeats the dislocation familiar in the plots of pastoral romance (180). Young's inquiry was composed of three elements: (a) the questions he asked about the pastoral mode; (b) the materials he interrogated or studied to answer his question, including the Italian scenari, Gonzalo's utopian vision, and Prospero's masque, among others; and (c) the conclusions he drew about the reconciliation of opposites within pastoral form. Shakespeare's pastoral, for Young, leaves the audience pondering questions about nature and art: "Like nature, art is many faceted; it is variously linked to music, order, illusion, entertainment, personal wisdom, dreams, wish fulfillment. Like nature it varies according to the viewpoint and situation. And like nature it is again and again a means of self-projection and idealization" (188).

Twenty-three years later Kim Hall examined *The Tempest* from a very different point of view. Hall observed that colonialist readings which explored race, cultural contest, and English authority in new world encounters had overlooked the role of women in colonial structures. Hall *asked* how the economic problem of "commerce and intercourse" informed representations of interracial desire in the early modern period. She *interrogated* Shakespeare's play, therefore, in contexts quite different than Young's pastoral preoccupations, including the first Virginia case law involving race in 1630 and matters concerning miscegenation and assimilation in Spenser's *A View of the Present State of Ireland*. Hall then argued that the various representations of "commerce and intercourse" in the play "draw attention to the increased fluidity" of the categories of race, class and gender and "question the future of dynastic alliance and succession in an Atlantic economy" (142). She found that these changes show up throughout the play: when, for example, Ferdinand's "seduction" of Miranda, orchestrated by Prospero, follows quickly after Caliban is reminded of his attempted rape (142); when "Caliban's threat 'to people the isle' with his offspring clearly suggests that he would control the island by creating a new 'mixed' race" through a patriarchal control over women (143); when Miranda responds to Caliban in a "tirade" against his ingratitude, reminding him of "his position in the web of economics, hegemonic control, and the linguistic exclusion that is common to discourses of race" (144); when Trinculo, a lower-class European, speculates about how to turn Caliban's monstrosity to his own profit (147); when Sebastian upbraids Alonso for

Claribel's marriage to the king of Tunis as the cause of their misfortune (149); and, finally, when in the face of Antonio's rebuke, Gonzalo's "insistence on Dido as widow authorizes her union as a marriage (since one must be wife to be a widow) and thereby legitimizes the foreign female's part in the creation of empire" (153).

Given the disparity between the readings of Hall and Young, many readers may agree with Stephen Orgel that: "*The Tempest* is a text that looks different in different contexts, and it has been used to support radically differing claims about Shakespeare's allegiances" (Introduction 11). While apparently agreeing with Hayden White, Orgel thinks: "all interpretations are essentially arbitrary, and Shakespearian texts are by nature open, offering the director or critic only a range of possibilities. It is performances and interpretations that are closed, in the sense that they select from and limit the possibilities the text offers in the interests of producing a coherent reading" (12). However, the examples of Young and Hall indicate that interpretation has a structure that interacts with the conditions of inquiry. Every interpretation consists of (a) texts which are read, (b) contexts in which those texts are placed, and (c) the implicit or explicit theories and assumptions which determine how the relations between texts and contexts are formed. Hall and Young may have different theories of the text; they certainly select different combinations of lexia (or textual fragments) from *The Tempest*; and the historical materials they bring to bear upon those lexia vary considerably. Yet, the informing structures of inquiry and interpretation are shared by both Young and Hall.

In his 1907 "Introduction" to *The Tempest* Henry James noticed "If the effect of [Shakespeare's] Plays and Poems," is apparently ." . .to mock our persistent ignorance of so many of the conditions of their birth and thereby to place on the rack again our strained and aching wonder," this difficulty is particularly characteristic of *The Tempest*. Unlike many readers who find the philosophical elements of Shakespeare's play baffling and exasperating, James found the enigmatic qualities of *The Tempest* "no unworthy tribute to the work" (79). He felt that for most commentary about *The Tempest* "the Questions" of Shakespeare's writing "convert themselves with comparatively small difficulty, into smooth and definite answers" (79). Commentary and criticism have missed the mark with their "affirmed conclusions, complacencies of conviction, full apprehensions of the meaning and triumphant pointings of the moral" (79). In this survey I will suggest that *Tempest* commentary is belated, deferred and delayed. By juxtaposing Young's reading with Hall's, one might be tempted to ask, for example: how does a distorted pastoral idealization within patriarchy work with the strategies of a disruptive and threatening interracial desire and vice versa? Literary criticism, therefore, may appear to be highly arbitrary or closed when it is actually governed by a rather complex set of variables that prevent it from ever achieving finality—in spite of its rhetoric of certainty. Questions emerge with the successive inadequacy of answers, which become somewhat implausible when faced with equally plausible, contradictory, or conflicting readings that will in turn be subject to their own imprecision and partialities.

A. Normative and Reductive Interpretations of *The Tempest*

Lytton Strachey thought in 1904 that Shakespearean criticism had been fundamentally altered because the chronological order of the plays had gradually become clearer through technical advances in assessing internal and external evidence. Vague speculations and random guesses were, Strachey noted, "reduced to a coherent law" as work like Fleay's tabulations, published in 1874, created new pressures and expectations for correctness. "It is no longer possible to suppose that *The Tempest* was written before *Romeo and Juliet*; that *Henry VI* was produced in succession to *Henry V*;" Stratchey wrote, "or that *Antony and Cleopatra* followed close upon the heels of *Julius Caesar*" (Strachey 51).

The relatively certain chronological succession of the plays led critics to draw conclusions about "the development of the mind of Shakespeare itself" (52). However, Strachey argued that these conclusions all assume "that the character of any given drama is, in fact, a true index to the state of mind of the dramatist composing it" (52). Strachey rightly thought that "the validity of this assumption has never been proved; it has never been shown, for instance, why we should suppose a writer of farces to be habitually merry . . ." (52). And in 1901 Ashley Thorndike had already suggested that Shakespeare turned to tragicomedy because Beaumont and Fletcher succeeded with romances, especially *Philaster* (168). Sometimes, Thorndike believed, Shakespeare "tried to outdo them at their own game" (169). Nevertheless, Strachey proceeded with the questionable assumption and arrived at a conclusion very different from Dowden's sense of a serene Shakespeare: "he was getting bored with himself. Bored with people, bored with real life, bored with drama, bored, in fact, with everything except poetry and poetical dreams." His proof was in "the singular carelessness" of Shakespeare's creation of secondary characters. Sebastian and Gonzalo, among others, "have not even the life of ghosts; they are hardly more than speaking names, that give patient utterance to involution upon involution" (64).

Having gestured to the relative stability of chronological facts, Strachey's essay raised the issue of selection, totality, and perspectivism. Dowden's critical claims about the whole of *The Tempest*, Strachey suggested, were grounded in a biased selection of its parts. Strachey thought that the "combination of charming heroines and happy endings" blinded critics to all of the other elements within the final plays. But he was compelled to ask: "In this world of dreams are we justified in ignoring the nightmares?" (11). Although Dowden accounted for the impatient service of

Caliban, Strachey's comment was one about proportions and emphasis. He implied that these are determined by the perspective of the reader, while he conjured the specter of relativism:

> To an irreverent eye, the ex-Duke of Milan would perhaps appear as an unpleasantly crusty personage, in whom twelve years' monopoly of the conversation had developed an inordinate propensity for talking. These may have been the sentiments of Ariel, safe at the Bermoothes; but to state them is to risk at least ten years in the knotty entrails of an oak, and it is sufficient to point out, that if Prospero is wise, he is also self-opinionated and sour, that his gravity is often another name for pedantic severity, and that there is no character in the play to whom, during some part of it, he is not studiously disagreeable. (68)

In a personal, perhaps homophobic, attack on Strachey (whose *ménage à trois* with Dora Carrington and Ralph Partridge was well known at the time), John Dover Wilson asserted "*The Tempest* is not a play for the Lytton Stracheys of this world, but for fathers!" (11). However, Wilson rightly noted that Strachey (also subject to the charge of partiality) neglected Ariel's advice to Prospero about empathy and did not consider the gestures in the play toward reconciliation and forgiveness (18).

Strachey's comments disturbed readers who had invested in sacred and sentimental readings of the play largely because he invested in their initial assumption—that the artwork is an index to the poet's mind, and he challenged their optimism with an equally normative pessimism. After quoting Caliban's "You taught me language, and my profit on't / Is, I know how to curse," Strachey asked: "Is this Caliban addressing Prospero, or Job addressing God? It may be either; but it is not serene, nor benign, nor pastoral, nor 'On the Heights'" (15). Readers eventually exploited Strachey's maneuvers: heightening identification with minor, neglected, or villainous characters. Yet, for all of its antithetical force and in spite of his own oppositional politics and values, Strachey's understanding of the play remained within the normative mode. Normative readings, according to Hayden White, unambiguously served "the causes of such higher values as culture, civilization, humanity, or life" (271). The critic's ability "to plumb the depths of meaning of a text, [to situate] a text within its historical contexts, and [to communicate] the features of the text's structure and content to the common reader" were unquestioned (270–271). For the most part, normative critics (including Strachey) never doubted the transparency of meaning, never questioned that there might be contexts relevant to the work other than Shakespeare's life and mind, his sources, and his other plays. Along with Coleridge, Hazlitt, and Lamb, Strachey accepted the idea that as a text *The Tempest* is a dramatic poem, but he selected different lexia for examination, and he approached these selections from a less optimistic perspective which did not challenge the idea that Shakespeare's work was most appropriately understood within the environs of his life and art. Unlike Daniel Wilson's reductive approach to the play, which (by drawing upon Darwin's writings) made art and morality answerable to evolution and theories about life, Strachey's essay did not require a (theoretical) dispute about the philosophical status of morality; instead, it worked within the normative assumption that art has an integrity apart from the restrictions and determinations of nature.

Normative readings of *The Tempest* often split over two conflicts: first, between historical and formalist interpretations of the play, and second, between readings that thought Shakespeare was writing *either* about the court of King James, on one hand, *or* the colonization of Virginia, on the other. Debates among Malone, Chalmers, and Hunter (and others) about the play's date of composition (which are amply quoted by Furness) are the nineteenth-century texts which at times determined the phrasing of this second conflict.

In his Preface to "Christabel" Coleridge had dismissed critics who tried to reduce every possible thought and image within a poem to tradition or to a source. Following Coleridge closely, Stopford Brooke, who imagined that on stage "Ariel should only be a voice, no one should represent him" (298), argued that Shakespeare needed no suggestions from books, his many (hypothetical) talks with captains and sailors were enough for his imagination (284–85). Kipling had suggested a similar idea in 1898. However, for others Shakespeare's use of sources was a confirmation of his genius. The debate between formalism and historicism in *Tempest* studies begins in part with these disputes, which were amplified among normative critics when E. E. Stoll strongly rejected any attempt to reduce *The Tempest* to historical (and particularly American) circumstances: "Literature, not history, sheds most light upon literature—drama upon drama; and often literature (and drama as well) is somewhat in opposition to the time" ("Certain" 490). When he applied this principle to Shakespeare's play, Stoll decided, *The Tempest* "stands like a tub on its own bottom, is a story in its own right and for its own sake . . ." ("*Tempest*" 699).

According to Virginia and Alden Vaughan, the early twentieth century was a period of rapprochement between England and the United States after strained diplomatic, social, and intellectual relations in the nineteenth century, and Sidney Lee (along with Frank Bristol, Walter Raleigh, Rudyard Kipling, and Edward Hale, Charles Mills Gayley, and Robert Ralston Cawley) all promoted *The Tempest*'s American affinities: "The times were propitious for seeing *The Tempest* as 'a veritable document of early Anglo-American history' (Lee's phrase), just as the times had not been conducive during the previous century" (130). Although the preference for reading *The Tempest* as a court play had momentarily faded, in 1920 Ernest Law published an article containing materials from his work in 1911 and 1918 that argued the play was performed like a masque and "originally produced at court." Orgel cautions, however, that "the evidence will not support these inferences" (Introduction 3). However, Law himself believed the play was first performed at Blackfriars (or perhaps the Globe), perfected there, and then produced at court (6–7). Although the structure of feeling that divided those who stressed colonial American materials from those who favored theories about the court performances persisted, Law sought some common ground between the "court party" and "the American school." Law attempted his rapprochement when he wrote for example:

> The great interest aroused in London by all this "Newes from Virginia," and "Newes from the Bermudas," can have moved no one more than young Prince Henry, who with his imagination already fired by the narratives of maritime adventure and stories of desert islands and the mysterious dangers of Western seas, was himself planning a project for a new expedition to the colony—a project mentioned by the Venetian Ambassador in a letter to the Doge and Seignory on the very day the play was produced at Whitehall. (9)

When the higher causes of culture, civilization, humanity, and life were threatened during the First World War, normative readers like Law, Gayley, and Lee used the play to invent a common Anglo-American culture. Law found Shakespeare's writings, particularly *The Tempest*, to be a place of "solace and distraction from overweighted thoughts" for those engaged in England's "struggle for existence and freedom" (1).

Influential reductive readings of *The Tempest* were not very common during the early part of the century. Nevertheless, in 1903 W. W. Newell in the *Journal of American Folk-lore* qualified the claims of Tieck, Cohen, and Bell that Ayer's *Fair Sidea* was Shakespeare's source for *The Tempest*. Instead, Newell suggested that the works of Shakespeare and Ayer shared a common yet distant source in "the most widely diffused and popular of all folktales" (240). Drawing upon work in the emerging human sciences, such as folklore studies, comparative mythology, psychoanalysis, and anthropology, reductive interpretations such as Newell's may not have directly opposed the normative concepts of both literature and criticism, but they eroded the belief in Shakespeare's genius as the independent origin of his art.

In 1914 Rachel Kelsey, observing that Morton Luce had overlooked colonial pamphlets and new world travel accounts written before 1608, noticed that Shakespeare probably used Rossier's 1605 ethnographic description of a native American dance (witnessed during the Weymouth expedition) to compose Ariel's song, "Come unto these yellow sands." She also compared Captain John Smith's "Virginian masque," reprinted in *Purchase, his Pilgrims*, to the elements of the vanishing banquet scene in act 3 scene 3. Kelsey did not speculate; yet, the juxtaposition of native dances with court masques quietly retrieved the pre-aesthetic and premoral forms of human impulses sublimated, obscured, or reinforced by art—clearly a reductive task. In an essay reprinted in this volume, Arthur Kinney has recently used Rossier's account to challenge assumptions readers have made about the textuality of *The Tempest* while they remain fixated upon the Strachey account, even though the case for it remains seriously flawed. Many new historicist commentators, including John Gillies, have also been preoccupied with Smith's "Virginian masque" and the contextual challenges it poses to the hegemonic readings of the play in the past as it conjures old world, Ovidian motifs.

In 1921, Colin Still observed resemblances between *The Tempest* and mystic rites of initiation and then tried to explain why and to what extent those resemblances were caused by an "inherent necessity" rather than by "deliberate design" or "sheer coincidence" (*Mystery* 83). Kermode dismissed Still's reading as "improbable," and, while citing the work of Jung and Butler on Neo-Platonic ceremonial magic and the magus legend, called for "some better account of the provenance of these ritual patterns which might explain their presence in Shakespeare" (lxxxiii). However, Kermode overlooked the way Still traced archaic Eleusinian patterns through a plentitude of literary texts, including Dante's *Divine Comedy* and Virgil's *Aeneid*, which is considered by Orgel, Pitcher, Hamilton, and Fuller to be an important anterior text for Shakespeare's play. In his lectures and essays on Shakespeare, Northrop Frye built upon Still's suggestion that Stephano and Trinculo, the court party, and Ferdinand undergo three different quests with corresponding ordeals and visions, and each party perceives the island differently depending upon their psychological and moral state (*"Tempest"* 171, "Shakespeare's" 45). For Still, Stephano and Trinculo represent a failure to achieve Initiation; the court party passes through purgatory in a "lesser initiation"; and in his "Greater Initiation" Ferdinand attains paradise through Miranda, his Beatrice and Persephone (14, 45, 217). Prospero is the hierophant and sometimes represents the supreme being (202–208). While Caliban functions as "the Tempter who is Desire" (170), Ariel is Hermes, or the Angel of the Lord, or Conscience, "the impelling, guiding and accusing messenger of God, which urges and sustains mankind in the long pilgrimage of religious endeavour" (*Mystery* 211).

In his attempt to interpret *The Tempest* Still altered expectations about what constitutes an adequate and complete reading. He found unconvincing Garnett's conclusion that Esclava's *Noches de Invierno* was "unquestionably the groundwork for the plot" (5) because it could not explain the peculiarities within the text that his allegorical theory rendered intelligible (6–7). For Still, "... every authentic initiation ritual is based upon certain permanent realities which are familiar to all the world in art, mythology, and experience" (84). Moreover, the initiation ritual "corresponds exactly with what may be called empirical initiation. For this detachment of consciousness from material and passional concerns is precisely what every philosopher must achieve before the Truth he seeks can be heard in inspiration . . ." (116).

For Walter Clyde Curry, Prospero's theurgical practices "represent no more than a means of preparation for the intellectual soul in its upward progress; union with the intelligible gods is the theurgists's ultimate aim" (196). Curry insisted upon preserving distinctions among medieval, scholastic, and Christian work, on one hand, and classical myth and pagan philosophy, on the other. Still's analysis conflated these differences into his larger allegorical pattern; however, both critics find the meaning of *The Tempest* located in metaphysical realities that determine the shape, the details, and the interconnections among characters within the play. The aim of the reductive critic, according to Hayden White, was to establish some distance from the artwork in order to illuminate "the revelation of its hidden, more basic, and preliterary content" (271). The few reductive critics at the start of the century eventually influenced subsequent discussions of the play, including the work of G. Wilson Knight, Frances Yates, John Mebane, C. J. Sisson, Barbara Mowatt, Michael Srigley, and Alvin Kernan's work on the playwright as magician. In an article that asks very good questions about Prospero's abjuration of his "rough magic," Cosmo Corfield used Curry's reading to suggest that Prospero has failed in his project to achieve "theurgic dignity" (largely due to his black or goetic preoccupation with revenge). Like Jaques whose melancholy separates him from the spirit of comedy, "Prospero ultimately fails to reintegrate" (48).

B. The Inflationary and Generalized Modes of Interpretation

Reductive strategies made the purposes of *The Tempest* dependent upon conditions beyond Shakespeare's own design. To oppose that trend, the inflationary readings of Tillyard, Knight, Traversi, Brower, and Frye for instance, while carving out a unique, disciplinary space for literary criticism, attempted to keep Shakespeare's art from being grounded in the reductive conditions identified by the human sciences: "New criticism, practical criticism, and formalism concentrated on the aesthetic, moral, and epistemological significance of the literary artwork, respectively, but in what was intended to be a nonreductive way . . ." (White 272). L. C. Knights, while gesturing to I. A. Richards, thought the art of *The Tempest* helped us to face "the intractabilities and the limitations of our lives" (30); however, at some distance from him, M. C. Bradbrook, thinking "the whole play is like a great chamber, full of echoes" (245), suggested, while commenting on the final scenes of chess and Prospero's plea, *The Tempest*'s art returns to art: "The devil's chapel of the theatre (so its early opponents had termed it) had been replaced by a scene at the court of a double new-joined kingdom, where royalty itself would enact the shows. . . . [Prospero's] epilogue raises the curtain on the drama—and the poetry of modern times" (249).

    Readings in the generalized mode, however, tried to be neither reductive nor inflationary while they maintained affiliations with both groups. These interpretations emerged from existentialist concerns with being and language as well as with consciousness and meaning—, ideas and concepts amplified in turn by phenomenology, structuralism, psychoanalysis. Often building upon the insights of the inflationary critics (while seriously qualifying their sense of the value of Shakespeare's play), writers like Clifford Leech, Jan Kott, Harry Berger, Norman Holland, and Bruce Erlich tried to balance textual autonomy and contextual circumstances—even though they often asked quite different questions of *The Tempest* and, therefore, selected different contexts, *lexia*, and theoretical positions to frame and phrase their answers.

Generalized readings of the play were often written by persons with specific personal and institutional allegiances to new critical, formalist, or practical approaches, and, because of its treatment as a dramatic poem by the Romantic tradition, *The Tempest* (especially given its place within the Shakespearean canon) frequently functioned as a signal text. While thinking about Prospero's plea to be relieved "by prayer, / Which pierces so that it assaults / Mercy itself, and frees all faults" (Epi. 13–18), C. L. Barber and Richard Wheeler suggested that Prospero and Shakespeare are perhaps concerned with the faults in the play, with the blame for using magic, and "the guilt attaching to the aggressiveness of the fable of an artist as mercifully avenging prince." Then Barber and Wheeler registered the tension (characteristic of the generalized mode) between art and life in Shakespeare's development: "perhaps also there is a need for expiation after having bodied forth, in *The Tempest* and throughout the unprecedented diversity and power of the work prior to it, *motives underlying life*—'this thing of darkness I / Acknowledge mine' (5. 1. 275–75)—even though they have been brought under *the control of art*" (emphasis added, 342).

The differences between Knight and Tillyard repeated the pattern between Coleridge, who perceived visionary and organic movement in the play, and Schlegel, who saw little action or progressive movement. For Knight the play was "a dynamic and living act of the soul" ("Myth" 27). For Tillyard, since Prospero's reconciliation has already happened before the play begins, *The Tempest* was a static work. Traversi tried to reconcile Knight's sense that the play was a logical development of Shakespeare's symbolic techniques with Tillyard's sense that the late romances supplemented the tragedies, by distinguishing, for instance, between Prospero's static, opening monologue and Miranda's gradual growth towards full comprehension of the past (196). Brower's solution to the difficulty of dramatic action was to transform the play into "a Metaphysical poem of metamorphosis" (121). Seen from this perspective, these interpretations of *The Tempest* generally agreed that the chronological order of Shakespeare's work, his purposes as a writer, and their contemporary preoccupations with the nature and purposes of art were the proper contexts for interpretation. However, the (sometimes slight) differences among these inflationary readings also revealed certain fractures concerning the nature of textuality that would become the basis for later exploration by readers working in the generalized and absurdist modes. Knight, Tillyard, Traversi, and Brower were preoccupied with the nature of art. The questions that moved beneath the surface of their inquiries were: how does the experience of an art work differ from historical experience or philosophical reflection; what kind of knowledge does it provide; how does art differ from religion; how does it transcend its own conditions while working within established analogical forms and metaphorical conventions? These critics found *The Tempest* to be a significant place to answer their particular versions of these questions. But the play also placed its own restrictions and uncertainties upon each writer's interpretation as well, once again turning their smooth and definite answers into perplexity by "[placing] on the rack again [their] strained and aching wonder" (Henry James 79).

In "Myth and Miracle," written 1929, G. W. Knight sketched an argument that he developed more fully in *The Shakespearian Tempest*, written 1932. Later, in *The Crown of Life* (published in 1947), Knight expanded his ideas about the play in "The Shakespearian Superman," a comprehensive catalog of *The Tempest*'s connections to the rest of Shakespeare's work as well as a recapitulation of his visionary reading of the play. Knight tried to answer reductive interpretations by turning Still's insights, for instance, back into the service of literature and art. "Still's centre of reference," Knight wrote in 1947, "is less in the poetry than in a rigid system of universal symbolism deliberately, but quite legitimately, applied to it" (*Crown* 230).

G. W. Knight's visionary reading in "Myth and Miracle" transformed the textuality of *The Tempest* into "a *record* of Shakespeare's spiritual progress and a *statement* of the vision to which that progress had brought him" (emphasis added, 27). Ariel and Caliban represent Shakespeare's own overcoming of a mental division visible in the problem plays between beauty, romance, and poetry, on one hand, and the hate-theme ("loathing of the impure, aversion from the animal kinship of man, disgust at the decaying body of death" [23]). The song, music, and poetry of the island, according to Knight, make powerless the hostile and evil impulses driven to the island by the storm, the recurrent poetic symbol of the tragic phase: Alonzo contains "traces" of *King Lear*; Antonio and Sebastian recall *Macbeth* (24). Miranda and Ferdinand repeat "the child-theme" of the final plays. When Prospero, like Cerimon over Thaisa, "revives, with music, the numbed consciousness of Alonso and his companions," his former enemies wake "as though mortality were waking into eternity" (25). The poetic symbolism developed throughout Shakespeare's career becomes the key for understanding the spiritual vision of *The Tempest*. If the shipwreck suggests the tragic destiny of man, Knight thought, then the survival of the passengers, who land unharmed and with fresh garments, and Ariel's songs for Ferdinand about suffering "a sea-change into something rich and strange" and kissing the wild waves into silence after coming "unto these yellow sands" signal a "triumphant mysticism of the dream of love's perfected fruition in eternity stilling the tumultuous waves of time" (26). For Knight, *The Tempest* is "a dynamic and living act of the soul, containing within itself the record of its birth: it is continually re-writing itself before our eyes" (27). Knight's approach toward the play "chalk'd forth the way" for future *Tempest* interpretations. He developed the idea that Shakespeare's plays could be thought of as a logical and predictable *series* that reaches a culmination ("Myth" 9). He also helped to erode the simple notion of character that had dominated Shakespeare criticism since the eighteenth century, finding each personage of *The Tempest* a "composite" of previous Shakespearean figures and ideas. Knight also borrowed terms from the lexicon of psychoanalysis, linking them to phrases drawn from Coleridge: "Art is an extraverted expression of the creative imagination which, when introverted, becomes religion" ("Myth" 22–23).

Tillyard was preoccupied with tragedy rather than religion—with the way one genre may complete what an earlier form cannot include or resolve. While strongly disagreeing with E. K. Chambers's conjecture that Shakespeare suffered from either a spiritual crisis or a nervous breakdown after writing *Timon* and before composing *Pericles* (14–15), Tillyard suggested, "the romances supplement the tragedies" (15). However, turning away from Dover Wilson's idea that the storm scene re-enacts a tragic plot, Tillyard thought the scene where Antonio persuades Sebastian to murder Alonso draws the earlier tragedy out of the past and places it in the present (51). Like Iago who wakes from "churlish 'honesty' to brilliant machinations," Antonio is transformed from "the cynical and lazy badgerer of Gonzalo's loquacity to the brilliantly swift and unscrupulous man of action" (51). Often overlooking the role of Ariel, Tillyard suggested, "Prospero is the agent of his own regeneration, the parent and tutor of Miranda; and through her and through his own works he changes the minds of his enemies" (50). Tillyard's Prospero is neither seriously intent upon vengeance, nor does he fundamentally change during the play, since apparently the need for change would belong to destructive portion of the tragic pattern left in the background (53–54). For Tillyard *The Tempest* finally has a "supplementary function": "Not only does it give Shakespeare's fullest sense of the different worlds we can inhabit; it is also the necessary epilogue to an already apprehended series of tragic masterpieces" (85).

Although Derek Traversi and Rueben Brower used inflationary conventions, their readings were remarkably different. They disagreed, for instance, about where to place the keystone moment of *The Tempest*. For Brower the shift takes place when "Prospero describes the behavior of the King and the courtiers as they slowly return from madness to sanity" (117). However, Traversi suggested Ariel's reprimand of Alonso and the court party, is "an explicit statement of what *The Tempest* is about" (248). Brower's *Tempest* consists of a harmonious, metaphorical design created by analogies between six recurrent connections or "continuities" ("strange-wondrous, sleep-and-dream, sea-tempest, music-and-noise, earth-air, slavery-freedom, and sovereignty-conspiracy") that are linked through the key metaphor of "the sea-change," understood as magical transformation or metamorphosis (97). For Traversi, the play is about *judgment*. "Only when the good and evil in human nature have been understood and separated . . . will the final reconciliation and restoration of harmony take place" (251). The movement of the play is choreographed to assure moral reconciliation. Brower's *Tempest* is metaphorically protean; yet, it is paradoxically under the control of a "total design" where the union of dramatic action and metaphor combine to create for the spectator "a shimmering transformation of disorder" (121). Traversi's play is static and divisive: its art stands in the service of a vague morality, destiny, and judgment tutored by an imprecise transcendental rationality.

In 1964 William Empson pointed to the cruelty in Traversi's suggestion that Stephano and Trinculo will be marooned since there is no reason to anticipate it, "except that [Traversi] felt spiteful, and believed that this was a moral way to feel" (239). Since Traversi wrote that " 'Caliban is bound by his nature to service,' " Empson was blunt: "Traversi is expressing here the pure milk of the master-race doctrine, and it is presented with the usual glum sanctimoniousness as a traditional Christian moral, with no sign that it has ever been questioned" (239). Northrop Frye found moral and intellectual themes in the play but insisted it was neither an allegory nor a religious drama. He suggested in *A Natural Perspective* that "drama is born in the renunciation of magic, and in *The Tempest* and elsewhere it remembers its inheritance" (59). Noting the title of the play means time as well as tempest and that "timing was important to a magician," Frye believed the play moves from Prospero's zenith to "the sense of the nothingness of all temporal things" (Introduction 1371). Because of his inflationary concerns with archetypal patterns of initiation, rebirth, and festivity, Frye redescribed these pre-aesthetic forms as literary genres rather than psychic categories or social rituals: "The masque shows the meeting of the fertile earth and a gracious sky introduced by the goddess of the rainbow, and leads up to a dance of nymphs representing the spring rains with reapers representing the autumnal harvest" (Introduction 1370).

In a manner that distinguishes a generalized interpretive stance from Frye's archetypal, inflationary approach, C. L. Barber and Richard Wheeler argued that Shakspeare's ironic use of the saturnalian rhythm of holiday festivals in *A Midsummer Night's Dream* is not repeated in *The Tempest* which reckons with "the power of the theater as an established institution" (337). Relying upon Enid Welsford's idea that Shakespeare's play is designed like a masque in which court members would disguise themselves as visiting monarchs from a distant world who voluntarily came to salute the reigning monarch, Barber and Wheeler noted: "Of course in this instance the visit is involuntary, and the Prince who receives the visitors has been wronged by them; the anti-masque itself is a threat to the Prince as well as a burlesque of the serious threat posed by Antonio and Sebastian." Shakespeare uses the masque to be "critical of monarchs in ways that the courtly form would not allow" (337). When Prospero makes Alonso one of the visitors, the monarch is placed totally within the artist's power: "Shakespeare uses the play to test what a dramatist might do, how far his power might extend . . . and then [to] see how much these subjects can be changed at deep levels by putting them inside the plot the dramatist invents for them" (338).

"*The Tempest* is a pastoral drama," Frank Kermode wrote in an effort to forestall interpretations that resorted to the "desperate expedients" of "assuming" the play was a political, autobiographical, or religious allegory. Serious pastoral poetry, according to Kermode, "is concerned with the opposition of Nature and Art," represented by the opposition between Prospero's and Caliban's worlds (xxiv). This position may be equally allegorical, but Kermode shifted the discussion by subordinating ideas to form, even though he insisted that *The Tempest* "is deeply concerned with difficult ideas, and with the philosophic genres of masque and pastoral" (lxxxviii). For Kermode Caliban is the "core" and the "ground" of the play: "like the shepherd in formal pastoral, he is the natural man against whom the cultivated man is measured" (xxiv). After gathering together a wide-range of materials from the Bermuda pamphlets, Montaigne, Neo-Platonic traditions of the mage, Spenser's *Faerie Queene*, and Castiglione's *Courtier* among others, Kermode demonstrated how Shakespeare assembled these materials in a unique manner, beyond the analytic grasp of criticism. Romance is one of the mechanisms for this process; however, Kermode defined it differently than Frye as "a mode of exhibiting the action of magical and moral laws in a version of human life so selective as to obscure, for the special purpose of concentrating attention on these laws, the fact that in reality their force is intermittent and only fitfully glimpsed" (liv). Given this definition, Kermode thought romance may inspire belief in the forces of fertility, but rational conviction shows this is not so in every case. Kermode foreshadowed approaches that would emphasize the play's scattered discursivity rather than its control and mastery. By emphasizing Shakespeare's use of the difference between generic forces that insist upon belief (as comic affirmation) and intellectual traditions that require a rational deliberation (and perhaps a suspension of judgment), Kermode identified, without signaling it as such, an epistemological faultline within the text.

Noting that the pastoral concern with the conflict between art and nature preoccupied Theocritus and Virgil as well as Shakespeare, Leo Marx believed: "the theme is one of which American experience affords a singularly vivid instance: an unspoiled landscape suddenly invaded by advance parties of a dynamic, literate, and purposeful civilization. It would be difficult to imagine a more dramatic coming together of civilization and nature" (35–36). However, Marx remained rather silent about the Native Americans who populated that landscape. Working against the pattern established by Leo Marx, in an essay written for this volume, Christopher Felker proposes that *The Tempest* in early America would have been read as an instance of a providential history which accounted for the differences between nature and culture by seeing both as a matter of creation. Yet, according to Felker, evidence (drawn from the archives and interpreted from the perspective of the history of the book) reveals that Shakespeare was apparently not read very often in colonial America.

Felker's essay provides some convincing evidence for Michael Dobson's claim that before and shortly after the American Revolution there was considerable resistance to Shakespeare's writing. Dobson thinks Michael Bristol mistaken in his "lament" that the "Shakespearizing" of America defeated its revolutionary ideals. "By the time of the drafting of the Constitution," Dobson argues, "it appears. . . the United States, claiming Shakespeare's magic book as its right, was already committed to the role of Prospero" ("Fairly" 203). Felker's observations, however, challenge this step in Dobson's work by suggesting that Cotton Mather in Boston, James Logan and Benjamin Franklin in Philadelphia, and the founders at the College of William and Mary had deliberately drifted away from Shakespeare specifically and from England in general in order to create an American (and at times Puritan) identity different from its European beginnings. A pre-Shakespearean America, according to Felker, did not exist; it had to be invented. In a way this is Dobson's point. His focus, however, is upon how Shakespeare was lifted from his historical context (and made universal by Americans who would make use of his work in order to be imported into America) and not upon how other (earlier) colonial Americans had to drift away from representations of monarchical and magical power, as Felker suggests, to assert democratic principles and scientific learning in opposition to authority and magic.

Many readers working in the generalized mode took their cue from the differences among inflationary readings of *The Tempest*. The tensions between Knight and Tillyard on the play's dynamic or static nature not only received further development with Frye's inflationary concerns about the temporality of archetypal cycles and fertility rituals, it also gave way to Clifford Leech's existential preoccupation with the interplay between unique and recurring events: "The experience of time make us aware of both cycle and crisis" (19). Leech accommodated Frye's archetypal position, yet, realized its partiality, and unlike Frye, Leech felt the play was dominated by a sense of incompletion as it makes its re-entry into the flux of time.

When he published *The Dream of Prospero* in 1967, D. G. James refuted the idea that Prospero was tired by noticing when Prospero says he will "*retire* me to my Milan," the word had "the meaning of removing or betaking oneself merely" (125). James suggested instead that Prospero returns at the height of his powers, "addressing himself again, with renewed energy, to the labours of government; and doing so not at all at the expense of the cultivation of his interior life" (126). Synthesizing materials on magic and the Bermuda pamphlets, James relied upon Frazer's *Golden Bough* to suggest that Prospero functions like a kingly priest, and his character draws upon "primitive thought and practice" to negotiate the tensions between public duty and visionary contemplation (127). Yet, James folds these reductive materials into an imaginative reading that may have anticipated Peter Greenaway's film, *Prospero's Books*: ". . . Prospero in truth never left Milan" and "the island and all that we see happen on it was a dream of Prospero's only" (149). Derek Jarman's film version of Prospero, however, might reflect the vigor James imagined in a way not matched by Gielgud's Prospero in Greenaway's production.

Norman Holland's essay "Caliban's Dream" shows how the introduction of Freudian concepts and terminology redescribed the textuality of the play by linking psychoanalytic phrases to the pastoral reading of Frank Kermode. While discussing how the isle is full of "Sounds and sweet airs that give delight, and hurt not," Caliban tells Stephano his dream about clouds that "would open and show riches / Ready to drop upon me, that, when I wak'd / I cried to dream again" (3.2.144–45, 150–52). By reading Caliban's speech as Erik Erickson would read the manifest content of a dream, Holland suggested that Caliban "expresses three levels of wish" (124). Holland amplified D. G. James's reading by transferring the focus from the dream that vanishes to the wish that expresses (through traces of infantile sexuality) the vulnerability that constitutes Prospero and Caliban as composite figures. "The play's moral contrast of Art and Nature acts out in an intellectual way the contrast between the integrity of age and the dependency of childhood, as in all art—and life, too—mature significances fulfil and inherit the conflicts of infancy" (124). Wondering why Shakespeare "endows Prospero with such extraordinary dominion," David Sundelson found traces of King Lear in a Prospero who "wants both the status of a father and the security and ease of a child" (105). By identifying with Ferdinand, Prospero satisfies his instincts by sharing them and "transforms a loss into a gratification" (120).

In 1969 Harry Berger also came to Freudian conclusions about Prospero's insights into the vanity of his art. Similarly, while Coppélia Kahn and David Sundelson may have agreed that "Prospero's identity is based entirely on his role as father," where Sundelson found the achievement of deep harmony, Kahn saw a family "never united or complete" (240). Kahn argued that in *The Tempest* woman is most strongly repressed; Prospero plays out rivalries and unresolved conflicts that he never fully confronted before; and he breaks free of repetition and his oedipal past, but by giving Miranda to "the son of his brother's partner in crime," he preserves a compromise that prevents him from acknowledging his sexuality and uniting with the feminine (239).

Berger believed that the sentimental readings of Madeline Doran, Stephen Orgel (in his early "New Uses of Adveristy"), Derek Traversi, Ruben Brower, and Northrop Frye (among others) were not wrong but that they did not "hit the play where it lives" (254). He noticed that the dominant reading of the play has to overlook certain details: Prospero's description of the usurpation implies he was responsible in some way; yet, *he* never seems to take that into account. Gonzalo was Antonio's accomplice, and is also likened to Prospero through verbal and ideological echoes, while Gonzalo's epilogue is badly timed. Berger asked questions he felt the sentimental reading could not ask, including: "Why do we respond to certain qualities in Caliban which Prospero ignores, and why are we made to feel that the magician is more vindictive than he needs to be?" and "Why the twenty-line epilogue, in which Prospero asks the audience for applause, sympathy, and release?" (255).

Berger suggested that Prospero is troubled by both the radical persistence of evil and the persistence of his "idealistic separation of Ariel from Caliban," or "of the liberal arts from servile labor" (270). Prospero's sudden reversal in the revels speech, which Kermode found inadequately motivated, is meant to be sudden:

> What he feels this time, and for the first time, is that everything golden, noble, beautiful and good—the works of man, the liberal arts, the aspirations variously incarnated in towers, palaces, temples, and theaters—that all these are insubstantial and unreal compared to the baseness of man's old stock. And not merely as vanities; but as deceptions, fantasies which lure the mind to escape from its true knowledge of darkness and which, dissolving, leave it more exposed, more susceptible, more disenchanted than before. (270–71)

Along with Leech's essay, Berger's "Miraculous Harp" prepared the ground for many of the tough-minded, late-twentieth century interpretations of the play. The sentimental reading often perceived the masque as Prospero's preparation for return to Milan; however, Berger believed: "Prospero's desire is to protract the entertainment and delay the return to actuality" (272). Similarly, the epilogue becomes more than a matter of "scene stealing," as well as a strategy of delay and deferral (277). "At the end he seems more unwilling to leave than ever" (277). Perhaps Berger could not free himself entirely from sentimental themes of resignation (as discovery) for he continued: "Although he knows his word is less than the miraculous harp, he lays the harp aside" (279).

Tempest criticism in the middle to late nineteen-seventies witnessed a major shift in the generalized mode that would eventually give rise to a mixture of poststructuralist and materialist readings. Although interpretations continue to this day to discuss the play in aesthetic (often inflationary) terms, the influential work of Fiedler, Erlich, Kott, Leininger, and Greenblatt (in "Learning to Curse"), for example, began to integrate intellectual developments in psychoanalysis and structuralism, while taking account of the ways the ideology of traditional humanism (with its sense of a universal human nature) had neglected and often oppressed non-European others. The change was significantly driven by political forces, summarized by Rob Nixon:

> Between 1957 and 1973 the vast majority of African and the larger
> Caribbean colonies won their independence; the same period witnessed the
> Cuban and Algerian revolutions, the latter phase of the Kenyan "Mau Mau"
> revolt, the Katanga crisis in the Congo, the Trinidadian Black Power upris-
> ing, and, equally important for the atmosphere of militant defiance, the civil
> rights movement in the United States, the student revolts of 1968, and the
> humbling of the United States during the Vietnam War. (557)

These historical and geopolitical changes, while placing stress upon traditional expectations about the force and value of criticism, fundamentally
altered the questions readers asked of *The Tempest* and changed their focus
concerning the play's details or *lexia*. As Rob Nixon has indicated, passages
from the play that had received little attention (for example: "My foot, my
tutor") derived a new significance and weight, reassigning to the standard
selections about visions and retirement a different value and purport. For a
while answers continued to link readers' insights into power and colonialism
to the phrases of the inflationary and generalized modes of interpretation.
However, it gradually became clear that criticism of *The Tempest*'s involvement with the expansion of colonial domination, with the persistence of
racism, and with patriarchal systems of exchange at times repeated the patterns of domination that structured colonial exploitation.

In 1950 Octave Mannoni published his controversial *Prospero and Caliban: The Psychology of Colonization*, which shaped the radical, critical reactions of Aimé Césaire and Franz Fanon. In an attempt to understand the
Madagascan uprising of 1947–1948 (in which, according to Nixon, "sixty
thousand Madagascans, one thousand colonial soldiers, and several hundred
settlers were killed"), Manoni used Prospero and Caliban as prototypes for the
idea that colonialism is advanced by the opposition between an inferiority
complex, represented in Prospero, and a dependence complex, represented by
Caliban (562–63). Clearly Caribbean and African intellectuals who anticipated their own freedom and independence rejected Manoni's theory and his
appropriation of *The Tempest*, (although his idea found some currency among
Tempest critics who sometimes attribute a similar view to Shakespeare himself). Nixon astutely suggested that Manoni's *Tempest* was the spur that
mounted "adversarial interpretations of the play which rehabilitated Caliban
into a heroic figure, inspired by noble rage to oust the interloping Prospero
from his island" (564). Fanon and Aimé Césaire noted Manoni neglected the
fact that colonialism was fundamentally economic exploitation; therefore, his
position could be used to undermine and contain revolutionary movements
(564–65).

When George Lamming, the first Caribbean writer to identify with Caliban, appropriated (or as Nixon says, annexed) Shakespeare's play, he created
a "prototype for successive Caribbean figures in whom cultural and political
activism were to cohere," including Toussaint Louverture, C. L. R. James, and

Fidel Castro (Nixon 569). Later Retamar would add others to the list, including Jose Marti, Césaire, and Fanon (Nixon 575). In *A Tempest* Aimé Césaire thought of Prospero as the complete totalitarian, "the man of cold reason, the man of methodical conquest." Caliban, however, "can still *participate* in a world of marvels, whereas his master can merely 'create' them through his acquired knowledge" (Césaire, qtd. in Nixon 571).

According to Nixon, "*Une Tempête* self-consciously counterpoises the materialist Prospero with an animistic slave empowered by a culture that coexists empathetically with nature" (571). The Cuban Roberto Fernández Retamar's Caliban, unlike Césaire's negritudist version which emphasized race, is focused on matters of class (Nixon 576). Retamar used Caliban to name (and project) "our America" as an inclusive society of mulattos, and he used oppressive interpretations of the play, for instance, in Renan's antidemocratic, aristocratic, and prefascist version, to solicit the ambivalence within Shakespeare's work (Retamar 9).

Jan Kott created common ground between new world experiences and old world concepts by loosely applying Edmund Leach and Levi-Strauss's theories concerning the structure of myths. By using Levi-Strauss' structural anthropology rather than Jung's archetypal theory of myth, Kott may have been establishing some distance from Leslie Fiedler's archetypal discussion of the east-west axis that disturbs and challenges Shakespeare's northern-southern orientation. Fiedler's Prospero bids farewell to "the anima-actor," Ariel, which should also mean, he is "leaving the shadow-clown behind" (247). Fiedler felt that because Césaire's revision included "the epiphany of a Congolese god," he left out "what is specifically Indian rather than African in Caliban" and therefore ignored the ways all Americans are disturbing strangers to Europe (248).

For Jan Kott it is a matter of signification rather than archetypes: "Shakespeare presents Caliban through two linguistic codes: one associated with his being a monster of the old world and the other with being a slave of the new." According to Kott, "A monster, a deformed creature, is always a hybrid" (12). Yet, the name for the hybrid is always a mediation between two terms of a binary opposition: Caliban is both mythic monster and new world savage; Ariel both imprisoned spirit and presenter of cruel spectacles; Prospero both exile and usurper (13). Only the names of the hybrid creature change in the mythic code, the structure, for Kott, endures and makes it possible to fuse widely disparate materials from vastly different cultures and epochs (14). Since myths shape the language of the chroniclers as well as the images and icons of artists, according to Kott, "we find a striking mixture of images and paraphrases from Virgil, Horace, and Ovid with the new language of mariners and colonizers" (10). Kott fundamentally redescribed the textuality of *The Tempest*, and he hit upon a semiotic resolution to the conflict (represented in the differences between Stoll and Cawley, for example) which had driven the previous (now somewhat futile) critical disputes about *The Tempest*'s new and old world contexts.

For Bruce Erlich, who used the play to demonstrate the nature of Marxist inquiry and interpretation, Ferdinand and Miranda's marriage reconciles "feudal legitimacy with capitalist striving" (52). Erlich read Prospero as a composite: as a European, he is "unseated by Machiavellian wiles," as a Virginian, he wins "his new realm twelve years earlier by kindness to the native inhabitant" but holds it "ever since by force of magic. His 'Art' suppresses rebellion, as Henry VI could not (IV.i.194–266); reconciles enemies (impossible for Richard II); and successfully institutes dynastic marriage (which escaped Lear): he thus prepares the personal, familial, and political harmony to accede upon return to Milan" (45).

Erlich concluded with the highly controversial view (associated with Manoni) that Shakespeare "uncannily confirms" the modern position that "colonialism demands that the native *willfully* repudiate himself and acknowledge European spiritual and political order" (62). He also accepted G. Wilson Knight's colonialist view that *The Tempest* celebrates England's duty to raise savage peoples from superstition, taboos, and witchcraft: "Shakespeare's insight exceeded his sympathies" and "he is great for what he recognized, and not for what he knowingly argued" (63). Erlich kept his argument within the inflationary phrasing of Knight; therefore, his work—in spite of its Marxist affiliations—did not break from the generalized mode. However, in 1976, one year before Erlich's essay, Stephen Greenblatt (a student of both W. K. Wimsatt's formalism and Raymond Williams's materialism) published "Learning to Curse: Aspects of Linguistic Colonialism in the Sixteenth Century"—an essay that signaled a change in *Tempest* scholarship.

Greenblatt used *The Tempest* as part of a larger argument about the strategies of a "linguistic colonialism" that operated with two contradictory beliefs: first, that native Americans had no language at all, and second, that there was no significant language barrier between Europeans and savages (26). The first belief results in thinking of native peoples as wild non-human creatures; the second, in the belief that native peoples are just like Europeans. According to Greenblatt, "both positions reflect a fundamental inability to sustain the simultaneous perception of likeness and difference, the very special perception we give to metaphor. Instead they either push the Indians toward utter difference—and thus silence—or toward utter likeness—and thus the collapse of their own, unique identity" (31). Native languages and cultures are consequently reduced to transparency either by denying their existence or by dismissing their significance. Greenblatt's *Tempest* opposed these European strategies for appropriating new world natives. The very opacity of Caliban's language resists both tendencies toward utter likeness or difference, while Shakespeare "does not shrink from the darkest European fantasies about the Wild Man" (26). These fantasies, according to the Vaughans, may have begun with Homer's Cyclops and developed through the medieval figure of the wodewose, while surfacing later in *Mucedorus* and *The Faeire Queene* (56–75). Greenblatt's Shakespeare adds a political dimension to the wodewose tradition "by having Caliban form an alliance with the lower-class Stephano and Trinculo to overthrow the noble Prospero" (38 n. 46).

As Erlich's reading demonstrates, not all readers share Greenblatt's confidence concerning Shakespeare's intentions or the play's clear function as a (metaphorical) resistance to dominant ideology. For Greenblatt "the audience achieves a fullness of understanding before Prospero does, an understanding that Prospero is only groping toward at the play's close" ("Learning" 31). Twelve years later in his "Martial Law in the Land of Cockaigne" Greenblatt's residual formalism will be rethought. The resistance of *The Tempest* gives way to an "unresolved and unresolvable doubleness" (158) between pure fantasy and pure power, as the material conditions of the theatrical joint-stock company create a commercial space that simultaneously appropriates and swerves from the discourse of power (*Shakespearean* 159).

In 1985 David Suchet described his own rediscovery of Caliban's humanity while he prepared the role (next to Michael Hordern's Prospero) for the 1978–79 RSC production directed by Clifford Williams. Suchet became depressed when Williams told him that he might be "half-fish, half-man (presumably I would wear fins) or possibly something deformed, like a thalidomide child" (169). Fearing that he had been badly miscast, Suchet returned to the text and discovered that Prospero says the island (not Caliban) was "not honored with / A human shape" before he arrived with his daughter. Moreover, when Miranda tells Ferdinand that he is "the third man that e'er I saw," Suchet noted, "Caliban is or can be the only other man she could have met" (170). Reading the scene of Trinculo's first encounter with Caliban, Suchet determined that "Shakespeare had obviously gone to great pains (not without tongue in cheek) to describe the popular concept of the 'native.'" (171). Realizing that Caliban fears Prospero might change him into ape with a villainous low forehead and that Caliban also "carries logs, makes fires, builds dams for catching fish, and is Prospero's slave," Suchet concluded that Shakespeare provided deliberate clues so that everyone would see beyond their confused perceptions: "'The monster' was in the eyes of the beholder" (172).

In an attempt to reconcile the postcolonial readings of Caliban with traditional interpretations, Paul Franssen has recently extended Suchet's insight, examining in detail how the other characters view Caliban from their own perspectives. In the same anthology, *Constellation Caliban: Figures of a Character*, Dirk Delabastita addressed the tension between historical and anachronistic readings of Caliban and *The Tempest*. Examining conflicting attitudes about Caliban's (human) love of music or (animal) response to noise, Delabastita proposed that a semiotic square (using the terms: life-giving/life-taking; order, self-control/chaos, savagery) enables "a more refined comparison of different versions of Caliban by raising the question whether Caliban is trapped in a single category, or is allowed to partake of different ones and/or to undergo a transformation in the course of the play" (15). Taking issue with the Vaughans' analysis of Caliban as a "departure" from the wild man, Barbara Baert has also suggested, by examining the visual arts, that Caliban's complexity is "essential to the very genre of the wild-man itself" (44). Baert demonstrated, in a manner that resonates with Gillies work on cartography, that the typology of Caliban remains hidden "without the study of non-textual material" (56), including Durer's *Meerwunder* (ca. 1498), based in Ovid and showing "a man with the tail of a fish, who has abducted a woman. He carries a tortoise as a shield" (52).

Peter Hulme has a slightly different sense of the problem. "Discursively, it could be said, Caliban is the monster all the characters make him out to be. . . . Caliban, as a compromise formation, can exist only within discourse: he is fundamentally and essentially beyond the bounds of representation" (*Colonial* 108). Suchet's comment, however, continues to solicit trouble. There is also Caliban's and the actor's body, no matter how chaotically crossed by a plurality of discursive significations.

C. The Poststructuralist and Materialist Modes

Interpretation of *The Tempest* since 1976 has been preoccupied with about five interrelated concerns which have been shaped largely by the poststructuralist criticism of Barthes, Foucault, and Derrida; by the materialist and cultural critiques of Raymond Williams, Immanuel Wallerstein, and Michel de Certeau; and by postcolonial discussions of Edward Said, Gayatri Spivak, and Homi Bhabha: the desire and subjectivity of the other (often in terms of race, class, and gender); the discursivity and plurality of the text; the coercive nature of power and knowledge; the circulation of social energy, shaped by a poetic geography, involving an economics of exchange; and the problem of a distinctively human agency and its acts of repetition. Readers have brought a wide-range of historical materials to bear upon these concerns, drawing upon past discussions of sources and anterior texts (including the Bermuda pamphlets and other accounts of new world voyages, Montaigne's *Essays*, Virgil's *Aeneid*, Ovid's *Metamorphoses*, and Shakespeare's own earlier work), while integrating recent studies in cultural anthropology; the history of capitalism, imperialism, and colonialism in both Atlantic and Mediterranean regions; accounts of native peoples after the arrival of Columbus in the Caribbean; and revisionist work on the English court, the royal family, early modern domestic situations, and the economic practices of the theater. The interaction among these materials has, furthermore, situated *The Tempest* at the site of significant controversy regarding the play's authority as a Shakespearean statement. Earlier concerns are not necessarily resolved or abandoned. They are, however, often *phrased* differently, as readers try to supply the adequate answer that typically eludes responses to the play.

For the last thirty years interpretations of *The Tempest* which privileged either historical, formalist, or theoretical approaches have been engaged in a struggle for dominance that has paradoxically revealed the indebtedness of each position to the other. It has gradually become clear that the struggle was not among history, formalism, and theory, since every interpretation must make some implicit or explicit use of these elements. Instead, disagreements about *The Tempest* result from interactions among competing versions of history, competing understandings of textuality, and competing senses of theory. The specific configurations of these interpretive elements determine the reading's rhetorical force and political affiliations.

In 1979 Charles Frey suggested that "we must go 'outside' the play to apprehend and create meanings for words and passages within it" (33). After examining Francis Fletcher's account of Drake's encounter with the Patagonians and other travel literature, Frey understood the play to be an imaginative site where history and romance are transformed into a work with both retrospective and prospective dimensions: "In melding history and romance, therefore, Shakespeare merely dramatized what his contemporaries enacted" (39). However, Frey's position in 1979 focused upon the enduring formal properties of the work; he stressed the universality of Shakespeare's poetry and its reduction of experience to the same: "As Shakespeare saw, our imaginations project in every world, old and new, the same surpassing story of a will to make a garden in a wilderness, to find the human fellowship that lies beyond all storm" ("*Tempest*" 39).

In 1995 Frey slightly altered his formalist commitment. Using phrases that recall the normative preoccupation (of the early twentieth century) with the higher causes of culture, humanity, and life, Frey insisted upon a second immediacy: "To rediscover through art that we live like winds and waters of the earth (melting into thin air, dissolving, minding our coursing blood) is to gain access to sensory being and beauty" (91). According to Frey, theoretically informed readings ignore "most of the concreteness—the material, sensuous, time-bound reality—of any specific practice of the play" ("Embodying" 90). The differences in phrasing between Frey's first essay in 1979 and his second in 1995 are telling. His use of the pastoral phrases of Kermode and Marx and the theme of human fellowship, which began with Hazlitt and was reformulated by Brower, are replaced by words that acknowledge cultural materialism ("social meaning" and "discursive capture") and deconstruction ("significance" and "supplement"). Yet, Frey turns these words against their theoretical positions by insisting upon an identity between the immediacy of experience and the sensuous presence of the signifier. Frey's insistence upon presence negates difference; however, he is not completely mistaken. There is *something* about *The Tempest* which refuses any kind of formal, theoretical, or historical reduction to the present, the past, or (possibly) the future.

Russ McDonald and Howell Chickering (172) believe that *something* to be the verse and song of *The Tempest*. McDonald agrees with Anne Barton's observation about the play's spiked use of spontaneous compounds (sea-change, cloud-capped, hag-seed, and man-monster) which drive toward linguistic compression while Shakespeare's disjunctive characterization, use of the unities, and strategic omission of details create the impression that the play is bigger than it is (McDonald 19). The verse is interlocked for McDonald, woven as if it were, etymologically speaking, a textile—or a baseless fabric. *The Tempest* is "uncommonly meaningful" for McDonald because its verbal music relates to the oneiric and unreal atmosphere of the text; yet, "it promises much and delivers little" (24). Although McDonald's essay promised a political reading of *The Tempest* in opposition to new historical readings (18), it reasserts positions similar to Paul Brown's and Terence Hawkes's: namely, that the play foregrounds undecidabilities that undermine ideological certainties. He differs from them in shaping his response to that uncertainty. *The Tempest* for McDonald "is one of the most knowing, most self-conscious texts in the canon" (27). However, because of his use of Brooks and Barthes, McDonald cannot assign this knowledge to Shakespeare. So we are left to ask: what kind of a play is it that, while it knows and promises to tell, also refuses to speak its knowledge?

Russ McDonald's attention to the pleasure of narrative delay (25–26) and Charles Frey's emphasis upon the "immersion in *now*" ("Embodying" 91) raise questions about the narrative temporality and dramatic design of *The Tempest* which were also addressed in essays by Stephen Miko in 1982, by Julian Patrick in 1983, and by John Turner in 1995. These discussions, like Frey's, use some deconstructive strategies; however, each essay in its own way, returned to a somewhat stable notion of the text or the author, often by repeating phrases from the normative, reductive, inflationary, or generalized modes. Miko proposed a skeptical and unsentimental reading of *The Tempest* as an experimental work which deliberately frustrates readers' expectations for poetic justice, symbolic neatness, and resolved endings (2). Relying upon the author as the site of a permissible incoherence, Miko wrote: "Shakespeare will not allow either unequivocal idealization or consistent 'realistic' parody" (15). While trying to understand why *The Tempest* has been so often adapted and retold, Julian Patrick's generic argument about romance usefully invokes Derrida's notion of the supplement, but his reading (which emphasizes shared patterns more than their displacement) is ultimately more formal than deconstructive. (The problem of *The Tempest*'s repetitive, generative capacity has also been usefully addressed from radically different perspectives by M. C. Bradbrook, Lorie Leininger, and Ruby Cohn.) By joining the apparently incompatible strategies of Bettelheim and Malinowski, John Turner expected to describe how "*The Tempest* performs its healing work—within the individual and within society"; he also hoped to suggest "how the historically specific form of Shakespearian drama brings history itself into play, offering us provisional readings of our common human destiny in no matter what society we find ourselves" (106). No matter how antithetical or undecidable its design, *The Tempest*—for Miko, Patrick, and Turner—is not as radically plural (and, therefore, indeterminate) as it is in the influential cultural materialist scholarship of Terence Hawkes, Francis Barker and Peter Hulme, and Paul Brown.

"What we actually have in the play," James Stephens suggests in an essay commissioned for this volume, "is a series of spectacles, all profound, none interpretable, despite the words" (532). For Stephens the artificial spectacle of the storm does not annihilate as a natural tempest might; instead, it merely pinches the passengers because it is Prospero's artifice. Similarly, while Miranda's empathic appeal "waylays perdition and pinches us all" (533) the miracle of her natural existence saves her father. Ferdinand and Miranda combine, like the double helix, the attributes of nature and providence that are kept separate in Caliban and Ariel (533). When Ariel interrupts Antonio and Sebastian conspiring against Alonso and Gonzalo, who has a "tendency to 'cram words' against the 'stomach' of sense" (534), Stephens thinks in a carefully qualified way that "it appears at this point that providence, thanks to art, is winning over human nature" (535). Designed like a ballet or a neatly-stitched fabric, the play has clowns (who mistake nature for providence) follow politicians (for whom living is plotting while they are uncertain if their salvation is like that of creatures in a Resurrection pageant). Prospero too is pinched by his own device when he sees Gonzalo weep tears "like winter's drops" (540–41). In contrast to Miko's, Patrick's and Turner's interpretations, nature, love, providence, art, and the great mysteries of human existence all displace one another in Stephens' version of this play, as Shakespeare dramatizes that "As we age, as our experience accumulates, as we gradually take in a lifetime of living, we find that we cannot utter what we know" (532).

Hayden White proposed that the absurdist (or poststructuralist) mode of literary criticism began in the 1960s when the ideas of Roland Barthes, Michel Foucault, and Jacques Derrida reduced literature to writing, while they used structuralist theories of the sign to redescribe writing as an arbitrary system of signification that will always defer, delay, and displace meaning (268–69, 278–82). Moreover, poststructuralists also proposed that "by their very nature as social products, art and literature are not only complicit in the violence which sustains a given form of society, they even have their own dark underside and origin in criminality, barbarism, and will-to-destruction" (269). As we have seen, a reductive trend within *Tempest* criticism preceded the poststructualist turn. Empson questioned the fascism in Traversi's view of Caliban; Leech continued Strachey's attack upon a serene Prospero and Shakespeare; Berger used the reductive ideas of Freud to stress Prospero's entrapped disillusionment with art; Kott used the structuralism of Levi-Strauss to demonstrate how *The Tempest* was able to connect widely disparate mythological systems, ritual practices, and historical narratives; Erlich provided a Marxist reading that ironically reasserted that Shakespeare held the colonialist view of G. Wilson Knight. Yet, most of these readings (by repeating phrases from earlier interpretations) linked themselves to modes of criticism that believed historical materials provided background for a stable work which possessed a meaning (determined by the author's intention) that paradoxically freed the work from historical limitations because it would remain identical with itself for all time.

Marxist and politically subversive interpretations of *The Tempest* required strategies of interpretation that could free them from the constraints of these earlier reductive positions while offering their position a concept of the materiality and iterability of the signfier. However, the poststructuralist solution came at some cost: referentiality and history also appeared to vanish. As the interpretations of McDonald, Miko, Patrick, and Turner indicate, poststructuralist readings found it very difficult to remain rigorously consistent to deconstructive strategies. The most rigorous attention to textual indeterminacy is found in the materialist reading of Terence Hawkes. Reactions to Hawkes often turned to the work of Raymond Williams, whose *Marxism and Literature*, published in 1977, wrestled with the poststructuralist discussion of the sign and its consequences for history, and his work became central for the development of cultural materialist readings of *The Tempest*. Similar to C. L. Barber's notion of the interaction between dramatic form and social custom in *Shakespeare's Festive Comedy*, Williams described the work of art as a social practice. Williams's theory is neither reductive nor inflationary since it accounts for the way the art work represents (*mimesis*) and shapes (*poiesis*) history and culture. Nor is the materialist idea fully compatible with Jonathan Goldberg, whose discussion of the Jonsonian masque reduced historical experience to textuality (57–58, 65).

Relying upon an idea of Levi-Strauss, which was then complicated by Derrida, Terence Hawkes noted: "All cultures find themselves impelled to divide the world into the fundamental categories of human and non-human, and when the division between these becomes blurred or uncertain, the effect is undoubtedly troubling" (26). *The Tempest* makes this trouble, specifically when Trinculo, upon first seeing Caliban, worries whether he is monster or man: "should Caliban cross that boundary, it would mean that the category of 'man' is not the closed, finished and well-defined entity that sustains and is sustained by a European taxonomy" (26). Hawkes deconstructed Trinculo's comments about Caliban to notice that the economic and cultural senses of the word *make* destablize each other: "the slippage between signifier and signified proves as difficult to control here as it does in the terms 'man' and 'monster.' If any strange beast can make a man, the distinction between these is no simple matter" (27). By following through on these observations, for Hawkes *The Tempest* becomes "a text whose plurality makes it an arena for the sifting of the immense issue: what makes a man?" (29). "To make a man is to make sense. And who makes sense, makes history" (30).

Hawkes contrasted Walter Raleigh's reading of *The Tempest* in a lecture on July 4, 1918 with his use of the play some fourteen years earlier in a 1905 edition of Hakluyt's *Principal Navigations*. Hawkes thought that "both readings are of course partial, harshly reducing what we have readily recognized as the text's plurality to the dimensions of a single, coherent statement" (39–40). Raleigh's Trinculo in 1904 was a drunken butler, and Caliban an example of Shakespeare's sympathetic understanding of uncivilized man. Under the quite different ideological pressures of American entry into World War I, Raleigh's Caliban becomes a German and Trinculo "a sturdy, good-natured 'non-commissioned officer'" (39). When Walter Raleigh opposed the denigration of *all* Germans into Calibans and orang-outangs, he was attacked by a *Times* reporter for "outrageously extolling the virtues of our enemies" (42). "My point is not that [Raleigh] was engaged in any illicit importation into Shakespeare of the extraneous political considerations in that, beyond those, there lies a comforting, unchanging, permanent Shakespearean play to which we can finally turn" (Hawkes 42). Unlike Stoll who preserved a place for opposition by insisting upon the author's intentions as the final arbiter, Hawkes does not appear to have a conceptual language for the ways the radical plurality of *The Tempest* resists ideological appropriation—except when readers or actors use it differently and in different historical or political contexts. Textuality is almost entirely reduced to subjectivity: the play apparently means whatever any reader can make it mean on any particular occasion. "Shakespeare's texts always yield to, though they never can be reduced to, the readings we give them: their plurality makes Walter Raleighs of us all" (42–3).

Barker and Hulme, while building upon Hawkes's insights, also tried to avoid the difficulty of his position by thinking of the text as an "historical utterance" which must be read "with and within a series of *con-texts*" (194–95). These con-texts have been paradoxically concealed and forgotten by a literary criticism which has recognized and abolished history through various processes of mystification, including the use of source study (preoccupied with Shakespeare's knowledge and intentions) and literary-historical accounts of developing traditions and genres. Frank Kermode, who serves as their example for this process, placed Caliban at the core of the play's preoccupations with the nature/art debate; however, he also occluded Caliban's political claims. Similarly, Kermode's discussion of the Bermuda pamphlets as sources for Shakespeare's language in the text paradoxically marginalizes them from any relevance for the play's structure of ideas (195). Therefore, Barker and Hulme proposed an *alternative* to the ways *Tempest* criticism has located the play "*over against* its contexts" by describing it in a Saussurean fashion: "no text is intelligible except in its differential relations with other texts" (192). However, since an alternative criticism, according to Barker and Hulme, risks surrendering historical ground to poststructuralist textuality, they suggest that "successive textual inscriptions" must not abandon the "no longer privileged but still crucially important *first* inscription of the text" (194).

By examining Prospero's "version of true beginnings" as he provides *authoritative* but nevertheless shaky versions of Ariel's and Caliban's past, Barker and Hulme argued that Prospero refuses to engage in a debate about Caliban's claim to own the island. Instead, the displaced Italian duke engages in an "indirect denial" by calling Caliban a "lying slave," and then moves to a counter accusation charging Caliban with the attempted rape of Miranda. Indirect denial and counter accusation "together foreclose the exchange and serve in practice as Prospero's only justification for the arbitrary rule he exercises over the island and its inhabitants. At a stroke he erases from . . . Prospero's play all trace of the moment of his reduction of Caliban to slavery and appropriation of his island" (199–200). This play about usurpation, argued Barker and Hulme, is "systematically silent about Prospero's own act of usurpation" (200). "Through its very occulsion of Caliban's version of proper beginnings, Prospero's disavowal is itself performative of the discourse of colonialism," Barker and Hulme suggested, since indirect denial and counter accusation was the trope used by European colonial regimes to assert "their authority over land to which they could have no conceivable legitimate claim" (200).

According to Paul Brown, *The Tempest* "declares no all-embracing triumph for colonialism" (68). Instead, when Shakespeare's play ends with gestures of renunciation and restoration, the text's colonialist discourse struggles ambivalently among apotheosis, mystification, and potential erosion: "the narrative ultimately fails to deliver that containment and instead may be seen to foreground precisely those problems which it works to efface or overcome" (48). Shakespeare's play (now more than an "historical utterance") is an *intervention* in a colonial project—that operated (according to Wallerstein's terminology) upon the English-Welsh mainland at its "core"; in Ireland at the "semi-periphery"; and in America at the "periphery" (51–52). Brown observed that the colonial project conflated various discourses of class, race, gender, and courtly politics in order to *produce* continually an apparent triumph of civility, which "seeks at once to harmonize disjunction, to transcend irreconcilable contradictions and to mystify the political conditions which demand colonialist discourse" (48).

Brown identified several places where these interventions are staged in the work, and the ambivalence of colonial discourse is exposed through various repetitions. In speaking to Miranda Prospero is forced to remember his own forgetfulness concerning his loss of Milan (59). Prospero must remind Ariel every month of his indebtedness, an act which continually reminds Prospero of his promises to release and his threats to incarcerate Ariel (60). Prospero's account also becomes vulnerable to subversion when he becomes identified with Sycorax: "both rulers are magicians, both have been exiled because of their practices, both have nurtured children on the isle" (61). Caliban incites Prospero's anger by not coming when called, by greeting the colonizers with a curse, and by designating Prospero as a usurper of his isle and his hospitality (61). Brown believes Caliban masters enough of the lessons of civility to ensure that his interpellation within it remains inadequate. "Whatever Caliban does with this gift [of language] announces his capture by it" (61). Caliban is capable of resistance, since he is both a *producer* of his own counter-narratives and the *produced* other used by the colonizer to enforce his rule. Colonial discourse is vulnerable to Caliban's efforts, because it undertakes "to represent seamlessly and palatably what in reality is a contest between a censorship and a latent drive" (66). That is, in his attempt to describe for historical purposes the play's use of colonial discourse, Brown deploys Freud's description of the dreamwork's strategies of displacement, condensation, symbolization, and secondary revision (66, 71 n.35).

For Deborah Willis "Brown's representation of otherness in colonial discourse seems one-dimensional and, at times, ahistorical" (288 n. 11). Willis also thought Brown overlooked that Shakespeare's *positive* treatment of "colonialism at the core" differs from his *problematic* understanding of it at the periphery. The colonial venture, for Willis, is subordinate to the play's engagement with oligarchy and division: "the play's true threatening 'other' is not Caliban, but Antonio" (280). Cynthia Lewis's recent book retrieves hagiographic and theatrical traditions that support Willis's claim. In *Shakespearean Eschatology* Cynthia Marshall also qualified Brown's view by noticing that colonialist discussions were "deeply ambiguated by eschatological rhetoric" (87). Drawing upon Shannon Miller's idea that Spenser "reinvents Ireland as a 'colony' that is like the Spanish possessions in the New World," David J. Baker thinks that in early modern England Miranda's condemnation of Caliban would have echoed debates about England's domination of the Gaels (71). And, by drawing upon Jeffrey Knapp's idea that Shakespeare used *The Tempest* to distract the English from the distractions and magical amusements of their colonial enterprises, Baker suggests Shakespeare "would have had a shrewd sense of the implications of New World discoveries for more familiar domains such as Ireland" (80). Therefore, Baker challenges Willis's attack upon Paul Brown, while qualifying his use of Wallerstein, since Brown "located the play within an expanded geo-political field" (82).

Gonzalo's comment that "This Tunis, sir, was Carthage" has become a touchstone for revisionist European readings of the play that take account of colonial concerns. Troubled at times by a naive topicality reminiscent of Frances Yates's view that Shakespeare's magus was John Dee, Richard Wilson recently made a persuasive case that Prospero was modeled after Robert Dudley, a transatlantic voyager and the most important Englishman in Italy, "pirate, redemptor, and renegade Lord of Shakespeare's Stratford" (352). By returning *The Tempest* to its Mediterranean contexts involving English piracy, white slavery, the redemptionist orders of the Trinitarians and the Knights of San Stephano, and the diplomacy over the proposed marriage between Prince Henry and Caterina, the daughter of the Grand Duke of Tuscany—, Wilson tried to restore some ambivalence to the ethical debate surrounding post-colonial readings. Drawing upon Wilson while remaining affiliated with a post-colonial politics, in 1998 Jerry Brotton argued that "Colonial readings have persistently elided Prospero's Italian identity" (30). The colonial American emphasis also concealed the play's direct inversion of Aeneas's voyage to Carthage and Caliban's specifically African lineage, including a possible allusion to the Italian town of Calibria on the African coastline, prominently featured on maps and atlases since 1529 (40 n. 21). Brotton recalls that "North Africa became the geographical point of military and political confrontation" between the Ottoman and Hapsburg Empires: "the voyage undertaken by Alonso and his retinue from Naples to Tunis in *The Tempest* was a voyage that traversed one of the most contested stretches of water within the Mediterranean World" (34). The "first organized English forays into the eastern Mediterranean took place" after the Ottomans recaptured Tunis in 1574, forcing the Hapsburg authorities "to pursue more fruitful expansion in the Americas" (35). When "refracted through the lens" of post-colonial theory, *The Tempest*, according to Brotton, "ultimately reflects the belatedness and subsequent subordination of English forays into the Mediterranean, and not the rise of English colonialism" (37). David Scott Kastan, while suggesting Prospero was drawn from Rudolph II, has also recently proposed that "the critical emphasis upon the New World not only obscures the play's more prominent discourses of dynastic politics but also blinds us to disturbances in the text that should alert us to this aspect of the play's engagement with its own historical moment" (95). Kastan finds the play's anchoring historical moment in King James's need to strengthen his alliance with the Protestant Evangelical Union and his desire to "counterbalance the destablizing aggressions of the Hapsburg monarchy" (98).

While considering apparently all relevant colonial contexts simultaneously, Barbara Fuchs has perhaps come the closest to resolving the false choices among these historical debates over the relevance of Ireland, America, Northern Africa, Europe, the Atlantic, the Mediterranean, and the Levant and the various contact zones among native Americans, the Irish, the English, the Hapsburgs, and the Ottomans among others. Fuchs thinks that just like metaphors or puns, "context, too, may be polysemous" (45). Following up on Cheyfitz's discussion of Caliban's (Jewish) gabardine, she noticed how colonialist ideology was "quoted" when early modern writers referred to the works of earlier planters and explorers. For example, Fuchs writes: "Even Powhattan's dress was described by one of John Smith companions as 'a faire Robe of skins as large as an Irish mantle'" (51). For Fuchs "the metonymic reduction of Islam to the figure of the witch is perverse, for what is at stake in the Mediterranean is not the 'Satanic' side of Islam—which Sycorax might represent—but its military might" (61). Claribel is placed at considerable distance by Antonio and Sebastian, and she becomes "Tunis" in order "to fix Islam firmly in Africa" (59) so that "In *The Tempest* gender does the work of imperialism rather than of discovery" (60).

In "Peopling, Profiting, and Pleasure in *The Tempest*" Barbara Ann Sebek examines the ideological requirements of proto-capitalist economic configurations and their intersection with the regulation of sexual relations. Her essay, specifically written for this volume, navigates the sometimes turbulent, often too calm, channels between Marxist and feminist modes of analysis by focusing on how the play's depiction of Miranda troubles binaries between ruler and laborer, gift and commodity, gender and class. For Sebek "Aristocratic Miranda is to be among those profiting from, not coupling with, the natives" (468). Many feminist readings overlook Ferdinand's pleasure in log-bearing, according to Sebek, which separates him from Caliban for whom it is painful and enforced. "For Ferdinand labor *is* pleasure" because he desires Miranda. Sebek thinks about how the conceptual status of persons and goods in commodity exchange becomes confused, and how the play's treatment of the courtship of Miranda registers this confusion. And Sebek successfully complicates what is too often taken as a conceptual given by other feminist readings of the play—that early modern women functioned as mere objects of exchange between men. For Sebek Miranda herself is an active, pleasure-taking subject who gives herself away before Prospero hands her over to Ferdinand. By offering to perform Ferdinand's labor, Miranda unsettles the paradigm: she becomes aligned with the labor pool, yet she also "resists being positioned as the prize that is labored for"—a logic that threatens the logic of a commodity economy (470). Sebek's essay stands apart from other feminist readings of the play (including work by Lorie Leininger, Frances Dolan, Kim Hall, Jyotsna Singh, and Denise Albanese) by following through on the ways class and labor issues complicate matters of gender and race.

In 1980 Leininger found that *The Tempest* continued to reproduce oppressive patriarchal confusions, and she tried to imagine a Miranda who would join with Caliban to reject Prospero's authority, the fantasy of slaves as subhuman, and any sense of herself as subservient. In 1992 Frances Dolan read *The Tempest* (as an early modern representation that shed light upon "petty treason," the interdependency of superiors and subordinates, and the precariousness of the master's authority) along with the narratives from the rape and sodomy trial of the earl of Castlehaven and the anonymous *Arden of Faversham* in her study of "dangerous familiars." Disagreeing with Curt Breight's notion that "'in structural terms Prospero always needs a demonic 'other'," Dolan suggests: "Prospero needs not an *other* as much as a servant . . . who while he may be demonic, is also domestic" (67). Caliban for Dolan threatens because he is the outsider-within who knows Prospero too well. Dolan's argument finally stresses containment: "Shakespeare's masterful manipulation of form in *The Tempest* results from his privileging the master's story over the slave's" (*Dangerous* 70). Kim Hall (discussed earlier on) and Jyotsna Singh demonstrate how post-colonial uses of the play continued to ignore or keep women in a subordinate place while overlooking the potential alliance between Miranda and Caliban that was seen by Leininger. Using Levi-Strauss, Mauss, and Rubin, Singh notes: "Though Miranda has a position of colonial superiority over Caliban, she nonetheless has a marginal role within a *kinship* system in which all three males [Prospero, Caliban, and Ferdinand] are bonded through their competing claims on her" (198). As a gift subject to exchange among men, Miranda confers solidarity as well as incites competition. Singh argues that Césaire's *A Tempest* only reversed the Hegelian roles of master and slave while doing little to question hierarchical structures (193–94). Césaire and Lamming posited revolutionary utopias which marginalize Miranda and Sycorax, and Fanon used the metaphor of the white woman as representative of white culture while never giving serious consideration to a fruitful partnership with a native woman (195). Denise Albanese supplements the colonialist reading of *The Tempest* with a reading that examines the "New Science" and its reciprocal interventions upon race and gender in the play. Using the work of Donna Haraway and the phrases of Foucault and Lacan, Albanese studies Miranda (by placing her among women primatologists such as Jane Goodall and Sara Blaffer Hrdy) to examine various continguities among the discourses of race, gender, science, nature, and art that are figured in the play as the play figures in the early modern construction of the "New Science."

Just as Willis, Lewis, Marshall, Baker, Wilson, Brotton, and Kastan return the play to old world contexts, a New World emphasis also persists—often seeking ways to identify the interactions among familiar and unfamiliar worlds and cultures. Finding no justification for the claim that English colonialism provides *the* dominant discursive context for *The Tempest*, in 1995 William M. Hamlin situated the play within the context of early modern ethnographic discourses he found in Alvar Nunez Cabeza de Vaca, Jean de Léry, José de Acosta, Walter Raleigh, William Strachey, and John Smith. This discourse qualifies Greenblatt's views to suggest certain early modern voyagers and ethnographers could "[acknowledge] *difference* without immediately concluding inferiority or [acknowledge] *equality* without positing identity" (107). In a similar (but reversed) effort in 1992, Jeffrey L. Hantman created a "Virginian Indian" context for reading Caliban's character by adding "the voices of three Calibans—Powhatan, Opechancanough, and Amoroleck—to the continuing discourse on otherness (79).

Significant work, however, continues to recover the complicated ways the old and the new world were materially and ideologically connected. While Greenblatt's early work focused on linguistic colonialism in the new world, his later writing has traced the negotiations among European and American materials. The reverse is true for Orgel, who began by examining the role of the court masque in Shakespeare's plays (*Illusion*) and later studied the iconographic old world representations of new world natives ("Shakespeare"). John Gillies's *Shakespeare and the Geography of Difference* reads Prospero as a voyager, shaped by cartographic discourses and their exotic margins. And Jonathan Baldo has examined new and old world materials in light of the discourse of forgetfulness. In an essay written for this volume, Geraldo U. de Sousa thinks *The Tempest* speaks more fundamentally to the problem of context as "History, ecology, and romance converge in the play's exploration of our relationship to place" ("Alien" 440). In earlier work on the play Sousa had suggested "The absence of the wife casts Prospero into the role of a woman— the role of the Other" (55): ". . . Prospero represents the battleground of a culture made uncomfortable when it senses the presence of its Other" ("*Tempest*" 54). And Sousa had also studied how the masque demonstrates the play's roots in romance and its generic ability to resist closure and break boundaries ("Closure"). In highly original work for this volume, Sousa asserts that *The Tempest*'s performances coincided with a period of intense preoccupation with domestic environmental policy and widespread deforestation in England. Addressing Parliament at Whitehall on March 21, 1609/10, King James urged passage of a new Statute for preservation of woods. Sousa proposes that this environmental concern resonates in *The Tempest* along with the Bermuda pamphlets and other New World travel literature.

Two other essays written specifically for this volume demonstrate how a reader's contextual choices and interpretive questions shape one's sense of the text and vice versa. Drawing upon her experience as an international theater critic, Claudia Harris explores several experimental productions of the play (including ones in the Netherlands and China, as well as ones by Peter Brook, Giorgio Strehler, and more recently by the Island Theatre Company at Kilmainham Gaol during the 1993 Dublin Theatre Festival and by the Royal Shakespeare Company at Stratford in the same season). Harris demonstrates how each new production comments upon its predecessors and how the social and political implications of these performances cross a spectrum from mere happenstance to a deliberate intention to change an audience's beliefs and behavior. "The power and popularity of *The Tempest*," Harris suggests, "rests in how well it invites exploration of [quoting Brook] 'the whole condition of man,' in how well it taps into intercultural root paradigms" (566). In a personal interview with Declan Donnellan, Harris learned about the theatrical genealogy surrounding Sam Mendes's decision in the RSC production to have Ariel at the moment of his release spit upon Prospero. The effect was borrowed from a 1988 Cheek by Jowl production Donnellan directed. On the evening

Harris was present for the RSC performance it happened that Prince Charles and Prince William were in audience—the gesture's significance was altered through the contingent interaction of art and politics, actors and audience.

Edward O'Shea, in an essay also written for this volume, examines the interplay between the cultural formation of late Anglo-American modernism and three modernist adaptations of *The Tempest*: W. H. Auden's *The Sea and The Mirror*, Virginia Woolf's *Between the Acts*, and Sir Michael Tippett's opera, *The Knot Garden*. Auden, Woolf, and Tippett share a sense of impasse or an experience of exhaustion, and they each turn to *The Tempest* (and to the ways it was commonly used during the modernist period) to fashion their unique responses to that exhaustion: Auden writes a poetic "commentary"; Woolf makes use of the pageant or masque in Miss Latrobe's attempt at a "total theater" which enacts English history from Chaucer to the present; and Tippett, while making direct use of Woolf's last novel, recasts *The Tempest* as an opera that eschews "Shakespeare's masque with its associations with ceremony, panoply and potential historical reference" (553).

O'Shea's essay suggests that *The Sea and the Mirror* documents a crucial moment in Auden's personal retreat from the idea that poetry can effect social change while he rejects performance practices that emphasized the unified effects and homogeneous illusions of *total theater*, represented by Orson Welles's 1937 production of *Julius Caesar*. O'Shea also proposes that Auden reversed the pattern G. Wilson Knight found in *The Tempest*, drawn from Dante, of a "serene and mystic joy": Caliban anchors *The Sea and the Mirror*, and Prospero's epilogue is replaced by Ariel's brief postscript; the action takes place after the play is completed; and the laconic, sometimes mute characters do not interact at all. Auden's Miranda comes the closest to romance; yet, she speaks the language of nursery rhyme, fairy tale and ballad and seems immature, fixated at a narcissistic stage.

D. Shakespeare's Agency

While providing direction for interpretations of *The Tempest* that displace the sentimental and valedictory readings which often identify Prospero with Shakespeare, Stephen Greenblatt and Stephen Orgel will acknowledge the need to reassess Shakespeare's agency as a writer and artist, but they do not always allow for readings that see *The Tempest* as *either* Shakespeare's own commentary (upon his sources or his contemporaries, for instance) *or* as his own deliberate, formal reflection upon the pressures of his time as well as upon his own, often distinctively human, preoccupations.

In *Shakespearean Negotiations* Greenblatt redescribed textuality as the circulation of social energy. He replaced "a total artist," who "through training, resourcefulness, and talent, is at the moment of creation complete unto himself" (2) with "a subtle, elusive set of exchanges, a network of trades and trade-offs, a jostling of competing representations, a negotiation between joint-stock companies" (7). However, some readers (like Meredith Skura, John Turner, and Richard Wheeler) wonder if there may be a mediating position between these extremes that would neither reduce human agency to exchange nor posit an artist "complete unto himself." For Orgel, who follows through on the idea that *The Tempest* is like a psychoanalytic case history, the text and its performances are not stable, objective accounts but collaborative fantasies which erode the boundaries between the text as an historical utterance and any particular reader's or culture's use of the work ("Prospero's" 218). For Stephen Orgel, *The Tempest* is, "both less and more than literature"—a script, poetry, drama, a printed text, and a series of performances real and imagined: "For all our intuitions of autobiography, the author in it is characteristically unassertive, and offers little guidance in questions of interpretation or coherence" (Introduction 12). In another context, however, Orgel *cannot* refrain from speculating about Shakespeare's intentions: "Since Shakespeare was free to have Antonio repent if that is what he had in mind—half a line would have done for critics craving a reconciliation—we ought to take seriously the possibility that that is not what he had in mind. Perhaps, too, penitence is not what Prospero's magic is designed to elicit from his brother" ("Prospero's" 226).

Clearly, some conceptual adjustments are needed to provide alternatives and, if possible, to resolve the contradictions Orgel's positions entail. How can interpreters identify a writer's choices while continuing to describe the text as unassertive? The answer may be that some writer's choices are not assertive, but this is difficult to imagine given Orgel's example of Shakespeare's Antonio). For Paul Yachnin Shakespeare's presence for biographical readings "exists only in the interstices between the text and the act of interpretation" (122). Finding that "unrevealed meaning is far more suggestive of authorial presence than meaning which is both revealed and easily comprehended" (122), Yachnin thinks Shakespeare's presence in the play is based upon the same techniques of ambiguity, inconsistency, and overdetermination which make his three-dimensional characters like Macbeth and Claudius appear convincingly self-conscious; however, in *The Tempest* Shakespeare designs two-dimensional characters in order to deploy his techniques over the play as a whole "so that we are made aware of an authorial presence above or behind the whole play" (122, 127). Yachnin thinks, ". . . Prospero is not Shakespeare. Prospero is rather Shakespeare's progenitor, the artificial person who summons his own creator into being" (128). Another alternative may be that the work of art reciprocally shapes (or works upon) a writer's decisions—allowing the writer to make use of assertions, while the text is not fully determined by them. Given Prospero's association with Shakespeare, the history of the play's interpretations shows that attempts to repress the agency of writers must suffer their return, while any insistence upon total authorial control will eventually find the work either isolated in a meaningless past or fully merged with (and indistinguishable from) each reader's passing bias. Reminiscent of Terence Hawkes's indeterminate text, Orgel's position is a variation upon Roland Barthes's notion of a plural *text* that operates as an open, methodological field:

> The text, in its mass, is comparable to a sky, at once flat and smooth, deep, without edges and without landmarks; like the soothsayer drawing on it with the tip of his staff an imaginary rectangle wherein to consult, according to certain principles, the flight of birds, the commentator traces through the text certain zones of reading, in order to observe therein the migration of meanings, the outcropping of codes, the passage of citations. (14)

This image of the commentator as soothsayer, however, only partially (and inadequately) describes the situation. If Orgel's contradictory comments are going to be reconciled, two problems with Barthes's image need to be considered. *First*, writers (especially those who use sources) are also commentators; they are soothsayers in their own right. *Second*, commentators not only interact with the text and the writer but also with other commentators and the history of their phrasing. That is, each person is caught up (with others) in the problematic play of inquiry and interpretation. These interactions continually redescribe the relations among the purposes, the materials, and the formal properties of the writer's work, advancing (sometimes in a discontinuous, contentious manner) intractable questions often under the guise of "smooth and definite answers," while the critical conversation advances a knowledge which remains open to revision.

In "Martial Law in the Land of Cockaigne" Greenblatt's Shakespeare, "near the close of his career" and reflecting upon "his own art with still greater intensity and self-consciousness than in *Measure for Measure*," conceived of the playwright as "a princely creator of anxiety" (*Shakespearean* 142). While there was perhaps a residual formalism in Greenblatt's "Learning to Curse," (as he distinguished what the play and Shakespeare actually *do* apart from Prospero's actions), this distinction collapsed at times in the later essay when Greenblatt fused Shakespeare's role with Prospero's. Revealing that a salutary anxiety is his to create and allay, Prospero not only "harrows the other characters with fear and wonder" (142); he also "puts himself through the paralyzing uneasiness with which he has afflicted others" (*Shakespearean* 144).

Using Foucault's phrases about power, knowledge, surveillance, and disciplinary technologies of the self, as well as anecdotes taken from William Strachey's account of the Gates expedition; a sermon by Hugh Latimer; accounts of James's execution of Watson, Clarke, and Brooke for their role in the Bye Plot, and of James's last minute pardon of Lords Grey, Cobham and Markham; as well as Shakespeare's appropriation of these techniques in the disguised Duke Vincentio's conversations with Claudio and Juliet—, Greenblatt redescribed a common distinction within *Tempest* criticism. Although it is customary to say that Prospero could use his magic to coerce the bodies of his enemies, it is often thought (by Miko and Turner, for instance) that Prospero could not control the minds of others. For Margreta de Grazia the question of what causes men to act arises repeatedly in the play. "As a result of virtually nothing," she writes, "a momentous change occurs in *The Tempest*" (249). That is, the play holds out the hope, (embodied in the figures of Ariel, Miranda, and Gonzalo) that persons "can act in response to what does not [physically] touch them personally . . ." ("*Tempest*" 249). More tough-minded than de Grazia, Orgel thinks the play presents "a fantasy about controlling other people's minds"; yet, the magic only works "indifferently well" (225). Prospero's power will achieve "a final assertion of authority and control: he has now arranged matters so that his death will remove Antonio's last link with the ducal power" ("Prospero's" 228). In an essay written for this volume, Robert Hapgood finds Prospero "prescient but not omniscient and certainly not omnipotent"; unlike Oberon, "he cannot finally control the fundamental attitudes of others, cannot compel those who resist his influence to submit to it willingly" (422). Greenblatt found instead that Prospero treats both his enemies and Miranda to an intense experience of suffering in the storm:

> Her suffering is the prelude to the revelation of her identity, as if Prospero believes that this revelation can be meaningful only in the wake of amazement and pity he artfully arouses. He is setting out to fashion her identity, just as he is setting out to refashion the inner lives of his enemies, and he employs comparable disciplinary techniques. (*Shakespearean* 142–43)

By accusing Ferdinand of treason and by using his magic "to cause a kind of paralysis," Prospero has the lovers pass through a ritual of humiliation and suffering which achieves its desired effect (*Shakespearean* 144).

According to Greenblatt, Strachey's Bermuda narrative tells of a state of emergency and a crisis of authority that results in a collapse of social distinctions between laborers and rulers. Strachey's and Shakespeare's account share—"a violent tempest, a providential shipwreck on a strange island, a crisis in authority provoked by danger and excess, a fear of lower-class disorder and upper-class ambition, a triumphant affirmation of absolute control linked to the manipulation of anxiety and to a departure from the island" (154). Yet, Shakespeare's play ends with an abjuration of authority, and his island is not uninhabited, is in the Mediterranean, and is not part of a colonial adventure. These differences foreground the play's swerve away from Strachey's materials:

> Detached from their context in Strachey's letter, these elements *may be transformed and recombined* with materials drawn from other writers about the New World who differ sharply from Strachey in their interests and motives—Montaigne, Sylvester Jourdain, James Rosier, Robert Eden, Peter Martyr—and integrated into a dramatic text that draws on a wide range of

discourse, including pastoral and epic poetry, the lore of magic and witchcraft, literary romance, and a remarkable number of Shakespeare's own earlier plays. (emphasis added, 155)

By observing *The Tempest*'s similarities and differences from Strachey's
account, Greenblatt traced the process whereby the Bermuda narrative "is
made negotiable, turned into a currency that may be transferred from one
institutional context to another" (*Shakespearean* 155). However, Greenblatt
elides the distinctively human agency of Shakespeare, the writer or commentator who, participating in the event of *The Tempest*, "transforms and recom-
bines" the materials within the play.

   Finding that new historicist readings are set into motion by the collapse
of a distinction between a (fictional, authored) work and a (factual, non-
authored) document, Margreta de Grazia makes it possible to see, first, that a
change in one's theory of the text alters both the contextual materials one may
consider relevant and the interpretive outcome. Second, she implies that
Greenblatt's view (concerning how materials are transformed and recombined
in the play) reduces Shakespeare's humanity to an economic principle of
selection and circulation.

   Indeed *history* for Greenblatt is mainly comprised of stories, homologous
   stories that can be paratactically juxtaposed. No discrimination need be
   made between testimony, eyewitness account, official report, letter, play,
   journal entry: all qualify as social practices demonstrating the same strategy.... The authenticity of the documents (a crucial consideration for Malone) is never at issue. No longer is it necessary to ask whether the accounts
   are factual or fictional, for all collapse into the intermediary category of the
   anecdote. ("What" 202)

De Grazia notes that Malone (discussed in detail in her *Shakespeare Verbatim*)
was aware of the period's deep investment in the expedition to Virginia and in
controlling propaganda about establishing a settlement. Yet, *The Tempest* (in
Malone's words, "converted by the magical hand of Shakespeare almost into
Fairy Tale" [qtd. in de Grazia]) remained "resistant to the incursions of its topical source as documented by Jourdain's eyewitness and Strachey's authoritative pamphlets" (201). Although de Grazia's distinction between a text and a
document is problematic, she concludes (in a manner which echoes Barker's
and Hulme's position about source study) that Malone "demonstrates how historical documentation can work to sequester the play from rather than involve
it in historical process" (201). Yet, she assigns a very different value to this
sequestration: "Knowing the date of the seastorm and calculating the time
when news of it would reach Shakespeare, [Malone] situates the play not in
global history, but in Shakespeare's unique history, that is, the history of his
artistic development, his chronology" ("What" 201).

Richard Wheeler, following directions suggested in his own earlier work on *The Tempest* in *Shakespeare's Development and the Problem Comedies* and *The Whole Journey* (written with C. L. Barber), is not as concerned with how Prospero remembers his past as he is concerned "with how the play remembers its past, with how *The Tempest* looks back on, and takes its place within, Shakespearean history" ("Fantasy" 128). Written for the Open University's "Theory in Practice" series, Wheeler's essay, "Fantasy and History in *The Tempest*," foregrounds the three reciprocal, interpretive categories that any adequate reading requires—theory, context, and textuality. Using Hans Loewald's psychoanalytic description of repression, individuation, and repetition, Wheeler suggests the "historicity that is built into individual development" is missing from cultural materialist discussions of *The Tempest* which submerge the individual and the human beneath the ideological and political. That is, Wheeler understands individual historicity as a psychoanalytic process as the subject separates and distinguishes itself from the undifferentiated maternal environment by passing through psychosexual developmental stages culminating in the Oedipus complex and its dissolution—a process of estrangement or repression. Wheeler's work shares some of the same theoretical values as Greenblatt's (given their mutual use of C. L. Barber's work, discussed by Wheeler in his introduction to Barber's *Creating Elizabethan Tragedy*); however, Wheeler's psychoanalytic reading of the play tries to name what is "distinctive to Shakespeare within his own age" while attempting "to bridge the gap between his historical moment and ours" (160).

Finding that *The Tempest* dramatizes "a father's relinquishing to another, younger man, the daughter upon whom his life has been centered ever since his exile to the island, and whose entry into adult sexuality must be her exit from his world," Wheeler asks: "But what enables Prospero to do what Lear could not? Or, what enables Shakespeare to move from the destructive exploration of Lear's love for Cordelia to the comic outcome of Prospero's love for Miranda?" (139).

Wheeler's complex answer finds parallels for Caliban's lyricism and Prospero's aggressive theatricality, on one hand, with Shakespeare's own potentiality for adoring self-surrender embodied in many of the sonnets and the distancing control he achieves through the drama, on the other. In Prospero's image of Antonio as "The ivy which had hid my princely trunk, / And sucked my verdure out on't" (1. 2. 85–87), Wheeler discovers "a base in the negative register of early infantile experience" (137). That experience, shaped by the activities of holding and sucking, Wheeler thinks "will countenance the emergence of polarized fantasies of omnipotence and of total helplessness; of fusion with a benign nurturant world and of annihilation by a hostile, rejecting world. . .of being loved unconditionally, and returning it in bliss, and of being hated without limit, and of returning that in rage" (137).

Wheeler traces several "Shakespearean genealogies" that mark the gradual emergence of Caliban and Prospero. For Caliban, Wheeler finds precedents in Bottom, Richard II, and Falstaff. "Characters who open themselves most fully to those inner dimensions of psychic experience often speak the most widely and vividly expressive poetry in the plays, the poetry that conveys the texture of joy or agony, of rage or bliss, of a self fulfilled or left desolate" (146). Prospero's predecessors, on the other hand, resist merger with the world and others and therefore have difficulty coming to terms with trusting relationships. These characters "who distance themselves from, or carefully mediate their relationship to, the force of such inner impulses" are, respectively, Oberon, Bullingbrook, and Henry V (147). Nevertheless, Wheeler also finds speeches by Jaques, Duke Vincentio, Macbeth, and Prospero where "the immediacy of social accommodation and mastery recede behind the trope of life as a dream, or as theater, or as both" (147). These very different characters—drawn from a comedy, a problem comedy, a tragedy, and romance—have distanced themselves from human intimacy and from a direct responsiveness to powerful inner feelings. Their speeches "do not demonstrate theatrical control over an action, but something of how the world looks from the vantage point of Shakespearean drama when it is fully theatricalized" (148).

While Prospero's magical recovery of his dukedom seems driven by "bountiful Fortune" and a "most auspicious star," for Wheeler "the deeper necessity for the events of the play is Miranda's maturation (152). The marriage masque reflects Prospero's idealized fantasies that have repressed the unconscious dimension of his fantasies, represented by Caliban and his sexual desire for Miranda. When the masque is interrupted and the dancers vanish to a strange hollow and confused noise, "what is dramatized is the disruptive convergence of what Prospero has worked so hard to keep separate" (153). By the time the play ends, Wheeler thinks Prospero is able ("following his recognition of his helplessness before his own desires and developments in his world, and in the course of an imaginative vision of universal emptiness") to touch base with a repressed wish (comparable to Caliban's psychological orientation toward a nurturant world) "to turn oneself over in trust to a world understood as the heritage of the infantile world of oneness with maternal bounty" (157).

Robert Hapgood, in essay written specifically for this volume, questions Orgel's view that all interpretations are "essentially arbitrary," by using a formalist approach to show how Shakespeare guides his interpreters while accommodating a free play of imagination. Building upon his work in *Shakespeare the Theatre-Poet*, Hapgood carefully examines *The Tempest* from the moment of the masque's interruption ("our revels now are ended") through Prospero's acknowledgement that "the rarer action is in virtue" and his decision to break his charms and restore the senses of Alonso and his followers. While giving his interpreters a large degree of freedom, Hapgood's Shakespeare also places limits and emphases within his play by using several large elements through which "the playwright's voice is most clearly audible" (including: the play's action—that is, what the characters do; patterns in stage movement; and dialogue). Further elements (including characterization, individual line-readings, and the overall meaning) are more open to interpretation and varying judgments. Reading the play in this way, enables Hapgood to show convincingly how Shakespeare, "with his keen eye for finely graduated emotional progressions," creates a superstructure of limits and emphases that allows him "a large measure of freedom from literal-mindedness" (436).

When Hapgood applies his sense of how the playwright guides his interpreters through *The Tempest* (from 4.1.139—5.1.32), he notices that the action after the masque moves from surprise at Prospero's interruption, to suspense about the extent of his retaliation, to a sudden reversal as his fury turns to self-restraint. The play is choreographed so that two groups (the mainlanders and the islanders) are subdivided, separated, and eventually converge while the dialogue gestures to specific themes involving art and nature, illusion and appearance, time and timing, public and personal conduct. "In particular," Hapgood notes, "each of Prospero's speeches of revelation takes part in a motif extensively developed in the dialog, concerning respectively the change-ableness of existence and the importance of fellow feeling" (421). Characters, for Hapgood, find themselves in others. The Neopolitans are "suggestible" for good or ill; Ferdinand and Miranda are in each other's power; Prospero finds himself too trusting and must struggle to assert his authority even as he is tempted to withdraw. Hapgood reads the text as a script and reveals many of the subtle choices directors and actors must consider—as Shakespeare's practice, through the interplay of character and action, invites both freedom and responsiveness in his interpreters.

While noticing a parallel between Prospero's comment that "the rarer action is / In virtue than in vengeance" and Montaigne's essay "Of Crueltie," Eleanor Prosser asserted that "Shakespeare's point is slightly different from Montaigne's" (263). According to Prosser, Montaigne described a choice between patience (arising from rational control) and passivity (arising from an amiable nature). However, Shakespeare exemplifies Montaigne's point while giving Prospero a choice between patience and vengeance. Prosser thought this use of Montaigne "suggests that Shakespeare did read Florio's translation and read it closely" (263). As a close reader, Shakespeare comments upon Montaigne's ideas—, a fact that calls into question the status of *The Tempest* as an unassertive or open text while implying that Shakespeare's art is deliberately critical; however, Shakespeare's response to Montaigne is difficult to characterize and clearly open to interpretation. Unlike Orgel's position, Greenblatt's sense of the author as a site of these *transformations* and *recombinations* can better account for Prosser's observations since Greenblatt emphasizes "that an individual play mediates between the mode of theater, understood in its historical specificity, and elements of the society out of which that theater has been differentiated" (*Shakespearean* 14). Yet, some readers find that Greenblatt's model cannot describe the specific quality of Shakespeare's uniquely personal deliberations upon Montaigne or any of his other materials—including, as Wheeler's reading indicates, Shakespeare's own individual historicity.

In an essay written for this volume, Alan de Gooyer recalls "that both Montaigne's essays and the plot of *The Tempest* are set in motion by the withdrawal from public life to the shelter of the study" (509). Both the *Essais* and *The Tempest* share a preoccupation with "a complicated sense of the 'kindness' of all humans, and a sadly tempered recognition of human frailty that entreats us to give up any pretensions we may have of escaping ourselves, our weaknesses, our places" (511). Both Montaigne and Shakespeare roughly present "a paradigm of self-exile involving some kind of 'transport' or ecstasy, a subsequent rebellion and loss, and eventually a chastened recovery that is achieved through the practice of their respective arts" (511–12). Building upon Arthur Kirsh's idea that Shakespeare's organization of the action of the play is informed by Montaigne's interrogative, anti-sentimental, and tragi-comic thinking, de Gooyer finds the play constantly tests its characters with new experiences, choices, and opportunities while raising fundamental ethical and epistemological questions: for instance, by forcing "the marooned characters to face up to questions about who they are and what they know" (515).

Like Hawkes, de Gooyer sees concerns about culture and ontology in Trinculo's and Stephano's recognition of Caliban, but he also hears questions about empathy in Stephano's puzzlements. Even Miranda, who seems most prepared to acknowledge the reality of others' feelings, is at times baffled by Prospero's motives, reactions, and anger toward Ferdinand. Free to respond to the island's invitation to philosophic self-reflection, the shipwrecked parties, according to de Gooyer, fail to abate their strong desires as they allow "their imaginations to revert to fantastical (and yet predictable) 'chimeras' of monarchical power and colonial rule, or to descend into suicidal grief or out-and-out drunkenness" (521). Finding parallels between the play and Montaigne's suspicions of all ecstasy (whether madness, melancholy, sexual passion, drunkenness, or ambition), de Gooyer believes that *The Tempest* keeps us wondering while "it does not keep us in a state of wonder or ecstasy" (717). Alonso, Ferdinand, and Caliban benefit from the wonders of the island by recovering from the ecstasies managed and observed by Ariel and Prospero. "Preparation for reality is Montaigne's objective, and for him reality means, simply, becoming more oneself" (522). In this way de Gooyer answers the question about Prospero's motives for surrendering his robe, staff, and book. Prospero acts in a manner that brings himself and the others back to themselves while admitting guilt and affliction without allowing cynicism advantage nor innocence its simplicity (527).

Criticism for de Gooyer always vacillates between the poles of annotation and speculation (705), and he agrees with Orgel that Shakespeare, in dramatizing both sides of a debate, frustrates any interpretive resolution that would appeal to authorial intentions. Nevertheless, de Gooyer's interpretation of *The Tempest* delivers on the promise embedded within Prosser's observation about Shakespeare as Montaigne's commentator. While on the surface Orgel's and Prosser's positions about authorship are irreconcilable, de Gooyer demonstrates that Shakespeare's commentary sets into play (with a variety of theatrical practices) the phrases of Montaigne's essays. If we read, for instance, the work of Donna Hamilton (which argues that Shakespeare imitated Virgil while pursuing a constitutionalist political agenda) and Jonathan Bate (which finds *The Metamorphoses* and Heywood's *The Silver Age* to be more compelling sources than *The Aeneid* [Ovid 239–270]), as we also think about Peter Hulme's recovery of colonial encounters in the Carribean in contrast with Gary Schmidgall's arguments for the developing courtly aesthetic that replaced Macbeth's bare stage with the magnificent splendor of Prospero's cloud-capp'd towers (perhaps suggested by the source text *Primaleon*)—, we may begin to understand how critical propositions are mutually (and often antagonistically) reciprocal: they follow contradictory traces that lead to their own erasure and repetition. In *The Tempest* Shakespeare writes a different kind of commentary, which provides, as de Gooyer says, an "experiential rather than propositional knowledge" (521n.22).

WORKS CITED

Addison, Joseph. *The Spectator*. Ed. and introd. by Donald F. Bond. 5 Vols. Oxford: Clarendon P, 1965.

Albanese, Denise. *New Science, New World*. Durham and London: Duke UP, 1996.

Baert, Barbara. "Caliban as Wild-Man: An Iconographical Approach." *Constellation Caliban: Figurations of a Character*. Ed. Nadia Lie and Theo D'haen. Atlanta and Amsterdam: Rodopi, 1997. 43–59.

Baker, David J. "Where is Ireland in *The Tempest*?" *Shakespeare and Ireland: History, Politics, Culture*. Ed. Mark Thornton Burnett and Ramona Wray. London: Macmillan; and New York: St. Martins P, 1997. 68–88.

Baldo, Jonathan. "Exporting Oblivion in *The Tempest*." *Modern Language Quarterly* 56.2 (1995): 111–44.

Barber, C. L. "A Mask Presented at Ludlow Castle: The Masque as a Masque." *A Maske at Ludlow*: Essays on Milton's *Comus*. Ed. John S. Diekhoff. Cleveland: Case Western UP, 1968. 188–206.

Barber, C. L. and Richard P. Wheeler. *The Whole Journey: Shakespeare's Power of Development*. Berkeley, Los Angeles, London: U of California P, 1986.

Barber, C. L. *Shakespeare's Festive Comedy: A Study of Dramatic Form and Its Relation to Social Custom*. 1959. Princeton: Princeton UP, 1972.

Barker, Francis, and Peter Hulme. "Nymphs and Reapers Heavily Vanish: the Discursive Con-texts of *The Tempest.*" *Alternative Shakespeares.* Ed. John Drakakis. London and New York: Methuen, 1985. 191–205, 235–237.

Barthes, Roland. *S/Z: An Essay.* 1970. Trans. Richard Miller. New York: Hill and Wang, 1974.

Barton, Anne. Introduction. *The Tempest.* 1968. Harmondsworth and New York: Penguin Books, 1979. 7–51.

Bate, Jonathan. *Shakespeare and Ovid.* 1993. Oxford: Clarendon P, 1994.

Bate, Jonathan. *Shakespeare and the English Romantic Imagination.* 1986. Oxford: Clarendon P, 1989.

Berger, Jr., Harry. "Miraculous Harp: A Reading of Shakespeare's *Tempest.*" *Shakespeare Studies* 5 (1969): 253–83.

Birch, W. J. *An Inquiry into the Philosophy and Religion of Shakspere.* n.d. [1848]. New York: Haskell House Publishers Ltd., 1972.

Bradbrook, M. C. "Romance, Farewell!: *The Tempest.*" *English Literary Renaissance* 1.3 (1971): 239–249.

Breight, Curt. "'Treason doth never prosper': *The Tempest* and the Discourse of Treason." *Shakespeare Quarterly* 41.1 (1990): 1–28.

Bristol, Michael. *Shakespeare's America, America's Shakespeare: Literature, Institution, Ideology in the United States.* New York: Routledge, 1990. 15–119.

Brooke, Stopford A. 1905. *On Ten Plays of Shakespeare.* New York: Barnes and Noble, 1961.

Brotton, Jerry. "'This Tunis, sir, was Carthage': Contesting Colonialism in *The Tempest.*" *Post-Colonial Shakespeares.* Ed. Ania Loomba and Martin Orkin. London and New York: Routledge, 1998. 23–42.

Browning, Robert. "Caliban Upon Setebos; Or, Natural Theology in the Island." Vol.6 *The Complete Works of Robert Browning.* Ed. John C. Berkey, Allan C. Dooley, and Susan E. Dooley. Waco, Texas: Baylor UP; Athens, Ohio: Ohio UP, 1996. 259–270.

Brower, Reuben Arthur. "The Mirror of Analogy: *The Tempest.*" *The Fields of Light: An Experiment in Critical Reading.* 1951. London, Oxford, New York: Oxford UP, 1968. 95–122.

Brown, Paul. "'This thing of darkness I acknowledge mine': *The Tempest* and the Discourse of Colonialism." *Political Shakespeare: New Essays in Cultural Materialism.* Ithaca and London: Cornell UP, 1985. 48–71.

Bruster, Douglas. *Drama and the Market in the Age of Shakespeare.* 1992. Cambridge: Cambridge UP, 1994.

Bruster, Douglas. "Local *Tempest*: Shakespeare and the Work of the Early Modern Playhouse." *Journal of Medieval and Renaissance Studies* 25.1 (1995): 33–53.

Butler, E. M. *The Myth of the Magus.* Cambridge: Cambridge UP; New York: Macmillan, 1948.

Cartelli, Thomas. "*Bartholomew Fair* as Urban Arcadia: Jonson Responds to Shakespeare." *Renaissance Drama* n.s. 14 (1983): 151–172.

Cawley, Robert Ralston. "Shakespeare's Use of the Voyagers in *The Tempest.*" PMLA 41 (1926): 688–726.

Césaire, Aimé. *A Tempest*. 1985. Translated by Richard Miller. Ubu Repertory Theater Publications. Rpt. 1990. *Une Tempête*. Paris: Editions de Seuil, 1969.

Cheyfitz, Eric. *The Poetics of Imperialism: Translation and Colonization from* The Tempest *to* Tarzan. New York and Oxford: Oxford UP, 1991.

Chickering, Howell. "Hearing Ariel's Songs." *Journal of Medieval and Renaissance Studies*. 24.1 (1994): 131–172.

Cohn, Ruby. *Modern Shakespeare Offshoots*. Princeton: Princeton UP, 1976.

Coleridge, Samuel Taylor. "Notes on *The Tempest*." *The Literary Remains of Samuel Taylor Coleridge*. Collected and ed. by Henry Nelson Colderidge. London: William Pickering, 1836; New York: AMS P, 1967.

Coleridge, Samuel Taylor. "The Transcript of Lecture 9." *Coleridge on Shakespeare: The Text of the Lectures of 1811–12*. Ed. R. A. Foakes. Charlottesville: U P of Virginia, 1971.

Corfield, Cosmo. "Why Does Prospero Abjure His 'Rough Magic'?" *Shakespeare Quarterly* 36.1 (1985): 31–48.

Curry, W. C. *Shakespeare's Philosophical Patterns*. 1939. 2nd Ed. Baton Rouge: Louisiana UP, 1959.

de Gooyer, Alan. "'Their senses I'll restore': Montaigne and *The Tempest* Reconsidered." *The Tempest: Critical Essays*. Ed. Patrick M. Murphy. New York: Garland P, 2000. 509–31.

de Grazia, Margreta. *Shakespeare Verbatim: The Reproduction of Authenticity and the 1790 Apparatus*. Oxford: Clarendon P, 1991.

de Grazia, Margreta. "*The Tempest*: Gratuitous Movement or Action Without Kibes and Pinches." *Shakespeare Studies* 14 (1981): 249–265.

de Grazia, Margreta. "What is a Work? What is a Document?" *New Ways of Looking at Old Texts*. Ed. Speed W. Hill. Papers of Renaissance Text Society 1985–1991. Binghamton, NY: Medieval & Renaissance Texts and Studies, 1993. 199–207.

Delabastita, Dirk. "Caliban's Afterlife: Reading Shakespeare's Readings." *Constellation Caliban: Figurations of a Character*. Ed. Nadia Lie and Theo D'haen. Atlanta and Amsterdam: Rodopi, 1997. 1–22.

Dobson, Michael. "'Remember/First to Possess His Books': The Appropriation of *The Tempest*." *Shakespeare Survey* 43 (1991): 99–107.

Dobson, Michael. "Fairly Brave New World: Shakespeare, the American Colonies, and the American Revolution." *Renaissance Drama* 23 (1992): 189–207.

Dobson, Michael. *The Making of the National Poet: Shakespeare, Adaptation, and Authorship, 1660–1769*. 1992. Oxford: Clarendon P, 1995.

Dolan, Frances E. "The Subordinate('s) Plot: Petty Treason and the Forms of Domestic Rebellion." *Shakespeare Quarterly* 43.3 (1992): 317–40. Rev. *Dangerous Familiars: Representations of Domestic Crime in England 1550–1700*. Ithaca: Cornell UP, 1994. 59–88.

Doran, Madeline. *Endeavors of Art: A Study of Form in Elizabethan Drama*. Madison: U of Wisconsin P, 1954.

Dowden, Edward. *Shakespere: A Critical Study of his Mind and Art*. 3rd Ed. New York and London: Harper & Brothers Publishers, 1905.

Dryden, John. *The Tempest or The Enchanted Island*. Vol. 10 *The Works of John Dryden*. Ed. Maximillian E. Novak and George Robert Guffey. General Ed. H. T.

Swedenberg, Jr. Berkeley, Los Angeles, and London: U of California P, 1970. 1–103, 319–379.

Dryden, John. "The Preface to the Play." *Troilus and Cressida or, Truth Found Too Late*. The Preface to the Play. Vol. 13 *The Works of John Dryden*. Ed. Maximillian E. Novak and George Robert Guffey. General Ed. Alan Roper. Berkeley, Los Angeles, and London: U of California P, 1984. 225–250.

Dupras, Joseph A. "The Tempest of Intertext in 'Caliban upon Setebos.'" *Concerning Poetry* 19 (1986): 75–82.

Empson, William. "Hunt the Symbol." *The Times Literary Supplement*, 23 April 1964. *Essays on Shakespeare*. 1986. Ed. David B. Pirie. Cambridge: Cambridge UP, 1987. 231–243.

Erlich, Bruce. "Shakespeare's Colonial Metaphor: On the Social Function of Theatre in *The Tempest*." *Science and Society* 41 (1977): 43–65.

Fanon, Frantz. *Black Skin, White Masks*. 1952. Trans. Charles Lam Markmann. New York: Grove P, 1967.

Felker, Christopher. "Print History of *The Tempest* in Early America, 1623–1787. *The Tempest: Critical Essays*. Ed. Patrick M. Murphy. New York: Garland P, 2000. 482–508.

Felperin, Howard. "Political Criticism at the Crossroads: The Utopian Historicism of *The Tempest*." *The Tempest*. Theory in Practice Series. Ed. Nigel Wood. Buckingham and Philadelphia: Open UP, 1995. 29–66; 175–178; 188–89.

Felperin, Howard. *Shakespearean Romance*. Princeton: Princeton UP, 1972.

Fiedler, Leslie A. *The Stranger in Shakespeare*. 1972. New York: Stein and Day, 1973.

Foakes, R. A., ed. Vol. 5:1 *The Collected Works of Samuel Taylor Coleridge Lectures 1808–1819 On Literature*. London: Routledge & Kegan Paul; Princeton: Princeton UP, 1987.

Franssen, Paul. "A Muddy Mirror." *Constellation Caliban: Figurations of a Character*. Ed. Nadia Lie and Theo D'haen. Atlanta and Amsterdam: Rodopi, 1997. 23–42.

Frey, Charles H. "Embodying the Play." *The Tempest*. Theory in Practice Series. Buckingham and Philadelphia: Open UP, 1995. 67–96.

Frey, Charles. "*The Tempest* and the New World." *Shakespeare Quarterly* 30.1 (1979): 29–41.

Frye, Northrop. Introduction. *The Tempest*. 1959. Ed. by Northrop Frye. *William Shakespeare: The Complete Works*. General ed. Alfred Harbage. The Pelican Text Revised. 1969. Baltimore: Penguin, 1970. 1369–1372.

Frye, Northrop. *A Natural Perspective: The Development of Shakespearean Comedy and Romance*. New York and London: Columbia UP, 1965.

Frye, Northrop. "Shakespeare's *The Tempest*." *Shenandoah* 42.4 (1992): 36–50.

Frye, Northrop. "*The Tempest*." *Northrop Frye on Shakespeare*. Ed. Robert Sandler. New Haven and London: Yale UP, 1986. 171–186.

Fuchs, Barbara. "Conquering Islands: Contextualizing *The Tempest*." *Shakespeare Quarterly* 48.1 (1997): 45–62.

Fuller, Mary. "Forgetting the *Aeneid*." *American Literary History* 4.3 (1992): 517–38.

Furness, Horace Howard. *The Tempest*. Vol. 9 *A New Variorum Edition of Shakespeare*. Philadelphia: J. B. Lippincott Company, 1895.

Gaines, Barry. "What Did Caliban Look Like?" *Shakespeare Yearbook* 1 (1990): 50–58.

Gildon, Charles. "Remarks on the Plays of Shakespear." *The Works of Mr. William Shakespear*. Ed. Nicholas Rowe. 1710. Rpt. New York: AMS P, 1967.

Gillies, John. *Shakespeare and the Geography of Difference*. Cambridge: Cambridge UP, 1994.

Gillies, John. "Shakespeare's Virginian Masque." *ELH* 53.4 (1986): 673–707.

Goldberg, Jonathan. *James I and the Politics of Literature: Jonson, Shakespeare, Donne and Their Contemporaries*. 1983. Baltimore: Johns Hopkins UP. Reissued. Stanford: Stanford UP, 1989.

Graef, Ortwin de. "Browning Born to Wordsworth: Intimations of Relatability from Recollections of Early Monstrosity." *Constellation Caliban: Figurations of a Character*. Ed. Nadia Lie and Theo D'haen. Atlanta and Amsterdam: Rodopi, 1997. 113–143.

Greenblatt, Stephen. "Learning to Curse: Aspects of Linguistic Colonialism in the Sixteenth Century." 1976. Rpt. *Learning to Curse: Essays in Early Modern Culture*. 1990. New York and London: Routledge, 1992. 16–39.

Greenblatt, Stephen. *Shakespearean Negotiations: The Circulation of Social Energy in Renaissance England*. Berkeley and Los Angeles: U of California P, 1988.

Greg, W. W. *The Shakespeare First Folio*. Oxford: Clarendon P, 1955.

Griffiths, Trevor. "'This Island's Mine': Caliban and Colonialism." *Yearbook of English Studies* 13 (1983): 159–180.

Gurr, Andrew. "*The Tempest*'s Tempest at Blackfriars." *Shakespeare Survey* 41 (1989): 91–102.

Hall, Kim. *Things of Darkness: Economies of Race and Gender in Early Modern England*. Ithaca: Cornell UP, 1995.

Hamilton, Donna B. "Shakespeare's Romances and Jacobean Political Discourse." *Approaches to Teaching Shakespeare's* The Tempest *and Other Late Romances*. Ed. Maurice Hunt. New York: Modern Language Association of America, 1992. 64–71.

Hamilton, Donna B. *Virgil and The Tempest: The Politics of Imitation*. Columbus: Ohio State UP, 1990.

Hamlin, William M. *The Image of America in Montaigne, Spenser, and Shakespeare: Renaissance Ethnography and Literary Reflection*. New York: St. Martin's P, 1995.

Hantman, Jeffrey L. "Caliban's Own Voice: American Indian Views of the Other in Colonial Virginia." *New Literary History* 23.1 (1992): 69–81.

Hapgood, Robert. "Listening for the Playwright's Voice: *The Tempest*, 4.1.139–5.1.32." *The Tempest: Critical Essays*. Ed. Patrick M. Murphy. New York: Garland P, 2000. 417–37.

Hapgood, Robert. *Shakespeare the Theatre-Poet*. Oxford: Clarendon P, 1990.

Harris, Claudia. "*The Tempest* as Political Allegory." *The Tempest: Critical Essays*. Ed. Patrick M. Murphy. New York: Garland P, 2000. 560–86.

Hawkes, Terence. "Swisser-Swatter: Making a Man of English Letters." *Alternative Shakespeares*. Ed. John Drakakis. London and New York: Methuen, 1985. 26–46, 228.

Hazlitt, William. "Characters of Shakespear's Plays." *The Complete Works of William Hazlitt*. Ed. P. P. Howe. New York: AMS P, 1967.

Holland, Norman. "Caliban's Dream." *Psychoanalytic Quarterly* 37 (1968): 114–25.

Hulme, Peter. *Colonial Encounters: Europe and the Native Caribbean 1492–1797*. 1986. London and New York: Routledge, 1992.

James, D. G. *The Dream of Prospero*. Oxford: Clarendon P, 1967.

James, Henry. "Introduction to *The Tempest*." 1907. *Shakespeare* The Tempest *A Casebook*. Ed. D. J. Palmer. London: Macmillan, 1968. 79–95.

Johnson, Samuel. "Notes on Shakespeare's Plays." Vol. 7 *Jonson on Shakespeare. Yale Edition of the Works of Samuel Johnson*. Ed. Arthur Sherbo. New Haven: Yale UP, 1968.

Jonson, Ben. *Bartholomew Fair*. Vol. 6 *Ben Jonson*. 1938. Ed. C. H. Herford, Percy and Evelyn Simpson. Oxford: Clarendon P, 1966. 1–141.

Kahn, Coppélia. "The Providential Tempest and the Shakespearean Family." *Representing Shakespeare: New Psychoanalytic Essays*. Ed. M. M. Schwartz and Coppélia Kahn. Baltimore and London: Johns Hopkins UP, 1980. 217–43.

Kastan, David Scott. "'The Duke of Milan/And His Brave Son': Dynastic Politics in *The Tempest*." *Critical Essays on Shakespeare's* The Tempest. Ed. Virginia Mason Vaughan and Alden T. Vaughan. *Critical Essays on British Literature*. Ed. Zack Bowen. New York: G. K. Hall. An Imprint of Simon & Schuster Macmillan; London: Prentice Hall International, 1998. 91–103.

Kelsey, Rachel. M. "Indian Dances in *The Tempest*." *Journal of English and Germanic Philology* 13 (1914): 98–103.

Kermode, Frank. Introduction. *The Tempest*. 6th ed. 1958. The Arden Edition of the Works of William Shakespeare. London and New York: Methuen, 1985.

Kernan, Alvin. *The Playwright as Magician*. New Haven. 1979. 129–145, 146–159.

Kinney, Arthur. "Revisiting *The Tempest*." *Modern Philology* 95.2 (1995): 161–177.

Kipling, Rudyard. Letter. *The Spectator* 2 July, 1898, 15–16.

Knapp, Jeffrey. *An Empire Nowhere: England, America, and Literature from Utopia to* The Tempest. Berkeley, Los Angeles, Oxford: U of California P, 1992. 220–242, 330–339.

Knight, G. W. *The Crown of Life: Essays in Interpretation of Shakespeare's Final Plays*. 1947. London: Methuen & Co. Ltd., 1961.

Knight, G. W. "Myth and Miracle (1929)." *The Crown of Life: Essays in Interpretation of Shakespeare's Final Plays*. 1947. London: Methuen & Co. Ltd., 1961. 9–31.

Knight, G. W. *The Shakespearian Tempest*. 1932. London: Methuen & Co. Ltd., 1960.

Knights, L. C. "*The Tempest*." *Shakespeare's Late Plays*. Athens, Ohio: Ohio UP, 1974.

Kott, Jan. "*The Tempest*, or Repetition." Trans. Daniela Miedzyrzecka. *Mosaic* 10.3 (1977): 9–36. Rpt. *The Bottom Translation: Marlowe and Shakespeare and the Carnival Tradition*. Trans. Daniela Miedzyrzecka and Lillian Vallee. Evanston, Illinois: Northwestern UP, 1987. 107–132.

Law, Ernest. *Shakespeare's* "Tempest" *as Originally Produced at Court*. Shakespeare Association Pamphlet. London: Chatto and Windus, 1920.

Leech, Clifford. "The Structure of the Last Plays." *Shakespeare Survey* 11 (1958): 19–30.

Leininger, Lorie Jerrell. "Cracking the Code of *The Tempest.*" *Shakespeare: Contemporary Critical Approaches.* Ed. Harry R. Garvin. Lewisburg: Bucknell UP; London and Toronto: Associated UP, 1988. *Bucknell Review* 25.1 (1980): 121–131.

Leininger, Lorie Jerrell. "The Miranda Trap: Sexism and Racism in Shakespeare's *Tempest.*" *The Woman's Part: Feminist Criticism of Shakespeare.* Ed. Carolyn Lenz, Gayle Greene and Carol Thomas Neely. Urbana and Chicago: U of Illinois P, 1980. 285–94.

Levin, Harry. "Two Magian Comedies: *The Tempest* and *The Alchemist.*" *Shakespeare Survey* 22 (1969): 47–58.

Lewis, Cynthia. *Particular Saints: Shakespeare's Four Antonios, Their Contexts, and Their Plays.* Newark: U of Delaware P; London: Associated UP, 1997.

Loeffelholz, Mary. "Two Masques of Ceres and Proserpine: *Comus* and *The Tempest.*" *Re-Membering Milton: Essays on the Texts and Traditions.* Eds. Mary Nyquist and Margaret Ferguson. New York: Methuen, 1987. 25–42.

Luce, Morton. Introduction. *The Tempest.* 3rd ed. rev. The Arden Shakespeare. London: Methuen and Co. Ltd., 1926. ix–lxx.

Major, John M. "*Comus* and *The Tempest.*" *Shakespeare Quarterly* 10 (1959): 177–83.

Mannoni, O[ctave]. *Prospero and Caliban: The Psychology of Colonization.* Trans. Pamela Powesland. Foreword by Philip Mason. New York: Frederick A. Praeger, 1956.

Marshall, Cynthia. *Last Things and Last Plays: Shakespearean Eschatology.* Foreword by Arthur Kinney. Carbondale and Edwardsville: Southern Illinois UP, 1991.

Marx, Leo. *The Machine in the Garden: Technology and the Pastoral Ideal in America.* 1964. London, Oxford, New York: Oxford UP, 1974.

Masten, Jeffrey. *Textual Intercourse: Collaboration, Authorship, and Sexualities in Renaissance Drama.* Cambridge: Cambridge UP, 1997.

Maus, Katharine Eisaman. "Arcadia Lost: Politics and Revision in the Restoration *Tempest.*" *Renaissance Drama* n.s. 13 (1982): 189–209.

McDonald, Russ. "Reading *The Tempest.*" *Shakespeare Survey* 43 (1991): 15–28.

Mebane, John S. "Metadrama and the Visionary Imagination in *Dr. Faustus* and *The Tempest.*" *South Atlantic Review* 53.2 (1988): 25–45.

Mebane, John S. *Renaissance Magic and the Return of the Golden Age: The Occult Tradition and Marlowe, Jonson, and Shakespeare.* Lincoln: U of Nebraska P, 1989.

Miko, Stephen J. "Tempest." *ELH* 49.1 (1982): 1–17.

Morgann, Maurice. *Shakespearian Criticism.* Ed. with introd. and notes by Daniel A. Fineman. Oxford: Clarendon P, 1972.

Mowat, Barbara A. "Prospero, Agrippa, and Hocus Pocus." *English Literary Renaissance* 11.3 (1981): 281–303.

Newell, W. W. "Sources of Shakespeare's *Tempest.*" *Journal of American Folk-lore* 16 (1903): 234–57.

Nilan, Mary M. "Shakespeare Illustrated: Charles Kean's 1857 Production of *The Tempest.*" *Shakespeare Quarterly* 26 (1975): 196–204.

Nilan, Mary M. "*The Tempest* at the Turn of the Century: Cross Currents in Production." *Shakespeare Survey* 25 (1972): 113–23.

Nixon, Rob. "Caribbean and African Appropriations of *The Tempest*." *Critical Inquiry* 13.3 (1987): 557–78.

O'Shea, Edward. "Modernist Versions of *The Tempest*." *The Tempest: Critical Essays*. Ed. Patrick M. Murphy. New York: Garland P, 2000. 543–59.

Orgel, Stephen. Introduction. *The Tempest*. By William Shakespeare. Oxford and New York: Oxford UP, 1987. 1–87.

Orgel, Stephen. "New Uses of Adversity: Tragic Experience in *The Tempest*." *In Defense of Reading*, ed. Reuben A. Brower and Richard Poirier. New York: E. P. Dutton, 1962. 110–132.

Orgel, Stephen. "Prospero's Wife." *Representations* 8 (1984): 1–13.

Orgel, Stephen. "Shakespeare and the Cannibals." *Cannibals, Witches, and Divorce: Estranging the Renaissance*. Ed. Marjorie Garber. Selected Papers from the English Institute, 1985. n. s. 11. Baltimore and London: Johns Hopkins UP, 1987. 40–66.

Orgel, Stephen. *The Illusion of Power*. Berkeley and Los Angeles: U of California P, 1975.

Patrick, Julian. "*The Tempest* as Supplement." *Centre and Labyrinth: Essays in Honour of Northrop Frye*. 1983. Ed. Eleanor Cook, et al. Toronto: U of Toronto P, 1985. 162–180.

Paulson, Ronald. *Book and Painting. Shakespeare, Milton, and the Bible: Literary Texts and the Emergence of English Painting*. Knoxville: U of Tennessee P, 1982.

Pitcher, John. "A Theatre of the Future: *The Aeneid* and *The Tempest*." *Essays in Criticism* 34.3 (1984): 193–215.

Prosser, Eleanor. "Shakespeare, Montaigne, and the *Rarer Action*." *Shakespeare Studies* 1 (1965): 261–64.

Retamar, Roberto Fernández. "Caliban: Notes Toward a Discussion of Culture in Our America." *Caliban and Other Essays*. Trans. Edward Baker. Foreword by Fredric Jameson. Minneapolis: U of Minnesota P, 1989. 3–45.

Richardson, William. *Essays on Shakespeare's Dramatic Character of Sir John Falstaff, and on his Imitation of Female Characters*. 1789. Facsimile rpt. New York: AMS P Inc., 1973.

Roberts, Jeanne Addison. "Ralph Crane and the Text of *The Tempest*." *Shakespeare Studies* 13 (1980): 213–33.

Schanzer, Ernest. "Shakespeare and the Doctrine of the Unity of Time." *Shakespeare Survey* 28 (1975): 57–61.

Schlegel, August Wilhelm [Von]. *Lectures on Dramatic Art and Literature*. Trans. John Black. 2nd Ed. Rev. by A. J. W. Morrison. London: George Bell & Sons, 1889.

Schmidgall, Gary. *Shakespeare and the Courtly Aesthetic*. Berkeley, Los Angeles, London: U of California P, 1981.

Schmidgall, Gary. "*The Tempest* and *Primaleon*: A New Source." *Shakespeare Quarterly* 37.4 (1986): 423–439.

Schoenbaum, S[amuel]. *Shakespeare's Lives*. Oxford: Clarendon P and New York: Oxford UP, 1970.

Sebek, Barbara Ann. "Peopling, Profiting, and Pleasure in *The Tempest*." *The Tempest: Critical Essays*. Ed. Patrick M. Murphy. New York: Garland P, 2000. 462–81.

Shapiro, Arnold. "Browning's Psalm of Hate: 'Caliban upon Setebos," Psalm 50, and *The Tempest.*" *Papers on Language and Literature* 8 (1972): 53–62.

Shakespeare, William. *The Tempest.* Ed. Stephen Orgel. Oxford and New York: Oxford UP, 1987.

Simon, Robin. "Hogarth's Shakespeare." *Apollo* 109 (March 1979): 213–220.

Singh, Jyotsna G. "Caliban Versus Miranda: Race and Gender Conflicts in Postcolonial Rewritings of *The Tempest.*" *Feminist Readings of Early Modern Culture: Emerging Subjects.* Ed. Valerie Traub, M. Lindsay Kaplan, and Dympna Callaghan. Cambridge: Cambridge UP, 1996. 191–209.

Sisson, C. J. "The Magic of Prospero." *Shakespeare Survey* 11 (1958): 70–77.

Skura, Meredith. "Discourse and the Individual: The Case of Colonialism in *The Tempest.*" *Shakespeare Quarterly* 40.1 (1989): 42–69.

Sousa, Geraldo U. de. "Alien Habitats in *The Tempest.*" *The Tempest: Critical Essays.* Ed. Patrick M. Murphy. New York: Garland P, 2000. 438–61.

Sousa, Geraldo U. de. "Closure and the Antimasque of *The Tempest.*" *Journal of Dramatic Theory and Criticism* 2 (1987): 41–51.

Sousa, Geraldo U. de. "*The Tempest,* Comedy, and the Space of the Other." *Acting Funny: Comic Theory and Practice in Shakespeare's Plays.* Ed. Frances Teague. Rutherford, NJ; Fairleigh Dickinson UP; Associated UP, 1994. 52–71.

Srigley, Michael. *Images of Regeneration: A Study of Shakespeare's The Tempest and Its Cultural Background.* Acta Universitatis Upsaliensis. Studia Anglistica Upsaliensia 58. Stockholm: Almqvist & Wiksell International, 1985.

Stephens, James. "Drama's 'Inward Pinches': *The Tempest.*" *The Tempest: Critical Essays.* Ed. Patrick M. Murphy. New York: Garland P, 2000. 532–42.

Still, Colin. *Shakespeare's Mystery Play: A Study of* The Tempest. London, 1921. Enlarged as *The Timeless Theme.* London, 1936.

Stoll, E. E. "Certain Fallacies and Irrelevancies in the Literary Scholarship of the Day." *Studies in Philology* 24.4 (1927): 485–508.

Stoll, E. E. "*The Tempest.*" *PMLA* 47 (1932): 699–726.

Strachey, Lytton. "Shakespeare's Final Period." 1906. Rpt. *Books and Characters: French and English.* New York: Harcourt, Brace and Company, 1922. 51–69.

Suchet, David. "Caliban in *The Tempest.*" *Players of Shakespeare: Essays in Shakespearean Performance by Twelve Players with the Royal Shakespeare Company.* Ed. Philip Brockbank. Cambridge: Cambridge UP, 1985. 167–179.

Sundelson, David. *Shakespeare's Restorations of the Father.* New Brunswick, New Jersey: Rutgers UP, 1983.

Tennyson, Alfred Lord. "Lucretius." Victorian Poetry and Poetics. 1959. 2nd Ed. Ed. Walter E. Houghton and G. Robert Stange. New York: Houghton Mifflin Co., 1968. 148–152.

Thorndike, Ashley H. *The Influence of Beaumont and Fletcher on Shakespere.* 1901. New York: Russell & Russell, 1965.

Tillyard, E. M. W. *Shakespeare's Last Plays.* (Based on a lecture delivered at the Sorbonne, 1936.) New York: Barnes and Noble, Inc., n.d.

Traversi, Derek. "*The Tempest.*" *Scrutiny* (1949). Rev. in *Shakespeare: The Last Phase.* New York: Harcourt, Brace & Company, n.d [c. 1953]. 193–272.

Turner, John. "Reading by Contraries: *The Tempest* as Romance." *The Tempest.* Theory in Practice Series. Ed. Nigel Wood. Buckingham and Philadelphia: Open UP, 1995. 97–126; 178–79; 189.

Vaughan, Alden T. and Virginia Mason Vaughan, *Shakespeare's Caliban: A Cultural History.* 1991. Cambridge: Cambridge UP, 1996.

Warton, Joseph. *The Adventurer.* Number 97. 1754. Facsimile rpt. New York: AMS P, 1968.

Welsford, Enid. *The Court Masque.* Cambridge: Cambridge UP, 1927. 335–49.

Wheeler, Richard P. "Fantasy and History in *The Tempest.*" *The Tempest.* Theory in Practice Series. Ed. Nigel Wood. Buckingham and Philadelphia: Open UP, 1995. 127–164; 179–180; 190–192.

Wheeler, Richard P. Introduction. *Creating Elizabethan Tragedy: The Theater of Marlowe and Kyd.* Ed. Richard P. Wheeler. Chicago and London: U of Chicago P, 1988. 1–44.

Wheeler, Richard P. *Shakespeare's Development and the Problem Comedies: Turn and Counter-Turn.* Berkeley, Los Angeles, London: U of California P, 1981.

White, Hayden. "The Absurdist Moment in Contemporary Literary Theory." *Tropics of Discourse: Essays in Cultural Criticism.* 1978. Baltimore and London: Johns Hopkins UP, 1987. 261–282.

Wickham, Glynne. "Masque and Anti-Masque in *The Tempest.*" *Essays and Studies* 28 (1975): 1–14.

Wikander, Matthew H. " 'The Duke My Father's Wrack': The Innocence of the Restoration *Tempest.*" *Shakespeare Survey* 43 (1991): 91–98.

Wilde, Oscar. "The Preface." *The Picture of Dorian Gray.* Ed. Donald L. Lawler. New York and London: W. W. Norton & Company, 1988. 3–4.

Williams, Raymond. *Keywords: A Vocabulary of Culture and Society.* 1976. Rev. and expanded ed. New York: Oxford UP, 1983.

Williams, Raymond. *Marxism and Literature.* Oxford and New York: Oxford UP, 1977.

Willis, Deborah. "Shakespeare's *Tempest* and the Discourse of Colonialism." *Studies in English Literature* 29.2 (1989): 277–289.

Wilson, Daniel. *Caliban: The Missing Link.* London: Macmillan and Company, 1873.

Wilson, John Dover. *The Meaning of* The Tempest. 1936. Folcroft Library Editions, 1972.

Wilson, Richard. "Voyage to Tunis: New History and the Old World of *The Tempest.*" *ELH* 64 (1997): 333–357.

Yachnin, Paul. " 'If by your art': Shakespeare's Presence in *The Tempest.*" *English Studies in Canada* 14.2 (1988): 119–134.

Yates, Frances A. *Majesty & Magic in Shakespeare's Last Plays: New Approaches to Cymbeline, Henry VIII, and* The Tempest. Boulder: Shambhala, 1978. First published as *Shakespeare's Last Plays: A New Approach.* London: Routledge & Kegan Paul, 1975.

Young, David. *The Heart's Forest: A Study of Shakespeare's Pastoral Plays.* New Haven and London: Yale UP, 1972.

PART II

The Tempest and the Critics

Preface to *The Tempest,*
*or The Enchanted Island**

JOHN DRYDEN

The writing of Prefaces to Plays was probably invented by some very ambitious Poet, who never thought he had done enough: Perhaps by some Ape of the *French* Eloquence, who uses to make a business of a Letter of gallantry, an examen of a Farce; and in short, a great pomp and ostentation of words on every trifle. This is certainly the talent of that Nation, and ought not to be invaded by any other. They do that out of gayety which would be an imposition upon us.

We may satisfy ourselves with surmounting them in the Scene, and safely leave them those trappings of writing, and flourishes of the Pen, with which they adorn the borders of their Plays, and which are indeed no more than good Landskips to a very indifferent Picture. I must proceed no farther in this argument, lest I run my self beyond my excuse for writing this. Give me leave therefore to tell you, Reader, that I do it not to set a value on any thing I have written in this Play, but out of gratitude to the memory of *Sir William D'avenant* who did me the honour to joyn me with him in the alteration of it.

It was orginally *Shakespear's*: a Poet for whom he had particularly a high veneration, and whom he first taught me to admire. The Play it self had formerly been acted with success in the *Black-Fryers*: and our excellent Fletcher had so great a value for it, that he thought fit to make use of the same Design, not much varied, a second time. Those who have seen his *Sea-Voyage*, may easily discern that it was a Copy of *Shakespear's Tempest*: the Storm, the desart Island, and the Woman who had never seen a Man, are all sufficient tes-

*Originally printed in *The Tempest, or The Enchanted Island, A Comedy* (London, 1670). Reprinted in Vol 10 *The Works of John Dryden*, eds., Maximillian E. Novak and George Robert Guffey; General Ed., H. T. Swedenberg, Jr., (Berkeley, Los Angeles, and London: U of California P, 1970), 3–5. Reprinted with the permission of University of California Press.

timonies of it. But *Fletcher* was not the only Poet who made use of *Shake-spear's* Plot: *Sir John Suckling*, a profess'd admirer of our Author, has fol-low'd his footsteps in his *Goblins*; his Regmella being an open imitation of *Shakespear's* Miranda; and his Spirits, though counterfeit, yet are copied from *Ariel*. But Sir *William D'avenant*, as he was a man of quick and piercing imag-ination, soon found that somewhat might be added to the Design of *Shake-spear*, of which neither *Fletcher* nor *Suckling* had ever thought: and therefore to put the last hand to it, he design'd the Counterpart to Shakespear's Plot, namely that of a Man who had never seen a Woman; that by this means those two Characters of Innocence and Love might the more illustrate and commend each other. This excellent contrivance he was pleas'd to communicate to me, and to desire my assistance in it. I confess that from the very first moment it so pleas'd me, that I never writ any thing with more delight. I must likewise do him that justice to acknowledge, that my writing received daily his amend-ments, and that is the reason why it is not so faulty, as the rest which I have done without the help or correction of so judicious a friend. The Comical parts of the Saylors were also his invention, and for the most part his writing, as you will easily discover by the style. In the time I writ with him I had the oppor-tunity to observe somewhat more neerly of him than I had formerly done, when I had only a bare acquaintance with him: I found him then of so quick a fancy, that nothing was propos'd to him, on which he could not suddenly pro-duce a thought extreamly pleasant and surprizing: and those first thoughts of his, contrary to the old *Latine* Proverb, were not alwaies the least happy. And as his fancy was quick, so likewise were the products of it remote and new. He borrowed not of any other; and his imaginations were such as could not eas-ily enter into any other man. His corrections were sober and judicious: and he corrected his own writings much more severely than those of another man, bestowing twice the time and labour in polishing which he us'd in invention. It had perhaps been easie enough for me to have arrogated more to my self than was my due in the writing of this Play, and to have pass'd by his name with silence in the publication of it, with the same ingratitude which others have us'd to him, whose Writings he hath not only corrected, as he has done this, but has had a greater inspection over them, and sometimes added whole Scenes together, which may as easily be distinguish'd from the rest, as true Gold from counterfeit by the weight. But besides the unworthiness of the action which deterred me from it (there being nothing so base as to rob the dead of his reputation) I am satisfi'd I could never have receiv'd so much hon-our in being thought the Author of any Poem how excellent soever, as I shall from the joining my imperfections with the merit and name of *Shakespear* and Sir *William D'avenant*.

Decemb. 1.1669.

Comment on Caliban*

JOHN DRYDEN

To return once more to *Shakespear*; no man ever drew so many characters, or so generally distinguised 'em better from one another, excepting only *Johnson*: I will instance but in one, to show the copiousness of his Invention; 'tis that of *Caliban*, or the Monster in the *Tempest*. He seems there to have created a person which was not in Nature, a boldness which at first sight would appear intolerable: for he makes him a Species of himself, begotten by an Incubus on a Witch; but this as I have elsewhere prov'd, is not wholly beyond the bounds of credibility, at least the vulgar still believe it. We have the separated notions of a spirit, and of a Witch; (and Spirits according to *Plato*, are vested with a subtil body; according to some of his followers, have different Sexes) therefore as from the distinct apprehensions of a Horse, and of a Man, Imagination has form'd a *Centaur*, so from those of an Incubus and a Sorceress, *Shakespear* has produc'd his Monster. Whether or no his Generation can be defended, I leave to Philosophy; but of this I am certain, that the Poet has most judiciously furnish'd him with a person, a Language, and a character, which will suit him, both by Fathers and Mothers side: he has all the discontents, and malice of a Witch, and of a Devil; besides a convenient proportion of the deadly sins; Gluttony, Sloth, and Lust, are manifest; the dejectedness of a slave is likewise given him, and the ignorance of one bred up in a Desart Island. His person is monstrous, as he is the product of unnatural Lust; and his language is as hob-

*Originally printed in "The Preface to the Play," *Troilus and Cressida, or Truth Found Too Late* (London, 1679). Reprinted in Vol. 13 *The Works of John Dryden*, ed., Maximillian E. Novak, George Robert Guffey, and Alan Roper (Berkeley, Los Angeles, and London: University of California Press, 1984), 239–40. Reprinted with permission of the University of California Press.

goblin as his person: in all things he is distinguish'd from other mortals. The characters of *Fletcher* are poor & narrow, in comparision with *Shakespears*; I remember not one which is not borrow'd from him; unless you will except that strange mixture of a man in the *King and No King*: So that in this part *Shakespear* is generally worth our Imitation; and to imitate *Fletcher* is but to Copy after him who was a Copyer.

The Adventurer, Number 93 [*]

Tuesday, September 25, 1753.

JOSEPH WARTON

Irritat, mulcet, falsis terroribus implet
Ut Magus; & modo me Thebis, modo ponit Athenis.
—HORACE

WRITERS of a mixed character, that abound in transcendent beauties and in gross imperfections, are the most proper and most pregnant subjects for criticism. The regularity and correctness of Virgil or Horace, almost confine their commentators to perpetual panegyric, and afford them few opportunities of diversifying their remarks by the detection of latent blemishes. For this reason, I am inclined to think, that a few observations on the writing of Shakespeare, will not be deemed useless or unentertaining, because he exhibits more numerous examples of excellencies and faults, of every kind, than are, perhaps, to be discovered in any other author. I shall, therefore, from time to time, examine his merit as a poet, without blind admiration, or wanton invective.

As Shakespeare is sometimes blameable for the conduct of his fables, which have no unity; and sometimes for his diction, which is obscure and turgid; so his characteristical excellencies may possibly be reduced to these three general heads: "his lively creative imagination; his strokes of nature and passion; and his preservation of the consistency of his characters." These excellencies, particularly the last, are of so much importance in the drama, that they amply compensate for his transgressions against the rules of time and place, which being of a more mechanical nature, are often strictly observed by a genius of the lowest order; but to portray characters naturally, and to preserve them uniformly, requires such an intimate knowledge of the heart of

*Originally printed in *The Adventurer* 25 September (London, 1753). Reprinted by AMS Press (New York, 1968).

man, and is so rare a portion of felicity, as to have been enjoyed, perhaps, only by two writers, Homer and Shakespeare.

Of all the plays of Shakespeare, *The Tempest* is the most striking instance of his creative power. He has there given the reins to his boundless imagination, and has carried the romantic, the wonderful, and the wild, to the most pleasing extravagance. The scene is a desolate island; and the characters the most new and singular that can well be conceived: a prince who practices magic, an attendant spirit, a monster the son of a witch, and a young lady who had been brought to this solitude in her infancy, and had never beheld a man except her father.

As I have affirmed that Shakespeare's chief excellence is the consistency of his characters, I will exemplify the truth of this remark, by pointing out some master-strokes of this nature in the drama before us.

The poet artfully acquaints us that Prospero is a magician, by the first words which his daughter Miranda speaks to him:

> If by your art, my dearest father, you have
> Put the wild waters in this roar, allay them:

which intimate that the tempest described in the preceding scene, was the effect of Prospero's power. The manner in which he was driven from his dukedom of Milan, and landed afterwards on this solitary island, accompanied only by his daughter, is immediately introduced in a short and natural narration.

The offices of his attendant Spirit, Ariel, are enumerated with amazing wildness of fancy, and yet with equal propriety: his employment is said to be,

> ——To tread the ooze
> Of the salt deep;
> To run upon the sharp wind of the north;
> To do——business in the veins o' th' earth,
> When it is bak'd with frost;
> ——to dive into the fire; to ride
> On the curl'd clouds——

In describing the place in which he has concealed the Neapolitan ship, Ariel expresses the secrecy of its situation by the following circumstance, which artfully glances at another of his services;

> ——In the deep nook, where once
> Thou call'st me up at midnight, to fetch dew
> From the still-vext Bermudas——

Ariel, being one of those elves or spirits, "whose pastime is to make midnight mushrooms, and who rejoice to listen to the solemn curfew"; by whose assistance Prospero has "bedimm'd the sun at noon-tide,"

> And 'twixt the green sea and the azur'd vault,
> Set roaring war;——

has a set of ideas and images peculiar to his station and office; a beauty of the same kind with that which is so justly admired in the Adam of Milton, whose manners and sentiments are all paradisical. How delightfully and how suitably to his character, are the habitations and pastimes of this invisible being, pointed out in the following exquisite song!

> Where the bee sucks, there lurk I:
> In a cowslip's bell I lie;
> There I couch when owls do cry.
> On the bat's back I do fly,
> After sun-set, merrily.
> Merrily merrily shall I live now,
> Under the blossom that hangs on the bough.

Mr. Pope, whose imagination has been thought by some the least of his excellencies, has, doubtless, conceived and carried on the machinery in his "Rape of the Lock," with vast exuberance of fancy. The images, customs, and employments of his sylphs, are exactly adapted to their natures, are peculiar and appropriated, are all, if I may be allowed the expression, sylphish. The enumeration of the punishments they were to undergo, if they neglected their charge, would, on account of its poetry and propriety, and especially the mixture of oblique satire, be superior to any circumstances in Shakespeare's Ariel, if we could suppose Pope to have been unacquainted with the *Tempest*, when he wrote this part of his accomplished poem.

> ——————She did confine thee
> Into a cloven pine; within which rift
> Imprison'd, thou didst painfully remain
> A dozen years: within which space she dy'd,
> And left thee there; where thou didst vent thy groans,
> As fast as mill-wheels strike.——

> If thou more murmur'st, I will rend an oak,
> And peg thee in his knotty entrails, 'till
> Thou'st howl'd away twelve winters.

> For this, be sure, to-night thou shalt have cramps,
> Side-stitches that shall pen thy breath up: urchins
> Shall, for that vast of night that they may work,
> All exercise on thee; thou shalt be pinch'd
> As thick as honey-combs, each pinch more stinging
> Than bees that made 'em.

If thou neglect'st or dost unwillingly
What I command, I'll rack thee with old cramps;
Fill all thy bones with aches; make thee roar,
That beasts shall tremble at thy din.

SHAKESPEARE

WHATEVER spirit, careless of his charge,
Forsakes his post or leaves the Fair at large,
Shall feel sharp vengeance soon o'ertake his sins,
Be stopp'd in vials, or transfix'd with pins;
Or plung'd in lakes of bitter washes lie,
Or wedg'd whole ages in a bodkin's eye;
Gums and pomatums shall his flight restrain,
While clog'd he beats his silken wings in vain;
Or alom styptics with contracting pow'r,
Shrink his thin essence like a shrivell'd flow'r:
Or as Ixion fix'd, the wretch shall feel
The giddy motion of the whirling wheel;
In fumes of burning chocolate shall glow,
And tremble at the sea that froths below!

POPE.

The method which is taken, to induce Ferdinand to believe that his father was drown'd in the late tempest, is exceedingly solemn and striking. He is sitting upon a solitary rock, and weeping over against the place where he imagined his father was wrecked, when he suddenly hears with astonishment aerial music creep by him upon the waters, and the Spirit gives him the following information in words not proper for any but a Spirit to utter:

Full fathom five thy father lies:
    Of his bones are coral made;
Those are pearls that were his eyes:
    Nothing of him that doth fade,
But doth suffer a sea-change,
Into something rich and strange

And then follows a most lively circumstance;

Sea-nymphs hourly ring his knell.
Hark! now I hear them——Ding-dong-bell!

This is so truly poetical, that one can scarce forbear exclaiming with Ferdinand,

> This is no mortal business, nor no sound
> That the earth owns!——

The happy versatility of Shakespeare's genius enables him to excel in lyric as well as in dramatic poesy.

But the poet rises still higher in his management of this character of Ariel, by making a moral use of it, that is, I think, incomparable, and the greatest effort of his art. Ariel informs Prospero, that he has fulfilled his orders, and punished his brother and companions so severely, that if he himself was now to behold their sufferings, he would greatly compassionate them. To which Prospero answers,

> ——Dost thou think so, Spirit?
> ARIEL.   Mine would, Sir, were I human.
> PROSPERO. And mine shall.

He then takes occasion, with wonderful dexterity and humanity, to draw an argument from the incorporeality of Ariel, for the justice and necessity of pity and forgiveness:

> Hast thou, which art but air, a touch, a feeling
> Of their afflictions; and shall not myself,
> One of their kind, that relish all as sharply,
> Passion'd as they, be kindlier mov'd than thou art?

The poet is a more powerful magician than his own Prospero: we are transported into fairy land; we are rapt in a delicious dream, from which it is misery to be disturbed; all around is enchantment!

> ——The isle is full of noises,
> Sounds, and sweet airs, that give delight and hurt not.
> Sometimes a thousand twanging instruments
> Will hum about mine ears, and sometimes voices;
> That if I then had wak'd after long sleep,
> Will make me sleep again: and then in dreaming,
> Ready to drop upon me:—when I wak'd,
> I cry'd to dream again!

The Transcript of Lecture 9[*]

SAMUEL TAYLOR COLERIDGE

He observed that it is a known and unexplained phenomenon that among the ancients Statuary rose to such a degree of perfection as to leave almost the hope of imitating it baffled, and mingled with despair of excelling it; while Painting, at the same time, notwithstanding the admiration bestowed upon the ancient paintings by Apelles[1] by Pliny and others, had been proved to be an excellence of much later growth, and to have fallen far short of Statuary. He remembered a man, equally admirable for his talents and his rank, [who,] pointing to a sign-post, observed that, had Titian not lived, the richness of representation by colour even there could never have existed. In that mechanical branch of painting, perspective, the ancients were equally deficient, as was proved by the discoveries at Herculaneum and the Palace of Nero,[2] in which such blunders were to be found as to render plausible the assertions of those who maintained that the ancients were wholly ignorant of it. That they were not totally destitute of it is proved by Vitruvius[3] in the introduction to his second book.

Something of the same kind appears to have been the case with regard to their dramas. Early in the lectures the Greek stage had been noticed, which had been imitated by the French, and by the writers of England since the reign of Charles II. Their scheme[4] allowed nothing more than a variation of the same note, and admitted nothing of that which is the true principle of life, the attaining of the same end by an infinite variety of means.

*Collier's transcript of Coleridge's lecture on Monday, 16 December 1811, edited by R. A. Foakes, *Coleridge on Shakespeare: The Text of the Lectures of 1811–12* (Charlottesville: Univeristy Press of Virginia for the Folger Shakespeare Library, 1971), 98–115. Copyright © 1971 R.A. Foakes. Reprinted with the permission of R.A. Foakes. For fuller notes and textual apparatus readers should consult Vol. 5:1 *The Collected Works of Samuel Taylor Coleridge Lectures 1808–1819 On Literature*, ed., R. A. Foakes (London: Routledge & Kegan Paul; Princeton: Princeton University Press, 1987), 343–369.

It is true that the writings of Shakespeare are not likenesses of the Greek: they are analogies, because by very different means they produce the same end; whereas the greater part of the French Tragedies and the English plays on the same plan cannot be called likenesses, but may be called the failing of the same end by adopting the same means under most unappropriate circumstances.

This had led Coleridge to consider that the ancient drama, meaning the works of Aeschylus, Euripides, and Sophocles (for the miserable rhetorical works by the Romans are scarcely to be mentioned as dramatic poems) might be contrasted with the Shakespearian Drama: he had called it Shakespearian, because he knew no other writer who had realized the same idea, although he had been told that the Spanish Poet Calderon[5] had been as successful. The Shakespearian drama might be compared to painting and statuary.[6] In the latter, as in the Greek drama, the characters must be few, because the very essence of statuary was a high degree of abstraction, which would prevent a great many figures from being combined into the same effects. In a grand group of Niobe, or any other ancient heroic subject, how disgusting it would appear were an old nurse introduced. The numbers must be circumscribed, and nothing undignified must be brought into company with what is dignified; no one personage must be brought in but what is abstraction: all must not be presented to the eye, but the effect of multitude must be produced without the introduction of anything discordant.

Compare this group with a picture by Raphael or Titian—where an immense number of figures might be introduced, even a dog, a cat, or a beggar, and from the very circumstance of a less degree of labour and a less degree of abstraction, an effect is produced equally harmonious to the mind, more true to nature, and in all respects but one superior to Statuary; the perfect satisfaction in a thing as a work of art. The man of taste feels satisfied with what, out of his mixed nature, he cannot produce, and to that which the reason conceives possible a momentary reality was given, by the aid of the imagination.

He had before stated the circumstances which permitted Shakespeare to make an alteration so suitable to his age, and so necessitated by the circumstances of the age. Coleridge here repeated what he had before said regarding the distortion of the human voice by the size of the ancient theatres, and the attempt introduced of making everything on the stage appear reality. The difference between an imitation and a likeness is the mixture of a greater number of circumstances of dissimilarity with those of similarity: an imitation differs from a copy precisely as sameness differs from likeness in that sense of the word in which we imply a difference conjoined with that sameness.

Shakespeare had likewise many advantages: the great at that time, instead of throwing round them the Chevaux de frise[7] of mere manners, endeavoured to distinguish themselves by attainments, by energy of thought, and consequent powers of mind. The stage had nothing but curtains for its scenes, and the Actor as well as the author were obliged to appeal to the imagination, and not to the senses, which gave the latter a power over space and time which in the ancient theatre would have been absurd simply because it was contradictory. The advantage is indeed vastly on the side of the modern; he appeals to the imagination, to the reason, and to the noblest powers of the human heart: he is above the iron compulsion of space and time. He appeals to that which we most wish to be when we are most worthy of being, while the ancient dramas bind us down to the meanest part of our nature, and its chief compensation is a simple acquiescence of the mind that what the Poet has represented might possibly have taken place—a poor compliment to a Poet who is to be a creator, to tell him that he has all the excellences of a historian! In dramatic composition, the Unities of Time and Place so narrowed the space of action, and so impoverished[8] the sources of pleasure, that of all the Athenian dramas there is scarcely one which has not fallen into absurdity by aiming at an object and failing, or which has not incurred greater absurdity by bringing events into a space of time in which it is impossible for them to have happened; not to mention that the grandest effort of the Dramatist to be the mirror of life is completely lost.

The limit allowed by the Greeks was twenty-four hours, but we might as well take twenty-four months, because it has already become an object of imagination. The mind is then acted upon by such strong stimulants that the one and the other are indifferent; when once the limit of possibility is passed there are no bounds which can be assigned to imagination. We soon find that such effects may arise from such causes. Above all, in reading Shakespeare, we should first consider in what plays he means to appeal to the reason or imagination, faculties which have no relation to time and place, excepting as in the one case they imply a succession of cause and effect, and as in the other they form a harmonious picture so that the impulse given by reason is carried on by the imagination.

Shakespeare was often spoken of as a Child of Nature, and many had been his imitators, and [they] attempted to copy real incidents, and some of them had not even genius enough to copy nature, but still they produced a sort of phenomenon of modern times, neither tragic, nor comic, nor tragicomic, but the Sentimental. This sort of writing consisted in taking some very affecting incidents, which in its highest excellence only aspired to the genius of an onion, the power of drawing tears, and in which the Author, acting like a Ventriloquist, distributed his own insipidity. Coleridge had seen plays, some translated, and some the growth of our own soil, so well acted and so ill written that, if the auditor could have produced an artificial deafness, he would have been much pleased with the performance as a pantomime.

Shakespeare's characters from Othello or Macbeth down to Dogberry are ideal: they are not the things, but the abstracts of the things which a great mind may take into itself and naturalize to its own heaven. In the character of Dogberry itself some important truths are conveyed, or some admirable allusion is made to some folly reigning at the time, and which the Poet saw must forever reign. The enlightened readers of Shakespeare may be divided into two classes:

1. Those who read with feeling and understanding.
2. Those who, without affecting to understand or criticize, merely feel and are the recipients of the poet's power.

Between the two no medium could be endured. The reader often feels that some ideal trait of our own is caught, or some nerve has been touched of which we were not before aware, and it is proved that it has been touched by the vibration that we feel, a sort of thrilling, which tells us that we know ourselves the better for it. In the plays of Shakespeare every man sees himself without knowing that he sees himself, as in the phenomena of nature, in the mist of the mountain, a traveller beholds his own figure, but the glory round the head distinguishes it from a mere vulgar copy; or as a man traversing the Brocken in the north of Germany at sunrise, when the glorious beams are shot askance the mountain; he sees before him a figure of gigantic proportions and of such elevated dignity, that he only knows it to be himself by the similarity of action—or as the [Fata Morgana][9] at Messina in which all forms at determined distances are presented in an invisible mist, draped in all the gorgeous colours of prismatic imagination, and with magic harmony uniting them and producing a beautiful whole in the mind of the Spectator.

It is rather humiliating to find that since Shakespeare's time none of our Critics seems to enter into his peculiarities. Coleridge would not dwell on this point, because he intended to devote a lecture more immediately to the prefaces of Pope and Johnson. Some of his contemporaries appear to have understood him, and in a way that does him no small honour: the moderns in their prefaces praise him as a great genius, but when they come to their notes on his plays they treat him like a Schoolboy. Coleridge went on to ridicule the modern commentators still further, asserting that they only exercised the most vulgar of all feeling—that of wonderment. They had maintained that Shakespeare was an irregular poet, that he was now above all praise, and now if possible below contempt, and they reconciled it by saying that he wrote for the mob. No man of genius ever wrote for the mob; he never would consciously write that which was below himself. Careless he might be, or he might write at a time when his better genius did not attend him, but he never wrote anything that he knew would degrade himself. Were it so, as well might a man pride himself of acting the beast, or a Catalani, because she did not feel in a mood to sing, begin to bray.[10]

Yesterday afternoon a friend had left for him a Work by a German writer,[11] of which Coleridge had had time only to read a small part, but what he had read he approved and he should praise the book much more highly, were it not that in truth it would be praising himself, as the sentiments contained in it were so coincident with those Coleridge had expressed at the Royal Institution. It was not a little wonderful that so many ages had elapsed since the time of Shakespeare and that it should remain so for *foreigners* first to feel truly, and to appreciate properly his mighty genius. The solution of this fact must be sought in the history of the nation. The English had become a busy commercial people, and had unquestionably derived from it many advantages moral and physical: we had grown into a mighty nation; one of the giant nations of the world, whom moral superiority still enables to struggle with the other, the evil genius[12] of the Planet.

The German nation on the other hand, unable to act at all, have been driven into speculation; all the feelings have been forced back into the thinking and reasoning mind. To do was impossible for them, but in determining what ought to be done, they perhaps exceeded every people of the globe. Incapable of acting outwardly, they have acted internally. They first rationally recalled the ancient philosophy; they acted upon their own spirits with an energy of which England produces no parallel since those truly heroic times in body and in soul, the days of Elizabeth.

If all that had been written upon Shakespeare by Englishmen were burnt for want of candles merely to read half of the works of Shakespeare, we should be gainers. Providence had given us the greatest man that ever lived, and had thrown a sop to Envy by giving us the worst critics upon him. His contemporaries were not so insensible: a poem of the highest merit had been addressed to him, and Coleridge knew nowhere, where a more full [description] or contra-distinguishing of great genius could be found than in this Poem.[13] It was as follows:

> A mind reflecting ages past, whose clear
> And equal surface can make things appear
> Distant a thousand years, and represent
> Them in their lively colours just extent
> To outrun hasty Time; retrieve the Fates,
> Roll back the Heavens: blow ope the iron gates
> Of Death and Lethe, where confused lie
> Great heaps of ruinous mortality
> In that deep husky dungeon to discern
> A Royal Ghost from churls; by art to learn
> The [physiognomy] of shades, and give
> Them sudden birth, wondering how [oft they live,]
> What story coldly tells, what Poets feign
> At second hand, and picture without brain,
> [Senseless and soul-less shows: to give a stage
> (Ample and true with life) voice, action, age,
> As Plato's year, and new scene of the world,

Them unto us, or to us them had hurl'd:]
To raise our ancient Sovereigns from their hearse,
Make Kings his subjects; by exchanging verse
[Enlive] their pale trunks; that the present age
Joys at their joy, and trembles at their rage:
Yet so to temper passion, that our ears
Take pleasure in their pain, and eyes in tears
Both weep and smile; fearful at plots so sad,
Then laughing at our fear; abus'd, and glad
To be abus'd; affected with that truth
Which we perceive is false, pleas'd in that ruth
At which we start, [and, by elaborate play,
Tortur'd and tickl'd; by a crab-like way
Time past made pastime; and in ugly sort
Disgorging up his ravin for our sport:—
—While the plebeian imp, from lofty throne,
Creates and rules a world, and works upon
Mankind by secret engines; now to move
A chilling pity, then a rigorous love;
To strike up and stroke down, both joy and ire
To steer th'affections; and by heavenly fire
Mold us anew, stol'n from ourselves:—]
This, and much more, which cannot be express'd
But by himself, his tongue and his own breast
Was Shakespeare['s freehold;] which his cunning brain
Improv'd by favour of the nine-fold train.

Never was anything characteristic of Shakespeare more happily expressed.

It is a mistake, Coleridge maintained, to suppose that any of Shakespeare's characters strike us as Portraits. They have the union of reason perceiving and the judgment recording actual facts, and the imagination diffusing over all a magic glory, and while it records the past, [it] projects in a wonderful degree to the future, and makes us feel, however slightly, and see, however dimly, that state of being in which there is neither past nor future, but which is permanent, and is the energy of nature.

Though Coleridge had affirmed, and truly, that all Shakespeare's characters were ideal, yet a just division may be made, [firstly], of those in which the ideal is more prominent to the mind; where it is brought forward more intentionally, where we were made more conscious of the ideal, though in truth they possessed no more or less reality; and secondly, of those which, though equally idealized, the delusion upon the mind is that of their being real. Shakespeare's plays might be separated into those where the real is disguised in the ideal, and those where the ideal is hidden from us in the real. The difference is made by the powers of the mind which the Poet chiefly appeals to.

At present the Lecturer would speak only of those plays where the ideal is predominant, and chiefly for this reason, that those plays had been objected to with the greatest violence; they are objections not the growth of our own Country but the production of France:[14] the judgment of Monkies by some wonderful phenomenon put into the mouths of men. We were told by these creatures that Shakespeare was some wonderful monster in which many heterogeneous components were thrown together, producing a discordant mass of genius and irregularity of gigantic proportions.

Among the ideal Plays was the Tempest, which he would take as an example. Many others might be mentioned but it was impossible to go through every separate piece and what was said on the Tempest would apply to all.—

In this Play Shakespeare has appealed to the imagination, and he constructed a plan according to it: the scheme of his drama did not appeal to any sensuous impression (the word sensuous was authorized by Milton) of time and space, but to the imagination, and it would be recollected that his works were rather recited than acted.

In the first scene was introduced a mere confusion on board a ship; the lowest characters were brought together with the highest, and with what excellence! A great part of the Genius of Shakespeare consisted of these happy combinations of the highest and lowest, and of the gayest and the saddest. He was not droll in one scene and melancholy in another, but both the one and the other in the same scene: laughter is made to swell the tear of sorrow, and to throw as it were a poetic light upon it, and the tear mixes a tenderness with the laughter that succeeds. In the same scene Shakespeare has shown that power which above all other men he possessed, that of introducing the profoundest sentiments of wisdom just where they would be least expected, and yet where they are truly natural; and the admirable secret of his drama was that the separate speeches do not appear to be produced the one by the former, but to arise out of the peculiar character of the speaker.

Coleridge here explained the difference between what he called mechanic and organic regularity.[15] In the former the copy must be made as if it had been formed in the same mould with the original. In the latter there is a law which all the parts obey, conforming themselves to the outward symbols and manifestations of the essential principle. He illustrated this distinction by referring to the growth of Trees, which from peculiar circumstances of soil, air, or position, differed in shape even from trees of the same kind, but every man was able to decide at first sight which was an oak, an ash, or a poplar.

This was the case in Shakespeare: he shewed the life and principle of the being, with organic regularity. Thus the Boatswain in the storm, when a sense of danger impressed all, and the bonds of reverence are thrown off, and he gives a loose to his feelings, and thus to the old Counsellor pours forth his vulgar mind:

"Hence! What care these roarers for the name of King? To cabin—Silence! trouble us not." Gonzalo observes—"Good; yet remember whom thou hast aboard!"

The Boatswain replies, "None that I more love than myself.—You are a Counsellor; if you can command these elements to silence, and work the peace of the present, we will not handle a rope more; use your authority: if you cannot, give thanks you have lived so long, and make yourself ready in your Cabin for the mischance of the hour, if it so hap—Cheerly good hearts!—Out of our way I say."

An ordinary dramatist would, after this speech, have introduced Gonzalo moralizing or saying something connected with it; for common dramatists are not men of genius: they connect their ideas by association or logical connection, but the vital writer in a moment transports himself into the very being of each character, and instead of making artificial puppets, he brings the real being before you. Gonzalo replies therefore,

"I have great comfort from this fellow: methinks he hath no drowning mark upon him, his complexion is perfect gallows. Stand fast, good fate, to his hanging; make the rope of his destiny our cable, for our own doth little advantage. If he be not born to be hanged our case is miserable."

Here is the true sailor, proud of his contempt of danger, and the high feeling of the old man who, instead of condescending to reply to the words addressed to him, turns off and meditates with himself, and draws some feeling of comfort to his own mind by trifling with his fate, founding upon it a hope of safety.

Shakespeare had determined to make the plot of this play such as to involve a certain number of low characters, and at the beginning of the piece pitched the note of the whole. It was evidently brought in as a lively mode of telling a story, and the reader is prepared for something to be developed, and in the next scene he brings forward *Prospero and Miranda*.

How was it done? By first introducing his favourite character Miranda by a sentence which at once expresses the vehemence and violence of the storm, such as it might appear to a witness from the land, and at the same time displays the tenderness of her feelings; the exquisite feelings of a female brought up in a desert, yet with all the advantages of education, all that could be given by a wise, learned, and affectionate father: with all the powers of mind, not weakened by the combats of life, Miranda says—

> Oh, I have suffered
> With those I saw suffer! a brave vessel,
> Which had *no doubt* some noble creatures in her,
> Dashed all to pieces,

The Doubt here expressed could have occurred to no mind but to that of Miranda, who had been bred up with her father and a Monster only: she did not know as others do what sort of creatures were in a ship: they never would have introduced it as a conjecture. This shows that while Shakespeare is displaying his vast excellence he never fails to introduce some touch or other which not only makes characteristic[16] of the peculiar person but combines two things, the person and the circumstances that acted upon the person. She proceeds,

> —Oh, the cry did knock
> Against my very heart—Poor souls, they perished;
> Had I been any God of power, I would
> Have sunk the sea within the earth or ere
> It should the good ship so have swallowed, and
> The freighting souls within her—

Still dwelling on that which was most wanting in her nature: these fellow-creatures, from whom she appeared banished, with only one relict to keep them alive not in her memory but in her imagination.

Another instance of excellent judgment (for Coleridge was principally speaking of that) was the preparation. Prospero is introduced first in his magic robes, which, with the assistance of his daughter, he removes, and it is the first time the reader knows him as a being possessing supernatural powers. Then he instructs his daughter in the story of their arrival in that Island, and it is done in such a manner that no reader ever[17] conjectures the technical use the poet has made of the relation, viz., informing the audience of the story.

The next step is that Prospero gives warning that he means for particular purposes to lull Miranda to sleep, and thus he exhibits his first and mildest proof of his magical power. It was not as in vulgar plays, where a person is introduced that nobody knows or cares anything about, merely to let the audience into the secret. Prospero then lulls his Daughter asleep, and by the sleep stops the relation at the very moment when it was necessary to break if off in order to excite curiosity, and yet to give the memory and understanding sufficient to carry on the progress of the fable uninterruptedly.

Coleridge could not help here noticing a fine touch of Shakespeare's knowledge of human nature, and generally of the great laws of the mind: he meant Miranda's infant remembrance. Prospero asks her

> —Canst thou remember
> A time before we came unto this cell?
> I do not think thou canst; for then thou wast not
> But three years old.—

Miranda answers

> Certainly sir, I can.

Prospero inquires

> By what?—By any other house or person?
> Of anything the image tell me that
> Hath kept with thy remembrance.

Miranda replies

> 'Tis far off—
> And rather like a dream than an assurance
> That my remembrance warrants. Had I not
> Four or five women once that tended me?

This is exquisite.—In general our early remembrances of life arise from vivid colours, especially if we have seen them in motion: persons, when grown up for instance, will remember a bright green door seen when they were young: but in Miranda, who was somewhat older, it was by 4 or 5 women. She might know men from her father, and her remembrance of the past might be worn out by the present object, but women she only knew by herself, the contemplation of her own figure in the fountain, and yet she recalled to her mind what had been. It is not that she saw such and such Grandees, or such and such peeresses but she remembered to have seen something like a reflection of herself, but it was not herself, and it brought back to her mind what she had seen most like herself: it was a constant yearning of fancy re-producing the past, of what she had only seen in herself, and could only see in herself.

The Picturesque power of Shakespeare, in Coleridge's opinion, of all the poets that ever lived was only equalled by Milton and Dante.[18] The power of genius was not shown in elaborating a picture, of which many specimens were given in Poems of modern date, where the work was so dutchified by minute touches that the reader naturally asked why words and not painting were used? The Lecturer knew a young Lady of much taste who, on reading the recent versifications of voyages and travels that had been published, observed that by a sort of instinct she always cast her eyes on the opposite page for coloured prints.

The power of Poetry is by a single word to produce that energy in the mind as compels the imagination to produce the picture. Thus when Prospero says,

> one midnight
> Fated to his purpose did Antonio open
> The gates of Milan, and i' the dead of darkness
> The Ministers for his purpose hurried thence
> Me and thy crying self.

Thus, by introducing the simple happy epithet *crying* in the last line, a complete picture is present to the mind, and in this the power of true poetry consists.

Coleridge would next mention the preparation of the reader, first by the storm, as before mentioned. The introduction of all that preceded the tale, as well as the tale itself, served completely to develop the main character and the intention of Prospero. The fact of Miranda being charmed asleep fits us for what goes beyond our ordinary belief, and gradually leads us to the appearance and disclosure of a being gifted with supernatural powers.

Before the introduction of Ariel too, the reader was prepared by what preceded: the moral feeling called forth by the sweet words of Miranda, "Alack what trouble was I then to you"—in which she considered only the sufferings and sorrows of her parent; the reader was prepared to exert his imagination for an object so interesting. The Poet made him wish that if supernatural agency were employed, it should be used for a being so lovely.—"The wish was father to the thought."[19]

In this state of mind was comprehended what is called Poetic Faith, before which our common notions of philosophy give way: This feeling was much stronger than historic faith, in as much as by the former the mind was prepared to exercise it. He made this remark, though somewhat digressive, in order to lead to a future subject of these Lectures, the Poems of Milton.

Many scriptural Poems had been written, with so much of scripture in them, that what was not scripture appeared not to be true: it seemed like mingling lies with the most sacred truths. It was for this reason that Milton has taken as the subject of his work that one point of scripture of which we have the mere fact recorded. A few facts were only necessary, as in story of King Lear, to put an end to all doubt as to their credibility. It is idle to say then that this or that is improbable because history says that the fact is so. The story on which Milton has founded his Paradise Lost[20] is comprized in the Bible in four or five lines, and the Poet has substituted the faith of the mind to regard as true what would otherwise have appeared absurdity.

Coleridge now returned to the introduction of Ariel, prepared as he had explained. If ever there could be a doubt that Shakespeare was a great Poet acting by Laws arising out of his own nature, and not acting without law as had been asserted, it would be removed by the character of Ariel. The very first words spoken by Ariel introduced him not as an Angel above men, not as a Gnome or a Fiend, but while the Poet gives him all the advantages, all the faculties of reason, he divests him of all moral character, not positively but negatively. In air he lives, from air he derives his being. In air he acts, and all his colours and properties seem to be derived from the clouds. There is nothing in Ariel that cannot be conceived to exist in the atmosphere at sunrise or sunset: hence all that belongs to Ariel is all that belongs to the delight the mind can receive from external appearances abstracted from any inborn or purpose.[21] His answers to Prospero are either directly to the question and nothing beyond, or if he expatiates, which he does frequently, it is upon his own delights, and the unnatural situation in which he is placed, though under a good power and employed to good ends. Hence Shakespeare has made his very first demand characteristic of him. He is introduced discontented from his confinement, and being bound to obey anything that he is commanded: we feel it almost unnatural to him, and yet it is delightful that he is so employed. It is as if we were to command one of the winds to blow otherwise than nature dictates, or one of the waves, now sinking away and now rising, to recede before it bursts upon the shore. This is the sort of feeling we experience.

But when Shakespeare contrasts the treatment of Prospero with that of Sycorax, instead of producing curses and discontent, Ariel feels his obligation; he immediately assumes the airy being, with a mind in which, when one feeling is past, not a trace is left behind.

If there be anything in nature from which Shakespeare caught the idea of Ariel [it is] from the child to whom supernatural powers are given; he is neither born of Heaven, nor of earth, but between both: it is like a may blossom kept by the fanning breeze from falling to the ground, suspended in air, and only by violence of compulsion touching the earth. This aversion of the Sylph is kept up through the whole, and Shakespeare, in his admirable judgment, has availed himself of this circumstance to give Ariel an interest in the event, looking forward to that moment when he was to gain his last and only reward, simple liberty.

Another instance of admirable judgment and preparation is the being contrasted with Ariel, Caliban, who is described in such a manner by Prospero as to lead the Reader to expect and look for a monstrous unnatural creature. You do not see Caliban at once—you first hear his voice: it was a sort of preparation, because in nature we do not receive so much disgust from sound as from sight. Still Caliban does not appear, but Ariel enters as a Water Nymph: all the strength of contrast [is] thus acquired, without any of the shock of abruptness, or of the unpleasant feeling which surprise awakes when the object is a being in any way hateful to our senses.

The character of Caliban is wonderfully conceived: he is a sort of creature of the earth,[22] partaking of the qualities of the brute, and distinguished from them in two ways: I. By having mere understanding without moral reason; 2. By not having the instincts which belong to mere animals.—Still Caliban is a noble being: a man in the sense of the imagination, all the images he utters are drawn from nature, and are all highly poetical; they fit in with the images of Ariel: Caliban gives you images from the Earth—Ariel images from the air. Caliban talks of the difficulty of finding fresh water, the situation of Morasses, and other circumstances which the brute instinct not possessing reason could comprehend. No mean image is brought forward, and no mean passion, but animal passions, and the sense of repugnance at being commanded.

The manner in which the Lovers are introduced is equally excellent, and the last point the Lecturer would mention in this wonderful play: in every scene the same judgment might be pointed out, still preparing and still recalling like a lively piece of music. One thing, however, he wished to notice before he concluded, and that was the subject of the Conspiracy against the life of Alonzo, and how our Poet had so well prepared the feelings of his readers for their plot, which was to execute the most detestable of all crimes, and which in another play Shakespeare had called "the murder of sleep."[23]

These men at first had no such notion; it was suggested only by the magical sleep cast on Alonzo and Gonzalo: but they are previously introduced as scoffing and scorning at what was said, without any regard to situation or age; without any feelings of admiration of the excellent truths, but giving themselves up entirely to the malignant and unsocial feeling, that of listening to everything that is said, not to understand and to profit by the learning and experience of others, but to find something that may gratify vanity, by making them believe that the person speaking is inferior to themselves.

This was [the] grand characteristic of a villain, and it would be not a presentiment, but an anticipation of Hell, for men to suppose that all mankind was either as wicked as themselves, or might be if they were not too great fools to be so.

It was true that Mr Pope[24] objected to this conspiracy, and yet it would leave in Coleridge's opinion a complete chasm if it were omitted.

Many, indeed innumerable, beauties might be quoted, particularly the grandeur of the language of Prospero in that divine speech where he takes leave of his magic art, but were he to repeat them, he should pass from the character of a lecturer into a mere reciter. Before he terminated, however, he would take notice of one passage which had fallen under the very severe censure of Pope and Arbuthnot,[25] who had declared it to be a piece of the grossest bombast. It was this,—Prospero addressing himself to his Daughter, directing her attention to Ferdinand:

> The fringed curtains of thine eye advance,
> And say, what thou seest yond.

Putting this passage as a paraphrase of "Look what is coming," it certainly did appear ridiculous, and seemed to fall under the rule Coleridge had laid down, that whatever without injury could be translated into a foreign language in simple terms ought to be so in the original or it is not good.

But the different modes of expression, it should be remembered, frequently arose from dif[ference] of situation and education: a blackguard would use very different words to express the same thing, to those a gentleman would employ, and both would be natural and proper: the difference arose from the feeling; the gentleman would speak with all the polished language and regard to his own dignity which belonged to his rank, while the blackguard, who must be considered almost a half-brute, would[26] speak like a half-brute, having respect neither for himself or others.

But Coleridge was content to try this passage by its introduction: How does Prospero introduce it? He has just told Miranda a story which deeply affects her, and afterwards for his own purposes lulled her to sleep, and Shakespeare [makes her] wholly inattentive to the present when she awakes, and dwelling only on the past. The Actress who truly understands the character should have her eyelids sunk down, and living as it were in her dreams. Prospero then sees Ferdinand, and wishes to point him out to his daughter, not only with great but almost scenic solemnity, himself always present to her, and to the spectators as a magician. Something was to appear on a sudden, which was no more expected than we should look for the hero of a Play to be on the stage when the Curtain is drawn up: it is under such circumstances that Prospero says,

> The fringed curtains of thine eye advance,
> And say, what thou seest yond.

This solemnity of phraseology was, in Coleridge's opinion, completely in character with Prospero, who was assuming the Magician, whose very art seems to consider all the objects of nature in a mysterious point of view, and who wishes to produce a strong impression on Miranda at the first view of Ferdinand.

It is much easier to find fault with a writer merely by reference to former notions and experience, than to sit down and read him, and to connect the one feeling with the other, and to judge of words and phrases in proportion as they convey those feelings together.

Miranda possessed in herself all the ideal beauties that could be conceived by the greatest Poet, although it was not Coleridge's object so much to point out the high Poetic powers of Shakespeare as his exquisite judgment. But to describe one of the female characters of Shakespeare was almost to describe the whole, for each possessed all the excellences with which they could be invested.

Coleridge concluded by a panegyric upon Shakespeare, whom he declared to be the wonder of the ignorant part of mankind, but much more the wonder of the learned, who, at the same time that he possessed profundity of thought, could be looked upon as no less than a Prophet—Yet at the same time, with all his wonderful powers, making us feel as if we were unconscious of himself and of his mighty abilities; disguising the half-god in the simplicity of a child, or the affection of a dear companion.

NOTES

1. *Apelles*] Written out in the short-hand notebook, but omitted from the 1856 text.
2. *Herculaneum and the Palace of Nero*] Herculaneum, near Naples, destroyed by an eruption of Vesuvius in A.D. 79, was excavated over a long period beginning in 1738; the discoveries there, including some remarkable paintings, were widely reported. Nero's great palace in Rome, the *domus aurea*, was largely demolished by Vespasian, but parts including some paintings, survive.
3. *Vitruvius*] Coleridge was perhaps thinking of the preface and first chapter of Bk. 3 of Vitruvius *On Architecture*; or the preface to Bk. 7, para. 11, where a principle of perspective in stage scenery is described.
4. *scheme*] In 1856 Collier altered this word to "theme," adding a note saying he misheard the lecturer and mistakenly wrote "scheme" in his "original short-hand note" (Raysor, II, 158 (121)). [Foakes uses short, self-explanatory titles in his notes. His references to T. M. Raysor's *Coleridge's Shakespearean Criticism* 2 vols (1930) and revised in 2 vols. for the Everyman edition (1960) provide page numbers for both editions.—ed.]
5. *he had been told ... Calderon*] In his Lecture XII, Schlegel moves from a consideration of Greek tragedy (he mentions Aeschylus and Sophocles), via a slighting reference to Roman drama, to an account of Shakespeare, who is ranked with Calderon as one of the two great modern original dramatists. In the course of this discussion, Schlegel also distinguishes between organic and mechanical form, and compares ancient drama with sculpture, modern drama with painting (*Lectures*, translated Black, II, 92–100; *Vorlesungen*, II, ii, 4–15). The name "Calderon" is written out in the short-hand notebook, but not "Lopez de Vega," whose name is added in the corresponding passage in the 1856 text (Raysor, II, 159, (122)).
6. *painting and statuary*] A comparison developed from Schlegel's Lecture XII; see Black, II, 99–101 (*Vorlesungen*, II, ii, 15–17), "we compared the antique tragedy to a group in sculpture, ... the romantic drama must be viewed as a large picture, where not merely figure and motion are exhibited in richer groups, but where even what surrounds the person is also portrayed."
7. *Chevaux de frise*] i.e. entanglement.
8. *impoverished*] "impoverishes" in MS.
9. *Fata Morgana*] The name by which the mirage-effect Coleridge describes is known; he may have seen it when he visited Messina in 1805. The words are not in the MS., which leaves a blank space, but in the short-hand notebook "phata Morgana" is written out, confirming that this is what Coleridge said. Collier may have left a blank in the transcription because he did not understand the phrase; it has disappeared from the 1856 text, which simply reads "near Messina" (Raysor, II, 163 (125)).
10. *as well ... bray*] Angelica Catalani, an Italian soprano, had a great vogue in London after her début there in 1806; Coleridge seems to have dined with her in 1811 (see *The Letters of Charles Lamb*, ed. E. V. Lucas (1935), II, 115). This passage is much changed in the 1856 text, and the reference to Catalani is omitted. Collier added a curious footnote, as if to lend authenticity to his text, which runs as

follows (Raysor, II, 164 (126)): "because Shakespeare could not always be the greatest of poets, was he therefore to condescend to make himself the least?" In the footnote, Collier adds that his short-hand note reads "beast" for "least," but this must be an error, "the antithesis being between 'greatest' and 'least,' and not between 'poet' and 'beast.'" See R.A. Foakes, Introduction, *Coleridge on Shakespeare: The Text of the Lectures of 1811–12*, ed. by R. A. Foakes (Charlottesville: U P of Virginia, 1971), 17.

11. *German writer*] In a letter of 6 November 1811, to Henry Crabb Robinson, Coleridge said he was anxious to see a copy of "Schlegel's Werke," and the *Vorlesungen ueber dramatische Kunst und Litteratur* were presented to him by a German, Bernard Krusve, the day after he delivered Lecture 8 on 12 December; see *Collected Letters*, III, 343, 359–60. Lecture 9 was given on 16 December, so "Yesterday afternoon" would have been the 15th. The discrepancy in dates is not really significant; it seems clear that Coleridge first read Schlegel on Shakespeare between delivering Lectures 8 and 9 in this series. The *Vorlesungen* were published in three volumes; Vols. I and II, part i, appeared in 1809; vol. II, part ii, was published in 1811. This third volume contains (in the original division of the lectures, changed in later editions), Lectures XII to XV. Lecture XII is on Shakespeare, and Lecture XIII on other English dramatists. Coleridge certainly refers to these two lectures in his own Lecture 9 in December 1811.

12. *evil genius*] Napoleon (so Raysor).

13. *Poem*] In the 1856 text, Collier printed the whole of the poem, but in the MS., as printed here, the last thirty-four lines are omitted. Collier also added in 1856 a short paragraph, perhaps his own invention, noting and approving the ascription of the poem to Milton. The full text, first printed in the Second Folio of Shakespeare's plays (1632), together with an account of the controversy over the authorship of it, may be found in the *Shakspere Allusion—Book* (1932), I, 364–8. Schlegel praises the poem as having "some of the most beautiful and happy lines that ever were applied to any poet" (*Vorlesungen* II, ii, 23; trans. Black, II, 105).

   The MS. omits those lines in square brackets. The short-hand notebook contains notes of a few more lines than appear in the MS.; the names "Clio" and "Calliope" are written out, and these occur in the five lines following the last line in the MS. I do not know why Collier did not transcribe them in the MS. The text as printed in 1856 was presumably taken by Collier from a printed source.

14. *France*] Schlegel glances at the objections of "Frenchmen in particular" to Shakespeare (Black, II, 106–7; *Vorlesungen*, II, ii, 24–5) but in quite different terms from Coleridge here, and without reference to particular plays.

15. *mechanic and organic regularity*] Schlegel makes this distinction (Black, II, 94–5; *Vorlesungen*, II, i, 8–9), and observes that we find organic forms "in nature throughout the whole range of living powers, from the crystallization of salts and minerals to plants and flowers, and from them to the human figure."

16. *makes characteristic*] sic; changed to "is not merely characteristic" in 1856 (Raysor, II, 172, (133)).

17. *ever*] "Never" in MS.

18. *Milton and Dante*] So in the 1856 text; in the short-hand notebook there is written out "Pindar and Dante."

19. *wish ... thought*] Perhaps Coleridge is recalling *2 Henry IV*, 4.5.93. The quotation marks were omitted in the 1856 text.
20. *Paradise Lost*] Altered in 1856 to "Milton's story"; but "Lost" is written out in the short-hand notebook.
21. *abstracted ... purpose*] A space for the word is left in the MS. In the 1856 text, this sentence, rather altered, ends with the word "appearances," and this final phrase is simply omitted.
22. *Caliban ... earth*] Schlegel makes the same comment, as Raysor notes: see *Vorlesungen*, II, ii, 129, translated Black, II, 180, "In the Zephyr-like Ariel the image of air is not to be mistaken ... as, on the other hand, Caliban signifies the heavy element of earth."
23. *"the murder of sleep"*] *Macbeth* 2.2.36.
24. *Pope*] Pope notoriously objected to the long interchange at the opening of 2.1 of *The Tempest*, including the satirical comments of Antonio and Sebastian upon Gonzalo, but not to the conspiracy itself.
25. *Pope and Arbuthnot*] In the *Art of Sinking in Poetry* (1727), Ch. 12; see the edition by Edna L. Steeves (1952), 69.
26. *would*] "And would," MS.

Notes on *The Tempest**

SAMUEL TAYLOR COLERIDGE

There is a sort of improbability with which we are shocked in dramatic representation, not less than in a narrative of real life. Consequently, there must be rules respecting it; and as rules are nothing but means to an end previously ascertained—(inattention to which simple truth has been the occasion of all the pedantry of the French school),—we must first determine what the immediate end or object of the drama is. And here, as I have previously remarked, I find two extremes of critical decision;—the French, which evidently presupposes that a perfect delusion is to be aimed at,—an opinion which needs no fresh confutation; and the exact opposite to it, brought forward by Dr. Johnson, who supposes the auditors throughout in the full reflective knowledge of the contrary. In evincing the impossibility of delusion, he makes no sufficient allowance for an intermediate state, which I have before distinguised by the term, illusion, and have attempted to illustrate its quality and character by reference to our mental state, when dreaming. In both cases we simply do not judge the imagery to be unreal; there is a negative reality, and no more. Whatever, therefore, tends to prevent the mind from placing itself, or being placed, gradually in that state in which the images have such negative reality for the auditor, destroys this illusion, and is dramatically improbable.

Now the production of this effect—a sense of improbability—will depend on the degree of excitement in which the mind is supposed to be. Many things would be intolerable in the first scene of a play, that would not at all interrupt our enjoyment in the height of the interest, when the narrow cockpit may be made to hold

*Originally published in Vol. 2 *The Literary Remains of Samuel Taylor Coleridge*, collected and ed. Henry Nelson Coleridge, (London, 1836). Reprinted by AMS Press (New York, 1967), 92–102.

> The vasty field of France, or we may cram
> Within its wooden O, the very casques,
> That did affright the air at Agincourt.

Again, on the other hand, many obvious improbabilities will be endured, as belonging to the ground-work of the story rather than to the drama itself, in the first scenes, which would disturb or disentrance us from all illusion in the acme of our excitement; as for instance, Lear's division of the kingdom, and the banishment of Cordelia.

But, although the other excellencies of the drama besides this dramatic probability, as unity of interest, with distinctness and subordination of the characters, and appropriateness of style, are all, so far as they tend to increase the inward excitement, means towards accomplishing the chief end, that of producing and supporting this willing illusion,—yet they do not on that account cease to be ends themselves; and we must remember that, as such, they carry their own justification with them, as long as they do not contravene or interrupt the total illusion. It is not even always, or of necessity, an objection to them, that they prevent the illusion from rising to as great a height as it might otherwise have attained;—it is enough that they are simply compatible with as high a degree of it as is requisite for the purpose. Nay, upon particular occasions, a palpable improbability may be hazarded by a great genius for the express purpose of keeping down the interest of a merely instrumental scene, which would otherwise make too great an impression for the harmony of the entire illusion. Had the panorama been invented in the time of Pope Leo X., Raffael would still, I doubt not, have smiled in contempt at the regret, that the broom-twigs and scrubby bushes at the back of some of his grand pictures were not as probable trees as those in the exhibition.

The Tempest is a specimen of the purely romantic drama, in which the interest is not historical, or dependent upon fidelity of portraiture, or the natural connexion of events,—but is a birth of the imagination, and rests only on the coaptation and the union of the elements granted to, or assumed by, the poet. It is a species of drama which owes no allegiance to time or space, and in which, therefore, errors of chronology and geography—no mortal sins in any species—are venial faults, and count for nothing. It addresses itself entirely to the imaginative faculty; and although the illusion may be assisted by the effect on the senses of the complicated scenery and decorations of modern times, yet this sort of assistance is dangerous. For the principal and only genuine excitement ought to come from within,—from the moved and sympathetic imagination; whereas, where so much is addressed to the mere external senses of seeing and hearing, the spiritual vision is apt to languish, and the attraction from without will withdraw the mind from the proper and only legitimate interest which is intended to spring from within.

The romance opens with a busy scene admirably appropriate to the kind of drama, and giving, as it were, the key-note to the whole harmony. It prepares and initiates the excitement required for the entire piece, and yet does not demand any thing from the spectators, which their previous habits had not fitted them to understand. It is the bustle of a tempest, from which the real horrors are abstracted;—therefore it is poetical, though not in strictness natural—(the distinction to which I have so often alluded)—and is purposely restrained from concentering the interest on itself, but used merely as an induction or turning for what is to follow.

In the second scene, Prospero's speeches, till the entrance of Ariel, contain the finest example, I remember, of retrospective narration for the purpose of exciting immediate interest, and putting the audience in possession of all the information necessary for the understanding of the plot.[1] Observe, too, the perfect probability of the moment chosen by Prospero (the very Shakspeare himself, as it were, of the tempest) to open out the truth to his daughter, his own romantic bearing, and how completely anything that might have been disagreeable to us in the magician, is reconciled and shaded in the humanity and natural feelings of the father. In the very first speech of Miranda the simplicity and tenderness of her character are at once laid open;—it would have been lost in direct contact with the agitation of the first scene. The opinion once prevailed, but, happily, is now abandoned, that Fletcher alone wrote for women;—the truth is, that with very few, and those partial, exceptions, the female characters in the plays of Beaumont and Fletcher are, when of the light kind, not decent; when heroic, complete viragos. But in Shakespeare all the elements of womanhood are holy, and there is the sweet, yet dignified feeling of all that *continuates* society, as sense of ancestry and of sex, with a purity unassailable by sophistry, because it rests not in the analytic processes, but in that sane equipoise of the faculties, during which the feelings are representative of all past experience,—not of the individual only, but of all those by whom she has been educated, and their predecessors even up to the first mother that lived. Shakespeare saw that the want of prominence, which Pope notices for sarcasm, was the blessed beauty of the woman's character, and knew that it arose not from any deficiency, but from the more exquisite harmony of all the parts of the moral being constituting one living total of head and heart. He has drawn it, indeed, in all its distinctive energies of faith, patience, constancy, fortitude,—shown in all of them as following the heart, which gives its results by a nice tact and happy intuition, without the intervention of the discursive faculty,—sees all things in and by the light of affections, and errs, if it ever err, in the exaggerations of love alone. In all the Shakespearian women there is essentially the same foundation and principle; the distinct individuality and variety are merely the result of the modification of circumstances, whether in Miranda the maiden, in Imogen the wife, or in Katharine the queen.

But to return. The appearance and characters of the super or ultra-natural servants are finely contrasted. Ariel has in every thing the airy tint which gives the name; and it is worthy of remark that Miranda is never directly brought into comparison with Ariel, lest the natural and human of the one and the supernatural of the other should tend to neutralize each other; Caliban, on the other hand, is all earth, all condensed and gross in feelings and images; he has the dawnings of understanding without reason or the moral sense, and in him, as in some brute animals, this advance to the intellectual faculties, without the moral sense, is marked by the appearance of vice. For it is in the primacy of the moral being only that man is truly human; in his intellectual powers he is certainly approached by the brutes, and, man's whole system duly considered, those powers cannot be considered other than means to an end, that is, to morality.

In this scene, as it proceeds, is displayed the impression made by Ferdinand and Miranda on each other; it is love at first sight;—

> at the first sight
> They have chang'd eyes:—

and it appears to me, that in all cases of real love, it is at one moment that it takes place. That moment may have been prepared by previous esteem, admiration, or even affection,—yet love seems to require a momentary act of volition, by which a tacit bond of devotion is imposed,—a bond not to be thereafter broken without violating what should be sacred in our nature. How finely is the true Shakespearian scene contrasted with Dryden's vulgar alteration of it, in which a mere ludicrous psychological experiment, as it were, is tried—displaying nothing but indelicacy without passion. Prospero's interruption of the courtship has often seemed to me to have no sufficient motive; still his alleged reason—

> lest too light winning
> Make the prize light—

is enough for the ethereal connexions of the romantic imagination, although it would not be so for the historical.[2] The whole courting scene, indeed, in the beginning of the third act, between the lovers is a masterpiece; and the first dawn of disobedience in the mind of Miranda to the command of her father is very finely drawn, so as to seem the working of the Scriptural command, *Thou shalt leave father and mother*, &c. O! with what exquisite purity this scene is conceived and executed! Shakespeare may sometimes be gross, but I boldly say that he is always moral and modest. Alas! in this our day decency of manners is preserved at the expense of morality of heart, and delicacies for vice are allowed, whilst grossness against it is hypocritically, or at least morbidly, condemned.

In this play are admirably sketched the vices generally accompanying a low degree of civilization; and in the first scene of the second act Shakespeare has, as in many other places, shown the tendency in bad men to indulge in scorn and contemptuous expressions, as a mode of getting rid of their own uneasy feelings of inferiority to the good, and also, by making the good ridiculous, of rendering the transition of others to wickedness easy. Shakespeare never puts habitual scorn into the mouths of other than bad men, as here in the instances of Antonio and Sebastian. The scene of the intended assassination of Alonzo and Gonzalo is an exact counterpart of the scene between Macbeth and his lady, only pitched in a lower key throughout, as designed to be frustrated and concealed, and exhibiting the same profound management in the manner of familiarizing a mind, not immediately recipient, to the suggestion of guilt, by associating the proposed crime with something ludicrous or out of place,—something not habitually matter of reverence. By this kind of sophistry the imagination and fancy are first bribed to contemplate the suggested act, and at length to become acquainted with it. Observe how the effect of this scene is heightened by contrast with another counterpart of it in low life,—that between the conspirators Stephano, Caliban, and Trinculo in the second scene of the third act, in which there are the same essential characteristics.

In this play and in this scene of it are also shown the springs of the vulgar in politics,—of that kind of politics which is inwoven with human nature. In his treatment of this subject, wherever it occurs, Shakespeare is quite peculiar. In other writers we find the particular opinions of the individual; in Massinger it is rank republicanism; in Beaumont and Fletcher even *jure divino* principles are carried to excess;—but Shakespeare never promulgates any party tenets. He is always the philosopher and the moralist, but at the same time with a profound veneration for all the established institutions of society, and for those classes which form the permanent elements of the state—especially never introducing a professional character, as such, otherwise than as respectable. If he must have any name, he should be styled a philosophical aristocrat, delighting in those hereditary institutions which have a tendency to bind one age to another, and in that distinction of ranks, of which, although few may be in possession, all enjoy the advantages. Hence, again, you will observe the good nature with which he seems always to make sport with the passions and follies of a mob, as with an irrational animal. He is never angry with it, but hugely content with holding up its absurdities to its face; and sometimes you may trace a tone of almost affectionate superiority, something like that in which a father speaks of the rogueries of a child. See the good-humoured way in which he describes Stephano passing from the most licentious freedom to absolute despotism over Trinculo and Caliban. The truth is, Shakespeare's characters are all *genera* intensely individualized; the results of meditation, of which observation supplied the drapery and the colors necessary to combine them with each other. He had virtually surveyed all the great component powers and impulses of human nature,—had seen that their different combinations and subordinations were in fact the individualizers of men, and showed how their harmony was produced by reciprocal disproportions of excess or deficiency. The language in which these truths are expressed was not drawn from any set fashion, but from the profoundest depths of his moral being, and is therefore for all ages.

NOTES

[These are the notes provided by Henry Nelson Coleridge.—ed.]

1.

> PRO. Mark his condition, and th' event; then tell me,
> If this might be a brother.
> MIRA. I should sin,
> To think but nobly of my grandmother;
> Good wombs have bore bad sons.
> PRO. Now the condition, &c.

Theobald has a note upon this passage, and suggests that Shakespeare placed it thus:—

> PRO. Good wombs have bore bad sons,—
> Now the condition.

Mr. Coleridge writes in the margin: "I cannot but believe that Theobald is quite right."—*Ed.*

2.

> FER. Yes, faith, and all his Lords, the duke of Milan,
> And his brave son, being twain.

Theobald remarks that no body was lost in the wreck; and yet that no such character is introduced in the fable, as the Duke of Milan's son. Mr. C. notes: "Must not Ferdinand have believed he was lost in the fleet that the tempest scattered?"—*Ed.*

The Tempest*

WILLIAM HAZLITT

There can be little doubt that Shakespear was the most universal genius that ever lived. "Either for tragedy, comedy, history, pastoral, pastoral-comical, historical-pastoral, scene individable or poem unlimited, he is the only man. Seneca cannot be too heavy, nor Plautus too light for him."[1] He has not only the same absolute command over our laughter and our tears, all the resources of passion, of wit, of thought, of observation, but he has the most unbounded range of fanciful invention, whether terrible or playful, the same insight into the world of imagination that he has into the world of reality; and over all there presides the same truth of character and nature, and the same spirit of humanity. His ideal beings are as true and natural as his real characters; that is, as consistent with themselves or if we suppose such beings to exist at all, they could not act, speak, or feel otherwise than as he makes them. He has invented for them a language, manners, and sentiments of their own, from the tremendous imprecations of the Witches in *Macbeth*, when they do "a deed without a name," [2] to the sylph-like expressions of Ariel, who "does his spiriting gently";[3] the mischievous tricks and gossiping of Robin Goodfellow, or the uncouth gabbling and emphatic gesticulations of Caliban in this play.

The Tempest is one of the most original and perfect of Shakespear's productions, and he has shewn in it all the variety of his powers. It is full of grace and grandeur. The human and imaginary characters, the dramatic and the grotesque, and blended together with the greatest art, and without any appearance of it. Though he has here given "to airy nothing a local habitation and a name,"[4] yet that part which is only the fantastic creation of his

*Originally printed in *Characters of Shakespear's Plays* (London, 1817). Reprinted in Vol. 4 *The Complete Works of William Hazlittt*, ed., P. P. Howe (New York: AMS Press, Inc., 1967), 238–244.

mind, has the same palpable texture, and coheres "semblably"[5] with the rest. As the preternatual part has the air of reality, and almost haunts the imagination with a sense of truth, the real characters and events partake of the wildness of a dream. The stately magician, Prospero, driven from his dukedom, but around whom (so potent is his art) airy spirits throng number-less to do his bidding; his daughter Miranda ("worthy of that name")[6] to whom all the power of his art points, and who seems the goddess of the isle; the princely Ferdinand, cast by fate upon the haven of his happiness in this idol of his love; the delicate Ariel; the savage Caliban, half brute, half demon; the drunken ship's crew—are all connected parts of the story, and can hardly be spared from the place they fill. Even the local scenery is of a piece and character with the subject. Prospero's enchanted island seems to have risen up out of the sea; the airy music, the tempest-tossed vessel, the turbulent waves, all have the effect of the landscape backgound of some fine picture. Shakespear's pencil is (to use an allusion of his own) "like the dyer's hand, subdued to what it works in."[7] Every thing in him, though it partakes of "the liberty of wit,"[8] is also subjected to "the law" of the under-standing. For instance, even the drunken sailors, who are made reeling-ripe, share, in the disorder of their minds and bodies, in the tumult of the ele-ments, and seem on shore to be as much at the mercy of chance as they were before at the mercy of the winds and waves. These fellows with their sea-wit are the least to our taste of any part of the play: but they are as like drunken sailors as they can be, and are an indirect foil to Caliban, whose figure acquires a classical dignity in the comparison.

The character of Caliban is generally thought (and justly so) to be one of the author's master-pieces. It is not indeed pleasant to see this character on the stage any more than it is to see the god Pan personated there. But in itself it is one of the wildest and most abstracted of all Shakespeare's char-acters, whose deformity whether of body or mind is redeemed by the power and truth of the imagination displayed in it. It is the essence of grossness, but there is not a particle of vulgarity in it. Shakespear has described the brutal mind of Caliban in contact with the pure and original forms of nature; the character grows out of the soil where it is rooted, uncontrouled, uncouth and wild, uncramped by any of the meannesses of custom. It is "of the earth, earthy."[9] It seems almost to have been dug out of the ground, with a soul instinctively superadded to it answering to its wants and origin. Vulgarity is not natural coarseness, but conventional coarseness, learnt from others, con-trary to, or without an entire conformity of natural power and disposition; as fashion is the common-place affectation of what is elegant and refined with-out any feeling of the essence of it. Schlegel, the admirable German critic on Shakespear, observes that Caliban is a poetical character, and "always speaks in blank verse."[10] He first comes in thus:

CALIBAN   As wicked dew as e'r my mother brush'd
            With raven's feather from unwholesome fen,
            Drop on you both: a south-west blow on ye,
            And blister you all o'er!
PROSPERO   For this, be sure, to-night thou shalt have cramps, Side-stiches that
            shall pen thy breath up; urchins
            Shall for that vast of night that they may work,
            All exercise on thee: thou shalt be pinched
            As thick as honey-combs, each pinch more stinging
            Than bees that made them.
CALIBAN   I must eat my dinner.
            This island's mine by Sycorax my mother,
            Which thou tak'st from me. When thou camest first,
            Thou stroak'dst me, and mad'st much of me; would'st give me
            Water with berries in 't; and teach me how
            To name the bigger light and how the less
            That burn by day and night; and then I lov'd thee,
            And shew'd thee all the qualities o' th' isle,
            The fresh springs, brine-pits, barren place and fertile:
            Curs'd be I that I did so! All the charms
            Of Sycorax, toads, beetles, bats, light on you!
            For I am all the subjects that you have,
            Who first was mine own king; and here you sty me
            In this hard rock, whiles you do keep from me
            The rest o' th' island.[11]

And again, he promises Trinculo his services thus, if he will free him
from his drudgery.

            I will shew thee the best springs; I'll pluck thee berries,
            I'll fish for thee, and get thee wood enough.
            I pr'ythee let me bring thee where crabs grow,
            And I with my long nails will dig thee pig-nuts:
            Shew thee a jay's nest, and instruct thee how
            To snare the nimble marmozet: I'll bring thee
            To clust'ring filberds; and sometimes I'll get thee
            Young scamels from the rock.[12]

In conducting Stephano and Trinculo to Prospero's cell, Caliban shows the
superiority of natural capacity over greater knowledge and greater folly; and
in a former scene, when Ariel frightens them with his music, Caliban to
encourage them accounts for it in the eloquent poetry of the senses.

            —Be not afraid, the isle is full of noises,
            Sounds, and sweet airs, that give delight and hurt not.
            Sometimes a thousand twanging instruments
            Will hum about mine ears, and sometimes voices,

That if I then had waked after long sleep,
Would make me sleep again; and then in dreaming,
The clouds methought would open, and shew riches
Ready to drop upon me: when I wak'd,
I cried to dream again.[13]

This is not more beautiful than it is true. The poet here shews us the savage with the simplicity of a child, and makes the strange monster amiable. Shakespear had to paint the human animal rude and without choice in its pleasures, but not without the sense of pleasure or some germ of the affections. Master Barnardine in *Measure for Measure*, the savage of civilized life, is an admirable philosophical counterpart to Caliban.

Shakespear has, as it were by design, drawn off from Caliban the elements of whatever is ethereal and refined, to compound them in the unearthly mould of Ariel. Nothing was ever more finely conceived than this contrast between the material and the spiritual, the gross and delicate. Ariel is imaginary power, the swiftness of thought personified. When told to make good speed by Prospero, he says, "I drink the air before me."[14] This is something like Puck's boast on a similar occasion, "I'll put a girdle round about the earth in forty minutes."[15] But Ariel differs from Puck in having a fellow feeling in the interests of those he is employed about. How exquisite is the following dialogue between him and Prospero!

ARIEL   Your charm so strongly works 'em,
          That if you now beheld them, your affections
          Would become tender.
PROSPERO Dost thou think so, spirit?
ARIEL   Mine would, sir, were I human.
PROSPERO And mine shall.
          Hast thou, which art but air, a touch, a feeling
          Of their afflictions, and shall not myself,
          One of their kind, that relish all as sharply,
          Passion'd as they, be kindlier moved than thou art?[16]

It has been observed that there is a peculiar charm in the songs introduced in Shakespear, which, without conveying any distinct images, seem to recall all the feelings connected with them, like snatches of half-forgotten music heard indistinctly and at intervals. There is this effect produced by Ariel's songs, which (as we are told) seem to sound in the air, and as if the person playing them were invisible. We shall give one instance out of many of this general power.

Enter Ferdinand; *and* Ariel *invisible, playing and singing.*

                      Ariel's Song
               Come unto these yellow sands,
               And then take hands;
               Curt'sied when you have, and kiss'd,
               (The wild waves whist;)
               Foot it featly here and there;
               And sweet sprites the burden bear.
                                    [Burden dispersedly.
               Hark, hark! bowgh-wough: the watch-dogs bark,
                  Bowgh-wowgh.
Ariel   Hark, hark! I hear
               The strain of strutting chanticleer
                  Cry cock-a-doodle-doo.
Ferdinand Where should this music be? i' the air or the earth?
               It sounds no more: and sure it waits upon
               Some god of th' island. Sitting on a bank
               Weeping against the king my father's wreck,
               This music crept by me upon the waters,
               Allaying both their fury and my passion
               With its sweet air; thence I have follow'd it,
               Or it hath drawn me rather:—but 'tis gone.—
               No, it begins again.

                      Ariel's Song
               Full fathom five thy father lies,
                  Of his bones are coral made:
               Those are pearls that were his eyes,
                  Nothing of him that doth fade,
               But doth suffer a sea change,
               Into something rich and strange.
               Sea-nymphs hourly ring his knell—
               Hark! now I hear them, ding-dong bell.
                                   [Burden ding-dong.
Ferdinand The ditty does remember my drown'd father.
               This is no mortal business, nor no sound
               That the earth owes: I hear it above me.—[17]

The courtship between Ferdinand and Miranda is one of the chief beauties of the play. It is the very purity of love. The pretended interference of Prospero with it heightens its interest, and is in character with the magician, whose sense of preternatural power makes him arbitrary, tetchy, and impatient of opposition.

The Tempest is a finer play than the *Midsummer Night's Dream*, which has sometimes been compared with it; but it is not so fine a poem. There are a greater number of beautiful passages in the latter. Two of the most striking in the *Tempest* are spoken by Prospero. The one is that admirable one when the vision which he has conjured up disappears, beginning "The cloud-capp'd tower, the gorgeous palaces," etc.,[18] which has been so often quoted, that every school-boy knows it by heart; the other is that which Prospero makes in abjuring his art.

> Ye elves of hills, brooks, standing lakes, and groves,
> And ye that on the sands with printless foot
> Do case the ebbing Neptune, and do fly him
> When he comes back; you demi-puppets, that
> By moon-shine do the green sour ringlets make,
> Whereof the ewe not bites; and you whose pastime
> Is to make midnight mushrooms, that rejoice
> To hear the solemn curfew, by whose aid
> (Weak masters tho' ye be) I have be-dimm'd
> The noon-tide sun, call'd forth the mutinous winds,
> And 'twixt the green sea and the azur'd vault
> Set roaring war; to the dread rattling thunder
> Have I giv'n fire, and rifted Jove's stout oak
> With his own bolt; the strong-bas'd promontory
> Have I made shake, and by the spurs pluck'd up
> The pine and cedar: graves at my command
> Have wak'd their sleepers; oped, and let 'em forth
> By my so potent art. But this rough magic
> I here abjure; and when I have requir'd
> Some heavenly music, which even now I do,
> (To work mine end upon their senses that
> This airy charm is for) I'll break my staff,
> Bury it certain fadoms in the earth,
> And deeper than did ever plumment sound,
> I'll drown my book.—[19]

We must not forget to mention among other things in this play, that Shakespear has anticipated nearly all the arguments on the Utopian schemes of modern philosophy.[20]

GONZALO	Had I the plantation of this isle, my lord—
ANTONIO	He'd sow it with nettle-seed.
SEBASTIAN	Or docks or mallows.
GONZALO	And were the king on 't, what would I do?
SEBASTIAN	'Scape being drunk, for want of wine.
GONZALO	I' the commonwealth I would by contraries
	Execute all things: for no kind of traffic

Would I admit; no name of magistrate;
Letters should not be known; wealth, poverty,
And use of service, none; contract, succession,
Bourn, bound of land, tilth, vineyard, none;
No use of metal, corn, or wine, or oil;
No occupation, all men idle, all
And women too; but innocent and pure:
No sovereignty.

SEBASTIAN   And yet he would be king on 't.

ANTONIO   The latter end of his commonwealth forgets the beginning.

GONZALO   All things in common nature should produce
Without sweat or endeavour. Treason, felony,
Sword, pike, knife, gun, or need of any engine
Would I not have; but nature should bring forth,
Of its own kind, all foizon, all abundance
To feed my innoncent people!

SEBASTIAN   No marrying 'mong his subjects?

ANTONIO   None, man; all idle; whores and knaves.

GONZALO   I would with such perfection govern, sir,
To excel the golden age.

SEBASTIAN   Save his majesty![21]

NOTES

1. *Hamlet*, 2.2.423.
2. *Macbeth*, 4.1.49.
3. *Tempest*, 1.2.298.
4. *A Midsummer Night's Dream*, 5.1.16.
5. *2 Henry VI*, 5.3.21.
6. *Tempest* 3.1.36.
7. *Sonnet* 111
8. *Hamlet*, 2.2.421.
9. *St. John*, 3:31.
10. Schlegel, p. 395
11. *Tempest*, 1.2.321–343.
12. *Tempest*, 2.2.173–174 and 180–185.
13. *Tempest*, 3.2.147–155.
14. *Tempest*, 5.1.102.
15. *A Midsummer Night's Dream*, 2.1.175.
16. *Tempest*, 5.1.17–24.
17. *Tempest*, 1.2.375–404.
18. *Tempest*, 4.1.152.
19. *Tempest*, 5.1.33–57.
20. The passage, of course, is based on Florio's translation of Montaigne. See Chapter 30, Book I, *Of the Caniballes*.
21. *Tempest*, 2.1.150–175. "Wealth" for "riches" in line 157 is Pope's metrical improvement, followed by Warburton.

Tempest*

W. J. BIRCH

The Boatswain, in the storm, has no religion—neither reverence for God, or man, but a love of life, which he respects more in himself than others. He says you are to be thankful you have lived so long, and be ready for the mischance of death. Readiness is all, as Hamlet said, and Gloster in Lear.

The more pious old counsellor of Naples derives consolation from the idea that such a boatswain was rather fated to be hanged than drowned:—

> Stand fast, good fate, to his hanging! make the rope of his destiny our cable, for our own doth little advantage! if he be not born to be hanged, our case is miserable.

This appears to be rather an ill timed mockery of prayer. On the re-appearance of the royal party the Boatswain receives them no better, but asks what do they there? and Sebastian gives the character of him and his language, by which again we may know what is considered blasphemous and derogatory of men or gods:—

> A pox o'your throat! you bawling, blasphemous, incharitable dog!

The Boatswain tells them to work. And when the rest fly to prayers, deeming all lost, he says, what, must our mouths be cold? thinking of the different liquid and results when he should have to take in sea water instead of engulphing fiery spirits.

The moral of this appears to be that on such occasions it would be better to work and endeavour to save yourself than waste time in prayers and lamentations, when a common fate must embrace all who expose themselves to it—

*Originally printed in *An Inquiry into the Philosophy and Religion of Shakspere* (n. p. 1848), 523–533. Reprinted by Haskell House Publishers Ltd. (New York, 1972), 523–533.

the pious, the blasphemous, the good and the bad, the royal and the ignoble. Such has been the case in a wreck, when the only one saved has reported that whilst he stripped, committed himself to the waves, and the assistance of objects around him, the rest he left in supplication to heaven.

MIRA   O! I have suffer'd
              With those that I saw suffer.

This is a sentiment of morality coming from an unsophisticated child of nature. The love of humanity, which is at once awakened in the heart of one of the same species, though ignorant of her kind before. This love, or this pity, left to itself, or cherished, would not bear to do injury, or see it done.

MIRA   O! the cry did knock
              Against my very heart: poor souls, they perish'd!

The love of mankind and creatures of this earth, which she feels, she thinks ought to extend to heaven; and thus she passes judgment on the want of mercy in the higher powers, who permit shipwrecks and other mundane calamities.

MIRA.   Had I been any God of power, I would
              Have sunk the sea within the earth; or e'er
              It should the good ship so have swallow'd, and
              The fraughting souls within her.

Shakspere here does not spare to gird the gods, of whatever religion, for their want of mercy, which he represents, as he has done before, more an attribute of humanity. He puts it in comparison that higher powers, if there be such, are not so good as men; and he has often rated them for their cruelty. The inference to be drawn is, that as before, prayer or not prayer, piety or impiety, good or bad, were shown to be all alike before the causes of nature; so Shakspere, in Miranda, gives the conclusion that there was no interference of Providence, no instance of its exercise on earth. Enough we see in these introductory strokes, and from what we know of the end of the play, to suppose that Shakspere framed this drama on the moral of *Measure for Measure*, and other plays: a human system of love, mercy, and forgiveness here, greater in extent, than in any religious scheme, present, or to arrive hereafter.

Shakspere gives an instance in Prospero of mentioning, in the same breath, Providence and fortune.

MIRA.   How came we ashore?
PRO.   By Providence divine.
              Know thus far forth.
              By accident most strange, bountiful fortune,
              Now my dear lady, hath mine enemies

Brought to this shore; and, by my prescience
I find, my zenith doth depend upon
A most auspicious star; whose influence
If now I court not, but omit, my fortunes
Will ever after droop.

Thus Shakspere mixed at random causes with Providence or chance; sometimes revising one with the other, but adhering more to the one than the other,
showing to which he inclined; sometimes affirming it and then denying it,
which induces us to think that he sometimes introduced Providence in propriety with the times, whilst he adhered on the whole to Nature. Here, as in Hamlet, Providence is assumed immediately to be negatived; we think this is as
strong evidence of the direction of a man's mind, as if, from appearance, it was
all on one side. It shows that he was aware of the other side of the question; of
the religious belief in a Providence, that he held it up in deference to public
opinion, and to be opposed by his own opinion. As to speaking in character,
here is one declaring himself, as Hamlet did in opposition to himself; and of
the two ideas, it must be asked, which of them belongs to the writer? If it be
said that Shakspere only painted nature, as Shaftesbury has in his characteristics, declaring that men are visited with different and opposite ideas on the
subjects of religion, then Shakspere drew men as infidels, where in poetry he
might have made them uniform, showed that he had the same opinion of men
as another infidel, and that he was of that opinion in which he most often
declared himself—the test which Shaftesbury says is applicable to the discovery of a man's real private thoughts on questions of religion.

Prospero, having gone from Providence to accident, proceeds to account
for things present and to come from his own knowledge, and a star which presides over his fortunes.

Caliban says to Stephano, he will show him where he may knock a nail
into the head of Prospero sleeping. Why not have said where he might slay
him, instead of mentioning a particular sort of death to a man sleeping, which
occurs in the Bible, in the story of Sisera? Such an allusion in the mouth of
Caliban on the stage we do not think reverential. The case here was one of
folly and wickedness; whilst in the Scriptures there were extenuating circumstances in the commission of the deed, the death of an enemy to one's country, which Prospero was not, although so thought of by the half man and half
brute, Caliban. On the provocations of Ariel, Trinculo says:—

O, forgive me my sins.
STE.   He that dies pays all debts: I defy thee. Mercy upon us.

In this drunken party is a repetition of Cassio under the same circumstances, using the Lord's Prayer, with the joking response of Falstaff and

denial of a future state. The conversation between these drunken associates is otherwise not very reverential in its allusions. Where you might expect to find it there is no mention of a future state; and in the dialogue between Antonio and Sebastian, there seems the conviction, whatever might happen on earth, there was no reckoning after death, and that the sleep of death, into which they propose to put Gonzalo and Alonzo, would be eternal and material. We shall find it fully developed by Prospero. Prospero enacts a scene of spirits to please his future son-in-law; when finished, Prospero turns what has been witnessed into argument and philosophy. Perhaps exception may be made physically to the extent which he allows to the wearing out of matter; but, both with regard to the universe, and particularly with regard to man, his conclusions as to their existence are most mortal and material.

> PRO.   You look, my son, in a mov'd sort,
>   As if you were dismay'd; be cheerful, sir:
>   Our revels now are ended: these our actors,
>   As I foretold you, were all spirits, and
>   Are melted into air, into thin air;
>   And, like the baseless fabric of this vision,
>   The cloud-capt towers, the gorgeous palaces,
>   The solemn temples, the great globe itself,
>   Yea, all which it inherit, shall dissolve;
>   And, like this insubstantial pageant faded,
>   Leave not a rack behind! we are such stuff
>   As dreams are made on, and our little life
>   Is rounded with a sleep.——Sir, I am vexed;
>   Bear with my weakness, my old brain is troubled:
>   Be not disturb'd with my infirmity;
>   If thou be pleas'd, retire into my cell,
>   And there repose: a turn or two I'll walk,
>   To still my beating mind.

It will be observed that he speaks of thin air, matter yet, however attenuated. Whether does he mean by "all which it inherit," these things he has mentioned upon the earth, or in continuation of the idea, that what succeeds this globe will come to the same end, and leave not a rack behind? Nothing can be more conclusive of the end of all things, great and small. Perpetual change of matter is proclaimed—perpetual loss of identity, which is the case with ourselves: as those spirits vanished, so shall we disappear. There is nothing more immortal or eternal in us than in the rest of matter; what happens to them, in a shorter time, having a shorter life, must happen to us. As these illusions, so are our dreams, and as these dreams are rounded by a sleep, so are our lives. We slept and knew not before we came into the world, so we shall when we leave it, of such stuff as to identity and eternity are we made. As is a dream in a sleep, so is life in eternity. Of such "stuff," not a very ennobling term, are we made.

There is some interest attached to this speech, in the minds of those who think it the farewell play of Shakspere. Then there is a peculiar significance attached to these revels ended, actors, spirits, these dissolving views, the property of the globe, the globe itself—the name of Shakspere's theatre.

Johnson has remarked of Shakspere, "It is impossible for any man to rid his mind of his profession." This is, in fact, the third time that Shakspere has drawn the resemblance between actors and the lives of men, the stage and the world. In the mouth of Macbeth we have life a walking shadow, a poor player, that struts and frets his hour upon the stage and then is heard no more—a tale told by an idiot, full of sound and fury, signifying nothing—instead of revels ended, and the actors' spirits, melting into thin air—the world, their stage, fading and leaving not a rack behind—their lives as dreams, rounded with a sleep. The Duke and Jaques using the same words as in the speeches of Prospero and Macbeth—the world a theatre of pageants, divided into scenes. Yes, says Jaques, the world's a stage, men and women merely players, many parts to every individual, the last scene of life as the first, sans everything—nothing.

As a picture of life, more especially in its relation to death, without the illustration of the theatre, what more was the speech of the Duke in *Measure for Measure*? There the best of rest is sleep, and death is no more. There, too, he likened life to a dream, and thereby draws a distinction between the sleep of dreams and sleep without dreams. He says of the whole of life, youth and age, that it is, as it were, an after-dinner's sleep dreaming on both. What is this that bears the name of life? death makes all these odds even—no more, nothing.

What appeared to us so clear in itself, we should have thought it scarcely necessary to make clearer by comparing this speech with others on the same subject. It seems that others thought the same, that life rounded with a sleep meant terminated; but Mr. Knight, finding it affirmed, not by Johnson, but by his (Knight's) correspondents in this case, has taken upon himself, on the part of Shakspere, and as commentator, absolutely to deny this interpretation. "We have been asked," he says, "the meaning of this passage, rounded with a sleep, it being supposed that rounded was used in the sense of terminated; and that one sleep was the end of life. This was not Shakespeare's philosophy; nor would he have introduced an idea totally disconnected with the preceding description." As Shakspere has a philosophy, it would have been but fair to us and Shakspere to have told us what it was, and superseded the necessity of this inquiry. It is at least agreeable to us, who have heard so much about character, and Shakspere not being a man, to find it admitted that there was any philosophy discoverable in his works.

The philosophy of Shakspere, we are told, is not the philosophy which Johnson has assigned to him on a similar passage, where it is elaborately drawn out, given twice, as the point and moral of the speech, the whole of life—being there analysed morally and materially to produce this conclusion twice repeated. There the whole weight of circumstances go to prove it the philosophy of Shakspere: the character of the duke-priest, the character and sentiments of the patient Claudio to whom it is applied. The didactic nature of the lesson, the occasion and the person, the repetitions elsewhere of the same philosophy, all brought to an unmistakable focus in the Duke's speech, made Johnson, who entertained a very different philosophy, think it could not pass unobserved by the most casual reader, and must produce its impression. Johnson, therefore, in the character of a moralist and philosopher, denounced Shakspere. What he saw there, everybody, it seems, but Mr. Knight, saw, and regarded the words as having the same meaning as in Prospero.

We confess ourselves at a loss to see how the idea commonly affixed to the passage is totally disconnected with its preceding description. If introduced without propriety, it only the more shows the individual bias of Shakspere to turn everything to his own philosophy. But we do not see any disconnection in this speech, and find no disconnection in other speeches of a similar character. Mr. Knight, however, does, by mentioning Berkeley about dreams, wish to have it supposed that Shakspere had the same philosophy as the no-matter Bishop[.] *His* intention was avowed—it was to support religion, and points of faith; but we have no such spiritualism in Shakspere—all indicates materialism. However, they say the Bishop himself repented of his theory. Hume said, his works on matter "form the best lessons of scepticism which are to be found either among the ancient or modern philosophers, Bayle not excepted." Dr. Beattie, also, considers them as having a sceptical tendency.—*Vide* Chalmers' Bio. Dict.

To us it appears, "life rounded by a sleep" expresses exactly what Cicero said, and the poets of antiquity, that you returned in death to what you were before you were born: the beginning, middle, and end of existence, comprised in a circle of perpetual night. "A mind firm and enlightened is without inquietude; it despises death, which places man back in the same state where he was before he was born."—*Cicero de finibus.*

A French poet, Cyrano, had his tragedy of Aggrippina interdicted for introducing Sejanus answering her inquiries whether he did not fear death, or the uncertainty where death might lead—"An hour after death our vanquished soul will be what it was before life."

"Our revels ended," express the pleasures of life ended as well as the pangs. Life rounded with a sleep seems well expressed by Seneca in consolations to a friend, though, for the same purpose as Shakespere has in speaking of death, he makes the consolation to consist, as Shakspere does generally, in its being the termination of our pains. "Death finishes all our pains; beyond there remains nothing to suffer: it restores us to that profound tranquillity in which we were softly extended before that we saw the day."

Jean Jacques Rousseau, in a letter to Voltaire on his poem of Lisbon, says, "The question of Providence belongs to that of the immortality of the soul, which I have the happiness of believing, without being ignorant that reason may doubt it." Those have generally been considered atheists who have denied the immortality of the soul. Suidas, in his lexicon, vol. 1, p. 108, says "Atheum est immortalitatem animae non conservare." That is to say, "It is atheistical not to hold the doctrine of the immortality of the soul."

After this natural philosophy of Shakspere's, we have a splendid example of his morality, in theory and practice, quite in conformity with similar sentiments and actions of his dramas. Ariel relates to Prospero the afflictions of the royal party wrecked on his island:—

	Your charm so strongly works them,
	That if you now beheld them, your affections
	Would become tender.
PRO.	Dost thou think so, spirit?
ARI.	Mine would, sir, were I human.
PRO.	And mine shall.
	Hast thou, which art but air, a touch, a feeling
	Of their afflictions, and shall not myself,
	One of their kind, that relish all as sharply,
	Passion as they, be kindlier mov'd than thou art?
	Though with their high wrongs I am struck to the quick,
	Yet, with my nobler reason, 'gainst my fury
	Do I take part; the rarer action is
	In virtue than in vengeance; they being penitent,
	The sole drift of my purpose doth extend
	Not a frown further; go, release them, Ariel;
	My charms I'll break, their senses I'll restore,
	And they shall be themselves.
ARI.	I'll fetch them, sir.

The sight of evil, as we have said before, in a natural condition of humanity, is and would be a sufficient guarantee against the commission of injuries.

The consequences of one being like another, of whatever difference of opinion—of whatever different circumstances, which should result in mutual love, and which was so finely delivered by Shylock in the *Merchant of Venice*, are here repeated by Prospero. Reason properly exercised is a sufficient counterpoise to fury; the rarer, that is, the more excellent, action, is rather in forgiveness of injuries than in taking vengeance. Punishment should go no further than producing repentance, into which men should be led, and should not be given as retaliation, or as precluding repentance and reform.

Here is the moral of the play, which we remarked in the beginning.

Miranda has the sentiments of her father and Ariel, and she says if she had been a god of power she would have saved the crew. Prospero had acted on, and was proceeding to the practice of, these precepts of morality. Can we help, therefore, thinking that with so marked a reference to what a god ought to do, that Shakspere had in mind that neither man nor Providence should add to evil, but do all the good they could in this world, and that judgment in the next should exercise mercy and general pardon—that justice was not in eternal punishments, and should reach no further than repentance? These comparisons between a supposed god of power and man—the contrast between the feelings and practice of Miranda, Ariel, and Prospero—the introduction of spirits, and what they must be as well as man—the delivery of Prospero's prisoners to a momentary place of trivial torment, and their release from it at the intercession of a spirit agreeing with his own intentions—all seem to us strongly to mark intentions towards a system of divine and religious judgment, as well as human. We do not any the more admit that Shakspere believed in a future state; but how common it is for infidels to argue in the strain of Shakspere—that from the attributes given to the Deity, particularly benevolence, he must excel in this virtue more than his creature—that he is not worse, as he is represented, but must be better and more merciful than man. We have before remarked that the purpose exhibited in this is more or less seen in other plays—was the sole drift of his purpose in *Measure for Measure*, where, villany frustrated, Justice did not extend a frown further, to the penitent or not penitent—but, having rewarded the good, it left the bad to become better. The injuries past of Alonzo and Sebastian, and the recent intended murderers, Antonio and Sebastian, are alike forgiven, and absolution made of their offences.

Gonzalo addresses the re-appearance of the Boatswain, who had not suffered at all:—

> Now, blasphemy,
> That swear'st grace o'erboard, not an oath on shore?
> Hast thou no mouth by land? what is the news?

It appears blasphemy was none the worse, had got rid only of the wicked out of his ship, and having said no prayers, expressed no thanksgiving for his deliverence, no repentance of his blasphemy, in reply to the question of the pious Gonzalo, merely says:—

> The best news is, that we have safely found
> Our King and company; the next, our ship,
> Which is but three glasses since we gave out split,
> Is tight and yare, and bravely rigg'd, as when
> We first put out to sea.

There is no expression even of reverence for a miracle. Though Alonzo says—

> And there is in this business more than nature
> Was ever conduct of,

Caliban is pardoned, who is another Barnardine, though more a monster of fancy. Caliban being commmanded to do his duty as servant, with his drunken associate, says:—

> Ay, that I will; and I'll be wise hereafter,
> And seek for grace. What a thrice-double ass
> Was I, to take this drunkard for a god?
> And worship this dull fool?

Barnardine did not answer the exhortation of the Duke to repentance; and we say the idea given to this half-and-half beast and human of turning to grace, is done in ridicule of religion, and is plainly expressed to produce that effect. There is the additional satire, or what may be called the philosophy of religion, as the Shaftesburys and Humes have it, that man makes his religion: according to what he is, so will he construct his divinity. An ass will have a fool for his god.

The Monster Caliban*

DANIEL WILSON

Arise, and fly
The reeling Faun, the sensual feast;
Move upward, working out the beast,
And let the ape and tiger die.
[TENNYSON, *IN MEMORIAM* CXVIII 25–28]

The innate and seemingly instinctive aptitude of the human mind to conceive of the supernatural is so universal, and so intimately interwoven with that other conception of a spiritual life, the successor of this present corporeal existence,—which, far more than any supposed belief in a Supreme Being, seems the universal attribute of man,—that Shakespeare's whole conception of the supernatural may fitly come under review as a sequel to the more limited subject specially occupying our consideration. But it is sufficient for the present to bear in mind the originality and prolific powers revealed in his supernatural imaginings, in order the more clearly to appreciate the one portraiture of a being which, though in no sense spiritual, is so far as all experience goes, thoroughly supra-natural.

"'Tis strange, my Theseus," says Hippolyta to her ducal lover, as the fifth act of *A Midsummer Night's Dream* opens in a hall of his palace at Athens, where they hold discourse on the themes that lovers speak of. The previous scenes have been ripe with the sportive creations of the poet's fancy, with his Oberon, Titania, and all their fairy train; and now, in true dramatic fashion, he claims the shadowy beings as his own. "More strange than true," Theseus replies:—

Originally published as "Chapter 5: The Monster Caliban" in *Caliban: The Missing Link* (London: Macmillan, 1873), 67–91.

123

> I never may believe
> These antique fables, nor these fairy toys.
> Lovers and madmen have such seething brains,
> Such shaping fantasies, that apprehend
> More than cool reason ever comprehends;

and then, after quaintly coupling the lover and the lunatic as beings "of imagination all compact," he adds this other picture of the poet's fantasies:—

> The poet's eye, in a fine frenzy rolling,
> Doth glance from heaven to earth, from earth to heaven;
> And as imagination bodies forth
> The forms of things unknown, the poet's pen
> Turns them to shapes, and gives to airy nothing
> A local habitation and a name.
> Such tricks hath strong imagination.

As to the actual belief in the beings so dealt with, among the men of that
generation, it was vague and indeterminate as themselves. When, indeed, the
poet glanced to earth, and called up on the blasted heath, near by the scene of
Macbeth's great victory over the Norweyan host, those wild and withered
hags, that "looked not like the inhabitants o' the earth, and yet were on't," he
idealised a very harsh and deep-rooted belief of his age. When again he
glanced from earth, not to heaven, but to that intermediate spirit-world, with
all the ghostly or airy habitants with which fancy or superstition had favoured
it, he wrought with materials that had fashioned the creed of many generations. He had, himself, believed in fairies; and doubtless still regarded ghosts
with becoming awe. They had held mastery over his youthful imagination;
constituted the fancies and the terror of his childhood; and were in maturer
years translated into those supernatural beings which have proved so substantial to other generations.

But the poet's own age had been familiarised with ideal beings of a
wholly different kind, the reality of which seemed scarcely to admit of question. Of the new world of the West which Columbus had revealed, there was,
at any rate, no room for doubt; and yet when, nearly a century after its discovery, Spenser refers, in his *Faerie Queen*, not only to the Indian Peru and
the Amazon, but to that "fruitfullest Virginia" of which his friend Raleigh had
told him many a wondrous tale, it is obvious that to his fancy America was still
almost as much a world apart as if his "Shepherd of the Ocean" had sailed up
the blue vault of heaven, and told of the dwellers in another planet on which
it had been his fortune to alight. He is defending the verisimilitude of that
Fairyland in which Una and the Red Cross Knight, Duessa, Belphoebe,
Orgoglio, Malecastaes and so many more fanciful impersonations disport
them with King Arthur and the Faerie Queen herself: and he argues that since

Peru, Virginia, and all the wonders of that new-found hemisphere prove to be real, what marvel if this Fairyland of his fancy be no less substantial a verity. For even now, of the world the the least part is known to us; and daily through hardy enterprise new regions are discovered, as unheard-of as were the huge Amazon, the Indian Peru, or other strange lands now found true:—

> Yet all these were, when no man did them know,
> Yet have from wisest ages hidden been:
> And later times things more unknown shall show:
> Why then should witless man so much misween,
> That nothing is but that which he hath seen?
> What if, within the moon's fair shining sphere,
> What if, in every other star unseen
> Of other worlds he happily should hear?
> He wonder would much more; yet such to some appear.

For voyagers to return from that new world with stories of its being peopled with human beings like themselves was a kind of blasphemy intolerable to all honest Christians. The council of clerical sages which sembled in the Dominican Convent of St. Stephen, at Salamanca, in 1486, to take into consideration the theory of Columbus as to a Cathaya, or other world of humanity lying beyond the Atlantic, after bringing the science and philosophy of the age to bear on the subject, pronounced the idea of the earth's spherical form heterodox, and a belief in antipodes incompatible with the historical traditions of our faith: since to assert that there were inhabited lands on the opposite side of the globe, would be to maintain that there were nations not descended from Adam, it being impossible for them to have passed the intervening ocean. This would be, therefore, to discredit the Bible, which expressly declares that all men are descendants of one common pair.

It is amusing, but also instructive, thus to find an ethnological problem of our own day adduced by the orthodox sages of Salamanca in the fifteenth century to prove that America could not exist. It is obvious enough, that with such Dominican philosophers in the councils of science, it was safer for their orthodoxy as well as their credibility, for travelers to tell of "anthropophagi, and men whose heads do grow beneath their shoulders," than to hint of a race of ordinary men and women. This kind of union of skepticism and credulity belongs exclusively to no special epoch. A story is told of a Scottish sailor returning to his old mother, and greeting her with an account of the wonders he had seen in far-away lands and seas. But his most guarded narrations conflicted so entirely with her personal experience that they were repelled as wholly incredible. "Weel, mother," said the baffled traveller, "what will ye say when I tell you that, in sailing up the Red Sea, on pulling up our anchor, we fand ane o' Pharaaoh's chairot-wheels on the fluke?" "Ay, ay! Sandy, that I can weel believe," responded the old dame; "there's Scripture for that!" It was in a like critical spirit that the men of the fifteenth and sixteenth centuries refused all belief in the humanity of the antipodes, while they welcomed the most monstrous exaggerations for the very air of truthfulness they bore, tried by their own canons of credibility.

The reasoning of that age arranged itself in a very simple syllogism. All men were descended from Adam; the beings inhabiting the worlds beyond the ocean could not possibly be descended from Adam; therefore they were not human beings. Yet as truth slowly dawned through a whole century; it became more and more obvious that, whatever their pedigree might be, they had many points in common with humanity. They had a kind of speech of their own; and could be taught with no great difficulty that of their discoverers. They had arts, arms, architecture and sculpture, and even religious rites, though of a very horrible kind. So the Spanish Dominicans pronounced them to be devils; and yet did not wholly abandon the hope of converting them, and making them Christians after a sort. The English adventurers, having no love for the Spaniards of the New World, and a very special aversion to their priests, were the less likely to be guided by their estimation of the Carib or Mexican; and hence there grew up a vague idea of inhabitants of the strange islands reported from time to time by returned voyagers who, though they could not possibly be of the race of Adam, had yet a far nearer resemblance, in many ways, to our perfected humanity than any ape, baboon, or other anthropomorphous being with which older travellers had made them familiar.

On this ideal Shakespeare unquestionably wrought in the creation of that "freckled whelp," as disproportioned in manners as in shape, whom Prospero found sole habitant of the lonely island on which he and Miranda were cast. As to Caliban's maternity, the theories of man's descent, and the consequent transitional stages of an unperfected humanity, with which we are now familiar, are of very modern date, and did not at all lie in Shakespeare's vein, whatever Bacon might have said of them. Unless the poet had contented himself with simply letting Prospero find the strange monster on the island, he had, like more modern philosophers, to account in some way for his being; and so he vaguely hints at supernatural conception, known to Prospero only at second-hand. For the witch Sycorax had died, and Ariel had writhed and groaned for years, imprisoned in the rifted pine where she had left him, till Prospero arrived and set him free. "As thou report'st thyself," is accordingly the form in which Prospero alludes to Sycorax and all else that pertained to those prehistoric island-times before he set foot there. Sufficient for us, therefore, is it, that the Duke of Milan found on that strange island just such a monstrous being as travellers' tales had already made familiar to all men as natives of such regions. The terms Carib and Cannibal were synonymous. The edicts of Isabella expressly excluded the Carribeans from all the ordinary rights of humanity on this very ground. They therefore were the anthropophagi of travellers' tales; and Caliban is but an anagram of the significant name.

"Do you put tricks upon us with savages and men of Ind?" says Stephano;

while the drunken Trinculo, puzzling, in his besotted fashion, over Caliban, who
has fallen flat at his approach in the hope of escaping notice, exclaims: "What
have we here? a man or a fish? A strange fish! Were I in England now, as once
I was, and had but this fish painted, not a holiday fool there but would give a
piece of silver; there would monster make a man; any strange beast there makes
a man; when they will not give a doit to relieve a lame beggar, they will lay out
ten to see a dead Indian. Legged like a man! and his fins like arms! Warm, o'
my troth! I do now let loose my opinion; hold it no longer: this is no fish, but
an islander, that hath lately suffered by a thunderbolt." It would be curious to
recover an exact delineation of the Caliban of the Elizabethan stage. "This is a
strange thing as e'er I looked on," is the exclamation of the King of Naples,
when Caliban is driven in, along with the revellers who have been plotting who
should "be king o' the isle;" and on his brother, Sebastian, asking, "What things
are these, my Lord Antonio?" he replies: "One of them is a plain fish, and no
doubt marketable." There was obviously something marine, or fish-like, in the
aspect of the island monster. "In the dim obscurity of the past," says Darwin,
"we can see that the early progenitor of all the vertebrae must have been an
aquatic animal;" in its earliest stages "more like the larvae of our existing
marine Ascidians than any other known form," but destined in process of time,
through lancelot, ganoid, and other kindred transitions, to—

> Suffer a sea change
> Into something rich and strange.

In Caliban there was undesignedly embodied, seemingly, an ideal of the latest
stages of such an evolution. Mr. Joseph Hunter in dealing with this, as with
other details, in his "Disquisition on Shakespeare's Tempest," lets his learning
come into needless conflict with the idealisation of the poet. He will by no
means admit of so simple a solution of the name of Caliban as the mere
metathesis of *cannibal*, but goes in search for it among the many names by
which Gaspar, Melchior, and Balthazar, the three magi, were known throughout medieval Europe. In like fashion he finds his form to be of Hebraistic origin, and not at all "a pure creation of Shakespeare's own mind." He
accordingly proceeds to "compare him with the fish-idol of Ashdod, the
Dagon of the Philistines:—

> Sea-monster! upward man,
> And downward fish
> —P[aradise]. L[ost]., Bk. i.

"Here we have also a figure half-fish, half-man; and so the learned commentator proceeds to questions of Rabbinical literature; discusses how the two
elements of fish and man coalesced in the form of Dagon; quotes Abarbinel

and Kimchi; and finally arrives at this conclusion: "The true form of Dagon was a figure shaped like a fish, only with feet and hands like a man. Now this is precisely the form of Shakespeare's Caliban, "a fish legged like a man, and his fins like arms." Nothing can be more precise than the resemblance. The two are in fact one, as to form. Caliban is therefore a kind of tortoise, the paddles expanding in arms and hands, legs and feet. And accordingly, before he appears upon the stage, the audience are prepared for the strange figure by the words of Prospero:—

> Come forth, thou tortoise!

"How he became changed into a monkey, while the play is full of allusions to his fish-like form," the learned critic leaves to others to explain.

There is an amusing literalness in this application alike of the confused ideas of the drunken Trinculo, and of the invective of Prospero. The wrathful magician calls to the creature whom Miranda has been denouncing as a villain,—"What ho! slave! Caliban! Thou earth, thou!" and as he still lingers, muttering his refusal, Prospero shouts, "Come forth, I say; come, thou tortoise! when?" In a milder mood he might have said, "Come thou snail!" expressing thereby the same idea of tardy reluctant obedience, with equally little reference to his form.

In reality, though by some scaly or fin-like appendages, the idea of a fish, or sea-monster, is suggested to all, the form of Caliban is nevertheless, essentially human. In a fashion more characteristic of Milton's than of Shakespeare's wonted figure of speech, this is affirmed in language that no doubt purposely suggests the opposite idea to the mind, where Prospero says:—

> Then was this island—
> Save for the son that she did litter here,
> A freckled whelp, hag-born,—not honoured with
> A human shape.

The double bearing of this is singularly expressive:—save for this son of Sycorax, the island was not honoured with a human shape. And, having thus indicated that his shape was human, by the use of the terms "whelp" and "littered" the brutish ideal is strongly impressed on the mind. But his strictly anthropomorphic character is delicately suggested in other ways. When Miranda says of Ferdinand—

> This
> Is the third man that e'er I saw, the first
> That e'er I sigh'd for,

she can only refer to her father and Caliban. In this the poet purposely glances at the simplicity of the inexperienced maiden, to whom the repulsive monster had hitherto been the sole ideal of manhood presented to her mind, apart from the venerable Prospero. How far he falls short of all manly perfections is indicated immediately afterwards in the contrast instituted between him and Ferdinand:—

> Thou think'st there are no more such shapes as he,
> Having seen but him and Caliban. Foolish wench!
> To the most of men this is a Caliban,
> And they to him are angels.

This is, of course, the purposed exaggeration of Prospero, in his fear 'lest too light winning make the prize light." But so soon as Miranda has become thoroughly impressed with the image of her new-found lover, with "no ambition to see a goodlier man," she ceases to think of Caliban as a being to be associated with him in common manhood. When, accordingly, she responds to Ferdinand's admiring exclamation—

> But you, O you,
> So perfect and so peerless, are created
> Of every creature's best,

it is by a declaration which wholly ignores Caliban's claims to rank in the same order of beings with those among whom she had so recently classed him.

> I do not know
> One of my sex; no woman's face remember,
> Save, from my glass, mine own; nor have I seen
> More that I may call men, than you, good friend,
> And my dear father.

In this way the gradual expansion of the ideas of this innocent maiden are traced by the most delicate indications; until at length, when Alonzo and his company are introduced into Prospero's cell, where Ferdinand and Miranda are seated, playing at chess, she exclaims—

> Oh! wonder!
> How many goodly creatures are there here!
> How beauteous mankind is! O brave new world
> That has such people in't!

The development being thus completed, and the perfection of true man-hood fairly presented to her eye and mind, Caliban is then introduced, with the awe-struck exclamation—

O Setebos, these be brave spirits indeed!

and immediately thereafter we have the remark of Antonio—"One of them is a plain fish, and no doubt marketable." He is a "thing of darkness," as Pros-pero calls him; a being "as disproportioned in his manners as in his shape;" yet nevertheless so closely approximating, in the main, to ordinary humanity, that Miranda had associated him in her own mind, along with her father, as "honoured with a human shape."

Again we are furnished with a tolerably definite clue to the age which Caliban has attained at the date of his introduction to our notice. Littered on the island soon after the reputed arrival of Sycorax, we learn that the malig-nant hag, unable to subdue the delicate Ariel to the execution of her abhorred commands, imprisoned him in the cloven pine, where he groaned out twelve wretched years, till relieved from his torments by the art of Prospero. Next, it appears from the discourse of her father to Miranda that she has grown up on that lonely island for a like period. "Twelve years since, Miranda, thy father was the Duke of Milan, and a prince of power." But she was not then three years old, and so the memory of that former state, and of the maidens who tended her in her father's palace, has faded away, "far off," and like a dream;" while the banished Duke, "rapt in secret studies," his library "a dukedom large enough," had more and more perfected himself in occult science, until he learns by its aid that now the very crisis of their fates has come. Caliban is, therefore, to all appearance in his twenty-fifth year, as we catch a first glimpse of this pre-Darwinian realisation of the intermediate link between brute and man. It seems moreover to be implied that he has already passed his maturity. At an earlier age than that at which man is capable of self-support, the crea-ture had been abandoned to the solitude of his island-home, and learned with his long claws to dig for pig-nuts; and now, says Prospero, "as with age his body uglier grows, so his mind cankers." We may conceive of the huge canine teeth and prognathous jaws which in old age assume such prominence in the higher quadrumana. Darwin claims for the bonnet-monkey "the forehead which gives to man his noble and intellectual appearance;" and it is obvious that it was not wanting in Caliban: for when he discovers the true quality of the drunken fools he has mistaken for gods, his remonstrance is, "we shall all be turned to apes with foreheads villainous low." Here then is the highest developement of "the beast that wants discourse of reason." He has attained to all the maturity his nature admits of, and so is perfect as the study of a living creature distinct from, yet next in order below the level of humanity.

The being thus called into existence for the purposes of dramatic art is a creation well meriting the thoughtful study of the modern philosopher, whatever deductions he may have based on the hypotheses of recent speculation. Caliban's is not a brutalised, but a natural brute mind. He is a being in whom the moral instincts of man have no part; but also in whom the degradation of savage humanity is equally wanting. He is a novel anthropoid of a high type—such as on the hypothesis of evolution must have existed intermediately between the ape and man,—in whom some spark of rational intelligence has been enkindled, under the tutorship of one who has already mastered the secrets of nature. We must not be betrayed into a too literal interpretation of the hyperboles of the wrathful Duke of Milan. He is truly enough the "freckled whelp" whom Prospero has subdued to useful services, as he might break in a wild colt, or rear a young wolf to do his bidding, though in token of higher capacity he has specially trained him to menial duties peculiar to man. For not only does he "fetch in our wood," as Prospero reminds his daughter, "and serves in offices that profit us," but "he does make our fire."

No incident attending the discovery of the New World is more significant than that of Columbus stationed on the poop of the Santa Maria, his eye ranging along the darkened horizon, when the sun had once more gone down on the disappointed hopes of the voyagers. Suddenly a light glimmered in the distance, once and again reappeared to the eyes of Pedro Gutierrez and others whom the great admiral summoned to catch this gleam of realised hopes; and then darkness and doubt resumed their reign. But to Columbus all was light. That feeble ray had told of the presence of the fire-maker, man. The natural habits of Caliban, however, are those of the denizen of the woods. We may conceive of him like the pongoes of Mayombe, described by Purchas, who would come and sit by the travellers' deserted camp-fire, but had not sense enough to replenish it with fuel. We have no reason to think of him as naturally a cooking or fire-using animal; though, under the training of Prospero, he proves to be so far in advance of the most highly developed anthropoid as to be capable of learning the art of fire-making.

"We'll visit Caliban, my slave, who never yields us kind answers," Duke Prospero says to his daughter in the second scene of "The Tempest," where they first appear, and Caliban is introduced; but the gentle Miranda recalls with shuddering revulsion the brutal violence of their strange servitor, and exclaims with unwonted vehemence: " 'Tis a villain, sir, I do not love to look on." But repulsive as he is, his services cannot be dispensed with. "As 'tis, we cannot miss him," is Prospero's reply; and then, irritated alike by the sense of his obnoxious instincts and reluctant service, he heaps opprobrious epithets upon him: "What, ho! slave! Caliban! thou earth, thou! Come forth, I say, thou tortoise!" and at length, as he still lingers, muttering in his den, Prospero breaks out in wrath—"Thou poisonous slave, got by the devil himself upon thy wicked dam, come forth!" Schlegel and Hazlitt accordingly speak in nearly the same terms of "the savage Caliban, half brute, half demon;" while

Gervinus—although elsewhere characterising him with more appreciative acumen as "an embryonic being defiled as it were by his earthly origin from the womb of savage nature,"—does, with prosaic literalness, assume that his mother was the witch Sycorax, and the devil his father. Shakespeare assuredly aimed at the depiction of no such foul ideal. It is the recluse student of nature's mysteries, and not the poor island monster that is characteristically revealed in such harsh vituperations. Prospero habitually accomplishes his projects through the agency of enforced service. He has usurped a power over the spirits of air, as well as over this earth-born slave; and both are constrained to unwilling obedience. Hence he has learned to exact and compel service to the utmost; to count only on the agency of enslaved power: until an imperious habit disguises the promptings of a generous and kindly nature. With all his tenderness towards the daughter whose presence alone has made life endurable to him, he flashes up in sudden ire at the slightest interference with his plans for her; as when she interposes on behalf of Ferdinand, he exclaims—"Silence! One word more shall make me chide thee, if not hate thee." He is indeed acting an assumed part, "lest too light winning" should make the lover undervalue his prize; but it is done in the imperious tone with which habit has taught him to respond to the slightest thwarting of his commands. This is still more apparent in his dealings with the gentle Ariel, who owes to him delivery from cruellest bondage. The relations subsisting between them are indicated with rare art, and are as tender as is compatible with beings of different elements. The sylph is generally addressed in kindly admiring terms, as "my brave spirit," "my tricksy spirit," "my delicate, my dainty Ariel." Yet on the slightest questioning of Prospero's orders, he is told: "Thou liest, malignant thing!" and on the mere show of murmuring is threatened with durance more terrible than that from which he has been set free.

In all this the characteristics of the magician are consistently wrought out. According to the ideas of an age which still believed in magic, he has usurped the lordship of nature, and subdued to his will the spirits of the elements, by presumptuous, if not altogether sinful arts. They are retained in subjection by the constant exercise of this supernatural power, and yield him only the reluctant obedience of slaves. This has to be borne in remembrance, if we would not misinterpret the ebullitions of imperious harshness on the part of Prospero towards beings who can only be retained in subjection by such enforced mastery. That Caliban regards him with as malignant a hatred as the caged and muzzled bear may be supposed to entertain towards his keeper, is set forth with clear consistency. Nor is it without abundant reason. He is dealt with not merely as a "lying slave, whom stripes may move, not kindness;" but by his master's magical art, the most familiar objects of nature are made instruments of torture. They pinch, affright him, pitch him into the mire, as deceptive firebrands mislead him in the dark, grind his joints with convulsions, contort his sinews with cramp, and, as he says,

> For every trifle are they set upon me:
> Sometimes like apes, that mow and chatter at me,
> And after bite me: then like hedgehogs, which
> Lie tumbling in my barefoot way, and mount
> Their pricks at my footfall; sometimes am I
> All wound with adders, who with cloven tongues
> Do hiss me into madness.

To reconcile such harsh violence with the merciful forgiving character of Prospero in his dealings with those who, after having done him the cruellest wrongs, are placed in his power, we have to conceive of the outcast father and child compelled in their island solitude to subdue a gorilla, or other brute menial, to their service; and, after in vain trying kindness, driven in self-defence to protect themselves from its brutal violence. The provocation which had roused the inappeasable wrath of Miranda's father was indeed great; but recognising the "most poor credulous monster" as the mere brute that he is, it involved no more delinquency; and therefore he is not to be regarded as devilish in origin and inclinations, because he tells Stephano what is literally true— "I am subject to a tyrant, a sorcerer, that by his cunning hath cheated me of the island." He accordingly invites the drunken butler to be his supplanter:—

> If thy greatness will
> Revenge it on him,—for I know thou darest,—
> Thou shalt be lord of it, and I'll serve thee.

He gloats on the idea of braining the tyrant, just as an abused human slave might, and indeed many a time has done.

> Why, as I told thee, 'tis a custom with him
> I' the afternoon to sleep: there thou mayst brain him,
> Having first seized his books; or with a log
> Batter his skull, or paunch him with a stake,
> Or cut his weazand with thy knife. Remember
> First to possess his books; for without them
> He's but a sot, as I am, nor hath not
> One spirit to command: they all do hate him
> As rootedly as I.

All this would be hateful enough in a human being; but before we pronounce Caliban a "demi-devil," we must place alongside of him the butler Stephano, who, with no other provocation than that of a base nature, and with no wrongs whatever to avenge, is ready with the response—"Monster, I will kill this man; his daughter and I will be king and queen, and Trinculo and thyself shall be viceroys;" and so the poor servant monster already fancies his slavery at an end, and exclaims, "Freedom, hey-day! hey-day, freedom!"

He who undertakes to subdue the wild nature of ape, leopard, wolf, or tiger, must not charge it with moral delinquency when it yields to its native instincts. It may be, as modern science would teach us, that our most human characteristics are but developed instincts of the brute; for the churl

> Will let his coltish nature break
> At seasons through the gilded pale.

The savage, though familiarised with habits of civilisation, reverts with easy recoil to his barbarian licence; and the highest happiness which the tamed monster of the island could conceive of was once more to range in unrestrained liberty, digging up the pig-nuts with his long nails, or following the jay and the nimble marmoset over rock and tree. But there is nothing malignant in this; and that nothing essentially repulsive is to be assumed as natural to him is apparent from the very invectives of Prospero:—

> Thou most lying slave,
> Whom stripes may move, not kindness: I have used thee,
> Filth as thou art, with human care; and lodged thee
> In mine own cell, till thou didst seek to violate
> The honour of my child.

Leaving aside, then, the exaggerations of the incensed Prospero, which have their legitimate place in the development of the drama, let us study, as far as may be, the actual characteristics of the strange islander. His story is told, briefly indeed, yet with adequate minuteness. Prospero retorts on him the recapitulation of kindnesses which had been repaid with outrage never to be forgiven:—

> Abhorred slave,
> Which any print of goddness will not take,
> Being capable of all ill! I pitied thee,
> Took pains to make thee speak, taught thee each hour
> One thing or other: when thou didst not, savage,
> Know thine own meaning, but wouldst gabble like
> A thing most brutish, I endowed thy purposes
> With words that made them known. But thy vile race,
> Though thou didst learn, had that in't which good natures
> Could not abide to be with.

In other words, he proved to be simply an animal, actuated by the ordinary unrestrained passions and desires which in the brute involve no moral evil, and but for the presence of Miranda would have attracted no special notice. Situated as he actually is, he is not to be judged of wholly from the invectives of his master. With brute instincts which have brought on him the condign punishment of Prospero, and a savage nature which watches, like any wild creature under harsh restraint, for escape and revenge, his feelings are nevertheless rather those of the captive bear than of "one who treasures up a wrong." There is in him still a dog-like aptitude for attachment, a craving even for the mastership of some higher nature, and an appreciation of kindness not unlike that of the domesticated dog, though conjoined with faculties of intelligent enjoyment more nearly approximating to humanity. When compelled reluctantly to emerge from his den, he enters muttering curses; yet even they have a smack of nature in them. They are in no ways devilish, but such as the wild creature exposed to the elements may be supposed to recognise as the blight and mildew with which Nature gratifies her ill-will. He imprecates on his enslaver—

> As wicked dew as e'er my mother brushed
> With raven's feather from unwholesome fen
> Drop on you both! A south-west blow on ye
> And blister you all o'er!

Prospero threatens him with cramps, side-stitches that shall pen his breath up, urchins to prick him, and pinching pains more stinging than the bees; but his answer has no smack of fiendishness, though he does retort with bootless imprecations. He stolidly replies—

> I must eat my dinner.
> This island's mine, by Sycorax my mother,
> Which thou takest from me. When thou camest first,
> Thou strokedst me, and madest much of me; wouldst give me
> Water with berries in't; and teach me how
> To name the bigger light, and how the less,
> That burn by day and night; and then I loved thee,
> And shew'd thee all the qualities o' the isle,
> The fresh springs, brine-pits, barren place and fertile;
> Cursed be I that did so! All the charms
> Of Sycorax, toads, beetles, bats, light on you!
> For I am all the subjects that you have,
> Which first was mine own king; and here you sty me
> In this hard rock, whiles you do keep from me
> The rest o' the island.

Prospero replies to him as a creature "whom stripes may move, not kindness," who had been treated companionably, with human care, till his brute instincts compelled the subjection of him to such restraint. He describes the pity with which he at first regarded the poor monster whose brutish gabble he had trained to the intelligent speech which is now used for curses. In all this do we not realise the ideal anthropoid in the highest stage of Simian evolution, stroked and made much of like a favourite dog, fed with dainties, and at length taught to frame his brute cries into words by which his wishes could find intelligible utterance. The bigger and the lesser light receive names, and are even traced, as we may presume, to their origin. But the intellectual development compasses, at the utmost, a very narrow range; and when the drunken Stephano plies him with his bottle of sack, the dialogue runs in this characteristic fashion:—

STEPH.　How now, moon-calf? how does thine ague?
CAL.　Hast thou not dropt from heaven?
STEPH.　Out o' the moon, I do assure thee: I was the man in the moon, when time was.
CAL.　I have seen thee in her, and I do adore thee.
　　　My mistress shewed me thee, and thy dog, and thy bush.
STEPH.　Come, swear to that; kiss the book: I will furnish it anon with new contents: swear.
TRIN.　By this good light, this is a very shallow monster! I am afeard of him! A very weak monster! The man i' the moon! A most poor credulous monster! Well drawn, monster, in good sooth!
CAL.　I'll shew thee every fertile inch o' the island;
　　　And I will kiss thy foot: I pr'ythee, be my god.

But we presently see Caliban in another and wholly different aspect. Like the domesticated animal, which he really is, he has certain artificial habits and tastes superinduced in him; but whenever his natural instincts reveal themselves we see neither a born devil, nor a being bearing any likeness to degraded savage humanity. He is an animal at home among the sounds and scenes of living nature. "Pray you, tread softly, that the blind mole may not hear a footfall," is his exhortation to his drunken companions as they approach the entrance of Prospero's cell. When Trinculo frets him, his threatened revenge is, "He shall drink nought but brine; for I'll not show him where the quick freshes are;" and he encourages his equally rude companion with the assurance—

　　　Be not afeard; the isle is full of noises,
　　　Sounds, and sweet airs, that give delight and hurt not.
　　　Sometimes a thousand twangling instruments
　　　Will hum about mine ears; and sometimes voices,
　　　That, if I then had waked after long sleep,
　　　Will make me sleep again: and then, in dreaming,

> The clouds, methought, would open, and shew riches
> Ready to drop upon me; that, when I waked,
> I cried to dream again.

To the drunken butler and his comrade, Caliban is "a most poor credulous monster! a puppy-headed, scurvy, abominable monster! a most ridiculous monster!" and when, by their aid, he has drowned his tongue in sack, he is no more to them than a debauched fish. But Shakespeare has purposely placed the true anthropomorphoid alongside of these types of degraded humanity, to shew the contrast between them. He is careful to draw a wide and strongly-marked distinction between the coarse prosaic brutality of debased human nature, and the inferior, but in no ways degraded, brute nature of Caliban. "He is," says Prospero, "as disproportioned in his manners as in his shape." He had associated for years in friendly dependence, lodged with Prospero in his own cell; for we have to remember that Miranda was but three years old when her father took in hand the taming of the poor monster, and used him with human care, until compelled to drive him forth to his rocky prison. His narrow faculties have thus been forced into strange development; but though the wrathful Prospero pronounces him a creature "which any print of goodness will not take, being capable of all ill," that is by no means the impression which the poet designs to convey. Man, by reason of his higher nature which invites him to aspire, and his moral sense which clearly presents to him the choice between good and evil, is capable of a degradation beyond reach of the brute. The very criminality which has so hardened Prospero's heart against his poor slave, involves to himself no sense of moral wrong. "O ho! O ho! would it had been done!" is his retort to Prospero; "thou didst prevent me; I had peopled else this isle with Calibans."

The distinction between the coarse sensuality of degraded humanity, and this most original creation of poetic fancy, with its gross brute-mind, its limited faculties, its purely animal cravings and impulses, is maintained throughout. The first scene opens with the sailors, released from all ordinary deference and restraint by the perils of the storm, shouting and blaspheming in reckless desperation; and no sooner are they ashore than Caliban is brought into closest relations with the still more worthless topers who win his admiration, till experience teaches him—

> What a thrice-double ass
> Was I, to take this drunkard for a god,
> And worship this dull fool!

The dog-like attachment which had drawn him to Prospero, till harsh treatment and restraint eradicated this feeling, and utterly alienated him from his first master, is transferred to the next being who treats him with any appearance of kindness. "I'll shew thee every fertile inch o' the island," is the first form in which his gratitude finds utterance;

> I'll shew thee the best springs; I'll pluck thee berries;
> I'll fish for thee, and get thee wood enough.
> A plague upon the tyrant that I serve!
> I'll bear him no more sticks, but follow thee,
> Thou wondrous man.

The drunken butler, with his bottle of sack, seems to the poor monster to have dropped from heaven, or rather from the moon, where once his mistress showed him that favourite myth of old popular folk-lore, the man-in-the-moon, with his dog and bush: and so he fawns on him as a dog might on an old acquaintance. "A most ridiculous monster," thinks Trinculo, "to make a wonder of a poor drunkard;" but Caliban is ready to lavish all his dog-like fidelity on his new-found master.

> I prithee, let me bring thee where crabs grow;
> And I, with my long nails, will dig thee pig-nuts;
> Shew thee a jay's nest, and instruct thee how
> To snare the nimble marmoset; I'll bring thee
> To clustering filberts; and sometimes I'll get thee
> Young scamels from the rock. Wilt thou go with me?

If we can conceive of a baboon endowed with speech, and moved by gratitude, have we not here the very ideas to which its nature would prompt it. It is a creature native to the rocks and the woods, at home in the haunts of the jay and marmoset: a fellow-creature of like nature and sympathies with themselves. The talk of the ship's crew is not only coarse, but even what it is customary to call brutal; while that of Stephano and Trinculo accords with their debased and besotted humanity. Their language never assumes a rhythmical structure, or rises to poetic thought. But Caliban is in perfect harmony with the rhythm of the breezes and the tides. His thoughts are essentially poetical, within the range of his lower nature; and so his speech is, for the most part, in verse. He has that poetry of the senses which seems natural to his companionship with the creatures of the forest and the seashore. Even his growl, as he retorts impotent curses on the power that has enslaved him, is rhythmical. Bogs, fens, and the infectious exhalations that the sun sucks up, embody his ideas of evil; and his acute senses are chiefly at home with the dew, and the fresh springs, the clustering filberts, the jay in his leafy nest, or the blind mole in its burrow.

No being of all that people the Shakespearean drama more thoroughly suggests the idea of a pure creation of the poetic fancy than Caliban. He has a nature of his own essentially distinct from the human beings with whom he is brought in contact. He seems indeed the half-human link between the brute and the man; and realises, as no degraded Bushman or Australian savage can do, a conceivable intermediate stage of the anthropomorphous existence, as far above the most highly organised ape as it falls short of rational humanity. He excites a sympathy such as no degraded savage could. We feel for the poor monster, so helplessly in the power of the stern Prospero, as for some caged wild beast pining in cruel captivity, and rejoice to think of him at last free to range in harmless mastery over his island solitude. He provokes no more jealousy as the inheritor of Prospero's usurped lordship over his island home than the caged bird which has escaped to the free forest again. His is a type of development essentially non-human,—though, for the purposes of the drama, endued to an extent altogether beyond the highest attainments of the civilised, domesticated animal, with the exercise of reason and the use of language;—a conceivable civilisation such as would, to a certain extent, run parallel to that of man, but could never converge to a common centre.

Shakspere's Last Plays*

EDWARD DOWDEN

Over the beauty of youth and the love of youth there is shed, in these plays of Shakspere's final period, a clear yet tender luminousness not elsewhere to be perceived in his writings. In his earlier plays, Shakspere writes concerning young men and maidens—their loves, their mirth, their griefs—as one who is among them; who has a lively, personal interest in their concerns; who can make merry with them, treat them familiarly, and, if need be, can mock them into good sense. There is nothing in these early plays wonderful, strangely beautiful, pathetic, about youth and its joys and sorrows. In the histories and tragedies, as was to be expected, more massive, broader, or more profound objects of interest engage the poet's imagination. But in these latest plays, the beautiful pathetic light is always present. There are the sufferers, aged, experienced, tried—Queen Katharine, Prospero, Hermione. And over against these there are the children, absorbed in their happy and exquisite egoism—Perdita and Miranda, Florizel and Ferdinand, and the boys of old Belarius.

The same means to secure ideality for these figures, so young and beautiful, is in each case (instinctively, perhaps, rather than deliberately) resorted to. They are lost children—princes, or a princess, removed from the court and its conventional surroundings into some scene of rare, natural beauty. There are the lost princes—Arviragus and Guiderius—among the mountains of Wales, drinking the free air and offering their salutations to the risen sun. There is Perdita, the shepherdess-princess, "queen of curds and cream," sharing, with old and young, her flowers, lovelier and more undying than those that Proserpina let fall from Dis's wagon. There is Miranda (whose very name is significant of wonder), made up of beauty and love and womanly pity, neither courtly nor rustic, with the breeding of an island of enchantment, where

*Reprinted from *Shakspere: A Critical Study of his Mind and Art*, 3rd ed., (New York and London: Harper & Brothers Publishers, 1905), 369–382.

Prospero is her tutor and protector, and Caliban her servant, and the Prince of Naples her lover. In each of these plays we can see Shakspere, as it were, tenderly, bending over the joys and sorrows of youth. We recognize this rather through the total characterization, and through a feeling and a presence, than through definite incident or statement. But some of this feeling escapes in the disinterested joy and admiration of old Belarius when he gazes at the princely youths, and in Camillo's loyalty to Florizel and Perdita; while it obtains more distinct expression in such a word as that which Prospero utters when from a distance he watches with pleasure Miranda's zeal to relieve Ferdinand from his task of log-bearing: "Poor worm, thou art infected."[1]

It is not chiefly because Prospero is a great enchanter, now about to break his magic staff, to drown his book deeper than ever plummet sounded, to dismiss his airy spirits, and to return to the practical service of his Dukedom, that we identify Prospero in some measure with Shakspere himself. It is rather because the temper of Prospero, the grave harmony of his character, his self-mastery, his calm validity of will, his sensitiveness to wrong, his unfaltering justice, and, with these, a certain abandonment, a remoteness from the common joys and sorrows of the world, are characteristic of Shakspere as discovered to us in all his latest plays. Prospero is an harmonious and fully developed *will*. In the earlier play of fairy enchantments, *A Midsummer Night's Dream*, the "human mortals" wander to and fro in a maze of error, misled by the mischievous frolic of Puck, the jester and clown of Fairy-land. But here the spirits of the elements, and Caliban, the gross genius of brute matter—needful for the service of life—are brought under subjection to the human will of Prospero.[2]

What is more, Prospero has entered into complete possession of himself. Shakspere has shown us his quick sense of injury, his intellectual impatience, his occasional moment of keen irritability, in order that we may be more deeply aware of his abiding strength and self-possession, and that we may perceive how these have been grafted upon a temperment not impassive or unexcitable. And Prospero has reached not only the higher levels of moral attainment; he has also reached an altitude of thought from which he can survey the whole of human life, and see how small and yet how great it is. His heart is sensitive; he is profoundly touched by the joy of the children with whom, in the egoism of their love, he passes for a thing of secondary interest; he is deeply moved by the perfidy of his brother. His brain is readily set a-work, and can with difficulty be checked from eager and excessive energizing; he is subject to the access of sudden and agitating thought. But Prospero masters his own sensitiveness, emotional and intellectual:

> We are such stuff
> As dreams are made on, and our little life
> Is rounded with a sleep. Sir, I am vex'd;
> Bear with my weakness; my old brain is troubled:

> Be not disturb'd with my infirmity;
> If you be pleased, retire into my cell
> And there repose; a turn or two I'll walk,
> To still my beating mind.

"Such stuff as dreams are made on." Nevertheless, in this little life, in this dream, Prospero will maintain his dream rights, and fulfill his dream duties. In the dream, he, a Duke, will accomplish Duke's work. Having idealized everything, Shakespeare left everything real. Bishop Berkeley's foot was no less able to set a pebble flying than was a lumbering foot of Dr. Johnson. Nevertheless, no material substance intervened between the soul of Berkeley and the immediate presence of the play of Divine power.[3]

A thought which seems to run through the whole of *The Tempest*, appearing here and there like a colored thread in some web, is the thought that the true freedom of man consists in service. Ariel, untouched by human feeling, is panting for his liberty. In the last words of Prospero are promised his enfranchisement and dismissal to the elements. Ariel reverences his great master, and serves him with bright alacrity; but he is bound by none of our human ties, strong and tender, and he will rejoice when Prospero is to him as though he never were.[4] To Caliban, a land-fish, with the duller elements of earth and water in his composition, but no portion of the higher elements, air and fire, though he receives dim intimations of a higher world—a musical humming, or a twanging, or a voice heard in sleep—to Caliban, service is slavery.[5] He hates to bear his logs; he fears the incomprehensible power of Prospero, and obeys and curses. The great master has usurped the rights of the brute-power Caliban. And when Stephano and Tririculo appear, ridiculously impoverished specimens of humanity, with their shallow understandings and vulgar greeds, this poor earth-monster is possessed by a sudden *Schwärmerei*, a fanaticism for liberty!—

> 'Ban, 'ban, Ca'-Caliban,
> Has a new master:—get a new man.
> Freedom, heyday! heyday, freedom! freedom! heyday, freedom!

His new master also sings his impassioned hymn of liberty, the *Marseillaise* of the enchanted island:

> Flout 'em and scout 'em,
> And scout 'em and flout 'em;
> Thought is free.

The leaders of the revolution, escaped from the stench and foulness of the horse-pond, King Stephano and his prime-minister Trinculo, like too many leaders of the people, bring to an end their great achievement on behalf of liberty by quarrelling over booty—the trumpery which the providence of

Prospero had placed in their way. Caliban, though scarce more truly wise or
instructed than before, at least discovers his particular error of the day and
hour:

> What a thrice-double ass
> Was I, to take this drunkard for a god,
> And worship this dull fool!

It must be admitted that Shakspere, if not, as Hartley Coleridge asserted, "a
Tory and a gentleman," had within him some of the elements of English con-
servatism.

But while Ariel and Caliban, each in his own way, is impatient of service,
the human actors, in whom we are chiefly interested, are entering into
bonds—bonds of affection, bonds of duty, in which they find their truest freedom. Ferdinand and Miranda emulously contend in the task of bearing the
burden which Prospero has imposed upon the prince:

> I am in my condition
> A prince, Miranda; I do think, a king:
> I would, not so! and would no more endure
> This wooden slavery than to suffer
> The flesh-fly blow my mouth. Hear my soul speak:
> The very instant that I saw you, did
> My heart fly to your service; there resides,
> To make me slave to it; and for your sake
> Am I this patient log-man.

And Miranda speaks with the sacred candor from which spring the nobler
manners of a world more real and glad than the world of convention and pro-
prieties and pruderies:

> Hence, bashful cunning!
> And prompt me, plain and holy innocence!
> I am your wife, if you will marry me;
> If not, I'll die your maid: to be your fellow
> You may deny me; but I'll be your servant,
> Whether you will or no.
>   FER.   My mistress, dearest;
> And I thus humble ever.
>   MIR.   My husband, then?
>   FER. Ay, with a heart as willing
> As bondage e'er of freedom.

In an earlier part of the play, this chord which runs through it had been playfully struck in the description of Gonzalo's imaginary commonwealth, in
which man is to be enfranchised from all the laborious necessities of life. Here

is the ideal of notional liberty, Shakspere would say, and to attempt to realize
it at once lands us in absurdities and self-contradictions:

> For no kind of traffic
> Would I admit: no name or magistrate;
> Letters should not be known: riches, poverty,
> And use of service none; contract, succession,
> Bourn, bound of land, tilth, vineyard, none;
> No use of metal, corn, or wine, or oil;
> No occupation; all men idle, all,
> And women too, but innocent and pure;
> No sovereignty.
>   SEB.   Yet he would be king on't.[6]

Finally, in the Epilogue, which was written perhaps by Shakspere, perhaps by some one acquanted with his thoughts, Prospero, in his character of a
man, no longer a potent enchanter, petitions the spectators of the theatre for
two things, pardon and freedom. It would be straining matters to discover in
this Epilogue profound significances. And yet, in its playfulness, it curiously
falls in with the moral purport of the whole. Prospero, the pardoner, implores
pardon. Shakespere was aware—whether such be the significance (aside, for
the writer's mind) of this Epilogue or not—that no life is ever lived which does
not need to receive as well as to render forgiveness. He knew that every ener-
getic dealer with the world must seek a sincere and liberal pardon for many
things. Forgiveness and freedom: these are key-notes of the play. When it was
occupying the mind of Shakspere, he was passing from his service as artist to
his service as English country gentleman. Had his mind been dwelling on the
question of how he should employ his new freedom, and had he been enforcing upon himself the truth that the highest freedom lies in the bonds of duty?[7]

It remains to notice of *The Tempest* that it has had the quality, as a work
of art, of setting its critics to work as if it were an allegory; and forthwith it
baffles them, and seems to mock them for supposing that they had power to
"pluck out the heart of its mystery." A curious and interesting chapter in the
history of Shaksperian criticism might be written if the various interpretations
were brought together of the allegorical significances of Prospero, of Miranda,
of Ariel, of Caliban. Caliban, says Kreyssig, is the People. He is Understanding apart from Imagination, declares Professor Lowell. He is the primitive
man abandoned to himself, declares M. Mézières; Shakspere would say to
Utopian thinkers, predecessors of Jean Jacques Rousseau, "Your hero walks
on four feet as well as on two." That Caliban is the missing link between man
and brute (Shakspere anticipating Darwinian theories) has been elaborately
demonstrated by Daniel Wilson. Caliban is one of the powers of nature over
which the scientific intellect obtains command, another critic assures us, and
Prospero is the founder of the Inductive Philosophy. Caliban is the colony of

Virginia. Caliban is the untutored early drama of Marlowe.[8] Such allegorical interpretations, however ingenious, we cannot set much store by. But the significance of a work of art, like the character of a man, is not to be discovered solely by investigation of its inward essence. Its dynamical qualities, so to speak, must be considered as well as its statical. It must be viewed in action; the atmosphere it effuses, its influence upon the minds of men, must be noted. And it is certainly remarkable that this, the last, or almost the last, of Shakspere's plays, more than any other, has possessed this quality of soliciting men to attempt the explanation of it, as of an enigma, and, at the same time, of baffling their inquiry.

If I were to allow my fancy to run out in play after such an attempted interpretation, I should describe Prospero as the man of genius, the great artist, lacking at first in practical gifts which lead to material success, and set adrift on the perilous sea of life, in which he finds his enchanted island, where he may achieve his works of wonder. He bears with him Art in its infancy—the marvellous child, Miranda. The grosser passions and appetites—Caliban—he subdues to his service:

MIR.   'Tis a villain, sir,
     I do not love to look on.
PROS.   But as 'tis,
     We cannot miss him.

And he partially informs this servant-monster with intellect and imagination; for Caliban has dim affinities with the higher world of spirits. But these grosser passions and appetites attempt to violate the purity of art. Caliban would seize upon Miranda and people the island with Calibans; therefore his servitude must be strict. And who is Ferdinand? Is he not, with his gallantry and his beauty, the young Fletcher in conjunction with whom Shakspere worked upon *The Two Noble Kinsman* and *Henry VIII*? Fletcher is conceived as a follower of the Shaksperian style and method in dramatic art; he had "eyed full many a lady with best regard," for several virtues had liked several women, but never any with whole-hearted devotion except Miranda. And to Ferdinand the old enchanter will intrust his daughter, "a third of his own life." But Shakspere had perceived the weak point in Fletcher's genius—its want of hardness of fibre, of patient endurance, and of a sense of the solemnity and sanctity of the service of art. And therefore he finely hints to his friend that his winning of Miranda must not be too light and easy. It shall be Ferdinand's task to remove some thousands of logs and pile them according to the strict injunction of Prospero. "Don't despise drudgery and dryasdust work, young poets," Shakspere would seem to say, who had himself so carefully labored over his English and Roman histories; "for Miranda's sake such drudgery may well seem light." Therefore, also, Prospero surrounds the marriage of Ferdinand to his daughter with a religious awe. Ferdinand must honor her as sacred, and win her by hard toil. But the work of the higher imagination is not drudgery; it is swift and serviceable among all the elements—fire upon the topmast, the sea-nymph upon the sands; Ceres, the goddess of earth, with harvest blessings, in the masque. It is essentially Ariel, an airy spirit—the imaginative genius of poetry but recently delivered in England from long slavery to Sycorax. Prospero's departure from the island is the abandoning by Shakspere of the theatre, the scene of his marvellous works:

> Graves, at my command,
> Have waked their sleepers, oped, and let them forth,
> By my so potent art.

Henceforth Prospero is but a man—no longer a great enchanter. He returns to the dukedom he had lost, in Stratford-upon-Avon, and will pay no tribute henceforth to any Alonzo or Lucy of them all.[9]

Thus one may be permitted to play with the grave subject of *The Tempest*; and I ask no more credit for the interpretation here proposed than is given to any other equally innocent, if trifling, attempt to read the supposed allegory.

Shakspere's work, however, will, indeed, not allow itself to be lightly treated. The prolonged study of any great interpreter of human life is a discipline. Our loyalty to Shakspere must not lead us to assert that the discipline of Shakspere will be suitable to every nature. He will deal rudely with heart and will and intellect, and lay hold of them in unexpected ways, and fashion his disciple, it may be, in a manner which at first is painful and almost terrible. There are persons who, all through their lives, attain their highest strength only by virtue of the presence of certain metaphysical entities which rule their lives; and in the lives of almost all men there is a metaphysical period when they need such supposed entities more than the real presences of those personal and social forces which surround them. For such persons, and during such a period, the discipline of Shakspere will be unsuitable. He will seem precisely the reverse of what he actually is: he will seem careless about great facts and ideas; limited, restrictive, deficient in enthusiasms and imagination. To one who finds the highest poetry in Shelley, Shakspere will always remain a kind of prose. Shakspere is the poet of concrete things and real. True, but are not these informed with passion and with thought? A time not seldom comes when a man, abandoning abstractions and metaphysical entities, turns to the actual life of the world, and to the real men and women who surround him, for the sources of emotion and thought and action—a time when he strives to come into communion with the Unseen, not immediately, but through the revelation of the Seen. And then he finds the strength and sustenance with which Shakspere has enriched the world.

"The true question to ask," says the Librarian of Congress, in a paper read before the Social Science Convention at New York, October, 1869—"The true question to ask respecting a book is, *Has it helped any human soul?*" This is the hint, statement, not only of the great Literatus, his book, but of every great artist. It may be that all works of art are to be first tried by their art-qualities, their image-forming talent, and their dramatic, pictorial, plot-constucting, euphonious, and other talents. Then, whenever claiming to be first class works, they are to be strictly and sternly tried by their foundation in, and radiation (in the highest sense, and always indirectly) of, the ethic principles, and eligibility to free, arouse, dilate.[10]

What shall be said of Shakspere's radiation, through art, of the ultimate truths of conscience and of conduct? What shall be said of his power of freeing, arousing, dilating? Something may be gathered out of the foregoing chapters in answer to these questions. But the answers remain insufficient. There is an admirable sentence by Emerson: "A good reader can in a sort nestle into Plato's brain, and think from thence; but not into Shakspere's. We are still out of doors."

We are still out of doors; and, for the present, let us cheerfully remain in the large, good space. Let us not attenuate Shakspere to a theory. He is careful that we shall not thus lose our true reward: "The secrets of nature have not more gift in taciturnity."[11] Shakspere does not supply us with a doctrine, with an interpretation, with a revelation. What he brings to us is this—to each one, courage and energy and strength to dedicate himself and his work to that, whatever it be, which life has revealed to him as best and highest and most real.

NOTES

1. The same feeling appears in the lines which end act iii., sc 1: "*Prospero.* So glad of this as they I cannot be, / Who are surprised with all; but my rejoicing / At nothing can be more."

2. This point of contrast between *The Tempest* and *A Midsummer Night's Dream* is noticed by Mézières, "Shakspeare, ses Oeuvres et ses Critiques," pp. 441, 442.

3. See a remarkable article on Goethe and Shakspere by Professor Masson, reprinted among his collected Essays. On *The Tempest*, the reader may consult, as an excellent summary of facts, the article "On the Origin of Shakspeare's Tempest," *Cornhill Magazine*, October 1872. It is founded upon Meissner's "Untersuchungen über Shakespeare's Sturm" (1782). See also Meissner's article in the *Jahrbuch der deutschen Shakespeare-Gesellschaft*, vol. v. Jacob Ayrer's "Comedia von der schönen Sidea" will be found, with a translation, in Mr. Albert Cohn's interesting volume "Shakespeare in Germany" (Asher, 1865).

4. Ariel is promised his freedom after two days, act i., sc.2. Why two days? The time of the entire action of *The Tempest* is only three hours. What was to be the

employment of Ariel during two days? To make the winds and seas favorable during the voyage to Naples. Prospero's island, therefore, was imagined by Shakspere as within two days' quick sail of Naples.

5. The conception of Caliban, the "servant-monster," "plain fish, and no doubt marketable," the "tortoise," "his fins like arms," with "a very ancient and fish-like smell," who gabbled until Prospero taught him language—this conception was in Shakspere's mind when he wrote *Troilus and Cressida*. Thersites describes Ajax (act iii, sc. 3), "*He's grown a very land-fish, languageles, a monster.*"

6. Act ii, sc. 1. The prolonged and dull joking of Sebastian in this scene cannot be meant by Shakspere to be really bright and witty. It is meant to show that the intellectual poverty of the conspirators is as great as their moral obliquity. They are monsters more ignoble than Caliban. Their laughter is "the crackling of thorns under a pot."

7. Mr. Furnivall, observing that in these later plays breaches of the family bond are dramatically studied, and the reconciliations are domestic reconciliations in *Cymbeline* and *A Winter's Tale*, suggests to me that they were a kind of confession on Shakspere's part that he had inadequately felt the beauty and tenderness of the common relations of father and child, wife and husband; and that he was now quietly resolving to be gentle, and wholly just to his wife and his home. I cannot altogether make this view of the later plays my own, and leave it to the reader to accept and develop as he may be able.

8. This last suggestion is that of M. Émile Montégut, in the *Revue des Deux Mondes*. The following passage from Professor Lowell will compensate for its length by its ingenuity: "In *The Tempest* the scene is laid nowhere, or certainly in no country laid down on any map. Nowhere, then? At once nowhere and anywhere—for it is in the soul of man that still vexed island hung between the upper and the nether world, and liable to incursions from both. . . .Consider for a moment if ever the Imagination has been so embodied as in Prospero, the Fancy as in Ariel, the brute Understanding as in Caliban, who, the moment his poor wits are warmed with the glorious liquor of Stephano, plots rebellion against his natural lord, the higher Reason. Miranda is mere abstract Womanhood, as truly so before she sees Ferdinand as Eve before she was awakened to consciousness by the echo of her own nature coming back to her, the same, and yet not the same, from that of Adam. Ferdinand, again, is nothing more than Youth, compelled to drudge at something he despises, till the sacrifice of will and abnegation of self win him his ideal in Miranda. The subordinate personages are simply types: Sebastian and Antonio, of weak character and evil ambition; Gonzalo, of average sense and honesty; Adrian and Francisco, of the walking gentlemen, who serve to fill up a world. They are not characters in the same sense with Iago, Falstaff, Shallow, or Leontius; and it is curious how every one of them loses his way in this enchanted island of life, all the victims of one illusion after another, except Prospero, whose ministers are purely ideal. The whole play, indeed, is a succession of illusions, winding up with those solemn words of the great enchanter, who had summoned to his service every shape of merriment or passion, every figure in the great tragi-comedy of life, and who was now bidding

farewell to the scene of his triumphs. For in Prospero shall we not recognize the Artist himself—

> That did not better for his life provide
> Than public means which public manners breeds,
> Whence comes it that his name receives a brand—

who has forfeited a shining place in the world's eye by devotion to his art, and who, turned adrift on the ocean of life in the leaky carcass of a boat, has shipwrecked on that Fortunate Island (as men always do who find their true vocation) where he is absolute lord, making all the powers of Nature serve him, but with Ariel and Caliban as special ministers? Of whom else could he have been thinking when he says:

> Graves at my command,
> Have waked their sleepers, oped, and let them forth,
> By my so potent art"?
> —*Among My Books. Shakespeare Once More*, pp. 191–192.

9. Ulrici has recently expressed his opinion that a farewell to the theatre may be discovered in *The Tempest*; but he rightly places *Henry VIII* later than *The Tempest* (*Shakespeare-Jahrbuch*, vol. vi., p. 358).
10. Whitman, "Democratic Vistas," p. 67.
11. *Troilus and Cressida*, act iv., sc. 2.

Shakespeare's *Tempest* as Originally Produced at Court [1*]

ERNEST LAW

In these supreme days of our nation's struggle for existence and freedom, there is no direction in which we can more profitably turn for solace and distraction from our overweighted thoughts, and for support and inspiration in our hours of trial and strain, than to our great national poet, Shakespeare, in whose works, whether acted or read, while being lifted out of ourselves, we may find expressed more thoroughly and intensely than in those of any other Englishman the spirit and the feelings which animate us—his fellow countrymen—at this tremendous crisis in the fate of our—and his—beloved country.

This it is hoped, may be sufficient apology for submitting at such a time the results of the writer's researches into the mode in which one of Shakespeare's plays was presented in his life-time, and probably under his personal superintendence, before the Court of King James at Whitehall. Especially may this be so, perhaps—small as the subject may seem, beside the vast, and ever-expanding lore, that deals with Shakespeare and his art, and insignificant as may appear the present writer's contribution towards it—if, nevertheless, it should help us, however so little, towards arriving at the right solution of that ever-present and ever-pressing problem—equally pressing for play-goers, play actors, and play producers—namely, what is, with due regard to the dramatist's work, the best and most loyal, as well as the most effective and convincing mode of presenting his plays on the modern stage?

It is now just 306 years and a half since, on 1st November, 1611, in the old banqueting-house of Whitehall Palace, on the site where stands to-day Inigo Jones's later building, there was presented by Shakespeare's Company of His Majesty's Players, before King James and his Court, that most perfect

*Originally published for the Shakespeare Association (Papers, no. 5), St. Martin's Lane: Chatto and Windus, 1920.

and enchanting creation of our great dramatist—the crown of his life's work—
The Tempest.

Until recently the precise date of this composition and production of this
play had remained in doubt, notwithstanding the ceaseless discussion of the
problem by scholars of all nations during the last 160 years. Latterly it had
been round the famous theory of the German critic, Tieck, promulgated by
him at the beginning of the last century, that the controversy had mainly
raged—the theory that the play, with its hymeneal masque, was written by
Shakespeare in honour of the marriage of the Princess Elizabeth with the
Prince Palatine in 1613.

This ingenious idea, though rather discredited for a while by the publication in 1842 of Cunningham's "Extracts from the Revels at Court," quickly
received support again when the lists of plays in that book, which is now preserved in the Record Office, were soon after universally condemned as gross
and impudent forgeries. It was adopted, for instance, by, among others, Dr.
Brandes, the Danish critic, and it was the subject of a most interesting essay
in the "Universal Review" by the late Dr. Garnett, who, with a wonderful array
of illustration and suggestion, elaborated the theory in such a way as to bring
conviction to many minds. Even so recently as 1910 the late Mr. Henry James
gave it countenance in his introduction to the play in the "Caxton" edition.
Less imaginative writers have, however, been more cautious. In America, Dr.
Furness, after marshalling all the arguments on each side in some thirty-five
pages of closely-printed type in his great New Variorum edition, left the question still undetermined. In England, Sir Sidney Lee, whose cool judgment,
tested by recent discoveries, has been rarely found at fault, rejected Tieck's
and Garnett's attractive theory entirely, and pronounced decidedly for an earlier date. His view was followed, or shared, by Professor Gollancz, Professor
Herford, Professor Boas and others, and was reinforced by Mr. Morton Luce
in a most penetrating and exhaustive analysis of all that bore on the subject of
the origin of the play in the "Arden" edition. And then, at last, in support of the
conclusions arrived at by these critics, and finally to close the long controversy, came the universal acceptance by our leading palaeographers and
archivists—Dr Wallace, Professor Feuillerat, Sir George Warner, Sir Henry
Maxwell-Lyte, and others—and by all Shakespearean scholars throughout the
world, of the fact that the supposed "Cunningham Forgeries" were, after all no
forgeries at all, and that consequently the list of plays prefixed to the account
book of Sir George Buc, Master of the Revels in 1611, was an absolutely genuine document.

The bearing of this on the question of the date of *The Tempest* will at once
be made apparent by the following extracts from this "Book of Reuells" for
the year 1611–12. On page 2 is written: "The Chardges of those times, viz:
Betwine the last of Octobar 1611, Anno Reg. Regis Jacobi Nono untill the first
of Novembar, 1612 . . ." and on page 3 is the heading: "The names of the

Playes And by what cumpaney played them hearafter followethe . . . presented before the Kinge's Matie.," the first item in the list being: "By the King's Players: Hallowmas Nyght was presented att Whithall, before ye Kinges Matie. a play called 'The Tempest.'"

The accuracy of this information is confirmed by an entry in the accounts of the "Treasurer of the Chamber" of a payment made to Shakespeare's fellow-actors for a play on this very night (Audit Office. Declared Accounts: Bundle 389, Roll 49. For facsimiles, see the writer's, "Some Supposed Shakespeare Forgeries "and "More about Shakespeare Forgeries"):

> To John Hemynges for himselfe and his fellowes the Kinges Ma^tes Servauntes and Players upon the Councells warrante dated at Whitehall primo Junii, 1612, for presenting VI severall Playes before his Ma^ty, viz. one upon the laste of October, one upon the first of November (*The Tempest*) one on the vth of November (*A Winter's Tale*), one on the 26th of Decr. . . . at twenty nobles (£6 13s. 4d.) for every play, and five markes (£3 6s. 8d.) for a reward for every play.—LX.li. (£60).

Here then we have conclusively established for us the exact date and place of production before King James and his Court of that ever delightful and most poetic of plays—in Shakespeare's presence, as we may assume, if not under his personal superintendence.

So interesting an occasion seems to warrant an attempt at reconstructing, as far as is possible, with the fragmentary matter that remains to us, the scene and circumstances of that "first-night," when the creator of the enchanted island and its inhabitants held "spell-stopt" for "at least two glasses," by the magic of his imagination "the King and 's followers."

Our first inquiry must be directed to identifying the site and discovering the appearance of the chamber in which the piece was staged. For this purpose original documents in the Record Office, some of them apparently never searched through before, still less transcribed or published, provide us with what we seek. Among the accounts already cited is to be found this entry (folio 26a):

> To James Maxwell, gentleman usher daylie wayter to his Ma^ty for th' allowaunce of himselfe, one yeoman usher, three yeomen, two groomes of the chamber, two groomes of the warderobe, and one groome porter for making ready the Banquetting House there (at Whitehall) three several tymes for playes VI daies . . . mense Octobr et Novembr, 1611.

Now "the Banquetting House" here referred to was the one built by order of King James in 1606–7, but burnt down some ten years afterwards. References to it among the "Works and Buildings" accounts prove that it stood on the site of the famous building whence Charles I stepped forth to the scaffold.

This being so, one cannot but pause to think how impossible it would have been for the little Prince Charles, then just eleven years old, seated there that night listening to the play, with his father and mother and his elder brother, Henry Prince of Wales, beside him, to have imagined that thirty-eight years later he would, as King, be hurried across that very spot where he was then sitting, out into the street—to the block!

This earlier Banqueting House, though inferior in architecture to its successor, was yet a fine building. It was some 160 or 170 feet long by 50 or 60 feet wide; with a richly carved and decorated open roof, supported by columns, between which on both sides were galleries with raised tiers of seats for the spectators. It was reared expressly for the exhibition of plays and masques and shows, being in effect, though not in name, a theatre, differing in little from our modern public theatres, and still less from those of the later years of the seventeenth century as well as of the eighteenth century. Its stage was very large—larger than most of those of the public theatres of the time, such as the "Swan," the "Curtain," the "Rose," the "Blackfriars," or the "Globe," being 40 feet square, and standing 3 feet high. Moreover it seems to have had sides of solid partitions and something of a proscenium also; and being thus—unlike the open-air theatres—detached from the audience, which sat entirely in front of it, it must have afforded full scope for scenic illusion and the presentment of "tableaux" on a scale and in a setting of unprecedented splendour. It was thus in every way suitable for the presentation of such a play as *The Tempest*, with its frequent spectacular effects—storms with thunder and lighting and rain, spirit appearances and "monstrous shapes," phantom banquets, "marvellous sweet music."

Then at the disposal of the actors were all the properties, scenery, and dresses of the Revels Office, and all the resources and contrivances invented by Inigo Jones for the Royal Masques.

Not that we are to infer from all this that *The Tempest* was specially composed for performance, in the first instance, at Court. On the contrary, it seems certain, for many reasons, that none of Shakespeare's later plays were first produced on any other stage than that of one or other of the two theatres owned by his company—"The Globe" or "Blackfriars." Only after a piece had received the stamp of public approval and had undergone the perfecting process of frequent public acting was it presented before the Sovereign. There are many considerations, indeed, rendering it almost certain that it was at the "Blackfriars" which stood, as is well known, on the exact site of the present offices of "The Times" newspaper—that *The Tempest* was first put on the stage, in the spring or early summer of 1611. Little more than a year before this the Burbages, who were the freeholders, had bought out their lessee, "The Master of the Queen's Children of the Revels"—"The Boy Players"—and resumed possession and "placed in it," as their descendants phrased it some four-and-twenty years later, "men players"—"those worthy men"—which were Hemynges, Condall, Shakespeare, etc." Glad, indeed, must they all have

been to displace the "aëry of children, little eyases," who had so long trenched
on their profits, and to acquire a house affording fuller scope than "The
Globe," for gratifying the growing taste for spectacular display.

For this reason, if for no other, it is exceedingly probable that when
Shakespeare wrote *The Tempest* he did so with the view of its being acted
before the higher class of playgoers who frequented the "Blackfriars"—the
first of the closed, roofed-in houses, called "Private" Theatres, of which the
prototypes in structure and general conditions were the Great Halls of Green-
wich, Hampton Court and Whitehall. Already, in fact, it would seem, "The
Globe" on the Surrey side was beginning to be looked upon as the home of
transpontine, rather than of high-class drama.

It is likely enough, indeed, that *The Tempest*—with the *Winter's Tale*—
was Shakespeare's contribution towards the Burbages' new venture, and the
consideration for the "Founders' Shares"—as they were in effect—allotted to
the dramatist by his fellow shareholders—the "adventurers" as they were then
called, the "promoters," as we should call them now—if, indeed, he was not
himself the chief promoter and chairman of the syndicate—in the "Blackfriars sub-company," an off-shoot of the "Parent" Company of the King's Comedians. Put in this way, it will be seen that Shakespeare was up to, if he was not
the original inventor of, the most modern and astute of the devices of our
financial experts in the City of London.

Also, it may be noticed—though this is a mere piece of negative evidence—that Dr. Simon Forman, the astrologer and quack doctor, who
described in his note-book performances of four of Shakespeare's plays witnessed by him at "The Globe" in April and May, 1611, makes no mention of
The Tempest at all. More convincing, however, if not conclusively so, is the
statement of Dryden, writing in 1669, in the preface to his own mangled version of the play, that Shakespeare's original composition "had formerly been
acted with success at the Black Fryers." It seems probable, therefore, almost
to the point of certainty, that it was on the very spot where now stand the
offices of "The Times" newspaper that those immortal beings, Prospero and
Antonio, Miranda and Ferdinand, Ariel and Caliban, were first introduced to
the people of London by their creator, just about six months earlier than they
made their appearance at Whitehall before the King and Queen.

Apart from all its matchless qualities as a superb piece of dramatic invention, sublimated by poetic imagery, the play doubtless owed much of its
immediate success and popularity, not only to the musical and scenic effects
with which it was mounted, but also, and perhaps as much, to the topical
nature of many of its incidents and allusions—in which were reflected the
thoughts and feelings then uppermost in the mind of the public, equally with
the Court. For although, as has been already shown, its composition can have
had nothing to do with the wooing of the Princess Elizabeth by the Prince
Palatine, Royal marriages were in the air. Already suitors were numerous for

the hand of the little Princess, and many alliances were being offered also for the young Prince of Wales. This appears from the despatches of the foreign Ambassadors in England, which are full of the subject, especially in the few weeks previous to the play's being acted at Court. They are likewise full, as are also the private letters of the time, of the wrecking of Sir George Somers' flagship, bound for the plantation of Virginia, on the Bermudas—"the still-vexed Bermoothes." The ideas and phrases adopted by Shakespeare from several of the pamphlets about that event, which appeared in the autumn of 1610, prove that he shared the popular excitement, or at least made use of it for giving a topical flavour to his new play. That he was keenly interested, also, in every particular of the terrible tempest, and the adventures of the wrecked crew, for ten months castaways on the "Ile of Divils," is likewise proved by his having read, as we know he must, in the original manuscript now in the British Museum, William Strachey's journalistic letter—or "true reportory," as he termed it—written from Virginia on 15th July, 1610, to some "excellent lady" in London. For phrase after phrase that occurs in the play is to be found in the "reportory," though it was not printed until fifteen years after by Purchas in his "Pilgrimes."

When Strachey, who, by the way, was himself a bit of a poet, as well as a descriptive reporter, came back to London towards the end of 1611, he stayed in a "lodginge in the Blacke-friars," close to where *The Tempest* was then being acted, and close to where Shakespeare soon after purchased a house. It was, probably, therefore, by the courtesy of a common friend that Shakespeare was able to read Strachey's private letter about the great tempest of 1609 and the wreck off the Bermudas.

The great interest aroused in London by all this "Newes from Virginia," and "Newes from the Bermudas," can have moved no one more than the young Prince Henry, who, with his imagination already fired by the narratives of maritime adventure and stories of desert islands and the mysterious dangers of the Western seas, was himself planning a project for a new expedition to the colony—a project mentioned by the Venetian Ambassador in a letter to the Doge and Seignory on the very day the play was produced at Whitehall. No one, therefore, was more likely than him to desire to see *The Tempest* acted; and the Lord Chamberlain would have had this in mind when consulting about a suitable play for Hallowmas Night with the Master of the Revels and Burbage or Shakespeare. Between them, with the assistance of Inigo Jones and his men from the Office of Works, they would have made all the necessary arrangements in the Banqueting House, which, from its large size and regular stage and fittings—as already described—was just the sort of theatre required for a spectacular piece like this.

The general theatric conditions of the performance of one of Shakespeare's plays before the Court, and the particular circumstances of the staging of *The Tempest*, now require to be noticed.

To begin with, it may here be remarked that the fact of all representations of plays at Court taking place *at night*, is one of the chief and most pregnant of several differences, distinguishing them from performances in the public theatres; strongly influencing the subsequent development of the arts both of playwright and players; aiding, in fact, that gradual transformation of the "drama of rhetoric" into the more detached, emotional and pictorial presentations of modern times. In this process, the effect of the use of artificial lighting on the stage, resulting—as it surely must—in stimulating the senses and exalting the imagination of the spectator, while heightening the theatrical illusion, was the most obvious, if not one of the most potent of them all.

Moreover, there is the fact that the Banqueting House was—owing to its solid walls and reverberant roof—an admirable place for hearing; and, therefore, certain to modify the players' method of delivery, substituting for that loud, declamatory, blatant style of histrionics, so common on the public open theatres, that "tearing a passion to pieces," which so greatly distressed the Lord Hamlet, and which would have been as much out of place as ineffective in the refined atmosphere of a performance before the Court—a restrained and quieter style, wherewith the more delicate gradations of thought, and the subtler shades of feeling, could be more intimately suggested.

Finally, the oblong shape of the Banqueting House, with the stage at one end, and the audience in front of it, tended towards that shrinking of the platform towards the proscenium or inner stage, which thenceforth proceeded unremittingly until our day. Already, even in the time of Queen Elizabeth, as well as in the earlier years of James I, before the full influence of the elaborate spectacular Court Masques had made itself felt, the *mise-en-scène* at the Palace was the very antithesis of that mere platform, entirely bare of any scenery or accessories and devoid of all mechanism, imagined for us by some critics as the invariable condition under which all Shakespearian representations took place, until the suppression of the theatres in 1642. Disregarding other evidence, how should we otherwise explain the explicit statements of successive Masters of the Revels (*R.O. Audit Office Accounts—Various*. Bundles 1213, etc.) that among their chief duties was the:

> ffrurnishing, fitting and setting foorthe of sundry Tragedies, Playes, etc., with theier apte howses of paynted canvas and properties incident suche as mighte most lyvely expresse the effect of the histories plaied

and also the providing of:

> apt howses made of canvasse, fframed ffashioned and paynted accordingly as mighte beste serve theier severall purposes.

Can we suppose that among the "painted cloths for the Musick House and stage at Court" specially made and provided by the Master of the Revels in this particular year, there were not some that "might most lively express the effect of" *The Tempest*? Or that the vast collection of such "painted cloths" and "framed canvasses," as were stored in the Office-House of the Revels—including such things as trees, clouds, mountains, woods, forests, caves, rocks, etc.,—were not requisitioned, "as they might best serve the purpose" of exhibiting Prospero's enchanted island? When we find that in a play acted before Queen Elizabeth in the Great Hall of Hampton Court "a wilderness" was represented by three dozen forest trees, are we to believe that Shakespeare's *Tempest* put on the great stage of the Banqueting House at Whitehall 30 years later was not mounted with an equal regard for realism?

The truth, indeed, seems to be *not* so much that there was *no* scenery as that there was little, if any, change of scene—the various localities of the whole play being all shown simultaneously known as "multiple setting" or "Décor simultané"—so that the utmost adaptation that could be attempted was the occasional drawing of a "painted cloth," illustrative of a different place, in front of such portions of the setting as were not then applicable. In this respect, however, *The Tempest*—all its action going on in the open air on an island—can have offered but few difficulties to Shakespeare's or Sir George Buc's scene-shifters.

Turning now to describe the particular scenery set up for this play that night, we may say for certain that at the back of the main part of the stage was the usual "inner stage," which would have served for Prospero's cell; while overhead was probably the place where Prospero appeared in person more than once "above invisible"—as the stage direction puts it—perhaps through a transparency. Not far from it must have been the rock from which Caliban comes forth, and which was evidently a visible tangible thing; for it is referred to distinctly by Prospero—"wherefore thou art deservedly confined in this *rock*," and, pointedly, also, by Caliban;—"Here you sty me in this *hard rock*, while you do keep from me the rest of the island." On another side may have been represented "the lime-grove that weather fended his cell"—by practical trees. And the efforts of the Revels men may not have ended there; for they perhaps even showed a distant landscape, and "the rocky marge" and "yellow sands" of "the never surfeiting sea."

In this play, therefore, there would have been little need for those "locality boards" which frequently were put up for the information of the audience; and of which Mr. W. J. Lawrence has given us an account in his two exceedingly interesting volumes on "The Elizebethan Stage,"—one of the valuable publications, by the way, of the Shakespeare Head Press.

Scenes in "another part of the island" would have been quite sufficiently notified by drawing across the mouth of the cell or cave a "traverse," painted or plain. Such devices and "locality boards" were resorted to, as much owing to the absence of programmes as to the inadequacy of the scenery. To the King and Queen, however, were usually presented a fine illuminated "table," or synopsis of the characters and plot; and occasionly [sic], also, a copy of the words of the songs.

Across the top of the stage—"highest and aloft"—to use a phrase of the Revels men—would have been fixed a large title-board with the name of the play—*The Tempest*—decoratively painted on it.

Here again, I can claim the authority of Mr. Lawrence's admirable works in confirmation and amplification of my own researches.

Now, the suggestions just made made [sic] as to the scenic conditions under which Shakespeare's last play was presented at Court are so far rather presumptions than ascertained facts. But it is possible, I think, to arrive at a more precise and definite idea of the general setting of the stage on that night.

For we happen to have a description of a scenic arrangement for three masques acted a year and three months after in the same Banqueting House, and for one two years after, and on the same stage, which it seems highly probable was nearly the same, if not exactly the same, as that used for *The Tempest*. The masques were Thomas Campion's *Masque of Lords*, Chapman's of the *Middle Temple and Lincoln's Inn*, and Beaumont's of the *Inner Temple and Gray's Inn*, all three presented in February, 1613; and another of Campion's, at the end of the same year—on St. Stephen's night—in honour of the marriage of the Earl of Somerset to Lady Elizabeth Howard, the divorced wife of the Earl of Essex.

A full description of the scenery in this last is to be found in Campion's own preface. That in it we may see a picture of the stage as it appeared on Hallowmas night, 1611, is the more likely, in that a very similar scene is described in Prince Henry's masque of *Oberon*, by Ben Jonson, presented in the Banqueting House ten months *before The Tempest*—not to mention like similarities in the less important masques in the interval between these dates, affording us good reason for suspecting that the arrangements were more or less permanent, or, at any rate, that the scenery for each play or masque was made up from stock stuff belonging to the Office of Revels, there being in the descriptions of all of these masques mention of *rocks* and a *seashore*; *clouds*, a *cave* and a *wood*.

Campion, after noting that the upper part of the house, where the Royal dais or "state" was placed, was "theatred with pillars, scaffolds and all things answerable to the sides of the room," proceeds to describe how at the lower end

before the sceane, was made an arch tryumphall, passing beautifull, which enclosed the whole works—

evidently like a modern proscenium. He goes on to say:

The sceane itself, the curtaine being drawne, was in this manner divided—on the upper part there was formed a skye with cloudes very arteficially

shadowed; on either side of the scene below was set a high promontory . . .
one bounded with a rocke standing in the sea, the other with a wood; in the
midst betweene them appeared a sea in perspective with ships, some cunningly painted, some artifically sayling.

And now comes a rather remarkable thing. Campion was not by any
means satisfied with this scenery, so described by him, for his masque. He had
at first instructed an Italian architect, M. Constantine, to provide something
finer and more elaborate. But they fell out. The Italian "failed in the assurance
he gave," and declining "to be drawn to impart his intentions," the poet dispensed with his services and had to content himself with a less ambitious
scheme, falling back evidently on what was already at hand on the stage of the
Banqueting House, and which he describes in the words just quoted.

Significant, too, is it that in apologising for these shortcomings, as he
thought them, in the scenery, he gives as one of the causes:

That our modern writers have rather transferred their fictions to the persons
of Enchanters and Commanders of Spirits—

so that

in imitation of them he had founded his whole invention upon enchantments
and severall transformations.

Here, surely, is as plain a reference to the influence of Shakespeare's
Prospero and his enchanted island as one might very well expect to have. Further than this the speeches of Campion's masques abound in phrases and
ideas evidently inspired, if not copied, from *The Tempest*-such as "a storme
confus'd against our tackle beat, severing the ships" . . . "about our deckes and
hatches" . . . "all was husht, as storme had never beene" . . . "for while the
Tempest's fiery rage increast." There are even two or three words here and
there reminiscent of the stage directions in the First Folio, which, taken with
the parallel passages in the text, almost make one suspect the existence of an
unknown quarto of *The Tempest*, of which some lurking copy may yet be discovered.

Considering next the lighting of the auditorium and the stage: these were
alike brilliantly illuminated with candelabra, candle-rings and "fairy lights,"
"pendant by subtle magic" from invisible wires, stretched overhead, from
rafter to rafter, of the roof; and shedding a soft glow, "as from a sky"; though,
at the same time, we know that occasionally the whole house was darkened to
heighten the tragic effect. As it happened in this particular year, in view, perhaps, of this very production, and of that of *The Winter's Tale* four days after,
there was a complete renovation of all the lighting arrangements of the theatre
at a cost equivalent to about £400 at the present day.

Another important element in this first performance of *The Tempest* at

Whitehall was the "Musick-Howse" by the stage, in which were stationed the King's band of some thirty or forty musicians. Here they played not only during, but also between, the acts. For whatever may have been the custom in the public theatres, the evidence bearing on the acting of plays at Court gives as little countenance to the theory of invariable "continuous action" as it does to that of a scene-less stage. Sometimes this "inter-act music" was accompanied by the handing round of refreshments to the audience—especially when there were foreign guests present; some of whom, understanding little of the dialogue, probably enjoyed these interludes a good deal more than the play.

It may be observed, moreover, of *The Tempest*, that its divisions into acts, even scenes, are very far from being arbitrary or fortuitous: but that, on the contrary, they correspond with definite stages in the action and progress of the drama.

A more important function of the King's musicians in their "Musicke Howse" was to play all that incidental "solemn and strange music," "marvellous sweet music," "heavenly music," of which so much is interspersed in *The Tempest*. During most of the action of the play the musicians in their gallery were evidently curtained off and unseen, breathing low, murmuring music from "flutes and soft recorders" and lutes and "sagbuttes," thus enhancing the mysteriousness. In the Revels' Accounts, indeed, for this year (1611) in which *The Tempest* was produced at Court, there happens to be noted a special provision of "a curtain of silk for the Musick House at Whitehall"—silk because, while effectively screening the musicians and singers from view, it would have offered but little obstruction to those strains of magic melody, heard by Ferdinand as it crept by him "upon the waters," and afterwards above him: "those sounds and sweet airs that give delight and hurt not," those "thousand twangling instruments" that, humming about the slumbering ears of Caliban, made him—when waking—but "cry to dream again." All this music was doubtless composed by some of the King's musicians, among whom were several excellent composers, such as Ferrabosco and Nicholas Laniere, whose works are still delighted in by the lovers of old-time melodies.

An equally, if not more, important task of theirs was playing the accompaniment to those most exquisite lyrics, the very quintessence of poetry—Ariel's songs. Of two of these, it is interesting to note, that we may still hear the very airs sung that night three hundred years ago in Shakespeare's presence at Whitehall.

For there happen to have survived to us in Dr. John Wilson's "Cheerfull Ayres or Ballads," published in 1660, his harmonised scores of the beautiful original setting for "Full Fathom Five," and "Where the Bee sucks," attributed by him in his manuscript to Robert Johnson, a well-known lutenist, who was in the service of Prince Henry in this very year, 1611. These two facts have been already known for some little time, but I have discovered from a reference to Johnson in the accounts of the "Treasurer of the Chamber" that he became "one of the consortes of his Mat^{ies} musicyans" in this same year—affording confirmation, if any were needed, of Wilson's statement, and suggesting that he was taken into the King's service in connection with his music for this particular performance of *The Tempest*. Johnson's beautiful melodies, it may be noted, were sung at the meeting of the British Academy at Burlington House in July, 1910, when M. Jusserand, now the French Ambassador at Washington, delivered his address on Shakespeare.

The first Ariel to sing those enchanting songs was no doubt "the principal boy" at the new "Blackfriars," probably one of the "Children of the Queen's Majesty's Revels," taken over into Shakespeare's Company when they resumed possession of that theatre. This part, indeed, ought never to be played at all except by a boy in his early 'teens. Shakespeare and his fellow-actors, could they revisit the London stage, would probably have much more difficulty in understanding our modern ineptness of setting a grown-up young woman to personate that "spirit of air," than we can have in understanding their practice of entrusting Miranda's part to "a squeaking boy," for which could, at any rate, be pleaded the inexorable prejudices of the times—first broken down, be it remembered, at Court by the ladies performing in the Masques.

Of the "dressing" of the play that night we can form a very fair impression. Prospero's costume we get hints of from the text and stage directions—"Pluck my magic garment from me," "Resumes his mantle," "Enter Prospero in his magic robes,"—probably with cabalistic signs embroidered on it. That Trinculo's dress was the fool's conventional motley we likewise gather from the text: "What a *pied* ninny's this!" "Thou scurvey *patch*!" cries Caliban to the "jesting monkey." Stephano's, too, offers no great difficulty; nor the mariner's either; Caliban's clothing seems to have been traditionally a "bear's skin," and over it the "gabardine," which Trinculo creeps under to shelter himself from the storm, and which Cotgrave defines as "a Cloake of Felt for rainie weather."

As for the "garments . . . fresher than before" worn by Alonso and his followers, they would certainly have been of the Italian fashion, and not of the English of James's Court. Here again the records of the Revels come to prove that, contrary to the too generally accepted opinion, a great deal of care was devoted in all dramatic representations, to accuracy in costume, so as to make it accord with the nationality, as well as with the rank, profession or station, of each character, appearing in the piece. Not only were the ancients dressed in classical or "antick" attire—as it was called—but Venetians in their "Venetian weed," and senators and councillors in the robes appropriate to their offices; while "Almains," "Turks," "Moors," Patriarchs and such-like, appeared in distinctive "garmentes, vestures and apparell." Not, of course, that Shakespeare and his fellow actor-managers, or the Masters of the Revels-"The Producers" of the Court Performances—were as scrupulously archaeological in "dressing" a play as are our present-day stage artists; but they strove after the greatest correctness possible, with such knowledge and means as they found at their disposal. For this purpose there was available, in fact, an enormous assortment of "stuff" in the charge and custody of the Master of the Revels—"sundry garments of the store of the office"—as he phrased it—which were constantly being altered and *translated*, and which were always at the disposal of Shakespeare's company to supplement their own scarcely less rich and ample wardrobe.

From one or other of these "fripperies" would have been brought out some "glistering apparel" for Ariel. What his dress was on the night in question we may gather in a general way from Inigo Jones's sketch, now preserved at Chatsworth, of a costume for an "Aery Spirit" in some play or masque, and from Ben Jonson's description of a very similar costume for "Jophiel, an Airy Spirit," in his masque of "The Fortunate Isles" acted in 1626. These two authorities taken together suggest a close-fitting tunic of silk in rainbow colours, wings tinctured in harmony with it, a scarf over his shoulders, buskins or blue silk stockings, and on his head a chaplet of flowers—not unlike the costume worn by Charles I when as Duke of York, and only eleven years old, he acted the character of Zephirus in Daniel's "Tethy's Festival"—the great Masque of Britain's Sea-Power—presented the year before *The Tempest* on the same spot in the Banqueting House—to wit, green satin, embroidered with golden flowers, with silver wings and a garland of flowers on his head.

Of the actual acting of the play that night there is little else to record: and not much about the spectators either. Prominent among them were, of course, King James and his Queen, seated in the middle of the house in chairs of State on a daïs, covered with fine oriental carpets and under a rich canopy, and perhaps curtained off on either side. By them would have sat their children; and gathered around them all the most famous, great and illustrious men in England at that time—Bacon, Salisbury, Nottingham, Northampton, Pembroke, Montgomery, Southampton—whether resident in the Court or in their own houses in the Strand or about Holborn; with their wives also, of course; as well as all the most beautiful and fashionable women that London could then show. The best places were reserved for "the best people;" while for any guests who were specially favoured, there were the private boxes—for the foreign ambassadors, particularly, who eagerly competed for invitations for all the great shows at Court.

As to the appearance of the audience, needless to say that the gorgeousness of the costumes on the stage was more than matched by the splendour and extravagance of the dresses of the King and his courtiers. James I, who, as Wilson said of him "was ever of all men the moste taken with fyne clothes," and who loved above all things to see his minions—at that time James Hay, Earl of Carlisle and the infamous Robert Carr, Earl of Somerset—superbly clad in the richest silks and velvets, and resplendent in the jewels of fabulous price which he showered upon them, himself led the fashion. "The imagination"—wrote the Venetian ambassador a few days after this performance of *The Tempest*—"could hardly grasp the gorgeousness of the spectacle. The King's own cloak, breeches and jacket were all sewn with diamonds, a rope and jewel of diamonds also in his hat of inestimable value." The Queen, nothing loth to follow the lead of the men, "had in her hair a very great number of pear-shaped pearls, the largest and most beautiful in the world; and there were diamonds all over her person, so that she was ablaze." All her ladies, naturally, and the whole Court followed suit.

Besides all these leading courtiers there would also have been among the spectators the whole Royal Household, including the minor officials of the Court—gentlemen ushers, grooms of the chamber, even porters, yeomen, tiremen, etc.—together with such of their friends and relations as they could, by hook or by crook, and under the guise of all sorts of subterfuges, manage to smuggle into odd nooks and corners of the house or the stage—all eager to see, without having to pay for the privilege, the much-talked-of new play—"the latest and most excellent and pleasant conceited comedie"—as they would have called it—"made by that famous and most witty poet and player Master Shaxpere and his worthy fellow that renowned tragedian Dick Burbage."

We can imagine these denizens and hangers-on of the Court gathered together next day talking it all over, "sitting at a round table by a sea-coal fire" in the Watching Chamber of old Whitehall "on All Souls' night" in the year of our Lord, 1611.

We can imagine them telling their friends all about "the magician King and his Enchanted Island, and the terrible Tempest—like unto that which wrecked Sir George's Somers' great ship off the Bermoothes, with the thunder and the lightning and the rain, all like unto real thunder, and real lightning and real rain, and the mysterious spirits, which float about and then of a sudden vanish into air; and the monstrous shapes, which dance around the magic banquet with mops and mows, and many other phantom things, which awe and amaze; and the marvellous magical music, so sweet and beautiful, which seems to come from nowhere; and the dazzling lights and then the black darkness! And who has not heard of the wrecked King's ridiculous drunken butler, who thought to be himself King of the Island, and of the fool in his motley, with his witty sayings; and the strange wild man and his wicked imaginings—truely a fearsome monster with a face like a man, but claws like a bear and fins like a fish; and the talkings of these three together, which ever called forth shrieks of laughter, so that the players could scarce proceed!"

"Then how the rightful King gets back his throne and how his fair sweet daughter weds the bad old King's son and how all are happy ever after. Of a surety, never before was ever beheld scenes so fair, and dresses so comely, more like unto fairyland than any theatre's stage—rocks and trees and flowers, and glistering apparel of silk and velvet and broidery. They tell, indeed, at the Revels' Office at St John's, how worthy Sir George Buc and his men were at work both night and day, for many a day, making ready all things needful thereto—more as if 'twere one of the Queen's Majesty's Royal Masques than a mere common player's Comedy."

Thus "would, or could or should" have gossiped such of the hangers-on of the Court as had been lucky enough to be squeezed in by kind friends into the Banqueting House the night before.

That the play was received by every section of the audience with approval, applause and delight, we have every reason to believe, knowing that it was again produced at Court, if not very soon after, certainly fourteen or fifteen months later. This was at the beginning of February, 1613, in honour of the marriage of the Princess Elizabeth to the Elector Palatine, already referred to at the beginning of this article. In this connection it may be observed that I have found a note in the accounts of the Master of the Revels for this year, of a special charge "for rehearsalls and making choice of plaies and comedies, and for reforminge playes to be presented at the courte agaynst the marriadge of the Ladye Elizabeth to the Prince Palatine." Among these plays and comedies as many as twenty were acted by the King's Company, no less than eight of them being Shakespeare's; and as we happen to know that he was in London on private business in the early part of the year, it is likely enough that he personally superintended their production at Court—the longer ones, perhaps, being "reformed" by the Master of the Revels into shorter Court versions.

That among them *The Tempest* may have been subjected to some "reformation" is possible; through this would scarely have been in the way of curtailment, as has been suggested by Fleay and other commentators. For the play, as we have it in the First Folio, is so rigidly constructed, so compactly knit and so well-balanced, with no signs anywhere of any gaps in it—in this respect very unlike *Macbeth*—that there seems no ground for supposing any part of Shakespeare's original text to have dropped out of it and been lost, although it is the shortest but one of any of his plays. This is the more certain owing to the fact that *The Tempest* is almost the only one of them of which it can be said that the dramatic "unities" are strictly observed in it; still more so that this observance was evidently intentional and designedly made plain on the part of the dramatist, emphasized by him, as it is, several times in the course of the play, not only by the significance of the action being confined to a small island, but also by reiterated references to "What's the time of day," and the insistence by Prospero that the time-limit of his work, leading to the denouement of the drama, must not exceed "three glasses."

The "reforming" of *The Tempest*, however—if it was reformed at all—although unlikely to have been by way of abridgement, may well have been in that of addition. Indeed, there is every ground for suspecting that the masque in the fourth act as we have it now, ostensibly as an integral, though really a subsidiary part of the play, was an addition interpolated into the original text of 1611, for the performance at Court in 1613—interpolated, in fact, in honour of the nuptials of the young Princess and her affianced husband the Count Palatine. It was by that very acute critic Fleay, in his "Chronicle History of the Life and Works of Shakespeare," published in 1886, that currency was first given to this idea of the origin of the masque. To this extent, we may, indeed, admit that Tieck, Dr. Garnett and the rest were on the right tack: though this is, of course, a very different thing from accepting their theories as to the origin and date of the whole play.

On this point of the origin of the masque: I doubt whether any one interested in the question, who should take down Nichols' "Progresses of James I" and read through, in the second volume, the three several masques performed in honour of that marriage, with all the curious descriptions of them, and the letters of the time about them, could come to any other conclusion but this: that the masque in *The Tempest*—that is to say its spoken verse—is likewise connected with that event by the closest links. The similarities—not to say identities—in ideas, expressions, phrases, poor, indeed, as they are in all four masques, are unmistakeable: convincing one that whoever may have been the author of this particular masque worked on common lines of conventional compliment with the others. Moreover, many of the characters represented in these masques are the same classical deities, and their procedure actuated by the same devices. Everything, in fact, seems definitely to exclude any probability that this masque in Shakespeare's play—certainly the part of it in which Iris and the two goddesses converse—can have been composed in 1611, or indeed, for any occasion whatever, or for any purpose whatever, other than "a contract of true love to celebrate," ostensibly, no doubt, the one between Miranda and Ferdinand, but primarily and by plain implication, the one between Elizabeth and Frederick as well. That such a contract was of the very essence of the scheme and plot of the play as originally written, was, on this supposition, a mere coincidence, of which advantage was taken in 1613 to enhance the topical interest of the piece.

All this, however, does not answer the further question that has been raised, as to whether Shakespeare himself was really the author of this masque at all—a distinct and very much more difficult problem. Here again Fleay was the first formally to propound a doubt on the subject; and he was followed by the editors of the "Cambridge Shakespeare" in 1891. Before Fleay, however, a great many people, and since Fleay, a great many more, have felt that in its pointless, rather banal dialogue, and its halting, rhymed decasyllabics, we have something very far removed from any of Shakespeare's usual styles, altogether most unworthy and unlikely stuff to have come from the pen of the poet, who was capable, at the same time, of writing so superb and incomparably beautiful a dramatic poem as *The Tempest*.

Fleay's theory—often quoted with approval since by competent critics—was that Beaumont was the real author of this Tempest masque, citing in support of it several very striking parallel passages between it and that dramatist's "Inner Temple and Gray's Inn" masque, "whereof Sr Fra. Bacon was the chiefe contriver," written for Shrove Tuesday, 16th February, though not acted until Saturday, the 20th.

A more recent suggestion is that of the Right Hon. J. M. Robertson, M.P., who, in his remarkable book on "Shakespeare and Chapman" (published in 1917) puts forward a strong case for Chapman as the author. In support of it he analyses the sixty-eight rhymed lines of the masque, and finds no less than eighteen words, which do not occur anywhere else in the plays attributed to Shakespeare, though most of them are to be found in Chapman's works. Further, he finds similar coincidences and many singular resemblances in the compound words, which are so noticeable a peculiarity of this masque, and which, though not occurring anywhere else in any of the plays, are, many of them, paralleled if not exactly to be found, in Chapman's works. Further, he finds similar coincidences and many singular resemblances in the compound words, which are so noticeable a peculiarity of this masque, and which, though not occuring anywhere else in any of the plays, are, many of them, paralleled, if not exactly to be found, in Chapman's works.

This theory and these arguments of Mr. Robertson's may, I think, be reinforced by parallel passages—almost, if not quite, as remarkable as those in Beaumont's masque—in Chapman's "Memorable Masque of the Two Honourable Hovses or Innes of Court, the Middle Temple and Lyncolnes Inne," presented at Whitehall on Shrove Monday, the 15th of February, 1613.

Whatever weight—or whether any weight at all—should be given to these several points, the supposition on either of these theories would be that Chapman—or Beaumont—with or without Shakespeare's assent—even without his cognizance if he happened to be absent from London at that time—was employed, either by Hemynges or Burbage on behalf of the King's Company, or, otherwise, by the Master of the Revels when "reforming" *The Tempest*—to insert in it a topical masque in honour of the Royal nuptials. Then, once having formed part of the play, there would naturally have arisen among the "Blackfriars" audiences a desire to witness the masque, invested, as it would have been, with the prestige of having been acted before the Court. In this way it would have become permanently incorporated in the prompter's acting copy of the text. This, in brief, is the case for another hand but Shakespeare's.

Other distinguished scholars, however, such as Professor Morton Luce in his analysis of the play in the "Arden" edition, referred to at the beginning of this article, and Professor Boas, in his most cogent and illuminating study of the play in the "Warwick" edition, have not been disposed to endorse Fleay's scepticism, or to admit any other but Shakespeare's own handiwork in the masque—though, it must be remembered, they wrote before Mr. Robertson had put forward his claim for Chapman.

"Non nostrum inter vos tantas componere lites." But I may, perhaps, venture to submit with diffidence, a theory of my own, which, to a certain extent, would seem to reconcile the various divergent views of so many learned and acute commentators, leaving to them to determine what value it may possess.

Briefly, my proposition is this: that though the rhymed verses and the song in the Masque were interpolated in 1613 into the original text, there was at this point, in the fourth act, from the very first production of the play at the Blackfriars, revelling and dancing of spirits.

Fleay's idea was that "the mythological personages in the original play acted in dumb show"; and in support of it, he referred to the stage direction "Juno descends" at line 81, while in the added verses the words are "great Juno comes," and Ceres knows "her by her gait"—as if implying that originally Juno came down from the skies, lowered, he seems to suggest, "in a creaking throne the boys to please," while in the amended Masque she merely walked on. But in this Fleay betrays ignorance of the almost invariable procedure in masques with classical characters, which was that the gods or goddesses or other characters were beheld some little time before they came on to the stage proper, descending from on high at the extreme back of the Inner Stage by means of "winding staires by whose greeces (steps) the persons above might make their descents and all the way be seene." These words are taken from the descriptive introduction to Chapman's "Memorable Masque," and as there were such stairs at the back of the Inner Stage of the Banqueting House, they would apply equally well to the entry of Juno, if not to that of Ceres also, in the *Tempest* Masque.

The convention had its origin in the first true Jacobean Masque ever acted—Daniel's "Vision of the Twelve Goddesses" presented in the Great Hall at Hampton Court on Sunday, 8th January, 1604—a Masque, by the way, which Shakespeare must have witnessed, for he was staying in the Palace at the time; and which the writer of *The Tempest* Masque—whoever he may have been—must have been well acquainted with, especially as it had been printed and published in 1604, and because there are several points of marked resemblance between the two masques.

Altogether, there really seems no adequate reason for, nor any particular probability in, Fleay's suggestion that the classical characters in this masque were originally acted in dumb show: every reason, indeed, as I shall show, that they never did anything of the sort.

At the same time, it would not—even if proved—render in the least less likely the theory I have ventured to put forward, namely, that a show of spirits, revelling and dancing, formed part of the original play. Several phrases in

Prospero's and Ariel's speeches indeed seem clearly to point to this. Thus, Prospero, at the beginning of the fourth act, just before the masque, says to Ariel:

> Thou and thy *meaner fellows* your last service
> Did worthily perform; and I must use you
> In such another trick—

evidently referring to the bringing in and removing of the magic banquet at the end of the third scene in the third act, by "several strange shapes"—"of monstrous shape," says Gonzalo—who are there referred to by Prospero as "my *meaner ministers*" and by Ariel as "my *fellow ministers.*"

They appear, it will be remembered, twice in the third act, bringing the banquet in and dancing about it "with gentle actions of salutation,"—as the stage direction in the first folio says—and afterwards carrying the table out, and *dancing* with "mocks and mows." Now this exactly corresponds with the words in which Ariel in the fourth act receives Prospero's charge, just before the masque

> Each one, tripping on his toe
> Will be here with *mop and mow.*

Again, Prospero instructing Ariel how he is to perform "such another trick," says to him:

> Go bring *the rabble*,
> O'er whom I gave thee power, here to this place:
> Incite them to *quick motion.*

Can Prospero and Ariel, I would ask, have been anticipating in all this the solemn stately Masque of mythological characters that follows in the play as we now have it—the "most majestic vision," as Ferdinand afterwards calls it? Can they, when using these words and phrases, have been thinking—or rather can Shakespeare have been thinking when he put them into the mouths of his actors—of anything else, or of preparing his audience for anything else, but a dumb show of a rabble of "monstrous shapes," dancing in "quick motion" and with "mops and mows?"

Yet, as we now have the Masque, we have instead of a *rabble*—even if the meaning of the word is only a "crowd," a "gathering," or a "company," with no contemptuous implication in it—three stately characters; and instead of "quick motion" we have their dignified approach—Juno especially, "highest Queen of State," "known by her gait."

Again, at the end, after the Masque has been dissolved, Prospero says:

"Our *revels* now are ended." But masques, especially of the classical and stately sort, were not often, if ever, called "revels." The phrase was always "masques *and* revels." The word "revels," in fact, was applied rather to dancing, rollicking, "mops and mows" and such like; and of these but little survives in the "revels" in the fourth act, as we now have them, except perhaps the "Country footing"—of the "nymphs and reapers"—described in the stage directions, as "a graceful dance." Does not all this seem plainly to point to, and is it not all very simply explicable by, the theory that the masque was just botched into the play, and substituted for the original revellings, with scarcely any alteration of the text? If so, it would reinforce the supposition that there was another hand rather than that of Shakespeare, who, one would presume, would have adapted the old to the new less clumsily, when the "most majestic vision" was inserted out of compliment to the Lady Elizabeth's marriage in place of the "revels" of Shakespeare's own original conception, which would have been appropriate enough, while not interrupting, as does the existing Masque, the progress and action of the play.

Yet one more point: Prospero, just as the masque is beginning, says to Ferdinand, "No tongue, *all eyes*, be silent"—which seems to indicate that the show was to be something to *look at* only, not to listen to. Can such discrepancies between the dialogue before or during the masque, and the spoken masque itself, be explained on any other theory but the one just propounded?

Leaving, however, theories and literary problems to be pronounced upon by experts, let us turn to more material and positive problems. One of the first of these, which demand solution, is: on what part of the stage was the masque presented? As to this, there can be little doubt that it was presented on the Inner Stage, which, in the Banqueting House at Whitehall, at any rate, certainly had a regular proscenium, and was treated separately from the rest of the stage in the way of scenery and decoration; and was revealed by the drawing aside of "traverses" or curtains, or, perhaps, in this case, by a suddenly illuminated scene, perceived through a transparency.

It was, in fact, composed as a set-piece, though small, very like any of our modern solid-sided interiors. The development, in truth, of our present framed picture-stage may be traced quite as well by looking on it as an advance and encroachment of the Inner Stage on the old platform-stage—which it eventually absorbed altogether—as by considering it as a shrinking of the platform-stage backwards, until it was withdrawn entirely behind the proscenium, which is the usual way of presenting the case. This tendency first showed itself in the performances at Court, where it was originally and mainly due to the scenic exigences of the pictorial element in the spectacular masques.

Next, as to the floor of the Inner Stage, on which the masque was represented. This, it would seem, was raised two or three steps above the main stage; and it was, doubtless, covered, according to the usual practice in masques in the royal theatres, with some sort of green cloth or baize for the dancing. That this was so for the *Tempest* masque we have something more than custom to convince us. For the references in it to such a counterfeit plot of grass are too plain and frequent not to be unmistakeable. Thus:

> Here on this *grass-plot*, in this very place,

says Iris when summoning Ceres; who, in answer, enquires:

> Why hath thy Queen
> Summoned me hither to this *short-grassed* green ?

And Iris again, when calling the nymphs, bids them come to:

> This *green land.*

Such pointed expressions, three times repeated, would scarcely have been used except of a physical feature patent to the eyes of the audience.

Next, as to the probable "dressing" of the characters in the masque. These, there can be no doubt, appeared in appropriate costumes, something like those of the same personages in Daniel's "Vision of the Twelve Goddesses," already referred to. As described by that author himself, in his preface, Iris appeared "deckt like a rainbow," Ceres "in a straw-colour and silver imbroidery, with eares of corne," and a head-dress of the same and carrying a sickle. Juno was attired "in a skie-colour mantle imbroidered with gold and figured with peacocks' feathers, wearing a crown of gold on her head," set with jewelled stars, and carrying a sceptre.

Thus staged, the masque, though adding nothing to the dramatic interest or poetic beauty of the play, must have greatly delighted the not very discriminating Court audience of 1613.

And now all that gave life and brilliance to that night's scene more than 300 years ago have passed into "the dark backward and abysm of Time." Of those who witnessed that performance the very names of most of them are forgotten. Only those of a very few of the small group, who formed the centre of the bright throng, now evoke even a faint echo. The Earl of Pembroke and his brother Montgomery are, it is true, still remembered: but why? Merely because they were "the icomparable paire of brethren" to whom the First Folio was dedicated, and who share the eternal honour of having "favoured the authour living." Southampton was there: but who would trouble now about the comings and goings, or even the existence, of the Earl of Southampton, were he not known to have befriended the struggling actor and playwright William Shakespeare? And the King's son Henry—is he as much, or anything like as much to us to-day as that as "the King's son Ferdinand"? The Princess Elizabeth, indeed still awakens some thrill of emotion in us as that "Queen of Hearts," to whom sir Henry Wotton addressed his beautiful poem—"Ye meaner beauties." Yet how dim does her figure seem through the mists of the long years past, compared with her who through all ages will ever shine radiant—"so perfect and so peerless, created of every creature's best"—Miranda! King James, Salisbury and Northampton are gone, but Prospero, Gonzalo and Antonio still remain with us as living entities. As for Anne of Denmark, would not the world prefer that all memory of her should be bloted out, or that she had never lived, than that we should lose a single speech of Caliban's? Alone of that night's audience Bacon lives with us and speaks to us, in his own writings, with something of the vividness, with which Prospero lives with us and speaks to us though Shakespeare's deathless page.

And this our great dramatist's most wondrous triumph—that he has endowed these mere creatures of his imagination with a reality, a vividness, and a persistence, outliving and transcending the ever fading remembrance of all mortal beings.

Such, then, were the circumstances—so far as I have been able to reconstruct them from the old records—in which the *Tempest* was performed before the Court at Whitehall in the years 1611 and 1613. The indications may be considered to be slight, and not very precise. Yet, such as they are, they may, I hope, help towards the understanding of the problem to which I referred at the beginning of this article, and which is of great interest to all Shakespearean students, and of present practical moment to all those concerned—whether as spectators or producers or stage managers—in the acting of our great dramatist's plays to-day—namely, the mode of their presentation on the modern stage. Otherwise, in truth, what are all these old things and these ancient topics to us? Why go searching in musty records or faded parchments? Why go grubbing among the old foundations and broken walls of a long vanished palace, except that, by such means interpreting the past, we may be helped towards correct action in the present, which is ours, and which holds for us the priceless and ever-enduring treasures the poet has bequeathed to all mankind?

If then, by tracing out these exact circumstances, and, with such fragmentary matter as remains to us, we try to evoke a vision, as it were, of the surroundings in which Shakespeare's marvellous imaginings were originally set forth before the world, it is with the hope also that we may thereby the better apprehend the pregnant thoughts and the inspiring truths, which, more and more, all men of every race, and of every clime, acclaim in the pages of him, who, more intensely than any other poet, moves vibrating the most intimate chords of the soul of man; who deeper than any other mortal being, has sound the inmost recesses of the human heart. Halls and banquetting houses, stages and theatres, actors and spectators, what are they? They all

> Are melted into air, into thin air:
> And, like the baseless fabric of this vision,
> The cloud-capp'd towers, the gorgeous palaces,

> The solemn temples, the great globe itself,
> Yea, all which it inherit, shall dissolve
> And, like this insubstantial pageant faded,
> Leave not a rack beind—

—even as the hand that wrote those words, and the brain that conceived the whole wonderful fabric of the plays, with their multitudinous pageantry of life, are alike dust in a narrow grave at Stratford.

Yet the poet's thoughts live on—the penetrating truths, the wide philosophy, the exquisite felicities and fancies the enchanting rhythm and music of the verse—live on, and spread through all the nations of the globe; become, indeed, for ever the universal heritage, stamped on the mind of the man with an impress that will last as long as this world shall endure.

NOTES

1. Some of the information here published is an amplification of lectures delivered by the writer in February and March, 1918, to the "Shakespeare Association," and to the "Shakespeare Club" of Stratford-on-Avon; and part of it originally appeared in "The Times," 1st November, 1911.

The Tempest*

DON CAMERON ALLEN

Though *The Tempest* is a play, it is also a complicated masque or a narrative poem with lyric intervals. It is difficult to compare with Shakespeare's other plays, for it is briefer, more elaborate in fantasy, and in some respects more intensely personal than they. During the last century, it was thought to be confessional and Prospero's final speeches were associated with Shakespeare's retirement from the theater. The play does not permit this conclusion. Shakespeare is not forsaking his art. If *The Tempest* is to be read biographically at all, it must be seen as a poetical summary of the poet's life and its satisfactory achievements, as the poetic rendering of that bright moment at the end allowed to men of special favor, a moment that assures them that what they have loved will endure. *The Tempest*, like *Pericles*, *Cymbeline*, and *The Winter's Tale*, is one of a series of warm afternoons in the autumn of Shakespeare's life. It is mellow with the ripeness of knowledge, for its maker has discovered the right ritual for the marriage of the inner and the outer world, of the real and the ideal, the experienced and the imagined, the dream and the actuality.

With the writing of *Hamlet* Shakespeare begins to experiment with darkness, and the sun does not come again until Pericles, who is "music's master," hears, like no other character in Shakespeare's plays, the harmony of the heavenly spheres. This is the same harmonious end toward which Prospero looks: "When I have required / Some heavenly music—which even now I do." It is plain from the tragedies that an awakening from idealism into cold reality is the required preliminary experience to the search for celestial harmony. The distaste for life expressed by Hamlet, a distaste that helps to shape the succeeding tragedies, has been associated by biographical critics with the poet's

*Don Cameron Allen, "The Tempest," published in *Image and Meaning: Metaphoric Traditions in Renaissance Poetry* (Baltimore: Johns Hopkins University Press, 1960; rev., 1968), 77–101. ©1968 The Johns Hopkins University Press. Reprinted by permission.

private experience, with his increasing boredom with life and art, with an obsessing puritanical temper, with a disappointment in love or friendship, and with some sort of neurotic illness. None of this can be proved. All we know is that Shakespeare experimented with tragic circumstances, he led his creatures out of the world of darkness into eternal day.

In each of the three plays written before *The Tempest*, the dramatic premise is tragic, although the poet always forfends "the promised end." Pericles, a Hamlet-like seeker of truth, begins his search in a place of evil with the reek of incest and carnage. He wanders through storm upon storm over the wide map of the great lost world of antiquity. In the end, he hears the divine music, sees the vision of the celestial "goddess argentine," and finds at last his lost wife and child. The play follows an established legend, but the bareness of myth is made a living reality through the poet's restored belief. *Cymbeline*, which is drawn from the truth of history, shuns history so that Cymbeline may see the consequence of wrong, that Imogen may triumph in her love, that the lost princes may be found, that Posthumus, cured and forgiven, may have his dream made real, and that Iachimo, weak son of Iago, may be pardoned. With *The Winter's Tale* the miracle increases, for Greene, father of the story, could not believe in the resurrection of Hermione or the redemption of Leontes. Shakespeare, the poet, is alone able to distract the current that flows toward tragedy. The end is so miraculous that we, too, like the healed King Leontes, may say, "If this be magic, let it be an art / Lawful as eating." The ritual of restoration, the magic that transforms the stale world into the "brave new world," is presented to us in the last play, which interprets the mode of all these romances. We must go to *The Tempest* for this information and then we may understand what the wise, young poet Keats meant when he said that Shakespeare lived the life of allegory.

The Tempest, like the other last plays, is separated from the world of Elizabethans by an imaginative reach that is greater than the finite measurements of space and time. It is remote in time and it is out of time. The imaginative distances are enhanced by the mortal chronology of the text: the precise three hours of the action and the twelve-year island sojourn of Prospero and Miranda. Because of these exact statements the interior distance between us and the island is closer than are the external distances of time and space. We can almost find the island in the atlas of literary tradition: it is on or off the direct course to Carthage or Tunis, the capes where Aeneas, swept by storm, came into the realm of "widow Dido." The time may be any time, but it is more truly a constant present. All of these distinctions are made certain by the past, for it is not just that Shakespeare was an Englishman or read the sea adventures of Jourdan that put the island on the chart of his imagination.

We stand, at the play's beginning, watching a storm that we also see through the eyes of Prospero, the stormmaker, and of the admirable Miranda. It is a fairy storm, real only to the men returning from Carthage and to the spellbound girl. It is a storm similar to the one that Prospero may have known inwardly when twelve years before he and his infant daughter crossed the same waters on "a rotten carcass of a butt."

> There they hoist us,
> To cry to the seas, that roared to us; to sigh
> To the winds, whose pity sighing back again
> Did us but loving wrong.[1]

The storm that was then in Prospero's mind was not unlike the one that drove Lear mad, but now, except for occasional ripples of anger or impatience, it has blown itself out. Prospero had been tested and educated in his island; he has learned to control his passions' weather and so he can make storms in semblance. When Miranda asks how they came ashore, Prospero, grateful for the experience, can give her a serene answer, "By Providence divine." To reach this emotional shelter, one must pass through stormy weather to an island, and it is on the island, outside of known reality, that a symbolic miracle can occur.

To come across broad waters in a helpless boat and to find haven at last in a magic island is a symbolic motif that has found a place in the history of heroes since literature began. The storms that drove the Argonauts are poetically recorded;[2] we know in the same way the wracking tumult in which Ceyx drowned[3] and the monstrous gale that brought Aeneas to Carthage.[4] The accounts of the poets are sustained by the romantic historians, one of whom, Diodorus Siculus, gives us the tale of Iambulus, storm-driven for months in the Erythraean Sea and brought at last to an island where men lived happily in the earliest of Utopias.[5] The same romancer, in his book of islands, sets down a legend congenial with that of *The Tempest*. He writes that sailors from Carthage, exploring the sea beyond the Pillars of Hercules, were carried by strong winds far into the ocean. After many days, they were driven onto an island filled with springs, rivers, and beautiful orchards but unknown to men. Its climate was so felicitous that "it would appear. . .that it was a dwelling-place of gods."[6] But the master of storm, of shipwreck, and of enchanted islands is the wise son of Laertes, Odysseus of many counsels. To understand part of the tradition behind *The Tempest*, we should rehearse his Mediterranean journeys and understand what they mean.

The whole course of Odysseus from Troy to the high hall of King Alcinous is related by Homer in the central section of the epic. It is placed in the mouth of the great adventurer, who takes on himself a kind of "minstrelsy" ($\dot{\rho}\alpha\psi\omega\delta\iota\alpha$), as he words it, in order to offer the listening Phaeacians his real story as a counterwork to the artful myth recited by Demodocus. The storm begins to blow after the boats leave the beach at Ismarus; for nine days the ruinous winds carry the hero past Malea and Cythera to the Land of Lotus-Eaters. Even when the son of Hippotas gives the wanderers a wallet containing the ways of the winds, a triumph of ill-counsel brings the tempest again until further smash and bluster drive Odysseus with his single ship to the island of Circe. After she frees Odysseus and his companions and the dreaded rocks are avoided, the storms crash again, destroying all but the hero, who is carried after nine days to Ogygia "where dwelt Calypso of the braided hair." His release from this island at the request of the gods and his long and stormy voyage on the raft of his own making to the kingdom of Alcinous end the mighty story that he relates to the king and his white-armed wife, Arete. This is the way the topic begins: The hero crosses watery wastes impelled by power beyond his will; he arrives on islands or strands beyond the reach of the real; and there he finds a perfection of soul that makes actuality, when he returns to it, endurable. This is the ancient understanding of the travails of Odysseus, and it was not unknown to the Elizabethans. It seems possible to me that the story of Odysseus and its moral meaning may have colored for them the dramatic procedure of *The Tempest*.

To an Elizabethan who had the Greek and the stomach for the task, a number of commentaries explained the meaning that Homer hid beneath the literal fiction of Odysseus' wanderings in the islands. Armed with the popular notion that noble doctrine should be sugared with story, the Elizabethan might come to the labor of reading the Homeric commentaries of Heraclitus, Eustathius, Porphyrius, and the pseudo-Plutarch with more interest than these ancient exegetes can beget in us. The *De Vita et Poesi Homeri* of the pseudo-Plutarch argues that the Homeric poems are philosophical accounts of the physical nature of the world as well as ethical expositions of the vices and virtues.[7] Heraclitus demands that both epics be read as allegories. Only the ignorant, says he, who do not understand the language of allegory, who are incapable of recognizing truth, and who reject analogical interpretation, cling to the appearances of fiction. As a consequence, these ignoramuses are deaf to the voice of philosophy; but the wise, who hear the voice, go forward, accepting the *Iliad* and the *Odyssey* as guides to holy truth.[8] Some samples of this truth are apropos.

"All of the wanderings of Odysseus," writes Heraclitus, "if one regards them closely are great allegories. Homer invented this man in order to expound the nature of virtue and to serve the teaching of wisdom, because he detests the manifold vices that consume men."[9] The lotus is, consequently, a symbolic plant; it represents those pleasures and delights that cause men to forget their true home. The fact that Odysseus passes close to slaves of exotic barbarian pleasures and is not tempted makes a shrewd moral point.[10] His temperance is further illustrated when he refuses, though starving, to eat the cattle of Helios. The temptations of Circe's island are obvious, but the reader must also understand that Hermes, who aids Odysseus in subduing the goddess, is a symbol, not a god in presence. Hermes is reason and dwells in Odysseus. When they seem to be talking, it is Odysseus reflecting or conversing with himself. The magic moly is the sign of reason; hence it has black roots to represent the hard first steps of knowledge, but it terminates in a bright flower.[11] Such is the pagan reading; now we can continue this knotty explanation of Odysseus' wanderings by turning to Bishop Eustathius for the Christian message.

The island goddess Calypso, say Eustathius, is literally "the fair goddess," but she is also two abstract ideas. She is the body that confines the soul; and Odysseus, aided by Hermes-Reason, gives her up in order to return to Penelope, or Philosophy. There is a second meaning. Calypso is the child (the thought) of Atlas, so she is clearly the science of astronomy and astrology. Odysseus, we know from other places in the epic, was well versed in starlore; but after Calypso has furthered his education in this science, he, realizing that it is only a minor branch of learning, returns to his wife, whose daily weaving and unweaving of her web shows that she is Philosophy.[12] So Eustathius finds moral readings here and in other episodes in the epic to support his conviction that the poem is a treatise on the education of men.[13]

There is no question that the sixteenth century saw these moral meanings in the stormblown ventures not only of Odysseus but also of his Latin reflection, Aeneas. When Chapman inscribed his translation of the *Odyssey* to the Earl of Somerset, he stated that a moral reading of the poem was a requirement. The *Iliad*, he writes, begins with the word "wrath," the *Odyssey* with "man"; the latter poem is, consequently, superior in moral instruction.

> In one, Predominant Perturbation; in the other, overruling Wisedome; in one, the Bodie's fervour and fashion of outward Fortitude to all possible height of Heroical Action; in the other, the Mind's inward, constant and unconquerd Empire, unbroken, unaltered with any most insolent and tyrannous infliction. . . . Nor is this all-composing Poesie phantastique, or meere fictive, but the most material and doctrinall illations of Truth, both for all manly information of Manners in the yong, all prescription of Justice, and even Christian pietie, in the most grave and high-governd. To illustrate both which in both kinds, with all height of expression, the Poet creates both a Bodie and a Soule in them—wherein, if the Bodie (being the letter, or historie) seemes fictive and beyond Possibilitie to bring into Act, the sence then and Allegorie (which is the Soule) is to be sought—which intends a more eminent expressure of Vertue, for her lovelinesse, and of Vice, for her uglinesse, in their severall effects, going beyond the life than any Art within life can possibly delineate. Why then is Fiction to this end so hatefull to our true Ignorants?[14]

Heraclitus comes to life in the last sentence, but the tone of the whole passage implies that he was never really dead.

If Odysseus' journeys to the storm-set islands were allegories of the moral testing and education of men, we can, perhaps, assume that the voyage of Prospero and that of his enemies might have the same intent. We must notice at the start that the islands of the Greek epic and that of *The Tempest* are not exactly alike. The Greek islands are fantastic garden spots, direct mirrorings of the Isles of the Blest; they are not unlike the one that Diodorus' sailors found in the broad ocean. The Renaissance had not forgotten the Homeric islands, and we have only to turn to Ronsard's poem on Calypso to recapture their charm.

> Terre grasse et fertille,
> Lieu que les Dieux avoient pour eux esleu,
> Pour tes forests autrefois tu m'as pleu,
> Por tes jardins, pour tes belles fonteines,
> Et pour tes bords bien esmailles d'areines.[15]

Prospero's island, like Perdita's Arcadia, suffers intrusions from reality. In most instances we see the island through the eyes of Caliban, the only animal survivor now that its Circe (Sycorax) is dead. Through these banal eyes, we see that the island has fresh springs, brine pits, barren and fertile places, bogs, fens, flats. We learn through other eyes that there are desolate spots where there is "neither bush nor shrub." But it also has grassplots, "lush and lusty"; it produces berries, pignuts, crabapples, filberts, and limes. It is, however, no thornless Eden, for—once again Caliban tells us—it has "toothed briars, sharp furzes, pricking goss, and thorns."

When Prospero set foot on the island, it was not unlike Circe's Aeaea, not honored "with a human shape." The blue-eyed witch Sycorax (a true half-sister of the daughter of Helios), whose antiquity is attested by her ability to "control the moon," ruled the island with "earthly and abhorred commands." The child of this earthy enchantress is naturally earthy, an animal bent on animal pleasures, filled with animal desires, haunted by animal fears. Odysseus broke the spell of Circe; but Prospero, although he can undo the black magic of Sycorax, is unable to raise Caliban to human estate. The island has also some colors of Ogygia; but of Calypso, who sang with sweet voice while she wove on her loom with a golden shuttle, only the music and the knowledge are left. It is this music that Ferdinand hears—the singing of the invisible Ariel—before he sees Miranda, and so he speaks as Odysseus may have spoken when, fresh from Hell and sea-peril, he saw the humane goddess "who took him in and treated him kindly."

> Most sure, the goddess
> On whom these airs attend. Vouchsafe my prayer
> May know if you remain upon this island,
> And that you will some good instruction give
> How I may bear me here.[16]

The music that diabolic magic imprisoned in a tree, heavenly magic released, and now it has charms even for beast-hearted men. "The isle is full of noises," says Caliban, "sound, and sweet airs, that give delight and hurt not."[17] The two clowns, made beasts by wine, "lifted up their noses / As they smelt music."[18] If in these respects the island has recollections of Ogygia, there are reminders of Calypso in both Prospero and Miranda: her wisdom in the father, her beauty in the girl. In Miranda there is a further quality of the Greek woman—the pity that only a goddess can have for men. "For I have a proper mind," says Calypso as she walks to the beach with Odysseus, "and my heart is not iron but as pitiful as yours."[19]

Prospero's island also brings to mind other literary islands of later date. Honorius, who wrote two thousand years after Homer, tells about the island Perdita, charming, fertile, unknown to men. "Once you have found it by chance, if you leave it, you will never find it again."[20] This island like all lost islands—Atlantis, the island of the sybil who prophesied the birth of Christ, the islands of Delos unknown before the Flood—haunted the imagination of many generations. Sir John Mandeville knew many of these islands, and we can follow his sail from Crues to Lamary to Silha to the Isle of Bragman.[21] But the most popular legend which brought together saints, men of sin, and visions, is the story of Brendan, the Irish Odysseus, who found Island Perdita (lost by Honorius), the Island of Sheep, (where the kine of the Sun are remembered), and the "Paradisus Avium" (where a great white tree was filled with Ariels).[22] He who has visited the islands of antiquity and of the Middle Ages has no difficulty in finding his way to those of the Renaissance.

When we visit the islands of the sixteenth century writers of romances, we sometimes find that they are also inhabited by women who stand in the ranks of magic between Sycorax and Circe. Ariosto's Alcina and Tasso's Armida are superb island enchantresses; but a better link between the experiences of Odysseus and Prospero is supplied by Francesco Bello's Mambrino, who sailed from France in fair weather and was overtaken by storm.

> Con sì gran furia allor mugghiava il mare,
> Che se il patron commanda non è inteso;
> Più non si può col timon governare,
> Col qual gran pezzo già s'era difeso
> Il cìel altro non fa che balenare;
> De la tempesta ognor duplica il peso,
> E sopra il legno in modo balzan l'onde,
> Che ognun in sè medesimo si confonde.[23]

Flung into the sea, Mambrino swims to the Isle of Monte Faggio, a place charming in palace and gardens and ruled by Carandina, who is described as a woman more gifted in magic that Zoroaster, Circe, and Medea. The hero and his companion, bewitched by her arts, live a luxurious life until they are reminded of their forgotten duties by a divine vision. This island miracle is suggestive but the experiences of Ariosto's Ruggiero are even more helpful for the moral interpretation of *The Tempest*.

The sea storm during which Ruggiero's conversion begins was mentioned in the last century as Shakespeare's literary model. This artistic relationship is probably untrue, but the career of the hero after the storm may enable us to add meaning to Shakespeare's play. Until he was swept into the sea, Ruggiero was a pagan; but as he swims, he remembers his unfulfilled vows and the loss of time. It occurs to him that he is being baptized in bitter salt water because he refused the sweet water of Christ's mercy. He makes a vow. By miracle, "miracol fu," his swimming becomes easier and, like Prospero, he arrives at a providential island: "Nel solitario scoglio uscì Ruggiero, / Come all' alta Bontà divina piacque." Climbing a hill of juniper, laurel, myrtle, palm, and clear springs, he comes to the hermit's cell at the summit. Here the holy man greets him with the words that blind Saul heard on the Damascus road;[24] and Ruggiero's penitence, conversion, and religious education begin. These qualities of vision, conversion, penitence, and education—the archetypal influence of Patmos and the exiled St. John cannot be avoided—[25] attach themselves to the Christian island and may be transferred to the island that Shakespeare made in the Middle Sea.

The island of *The Tempest* is one in which pagan magic has been replaced by Christian miracle, and the maker of these miracles is a man who resembles to some degree an island saint. When we first encounter Prospero, he is "master of a full poor cell," not of the splendid palace surrounded by vast gardens of rare plants that once he may have possessed. The hermit who converted and instructed Ruggiero set fruit-bearing palms about his hut; and Prospero, equally modest, defends "this mouth o' the cell" with a grove of lime trees. In this place, the banished Duke lives and meditates; there are even periods when he shuts himself off, like an anchorite, from all human conversation. But this is credible because Prospero was something of an eremite before his scheming, worldly brother deprived him of the dukedom:

> I thus neglecting worldly ends, all dedicate
> To closeness, and the bettering of my mind.[26]

"Closeness" is a word that explains the Prospero whom we know; he is an aloof man, who stands apart or rises above (as if he were a playwright) the other characters in the drama that his secret powers have made.

On Shakespeare's lost island, Prospero was first his daughter's schoolmaster; it is here that she had her only education.

> Here in this island we arrived, and here
> Have I, thy schoolmaster, made thee more profit
> Than other princess can, that have more time
> For vainer hours, and tutors not so careful.[27]

The admirable and sympathetic Miranda has attempted, in turn, to teach Caliban the Italian language; but her lessons have been partially wasted, because, like so many poor linguists, the man-brute has only an ear for profanity. Prospero, too, has tried unsuccessfully to give lessons to the son of Sycorax. But while he was teaching others, Prospero taught himself, learning, first, about his own nature and, next, how to predict and control his inner weather. In this control, he surpasses his old foe Alonso, who is "cloudy" over the loss of Ferdinand until he, too, is educated by the man he helped to depose. There are occasions when the lightning still flashes in the sky of Prospero's anger, but he never inflicts, as he was quite able to do, another tempest on his storm-driven enemies.

> Though with their high wrongs I am struck to th' quick,
> Yet, with my nobler reason 'gainst my fury
> Do I take part. The rarer action is
> In virtue than in vengenance. They being penitent,
> The sole drift of my purpose doth extend
> Not a frown further.[28]

Though education is preliminary to conversion, it is only a preparative requirement, and Prospero, whose real change of heart may have begun when his raft reached the island, knows about that process, too.

Before the hapless wedding party arrived on the island—we should notice the difference between Prospero and Alonso as matchmakers—Prospero tried to dissuade Caliban from the worship of Setebos; but it is useless to attempt the conversion of those who are guided by the lowest levels of the soul.

> A devil, a born devil, on whose nature
> Nurture can never stick; on whom my pains,
> Humanely taken, all, all lost, quite lost,
> And as with age his body uglier grows,
> So his mind cankers.[29]

With the newcomers his task is easier, because they are supposedly Christians from a Christian land. Actually, only Gonzalo is a real Christian, who testifies to his faith on all occasions. He joins the King in prayers; he believes in "the miracle" of preservation; he comforts the suffering King; he plans, to the amusement of the scoffers, a Christian state; he trusts heaven; he calls on "the name of something holy"; he requests the guidance of "some heavenly power"; he asks the gods "to look down"; and his last speech in the play is "Be it so, Amen." There is plain piety in almost every word he utters, and everything he does explains his earlier act of dangerous charity to Prospero and the infant Miranda. Gonzalo has grace enough for sainthood, but he is associated with men whose need for spiritual rehabilitation is obvious.

The clowns, Trinculo and Stephano, are almost too stupid for salvation. They will run down the primrose path to the eternal bonfire, forever boisterous, forever drunk, forever singing the libertine's song: "Flout 'em and scout 'em, and scout 'em and flout 'em; / Thought is free!" Paired with them are the freethinking and worldly cynics, Sebastian and Antonio. The atheism of Antonio is made clear when he is asked, after proposing murder, about the state of his conscience.

> But I feel not
> This deity in my bosom. Twenty consciences
> That stand 'twixt me and Milan, candied be they,
> And melt ere they molest.[30]

It is only by a kind of angelic intervention through the miracle of music that the crime of murder is avoided. Conscience finally comes to Antonio, as it does to the other "men of sin," and it comes, as we might expect, because of the nature of islands, through a vision. In this case the vision is that of a banquet served by mysterious ministers. With the appearance of these harmonious servants, the doubting sinners begin to believe. Religious words fill the mouth of Alonso; the sceptical Sebastian and Antonio, smitten dumb by the spectacle, find their tongues with the word "believe." Gonzalo, true to his pious nature, thinks that he sees the realization of his Christian community, that he has arrived on Mandeville's Island of Bragman.

> For certes these people of the island—
> Who, though they are of monstrous shape, yet note,
> Their manners are more gentle-kind than of
> Our human generation you shall find
> Many, nay, almost any.[31]

Then, as speculation gives way to hunger, Ariel appears in the form of a harpy and the banquet vanishes like a dream.

To understand Ariel's appearance as a harpy and the nature of the banquet, we must go, as Shakespearean annotators have gone, to the third book of the *Aeneid*; but we must apply the speech of Celaeno, as it has not been applied, to the lecture of Ariel. "I, the eldest of the Furies," says the harpy Celaeno, "reveal it to you." "Vobis Furiarum ego maxima pando."[32] Harpies are Furies; they both bring divine vengeance. Valerius Flaccus affirms the testimony of Vergil when he writes that the harpies thrust the earned anger of the gods on men.[33] But harpies are more than this. Hesiod says that they are "beautiful creatures of the wind and air";[34] whereas Homer, who does not mention their beauty, identifies them with "the spirits of the storm." In the fourteenth book of the *Odyssey*, Eumaeus gives us a key text: "νῦν ςέ μιν ἀκλεεῶς ἄρέπνιαι ἀνηρείψαντο" (371). So Ariel, the beautiful spirit of the air, who made the storm of the first scene, is also a Harpy-Fury who troubles the minds of the three sinners. "Holy" Gonzalo, who observes the change in the countenance and manner of the three, cannot withhold his observation: "Their great guilt. . .'gins to bite the spirits." The effect of the lecture of Conscience is greater than biting; Antonio and Sebastian, who thought they had the power in pocket, twist in its mighty grasp.

> Thou art pinched for't now Sebastian. Flesh and blood,
> You brother mine, that entertained ambition,
> Expelled remorse and nature, who, with Sebastian—
> Whose inward pinches therefore are most strong—
> Would here have killed your King.[35]

Faithful to tradition, the island of education, saints, and visions, is also a place of repentance and conversion; but the visions do not end with one that produces a change of heart.

For the troth-plight of his daughter and Ferdinand, Prospero makes a pleasant, yet visionary, masque of spirits who are borrowed, except for the realistic British harvestmen, from the mythological records. To point the difference between two kinds of visions, Shakespeare makes Ferdinand say in the middle of the second:

> This is a most majestic vision, and
> Harmonious charmingly. May I be bold
> To think these spirits?[36]

Prospero admits that they are spirits, whom he has called forth to act his "present fancies." His fancies are worth noticing because they reveal the ultimate Shakespearean resolution of the fate of man. The theme of the masque is fertility in marriage, a theme annotated for us by Ferdinand's vow of prenuptial chastity. Such a condition is impossible for Caliban, the rapist, and his new-found human gods; they accept propagation, but sacraments are not for them. Because their sort of love is excluded from the idealism of the island, Venus and her son are omitted from Prospero's cast of characters. Iris informs us that the heroine of *Venus and Adonis* has departed with her son for Paphos.

> Here thought they to have done
> Some wanton charm upon this man and maid,
> Whose vows are, that no bed-right shall be paid
> Till Hymen's torch be lighted.[37]

So the goddess of marriage, Juno, and the goddess of fertility, Ceres, are the principal actors in this blessed vision, which concludes with the symbolic August scene of harvest and garner. The masque, it must be noticed, is structurally bound to the play through the character of Iris, who, in her mythological guises, is the messenger of the goddesses, a virgin,[38] and, bettter still, sister to the Harpies.[39] It is a part that Ariel could and did play with great skill.

The masque is one of the dramatic centers of the play, and in its simple theme of immortality through generation we have again the doctrine that lighted most of Shakespeare's days on earth. Though I shall return to this, I want first—now that the island is for the moment so plainly a place of vision—to ponder the secondary emphasis in this play, as in previous ones, on the world of vision and dream. This emphasis is finely stated when Prospero speaks his famous lines concluding the revels.

> These our actors,
> As I foretold you, were all spirits, and
> Are melted into air, into thin air;
> And like the baseless fabric of this vision,
> The cloud-capped towers, the gorgeous palaces,
> The solemn temples, the great globe itself,
> Yea all which it inherit, shall dissolve,
> And like this insubstantial pageant faded
> Leave not a rack behind. We are such stuff
> As dreams are made on; and our little life
> Is rounded with a sleep.[40]

Within the boundaries of this utterance, Shakespeare accepts the philosophy of mortal existence against which the dark plays protest. Because once again he accepts the promise of the masque, the benediction of Juno and the rewards of Ceres, he can also accept the necessary condition that men and their works, as he knew them, are only visions and will dissolve like summer clouds. If the world that each man has made is a vision, then life as each man possesses it is a dream. To expound this idea, sturdy tradition aids us mortals, who like Christopher Sly have only "an after-dinner's sleep" between youth and age, to comprehend the topics that Prospero's aria reveals.

First, it is interesting to scrutinize the dream metaphors in *The Tempest*. Miranda, mindful of her childhood, says that it was "rather like a dream than an assurance"; and Ferdinand, under the spell of both the girl and her father, finds his "spirits" all bound up "as in a dream." The Boatswain, no philosopher, thinks of dreams when he searches his mind for a figure to express the rapid course of time: "On a trice, so please you, / Even in a dream, were we divided from them." Even Caliban, earth and filth that he is, brings dream and music together to describe the island:

and then, in dreaming,
The clouds methought would open, and show riches
Ready to drop upon me, that when I waked
I cried to dream again.[41]

Throughout Shakespeare's plays—and the custom is not peculiar to him alone—*dream* is a metaphor of *life*, as if it were difficult to separate the life of dreams from conscious existence.

The origin of this imagistic comparison begins, I suppose, with human time. The Gentile hero, Job, whose poet almost got him canonized, says of the lot of man: "He shall fly away as a dream, and shall not be found: yea, he shall be chased away as a vision of night."[42] Across the lines of Jehovah's territory were less consecrated poets who would agree. For Pindar, "man is a shadow's dream,"[43] and Sophocles describes men in the Ajax as "dreams or shadows."[44] Aristophanes summons men, who "pass like dreams of sorrow," to listen to the singing of the *Birds*.[45] The Middle Ages improved on these images of the Greeks and the Romans to such an extent that its child and reformer, the optimistic Petrarch, could complain about the dreamlike quality of existence. He writes to Giacomo Colonna that life is a dream or shifting fancy. "Illa relegenti, totam mihi vitam meam, nihil videri aliud quam leve somnium, fugacissimumque phantasma."[46] It is interesting that this passage comes from a letter on the subject of the vanished glories of Rome, a city that had long been the subject of meditations on the transitoriness of mortal achievement.

Prospero's reverie about "cloud-capped towers," "gorgeous palaces," and "solemn temples" is a metropolitan intrusion into the primitive island realm. The former duke remembers the land across the waters, the cities of Carthage or of the Italian mainland. "The great globe itself" may be a playful allusion to the theater on the Bankside, and the whole speech may wave away the theatrical world of painted cloth and tinsel; but this is not a speech to father laughter or even smiles, for its conclusion is grave and its total import is serious. Man passes and so does what he makes. "My weakness . . . my old brain . . . my infirmity . . .my beating mind." The mind of the Renaissance reader is directed by Prospero's words not to the island or to England, but to Rome, the ruined imperial city, where man had pondered for many generations on the impermanence of life and art.[47]

The Middle Ages had two opinions about the fallen towers, palaces, and temples of Rome. One was that the material ruin that lay about the sojourner in the city was full evidence of its spiritual ruin.[48] Alcuin saw in the broken stones the great symbol of the foolishness of human glory. "Roma, caput mundi, mundi decus, aurea Roma / Hunc remanet tantum saeva ruina tibi."[49] To a second group, of which Hildebert of Larvardin[50] is a good representative, there are two Romes: the ruined center of paganism and the splendid capital city of the Christian world. For Dante the ruins are venerable;[51] and though Petrarch reads their lesson, he hopes to see splendor reborn from the debris that by itself filled him with adoration.[52] Some of the humanists agreed with the mediaeval sermons on the ruins, but most of them saw in the fallen arches and columns the fragility of all human effort. Poggio finds dignity and greatness in the ruin—"sola ruina praeteritam dignitatem ac magnitudinem ostentantem"—but he is also moved by them to speculate on the power of Fortuna, a non-Christian lady.[53] Traversari reads them as torn documents, to the same end,[54] and Urceus wanders through the decaying city to write an epigram on man's fate.

> Roma fuit periere patres periere quirites
> Restat deserto sola ruina solo
> Quaeque tamen restat doctorum poena virorum
> Hic labor; hic non sunt praemia: nulla quies.[55]

The poets of the vernacular follow the same themes, and the ruins, as symbols of man's tender hold on life and the world, haunt such lyrics as Castiglione's "Superbi colli, e voi sacre ruine," and Guidicconi's "Degna nutrice de le chiare genti." The sixteenth-century Italian poet, Bernardino Baldi, who wrote a sonnet sequence on Rome, likewise saw in the wreckage about him the eternal lesson of the "insubstantial pageant faded." A fragment of his poem on the Coliseum is sample enough of the mode and the mood.

> Da questo campo abbandonato ed ermo,
> Cui fanno alte ruine ampia corona,
> Prender può esempio ogni mortal persona
> Come contro l'eta perda ogni schermo.
> O fugaci bellezze, o mondo infermo,
> O nostra fama che sì breve suona,
> Ben sei nubilo ciel che splende e tuona
> Tutto in un punto, e nulla è 'n te di fermo.[56]

Although the Italian poets lamented the ruins of Rome, they also lived on them. The distance was not great enough for real nostalgia. It was French poet, Du Bellay, who built these broken stones into a giant European symbol of evanescence.

In the sonnets of *Les Antiquitez* and in the Latin "Romae Descriptio," Du Bellay proclaimed his love of the past and told his contemporaries what their future contained. These sonnets are separate and numbered, but they seem like stanzas in a long poem on the inconstant nature of life. In some the poet imitates Latin and Italian predecessors; in others he makes poetic excursions into history; but there is always the implication of decay, the sense of impermanence. Rome may seem to be renewing herself, but we may look at her broken body for the mortal lesson (XXVII). She resists time, but time will have her in the end (VII). Only the flowing Tiber is unchanged because only change endures in a world of change (III). Consolation is to be found, but it is the consolation of mutability.

> Ainsi quand du grand Tout le fuite retournée,
> Ou trentesix mil' ans ont sa course bornée,
> Rompra des elemens le naturel accord,
> Les semences qui sont meres de toutes choses,
> Retourneront encor' a leur premier discord,
> Au ventre du Chaos eternellement closes. (XXI)

When Prospero talks about ruined towers, temples, and palaces, he may be speaking in general terms, but a travelled Jacobean who listened to him would certainly think of the waste of Imperial Rome. No dream was ever greater than this imperial one; no dream ever passed more sadly and left grander evidence of its passing. The text for Prospero's speech was provided by *Lear*: "Oh ruined piece of nature; this great world / Shall so wear out to naught." But a world and a life that are dreams is a common enough theme for Shakespeare. The fate of the dreamer is a great topic in all the tragedies, whose heroes, dreams, in themselves, awaken from dreams unable to endure the reality in which they find themselves. The island is where they were born, and when they cross to the mainland, they learn that they "are the stuff that dreams are made on." With *The Tempest* Shakespeare returns to his old belief in the continuity of man—the heroes of the tragedies, even Lear, die childless. The doctrine is a simple one. Life will go on; only the individual passes. This is the "brave new world."

NOTES

1. *The Tempest* 1.2.148–51.
2. Apollonius of Rhodes, *Argonautica* IV.1228–1304; Valerius Flaccus, I.574–607.
3. *Metamorphoses* XI.481–534.
4. *Aeneid* I.81–141.
5. *Bibliotheca* II.55–60
6. Ibid., V.19–20. The same tale appears in the pseudo-Aristotle, *De Mirabilibus Auscultationibus*, in *Opera*, ed. Bekker (Berlin, 1831), II, 836.
7. Plutarch, *Opera*, ed. Dübner (Paris, 1875), V, 104.
8. *Quaestiones Homericae*, ed. Oelmann (Leipzig, 1910), p. 4.
9. Ibid., pp. 91–92.
10. Ibid, pp. 94–95.
11. Ibid., pp. 96–97; Alcinous is equated with the Epicurean philosophy; and hence, his kingdom has no charm for the Platonist Odysseus. Cf. pp. 105–106.
12. *Commentarii ad Homeri Odysseam* (Leipzig, 1825), I, 16–17.

13. Ibid., II.4–5; Odysseus listens to the sirens because it is good for a philosopher to hear the poets.

14. Homer, Chapman trans., ed. Nicoll (New York, 1956), II, 4–5.

15. *Oeuvres*, ed. Vaganay (Paris, 1924), IV, 218.

16. *Tmp.* 1.2.420–25.

17. *Tmp.* 3.2.144–45.

18. *Tmp.* 4.1.177–78.

19. *Odyssey*, V.190–91.

20. *De Imago Mundi* (*PL*, CLXXII, 132–33).

21. *The Travels*, ed. Pollard (London, 1915), pp. 108–15, 119–39, 192–98.

22. *The Anglo-Norman Voyage of St. Brendan by Benedeit*, ed. Waters (Oxford, 1928), pp. 23, 28–29; see also *St. Brandan*, ed. Wright (London, 1844); *Sanct Brandan*, ed. Schröder (Erlangen, 1871); *Les voyages merveilleux de Saint Brandan*, ed. Francisque-Michel (Paris, 1878); *Die alt-franzosische prosaüber-setzung von Brendans Meerfahrt*, ed. Wahlund (Upsala, 1900); *An old Italian version of the Nagvigatio Sancti Brendani*, ed. Waters (Oxford, 1931).

23. *Mambriano*, ed. Rua (Turin, 1926), I, 8.

24. *Orlando Furioso*, ed. Caretti (Milan-Naples, 1954), pp. 1061–64.

25. Though Erasmus had questioned whether or not St. John the Apostle was also the writer of the Book of The Revelation and was followed in this position by Sebastian Castellio, who called him "Joannes Theologus" as did some of the Fathers (see his *Biblia* [Basel, 1565], p. 486), the post-Trent Vulgate and the Protestant scholars thought of the two Johns as one man. The nature of their arguments is summed up by Beza in the prolegomena to the Apocalypse in the *Biblia* (Hanover, 1602). The usual legend read that John was exiled to Patmos by Diocletian and there not only preached the faith but had his vision: see J. Camerarius, *Historia Jesu Christi. . .Itemque de Apostolis* (Leipzig, 1581), p. 124; and Surius, *De Probatis Sanctorum Historiis* (Cologne, 1575), VI, 1013. The notion of an island saint is not too uncommon. In *Le Roman en Prose de Tristan* (ed. Löseth [Paris, 1890]), Sadoc is thrown overboard during a storm and swims to some rocks where he is saved by an eremite and where he lives for three years (pp. 4–5).

26. *Tmp.* 1.2.89–90.

27. *Tmp.* 1.2.171–74.

28. *Tmp.* 5.1.25–30.

29. *Tmp.* 4.1.188–92.

30. *Tmp.* 2.1.277–80.

31. *Tmp.* 3.3.30–34.

32. *Aeneid*, III.252

33. *Aeneid*, IV.428–61.

34. *Theogonia*, 265.

35. *Tmp.* 5.1.74–78.

36. *Tmp.* 4.1.118–20.

37. *Tmp.* 4.1.94–97.

38. Theocritus, *Eidyllion* XVII.134; Vergil, *Aeneid* V.610.

39. Hesiod, op. cit., 266, 780.

40. *Tmp.* 4.1.146–57.

41. *Tmp.* 3.2.149–52.

42. Job 20:8.

43. *Pyth.* 8.95–96.

44. *Ajax* 126.

45. *Birds* 686–87.

46. *Opera* (Basel, 1554), p. 667.

47. There was present in the imperial Romans, who looked on the ruins of Athens ("vacuae Athenae," says Horace in *Epistulae* II.2.81), a modest sense of personal unworthiness and the melting glory of man; nonetheless, they were equally possessed by a reassurance that man's material remainders contain and preserve him. An anonymous late Latin poet might write a poignant epitaph of the great city in which the autumnal music of the Middle Ages is audible (*Anthologia Latina*, ed. Riese [Leipzig, 1922], I, 267), yet the view of the mighty city stirred emotions far more deep. Propertius escapes from the obdurate Cynthia to *doctae Athenae* to purge himself of foul passions by seeing those places in which were stored recollections of noble emotions and of men healed of error (III.21.25–30). Cicero describes a walk among its ruins that, he says, made the persons of Sophocles, Plato, and Epicurus more vivid to him than their books (*De Finibus* V.1–6). Two centuries later, Dio Chrysostom pondered the ruined land, but he was certain that the ruins make manifest the greatness of Greece (*Orationes* VII.38–39) for the ruins are far more gracious than the living cities (XXXI.160).

48. "Versus Romae," in *Poetae Latini Aevi Carolini*, ed. Traube (Berlin, 1896), III, 555–56. This poem is discussed by A. Graf, *Roma nella Memoria e nelle Immaginazioni del Medio Evo* (Turin, 1882), I. 46–47. This pioneer work has been somewhat superseded by Schneider, *Rom und Romedanke im Mittelalter* (Munich, 1926), but it is still the best for literary texts.

49. *Opera*, ed. Dümmler (Berlin, 1891), I, 230.

50. B. Haureau, *Notices et Extraits des Quelques Manuscrits Latins de la Bibliothèque Nationale* (Paris, 1890–1893), pp. 330–36. The theme appears in Sedulius Scottus, *Carmina*, ed. Traube, *PLAC* (Berlin, 1896) III, 170–76; in a tenth-century poem in *Novati, L'Influsso del Pensiero Latino* (Milan, 1899), pp. 172–7; and in Neckham, *De Laudibus Divinae Sapientia*, ed. Wright (London, 1863), p. 445.

51. There have been numerous studies of Dante's attitude; for the most recent, see Davis, *Dante and the Idea of Rome* (Oxford, 1957).

52. *Opera* (Basel, 1554), pp., 731, 1169.

53. *De Fortunae . . . Romae et de Ruina Eiusdem*, in De sallengre, *Novus Thesaurus* (Hague, 1716), I, 502.

54. Graf, op. cit., I, 52.

55. *Silvae* (Venice, 1506), Li verso.

56. *Versi e Prose*, ed. Ugolini and Polidori (Florence, 1859), p. 258.

Romance, Farewell!
*The Tempest**

M.C. BRADBROOK

Characters whose life is in their action; adventures full of variety and always interweaving; such was the old romance. In *The Tempest*, encounter supplies all the action given to anyone; simply to meet suffices. The quest to find one's fellows is to regain society out of loneliness. For character exists without need for action—Miranda has no need to do anything—she has simply to appear "the goddess on whom these airs attend"[1] to gratify Ferdinand at his labors. The sublimation of romantic escape lies in the musician, Ariel, who finally escapes from man, as his songs escape, in perpetual holiday from "poor little talkative humanity"—its conflicts and loss—to somewhere on the other side of despair. "Full fadom five thy father lies; / Of his bones are coral made; / Those are pearls that were his eyes" (1.2.399–401). Grief is transmuted—as a medieval poet once too saw a girl with a coronet of pearls, through the separation of flowing water which he could not cross.

But if Ariel is free, his author is bound by strictest rules: the Unities. Prospero's charm also depends on an exact moment and much calculation, if to others it seems a blind maze and the action "more than nature was ever conduct of."[2]

The effect is paradoxical—a fantasy obeys strict canons of art, at the end of the play to become itself the matter of wondering words suspended between actors and audience. Prospero's first epilogue, "Our revels now are ended," with his second, the epilogue proper, unwinds the charm and yet leaves his mystery more mysterious.

The play, both a masterpiece and an enigma, where severity of control is balanced by freedom to use the language of show and of music, and by the

*M. C. Bradbrook, "Romance, Farewell!: *The Tempest*," originally published in *English Literary Renaissance* 1:3 (1971): 239–49. Reprinted by permission of *English Literary Renaissance*.

luminous depth of the character as idea, might stand as illustration of Puttenham's distinction between true and false fantasy. When it is misused, "then doth it breed chimeras and monsters in man's imaginations, and not only in his imaginations, but also in all his ordinary actions and life which ensues"; but when it is not confused, it represents to the soul "all manner of beautiful visions, whereby the inventive part of the mind is so much holpen, as without it no man could devise any new or rare thing. . . ."[3] The unusual severity of composition released the fantasy into a new world beyond nature.

Without offering the interlacing variety of *Cymbeline* or the depth of character in action of *The Winter's Tale*, after we have "founder'd" in Scene I the poet leaves the exploration of his brave new world to unfold in successive layers of illusion and revelation. He holds up a mirror in which each may see the image he himself casts, with exceptional clarity, so that at the end the treasures that each seeks are found, but also "all of us ourselves, / When no man was his own" (5.1.212–13). As in romances the story is distanced, the response unqualified, but it is an individual response, not a group response. The island setting provides the superlatives that romance exacts. Purity and isolation so great lie beyond any pastoral dream; this is Eden, an unfallen world where the air is full of music, the virgin sand bears no footprint as the spirits dance over it. Prospero's absolute dominion, however, is ruled by working through natural sympathies, by shock and hypnotic power over human sinew. Ferdinand thinks that Miranda (like her father) would have power to reanimate the dead; her charm is tested by setting the Prince of Naples to bearing logs like Hob or Dick. Caliban is no monster of brown paper to be subdued by the hero in combat; he curses and plots, and though subdued is not destroyed, but rather acknowledged in a deeper sense than the literal one: "This thing of darkness I acknowledge mine" (5.1.275). To the servants he is something to show at a fair, like the strange fish about which Autolycus hawked ballads.

The transformed elements of the old romances, though so numerous, do not seem to belong to communal tradition any more. The magician or conjuror, with his magic wand and book, seeming in some fashion related to the author of the play, is to be found in early drama.[4] Prospero begins with a long narrative of old adventures that sound like one of the romances of ordeal— indeed it has not a little resemblance to *Pericles*. Besides the new kind of monster and spirit, the Ship, the Cave, the Enchanted Banquet, the Masque of Goddesses, the coat to go invisible remain; there is a hunting with hounds upon the stage that recalls the hunt in the hall of early revels at the Inns of Court and the Universities (4.1.254), and Ariel's former imprisonment in the Hollow Tree looks back to a favorite device of Lyly's stage.[5] Echoes of old plays survive because an individual dramatist chooses to recall them, harmonized into the Jacobean play—these are not ghosts of a vanished stage, but the discoveries of a new one. *Pericles* erupted from a deep center and bore marks of the conflict that preceded; *The Tempest* builds up to an abdication of the play world, and also of the transient realm of magic, returning to a city that is as transient, though in another sense and dimension.

The childish magic of *John a Kent and John a Cumber* lies behind both *Midsummer Night's Dream* and *The Tempest*, as Professor Coghill made plain in *Shakespeare's Professional Skills*.[6] Here two rival magicians impersonate each other in turn, and everyone else changes shape, or becomes transformed in a magic mist. The action is gratuitously complicated by the magicians and treated as if it were a play. "Must the first Scene make absolute a play? / no crosse? no change? what? no varietie?"[7] The magician's apprentice, who can fly through a keyhole, reveals a conspiracy in a song which he puts into the mouth of clowns, who are blamed for it. He leads astray travellers by playing on an instrument, charms them asleep, leads them in a circle round a magic tree. Princes appear in antic form, darting in from all sides and from beneath the stage; the music and dancing present the state of enchantment in which no one is quite sure who is "shadow" and who is "substance"—"shadow" being a term used equally of actors and of apparitions. For in addition to the magic transformations, this play includes a troupe of rustic actors, led by a serving man named Turnop, who offers welcome to the bridegrooms and a scene of ritual abuse against one of the conjurors; him they dress in a fool's coat as part of their morris dance. These substantial and lively characters are sharply contrasted with the chameleon magicians and the sextet of lovers, rivals, ladies.

The play is set firmly in particular places—Chester and the country around—and may therefore have been commissioned for some great marriage in those parts. The manuscript was preserved in the library of a local magnate, Lord Mostyn. For it is a characteristic of the most fantastic romance to be given a particular setting—and though the precise locality of Prospero's isle is "somewhere in the Mediterranean," the basis of its adventures is quite definite and situated in very different waters.

The story of the *Sea Venture*'s wreck on the islands of Bermuda in July 1609 impressed itself on contemporaries, and is still the most important event that has ever happened there—a creation *ab initio*, the beginning of history. In an uninhabited island, such as this (or Iceland before the Norsemen) the first settlement acquires a mythic grandeur and scale; no half-obliterated story of the conquered blurs its pristine clarity. The image of the shipwreck forms the arms of the islands, for it was from the first a happy wreck. A rich coast had been shunned by all seamen as "the dangerous and dreaded island, or rather islands of the Bermuda . . . [since] they be so terrible to all that ever touched on them, and such tempests, thunders and other fearful objects are seen and heard about them that they be called commonly, The Devil's Islands."[8] Another writer speaks of them as by common belief "a most prodigious and enchanted place"; they turned out to be "the richest, healthfullest and pleasing land."[9] For nine months the party from the *Sea Venture* wintered there happily, before sailing on to Virginia, whither they had been bound.

No legend, but the latest exploit of the Virginia Company, furnished the groundwork of the plot—a venture in which Shakespeare's friends and his former patron, Southampton, were engaged. The colonists had exorcised the devils and disproved the marvels. The play's Neapolitans at first thought themselves on such a deadly coast—Ferdinand threw himself overboard as St. Elmo's fire burst from the ship's rigging, crying "Hell is empty, and all the devils are here" (1.2.214–15).

The Tempest does not seek to rouse the comic response of "delight" but the graver tragic one of "admiration." Through Ariel's shows, or the beauty of admired Miranda, or the wonder of the strange fish, astonishment strikes the characters of the play so that they are petrified or "made marble with too much conceiving."[10]

Caliban thinks the revellers must have dropped from the moon—in a court masque, it was expected that the masquers should arrive from Russia or Cathay or outer space, the *Vastus Vacuum*.[11] However much an entertainment of that kind had been planned, it was expected to look spontaneous. The surprises in this play are of a more theatrical kind. The opening presents a scene of genuine horror—cries of "All lost, to prayers, to prayers!" and "Farewell, my wife and children!" The mariners look to be as cold under water as those of *The Winter's Tale*—Gonzalo's humor hints ironically at survival.

The first words of Miranda dissolve this tragic moment: "If by your Art, my dearest father, you have / Put the wild waters in this roar, allay them" (1.2.1–2). The distancing of feeling was probably accompanied by a scene change. A bare stage would be an unsuitable prelude to the marvels following—at least the wave-machine and thunder-box, or some interesting variant of the medieval Ship Entry, is needed.

The Mock Banquet appears as a kind of show, introduced by the sort of pageant that excited more wonder, for even the cool Sebastian says:

> Now I will believe
> That there are unicorns; that in Arabia
> There is one tree, the phoenix' throne; one phoenix
> At this hour reigning there. (3.3.21–24)

The banquet vanished by a special trick, which actors termed a "secret,"[12] but the table was left behind. The wonders of the Neapolitans grow steadily, Prospero offering more rare sights as they tread the "maze." Prospero breaks off the second interlude, the Marriage Masque, with a single word—as a host indeed might do if displeased—and all vanish to a "strange, hollow, and confused noise." Designed to cover the exit, this is the very opposite of music, something like "the chimes of hell" muffled perhaps; there are other points where alarming noise is called for.[13] The Hunting Masque follows.

The illusions of this play belong in their conception to the lighted indoor theatre of the court and of Blackfriars. It was given as part of the marriage celebrations of the Princess Elizabeth, and though it need not have been specially composed for that occasion, its singleness of vision, with a kind of authority or security in the tone of utterance, suggests that it could be offered to the public as a special attraction. It is rather short for a full bill, but placed in the position of honor at the front of the Folio. Insofar as the island itself is one of the chief characters of the play, it is an enchanted ground with a good firm basis in theatrical machinery; *The Tempest* can even today be put on expensively as a showpiece. The play is both curious and costly and in a firm way assumes the compliance of the spectators until the very end.

Yet when Prospero, in his plumed hat and rapier, comes forward as Duke of Milan for his second epilogue—"Our revels now are ended" being epilogue to all shape-changing except the hunt, which follows it—he resumes the octosyllabics of Ancient Gower in *Pericles*. These Milton was also to use in a masque much indebted to *The Tempest*. The "beautiful vision" presented by a composed imagination as the device of "a new and rare thing" has vanished. Yet if the magician has abandoned his art, the player has not fully abandoned his role and finally addresses, perhaps, his royal master, whose badge he wore, in a mixture of play fancy and deep entreaty. Even a prayer for the King would not follow well on "As you from crimes would pardon'd be, / Let your indulgence set me free." It is Christian charity that is begged, not a contribution to the players' box.

Not only as actor of the main part but as director of the "shows" (and one who had begun with a long narrative like a minstrel's), the part of Prospero combines a multiplicity of older roles. In its complexity, it is set off by the flatness of other characters and by the "gaps" in the story. He himself breaks off the Masque of Ceres with all the curtness of royalty dismissing poor players. Even if their senses are not being charmed, characters do not communicate with each other; Miranda does not understand her father's story, since she has no experience of the kind of world inhabited by Sebastian and Antonio, whose sophistication enables them to communicate by cool hints and Machiavellian jests the project of a murder. They belong to a modern world—the world that Iachimo had also known.

Miranda answers Prospero therefore with the prim phrases of morality she has been taught; but when she meets Ferdinand, their communication, even more perfect than that of the conspiracy of evil, needs almost no words at all: "They have changed eyes." In the betrothal scene she offers herself to Ferdinand with a sweetness like that of the island, where Providence "hangs in shades the Orange bright, / Like golden Lamps in a green Night."[14] She looks out on the brave new world with a happy unguarded radiance which the poet Auden has caught perfectly in the Song he gives her: "He kissed me awake and no one was sorry; / The sun shone on sails, eyes, pebbles, anything, / And the high green hill sits always by the sea."[15] In its condensed poetry, *The Tempest* constantly invites such extensions of its own hints and guesses. The complex feelings of Prospero are themselves enigmatic; the whole play is like a great chamber, full of echoes. Many writers have been caught up to develop it—Dryden, absurdly, by doubling all the roles out of admiration for its mechanical beauties, loaded it with the mathematical symmetry of *John a Kent* and dubious innuendo of his own. Auden played with extending it beyond the conclusion, putting his ironic commentary, as Browning did, into the mouth of Caliban.

The offering carries almost the power of a rite; to foster openness of interpretation, it permits an immense number of mythical, personal, and social extrapolations, and is accommodating to them all. Sidney knew "the poet never affirmeth and therefore never lieth"; but by this very neutrality he drives others to passionate affirmations and denials. The play is among Shakespeare's shortest but it is his most elastic, most mutable composition.

Within the primary level of the action, Prospero as a white magician relies on invoking the cooperating powers of nature.[16] The natural sympathy and unity between all parts of the world, whereby the more powerful controlled the less (as the sea is governed by the moon), enabled the man of art to put himself in sympathy and in tune with the whole natural process. Even the ranges of power beyond the moon, and therefore beyond the mutability of sublunary objects, were accessible. By talismans, on which the appropriate signs were inscribed, the magician could as it were harness the power behind the sun; he could get "on the beam" of the supreme powers. Sycorax manipulated her black art to exert a physical compulsion on these heavenly spheres—for so I read the crux that she "could control the moon. . . / And deal in her command, without her power" (5.1.27–71). "Her command" is Sycorax's; "without her power" means "beyond the moon's range." The guilty Alonso hears the whole universe speak with one voice as Prospero works on him:

> O, it is monstrous, monstrous!
> Methought the billows spoke, and told me of it;
> The winds did sing it to me; and the thunder,
> That deep and dreadful organ-pipe, pronounc'd
> The name of Prosper. (3.3.95–99)

This power Prospero sums up in the torrential evocation that proclaims and abjures power at once (5.1.33–57). Ariel, half demon and half fairy, is tricksy and not wholly under Prospero's will—he too had his forerunners in old plays. His malleable shape-changing is the demonstration of Prospero's power. In this play Prospero is supreme. The Neapolitans say their prayers, and what Ariel in rebuking the "men of sin" terms "Destiny" or "Fate"—which uses the lower world as an instrument—Prospero and Ferdinand term "Providence."[17] But if Prospero has to work when the stars are auspicious, he is left to play the god in a world where the spirits obey him; he claims to have raised the dead, but begins to feel death working within himself where he cannot command it. The humility of the final epilogue seems a necessary retraction after the extraordinary arrogance of the claims within the part itself, which leave him almost beyond mortality.

An overruling Providence was strongly present in the original story of the discovery of the Bermudas, as it is in Marvell's later poem:

> What should we do but sing his Praise
> That led us through the watry Maze
> Unto an Isle so long unknown,
> And yet far kinder that our own?. . .
> He gave us this eternal Spring,
> Which here enamells everything. . .
> He makes the Figs our mouths to meet;
> And throws the Melons at our feet.
> But Apples plants of such a price,
> No Tree could ever bear them twice.[18]

Prospero too discovers a new self; it would seem—the story is not clear—that though he has planned the wedding of Ferdinand and Miranda, yet the arrival of his betrayers stirs up other thoughts that would not fit in with such plans. Only by attaining the self-mastery that knows "the rarer action is in virtue than in vengeance" (5.1.27–28) does Prospero, by this final ironical "rarity," become strong enough not only to accept his enemies, but to abjure the magic by which he had wielded Jove's thunder. The great transformation increases his power over others by increasing his power over himself.

His relation with Ariel (and with Caliban) is what really needs solving, even more than his relation with other mortals. The shipwrecked characters at first relate to Prospero only through their relation to his creatures. The King and his party encounter not the man, but Ariel; the servants meet not the master, but his deformed and savage slave. The play moves towards a final meeting; once this is achieved, the enchantments are dissolved.

When the trance of the King and the company is lifted, whole groups of statues come to life, and they return from the interior journey on which they have been sent by art; the wonder they feel grows greater and Alonso thinks only an oracle could resolve it. But Prospero, the director of shows, winds up with his last and best—the discovery of the lovers at chess.

This high and lofty game, used as the climax for more than one play,[19] casts, over the dispositions of followers and subjects, the cool and civilized grace of a mind that "knows now what magic is;—the power to enchant / That comes from disillusion."[20] The interweaving of different groups at last brought together, Prospero finishes his game. The theme of usurpation dissolves in a lovers' jest:

MIRANDA	Sweet lord, you play me false.
FERDINAND	No, my dearest love.
	I would not for the world.
MIRANDA	Yes, for a score of kingdoms you should wrangle,
	And I would call it fair play. (5.1.171–75)

If allegory be an interaction between the play and its audience, stage audience and greater audience watch a game with more than one level here. Alonso, after passing through a series of ordeals, finds that they lead to the doorway of a fellow man, where he meets his son, his servants, the familiarity of the common world. The same boatswain and sailors, who had bid the world goodbye, make their landfall to return with the rest to the world of men.

The abdication of the magician's power could be an impoverishing choice, yet the moment of abdication itself confers an increased power; the hero shows a knowledge of the world coupled with detachment, which is also the effect of the play. It is upon the final self-conscious reflection of art looking on itself that the last of the romances comes to rest: "We are such stuff / As dreams are made on" (4.1.156–57). Auden spins the mood out in Prospero's speech to Ariel:

> Stay with me, Ariel, while I pack. . . .
> Now our partnership is dissolved, I feel so peculiar:
> As if I had been on a drunk since I was born
> And suddenly now, and for the first time, am cold sober. . .
> I never suspected the way of truth
> Was a way of silence. . .even good music
> In shocking bad taste; and you of course never told me.[21]

The illusion that romance had so beguilingly indulged is carefully, layer on layer, penetrated, not simply as it would have been done in mimed narrative, but with the added depth and complexity of the developed stage arts. Romance, the least inherently dramatic of the forms that contributed to the Elizabethan stage, was the most powerful in terms of group response and group affirmation. Shakespeare's series of romances began with *Pericles*, directly invoking an archaic narrative form; he ended with a play where not only the narrative and its narrator, its leading figure, were identified at the opening, but the complex relations of life and the poor player, of magic and death and change, were articulated.

Perhaps a formal structure was necessary, the artifice of the Unities serving as a launching platform for this extremely difficult ascent to a unified speech, in Prospero's three great moments—the first epilogue, to Ferdinand, "Our revels now are ended"; the speech to Ariel, in which he renounces fury, leading into the evocation and renunciation of his magic power; and the final epilogue. There was surely also one climactic Occasion, one Rite, to elicit these words. The play may have been performed many times; it must have been performed once on some great ceremonial occasion when these great set pieces were authenticated, for the author and director at least.

The first epilogue ("Our revels now are ended") closes the last beautiful show and recalls in its imagery the dissolution of the body in death. From the heroic last speech of Antony's "Sometimes we see a cloud that's dragonish," the dissolving rack, the dissolving "shape" of a mortal, has become also the dissolving dream of a masque and the dissolving, finally, of the "great globe" in cosmic mutability, that includes all organic nature. The union of the life of the stage and the life of the world in a royal masque—where at court, royalty itself took part, sometimes—and the uncertainty of both, supplies Prospero's instruction in statecraft—by means of these toys—to his new son, his new heir, Prince Ferdinand. It precedes the Ovidian summary of Prospero's darker "shows," of which the opening scene had given a powerful impression. The darkening of the sun, the stirring up of winds and seas, and the tearing up of forests and shuddering of rocks crams more imagined action into a dozen lines than we are given in the rest of the play. The awesome and ominious power flashes a current back through the storms of *King Lear*, through Glendower to Oberon. It is, of course, a straight translation from Ovid, and it is written as an abdication of the power now invoked for the last time—the power to wield Jove's thunderbolt. The actor, the author and director, is absolved—at least he asks absolution—in the final epilogue, in the flat archaic language of Gower in *Pericles*, and something in the posture of Alonso appealing to Prospero.

The devil's chapel of the theatre (so its early opponents had termed it)[22] had been replaced by a scene at the court of a double new-joined kingdom, where royalty itself would enact the shows, as well as receiving the offerings, where the actors were royal servants. Ariel is out of his apprenticeship;[23] Prospero, though with a large area left unspoken in spectacle and song, in this last play closed his series. But it led forward to others, by other men. This epilogue raises the curtain on the drama—and the poetry—of modern times.

NOTES

1. This and subsequent quotations of *The Tempest* are from Frank Kermode's New Arden edition (London, 5th ed., 1954), 1.2.424–25.
2. Tmp. 5.1.243–44. For the "maze" see 3.3.2; a word used by Milton in *Comus*.
3. George Puttenham, *The Arte of Poesie*, ed. G. D. Willcock and A. Walker (Cambridge, England, 1936), 19.
4. *John a Kent and John a Cumber, Wyly Beguiled, Grim the Collier of Croydon, Friar Bacon and Friar Bungay*, and *The Old Wives' Tale; The Rare Triumphs of Love and Fortune* has a number of additional likenesses.
5. An antic comes out of a tree "if possible it may be" in *John a Kent*. William Percy, in *The Faery Pastoral*, gives a full description of how this property worked; here it has faded to something remembered. In the masque of Ceres, on

the other hand, some materials and dances from court performance may have been used again.

6. Neville Coghill, *Shakespeare's Professional Skills* (Cambridge, England, 1964), 41–60.

7. *John a Kent and John a Cumber*, ll. 530–31, quoted in Coghill, 44.

8. William Strachey, in his *True Reportory*, extracts from which are reprinted in the New Arden edition of the play, Appendix A; quotation on p. 137. The islands were uninhabited. Compare the sense of providential felicity in the poem "Bermudas" by Andrew Marvell, quoted below. Marvell's nephew Popple was Governor there; Marvell, as a tutor himself at John Oxenbridge's house, might have heard of the islands which Oxenbridge knew.

9. Sylvester Jourdain, *A Discovery of the Bermudas* (1610), quoted in ed. cit., p. 141.

10. Lines by Milton prefixed to the Second Folio.

11. Enid Welsford makes this point in *The Court Masque* (Cambridge, England, 1927), 133ff.

12. See A. M. Nagler, *Shakespeare's Stage* (New Haven, 1958), 100.

13. During the sea storm (1.1) and the clowns' scene (2.2) there is thunder; the voice of Ariel's warning may have sounded to Sebastian like the "hollow burst of bellowing" he speaks of (2.1.306); and again, in contrast with the soft music of the mock banquet (3.3.82), sounds strike Alonso fearfully (3.3.95–102).

14. Andrew Marvell, "Bermudas," in *Poems*, ed. H. M. Margoliouth (Oxford, 1927), 17. The luscious fruit that offers itself is detailed at length. See below.

15. W. H. Auden, "The Sea and the Mirror," in *For the Time Being* (London, 1945), 29.

16. The following passage is adapted from my British Academy Annual Shakespeare Lecture for 1965, "Shakespeare's Primitive Art," *Proceedings of the British Academy*, 51 (London, 1966), 232–33.

17. Providence is a powerful force in Marvell's poem on the Bermudas and was perhaps from the first invoked to explain the happy wreck. The order of the play is, of course, a pattern of providential control.

18. "Bermudas" in Margoliouth's edition of *Poems*, 17.

19. Yeats used it in his *Deirdre* tragically. Chess was a recognized form of "commoning" for young and noble courtiers.

20. Auden, "The Sea and the Mirror," ed. cit., 10.

21. "The Sea and the Mirror," ed. cit., 9, 14, 15.

22. William Rankin's *Mirror of Monsters* (1587) most fully developed the analogy of the Devil's Chapel—with papal images—being in the Theatre.

23. Young actors were serving an apprenticeship by now, and must have been pleased to be out of their time to their masters. Ariel would presumably have been played by someone's hopeful apprentice.

The Day of *The Tempest*[*]

JOHN B. BENDER

Pagan Halloween marking the end summer and the onset of winter, Christian Hallowmas inaugurating the Christmas season, ceremonial dramatics typified by court masques at Epiphany and Candlemas all refer in their distinctive ways to adjustments in mental perspective that occur as human imagination and desire annually confront winter, the season of death. To interpret *The Tempest* as an anatomy of this pervasive seasonal mentality—that is the project of this essay—is to employ criticism as a bridge between the profound emotions the play arouses and our comprehension of them. Such explication of *The Tempest*'s seasonal ceremonial status, far from trivializing the play by confining it to a single occasion, describes broad currents of meaning that account for its enduring power even among audiences in whom modernity has dimmed the awareness of what matters about the seasons. Although the present study has its inevitable archaeological features, its justification is to lend intellectual substance to the feeling, nurtured by many and for long, that this play is among Shakespeare's most profound—which is to say, one of the highest products of human endeavor.

What notable implications emerge from close attention to the day when *The Tempest* first appeared at court—November 1, that is All Saints' or Hallowmas, of the year 1611?[1] This is the question in its simplest form: what might the performance of *this play* on *this day* signify? The question assumes no more than the documentary fact that gives rise to it. We do not know that the premiere took place at court, though probably the recorded performance was a very early one. Nor do we know that the play was composed or altered for this occasion, though revisions were common for such appearances. We do not know that the King's Men ever presented a play composed uniquely for

*John B. Bender, "The Day of The Tempest," originally published in *ELH* 47 (1980): 235–258. © 1980 The Johns Hopkins University Press. Reprinted by permission.

the court, and so spectators at the Globe or Blackfriars have to be kept in view. On the other hand, the evidence allows us to speculate that when *Bartholomew Fair* was tried out at a public theatre on October 31, 1614 and then performed at court the next night it may well have followed the same pattern as *The Tempest* three years before.[2]

Thus warned, let us suppose that the date of the original court performance is meaningful—whether as the occasion for which the play was conceived or as one for which it was thought appropriate. Let us explore the interpretative consequences of reading *The Tempest* as Shakespeare's encounter with a ceremonial occasion in the annual cycle of holidays, and as his meditation on the scriptural liturgy of a seasonal Anglican feast. As C. L. Barber has shown, seasonal customs are so deeply embedded in some of Shakespeare's earlier comedies that the plays evoke the ethos of particular seasons. The date of a known performance, like a tag or title, can serve as a clue giving access to the play's inner life. Thanks to Barber, the festivities associated with the Lords of Misrule during the May-games and the Twelve Days, though not at Hallowmas of which he makes no mention, have been recognized as among the sources of mimetic energy that underlie Shakespeare's romantic comedies. Whatever the minute particulars, the idea that the festive or carnival spirit undergoes a dramatic reincarnation in these plays remains correct in general outline. And once Barber has helped us to recognize Falstaff as a holiday type, we can catch the implications of Hal's epithets as plump Jack leaves Poins to reason the Prince into joining the robbers at Gad's Hill. Like Indian or Allhallown summer, Falstaff is an "old fat man" out of season, a winter Lord of Misrule and indoor feasting who seeks to enjoy summer's last youthful warmth out-of-doors by moonlight: "Farewell, the latter spring! Farewell, All-hallown summer!" (*1 Henry IV*, 1.2 154–55).[3]

II. HALLOWMAS, THE CHRISTMAS REVELS, AND THE SCRIPTURES FOR ALL SAINTS'

Shakespeare clearly delineates Hallowmas as the feast of winter and contracting daylight when he characterizes Isabel toward the end of *Richard II*: "She came adorned hither like sweet May, / Sent back like Hollowmas or short'st of day" (5.1.79–80). The festivities gathered about Hallowmas are the symmetrical opposites of the May-games in the calendrical cycle. At both major seasonal junctures chaos temporarily breaks loose and the reign of established authority gives way for a time to supernatural powers symbolized by fairies, goblins, wandering souls and witches. Halloween, the night before Hallowmas, presages the cold, dark, short days of winter—the season of death and indoor confinement—as opposed to the green out-of-doors world of summer warmth, long light, and youthful fecundity. Hallowmas itself became a solemn day for praising all of the saints—tangible presentments of God's

power on earth—and for anticipating the Last Judgment. It figures forth a
sense of last chances, a sense of endings, for it was the time of the ancient
Celtic New Year. In Anglican sequence, it is the last special feast before the
liturgical cycle begins afresh with Advent, a season with which it came to have
vital associations.[4]

As the reign of James continued toward its apogee shortly before the
death of Prince Henry, the Christmas revels expanded into Lent on the one
flank and reached on the other to Hallowmas or All Saints' Day, the first of
November. Hallowmas traditionally marked the beginning of winter and was
the earliest legitimate starting point for the festivities accompanying Christmas. Accordingly, during James's reign the King's habitual return to residence
at Whitehall was often celebrated by a play. On November 1, 1611 that play
was *The Tempest*, and King James was present to witness it: "By the Kings
Players: Hallowmas nyght was presented att Whithall before y[e] Kinges Ma[tie]
a play called the Tempest."[5]

Even today persistent yuletide pageants, pantomimes and, for that matter,
the *Nutcracker*'s ceremonial recurrence, exist to stimulate our intuition of the
spirit that caused the Christmas Revels to be the festive high point of the
Jacobean winter season, indeed of the whole court year. The relatively commonplace idea that plays may replace individual ritual celebration or seasonal
games is confirmed by our own experience of anticipation and festive release
in the theatre. We do not go to see just any ballet because it is Christmas; the
ritual aspect is emphasized in the fact that it must be the *Nutcracker* every
year. Typically the twelve days of Jacobean Christmas overflowed with plays
at Whitehall, and after the culmination of a masque on or about Epiphany, the
plays spilled well into January. The Christmas Revels of 1608/09 called forth
twenty-three plays at court, in the midst of which Twelfth Night would have
been celebrated by the lavish splendors of the *Masque of Queens* but for a
postponement until Candlemas for reasons of diplomacy.[6]

In the political realm Hallowmas was naturally felt as an occasion to
transfer authority or to reaffirm its validity and presence. Therefore, it was the
last day on which both the old and the new Lord Mayors of London rode
together ceremonially. At the beginning of winter, following upon the night of
Halloween disorder, "both the Maiors weare their Veluet Hoods: but all Saints
day is the last day that the old Maior rideth with the new." It was also the first
of seven days of the year—all during the Christmas season and ending with
Candlemas—when the "Companies or Fellowships" attended in formal rank
upon the Lord Mayor "at his going to *Pauls*."[7] Such a day was obviously right
for King James's ritual return to establish winter court at Whitehall. Further,
just as it was a time for governmental authority to show itself, it was the occasion for the powers of chaos, demonic grotesquerie, and misrule that had been
unleashed on Halloween the night before, during the hiatus between the seasons, to be socialized, sanctioned, and assigned a formal place in the order of

things. Hallowmas was the first full day of the reign of the winter Lord of Misrule; here is the account from Stow's *Survay*:

> In the feast of Christmas, there was in the kings house, wheresoeuer he was lodged, a Lord of Misrule, or Master of merry disports, and the like had yee in the house of euery Noble-man of honour, or good worship, where he spiritual or temporall. Amongst the which, the Maior of *London*, and either of the Sheriffes had their seuerall Lords of Misrule, euer contending without quarrell or offence, who should make the rarest pastimes to delight the beholders. These Lords beginning their rule on Alhallon Eue, continued the same til the morrow after the Feast of the Purification commonly called, *Candlemas* day: In all which space, there were fine and subtill disguisings, Maskes and Mummeries. (Stowe, 149)

Such was the commitment of authority to these revels, which were also practiced at the Inns of Court, that at Gray's Inn under Henry VIII "there was an order made, that all the fellows . . . who should be present upon any Saturday at supper, betwixt the feasts of All Saints' and the Purification of our Lady; or upon any other day, at dinner or supper, when there are *revels*, should not depart out of the hall until the said *revels* were ended, upon the penalty of 12d."[8] Revelry could thus verge upon being a legal requirement; certainly the indoor revels of winter could be kept under closer watch than the out-of-door rites of May and Midsummer.

The popular customs of the Christian feasts that parenthetically enclose the Christmas season, as well as those of the Twelve Days proper, had an inextinguishably pagan flavor, though in England the paganism of Hallowmas or All Saints' Day was probably as much British as Roman. That the "Grand Christmas" was pagan from beginning to end William Prynne would show at tireless length, with citations to Polydore Virgil and other authorities. Says Prynne,

> Our Christmas Lords of misrule . . . together with dancing, Masques, Mummeries, Stage-players, and such other Christmas disorders now in use with Christians, were derived from these Roman Saturnalia, and Bacchanalian festivals; which should cause all pious Christians eternally to abominate them. If any here demaund, by whom . . . these disorderly Christmasses & Stageplayes were first brought in among the Christians? I answer that the paganizing Priests and Monks. . . were the cheife Agents in this worke: . . . they borrowed their Feast of All-Saints, from the heathen festival Pantheon; and then the feast of the Purification of the Virgin Mary, (which they have christned with the name of Candlemasse) from the festivall of the Goddesse Februa, the mother of Mars; to whom the Pagan Romans offered burning tapers. . . .[9]

Overstatement is Prynne's metier and Rome his obsession, but in general he is right. The Church had sought to Christianize pagan celebrations rather than setting the new feasts entirely apart and honoring them in distinctive ways (as Prynne and other Puritans would have liked).

All Saints' and All Souls' on the first two days of November "preserved at or near the original date one part of the old beginning-of-winter festival—the part concerned with the cult of the dead."[10] The Reformation left the English Church without All Souls', but it was partially assimilated to All Saints', the day before, and popular customs surrounding the cult of the dead survived. Although the pagan festivals ending summer and beginning winter could not be fully Christianized, the Church could respond to the seasonal pattern of emotions that engendered them. In Shakespeare's time the *Book of Common Prayer* set down for ordinary days a cycle of scriptural readings that systematically proclaimed virtually the entire Bible to parishioners each year. Omitted from the Old Testament were "certain books and chapters, which be least edifying," and, from the New Testament, the Apocalypse, "out of the which there be only certain Lessons appointed upon divers proper feasts." The Psalms were read from beginning to end each month starting with Morning Prayer on the first day and ending with Evening Prayer on the last. Feast days broke the cycle of scriptures (other than Psalms) in favor of specially chosen texts.[11]

The passages selected to honor the Anglican feast of All Saints' emphasized the reassertion or resurrection of God-given authority after its apparent demise during the chaotic explosion of disorder the night before. Contrasting the human perspective to the divine, they dwelt on the meaning of death and on the Last Judgment—particularly on the notion that the righteous dead shall miraculously confront those who despised them and shall be the instruments of judgment. It was one of only two days on which passages from the Apocalypse were read. These texts preach the verity of moral absolutes amid the confusion of daily existence, and the providential movement of natural forces. They assert that lives have final meanings, summary moments, last chances. They are scriptures, but from a literary point of view they are essentially Romantic: the literary consequence of their world-view is what we call Romance. Entirely consonant with the perspective of the All Saints' scriptures is *The Tempest*'s "Providence divine," which offers Prospero a unique chance to astonish enemies who thought him dead, to gain power over them, and to recoup a kingdom—meanwhile learning for himself the meaning of death without actually suffering it.

Anyone who awoke from Halloween night and went to chapel in England the morning of All Saints', 1611, would have heard a reading specified from the *Wisdom of Solomon*, 3:[12]

> But the soules of the righteous are in the hand of God, and there shall no torment touch them. *In the sight of the vnwise they seemed to die*: and their departure is taken for misery, And their going from vs to be vtter destruction:

but they are in peace. For though they bee punished in the sight men: yet is their hope full of immortalitie. *And hauing bene a little chastised, they shalbe greatly rewarded.... But the ungodly shalbe punished according to their owne imaginations*, which haue neglected the righteous, and forsaken the Lord. *For who so despiseth wisedome, and nurture, he is miserable*, and their hope is vaine, their labours vnfruitfull, and their works vnprofitable.

At Evening Prayer readings continued from the *Wisdom of Solomon*, 5:

Then shal the righteous man stand in great boldness, before face of such as haue afflicted him.... When they see it, they shalbe troubled with terrible feare, & shall be amazed at the strangenesse of his saluation, so farre beyond all that they looked for. *And they repenting, and groning for anguish of spirit*, shall say within themselues, This was he whom wee had sometimes in derision, and a prouerbe of reproch. We fooles accounted his life madnes, and his end to be without honour.... *We have gone through deserts, where there lay no way:* but as for the way of the Lord, we haue not knowen it. What hath pride profited vs? or what good hath riches with our vaunting brought vs? All those things are passed away like a shadow, and as a Poste that hasted by. *And as a ship that passeth ouer the waues of the water, which when it is gone by, the trace thereof cannot bee found:* neither the path way of the keele in the waues. Or when a bird hath flowen thorow the aire, there is no token of her way to be found, *but the light aire being beaten with the stroke of her wings, and parted with the violent noise and motion of them, is passed thorow, and therein afterwards no signe where she went, is to be found....* For the hope of the ungodly is like the dust that is blowen away with ye wind, like a thinne froth that is driuen away with ye storme: *like as the smoke which is dispersed here and there with a tempest, and passeth away as the remembrance a guest that tarieth but a day.* But the righteous liue for euermore.... Therefore shall they receiue a glorious kingdome, & a beautiful crowne from the Lords hande.

Temporality and finality, recognition and reversal, these are the cognates and the dominant tonality of the day. Although in the end Prospero leaves the awful burdens of vengeance to God, he revels, like these scriptural voices, in the pleasure of vindication occasioned by higher authority and contemplates vengeance as the comic denouement of a suffering existence. The point of view he shares with them is fundamentally paradoxical and tragicomic.

Psalm 149, selected for special repetition as the introit at Anglican Holy Communion on All Saints', represents the simplest possible distillation of this paradoxical sense of joy issuing out of a tragic past and out of the suffering of others—a form so schematic that the day's other Old Testament scriptures themselves constitute a substantial refinement of it.

Let the children of Zion bee ioyfull in their King. Let them praise his Name in the dance: let them sing praises vnto him with the timbrell and harpe. Lord taketh pleasure in his people: hee will beautifie the meeke with saluation. Let the Saints be ioyfull in glory: let them sing aloude vpon their beddes. Let the high praises of God be in their mouth: and a two edged sword in their hand: To execute vengeance vpon the heathen: and punishments vpon the people. To binde their Kings with chaines: and their Nobles with fetters of yron. To execute vpon them the iudgement written.

While the the *Book of Common Prayer* did not explicitly recognize All Souls' the next day, the Catholic feast reflecting the pagan day of the dead must have influenced the choice of scriptures from the Apocalypse for English All Saints'. The readings from Revelations at both evening prayer and Holy Communion are explicit reminders that this is a season of judgment, even though caution was necessary concerning the purgatorial implications of All Souls'.

Many scriptures for All Saints' remained the same in the English service as in the Roman, and though some were permanently dropped at the Reformation, one of the Psalms in the Catholic service provided such an exemplary summation of the day's scriptural atmosphere that it eventually crept back into the modern Anglican readings. While banished from the official Jacobean liturgy, to numbers of Shakespeare's audience—especially at court—it must yet have retained distinct associations with All Saints':

> The Lord raigneth, let the earth reioyce: *let the multitude of Isles bee glad thereof. Clouds and darkenesse are round about him:* righteousnesse and judgement are the habitation of his throne. *A fire goeth before him:* and burneth vp his enemies round about. His lightnings inlightned the world: the earth sawe, and trembled. . . . The heauens declaure his righteousnesse: and all the people see his glory. Confounded be all they that serue grauen images, that boast themselues of idoles: worship him all yee gods. (Psalm 97)

An epitome of the texts for All Saints', this great Psalm of Judgment Day scorifies the errant perpetrators of mere human, mischief in language at once apocalyptic, like that of the Old Testament scriptures quoted above, and full of joyful promise like that of the New Testament gospels.

Indeed, one scriptural passage from the Anglican Holy Communion on All Saints' stands in strongest possible contrast to the wrathful, authoritarian aspect of the day's other readings. It is the beginning of the Sermon on the Mount:

> Blessed are the poore in spirit: for theirs is the kingdome of heuen. Blessed are they that mourne: for they shall be comforted. Blessed are the meeke: for they shall inherit the earth. . . . Blessed are the mercifull: for they shall obtaine mercie. Blessed are the pure of heart: for they shall see God. Blessed are the peacemakers: for they shall bee called the children of God. Blessed are they which are persecuted for righteousnesse sake: for theirs is the kingdome of heuen. (Matthew 5)

Frank Kermode, the Arden editor, finds allusions to the Sermon on the Mount both in Prospero's climactic "revels" speech (4.1.154) and in his lines commencing the denouement: "the rarer action is / In virtue than in vengeance" (5.1.27–28). In Prospero, *The Tempest* posits a character whose supernatural powers and contradictory aspects savor as much of Judeo-Christian divinity as dramatic credibility will allow. The opposite poles of his quasi-divinity are set forth by the Hallowmas scriptures. Intimations that he is a "god of power" give him a special place among Shakespeare's heroes. The storm displays his elemental Jehovah-like wrath, and the middle of the play shows a balance of human traits with god-like omniscience. Only in the end does Prospero embrace simple humanity.

Yet I do not find the significance of these scriptures for *The Tempest* specifically religious: neither Judaic wrath, nor Christian redemption, nor their combination in apocalyptic eschatology, seems to me central to this play. The language of these religious modes figures throughout, but in service of a fundamentally secular world view. Their fields cross with those of many other polarities in the arena where human life takes form: white and black magic, virtue and vengeance, innocence and corruption, reverie and reality, wisdom and folly, youth and age, humanity and bestiality, sobriety and drunkenness, nature and supernature, humanity and divinity, rule and misrule, authority and liberty.

Shakespeare seems to take the absolutes of the Old and New Testament scriptures as radical opposites, even as fantasies, that cannot be realized in human life except perhaps at transcendent moments. Prospero's psychological three-dimensionality is sustained by his life near the center crossing of such opposite forces. All other characters in the play gravitate to this or that pole. Even the prudent Gonzalo ends with a summary of the action in which specific happy truths billow into a fantasy of general redemption.

> O, rejoice
> Beyond a common joy! and set it down
> With gold on lasting pillars: in one voyage
> Did Claribel her husband find at Tunis,
> And Ferdinand, her brother, found a wife
> Where he himself was lost, Prospero his dukedom
> In a poor isle, and all of us ourselves
> When no man was his own. (5.1.206–13)

The echo here of the fortunate fall (*felix culpa*) suggests an affinity between Gonzalo's sudden access of joy and salvation, but his fervent allusiveness provides no licence to reduce the play to a Christian allegory.

What I look to, then, is not so much the doctrinal content of the Hallowmas readings as their way of imagining men's relationships to one another, to authority, to nature, and to the finality of death. Although I cannot prove it, I postulate that these scriptures were chosen as communal responses to a recurrent seasonal mentality. The Celtic New Year figuratively embodies this same anxiety, and so do other ancient holidays not specifically relevant to *The Tempest*. To the Church of England, All Saints' Day was the name of this seasonal juncture. The more popular name used to be Hallowmas. While the word "hallow" means "holy" or "sainted" in Shakespeare's English, its etymology yields such meanings as "healthy," "whole," "complete," "full." These, of course, are the qualities of saints under the eye of eternity. They are also conditions to which humanity aspires while surviving the threatening winter season on earth, and which it hopes to attain during the season of fecundity that culminates at harvest. The Sermon on the Mount, the Psalms, Saints' Lives, and Romances are literary constructs for assuring us that human attainment within the seasonal cycle is stable and not merely ephemeral—or even illusory as Spenser's character Mutabilitie wrongly argues. In a religious matrix the promise is salvation. The literary matrix provides Gonzalo's romantic "set it down / With gold on lasting pillars" (5.1.205–13). *The Tempest* lets us join Ferdinand, Miranda, and Gonzalo in nurturing such hopes, but ends requesting our applause for a Prospero who has accepted the contradictions of mere humanity. If, like Alonso, we "long / To hear the story" of Prospero's former life (5.1.311–14), we remain "confin'd" with him in a Romantic fiction.

III. *THE TEMPEST* AT HALLOWMAS

Read as a play for Hallowmas, *The Tempest* becomes a conjuration against winter, a miniature reenactment of the annual endeavor to countermand the cold, dark, fearful out-of-doors through indoor revels. To the Renaissance, tempest-tossed ships were emblems of Fortune or Providence operating through Nature, but tempests are much more obviously and simply symbols of winter. In emblems and proverbs these ships were piloted by the Prudent or Temperate man caught making for port in autumn: "November take flail, let ships no more sail."[13] The play may be taken as a surrogate for ceremonials, charms or rites; the threatening season can be brought under human control through mimesis on the stage—an indoor stage since this was the time of year when players had to abandon their outdoor summer houses on the Bankside in favor of "enclosed space," just as the King and his court returned to Whitehall from the sports of the summer Royal Progress and the autumn hunts. *The Tempest* itself shifts from a beginning that might have suited a typical panoramic Shakespearean play to a firm assertion of the more studied Italianate unities appropriate indoors. It opens with an emblematic storm-driven ship and its center piece is a masque that seeks to realize the age-old human wish to omit winter from the calendar, while its denouement opposes summer to winter and equates emergence from the action with sailing in fair weather.

Prospero, in one respect, is a dramatic personification of our yearning to dominate nature through mimetic charms. Like his control of natural forces, his reign over human affections seems, for a time, providential. He nurtures love and regulates hate—so much of fantasy Shakespeare grants us through him. Indeed, Prospero's plot of vengeance against Antonio may be deflected into Alonso's conversion precisely because the grieving king fits the fantasy ideal whereas the traitorous brother does not. But death and human malevolence remain Prospero's obsessions, and though they are contained by fear of him and mocked by comedy, the intimation of death haunts the play to its end.

A similar ambivalence lives in the structure of celebration at the seasonal juncture of Hallowmas. As one looks back on autumn and summer and forward toward winter, anxiety and doubt take the shape of spirits, dubious in origin, reigning out-of-doors, and the future becomes a question. And so the strongest ritual impulses of the old Halloween were toward divinations about deaths to come during the imminent winter, and about marriages to follow in the next season of fertility. This is very ancient. The pagan feasts of the dead, including the Celtic New Year, became All Souls' (November 2) under the Catholic Church, and survived the English Reformation in the popular custom of baking and eating soul-cakes for the dead on the eve of the old Catholic feast. On Hallowmas, Prospero's "Every third thought shall be my grave" would have to be taken as an allusion to All Souls' and to customs predicting death. The other obsession, which perhaps enjoys a preponderance of entries in Brand's *Popular Antiquities*, is for maidens to discover omens about marriage—to divine the nature, shape or identity of their husbands to be, or even to see apparitions of their future spouses. We recall Miranda, who begins thinking her future husband, Ferdinand, "carries a brave form. But 'tis a spirit" (1.2.414), and persists in believing him an apparition—"for nothing natural / I ever saw so noble" (1.2.421–22)—even when Prospero has declared him to be human. Although Prospero mistreats Ferdinand, "lest too light winning / Make the prize light" (1.2.454–55), almost at once he announces his daughter's engagement to us in an aside. Ferdinand is a true apparition and also the real thing. The opposites of Hallowmas temporarily shift into balance during the masque for Ferdinand and Miranda, but, seething with echoes of the tragedies, the play as a whole is somber in tonality and Prospero's spectacle is cut off by the threat of murder. Shakespeare's imagination seems even more deeply enmeshed in Prospero's emotional and intellectual struggle with mortality than in Miranda's innocent promise of fecundity, generational renewal, and political stability. The ancient Celtic festivals contemplate these two perspectives more equally. Many possibilities for drama, of course, inhered in this holiday. Shakespeare distilled a peculiar extract of the winter mood that reached an intensity far beyond the demands of the occasion itself. Consider what a different catalyst the same holiday proved to Ben Jonson three years later when—evidently—he wrote *Bartholomew Fair* anticipating performance at court on Hallowmas.[14]

In *The Tempest*, the masque which constitutes Prospero's wedding gift to his children at first seems to strike a sunnier mood. It unfurls a pageant of the seasons which begins when Iris summons Ceres from the "banks with pioned and twilled brims, / Which spongy April at thy hest betrims," and proceeds from the "pole-clipt vineyard" of spring on through summer, to envision a fecundity that entirely passes over winter:

> Vines with clust'ring bunches growing;
> Plants with goodly burthen bowing;
> Spring come to you at the farthest
> In the very end of harvest! (4.1.112–15)

The moment invoked for the coming of spring, "the very end of harvest," would have been exactly the time of dramatic action in the real present when Prospero's masque was given on Hallowmas. On the other hand, the play taken as a whole presents the winter omitted from the masque: It begins with a tempest, and its central figure is a man in the late autumn or early winter of life.

Shakespeare has given explicit dramatic shape to those opposites present in Hallowmas itself. It is the season of short days and black vestments, but also when the court begins stately revels that are the antidote to winter; the time when nature is laid to chilly rest after Halloween chaos, but also one anticipating the festivities around the Advent of Christ. Divinations concerning death are its winter side, those concerning marriage and fertility its hope for spring. *The Tempest* as a whole is dominated by Prospero, Gonzalo, and Alonzo—by middle and old age symbolized even in Prospero's masque by the appearance of authoritative Juno. But the masque, like rites of divination, leaps time through imagination: from the stylized "grass plot" of green baize appropriate to indoor courtly dancing and revels during winter[15] to a formalized enactment of the spring and summer seasons when "this short-grass'd green" becomes "this green land"; when the young disport themselves, as in *A Midsummer Night's Dream*, with "demi-puppets that / By moonshine do the green sour ringlets make" (5.1.36–37). Prospero interrupts the masque just when Iris has invoked the "temperate Nymphs" and "sunburn'd sicklemen, of August weary," and just when "certain Reapers . . . join with the Nymphs in a graceful dance." Summer is giving way to the harvest merriment that precedes Hallowmas when Prospero's memory of Caliban's conspiracy plunges us back into the main action (equated in the play with reality) and back into the frame of winter. Once Prospero has put down Caliban's grotesque conspiracy, he will encounter Ariel's picture of the old Gonzalo, whose "tears runs down his beard, like winter's drops / From eaves of reeds" (5.1.16–17).[16] Earlier, before this approach to the limits of despair, Gonzalo's vision of spontaneous plenty in his ideal commonwealth had implied continuous warmth (2.1.143–64); and

Ariel himself, while dressing Prospero as Duke for the final scene, lyricizes the freedom he presently will gain as a pursuit of perpetual summer:

> Where the bee sucks, there suck I:
> In a cowslip's bell I lie;
> There I couch when owls do cry.
> On the bat's back I do fly
> After summer merrily.
> Merrily, merrily shall I live now
> Under the blossom that hangs on the bough. (5.1.88–94)

The counterposition of winter and spring, itself a commonplace, of course makes its debut much earlier in Shakespeare's career. *Love's Labour's Lost*, for example, ends with contrasting rustic personifications singing the chants of their seasonal birds: "This side is *Hiems*, Winter, this *Ver*, the Spring; the one maintained by the owl, the other by the cuckoo" (5.2.881–83). This conflict may once have been resolved at court in an epilogue that takes the Queen as muse of an orderly temporality and a productive seasonal cycle.

> As the diall hand tells ore/
> yᵉ same howers yt had before
> still beginning in yᵉ ending/
> circuler account still lending
> So most mightie Q. we pray/
> like yᵉ diall day by day
> you may lead yᵉ seasons on/
> making new when old are gon.[17]

In *A Midsummer Night's Dream*, a labyrinthine interchange of seasons arises from Oberon's and Titania's quarrel over precedence:

> And thorough this distemperature, we see
> The seasons alter: hoary-headed frosts
> Fall in the fresh lap of the crimson rose,
> And on old Hiems' thin and icy crown
> An odorous chaplet of sweet summer buds
> Is, as in mockery, set; the spring, the summer,
> The chiding autumn, angry winter, change
> Their wonted liveries; and the maz'd world,
> By their increase, now knows not which is which.
> And this same progeny of evils comes
> From our debate, from our dissension;
> We are their parents and original. (2.1.106–17)

Titania describes effects on the whole of Nature and human society, whereas Prospero's seasonal dislocations seem confined to an artificial span of revels at his daughter's betrothal. But the seasonal transformations that figure in the masque extend to every fiber of *The Tempest*, and apart from the storm which sets the play's seasonal frame, the masque is the most concentrated manifestation of Prospero's conjuration that we are called upon to witness. It inevitably reminds us that when Prospero was "transported / And rapt in secret studies" in Milan, studies which culminate in the storm and the masque, he occasioned Antonio's usurpation and his own exile to supposed death at sea. By interrupting the masque with Prospero's recollection of Caliban's "foul conspiracy," which itself parallels Antonio's, Shakespeare articulates this point. He then restates it by cutting summer short in Prospero's spectacle of masquing and exchanging it for a reverie on the transience of such diversions and the inexorability of death.

> Our revels now are ended. These our actors,
> As I foretold you, were all spirits, and
> Are melted into air, into thin air:
> And, like the baseless fabric of this vision,
> The cloud-capp'd towers, the gorgeous palaces,
> The solemn temples, the great globe itself,
> Yea, all which it inherit, shall dissolve,
> And, like this insubstantial pageant faded,
> Leave not a rack behind. We are such stuff
> As dreams are made on; and our little life
> Is rounded with a sleep. (4.1.148–58)

His prior reverie of "study" in Milan led from a library that "was dukedom large enough" to "a rotten carcass of a butt" which, furnished out by Gonzalo with "rich garments, linens, stuffs and . . . from mine own library with volumes that I prize above my dukedom," became Prospero's microcosmic second realm. "By Providence divine" the island became his third, a realm of dream fantasy that he will exchange—upon drowning his prized Book—for renewed ducal sway in Milan.

Library, butt, island: all are surrogates. The seasonal incompleteness of the masque shows that their romantic attractiveness is still alive to Prospero; his awakening shows that he realizes their partiality. The "revels" speech exhales such a perfume of bitter nostalgia that it has to be considered part of a recurrent threefold pattern which runs: fantasy, rude awakening, reverie. Prospero's study, his Art, and his fantasies of winterless fecundity appear to occasion ever reenacted conspiracy. Disorderly action is an effect rather than a cause. Prospero's reign is the obverse image of Titania's realm in which distemperature, seasonal dislocation, and fantasy arise from her dissension with Oberon. The action of the play, like its weather, is the tangible presentment of Prospero's mentality. When Prospero orders his own mind, he also redirects the ensuing action and ultimately establishes "calm seas, auspicious gales, and sail so expeditious that shall catch / Your royal fleet far off" (5.1.314–16). At that distant point in the Mediterranean, Prospero will rejoin the normal cycle of seasons, accept natural weather, and bring his newly ordered mind fully to bear on old realities. Ariel will "then to the elements," that is, to his free quest of perpetual summer.

When Prospero renounces magic, he invokes the "elves" and "demi-puppets"

> by whose aid—
> Weak masters though ye be—I have bedimm'd
> The noontide sun, call'd forth the mutinous winds,
> And 'twixt the green sea and the azur'd vault
> Set roaring war: to the dread rattling thunder
> Have I given fire, and rifted Jove's stout oak
> With his own bolt; the strong-bas'd promontory
> Have I made shake, and by the spurs pluck'd up
> The pine and cedar: graves at my command
> Have wak'd their sleepers, op'd, and let 'em forth
> By my so potent Art. (5.1.40–50)

Scholars have blessed many features of Prospero's magic as white, but this speech rejecting it is based directly on Medea's in Golding's Ovid. Such magic was no less black in Jacobean times than in Ovid's: under the witchcraft act of 1604 it was a capital crime to raise the dead.[18] Though possibly caught up in a frenzy of rejection in this speech, Prospero clearly stigmatizes himself as a witch who has distorted the frame of nature much as it is distorted on Halloween. Yet whether his magic was white or black is less important than his rejection of it as invalid. Viewed here as an instrument of "vengeance" rather than "virtue," it is incompatible with the mantle of authority he is about to reassume. He must abjure it to be Duke of Milan. In this respect, the cycle of his life mirrors the alternations of the seasonal year through authoritarian phases, festive abandon, and fresh dominion. Shakespeare displays a hero poised at the juncture that Hallowmas epitomizes in seasonal terms.

Shakespeare naturally characterizes so vital a juncture in other terms as well. To the same end, Prospero's famous speech to Ariel just before his renunciation of magic employs some other Renaissance commonplaces:

> Though with their high wrongs I am struck to th' quick,
> Yet with my nobler reason 'gainst my fury
> Do I take part: the rarer action is
> In virtue than in vengeance: they being penitent,
> The sole drift of my purpose doth extend
> Not a frown further. (5. 1. 25–30)

This speech has given some unnecessary trouble over the years, though we know that it is based on a passage in Montaigne's essay "Of Crueltie":

> Me thinkes vertue is another manner of thing, and *much more noble* than the inclinations vnto goodnesse, which in vs are ingendered. Mindes well borne, and directed by themselves, follow one same path, and in their actions represent the same visage, that the vertuous doe. But vertue importeth, and soundeth somewhat I wot not what greater and more active, then by an happy complexion, gently and peaceably, to suffer it selfe to be led or drawne, to follow reason. He that through a naturall facilitie & genuine mildnes, should neglect or contemne injuries received, should no doubt performe *a rare action*, and worthy commendation: But he who being *toucht & stung to the quicke*, with any *wrong* or offence received, should arme himselfe with *reason against* this *furiously* blinde desire of *revenge*, and in the end after a great conflict yeeld himselfe maister over-it, should doubtlesse *doe much more*. The first should doe well, the other *vertuously*: the one action might be termed goodnesse, the other *vertue*. For it seemeth, that the very name of vertue presupposeth difficultie, and inferreth resistance, and cannot well exercise it selfe without an enemie. It is peradventure the reason why we call God, good, mighty, liberall and just, but wee terme him not vertuous.[19]

Sources rarely solve all problems, but this passage from Montaigne does help us to see that Shakespeare conceives Prospero as continually governing his own intrinsically unstable nature. Unstable in the sense that a well-ridden, high-spirited thoroughbred is: Prospero's human nobility and virtue are attained through risk, and, for all his God-like attributes, they will have to be reattained over and over again. In him the noble life is itself conceived in a cyclical pattern where attainment implies past and future failure. It differs from tragic nobility, which is linear and defined by death, and from comic nobility which tends to the permanent and generalized. Paradoxically, Shakespeare arrives at something most like real life in this most self-consciously artificial of his plays.

Past and future in the play come together in the concept of Prudence. Traditionally it had three parts: memory, which contemplates the past; intelligence, which studies the present; and foresight or providence which looks to the future.[20] Prudence is the virtue which prevails when St. Augustine's three parts of the soul—memory, understanding, and will—function in proper harmonic balance; it is a dynamic concept that obtains but precariously in real human life. Perhaps it is over-inventive to parallel this topos with the elements of Hallowmas season, but the elements line up neatly and provocatively:

Time	*Prudence*	*Soul*	*Holiday*
Past	Memory	Memory	Halloween
Present	Reason-Intelligence	Understanding	Hallowmas
Future	Foresight-Providence	Will	All Souls'

The Tempest divides past, present, and future as clearly as dramatic art allows. In the past Prospero lost his authority through absorption in supernatural arts; in the present he regains his Dukedom by employing those arts at the apogee of their force—only to abandon them in favor of "nobler reason"; in the future he will contemplate death and final judgment. Having attained Prudence and being an old man, he finds that "Every third thought shall be my grave." This statement is not extreme, nor, as some have thought, is it a renunciation of the active life. Quite the contrary. It expresses Prospero's intention to keep the forces of his spirited mind in temperate balance.

In the Epilogue Prospero enlists our applause to fill his sails and send him back to Naples; this "gentle breath" is presumably one and the same with the "auspicious gales" he mentions in the play's last lines. Both are the favorable winds of All-hallow summer. Prospero's alternative is to "dwell / In this bare island by your spell": that is, to remain in the winter world of the play, and perhaps also on a dark, bare, unwarmed winter stage. The reason we ought to bless him is that he has attained virtue through his own strength, forsaken magic, and proffered mercy. If we do not agree, we declare him one of the "men of sin" and, like Alonso at the end of the Harpy scene, his threatened "ending is despair." That is, like Redcrosse Knight in the Despair episode of *The Faerie Queene* (I.ix), he will have lost all objective sense of how his being relates to absolute moral categories. In such case—if he has not attained "the rarer action" he aspires to as a condition of life—he can only be relieved through the intercession of prayer. Most numerous among the intercessors are the saints, and Hallowmas is their day. Through their "indulgence," souls in Purgatory are "set free."

Two of the sentences that habitually began both Morning and Evening Prayer leap out when considered along with Prospero's "rarer action" upon attaining Prudence:

(1) If we say that we have no sin, we deceive ourselves, and there is no truth in us. (1 John 1)
(2) Correct us, O Lord, and yet in thy judgment, not in thy fury, lest we should be consumed and brought to nothing. (Jerem. 2)

These sentences point up the largest concerns of *The Tempest*: to balance forces that constitute virtue; to judge wisely and to be judged well.[21]

These references to prayer return us, finally, to the scriptural, liturgical, and ritual context of Hallowmas. Prospero makes much of the play's happening in the mid-afternoon, and the Epilogue finishes with his mention of prayer. (Ours presumably is the company's usual acting version; the times, and possibly the Epilogue, probably would have differed at court.) Especially notable in point of clock time is that Evening Prayer in Shakespeare's day took place around four p.m.: that is, during the fictional time of the play and during its real time of enactment in the public theatre.[22] Since an audience at the Globe could not have heard this service in church, *The Tempest* can be imagined as a surrogate for a liturgy unconsciously deemed insufficient to the great seasonal junctures—such as midsummer and the beginning of winter—that demanded superabundant rites. In the case of Hallowmas, these comprehended not only Halloween but pagan customs that had attached themselves to the Catholic All Souls' and continued even after this feast had been officially abandoned at the Reformation. At the Globe the play could conjure the ethos of Hallowmas on any day of the year; any audience can feel this ceremonial impetus without necessarily recognizing the play's thematic appropriateness to its season or its affinities to the liturgy of All Saints'.

At Whitehall, where the Hallowmas audience would have had all of the appointed scriptures fresh in mind from services or from family prayers, the ceremonial ambience of *The Tempest* would have been more literal than at the Globe. When the court inaugurated Christmas on November 1, it anticipated genuine masques in the Jacobean fashion so artfully simulated by Prospero. These were *actual* ceremonies planned to occur on the annual religious feasts of Epiphany and Candlemas and involving fictional pilgrimages to greet a real king who sought to clothe himself in attributes of divinity.[23] Just as *The Tempest* bestows permanent form and universal meaning on ephemeral courtly spectacles that projected James's most ardent hopes for the future of his reign and kingdom, the play refers to the general truths of a liturgy that regulated the present life of its audience, and it reincarnates pagan rituals whose archetypal force survived Britain's most ancient past.

T.S. Eliot wrote *Murder in the Cathedral* for sanctified space, meaning it for churches but also implying that his play instigates a complex of feelings appropriate to such a setting. With this analogue in mind, I imagine *The Tempest* not merely as composed for Hallowmas at court but more broadly as a dramatic *summa* of the rituals, ceremonials, festivities and emotions appropriate to its day and occasion. Rites, ceremonies, and festivals attain meaning through the direct participation of their celebrants. They cannot survive their moment. Drama is vicarious—an imitation or mimesis of action—and so plays not only outlive specific occasions, they may let audiences relive those elusive hours. Again recalling Prospero's "rarer action," let us think of Bacon who says in "Of Ceremonies and Respects": "the occasion of any great vertue, commeth but on holie daies."

NOTES

1. A Study Fellowship from the American Council of Learned Societies provided initial support for my research; the writing accompanied further research while I held a Fellowship at the Huntington Library, where this paper was read in 1977.

I confine the notes to primary texts, to a few Shakespearean studies central
to my own, and to works outside the literary sphere. In particular, I avoid piling
up citations to standard books such as E. K. Chambers's great *Elizabethan
Stage*, 4 vols. (Oxford: Clarendon Press, 1923), on points that I take to be gen-
erally accepted or tangential to the argument. Texts of Shakespeare are from *The
Arden Shakespeare*, in which *The Tempest* is edited by Frank Kermode, 6th ed.
(London: Methuen & Co., 1962); *A Midsummer Night's Dream* is quoted from
The Riverside Shakespeare, ed. G. Blakemore Evans, et al. (Boston: Houghton
Mifflin Co., 1974).

The arguments concerning the customary dating of the play in 1611 are summarized in Kermode's introduction; old doubts about the authenticity of the
Revels Accounts for 1604–1605 and 1611–1612, on which our knowledge of
the Court performance depends, have been resolved by time and by scholarship.
On this point see Kermode, p. xxi; *Elizabethan Stage*, IV, 136–41; and E. K.
Chambers, *William Shakespeare* (Oxford: Clarendon Press, 1930), II, 330–31;
341–42.

2.   On topicality see David Bevington, *Tudor Drama and Politics* (Cambridge,
Mass.: Harvard UP, 1968); and Hallett Smith, *Shakespeare's Romances* (San
Marino, Calif.: Huntington Library, 1972), Appendix B, pp. 211–21. *The Tempest* is one of Shakespeare's few spontaneous dramatic inventions, and links to
accounts of the Virginia Plantation dating from 1609–10 suggest that its immediate inspiration may have been topical. Most likely, it is no coincidence that the
two other sourceless comedies, *Love's Labour's Lost* and *A Midsummer Night's
Dream*, also appear to be courtly, topical, and seasonal—nor that each of them
also contains a failed play within the play.

3.   Barber eloquently distinguishes between ceremony and drama when he says
that the Renaissance "was a moment when educated men were modifying a ceremonial conception of human life to create a historical conception. The ceremonial view, which assumed that names and meanings are fixed and final,
expressed experience as pageant and ritual—pageant where the right names
could march in proper order, or ritual where names could be changed in the
right, the proper way. The historical view expresses life as drama. . . . Shakespeare's plays are full of pageantry and of action patterned in a ritualistic way.
But the pageants are regularly interrupted; the rituals are abortive or perverted;
or if they succeed, they succeed against odds or in an unexpected fashion. The
people in the plays try to organize their lives by pageant and ritual, but the plays
are dramatic precisely because the effort fails. This failure drama presents as
history and personality; in the largest perspective, as destiny." *Shakespeare's
Festive Comedy* (Princeton: Princeton UP, 1959; reprinted, Cleveland & New
York: Meridian Books 1963), p.193. Barber's work is a vital point of departure
for this essay. My debt to him is large, though he denies the validity of his
scheme for the late comedies, and my concept of occasion extends beyond the
ancient folk-customs he emphasized to include rites of court and church as well.

A significant article concerning the seasonal context of *A Midsummer
Night's Dream* appeared when this essay was complete: Anca Vlasopolos, "The
Ritual of Midsummer: A Pattern for *A Midsummer Night's Dream*," *R[enais-
sance] Q[uarterly]*, 31 (1978), 21–29. Announced as forthcoming is R. Chris

Hassel, Jr., *Renaissance Drama and the English Church Year* (Lincoln, Nebraska: U of Nebraska P, 1979).

On the similarity of rites at the major seasonal junctures see Enid Welsford, *The Court Masque* (Cambridge: The Univ. Press, 1927), p.12 and citations.

4. Most sources on Halloween and Hallowmas are anecdotal, like John Brand, *Popular Antiquities of Great Britain*, ed. Henry Ellis (London: Henry G. Bohn, 1849), I, 377–96; T. F. Thiselton-Dyer, *British Popular Customs* (London: George Bell and Sons, 1876), pp. 394–408, and *Folk-Lore of Shakespeare* (London: Griffith & Farran, 1883), pp. 306–07; Sikes Wirt, *British Goblins* (London: Sampson Low, 1880), pp. 280–84; and F. Marian McNeill, *The Silver Bough...National and Local Festivals of Scotland* (Glasgow: William Maclellan, 1961), III, 11–39. More analytic are Alwyn Rees and Brinley Rees, *Celtic Heritage* (London: Thames and Hudson, 1961), pp. 89–93, and E. 0. James, *Seasonal Feasts and Festivals* (New York: Barnes & Noble, Inc., 1961), pp. 316–19. For a recent attempt to place a work of Shakespeare in Halloween context, see Jeanne Addison Roberts, " 'The Merry Wives of Windsor' as a Hallowe'en Play," *Shakepeare Survey* 25 (1972), 107–12. On the specifically Christian History of All Saints' and All Souls', which originally were celebrated on the same day, see, in addition to *The Catholic Encyclopedia*, Ethel L. Urlin, *Festivals, Holy Days, and Saints' Days* (London: Simpkin, Marshall, Hamilton, Kent & Co., n.d.), pp. 190–203; Francis X. Weiser, *The Holyday Book* (New York: Harcourt, Brace and Co., 1956), pp.121–36; and Victor W. Turner, *The Ritual Process: Structure and Anti-Structure* (Chicago: Aldine Publishing Co., 1969), pp. 181–82.

5. The most useful narrative account of Hallowmas as part of Christmas is Clement A. Miles, *Christmas in Ritual and Tradition* (London: T. Fisher Unwin, 1912; reprinted Detroit: Gale Research Co., 1968), pp. 161–98. On the association of Hallowmas with winter, and with the beginning of the masquing and mummery of the Christmas Revels see E. K. Chambers, *The Medieval Stage*, 2 vols. (Oxford: Oxford UP, 1903), Chapters XI and XII; also *Elizabethan Stage*, I, 21 and IV, 237; and Enid Welsford, *The Court Masque*, p.12. On drama in Lent see Gerald Eades Bentley, *The Jacobean and Caroline Stage* (Oxford: Clarendon Press, 1941–1968), VI, 194 and VII, 1–9. For documents on the court performance of 1 November 1611 see E. K. Chambers, *Elizabethan Stage*, IV, 125 and 177; also printed in *William Shakespeare*, II, 342.

6. *Letters of John Chamberlain*, ed. Norman Egbert McClure (Philadelphia: The American Philosophical Society, 1939), January 10, 1609, I, 281. Chamberlain had thought the plays a chief ornament of the rather poor season.

7. John Stow, *The Survay of London....corrected and much enlarged* (London, 1618), pp. 970 and 975; hereafter cited as "Stow."

8. W. Herbert, *Antiquities of the Inns of Court and Chancery* (London: Vernor and Hood, 1804), p. 335; also pp. 205–06, 231–35, 248–59, and 316–18. See in addition, Robert J. Blackham, *The Story of the Temple* (London: Sampson Low, Marston & Co., n.d.), pp. 35–38. The best modern history is by Wilfrid R. Prest, *The Inns of Court Under Elizabeth I and the Early Stuarts, 1590–1640* (London: Longman, 1972).

9. William Prynne, *Histrio-Mastix* (London, 1633), pp. 757–58 (italics omitted).
10. Clement A. Miles, *Christmas in Ritual and Tradition*, p. 190.
11. A convenient form in which to consult the prayer book is *The First Prayer-Book of Edward VI. Compared with the Successive Revisions of the Book of Common Prayer* (Oxford and London: James Parker and Co., 1877). This edition records the revisions of 1552, 1559, 1604, and 1662, as well as the Scotch Liturgy of 1637.

A table of scriptures follows for the various services according to the 1604 Prayer book, which revised the 1559 version in some respects. Since there are minor variations among Jacobean prayer books, any table such as this approximates what actually was read. I take the scriptures for All Saints' Eve to be of interest even though they were part of the regular sequence.

	All Saints' Eve. Evensong	All Saints' Day Matins	All Saints' Day Holy Communion	All Saints' Day Evensong
Psalms	147, 148, 149, 150	1, 2, 3, 4, 5.	149 (specially at Communion)	6, 7, 8.
First Lesson	Ecclesiasticus 13.	Wisdom 3 (to "If ye indure")	Epistle: Apoca- lypse 7 (to "God for euermore").	Wisdom 5 (to "His iealousie also").
Second Lesson	Colossians 1	Hebrews 11, 12 ("Saints by faith" to "If ye endure").	Gospel: Matthew 5 (to "Prophets which were before you").	Apocalypse 19 (to "And I saw an Angel stand").

Church was not the only place where Shakespeare and his audience encountered scriptures or even the liturgy. T. W. Baldwin, *William Shakspere's Small Latine & Lesse Greeke*, 2 vols. (Urbana: U of Illinois P, 1944), quotes a variety of sixteenth-century educators who recommended that Psalms, Ecclesiasticus, and Proverbs be used in school for exercises in Latin translation; Erasmus cited these books, as well as the Book of Wisdom, for this purpose. Further, in some families morning and evening prayers were conducted at home following the prayer book. For this last, as well as advice on certain points of Anglican liturgical history, I am indebted to the Rev. Massey Shepherd, Jr., Professor of Liturgics, Church Divinity School of the Pacific, Berkeley, California.

On the use of the Book of Common Prayer at home by George Herbert's family see Horton Davies, *Worship and Theology in England* (Princeton: Princeton Univ. Press, 1961–1975), II, 102–04; see also I, 442. Other useful works on the English liturgy include, F. E. Brightman, *The English Rite*, 2nd ed., 2 vols. (London: Rivingtons, 1921; reprinted Gregg International, 1970); Francis Procter and Walter Howard Frere, *A New History of the Book of Common Prayer*, 3rd Impression (London: Macmillan & Co., 1914); W. K. Lowther Clarke, ed., *Liturgy and Worship: A Companion to the Prayer Books of the Anglican Communion* (London: S.P.C.K., 1959). For a study of the broad patterns of liturgy and ritual in Shakespeare see Herbert R. Coursen, Jr., *Christian Ritual and the World of Shakespeare's Tragedies* (Lewisburg, Pa.: Bucknell Univ. Press, 1976); in his final chapter, about *The Tempest*, Coursen is especially concerned with the symbolism of penitence and communion.

12. In the following quotations from the Bible, the italics indicate passages that suggest some action, situation, or character in *The Tempest* when the scriptures and the play are simultaneously borne in mind. The italics are intended as guideposts to the reader, not as indications of direct source relationships. I have dropped the few original italics.

The scriptural quotations in this essay come from the first issue of the King James version, which is usually called the "folio 'He' Bible" of 1611. Its printing began in 1610 and stretched into 1611, when it was supposed to be on the lecterns by the spring. Certainly there are strong arguments for quoting the Bishops' Bible, perhaps alongside the popular Geneva version, in writings on Shakespeare. But since I have studied the All Saints' Day scriptures in each of the three versions, and in none of them have found sure verbal parallels with Shakespeare's language in *The Tempest*; since the King James Bible was the latest official version at the time of the play's earliest documented performance; and since the Bishops' Bible was, in any case, the basic text from which the translators of the new version were directed to work, I have chosen the King James. The key passages are similar in all three versions. For bibliographical information see A. S. Herbert, *Historical Catalogue of Printed Editions of the English Bible, 1525–1961* (London: British & Foreign Bible Society; New York: The American Bible Society, 1968).

13. The proverb is N348 in Morris P. Tilley, *A Dictionary of the Proverbs in England in the Sixteenth and Seventeenth Centuries* (Ann Arbor: Univ. of Michigan Press, 1950). Tilley's earliest citation for this proverb is 1557. Similar, and additional, proverbial wisdom appears in Nicholas Breton, *Fantasticks* (London, 1626), sigs. B3[r] Dl[r]; also in Matthew Stevenson, *The Twelve Moneths* (London, 1661), pp. 49, 51, and 54. The most convenient compendium of emblems, though incomplete, is Arthur Henkel and Albrecht Schöne, *Emblemata* (Stuttgart: J. B. Metzlersche, 1967). Relevant in this context are columns 1461–1470 of the section entitled "Menschenwelt/Schiff und Schiffsgerät" see especially columns 1469–1470.

14. For a provocative comparison see Alvin Kernan, "The Great Fair of the World and the Ocean Island: *Bartholomew Fair* and *The Tempest*," in *The Revels History of Drama in English*, eds. J. Leeds Barroll, Alexander Leggatt, Richard Hosley and Alvin Kernan (London: Methuen, 1975), III, 456–74; Kernan does not specifically concern himself with the Hallowmas occasion shared by the two plays. It is perhaps typical that Jonson recalls the dog days of late summer and sees marriage as a business deal, whereas Shakespeare looks forward to the burgeoning of spring and views marriage idealistically.

15. See C. H. Herford and Percy and Evelyn Simpson, eds., *Ben Jonson* (Oxford: Clarendon Press, 1925–1952), X, 406–07: before the stage "a green-carpeted space was kept clear for the nobles or ladies when they descended from the stage for the masquing-dance."

16. Shakespeare may have had in mind stanxas six and seven of "Januarye" in *The Shepheardes Calender*, especially: "And from mine eyes the drizling teares descend, / As on your boughes the ysicles depend." For a discussion of the pos-

sible scriptural reference in the name "Ariel" see Ann Pasternak Slater, "Variations Within a Source: From Isaiah XXIX to 'The Tempest,'" *Shakespeare Survey*, 25 (1972), 125–35.

17. William A. Ringler, Jr., and Steven W. May, "An Epilogue Possibly by Shakespeare, *M[odern] P[hilology]* 70 (1972-1973), 138–39. The manuscript heading
to this poem reads: "to yᵉ, Q. by yᵉ players 1598."

18. George L. Kittredge, *Witchcraft in Old and New England* (Cambridge, Mass.:
Harvard University Press, 1929), p.312: "There is a new provision in the statute
of 1604 (not found in Elizabethan law) imposing the death penalty on any one
who shall 'take up any dead man, woman, or child out of his, her, or theire
grave, or any other place where the dead bodie resteth, or the skin, bone or any
other parte of any dead person, to be imployed or used in any manner of Witch-
crafte, Sorcerie, Charme, or Inchantment.'"

19. Michel de Montaigne, *The Essayes, or Morall, Politike and Militarie Discourses. . .*, trans. John Florio (London, 1603), p. 243. I have suppressed Florio's
italics; the added italics are those used to point up the source relationship in
Eleanor Prosser, "Shakespeare, Montaigne, and *the Rarer Action*," *Shakespeare
Studies*, 1 (1965), 261–64.

20. The primary and secondary bibliographies on Prudence are vast. On Prudence
in *The Tempest*, see Douglas L. Peterson, *Time, Tide, and Tempest* (San Marino:
The Huntington Library, 1973), pp. 16–17, 54–55, *et passim*. Other studies of
Prudence in Shakespeare include Barry B. Adams, "The Prudence of Prince
Escalus," *ELH* 35 (1968), 32–50; Nigel Alexander, *Poison, Play and Duel: A
Study in Hamlet* (London: Routledge & Kegan Paul, 1971), Chapter 2; and Raymond B. Waddington, "Shakespeare's Sonnet 15 and the Art of Memory," pp.
96–122 in *The Rhetoric of Renaissance Poetry*, ed. Thomas O. Sloan and Raymond B. Waddington (Berkeley and Los Angeles: Univ. of California Press,
1974).

21. See *The First Prayer-Book of Edward VI. Compared with the Successive Revisions*, p. 66, for the sentences. The scriptures for Evening Prayer on Hallowmas
included the passage from Wisdom 5 quoted above, along with one of the Lec-
tionary's two annual selections from the Apocalypse. Prospero's emphasis on
penitence, prayer, and indulgence suggests at least a glancing reference to All
Souls' in the play—as in the Anglican scriptural choices. E. J. Devereux, "Sacra-
mental Imagery in *The Tempest*," *Humanities Association Bulletin*, 19 (1968),
50–62, believes that the Epilogue refers specifically to Catholic doctrine.

The survival in Renaissance England of All Souls' customs such as the baking of Soul Cakes to be left out for wandering spirits, suggests that ideas of Purgatory, officially rejected by the Church of England, were far from confined to
practicing Catholics. The preparation of meals to be served up for spirits on their
penitential journeys and left, at least ostensibly, untouched was the most common of All Souls' customs. When *The Tempest* is considered in a Hallowmas
context, the vanishing banquet that Ariel sets before the men of sin, who are
thought dead by at least some characters in the play and whom Prospero treats
as penitents, strongly suggests the rites of All Souls'. In view of *The Tempest*'s

fictional geography, one regional All Souls' Eve custom is of a certain tantalizing interest: "On the Adriatic coast, people go down to the seashore with lights
to evoke the dead; perhaps, in particular, those who were drowned" (Urlin, p.
197).

22. Horton Davies, *Worship and Theology in England*, II, 103, calls 4:00 p.m. the
"canonical" hour; see also, II, 468. John Stow reports that after the new lord
Mayor's first Evening Prayer at St. Pauls on All Saints' Day, "by the helpe of
Torchlight, at the Companies cost, the Aldermen bring the Lord Maior home,
where they haue Spicebread and Ipocras, and so take their leaue" (*Survay*, p.
970). If the service had begun significantly earlier than 4:00 p.m., torch light
would not have been needed at its conclusion; significantly later, and torch light
would have been needed both coming and going.

23. See Stephen Orgel, *The Illusion of Power: Political Theater in the English
Renaissance* (Berkeley, Los Angeles, London: Univ. of California Press, 1975);
and Stephen Orgel and Roy Strong, *Inigo Jones: The Theatre of the Stuart
Court*, 2 vols. (London, Berkeley, Los Angeles: Sotheby Parke Bernet and Univ.
of California Press, 1973).

The Miranda Trap
Sexism and Racism in Shakespeare's *Tempest**

LORIE JERRELL LEININGER

Shakespeare's *Tempest* was first performed before King James I at Whitehall in November of 1611. It was presented a second time at the court of King James early in 1613, as part of the marriage festivities of James's daughter Elizabeth, who, at the age of sixteen, was being married to Frederick the Elector Palatine. The marriage masque within *The Tempest* may have been added for this occasion. In any case, the Goddess Ceres' promise of a life untouched by winter (*"Spring come to you at the farthest / In the very end of harvest!"* IV. i. 114–15)[1] and all the riches the earth can provide (*"Earth's increase, foison plenty"*) was offered to the living royal couple as well as to Ferdinand and Miranda.

Elizabeth had fallen dutifully in love with the bridegroom her father had chosen for her, the youthful ruler of the rich and fertile Rhineland and the leading Protestant prince of central Europe. Within seven years Frederick was to become "Frederick the Winter King" and "The Luckless Elector," but in 1613 he was still the living counterpart of Ferdinand in *The Tempest*, even as Elizabeth was the counterpart of Miranda. Like Miranda, Elizabeth was beautiful, loving, chaste, and obedient. She believed her father to be incapable of error, in this sharing James's opinion of himself. Miranda in the play is "admired Miranda," "perfect," "peerless," one who "outstrips all praise"; Elizabeth was praised as "the eclipse and glory of her kind," a rose among violets.[2]

What was the remainder of her life to be like? Elizabeth, this flesh-and-blood Miranda, might have found it difficult to agree that "We are such stuff / As dreams are made on; and our little life / Is rounded with a sleep"

*Originally published in *The Women's Part: Feminist Criticism of Shakespeare*, eds., Carolyn Ruth Swift Lenz, Gayle Greene, and Carol Thomas Neely. Copyright 1980 by the Board of Trustees of the University of Illinois. Used with the permission of the University of Illinois Press and Lorie Jerrell Leininger.

(IV.i.156–58). The future held thirteen children for her, and forty years as a landless exile. Her beloved Frederick died of the plague at the age of thirty-six, a plague spreading through battle camps and besieged cities in a Europe devastated by a war which appeared endless—the Thirty Years War, in which whole armies in transit disappeared through starvation and pestilence. The immediate cause of this disastrous war had been Frederick and Elizabeth's foolhardy acceptance of the disputed throne of Bohemia. Politically inept, committed to a belief in hierarchical order and Neoplatonic courtliness, the new king and queen failed to engage the loyalty of the Bohemians or to prepare adequately for the inevitable attack by the previously deposed king.

While the happiness of the young lovers in *The Tempest* depended upon their obedience to Miranda's father, the repeated political and military failures of Elizabeth and Frederick were exacerbated by their dependence upon the shifting promises of King James. Elizabeth experienced further tragedy when two of her sons drowned, the eldest at the age of fifteen in an accident connected with spoils from the New World, the fourth son in a tempest while privateering in the New World. There was no Prospero-figure to restore them to life magically.

The Princess Elizabeth, watching *The Tempest* in 1613, was incapable of responding to clues which might have warned her that being Miranda might prove no unmixed blessing: that even though Miranda occupies a place next to Prospero in the play's hierarchy and appears to enjoy all of the benefits which Caliban, at the base of that hierarchy, is denied, she herself might prove a victim of the play's hierarchical values. Elizabeth would be justified in seeing Miranda as the royal offspring of a ducal father, as incomparably beautiful (her external beauty mirroring her inward virtue, in keeping with Neoplatonic idealism), as lovingly educated and gratefully responsive to that education, as chaste (her chastity symbolic of all human virtue), obedient and, by the end of the play, rewarded with an ideal husband and the inheritance of two dukedoms. Caliban, at the opposite pole, is presented as the reviled offspring of a witch and the Devil, as physically ugly (his ugly exterior mirroring his depraved inner nature), as racially vile, intrinsically uneducable, uncontrollably lustful (a symbol of all vice), rebellious, and, being defined as a slave by nature, as justly enslaved.

Modern readers have become more attentive than Elizabeth could have been in 1613 to clues such as Prospero's address to Miranda, "What! I say, / My foot my tutor?" (I.ii.471–72). The crucial line is spoken near the end of the scene which begins with Prospero's and Ariel's delighted revelation that the tempest was raised through Prospero's magic powers and then continues with the demonstration of Prospero's ability to subjugate the spirit Ariel, the native Caliban, and finally the mourning Prince Ferdinand to his will. Miranda's concern is engaged when Prospero accuses Ferdinand of being a spy, a traitor and usurper; Prospero threatens to manacle Ferdinand's head and feet together and to force him to drink salt water. When Ferdinand raises his sword to resist Prospero's threats, Prospero magically deprives him of all strength. Miranda, alarmed, cries,

> O dear father,
> Make not too rash a trial of him, for
> He's gentle, and not fearful. (I.ii.469–71)

Prospero's response is,

> What! I say,
> My foot my tutor? (I.ii.471–72)

Miranda is given to understand that she is the foot in the family organization of which Prospero is the head. Hers not to reason why, hers but to follow directions: indeed, what kind of a body would one have (Prospero, or the play, asks) if one's foot could think for itself, could go wherever it pleased, independent of the head?

Now it is true that Prospero is acting out a role which he knows to be unjust, in order to cement the young couple's love by placing obstacles in their way. Miranda, however, has no way of knowing this. Prospero has established the principle that stands whether a father's action be just or unjust: the daughter must submit to his demand for absolute unthinking obedience.

But might not being a "foot" to another's "head" prove advantageous, provided that the "head" is an all-powerful godlike father who educates and protects his beloved daughter? Some ambiguous answers are suggested by the play, particularly in the triangular relationship of Prospero, Miranda, and Caliban. When Prospero says to Miranda,

> We'll visit Caliban my slave, who never
> Yields us kind answer,

Miranda's response is,

> 'Tis a villain, sir,
> I do not love to look on.   (I.ii.310–12)

Miranda fears Caliban, and she has reason to fear him. The play permits either of two interpretations to explain the threat which Caliban poses. His hostility may be due to his intrinsically evil nature, or to his present circumstances: anyone who is forced into servitude, confined to a rock, kept under constant surveillance, and punished by supernatural means would wish his enslavers ill.[3] Whatever Caliban's original disposition may have been when he lived

alone on the isle—and we lack disinterested evidence—he must in his present
circumstances feel hostility toward Prospero and Miranda. Miranda is far
more vulnerable to Caliban's ill will than is her all-powerful father.

Prospero responds to Miranda's implicit plea to be spared exposure to
Caliban's hostility with the *practical* reasons for needing a slave:

> But, as 'tis,
> We cannot miss him: he does make our fire,
> Fetch in our wood, and serves in offices
> That profit us. What, ho! slave! Caliban! (I.ii.312–15)

A daughter might conceivably tell her loving father that she would prefer that
they gather their own wood, that in fact no "profit" can outweigh the uneasiness she experiences. Miranda, however, is not free to speak, since a father
who at any time can silence his daughter with "What! My foot my tutor?" will
have educated that "foot" to extreme sensitivity toward what her father does
or does not wish to hear from her. Miranda dare not object to her enforced
proximity to a hostile slave, for within the play's universe of discourse any
attempt at pressing her own needs would constitute both personal insubordination and a disruption of the hierarchical order of the universe of which the
"foot/head" familial organization is but one reflection.

Miranda, admired and sheltered, has no way out of the cycle of being a
dependent foot in need of protection, placed in a threatening situation which
in turn calls for more protection, and thus increased dependence and increased
subservience.

Miranda's presence as the dependent, innocent, feminine extension of
Prospero serves a specific end in the play's power dynamics. Many reasons are
given for Caliban's enslavement; the one which carries greatest dramatic
weight is Caliban's sexual threat to Miranda. When Prospero accuses Caliban
of having sought "to violate / The honour of my child" (I.ii.349–50), Caliban
is made to concur in the accusation:

> O ho, O ho! Would't had been done!
> Thou didst prevent me; I had peopled else
> This isle with Calibans. (I.ii.351–53)

We can test the element of sexual politics at work here by imagining, for a
moment, that Prospero had been cast adrift with a small son instead of a
daughter. If, twelve years later, a ship appeared bearing King Alonso and a
marriageable daughter, the play's resolution of the elder generation's hatreds
through the love of their offspring could still have been effected. What would
be lost in such a reconstruction would be the sexual element in the enslavement of the native. No son would serve. Prospero needs Miranda as sexual

bait, and then needs to protect her from the threat which is inescapable given his hierarchical world—slavery being the ultimate extension of the concept of hierarchy. It is Prospero's needs—the Prosperos of the world—not Miranda's, which are being served here.

The most elusive yet far reaching function of Miranda in the play involves the role of her chastity in the allegorical scheme. Most critics agree that the chastity of Miranda and Ferdinand in the fourth act symbolizes all human virtue ("Chastity is the quality of Christ, the essential symbol of civilization"[4]), while Caliban's lust symbolizes all human vice.

The first result of this schematic representation of all virtue and vice as chastity and lust is the exclusion from the field of moral concern the very domination and enslavement which the play vividly dramatizes. The exclusion is accomplished with phenomenal success under the guise of religion, humanism, and Neoplatonic idealism, by identifying Prospero with God (or spirit, or soul, or imagination), and Caliban with the Devil (or matter, body, and lust). Within the Christian-humanist tradition, the superiority of spirit over matter, or soul over body, was a commonplace: body existed to serve soul, to be, metaphorically, enslaved by soul. In a tradition which included the *Psychomachia*, medieval morality plays, and Elizabethan drama, the "higher" and "lower" selves existing within each person's psyche had been represented allegorically in the form of Virtues and Vices. A danger inherent in this mode of portraying inner struggle lay in the possibility of identifying certain human beings with the Vice-figures, and others (oneself included) with the representatives of Virtue. Such identification of self with Virtue and others with Vice led to the great Christian-humanist inversion: the warrant to plunder, exploit and kill in the name of God—Virtue destroying Vice.

It was "only natural" that the educated and privileged be identified with virtue and spirit, and that those who do society's dirty work, and all outsiders, be identified with vice and matter. Ellen Cantarow has analyzed the tendency of allegory to link virtue with privilege and sin with misfortune, making particular power relationships appear inevitable, "natural" and just within a changeless, "divinely ordained" hierarchical order;[5] Nancy Hall Rice has analyzed the manner in which the artistic process of embodying evil in one person and then punishing or destroying that person offers an ersatz solution to the complex problem of evil, sanctioning virulent attacks on social minorities or outcasts;[6] and Winthrop D. Jordan has discussed the tendency of Western civilization to link African natives, for example, with preconceived concepts of sexuality and vice. Jordan speaks of "the ordered hierarchy of [imputed] sexual aggressiveness": the lower one's place on the scale of social privilege, the more dangerously lustful one is perceived as being.[7]

Thus in *The Tempest*, written some fifty years after England's open participation in the slave trade,[8] the island's native is made the embodiment of lust, disobedience, and irremediable evil, while his enslaver is presented as a

God-figure. It makes an enormous difference in the expectations raised, whether one speaks of the moral obligations of Prospero-the-slave-owner toward Caliban-his-slave, or speaks of the moral obligations of Prospero-the-God-figure toward Caliban-the-lustful-Vice-figure. In the second instance (the allegorical-symbolic), the only requirement is that Prospero be punitive toward Caliban and that he defend his daughter Miranda's chastity—that daughter being needed as a pawn to counterbalance Caliban's lust. In this symbolic scheme, Miranda is deprived of any possibility of human freedom, growth or thought. She need only *be* chaste—to exist as a walking emblem of chastity. This kind of symbolism is damaging in that it deflects our attention away from the fact that real counterparts to Caliban, Prospero, and Miranda exist—that real slaves, real slave owners, and real daughters existed in 1613 for Shakespeare's contemporaries and have continued to exist since then.

To return to one of those daughters, Miranda's living counterpart Elizabeth Stuart, at whose wedding festivities *The Tempest* was performed: it appears likely that King James's daughter and her bridegroom were influenced in their unrealistic expectations of their powers and rights as future rulers by the widespread Jacobean attempt to equate unaccountable aristocratic power with benevolent infallibility and possibly by the expression of that equation in *The Tempest*. In our own century the play apparently continues to reflect ongoing societal confusions that may seduce women—and men—into complicity with those who appear to favor them while oppressing others. Can we envision a way out? If a twentieth century counterpart to Miranda were to define, and then confront, *The Tempest*'s underlying assumptions—as, obviously, neither the Miranda created by Shakespeare nor her living counterpart in the seventeenth century could do—what issues would she need to clarify? Let us invent a modern Miranda, and permit her to speak a new Epilogue:

"My father is no God-figure. No one is a God-figure. My father is a man, and fallible, as I am. Let's put an end to the fantasy of infallibility.

"There is no such thing as a 'natural slave.' No subhuman laborers exist. Let's put an end to *that* fantasy. I will not benefit from such a concept presented in any guise, be it Aristotelian, biblical, allegorical, or Neoplatonic. Three men are reminded of Indians when first they see Caliban; he might be African, his mother having been transported from Algiers. I will not be used as the excuse for his enslavement. If either my father or I feel threatened by his real or imputed lust, we can build a pale around our side of the island, gather our own wood, cook our own food, and clean up after ourselves.

"I cannot give assent to an ethical scheme that locates all virtue symbolically in one part of my anatomy. My virginity has little to do with the forces that will lead to good harvest or to greater social justice.

"Nor am I in any way analogous to a foot. Even if I were, for a moment, to accept my father's hierarchical mode, it is difficult to understand his concern over the chastity of his *foot*. There is no way to make that work. Neither my father, nor my husband, nor any one alive has the right to refer to me as his foot while thinking of himself as the head—making me the obedient mechanism of his thinking. What I do need is the opportunity to think for myself; I need practice in making mistakes, in testing the consequences of my actions, in becoming aware of the numerous disguises of economic exploitation and racism.

"Will I succeed in creating my 'brave new world' which has people in it who no longer exploit one another? I cannot be certain. I will at least make my start by springing 'the Miranda-trap,' being forced into unwitting collusion with domination by appearing to be a beneficiary. I need to join forces with Caliban—to join forces with all those who are exploited or oppressed—to stand beside Caliban and say,

> As we from crimes would pardon'd be,
> Let's work to set each other free."

NOTES

An earlier version of this essay was presented at a Special Session on Problems in Racism and Sexism as Reflected in Shakespeare at the MLA Annual Convention, December 1977, Chicago, Illinois.

1. This quotation and subsequent ones are from *The Tempest*, Arden Shakespeare, ed. Frank Kermode (Cambridge, Mass.: Harvard University Press, 1958).

2. "The eclipse and glory of her kind" is the closing line of Sir Henry Wotton's poem, "On His Mistress, The Queen of Bohemia," in *The Poems of Sir Walter Raleigh. . . with those of Sir Henry Wotton and other Courtly Poets from 1540–1650*, ed. John Hannah (London: Bell and Sons, 1892), pp. 95–96. "A rose among violets" is a paraphrase of the third verse of that poem; the compliment was often quoted.

3. That the spirit Ariel, the figure contrasted to Caliban in the allegorical scheme, is a purely imaginary construct for whom no human counterparts exist helps to obscure the fact that human counterparts for Caliban did indeed exist. A community of free blacks had been living in London for over fifteen years at the time of the writing of *The Tempest*. The first Indian to have been exhibited in England had been brought to London during the reign of Queen Elizabeth's grandfather, Henry VII. For a full discussion of the historical background see Chapter II of my dissertation, "The Jacobean Bind: A Study of *The Tempest*, *The Revenge of Bussy D'Ambois*, *The Atheist's Tragedy*, *A King and No King* and *The Alchemist*, the Major Plays of 1610 and 1611, in the Context of Renaissance Expansion and Jacobean Absolutism," University of Massachusetts at Amherst, 1975. For more on the effects of the ambiguity surrounding the definition of Caliban as an abstract embodiment of evil and as an inhabitant of a newly discovered island see Chapter III of the same work, which considers *The Tempest* in relation to seventeenth- and twentieth-century imperialism.

Four critics, among others, who have dealt with the colonial aspects of *The Tempest* and have focused upon Caliban and his enslavement as moral concerns are O. Mannoni, *Prospero and Caliban: The Psychology of Colonization*, trans. Pamela Powesland (New York: Praeger, 1956); Philip Mason, *Prospero's Magic: Some Thoughts on Class and Race* (London: Oxford University Press, 1962), pp.75–97; Roberto Fernández Retamar, "Caliban," *Massachusetts Review*, 15 (Winter-Spring 1974), 7–72; and Kermode, "Introduction," *The Tempest*. While Kermode observes that Shakespeare, and more generally Renaissance writers, held contradictory attitudes toward Indians, viewing them on one hand as inhabitants of a golden age, with no *meum* or *tuum*, and on the other hand as human beasts in whom one could place no trust, he nevertheless arrives at the conclusion that "the confusion of interests characteristic of the subject is harmoniously reflected in Shakespeare's play" (p. xxxi)—a "harmony" more likely to be acceptable to those who are at ease with the historical reality of conquest and enslavement than by those who, like Caliban's living counterparts, have been conquered, enslaved, or colonized. It is puzzling that even an article as sensitive as Harry Berger, Jr.'s "Miraculous Harp: A Reading of Shakespeare's *Tempest*," in *Shakespeare Studies*, 5 (1969), 253–83, in its exploration of the contradictory elements in Prospero's character—his tendency to see himself as a god, his limited knowledge of human nature, his pleasure in dominating others, and his preference for, and success in, dealing with projected embodiments of pure evil—falls short of focusing upon the dramatization of enslavement itself as an ethical concern. I explore this question, posed in general terms, in my "Cracking the Code of *The Tempest*," *Bucknell Review*, 25 (Spring 1979), issue on "Shakespeare: Contemporary Critical Approaches," ed. Harry R. Garvin and Michael D. Payne.

4.   Irving Ribner, "Introduction" to Shakespeare's *Tempest*, ed. George Lyman Kittredge, rev. Ribner (Waltham, Mass.: Blaisdell, 1966), p. xv.

5.   Ellen Cantarow, "A Wilderness of Opinions Confounded: Allegory and Ideology," *College English*, 34 (1972), 215–16.

6.   Nancy Hall Rice, "Beauty and the Beast and the Little Boy: Clues about the Origins of Sexism and Racism from Folklore and Literature," Diss. University of Massachusetts at Amherst 1974, p. 207.

7.   Winthrop D. Jordan, *The White Man's Burden: Historical Origins of Racism in the United States* (New York: Oxford University Press, 1974), p. 196.

8.   See, for example, accounts of the 1562–68 slaving voyages of Sir John Hawkins (one with Sir Francis Drake) which appear in Richard Hakluyt's *Principall Navigations Voiages and Discoveries of the English Nation* (London, 1589; facs. rpt. Cambridge: Cambridge University Press, 1965), Part Two, 521–22, 526–29, 531–32, 553–54, 562–64.

Prospero's Wife *

STEPHEN ORGEL

This essay is not a reading of *The Tempest*. It is a consideration of five related
moments and issues. I have called it "Prospero's Wife" because some of it centers on her, but in a larger sense because she is a figure conspicuous by her
absence from the play, and my large subject is the absent, the unspoken, that
seems to me the most powerful and problematic presence in *The Tempest*. In
its outlines, the play seems a story of privatives: withdrawl, usurpation, banishment, the loss of one's way, shipwreck. As an antithesis, a principle of control, preservation, re-creation, the play offers only magic, embodied in a single
figure, the extraordinary powers of Prospero.

Prospero's wife is alluded to only once in the play, in Prospero's reply to
Miranda's question, "Sir, are you not my father?"

> Thy mother was a piece of virtue, and
> She said thou wast my daughter; and thy father
> Was Duke of Milan; and his only heir
> And princess: no worse issued. (1.2.55–59)[1]

Prospero's wife is identified as Miranda's mother, in a context implying that
though she was virtuous, women as a class are not, and that were it not for her
word, Miranda's legitimacy would be in doubt. The legitimacy of Prospero's
heir, that is, derives from her mother's word. But that word is all that is
required of her in the play. Once he is assured of it, Prospero turns his attention to himself and his succession, and he characterizes Miranda in a clause
that grows increasingly ambivalent—"his only heir / And princess: no worse
issued."

*Reprinted from *Representations* 8 (1984): 1–13. Copyright 1984 by the Regents of
the University of California. Reprinted by the permission of the University of California Press and Stephen Orgel.

Except for this moment, Prospero's wife is absent from his memory. She is wholly absent from her daughter's memory: Miranda can recall several women who attended her in childhood, but no mother. The implied attitudes toward wives and mothers here are confirmed shortly afterward when Prospero, recounting his brother Antonio's crimes, demands that Miranda "tell me / If this might be a brother," and Miranda takes the question to be a charge of adultery against Prospero's mother:

> I should sin
> To think but nobly of my grandmother:
> Good wombs have borne bad sons. (1.2.118–20)

She immediately translates Prospero's attack on his brother into an attack on his mother (the best she can produce in her grandmother's defence is a "not proved"), and whether or not she has correctly divined her father's intentions, Prospero makes no objection.

The absent presence of the wife and mother in the play constitutes a space that is filled by Prospero's creation of surrogates and a ghostly family: the witch Sycorax and her monster child, Caliban (himself, as becomes apparent, a surrogate for the other wicked child, the usurping younger brother), the good child/wife Miranda, the obedient Ariel, the violently libidinized adolescent Ferdinand. The space is filled, too, by a whole structure of wifely allusion and reference: widow Dido, model at once of heroic fidelity to a murdered husband and the destructive potential of erotic passion; the witch Medea, murderess and filicide; three exemplary goddesses, the bereft Ceres, nurturing Juno and licentious Venus; and Alonso's daughter, Claribel, unwillingly married off to the ruler of the modern Carthage, and thereby lost to her father forever.

Described in this way, the play has an obvious psychoanalytic shape. I have learned a great deal from Freudian treatments of it, most recently from essays by David Sundelson, Coppélia Kahn and Joel Fineman in the volume called *Representing Shakespeare*.[2] It is almost irresistible to look at the play as a case history. *Whose* case history is a rather more problematic question, and one that criticism has not, on the whole, dealt with satisfactorily. It is not, obviously, that of the characters. I want to pause first over what it means to consider the play as a case history.

In older psychoanalytic paradigms (say Ernest Jones's) the critic is the analyst, Shakespeare is the patient, the plays his fantasies. The trouble with this paradigm is that it misrepresents the analytic situation in a fundamental way. The interpretation of analytic material is done in conjunction with, and in large measure by, the patient, not the analyst; what the analyst does is *enable* the patient, free the patient to interpret. An analysis done without the patient, like Freud's of Leonardo, will be revealing only about the analyst. A more recent paradigm, in which the audience's response is the principal analytic material, also seems to me based on fundamental misconceptions, first because it treats an audience as an entity, a unit, and in addition a constant one, and more problematically, because it conceives of the play as an objective event, so that the critical question becomes, "this is what happened: how do we respond to it?"

To take the psychoanalytic paradigm seriously, however, and treat the plays as case histories, is surely to treat them *not* as objective events but as collaborative fantasies, and to acknowledge thereby that we, as analysts, are implicated in the fantasy. It is not only the patient who creates the shape of his history, and when Bruno Bettelheim observes that Freud's case histories "read as well as the best novels,"[3] he is probably telling more of the truth than he intends. Moreover, the crucial recent advances in our understanding of Freud and psychoanalysis have been precisely critical acts of close and inventive reading—there are, in this respect, no limits to the collaboration. But if we accept this as our paradigm and think of ourselves as Freud's or Shakespeare's collaborators, we must also acknowledge that our reading of the case will be revealing, again, chiefly about ourselves. This is why every generation, and perhaps every reading, produces a different analysis of its Shakespearean texts. In the same way, recent psychoanalytic theory has replaced Freud's central Oedipal myth with a drama in which the loss of the seducing mother is the crucial infant trauma. We used to want assurance that we would successfully compete with or replace or supersede our fathers; now we want to know that our lost mothers will return. Both of these no doubt involve real perceptions, but they also undeniably serve particular cultural needs.

Shakespeare plays, like case histories, derive from the observation of human behavior, and both plays and case histories are imaginative constructs. Whether either is taken to be an objective report of behavior or not has more to do with the reader than the reporter, but it has to be said that Shakespearean critics have more often than not treated the plays as objective accounts. Without such an assumption, a book with the title *The Girlhood of Shakespeare's Heroines* would be incomprehensible. We feel very far from this famous and popular Victorian work now, but we still worry about consistency and motivation in Shakespearean texts, and much of the commentary in an edition like the Arden Shakespeare is designed to explain why the characters say what they say—that is, to reconcile what they say with what, on the basis of their previous behavior, we feel they ought to be saying. The critic who worries about this kind of consistency in a Shakespeare text is thinking of it as an objective report.

But all readings of Shakespeare, from the earliest seventeenth-century adaptations, through eighteenth-century attempts to produce "authentic" or "accurate" texts, to the liberal fantasy of the old Variorum Shakespeare, have been aware of deep ambiguities and ambivalences in the texts. The eighteenth century described these as Shakespeare's errors, and generally revised them through plausible emendation or outright rewriting. The argument was that Shakespeare wrote in haste, and would have written more perfect plays had he taken time to revise; the corollary to this was, of course, that what we want are the perfect plays Shakespeare did not write, rather than the imperfect ones that he did. A little later the errors became not Shakespeare's but those of the printing house, the scribe, the memory of the reporter or the defective hearing of the transcriber. But the assumption has always been that it is possible to produce a "perfect" text: that beyond or behind the ambiguous, puzzling, inconsistent text is a clear and consistent one.

Plays, moreover, are not only—and one might argue, not primarily— texts. They are performances too, originally designed to be read only in order to be acted out, and the gap between the text and its performance has always been, and remains, a radical one. There always has been an imagination intervening between the texts and their audiences initially the imagination of producer, director, actor (roles that Shakespeare played himself), and since that time the imagination of editors and commentators as well. These are texts that have always had to be *realized*. Initially unstable, they have remained so despite all our attempts to fix them. All our attempts to produce an authentic, correct, that is, *stable* text have resulted only in an extraordinary variety of versions. Their differences can be described as minor only if one believes that the real play is a Platonic idea, never realized but only approached and approximately represented by its text.

This is our myth: the myth of a stable, accurate, authentic, *legitimate* text, a text that we can think of as Shakespeare's legitimate heir. It is, in its way, a genealogical myth, and it operates with peculiar force in our readings of *The Tempest*, a play that has been, for the last hundred and fifty years, taken as a representation of Shakespeare himself bidding farewell to his art—as Shakespeare's legacy.

THE MISSING WIFE

She is missing as a character, but Prospero, several times explicitly, presents himself as incorporating her, acting as both father and mother to Miranda, and in one extraordinary passage describes the voyage to the island as a birth fantasy:

> When I have decked the sea with drops full salt,
> Under my burden groaned, which raised in me
> An undergoing stomach, to bear up
> Against what should ensue. (1.2.155–58)

To come to the island is to start life over again—both his own and Miranda's—with himself as sole parent, but also with himself as favorite child. He has been banished by his wicked, usurping, possibly illegitimate younger brother Antonio. This too has the shape of a Freudian fantasy: the younger child *is* the usurper in the family, and the kingdom he usurps is the mother. On the island, Prospero undoes the usurpation, recreating kingdom and family with himself in sole command.

But not quite, because the island is not his alone. Or if it is, then he has repeopled it with all parts of his fantasy, the distressing as well as the gratifying. When he arrives he finds Caliban, child of the witch Sycorax, herself a victim of banishment. The island provided a new life for her too, as it did literally for her son, with whom she was pregnant when she arrived. Sycorax died some time before Prospero came to the island; Prospero never saw her, and everything he knows about her he has learned from Ariel. Nevertheless, she is insistently present in his memory—far more present than his own wife—and she embodies to an extreme degree all the negative assumptions about women that he and Miranda have exchanged.

It is important, therefore, that Caliban derives his claim to the island from his mother: "This island's mine, by Sycorax my mother" (1.2.333). This has interesting implications to which I shall return, but here I want to point out that he need not make the claim this way. He could derive it from the mere fact of prior possession: he was there first. This, after all, would have been the sole basis of Sycorax's claim to the island, but it is an argument that Caliban never makes. And in deriving his authority from his mother, he delivers himself into Prospero's hands. Prospero declares him a bastard, "got by the devil himself / Upon thy wicked dam" (1.2.321-22), thereby both disallowing any claim from inheritance and justifying his loathing for Caliban.

But is it true that Caliban is Sycorax's bastard by Satan? How does Prospero know this? Not from Sycorax: Prospero never saw her. Not from Caliban: Sycorax died before she could even reach her son to speak. Everything Prospero knows about the witch he knows from Ariel—her appearance, the story of her banishment, the fact that her pregnancy saved her from execution. Did Sycorax also tell Ariel that her baby was the illegititnate son of the devil? Or is this Prospero's contribution to the story; an especially creative piece of invective, and an extreme instance of his characteristic assumptions about women? Nothing in the text will answer this question for us, and it is worth pausing to observe first that Caliban's claim seems to have been designed so that Prospero can disallow it, and second that we have no way of distinguishing the facts about Caliban and Sycorax from Prospero's invective about them.

Can Prospero imagine no good mothers, then? The play, after all, moves toward a wedding, and the most palpable example we see of the magician's powers is a betrothal masque. The masque is presided over by two exemplary mothers, Ceres and Juno, and the libidinous Venus with her destructive son Cupid has been banished from the scene. But the performance is also preceded by the most awful warnings against sexuality—male sexuality this time: all the libido is presumed to be Ferdinand's, while Miranda remains Prospero's innocent child. Ferdinand's reassuring reply, as David Sundelson persuasively argues,[4] includes submerged fantasies of rape and more than a hint that when the lust of the wedding night cools, so will his marital devotion:

> ... the murkiest den,
> The most opportune place, the strong'st suggestion
> Our worser genius can, shall never melt
> Mine honor into lust, to take away
> The edge of that day's celebration.... (4.1.25–29)

This is the other side of the assumption that all women at heart are whores: all men at heart are rapists—Caliban, Ferdinand, and of course that means Prospero too.

THE MARRIAGE CONTRACT

The play moves toward marriage, certainly, yet the relations it postulates between men and women are ignorant at best, characteristically tense, and potentially tragic. There is a familiar Shakespearean paradigm here: relationships between men and women interest Shakespeare intensely; but not, on the whole, as husbands and wives. The wooing process tends to be what it is here: not so much a prelude to marriage and a family as a process of self-definition—an increasingly unsatisfactory process, if we look at the progression of plays from *As You Like It*, *Much Ado about Nothing*, *Twelfth Night* through *All's Well That Ends Well*, *Measure for Measure*, *Troilus and Cressida* to *Antony and Cleopatra* and *Cymbeline*. If we want to argue that marriage *is* the point of the comic wooing process for Shakespeare, then we surely ought to be looking at how he depicts marriages. Here Petruchio and Kate, Capulet and Lady Capulet, Claudius and Gertrude, Othello and Desdemona, Macbeth and Lady Macbeth, Cymbeline and his queen, Leontes and Hermionie will not persuade us that comedies ending in marriages have ended happily, or if they have, it is only because they have ended there, stopped at the wedding day.

What happens after marriage? Families in Shakespeare tend to consist not of husbands and wives and their offspring, but of a parent and a child, usually in a chiastic relationship: father and daughter mother and son. When there are two children, they tend to be represented as alternatives or rivals: the twins of *The Comedy of Errors*, Sebastian and Viola, infinitely substitutable for each other, or the good son-bad son complex of Orlando and Oliver, Edgar and Edmund. We know that Shakespeare himself had a son and two daughters, but that family configuration never appears in the plays. Lear's three daughters are quite exceptional in Shakespeare, and even they are dichotomized into bad and good. We might also recall Titus Andronicus's four sons and a daughter and

Tamora's three sons, hardly instances to demonstrate Shakespeare's convictions about the comforts of family life.

The family paradigm that emerges from Shakespeare's imagination is a distinctly unstable one. Here is what we know of Shakespeare's own family: he had three brothers and three sisters who survived beyond infancy, and his parents lived into old age. At eighteen he married a woman of twenty-four by whom he had a daughter within six months, and a twin son and daughter a year and a half later. Within six more years he had moved permanently to London, and for the next twenty years—all but the last three years of his life—he lived apart from his wife and family. Nor should we stop here: we do not in the least know that Susanna, Hamnet and Judith were his only children. He lived in a society without contraceptives, and unless we want to believe that he was either exclusively homosexual or celibate, we must assume a high degree of probability that there were other children. The fact that they are not mentioned in his will may mean that they did not survive, but it also might mean that he made separate, non-testamentary provision for them. Certainly the plays reveal a strong interest in the subject of illegitimacy.

Until quite late in his career, the strongest familial feelings seem to be expressed not toward children or wives but toward parents and siblings. His father dies in 1601, the year of *Hamlet*, his mother in 1608, the year of *Coriolanus*. And if we are thinking about usurping, bastard younger brothers, it cannot be coincidental that the younger brother who followed him into the acting profession was named Edmund. There are no dramatic correlatives comparable to these for the death of his son Hamnet in 1596. If we take the plays to express what Shakespeare thought about himself (I put it that way to indicate that the assumption strikes me as by no means axiomatic) then we will say that he was apparently free to think of himself as a father—to his two surviving daughters—only after the death of both his parents. 1608 is the date of *Pericles* as well as *Coriolanus*.

One final biographical observation: Shakespearean heroines marry very young, in their teens. Miranda is fifteen. We are always told that Juliet's marriage at fourteen is not unusual in the period, but in fact it *is* unusual in all but upper class families. In Shakespeare's own family, his wife married at twenty-four and his daughters at twenty-four and thirty-one. It was Shakespeare himself who married at eighteen. The women of Shakespeare's plays, of course, are adolescent boys. Perhaps we should see as much of Shakespeare in Miranda and Ariel as in Prospero.

POWER AND AUTHORITY

The psychoanalytic and biographical questions raised by *The Tempest* are irresistible, but they can supply at best partial clues to its nature. I have described the plays as collaborative fantasies, and it is not only critics and readers who are involved in the collaboration. It is performers and audiences too, and I take these terms in their largest senses, to apply not merely to stage productions, but to the theatrical dimension of the society that contains and is mirrored by the theater as well. Cultural concerns, political and social issues, speak through *The Tempest*—sometimes explicitly; as in the open-ended discussion of political economy between Gonzalo, Antonio and Sebastian in Act II. But in a broader sense, family structures and sexual relations become political structures in the play, and these are relevant to the political structures of Jacobean England.

What is the nature of Prospero's authority and the source of his power? Why is he Duke of Milan and the legitimate ruler of the island? Power, as Prospero presents it in the play, is not inherited but self-created. It is magic, or "art," an extension of mental power and self-knowledge, and the authority legitimizing it derives from heaven—"Fortune" and "Destiny" are the terms used in the play. It is *Caliban* who derives his claim to the island from inheritance, from his mother.

In the England of 1610, both these positions represent available, and indeed normative ways of conceiving of royal authority. James I's authority derived, he said, both from his mother and from God. But deriving one's legitimacy from Mary Queen of Scots was an ambiguous claim at best, and James always felt exceedingly insecure about it. Elizabeth had had similar problems with the sources of her own authority, and they centered precisely on the question of her legitimacy. To those who believed that her father's divorce from Katherine of Aragon was invalid (that is, to Catholics), Elizabeth had no hereditary claim; and she had, moreover, been declared legally illegitimate after the execution of her mother for adultery and incest. Henry VIII maintained Elizabeth's bastardy to the end. Her claim to the throne derived exclusively from her designation in the line of succession, next after Edward and Mary, in her father's will. This ambiguous legacy was the sole source of her authority. Prospero at last acknowledging the bastard Caliban as his own is also expressing the double edge of kingship throughout Shakespeare's lifetime (the ambivalence will not surprise us if we consider the way kings are represented in the history plays). Historically speaking, Caliban's claim to the island is a good one.

Royal power, the play seems to say, is good when it is self-created, bad when it is usurped or inherited from an evil mother. But of course the least problematic case of royal descent is one that is not represented in these paradigms at all, one that derives not from the mother but in the male line from the father: the case of Ferdinand and Alonso, in which the wife and mother is totally absent. If we are thinking about the *derivation* of royal authority, then, the absence of a father from Prospero's memory is a great deal more significant than the disappearance of a wife. This has been dealt with in psychoanalytic terms, whereby Antonio becomes a stand-in for the father, the real usurper of the mother's kingdom;[5] but here again the realities of contemporary kingship seem more enlightening, if not inescapable. James in fact had a double claim to the English throne, and the one through his father, the Earl of Darnley, was in the strictly lineal respects somewhat stronger than that of his mother. Both Darnley and Mary were direct descendants of Henry VII, but under Henry VIII's will, which established the line of succession, descendants who were not English-born were specifically excluded. Darnley was born in England, Mary was not. In fact, Darnley's mother went from Scotland to have her baby in England precisely in order to preserve the claim to the throne.

King James rarely mentioned this side of his heritage, for perfectly understandable reasons. His father was even more disreputable than his mother; and given what was at least the public perception of both their characters, it was all too easy to speculate about whether Darnley was even in fact his father.[6] For James, as for Elizabeth, the derivation of authority through paternity was extremely problematic. In practical terms, James's claim to the English throne depended on Elizabeth *naming* him her heir (we recall Miranda's legitimacy depending on her mother's word), and James correctly saw this as a continuation of the protracted negotiations between Elizabeth and his mother. His legitimacy, in both senses, thus derived from two mothers, the chaste Elizabeth and the sensual Mary, whom popular imagery represented respectively as a virgin goddess ("a piece of virtue") and a lustful and diabolical witch. James's sense of his own place in the kingdom is that of Prospero, rigidly paternalistic, but incorporating the maternal as well: the King describes himself in *Basilicon Doron* as "a loving nourish father" providing the commonwealth with "their own nourish-milk."[7] The very etymology of the word "authority" confirms the metaphor: *augeo*, "increase, nourish, cause to grow." At moments in his public utterances, James sounds like a gloss on Prospero: "I am the husband, and the whole island is my lawful wife; I am the head, and it is my body."[8] Here the incorporation of the wife has become literal and explicit. James conceives himself as the head of a single-parent family. In the world of *The Tempest*, there are no two-parent families. All the dangers of promiscuity and bastardy are resolved in such a conception—unless, of course, the parent is a woman.

My point here is not that Shakespeare is representing King James as Prospero and/or Caliban, but that these figures embody the predominant modes of conceiving of royal authority in the period. They are Elizabeth's and James's modes too.

THE RENUNCIATION OF MAGIC

Prospero's magic power is exemplified, on the whole, as power over children: his daughter Miranda, the bad child Caliban, the obedient but impatient Ariel, the adolescent Ferdinand, the wicked younger brother Antonio, and indeed, the shipwreck victims as a whole, who are treated like a group of bad children. Many critics talk about Prospero as a Renaissance scientist, and see alchemical metaphors in the grand design of the play. No doubt there is something in this, but what the play's action presents is not experiments and empiric studies but a fantasy about controlling other people's minds. Does the magic work? We are given a good deal of evidence of it: the masque, the banquet, the harpies, the tempest itself. But the great scheme is not to produce illusions and good weather, it is to bring about reconciliation, and here we would have to say that it works only indifferently well. "They being penitent," says Prospero to Ariel, "The sole drift of my purpose doth extend / Not a frown further" (5.1.28–30). The assertion opens with a conditional clause whose conditions are not met: Alonso is penitent, but the chief villain, the usurping younger brother Antonio, remains obdurate. Nothing, not all Prospero's magic, can redeem Antonio from his essential badness. Since Shakespeare was free to have Antonio repent if that is what he had in mind—half a line would have done for critics craving a reconciliation—we ought to take seriously the possibility that that is not what he had in mind. Perhaps, too, penitence is not what Prospero's magic is designed to elicit from his brother.

Why is Prospero's power conceived as magic? Why, in returning to Milan, does he renounce it? Most commentators say that he gives up his magic when he no longer needs it. This is an obvious answer, but it strikes me as too easy, a comfortable assumption cognate with the view that the play concludes with reconciliation, repentance, and restored harmony. To say that Prospero no longer *needs* his magic is to beg all the most important questions. What does it mean to say that he needs it? Did he ever need it, and if so, why? And does he in fact give it up?

Did he ever need magic? Prospero's devotion to his secret studies is what caused all the trouble in the first place—this is not an interpretation of mine, it is how Prospero presents the matter. If he has now learned to be a good ruler through the exercise of his art, that is also what taught him to be a bad one. So the question of his *need* for magic goes to the heart of how we interpret and judge his character: is the magic a strength or a weakness? To say that he no longer needs it is to say that his character changes in some way for the better, that by renouncing his special powers he becomes fully human. This is an important claim: let us test it by looking at Prospero's renunciation.

What does it mean for Prospero to give up his power? Letting Miranda marry and leaving the island are the obvious answers, but they can hardly be right. Miranda's marriage is *brought about* by the magic: it is part of Prospero's plan. It pleases Miranda, certainly, but it is designed by Prospero as a way of satisfying himself. Claribel's marriage to the King of Tunis looks less sinister in this light: daughters' marriages, in royal families at least, are designed primarily to please their fathers. And leaving the island, reassuming the dukedom, is part of the plan too. Both of these are presented as acts of renunciation, but they are in fact what the exercise of Prospero's magic is intended to effect, and they represent his triumph.

Prospero renounces his art in the great monologue at the beginning of Act V, "Ye elves of hills, brooks, standing lakes and groves," and for all its valedictory quality, it is the most powerful assertion of his magic the play gives us. It is also a powerful literary allusion, a close translation of a speech of Medea's in Ovid,[9] and it makes at least one claim for Prospero that is made nowhere else in the play: that he can raise the dead. For Shakespeare to present this as a *renunciation* speech is upping Prospero's ante, to say the least.

In giving up his magic, Prospero speaks as Medea. He has incorporated Ovid's witch, prototype of the wicked mother Sycorax, in the most literal way—verbatim, so to speak—and his "most potent art" is now revealed as translation and impersonation. In this context, the distinction between black and white magic, Sycorax and Prospero, has disappeared. Two hundred lines later, Caliban too is revealed as an aspect of Prospero: "This thing of darkness I acknowledge mine."

But Caliban is an aspect of Antonio, the evil child, the usurping brother. Where is the *real* villain in relation to Prospero now? Initially Antonio had been characterized, like Caliban and Sycorax, as embodying everything that is antithethical to Prospero. But in recounting his history to Miranda, Prospero also presents himself as deeply implicated in the usurpation, with Antonio even seeming at times to be acting as Prospero's agent: "The government I cast upon my brother"; "[I] to him put the manage of my state"; "my trust. . .did beget of him / A falsehood," and so forth. If Prospero is accepting the blame for what happened, there is a degree to which he is also taking the credit. Antonio's is another of the play's identities that Prospero has incorporated into his own, and in that case, what is there to forgive?

Let us look, then, at Prospero forgiving his brother in Act V. The pardon is enunciated ("You, brother mine, that entertain ambition. . . .I do forgive thee" [75–78])[10] and qualified at once ("unnatural though thou art"), reconsidered as more crimes are remembered, some to be held in reserve ("at this time I will tell no tales" [128–29]), all but withdrawn ("most wicked sir, whom to call brother / Would even infect my mouth" [130–31]), and only then confirmed through forcing Antonio to relinquish the dukedom, an act that is presented as something he does unwillingly. The point is not only that Antonio does not repent here: he also is not *allowed* to repent. Even his renunciation of the crown is Prospero's act: "I do. . .require / My dukedom of thee, which perforce, I know, / Thou must restore (131–34). In Prospero's drama, there is no room for Antonio to act of his own free will.

The crime that Prospero holds in reserve for later use against his brother is the attempted assassination of Alonso. Here is what happened. Prospero sends Ariel to put all the shipwreck victims to sleep except Antonio and Sebastian. Antonio then persuades Sebastian to murder Alonso—his brother—and thereby become King of Naples. Sebastian agrees, on the condition that Antonio kill Gonzalo. At the moment of the murders, Ariel reappears and wakes Gonzalo:

> My master through his art foresees the danger
> That you his friend are in: and sends me forth—
> For else his project dies—to keep them living. (2.1.293–95)

This situation has been created by Prospero, and the conspiracy is certainly part of his project—that is why Sebastian and Antonio are not put to sleep. If Antonio is not forced by Prospero to propose the murder, he is certainly acting as Prospero expects him to do, and as Ariel says, Prospero "through his art foresees" that he will. What is clearly taking place is Prospero restaging his usurpation and maintaining his control over it this time. Gonzalo is waked rather than Alonso so that the old courtier can replay his role in aborting the assassination.

So at the play's end, Prospero still has usurpation and attempted murder to hold against his brother, things that still disqualify Antonio from his place in the family. Obviously there is more to Prospero's plans than reconciliation and harmony—even, I would think, in the forthcoming happy marriage of Ferdinand and Miranda. If we look at that marriage as a political act (the participants are, after all, the children of monarchs) we will observe that in order to prevent the succession of his brother, Prospero is marrying his daughter to the son of his enemy. This has the effect of excluding Antonio from any future claim on the ducal throne, but it also effectively disposes of the realm as a political entity: if Miranda is the heir to the dukedom, Milan through the marriage becomes part of the kingdom of Naples, not the other way around. Prospero recoups his throne from his brother only to deliver it over, upon his death, to the King of Naples once again. The usurping Antonio stands condemned, but the effects of the usurpation, the link with Alonso and the reduction of Milan to a Neapolitan fiefdom are, through Miranda's wedding, confirmed and legitimized. Prospero has not regained his lost dukedom, he has usurped his brother's. In this context, Prospero's puzzling assertion that "every third thought shall be my grave" can be seen as a final assertion of authority and control: he has now arranged matters so that his death will remove Antonio's last link with the ducal power. His grave is the ultimate triumph over his brother. If we look at the marriage in this way, giving away Miranda is a means of preserving his authority, not of relinquishing it.

A BIBLIOGRAPHICAL CODA

The significant absence of crucial wives from the play is curiously emphasized by a famous textual crux. In Act IV Ferdinand, overwhelmed by the beauty of the masque Prospero is presenting, interrupts the performance to say,

> Let me live here, ever.
> So rare a wondered father and a wise
> Makes this place Paradise. (4.1.122–24)

Critics since the eighteenth century have expressed a nagging worry about the fact that in celebrating his betrothal, Ferdinand's paradise includes Prospero but not Miranda. In fact, what Ferdinand said, as Jeanne Addison Roberts demonstrated only six years ago,[11] reads in the earliest copies of the folio, "So rare a wondered father and a wife," but the crossbar of the *f* broke early in the print run, turning it to a long *s* and thereby eliminating Miranda from Ferdinand's thoughts of wonder. The odd thing about this is that Rowe and Malone in their eighteenth-century editions emended "wise" to "wife" on logical grounds, the Cambridge Shakespeare of 1863 lists "wife" as a variant reading of the folio, and Furnivall's 1895 photographic facsimile was made from a copy that reads "wife," and the reading is preserved in Furnivall's parallel text. Nevertheless, after 1895 the wife became invisible: bibliographers lost the variant, and textual critics consistently denied its existence until six years ago. Even Charlton Hinman with his collating machines claimed there were no variants whatever in this entire forme of the folio. And yet when Jeanne Roberts examined the Folger Library's copies of the book, including those that Hinman had collated, she found that two of them have the reading "wife," and two others clearly show the crossbar of the *f* in the process of breaking. We find only what we are looking for or are willing to see. Obviously it is a reading whose time has come.

NOTES

1. Line references throughout are to the Arden edition, edited by Frank Kermode. In this instance, I have restored the folio punctuation of line 59.
2. Edited by Murray M. Schwartz and Coppélia Kahn (Baltimore, 1980).
3. *The New Yorker*, March 1, 1982, p. 53.
4. "So Rare a Wonder'd Father: Prospero's *Tempest*," in *Representing Shakespeare*, p. 48.
5. Coppélia Kahn makes this point, following a suggestion of Harry Berger, Jr., in "The Providential Tempest and the Shakespearean Family," in *Representing Shakespeare*, p. 238. For an alternative view, see the exceptionally interesting

discussion by Joel Fineman, "Fratricide and Cuckoldry: Shakespeare's Doubles," in *Representing Shakespeare*, p. 104.

6. The charge that he was David Rizzio's child was current in England in the 1580s, spread by rebellious Scottish Presbyterian ministers. James expressed fears that it would injure his chance of succeeding to the English throne, and he never felt entirely free of it.

7. C. H. McIlwain, *Political Works of James I* (Cambridge, Mass., 1918), p. 24.

8. From the 1603 speech to Parliament; ibid., p. 272.

9. *Metamorphoses* 7.197–209, apparently at least partly refracted through Golding's English version.

10. Kermode and most editors read "entertained," but I have restored the folio reading, which seems to me unexceptionable.

11. "'Wife' or 'Wise'—The Tempest l. 1786," *University of Virginia Studies in Bibliography* 31 (1978).

"Remember/First To Possess His Books"

The Appropriation of *The Tempest*, 1700–1800[*]

MICHAEL DOBSON

The eighteenth century inherited two versions of *The Tempest*. One was an established classic, immensely popular in the theatre and the subject of countless allusions outside it: *The Tempest, or the Enchanted Island*, adapted by Dryden and Davenant in 1667 and provided with further operatic embellishments by Shadwell in 1674. The other was the play which appears first in the Shakespeare Folio, *The Tempest*, which had not been performed since its author's lifetime and would not be revived in anything like its original form until 1746. The history of these competing texts in eighteenth-century culture, which this paper will endeavour to illuminate, is not a simple matter of the Restoration's spurious, usurping *Enchanted Island* gradually succumbing to the inevitable rise of Bardolatry in favour of the true, Shakespearian *Tempest*, although this is how it has always tended to be represented. It is rather the history of how new concepts of Shakespeare—new ideas of the meanings and uses of Great English Literature conspire both with and against new readings of *The Tempest* to produce a series of new Prosperos, new Mirandas, and new Calibans over the course of the century—whether in fresh stage versions like Garrick's operetta of 1756, the puppet version of 1780 or Kemble's play of 1789, or in other media: novels, statues, poems, literary criticism. In this short essay I hope to suggest what issues were at stake for the eighteenth century's various appropriators of *The Tempest*, and quite why this text, frequently hailed from the nineteenth century onwards as perhaps the most artistically (and indeed typographically) reliable of all Shakespeare plays, should have been one of the most unstable in the repertory during precisely the period which both identified Shakespeare with Prospero and installed him as "the god

*Originally published in *Shakespeare Survey* 43 (1991): 99–107. © Cambridge University Press 1991. Reprinted with the permission of Cambridge University Press and Michael Dobson.

of its idolatry." In effect I shall be using eighteenth-century responses to *The Tempest* to sketch a history of the cultural pressures under which this text was enabled to function alternately as a fiction of gender relations and a fiction of racial mastery, developments which have been discussed with particular pertinence and urgency in the context of the twentieth century by Ania Loomba in *Gender, Race, Renaissance Drama*.[1]

On the stage, *The Tempest* entered the eighteenth century as a play which addressed the issue of power primarily in terms of patriarchal authority within the family. Davenant and Dryden's adaptation *The Enchanted Island* (first performed in 1667), perhaps as a result of its post-Restoration uncertainties about Prospero's political status within the state,[2] displaces the whole question of government on to the proper socialization of sexuality, compensating for its qualms about Prospero's authority as a father-king with a remarkable degree of enthusiasm for his authority as a father *tout court*. In its extended scenes between Ferdinand, Miranda, and the added characters Dorinda (Miranda's younger sister, equally ignorant of men) and Hippolito (Prospero's ward, "one that never saw Woman, right Heir of the Dukedom of *Mantua*")[3] *The Enchanted Island* sets out to prove, in a manner half way between that of a court masque and a Royal Society experiment, that patriarchal authority can be rationally deduced from nature; to demonstrate, in effect, that *Basilikon Doron* may not be entirely incompatible with *Leviathan*. Even the most cursory summary of Davenant and Dryden's additions to *The Tempest* may suggest the degree of insistence with which this enduringly popular play sets out to demonstrate the "naturalness" of contemporary gender rôles to an audience increasingly aware of the contingency of all social institutions. On their first appearance Miranda and Dorinda are represented as unpromptedly eager to be subjected to mates who will assume Prospero's paternal authority, even before they learn of Ferdinand and Hippolito's existence—"Methinks indeed it would be finer, if we two / Had two young Fathers" speculates Dorinda[4]—and Dryden goes so far as to have Miranda unconsciously consent to undergo labour pains as part of the cost—"I had rather be in pain nine Months, as my Father threatn'd, than lose my longing."[5] Having displayed these exemplary young women's innate aptness for precisely the functions to which contemporary society consigned them,[6] the play moves on to justify the ways of marriage to men. Hippolito, after his first forbidden meeting with Dorinda, seems unproblematically to embrace monogamy as the condition of possession—"I'd quit the rest o'the'world that I might live alone with / Her. .,"[7] he tells Prospero—but it transpires that this unprompted willingness to forsake all others is premised on his ignorance that any others exist. When Ferdinand lets this vital piece of information slip, Hippolito is overjoyed, declaring that "I'le have as many as I can, / That are so good, and Angellike as she I love. / And will have yours. . .,"[8] and the two young princes are soon engaged in a proto-Freudian primal struggle for dominion over the women. Ferdinand, defending his property rights in Miranda, kills Hippolito in a duel, and only a magic resurrection effected by Ariel prevents Prospero from executing him in revenge: after this solemn display of the disadvantages of the sexual "state of nature," the four young lovers, all together on stage at the start of the last act for the first time in the play, are able to deduce (even on purely mathematical grounds) that the adoption of conjugal fidelity on all sides is the best expedient to prevent further violence. At this convenient point in their experiments legitimate paternal authority arrives on the stage to ratify these agreements in the persons of Prospero and Alonzo, and thus despite its other principal subplot's dutiful attack on Hobbes (the mutinous and quarrelsome sailors repeatedly misquote *Leviathan*), the play can achieve comic resolution in a fashion surprisingly congruent with the emerging political doctrines of contractualism, patriarchal monogamy proving to be a rational contract made between men in a state of nature for their mutual self-preservation and the protection of their property.

So thoroughgoing is *The Enchanted Island* in its emphasis on gender that it virtually occludes Caliban altogether: in Davenant and Dryden's adaptation he gets drunk so thoroughly during his first encounter with the sailors that so far from leading an attempted coup against Prospero he neglects even to alert his new comrades to the Duke of Milan's existence. He is in effect rewritten as a potentially unruly woman by the provision of a sister, Sycorax, over the possession of whom Trinculo and Stephano struggle in a deliberate reiteration of the Hippolito / Ferdinand duel of the romantic subplot. Thomas Duffett's illuminating travesty of *The Enchanted Island*, *The Mock-Tempest* (1674), which transfers the action of the play to contemporary London low-life, is similarly uninterested in colonialism, translating Caliban perfunctorily into class terms (he features, briefly, as a lower-class hired bully, Hectoro), and preferring to gloss, in a strikingly Foucauldian fashion, Davenant and Dryden's overriding concern with gender politics by casting Prospero as the keeper of the Bridewell prison, the state's official punisher of prostitutes. Discussing Caliban in the preface to his subsequent adaptation *Troilus and Cressida; or, Truth Found Too Late* Dryden simply mystifies him as an example of the supernatural grotesque rather than a dispossessed native ("[Shakespeare] *there seems to have created a person who was not in Nature*"),[9] and this neglect of the racial issues raised by Shakespeare's "salvage and deformed Slave" seems to have persisted in the early eighteenth-century theatre, one production of *The Enchanted Island* at Drury Lane in 1729 having apparently omitted Caliban altogether.[10]

With or without Caliban, the first decades of the eighteenth century found *The Enchanted Island* achieving virtually annual revivals, reaching a level of popularity which, paradoxically, would ultimately be its undoing. Preserving what is virtually the sole potentially subversive aspect of Dryden and Davenant's adaptation—their original transvestite casting of Hippolito and Sycorax—and frequently compounding these disruptive aspects of its presentation by casting an actress as Ariel (so that at the play's conclusion Prospero appears to sanction two pairings of women, the cross-dressed Hippolito with Dorinda and the cross-dressed Ariel with her/his added spiritual partner Milcha), the play, acquiring new musical and visual accretions each season, became a carnivalesque holiday entertainment, a familiar set-piece revived (often for actors' benefits, a sure sign of broad popularity) for the socially heterodox audiences attracted to the theatre between New Year's Eve and Twelfth Night.[11] The English theatre now has a specific name for plays of this kind, spectacular Christmas performances of stories so familiar that they have come to constitute part of the ideology of their audiences, inexplicably featuring middle-aged men dressed as comic women: pantomime. Already equipped with a Principal Boy in Hippolito and a Dame in Sycorax, and possessing a Wizard in Prospero and a Good Fairy in Ariel, *The Enchanted Island*'s assimilation as the standard festive treat of the early eighteenth-century theatre identifies *The Tempest* as the ultimate source of Panto as the London stage still knows it. In the new cultural climate of the early 1700s, however, both the explicitly sexual content of *The Enchanted Island* and its "low," hybrid dramatic form could only result in its slow but inevitable demotion from the status of literature, and by the 1740s (during the early years of Garrick's reign at Drury Lane, as the Theatres Royal sought increasingly to present themselves as impeccably decorous social spaces) it was already on its way to being banished from the legitimate theatres altogether. After a few last Christmas revivals, the very last in the 1749–50 season, *The Enchanted Island* was driven out to less gentrified arenas, first to the illegal New Wells Theatre in Goodman's Fields for one production in 1745, and ultimately to that definitive site of lowness and transgression, Bartholomew Fair itself, where it was staged at Phillips's Great Theatrical Booth opposite Cow Lane from 1749 onwards.[12] After this the play was exiled to even darker fringes of the theatrical world, achieving regular revivals at the John Street Theatre in New York between 1774 and 1788, where its dramatization of the issues of absolutism and contractualism, and its admittedly attenuated interest in the structures of colonialism, must have seemed particularly to the point.[13]

Meanwhile, the return of the repressed colonial plot had to take place, for the time being, in other media. Alexander Pope, for example, follows Davenant and Dryden in appropriating *The Tempest* as a text about the policing of female sexuality, borrowing Ariel as the chief sylphic guardian of Belinda's chastity in *The Rape of the Lock* (1714), but his heroine is additionally a Miranda deeply implicated in the fate of offstage Calibans in that her beauty is conspicuously adorned, if not constructed, by a glittering catalogue of luxury items represented as the spoils of England's growing mercantile imperialism.[14] Five years later a text still more closely associated with the rise of capitalist imperialism would expel Miranda entirely to place the Prospero/Caliban relationship centre stage. In an article published nearly twenty years ago,

J. W. Loofbourow noticed some incidental similarities between *The Enchanted Island* and Defoe's *Robinson Crusoe* (1719),[15] and I would argue that Defoe's desert island episode constitutes in itself a radical bourgeois response to Davenant and Dryden's familiar play. Defoe simply deletes women as vigorously as the adaptors had imported them, enabling Crusoe and Friday, left alone on their conspicuously unenchanted island to get on with the serious business of the colonial plot (complete with its crucial language lessons), and although he grudgingly retains *The Enchanted Island*'s mutineers he carefully banishes them to the ship which finally comes to Crusoe's rescue.[16]

Neither of these printed derivatives of *The Enchanted Island* acknowledges Shakespeare by name: to be redeemed as a reputable, publishable Author in Augustan culture Shakespeare had to be cleared of his association with Davenant and Dryden's interpolated hanky-panky. Nicholas Rowe's pioneering six-volume edition of the Complete Works (1709) accordingly restores *The Tempest* to propriety (printing Shakespeare's unadulterated text following the Folio, as the first play in the canon) and identifies it as Shakespeare's exclusive literary property: the essay appended by Charles Gildon in a spurious seventh volume, "Remarks on the Plays of Shakespeare," opens fittingly with a scathing attack on *The Enchanted Island*, concluding with the remark that its additional scenes are "scarce guilty of a Thought, which we could justly attribute to *Shakespeare*."[17] Gildon's construction of a stable authorial presence behind and beyond the play, in his critical quest for such thoughts as we could justly attribute to Shakespeare, is entirely in tune with one of the most notable features of this edition, Rowe's provision of a biographical memoir by way of general preface. By 1746 it had become possible once more to stage *The Tempest* in something like its original form, only a few of Shadwell's added touches of pageantry remaining.[18]

Nevertheless, even the "original," Jacobean *Tempest* came to address similar contemporary issues to those canvassed in Defoe's demystified prose version of *The Enchanted Island*, Prospero the island colonist soon being adopted as an acutely timely figure for Shakespeare's "timeless" originality. The explicit adoption of Prospero as an unmediated Shakespearian self-presentation is initiated by Gildon just a year before *Crusoe*'s publication, when his "Shakespeariana: or Select Moral Reflections, Topicks, Similies and Descriptions from SHAKSPEAR,"[19] the first example of this particular way of commodifying Shakespearian drama for bourgeois home consumption, quotes the "Our revels now are ended. . ." speech under the tendentious heading beneath which it has been brandished so often since: it is offered as Shakespeare's own definitive statement on "*Humane Nature*." This now traditional stroke of biographical criticism was nationally institutionalized in 1741 by the chiselling of a garbled fragment of the same speech onto the scroll displayed by the statue of Shakespeare erected that February in Westminster Abbey:

> The Cloud cupt Tow'rs,
> The Gorgeous Palaces,
> The Great Globe itself
> Yea all which it Inherit,
>   Shall Dissolve;
> And like the baseless Fabrick of a Vision
> Leave not a wreck behind.

Although the committee which supervised the design and installation of this monument was predominantly aristocratic, if not positively Jacobite (it was led by Lord Burlington, and included Pope),[20] the impetus behind the project was chiefly mercantile: during the late 1730s Shakespeare had been proclaimed repeatedly, by bourgeois pressure-groups such as the Shakespeare Ladies' Club, as an exemplar of unfallen Elizabethan Protestantism, a cultural figurehead pressed into the service of the growing campaign for full-scale trade war against Spain.[21] The monument thus simultaneously identifes Shakespeare with Prospero the prince, a symbol of the lost splendour of the English monarchy (Burlington's committee insisted that the statue's pedestal should incorporate likenesses of Elizabeth I and Henry V), and with Prospero the private, magically creative proto-playwright, patron of a new and specifically culturally-based strain of nationalism. The latter perspective heavily predominates in the considerable number of mid eighteenth-century poems dedicated to celebrating Shakespeare as the type of home-grown British genius, poems which frequently both repeat the identification of Shakespeare with Prospero canonized by the Abbey monument and take a new pride in the Bard's humble market-town origins. *AVON, a Poem in Three Parts* (1758),[22] written by John Huckell (who characteristically accounts for Shakespeare's imaginative power by describing how as a youth he saw Nature bathing naked in the Avon), states that the Bard is "Possess'd of more than his own PROSP'RO'S skill";[23] the Scottish poet John Ogilvie's *Solitude: or, the Elysium of the Poets, A Vision* (1765)[24] presents Shakespeare, attended by Ariel, sharing poetic dominion over Britain with that other untaught native genius, Ossian. If Shakespeare is Prospero, the pastoral, provincial Britain he inhabits must be his island, a surmise confirmed in the "*VERSES on reading SHAKESPEAR*" printed in *The Gentleman's Magazine* for June 1753: here the Bard summons us

> to rove
> With humble nature, in the rural grove,
> Where swains contented own the quiet scene,
> And twilight fairies tread the circled green,
> Drest by *her* hand, the woods and valleys smile,
> And spring diffusive, decks th'inchanted isle.

More famously, Garrick's *An ode upon dedicating a building, and erecting a statue, to Shakespeare, at Stratford upon Avon*, recited in front of a copy of the

Westminster Abbey monument at the climax of the Stratford Jubilee of 1769, links the grammar-school prodigy with Prospero repeatedly, perhaps most remarkably in its opening patriotic rhetorical questions:

> To what blest genius of the isle,
> Shall Gratitude her tribute pay,
>   Decree the festive day,
> Erect the statue, and devote the pile?
>
> Do not your sympathetic hearts accord,
>   To own the "bosom's lord?"
> 'Tis he! 'tis he! that demi-god!
> Who Avon's flow'ry margin trod,
>   While sportive *Fancy* round him flew,
> Where *Nature* led him by the hand,
>   Instructed him in all she knew,
> And gave him absolute command!
>   'Tis he! 'tis he!
> "The god of our idolatry!"[25]

In the service of Prospero/Shakespeare, the genius of the isle, attended by sportive Fancy as Ariel, Garrick has here not only taken over the rhetoric of royal panegyric but outdone it: as the father of English Literature, Shakespeare is claimed as a national deity, whose special middle-class revision of absolutism is sanctioned by that quintessentially bourgeois virtue, sympathy.

If the identification of Shakespeare with Prospero serves here to claim *The Tempest* for what may look like a form of Little Englandism, it also presses it more strenuously than ever into the service of imperialism. Garrick's own version of *The Tempest*, an operatic abbreviation which ran for only six performances in 1756, was staged at the height of the Seven Years War, as Britain vied with France for control over vast colonized territories in India, the Far East, and the Americas; eschewing the interpolated pleasures of the Dorinda/Hippolito scenes, and cutting Sycorax, this adaptation restores the rebellion and punishment of Caliban to prominence in the subplot, and is additionally prefaced by a prologue which cites English opera as an ideal patriotic stimulus to its audience to commit deeds of valour against the French.[26] The Shakespeare Jubilee itself, staged in the interim between the colonial gains of the Seven Years War and the losses of the American War of Independence, featured reiterated boasts of Shakespeare's domination of World Literature, and it is hard not to regard the "gratitude" Garrick's climactic Ode showers so fulsomely upon the Bard as largely inspired by Britain's recent imperial acquisitions. A song in Garrick's subsequent pageant-play *The Jubilee* (1769) succinctly underlines this point: "Our Shakespeare compared to is no man / No Frenchman, nor Grecian, nor Roman."[27] Culturally superior to all major modern and classical competitors, Shakespeare's artistic triumph is here neatly congruent with the imperial triumph of his modern fellow Britons. Prospero, as both playwright and colonist, rules the waves.

Both *The Enchanted Island* and Garrick's operatic *Tempest* had by 1769 long been laid aside in the theatres in favour of Shakespeare's original text, and that this shift away from the adaptations, contemporary with the definitive appropriation of Shakespeare/Prospero as a figurehead for imperial expansion, is also a shift away from a gender-oriented and towards a race-orientated reading of *The Tempest* is perhaps suggested by the sole illustration of the play in performance which survives from this period. The frontispiece to the play in Bell's acting edition of 1774 ignores Miranda, Ariel, Ferdinand, and indeed Prospero to illustrate the moment in Act 2 when Trinculo and Stephano force the newly-drunk Caliban to swear allegiance—a primal scene of colonialism if ever there was one, and significantly the actor playing the kneeling Caliban is made up not as Dryden's supernatural freak but, perfectly representationally, as a Negro.[28] Garrick, too chooses this scene as the central moment of the play in the procession of Shakespearian characters which marks the climax of *The Jubilee*, having Prospero, preceded by Ariel "with a wand, raising a tempest" and a model "ship in distress sailing down the stage," march triumphantly downstage ahead of Miranda, and Caliban "with a wooden bottle and 2 Sailors all drunk":[29] contemporary engravings depicting this procession similarly record Caliban's representation as a black slave.[30] Prospero here serves as a living emblem of the proper jurisdiction of Englishmen over not only women and the incipiently mutinous lower classes (as he certainly does in *The Enchanted Island*) but also over the subject races newly compelled to pledge allegiance to the Empire.

This is not to say that Dryden and Davenant's adaptation, or the uses of *The Tempest* it initiates, had been forgotten. The editor of Bell's edition, Francis Gentleman, considered that Shakespeare's text was "*an odd, improbable, agreeable mixture. . .more nervous and chaste, but not so well supplied with humour or business, as* Dryden's," and opined that "*by properly blending. . .a better piece than either, might be produced.*"[31] In 1780 just such a hybrid, the anonymous puppet play *The Shipwreck*, enjoyed considerable success at the "Patagonian Theatre" on the Strand: more concerned with the disciplining of female sexuality than ever, this version pits Prospero against a whole team of insurgent witches in the main plot and, allowing Sycorax to upstage Caliban once more, expands the sailors' scenes to include a diatribe against masquerades.[32] More remarkably, another reworking of the old Davenant/Dryden adaptation would nine years later replace Shakespeare's original as the standard acting text employed in the Theatres Royal, namely *The Tempest; or the Enchanted Island. Written by Shakespeare; with additions from Dryden: as compiled by J.P. Kemble.*[33]

This "relapse" to what is in effect a slightly respectablized version of *The Enchanted Island*, more than four decades after the restoration of Shakespeare's original *Tempest*, has long puzzled stage historians, and I should like to close by suggesting some reasons why Kemble should have chosen to follow Gentleman's advice at this particular time. By the 1780s *The Tempest* was no longer the most prominent example in contemporary libraries of a text interested in describing the natural innocence of a woman brought up by an ideal guardian outside conventional society: it was competing as such against a text with potentially far more radical implications, namely Rousseau's *Emile*. Miranda is specifically held up as a counter-example to Rousseau's "child of nature," Sophie, in the most noteworthy piece of Shakespeare criticism published in the year of Kemble's adaptation, William Richardson's *On Shakespeare's Imitation of Female Characters*,[34] and in one of the acting editions of Kemble's adaptation she is contrasted with another Rousseauistic heroine of sensibility, Amanthis, the protagonist of the radical Elizabeth Inchbald's play *The Child of Nature*.[35] In the aftermath of the storming of the Bastille—and Kemble's *Tempest* was one of the first new productions mounted in London in the season which followed it—*The Tempest* was, in effect mobilized to discipline susceptible English womanhood and to warn the youth of Albion against the temptations of French libertinism. The reaction against the Revolution characteristically figures its enemy as female sexual transgression, and thus Dryden and Davenant's adaptation, with its redoubled pro-patriarchal love plot, was self-evidently better suited to Kemble's right-wing purposes than Shakespeare's original text. In effect the task of civilizing Caliban abroad was temporarily laid aside, the immediate threat of Revolution causing *The Tempest* once more to be deployed as a text enforcing law and order within the family.[36] A last example of this counter-revolutionary appropriation of the play is found in Mary Ann Hanway's conservative novel *Ellinor, or The World As It Is* (1798): here once more Shakespeare's play is invoked to police female sexual licence, when our heroine Ellinor is induced, like Sycorax in *The Shipwreck*, to attend a masquerade. Sir James Lavington, the upright member of the gentry who will prove to be Ellinor's rightful father, has been pressurized into attending the same masquerade by his wicked other daughter, Augusta: as a sign of his virtuous parental authority, and his true English moral superiority to such Continental excess, he comes dressed not mendaciously but as his true self: as Prospero.[37]

Obscure as Hanway's novel may be, Sir James Lavington provides in many ways a completely appropriate final incarnation of the late eighteenth-century Prospero. Over the course of the eighteenth century's transmission of *The Tempest*, Prospero's ambivalently royal prerogative has been used to sustain the changing versions of authority developed during the century's steady takeover by the merchant classes of the symbols of national power. Just as power relations themselves were being rewritten, so *The Tempest*, already deeply involved with them by 1700, had to be rewritten too. From sustaining Stuart patriarchy it had come to certify the enchantedness of Stratford and the cultural superiority of the English bourgeoisie, eventually being invoked to defend family life and property against the threat of Revolution. Deployed alternately as a figure for paternal jurisdiction, racial mastery and successful counter-revolution, Prospero, and by extension his creator, had been variously but securely appropriated as the defender of prosperity. Two centuries later, Miranda, Caliban and the mutineers have yet to depose him.

NOTES

This article began life as a paper presented to the Special session "Alternative Shake-speares: Adaptation and Interpretation, 1600–1900" at the MLA conference in New Orleans, 1988, and I am especially grateful to the panel's organizer, Professor Jean Marsden (University of Connecticut), and to my fellow panelists, notably Professor Nicola Watson (Northwestern University), for many valuable suggestions. Since then different versions have elicited further helpful advice from Professor Stanley Wells (Birmingham University) and Professors Marjorie Garber and Stanley Cavell (Harvard University).

1. Ania Loomba, *Gender, Race, Renaissance Drama* (Manchester: Manchester UP, 1989): see especially chapter 6, "Seizing the book," on colonial and post-colonial appropriations of *The Tempest* in India.
2. Persuasively analysed in Katharine Eisaman Maus, "Arcadia Lost: Politics and Revision in the Restoration *Tempest*," *Renaissance Drama* (new series) 13 (1982): 189–209, and further illuminated by Matthew Wikander, "'The Duke My Father's Wrack': The Innocence of the Restoration *Tempest*," *Shakespeare Survey* 43 (1991): 91–98.
3. Sir William Davenant and John Dryden, *The Tempest, or the Enchanted Island* (London, 1670), "Dramatis Personae."
4. Ibid, p. 13.
5. Ibid, p. 28. There is an interesting submerged pun at work here, as Miranda's willingness to undergo "labour" as the price of having Ferdinand takes the place of Ferdinand's Adamic labour (carrying logs) as the price of having Miranda in the original.
6. On empiricism and gender in *The Enchanted Island*, see Catherine Belsey, *The Subject of Tragedy: Identity and Difference in Renaissance Drama* (London and New York: Methuen, 1985), pp. 81–86.
7. *The Enchanted Island*, p. 47.
8. Ibid., p. 50.
9. John Dryden, *Troilus and Cressida; or, Truth Found Too Late* (London, 1679), "The Grounds of Criticism in Tragedy."
10. See Emmett L. Avery et al, eds., *The London Stage, 1660–1800* (5 pts. in 11 vols., Carbondale: Southern Illinois Univeristy Press, 1960–8), pt. 2 p. 1006.
11. See C. B. Hogan, *Shakespeare in the Theatre*, 1701–1800 (2 vols, Oxford: Clarendon Press, 1952), I, pp. 423–4.

12. See Mary Margaret Nilan, *The Stage History of The Tempest: A Question of Theatricality* (PhD thesis, Northwestern University, Evanston, Illinois 1967: Ann Arbor: Univeristy Microfilms International, 1980), Chapters 2–4: *The Daily Advertiser*, 23 August 1749.

13. See George C. D. Odell, *Annals of the New York Stage* (15 vols., New York: Columbia University Press, 1927–49), I, p. 163.

14. As Laura Brown remarks: "Of all the major works of its period, *The Rape of the Lock* does the most to match imperialism and commodity fetishism, and the most to place the commodification of English culture in the context of imperial violence." Laura Brown, *Alexander Pope* (Oxford: Blackwell, 1985), p. 22.

15. "Robinson Crusoe's Island and the Restoration *Tempest*" *Enlightenment Essays* 2 (1971), 201–7. Loofbourow notes that the polarizing of Crusoe's island into "garden" and "barren" areas, and the prominence of his cave, derive from the stage set of Dryden and Davenant's play, and adduces its Masque of Devils as a source for the earthquake and the accusing vision which follows it. The connections between Defoe's novel and the Davenant and Dryden adaptation are perhaps further suggested by *Robinson Crusoe*'s ultimate assimilation to the same pantomime tradition, from Sheridan's *Harlequin Friday* (1780: published anonymously, 1795) onwards.

16. For at least one other contemporary novelist, however, *The Enchanted Island* remained a text concerned almost exclusively with untutored sexuality: the desert island adventures which proliferated in the wake of Crusoe's success included *The Force of Nature; or the Loves of Hippollito and Dorinda. A Romance* (Northampton, 1720), which in keeping with its mildly salacious transcription of Davenant and Dryden's plot purports brazenly to be "Translated from the FRENCH Original, and never before printed in ENGLISH." Reprinted, with a short introduction, in Charles C. Mish, "An Early Eighteenth-Century Prose Version of *The Tempest*," in Shirley Strum Kenny, ed., *The British Theatre and the Other Arts* (London: Associated University Presses, 1984). On this novel's relation to *Robinson Crusoe* see p. 241.n.11.

17. Nicholas Rowe, ed., *The Works of Mr William Shakespear, in Six Volumes* (6 vols., London, 1709; 7 vols., London: Edmund Curll, "1709" [1710], vol. 7, p. 264.

18. See Nilan, *The Stage History of The Tempest*.

19. Published as part of his *Complete Art of Poetry* (2 vols., London, 1718).

20. On this statue, see Morris R. Brownell, *Alexander Pope and the Arts of Georgian England* (Oxford: Clarendon Press, 1978), pp. 354–6: David Piper, *The Image of the Poet: British Poets and their Portraits* (Oxford: Clarendon Press, 1982), pp. 78–82.

21. See especially the epilogue, addressed to the Shakespeare Ladies' Club, of George Lillo's Richardsonian adaptation of *Pericles, Marina* (London, 1738). On the Ladies's Club, see Emmett L. Avery, "The Shakespeare Ladies' Club," *Shakespeare Quarterly* (Spring 1956): 153–8.

22. Published anonymously (Birmingham, 1758).

23. Cf. Joseph Wharton's journal *The Adventurer*, no. 93, 25 Sept. 1753: "The poet is a more powerful magician than his own PROSPERO. . ."

24. (London, 1765).

25. David Garrick, *An Ode upon Dedicating a Building, and Erecting a Statue, to Shakespeare, at Stratford upon Avon. By D. G.* (London, 1769), p. 1.

26. See *The Plays of David Garrick*, ed. Harry William Pedicord and Frederick Lois Bergmann (6 vols., Carbondale and Edwardsville: Southern Illinois University Press, 1981), vol. 3, pp. 272–3.

27. David Garrick, *Songs, Choruses, &c. which are introduced in the New Entertainment of the Jubilee* (London, 1769), p. 4.

28. *Bell's Edition of Shakespeare's Plays* (9 vols., London, 1774), vol. 3, "The Tempest," frontispiece.

29. *The Plays of David Garrick*, vol 2, p. 116.

30. See for example, J. Johnson and J. Payne, publ., *The Principal Characters in the Procession of the Pageant Exhibited in the Jubilee at Drury Lane Theatre* (London, 1770). This and Bell's illustration tend to disprove Ania Loomba's assertion that "Not until 1934 was [Caliban] represented as black on the English stage." (Loomba, *Gender, Race, Renaissance Drama*, p. 143).

31. "Introduction" to *The Tempest* in *Bell's Edition of Shakespeare's Plays* (9 vols., London, 1774), vol. 3.

32. *The Shipwreck* (London, 1780). See George Speaight, *The History of the English Puppet Theatre* (London: Harrap, 1955), pp. 149ff. On the masquerade as a locus for anxieties about female sexual transgression, see Terry Castle, *Masquerade and Civilization* (Stanford: Stanford University Press, 1986).

33. (London, 1789).

34. Richardson's essay, largely devoted to the praise of Miranda, anxiously notes that "the history of modern Europe will attest, that even politics, a science of which men are particularly jealous, is not beyond the reach of adventurous females," and goes on to offer a terrible warning against the delusive attractions of free love:

    > In all situations whatever, where the tendency to extreme profligacy becomes very flagrant, the respect due to female virtues, and confidence in female affection, decline and decay. So great are the obligations of the fair sex to those institutions, which, more than any other, by limiting the freedom of divorce, and by other proper restrictions, have asserted the dignity of the female character.

    (Reprinted in *Essays on Shakespeare's Dramatic Characters*, 6th edn., London, 1812, pp. 342–3).

35. William Oxberry, ed., *The New English Drama*, vol. 17 (London, 1823), "The Tempest," p. vii. Oxberry hails Miranda as "the abstract of purity personified" (p. vii).

36. Racist readings of *The Tempest* would return emphatically in the early decades of the following century, first of all in the wake of the West Indian slave mutinies: J. H. Fawcett's ballet adaptation (1803), for example, endlessly replays Caliban's attempted rape of Miranda. The most striking such version remains the Brough brothers' travesty *Raising the Wind* (1848), which, conflating racism and counter-revolution, portrays Caliban as a caricatured Negro abolitionist who brandishes a red flag and sings the *Marseillaise*.

37. Mary Ann Hanway, *Ellinor, or The World As It Is* (4 vols., London, 1798), vol. II, p. 217.

Local *Tempest*

Shakespeare and the Work
of the Early Modern Playhouse[*]

DOUGLAS BRUSTER

If all the year were playing holidays,
To sport would be as tedious as to work.
                    —*1 HENRY IV*, 1.2.204–5

As much as it uses the theater to talk about colonialism, *The Tempest* (1611) uses colonialism to talk about the theater—particularly, about authority and work in certain early modern playhouses. Traditionally, when critics have spoken of the theater in *The Tempest*, it has been as an abstraction. In contrast, I take Shakespeare's theatrical experience to be a practical, not abstract, matter. Indeed it is not enough to say *The Tempest* is about the theater. We need to ask: Which theater or theaters? and Who and what *in* those theaters may have shaped the play? My primary claims are thus twofold, though related. First, that *The Tempest*, commonly acknowledged a play without a major literary source, looks to the Globe and Blackfriars playhouses, and to the realities of working in those structures, for its most salient sources. Its portrait of playhouse labor and experience includes not only Prospero as a playwright/director, but Miranda as a figure of an idealized spectatorship, and Ariel as a boy actor. My second major claim, one that builds on this playhouse allegory, is that Caliban derived from Shakespeare's experiences with Will Kemp, a celebrated Elizabethan clown known for his physical, even priapic comedy, his independent spirit, folk ethos, and intrusive ad libs. Kemp's tendency to ignore the lines playwrights had written translated, in fact, into Caliban's animosity toward Prospero's powerful books. Rewriting the relation of (among others) Theseus to Bottom as one of Prospero to Caliban, Shakespeare recollected an apparently

[*]Douglas Bruster, "Local *Tempest*: Shakespeare and the Work of the Early Modern Playhouse," Originally published in *Journal of Medieval and Renaissance Studies* 25.1 (1995): 33–53. Copyright 1995, Duke University Press. Reprinted with permission.

unwelcome interdependence of himself, as playwright and actor for what were then the Lord Chamberlain's Men, and the company's famous, if unruly, clown.

In situating *The Tempest* locally, I call into question a thoroughly colonialist interpretation of the play—an interpretation, that is, set in and about only the New World.[1] The play, in this reading, concerns European exploitation of the New World and its inhabitants. Here critics typically survey Montaigne's "Of Cannibals," Strachey's "True Reportory," Jourdain's *Discovery of the Bermudas*, and various passages from the extensive literature of European exploration. The play's island becomes Virginia, Ireland, or the Bermudas, Prospero a colonialist master, and Caliban an oppressed native. Perhaps not surprisingly, this reading, while available since Hazlitt, gained widespread acceptance in Anglo-American criticism during the governments of Thatcher and Reagan—themselves manipulative dramatists who, for this and other reasons, may have increased empathy for such an interpretation in politically alienated critics at the inauguration of post-colonialist studies.

To a large extent this colonialist *Tempest* still holds sway and is the reading my essay attempts to revise. Some might claim that, in arguing for a local *Tempest*, such an approach evades the political—political here meaning intercultural, if not transatlantic. As will become clear, however, my interpretation is less evading the political than in arguing that the politics of *The Tempest* are strongly local, identifying various objects of a play in the very structures and relations that produced it. Only when we think seriously about Shakespeare's lived history of playing and writing can we understand the energies of *The Tempest*.

A theatrical *Tempest* is, again, hardly new. Nearly everyone who writes on the topic agrees that Prospero is a playwright or director, whether symbolic or real, Machiavellian or benevolent. Fewer, however, have agreed as to the nature and location of the world this directing figure oversees, leading to what we might call the "Tempest question." The Tempest question is actually intertwined questions: Where is the play set? and Who or what is Caliban? Historically, where readers have seen *The Tempest* as located has influenced what they thought the play was about. Similarly, who or what readers have seen Caliban as representing—whether Native American, Caribbean, African, "missing link," or British wild man—has greatly affected their readings. Each of these decisions—location, and the significance of Caliban—bears on the other: a Virginian *Tempest*, for example, asks for one kind of Caliban; a Caribbean Caliban, another kind of *Tempest*. Despite disagreement about the local geography of the play, though, critics generally agree to answer the Tempest question in relation to the New World. Even Jeffrey Knapp, who fixes *The Tempest* in a tradition of utopias purposefully located "nowhere," sees this as underwriting the play's New World discourse.[2]

Yet is *The Tempest* about the New World? Neither the play nor its near contemporaries say so. Almost mischievously this "notoriously slippery" play believes itself to take place in the Mediterranean. The "still-vex'd Bermoothes," where Ariel has travelled to fetch dew, is a place elsewhere (1.2.229). Commenting on this, Frank Kermode suggests that "the fact that Shakespeare is at pains to establish his island in the Old World may be taken to indicate his rejection of the merely topical."[3] Certainly there is nothing "mere" about the topical; as the past decades of criticism have shown, the topical is always extremely complex. But it is significant, surely, that none of the playwrights who commented on, borrowed from, revised, or otherwise paid homage to *The Tempest* before the closing of the theaters seems to have been any more interested in colonialism than Shakespeare—or, for that matter, showed that he believed Shakespeare, in *The Tempest*, was talking about the New World. From Jonson's *Bartholomew Fair* (1614), folio *Every Man in His Humour* (1616), Tomkis's *Albumazar* (1615), and Fletcher's *Sea Voyage* (1622) to John Kirke's *Seven Champions of Christendom* (1635) and Suckling's *The Goblins* (1638), drama in the three decades following *The Tempest* saw it as a play about magic and illusion, not about the other end of English exploration.

In fact, decidedly local aspects of *The Tempest* were suggested in a later version of the story—a burlesque, in part, of Davenant's revision; this play locates the story in London. Thomas Duffett's *Mock Tempest; or The Enchanted Castle* (1674) opens with a tempestuous conflict in a brothel before moving to Bridewell prison, where Prospero—once "Duke of my Lord Mayor's Dog-kennel"—has become Keeper. Duffett's burlesque not only insists on the essential homeliness of *The Tempest*, but does so by reproducing, with slight variation, lines from that play, examples of which include: "This Miscreant, so dry he was for sway, betray'd me to *Alonzo*, Duke of Newgate; and in a stormy and dreadful Night open'd my Kenell Gates, and forc'd me thence with thy young Sister, and thy howling self" (Prospero: 1.2); "More toil—I pri'thee now let me mind thee of thy promise then—where is my Twopenny Custard?" (Ariel: 4.1). *The Mock Tempest* restages the opening storm of Shakespeare's title as an assault, by a Quaker and his friends, on a brothel. Duffett's burlesque mocks the enchantment of Davenant's "Enchanted Island"—and of Shakespeare's *Tempest*—by choosing to see the story's locale as London, its urban characters immersed in the politics of their place and time. Duffett's mockery—his vision of *The Tempest*'s homeliness—was itself close to home, for what he saw in Shakespeare's story was in many ways already there. Unlike Duffett's play, though, Shakespeare's drama concerns not a brothel, or Bridewell prison, but other structures of early modern London: the playhouses Shakespeare worked in and for.

"Playhouses" in the plural here, for in 1608 Shakespeare helped lease the Blackfriars theater, and by 1611 had routinely divided his time between the Blackfriars and Globe playing spaces. Because *The Tempest* relies on elements of and working histories associated with each theater, it is important to keep both in mind. To begin with the beginning: the opening scene of *The Tempest* incorporates Shakespeare's experiences of the Blackfriars playhouse, a private theater known for its elite, sometimes pretentious clientele. The confusion of authority and division of labor on the deck of the ship respond to what it must have been like to work as an actor on the Blackfriars' stage.

Why should a ship remind us of a playhouse? By 1611 the trope of theater as ship had become commonplace. Jonson would inveigh against this in the Prologue to the Folio version of *Every Man in His Humour*, where—in lines preceding his sneer at the sound effects of "roll'd bullet heard / To say, it thunders; [and] tempestuous drum [which] / Rumbles, to tell you when the storm doth come," and his equally caustic remark about his audience having "grac'd monsters" (presumably Caliban) (ll. 18–20; 30)—he speaks disparagingly of plays where the "Chorus wafts you o'er the seas." Both *Pericles* (1608) and *Henry V* (1599) feature these ship-like choruses, able to transport audiences overseas and back without wetting their clothing, as Ariel in *The Tempest* makes possible for that ship's passengers. Dekker's eighteen-line Prologue before *The Shoemakers' Holiday* (1599) is perhaps the most characteristic unfolding of a popular trope. A year before Shakespeare's romance the Prologue of Robert Daborne's *A Christian Turned Turk* (1610) says "Our Ship's afloat, we fear nor rocks nor sands, / Knowing we art environ'd with your helping hands" (ll. 23–24)— "hands," of course, used for applause, as well as for handling ropes and sails. The metaphor is in every way a natural one.

As Dekker, Daborne, and Shakespeare realized, playhouses are like ships in many ways. Both are wooden structures packed with people. Both are sites of labor where work is usually concentrated and frantic. Both rely on intensive cooperation: ships and their sailors' hands; actors and their audiences' hand-clapping-and, in a common trope, windy shouts of acclaim. Both can give one the impression of learning "what is happening abroad," as Thomas Platter said of English plays and playhouses in the 1590s, commenting on how the English "do not travel much, but prefer to learn foreign matters and take their pleasure at home."[4] In early modern London, people took boats to playhouses—the Blackfriars as well as the Globe. Middleton plays on this in *Father Hubburd's Tales* when he says that, after dinner, a gallant "must venture beyond sea, that is, in a choice pair of Nobelman's Oars, to the Bankside."[5] And plays (including *Hamlet*) were sometimes acted on seagoing ships. Therefore when Prospero says to the audience in the Epilogue of *The Tempest* that he will be "confin'd" to his "bare island" without "the help of your good hands," and that the "Gentle breath of yours my sails / Must fill, or else my project fails, / Which was to please" (ll. 4, 8, 11–13), he conflates the present, empty stage with the "bare island" of *The Tempest*, and the playhouse proper with the ship that is to return him to Naples, in a metaphor of unusual force.

But what was it about the Blackfriars that shaped this scene? A hallmark of the private theaters, and of the Blackfriars in particular, was the habit of sitting on stage—gallants perched on stools more to display themselves and their clothing than to gain a better view of the play. In the famous sixth chapter of *The Gull's Horn-book* (1609), Thomas Dekker advises "How a gallant should behave himself in a playhouse," suggesting, among other things, that "by spreading your body on the stage and by being a Justice in examining of plays you shall put yourself into such true scenical authority that some poet shall not dare to present his Muse rudely upon your eyes without having first unmasked her, rifled her and discovered all her bare and most mystical parts before you at a tavern, when you most knightly shall for his pains pay for both their suppers."[6] Dekker pictures a gallant's body spread egregiously over the stage, dominating the performance with "true scenical authority." Many resentful asides about the practice survive in plays of the period; playwrights and actors appear to have disliked stage sitting intensely.[7] As a dramatist subject to this form of criticism, Dekker recognizes that playwrights of Blackfriars plays compete with these voyeuristic, stage-sitting gallants for "authority."

Such competition, I would argue, was an important source of *The Tempest*'s opening scene. This scene frames the conflict between the laboring mariners and the Italian aristocrats and courtiers, for example, in terms of both "labor" and "authority." "You mar our labor," the Boatswain says to Antonio, "Keep your cabins; you do assist the storm" (1.1.13–14). When Gonzalo interrupts him, this Boatswain responds, "If you can command these elements to silence, and work the peace of the present, we will not hand a rope more. Use your authority" (1.1.21–23). The annoyance which actors undoubtedly felt when spectators at the Blackfriars marred their theatrical labor probably underlies a statement of Heminge and Condell in the First Folio (1623). The epistle "To the great Variety of Readers" says that "though you be a Magistrate of wit, and sit on the Stage at *Blackfriars*, or the *Cockpit*, to arraign Plays daily, know, these Plays have had their trial already, and stood out all Appeals; and do now come forth quitted rather by a Decree of Court, than any purchased Letters of commendation." Pitched to censorious stage sitters, this is also about them. When we remember that *The Tempest* and its opening storm scene initiate the dramatic moments of the First Folio, and read this scene in the context of the epistle's chastisement, it suggests that the conflict between playhouse laborers and unappreciative stage sitters was much on the mind of the King's Men from 1608 forward.

Read in the context of this remark, and in the context of contemporary sentiment against stage sitting, the first scene of *The Tempest* takes on a new cast. If it is about a ship at sea, it is also about working in a crowded playhouse. The Boatswain expresses his annoyance at the interference of a group of gazers who impede the working men in the performance of their roles. The ship's deck, like a stage circled by gallants, seems crowded; as the Boatswain apostrophizes the gale: "Blow till thou burst thy wind, if room enough!"

(1.1.7–8). Significantly, when Alonso gives unhelpful advice to the mariners, he tells them to "*Play* the men" (1.1.10; emphasis added), as though he, like a stage-sitting gallant, is offering the judgment of his "true scenical authority." It is relevant here that, in the same section of *The Gull's Horn-Book*, Dekker imagines such intrusive authority precisely in terms of the theater-as-ship metaphor: "By sitting on the stage you have a signed patent to engross the whole commodity of censure; may lawfully presume to be a girder; *and stand at the helm to steer the passage of scenes*."[8] This passage supports a reading which sees an analogy between, on the one hand, Alonso, Gonzalo, and the other passengers, and, on the other, stage-sitting gallants who "stand at the helm to steer the passage of scenes." Dekker's gallants are, in 1609—two years before *The Tempest*—already described as interfering with the ship-theater of a private playhouse very much like the Blackfriars. What we see in the tension between the laboring mariners, represented by the Boatswain, and the ship's higher-status passengers, I believe, is a translation of the experience that Shakespeare and the King's Men had in the handful of years that they had been playing at the Blackfriars. Dekker sees these gallants as "girder[s]"— that is, sneering wits. On them, the message of *The Tempest*'s opening scene, with its call for self-awareness and room in which to work, may well have been lost. But to those on stage doing the work of the performance, and to those in the audience who, like Dekker and many others, may have resented these stage sitters, the point must have been unmistakable: plays are hard work, and are hindered by nonlaboring, intrusive stage sitters.

The arrogance of these stage sitters—whom the epistle calls "Magistrate[s] of wit," and Dekker "girder[s]—is likely to have been the deep source of another sequence in *The Tempest*, the otherwise strange "widow Dido" passage in 2.1. There Gonzalo, old counsellor, and type of character Shakespeare typically played, slips and says that Tunis had not been graced with such a queen as Claribel since "widow Dido's time" (2.1.77). The following exchange occurs:

ANTONIO:	Widow? a pox o' that! How came that widow in? Widow Dido!
SEBASTIAN:	What if he had said "widower Aeneas" too? Good Lord, how you take it!
ADRIAN:	"Widow Dido," said you? You make me study of that. She was of Carthage, not of Tunis.
GONZALO:	This Tunis, sir, was Carthage.
ADRIAN:	Carthage?
GONZALO:	I assure you, Carthage.
ANTONIO:	His word is more than the miraculous harp.
SEBASTIAN:	He hath rais'd the wall, and houses too.
ANTONIO:	What impossible matter will he make easy next?

SEBASTIAN: I think he will carry this island home in his pocket, and give it his
               son for an apple.
ANTONIO: And sowing the kernels of it in the sea, bring forth more islands.

Like Dekker's stage-sitting girders, the mockers here offer their intrusive commentary on another's speech. They talk about Gonzalo's utterance as though
he is not a part of their group, as though he is an actor speaking the lines of a
playwright whose authority they question. Dido a widow? Carthage Tunis?
The "impossible matter" Gonzalo makes easy is the illusion of the theater—
moving place and object, transporting and reproducing, in the manner of a
playwright, fantasies like the present island.[9]
    Yet Gonzalo himself stands in for the playwright, for these impossible
matters are uncannily like the errors that Jonson would identify as quintessentially Shakespearean. To Jonson, Shakespeare was often poetically incor-
rect. Two statements by Jonson bear this out; the first from the *Conversations
with Drummond of Hawthorndon*, the second in his *Timber, or Discoveries*:

> Shakespeare in a play brought in a number of men saying they had suffered
> Shipwreck in Bohemia where there is no Sea near by some 100 Miles.
> (1.208–10)

> Many times he fell into those things, could not escape laughter: As when he
> said in the person of *Caesar*, one speaking to him; *Caesar, thou dost me
> wrong*. He replied: *Caesar never did never wrong, but with just cause*: and
> such like; which were ridiculous. (8.661–66)

This is Jonson the girder snickering at Shakespeare's infelicities. Many have
pointed out that nowhere in the *Julius Caesar* we have does Caesar say what
Jonson alleges; this may be an instance, it is further argued, of Jonson's critique affecting the version of the play ultimately printed. In any case, what
Jonson says here about "those things" that for him characterized Shakespeare—the impossible matters his rival insisted on raising, the violations of
fact and logic—are played out in Gonzalo's making Dido a widow, and Tunis
Carthage. In Jonson's view, such were errors typical of Shakespeare: "He
flowed with that facility," Jonson wrote in the *Discoveries*, "that sometime it
was necessary he should be stopped: *Sufflaminandus erat*; as *Augustus* said of
Haterius. His wit was in his own power; would the rule of it had been so too"
(8.658–61). Like the Shakespeare of Jonson's *Discoveries*, whose wit flows so
freely that others wish it might be stopped, Gonzalo's mouth and imagination
flow from "widow" to the awkward rhyme of "Dido," from an error of place
to geographical impossibility.
    Like Jonson, the critics within *The Tempest* step forward to mock this
flow. It is as if Shakespeare wrote both himself (as Gonzalo) and Jonson (as
Sebastian, Antonio, and Adrian) into *The Tempest*. To be sure, actors and poets

within the worlds of Shakespeare's plays are invariably at the mercy of their audiences and patrons. But where the nobles in *A Midsummer Night's Dream* (1596) seem physically distanced from the errors and actors they censure—though within earshot, they appear to be part of a great hall, or in the select boxes behind a public theater's stage—*The Tempest* imagines these Jonsonian girders as within arm's reach of the actor whose impossibilities they criticize; within, that is, a distance equivalent to that between stage sitters and actors. The space as well as the aesthetic politics of the scent speaks strongly of the Blackfriars.

Yet however much *The Tempest* draws from the Blackfriars, Shakespeare's career at the Globe must also have influenced the play. As playwright figure, Prospero is widely believed to be a double of Shakespeare—his version of the abilities and responsibilities of the dramatist written into and writing a dramatic plot. But if Prospero stands in at times for Shakespeare, we need to remember that playhouse correspondences in *The Tempest* are likely to have been multiple, something that requires that we look to Shakespeare's long history at the Globe as well. His associate Richard Burbage—leading actor of the King's Men, and perhaps of the early modern theater—is most likely to have played Prospero, just as he is likely to have played Vincentio, Macbeth, Lear, Hal, Othello, Hamlet, and Richard III. The controlling impulse and ability we see Shakespeare lend Prospero, then, may have much to say about Burbage's history as a senior member and shareholder of their acting company. As Charles Wallace first pointed out, Burbage's role in *The Tempest* was doubtless shaped by a directing role in the city pageant for Prince Henry on 1 May 1610, where he played "Amphion, the Father of Harmony or Music," a figure described as "a grave and judicious prophet-like personage, attired in his apt habits, every way answerable to his state and profession."[10] Burbage's abilities as a leading actor dovetailed with Shakespeare's image of a playwright figure leading characters through plays—from Richard III and Thomas More through Hamlet and Vincentio, a favorite Shakespeare type.[11]

As Prospero, the playwright figure positions Miranda as an ideal and idealized audience in the second scene of the play. Faced with narrating the complicated background of the plot, Shakespeare breaks up Prospero's exposition into units of less than twenty lines—in contrast with, for instance, the opening of his early comedy with "unity of time," *The Comedy of Errors* (1592), where Egeon's rambling, sixty-five-line exposition tends to bore audiences now. The difference between narration in this early comedy and *The Tempest* might be ascribed in part to Shakespeare's increased sophistication as a playwright. But Prospero's relation to Miranda during this famous exposition also works against a Jacobean trend toward the spectacular in drama—evidenced, for example, in the Masque of Ceres that Prospero arranges.[12]

For obvious reasons, we are used to thinking about Miranda in terms of the visual—she is, in *The Tempest*, both gazer ("O brave new world / That has such people in't!" [5.1.183–84]) and object of gazes ("Admir'd Miranda, / Indeed the top of admiration!" [3.1.37–38]). Her relation to Prospero as director, grounded both in the etymology of her name and in an inequality of knowledge and control, is as spectacle and spectatorship. These positions have a historical cause. The early modern theater in England increasingly relied on the visual, as opposed to the aural. The linguistically copious writing habits of the 1590s gradually gave way, after 1600, to a spectacular, masque-influenced practice—what Daniel called "Punctillos of Dreams and shows."[13] Accordingly, how Shakespeare described playgoers changed. "From 1610 onwards," Andrew Gurr notes, "Shakespeare abandoned the idea of an auditory in favour of spectators."[14] It may not have been a welcome change, however, for it is Prospero's task in the play's second scene to get his spectators—represented on stage by Miranda—to follow a story with their ears, to become, that is, an audience again. That it does not seem as easy as it had been in *The Comedy of Errors* is evident in Prospero's eight apparently impatient interjections: "I pray thee mark me" (l. 67); "Dost thou attend me?" (l. 78); "Thou attend'st not!" (l. 87); "I pray thee mark me" (l. 88); "Dost thou hear?" (l. 106); "Mark his condition" (l. 117); "Hear a little further" (l. 135); "Sit still, and hear" (l. 170). This is the impatience of a playwright. Perhaps what we have in the twenty years between *The Comedy of Errors* and *The Tempest*, then, is less Shakespeare learning to vary narration than Shakespeare's audiences having lost the patience to listen.

Where Miranda's relation to Prospero is in part that of an idealized spectatorship to what is perhaps an equally idealized playwright, Ariel relates to Prospero as boy actor to adult dramatist or stage director. Like Puck and Oberon, Ariel and Prospero collaborate in directing; the latter's actors, we are told, are inept, misguided, and lazy. Prospero calls Ariel, in contrast, "my industrious servant" (4.1.33). When Ariel successfully tantalizes Alonso, Sebastian, and the other hungry newcomers with the magical banquet during act 3, scene 3, Prospero sounds exactly like an older actor, one who has spent a life in the theater, praising a boy actor: "Bravely the figure of this harpy hast thou / Perform'd, my Ariel; a grace it had, devouring. / Of my instruction hast thou nothing bated / In what thou hadst to say; so with good life, / And observation strange, my meaner ministers / Their several kinds have done" (3.3.83–88). Throughout *The Tempest*, the relations between Prospero and his industrious servant are deeply analogous to the relations among mature players and boy actors in the early modern playhouse. We often find these playhouse relations embedded in plays, as, for example, in the Lord's advice to Bartholomew, his page, in *The Taming of the Shrew* (1592), the aristocrats to Moth in *Love's Labour's Lost* (1595), Oberon to Puck in *A Midsummer Night's Dream*, and Clerimont to the Boy in *Epicoene* (1609). It matters to Prospero that his spirit is a particularly good actor. Ariel's acting talents, in fact, are consonant with—even a sign of—his closeness to the human in *The*

Tempest. Indeed, when Ariel teaches Prospero charity—"Mine would, sir, were I human," he tells his master (5.1.20)—the difference between them is simultaneously suggested and questioned.

In contrast to Ariel, Caliban is both a bad actor and—at least to Prospero—decidedly subhuman. These attributes appear to have been connected in Shakespeare's mind. To say that Shakespeare saw the difference between good actors and bad actors as equivalent to the difference between the human and the subhuman might seem a drastic claim. We can see that such a belief was at least available to him, however, in Hamlet's injunctions to the Players, often thought to represent Shakespeare's opinions on the contemporary acting scene:

> HAMLET: O, there be players that I have seen play—and heard others praise,
> and neither having th' accent of Christians nor the gait of Christian,
> pagan, nor man, have so strutted and bellow'd that I have thought
> some of Nature's journeymen had made men, and not made them
> well, they imitated humanity so abominably.
> 1. PLAYER: I hope we have reform'd that indifferently with us, sir.
> HAMLET: O, reform it altogether. And let those that play your clowns speak no
> more than is set down for them, for there be of them that will them-
> selves laugh to set on some quantity of barren spectators to laugh
> too, though in the mean time some necessary question of the play be
> then to be consider'd. That's villainous, and shows a most pitiful
> ambition in the fool that uses it. (3.2.28–45)

What Harold Jenkins calls Hamlet's excursus on acting appears to change directions with the First Player's interjection.[15] Yet we can see that his critique is continuous. Hamlet begins by saying that some players are such bad actors that, though they have drawn praise from others, they seem nonhuman when on stage. The descending hierarchy of these actors' "gait" runs first Christian, then pagan, then not "man." The punning phrase "they imitated humanity so abominably" relies, of course, on an Elizabethan understanding of "abominable" as deriving from Latin *ab homine*, "away from man(kind)." The word is always spelled with the medial *h* in Shakespeare. That he was aware of these valences—in the air whenever the word was used—is perhaps shown in Holofernes's pedantic insistence on the aspirate form in *Love's Labour's Lost*: "This is abhominable—which he would call 'abbominable'" (5.1.24–25). The allegation that certain actors possess an accent not Christian, pagan, or human spirals down to the word *abhominable*: to act badly is to be less than human.

Hamlet, then, only appears to change topics when he inveighs against the clown who speaks more than has been written in the playbook. For when he uses the adjective "villainous" (1.44), calling upon a word that could imply moral or ethical corruption, and (from "vilein") lower class and rank as well, he continues to associate bad acting with the subhuman. Thus Caliban says that Prospero can turn the subplot's conspirators "to apes / With foreheads villainous low" (4.1.248–49). Not surprisingly, perhaps, Shakespeare several times uses "abominable" with "villain." In *King Lear*, for instance, we hear Gloucester call Edgar a "brutish villain," then "worse than brutish," until finally settling on "abominable villain" (1.2.76–78)—indicating that "abominable" is "worse than brutish." Playacting in *1 Henry IV*, Hal calls Falstaff "that villainous abominable misleader of youth" (2.4.462–63). Because Hamlet's remarks on the subhuman nature of certain accents and gaits jibe ethically with his critique of the villainous behavior of the bad clown, these apparently separate statements form a single diatribe. This diatribe is based on the conviction that bad actors, whether egotistical improvisers or bellowing stompers, are something less than human.

The improvising clowns Hamlet decries were undoubtedly suggested by Will Kemp, famous comedian of the Lord Chamberlain's Men. In *An Almond for a Parrat* (1590), Nashe calls Kemp "That Most Comical and Conceited Cavalier *Monsieur du Kemp, Jestmonger and* Vice-gerent general to the Ghost of Dick Tarlton."[16] As this genealogy from Tarlton might suggest, Kemp was known for, among other things, the folk obscenity of his nonrepresentational jigs and merriments, and for breaking the illusional boundaries of the plays he acted in by directly addressing audiences with ad hoc banter.[17] His reputation for ignoring the authoritative *locus* areas of the dramatic action to engage the audience from the imaginary *platea*, the no man's land between spectacle and spectator, lived long after him.[18] Kemp left the Chamberlain's Men under mysterious circumstances sometime in 1599, this after becoming one of the seven original shareholders in the new Globe playhouse. Even if he had not done so, this passage from *Hamlet* would suffice to show a tension between Shakespeare and Kemp, one perhaps partly responsible for Kemp's departure from the company.

This tension between what Kemp appears to have represented in the economy of work in the Globe playhouse and what Shakespeare may have imagined as an ideal appears in *The Tempest* in the relation between Prospero and Caliban. Shakespeare invokes the human/subhuman distinction when it comes to the differences between them. In an infamous phrase, Prospero calls Caliban "this thing of darkness" (5.1.275). Elsewhere he uses the animalistic to describe Caliban in recounting for Ariel how uninhabited the island was before they came: "Then was this island / (Save for the son that she did litter here, / A freckled whelp, hag-born) nor honor'd with / A human shape" (1.2.281–84). Jonson would be equally blunt, speaking of "a *Servant-monster*" just before slighting "*Tales, Tempests,* and such like *Drolleries*" in the Induction to *Bartholomew Fair* (6.127, 130). Like Hamlet the playwright, who contrives to interpolate "a speech of some dozen lines, or sixteen lines" as part of his rewriting of *Hamlet*, Prospero consciously "directs" the island world of *The Tempest*. He owns the "trumpery" and "glistering apparel,"[19] steers the actions of Ariel, his boy actor, cues the weather effects that Jonson would sneer at, and controls the shape and pace of the plot generally. The word Shakespeare uses here is "project," one that typically referred to plots and intrigtues within plays: one might note Ariel's "My master ... sends me forth / (For else his project dies) to keep them living" (2.1.297–99), his description of the subplot's conspirators "always bending / Towards their project" (4.1.174–75), and the Epilogue's "my project...was to please" (ll.12–13). Most important to Caliban's improvised project, however, is Prospero's "book."

Indeed Prospero is defined by books, speaking early of how Gonzalo, "knowing I lov'd my books," had stored several prized volumes in his boat (1.2.166–68). Caliban is in every way outside Prospero's book, and books in general, from the parody of kissing the Bible/bottle at 2.2.130–59 to his repeated injunctions, to Stephano and Trinculo, to seize and destroy Prospero's books: "There thou mayst brain him, / Having first seiz'd his books. . . . / Remember / First to possess his books; for without them / He's but a sot, as I am; nor hath not / One spirit to command: they all do hate him / As rootedly as I. Burn but his books" (3.2.88–95). Caliban's animosity to Prospero's books and his language contrasts with Prospero's reliance on them. Yet where Caliban resents Prospero's *books*, Prospero speaks of "book" in the singular. "I'll to my book," he says; later "I'll drown my book" (3.1.94; 5.1.57). It is as though Caliban, like an actor prone to interpolation, is thinking of a cache of playbooks—a collection of oppressive works owned by an acting company and stored in their "house." In contrast, Prospero, like an actor/writer/director/producer focused on the production at hand, refers to the actual promptbook of the current performance. In making Caliban resent books, and having him speak of spirits who hate working for Prospero, Shakespeare may well have been describing the local relations of actors at the playhouses he was associated with, and his theatrical experience over the past several decades.

From at least 1599, when Kemp left the Chamberlain's Men, Shakespeare and Burbage would have been in a position over the junior and part-time actors at the Globe and Blackfriars playhouses similar to that of Prospero over the theatrical "spirits" and others on "his" island. Even as Kemp apparently stepped outside the scripts of Shakespeare's plays, Caliban has ideas and desires of his own that run contrary to the plot Prospero writes. In this Caliban differs from Ariel, the "industrious servant" who follows the orders Prospero gives. To Prospero's "Thou shalt be as free / As mountain winds; but then exactly do / All points of my command," Ariel replies: "To th' syllable" (1.2.499–501). Besides his machinations within the play to murder Prospero and burn his books, Caliban's improvised plots include the attempted rape of Miranda before the action of *The Tempest* begins. Kemp's notorious obscenity, his lewd jigs and songs, may well have contributed to this narrative. For if Prospero relates to Miranda as a playwright and leading actor imagined themselves in relation to their spectators, so may have Kemp's theatrical praxis, his lewdness and his willingness to violate theatrical decorum, functioned as a deep source of the narrated rape in *The Tempest*. Called "an abominable monster" by Trinculo (2.2.158–59), Caliban, by trying to take the plot his way, embodies the abominable and villainous acting that Hamlet complained of shortly after Kemp left Shakespeare's company.

Caliban seems linked to Kemp through Kemp's physical habits as well. Caliban's joy upon conspiring with the bad actors Stephano and Trinculo, for example, is capped with a song—"Sings drunkenly" is the stage direction:

> Farewell, master; farewell, farewell!
> . . . .
> No more dams I'll make for fish,
>   Nor fetch in firing
>   At requiring,
> Nor scrape trenchering, nor wash dish
>   'Ban, Ban, Ca-Caliban
>   Has a new master, get a new man.
> Freedom, high-day! high-day, freedom! freedom, high-day,
> freedom! (2.2.178–87)

"O brave monster! lead the way," Stephano rejoins, and it seems probable that Caliban's song is a song and dance—a jig with which he leads Stephano and Trinculo off stage. The "high-day!" that closes his song is almost never glossed by editors, but it is crucial to understanding what the passage is about. "High-day" is a variant of a folksy exclamation which appears, variously, as *hey-day, heyday, heyda, hayday, hay day, hoighdagh, hoy day, hoyda, hoida, hay da, ha day, heigh-day*. Added to this complex was *hey-day guise* (sometimes *hay-de-gay*), a rural folk dance for which the "hay" (a synonym for jig), Nares suggests, "was only an abbreviation."[20] That such terms were interchangeable to Shakespeare can be seen, perhaps, in the use of "hoy-day" in both *Richard III* (4.4.459) and *Timon* (1.2.131), and "hey day" in *Troilus* (5.1.66). Defined by the *OED* as "an exclamation denoting frolicsomeness, gaiety, surprise, wonder, etc.," the "hey-day"/"high-day" complex was often used in jigs and morris dances.

Will Kemp, of course, was famous for his jigs; in fact he danced a celebrated marathon morris from London to Norwich the year he left the Chamberlain's men. When he wrote his account of this stunt—*Kemp's Nine Days' Wonder* (1600)—he punned on the Globe when he mentioned that some had alleged he had "danced myself out of the world." In this pamphlet Kemp calls himself "High Headborough of heighs" dancing his "hey de gaies" to Ilford, and interjects both a "hey" and a "*hey de gay!*" into his songs.[21] It is impossible, of course, to establish that Shakespeare was "quoting" Kemp when he gave Caliban the "high-days" of this sequence. But it is clear that the genre of lusty self-assertion was an important part of Kemp's character. And this seems precisely what Shakespeare sought to make suspect in lending Caliban the "high-days" of his song.

Despite the celebratory picture of folk culture we see in critics such as C. L. Barber and François Laroque, Shakespeare seems suspicious of the traditionalistic *homo gloriosus* throughout his plays.[22] Though there are obviously things to like about all his clown figures, if one looks closely at Bottom—almost certainly a portrait of Kemp—and Peter in *Romeo and Juliet* (1596)—where textual evidence (in Q1 and Q2, respectively) shows that Kemp acted the part—it is difficult not to find an uneasiness over Kemp's style of humor." However much he enjoyed Falstaff—again, probably played by Kemp—it is the more calculating Hal that Shakespeare ultimately endorses. This ran deep in Shakespeare. Empson was surely right, in his reading of the word *honest* in *Othello*, to suggest that "what Shakespeare hated in the word. . .was a peculiar use, at once hearty and individualist," and that *honest* eventually "came to have in it a covert assenion that the man who accepts the natural desires, who does not live by principle, will be fit for such warm uses of *honest* as imply 'generous' and 'faithful to friends', and to believe this is to disbelieve the Fall of Man."[24] While this may seem a heavy burden to place on a word, Empson's reading of *honest* in *Othello* bears out his claim. That the characters in Shakespeare who use "hey-day" and "hoy-day" are Thersites, Apemantus, and Richard III likewise indicates that Shakespeare may well have had the same impatience with its untrustworthy folkishness that he had for words such as *honest* in *Othello*.

Thus giving Caliban a song that ends with "high-day, freedom!" calls up not only the specter of rioting apprentices in early modern London—apprentices who routinely vandalized theaters during moments of drunken holiday (compare "freedom")—but, with its implied hearty individualism, an aggressive and questionable ethos. Kemp embraced this ethos and made it his public persona. We can see it as something like rite expression of a folk id. And in Caliban, I believe, this id looks for its primary source not to the New World, which Shakespeare never saw but to Will Kemp, whom Shakespeare appears to have seen too much of. Why, we may ask, should this portrait appear in *The Tempest* and not earlier? One answer is that, along with *Hamlet*, *The Tempest* is a play in which Shakespeare appears to have thought the hardest about playing. Even more than *Hamlet*, perhaps, it is a play about his life in the theater. Another answer has to do with a personal decorum that saw Shakespeare wait before mocking his dead contemporaries. Yet where he waited six years to deal with Marlowe's memory through an unfortunate joke in *As You Like It* (3.3.12–15), with Burghley as Polonius in *Hamlet* and with Kemp—who died in 1608/9—he waited barely three.

From individual actors to specific stages and rival playwrights, London's local scene shaped *The Tempest* in important ways. The playhouse relations uncovered here ask us to reconsider a critical trend that has made Shakespeare, variously, the anthropologist, chronicler, critic, jingoist, prophet, and poet of colonialism. To be sure, *The Tempest* is interested even invested—in what we have come to call colonialism. But much of its content is Shakespeare's lived history of work in the Globe and Blackfriars playhouses. If I have responded to the *Tempest* question with a local answer, this does not mean that the play is not simultaneously about the New World. We have learned too much from colonialist readings of the play—and from histories of colonialism—to believe that. But *The Tempest* also concerns itself with a more homely topic: the theatrical experiences of Shakespeare and his company. We need to take into account how this affected the drama to adequately understand it.

The tension between Prospero and Caliban, I have argued, embodies that between Shakespeare (and perhaps Burbage) and Will Kemp. It is perhaps not surprising to find Shakespeare suspicious of the uncontrolled, traditionalistic energy of Will Kemp and the anarchic aspects of the folk structures Kemp represented. For Shakespeare was something like the type of the calculating, legal-rational individual in early modern England—a man who made considerable money from words, from lending money, from speculating in real estate, and through his entrepreneurial activities in the early modern playhouse. To Shakespeare, as to Prospero, dramatic projects are serious work. And however much he endorsed the vital, Shakespeare was, in matters of business, puritanically thrifty. Thus *The Tempest* reverberates with Prospero's endorsement of obedience, discipline, and patience, of waiting to have one's toil and suffering recognized, of doing things, literally, by the book. *The Tempest* is a play about art, but it is deeply about the work that art requires. As such, it was perhaps the right play with which to open the First Folio. For if this 1623 magnum opus of Renaissance England is a collection of Shakespeare's theatrical labors, *The Tempest* is among the deepest of his meditations on laboring in the theater, and the latest of his serious thoughts about the business of playing. Shakespeare's double, Prospero haunts the island world like a playhouse director. One could say that, as *The Tempest* allegorizes Shakespeare's life and work in the theater, Prospero is the phantom of his opera.

NOTES

I am grateful to Glenn Clark, Scott Paul Gordon, and John G. Norman for their insightful comments on earlier versions of this essay.

Approximate dates for plays in this essay are given in Alfred Harbage, ed. *Annals of English Drama, 975–1700*, 3rd ed. (London: Routledge, 1989). All references to Shakespeare in this essay are from *The Riverside Shakespeare*, ed. G. Blakemore Evans (Boston: Houghton Mifflin, 1974). All references to Jonson are to *Ben Jonson*, ed. C. H. Herford, Percy Simpson, and Evelyn Simpson, 11 vols. (Oxford: Clarendon, 1925–50). Unless otherwise noted, I have modernized spelling and punctuation in quotations from early modern texts.

1. Recently Meredith Skura and Frances Dolan have, in separate essays, challenged the foundations on which a singularly colonialist *Tempest* rests. Skura points out that the play remains a "notoriously slippery" document, and contains much that an intensively postcolonialist hermeneutics cannot account for. The word "discourse" Skura demonstrates, has licensed many arguments even as— perhaps because—it fails to account for the variety of ideological positions about the New World available in Jacobean England. These positions varied not only from person to person and text to text, but even from year to year, something that a nebulous "colonialist discourse" does not acknowledge; Meredith Anne Skura, "Discourse and the Individual: The Case of Colonialism in *The Tempest*," *Shakespeare Quarterly* 40 (1989): 42–69. Skura's article contains an extensive bibliography of colonialist readings of the play.

   Similarly, Dolan has changed the way we see the drama by arguing for an inherently small *Tempest*, one in which the crime of petty treason steers a counterplot in this "shrunken, enclosed world. . .in which Prospero's household is the commonwealth"; Frances E. Dolan, "The Subordinate('s) Plot: Petty Treason and the Forms of Domestic Rebellion," *Shakespeare Quarterly* 43 (1992): 317–40. By reminding us that Prospero governs a household, and that the drama's plot is more domestic than critics have acknowledged, Dolan give us reason to think of the play in more homely terms. Both readings ask us to revise a generally accepted set of beliefs about *The Tempest*.

2. Jeffrey Knapp, *An Empire Nowhere: England, America, and Literature from "Utopia" to "The Tempest"* (Berkeley: U of California P, 1992), chap. 6, "Distraction in *The Tempest*," 220–42. Compare the following: "Part of what causes the rather rigorous exclusion of colonialism in a play so strongly suggesting the issue is, I will maintain, Shakespeare's skeptical mimicry of a brand of imperialism I have associated particularly with Spenser's Fairyland, an antimaterialism holding that the best way to win America is to raise the minds of one's insular nation above the low thought of mere earthly possession" (221).

3. *The Tempest*, ed. Frank Kermode, New Arden Shakespeare (London: Methuen, 1954), xxv-xxvi.

4. See *Thomas Platter's Travels in England*, trans. Clare Williams (London: Jonathan Cape, 1937), 170.

5. Thomas Middleton, *Father Hubbard's Tales* (London: W. Cotten, 1604) sig. D1^r.

6. Thomas Dekker, *Selected Prose Writings*, ed. E. D. Pendry (Cambridge: Harvard UP, 1968), 99.

7. On the practice of stage sitting, see Irwin Smith, *Shakespeare's Blackfriars Playhouse: Its History and Its Design* (New York: New York UP, 1964), 148, 220–23, 297–98, 308–11, 330.

8. Dekker, *Selected Prose Writings*, 99; emphasis added.

9. I have characterized this passage as a metatheatrical moment in *Drama and the Market in the Age of Shakespeare* (Cambridge: Cambridge UP, 1992), 32–33.

10. See C. W. Wallace, *Times* (London), 28 March 1913, 6. Quotations from *London's Love to the Royal Prince Henrie, Meeting Him on the River of Thames, at His Return from Richmonde, with a Worthy Fleet of Her Citizens, on Thursday the Last of May 1610. With a Briefe Reporte of the Water-Fight and Fire-Workes* (London: N. Fosbrooke, 1610), reprinted in *The Progresses, Processions, and Magnificent Festivities of King James the First*, ed. John Nichols, 4 vols. (London: J. B. Nichols, 1828; reprint New York: Burt Franklin, 1960–69), 2:319, 321.

11. See Douglas Bruster, "Comedy and Control: Shakespeare and the Plautine *Poeta*," *Comparative Drama* 24 (1990): 217–31; reprinted in Clifford Davidson, Rand Johnson, and John H. Stroupe, eds., *Drama and the Classical Heritage: Comparative and Critical Essays*, AMS Ancient and Classical Studies 1 (New York: AMS Press, 1993), 117–31. On the role of the directing actor-manager in Shakespeare, see also Meredith Anne Skura, *Shakespeare the Actor and the Purposes of Playing* (Chicago: U of Chicago P, 1993).

12. On the growing reliance on the visual in Shakespeare, see Gary Schmidgall, *Shakespeare and the Courtly Aesthetic* (Berkeley: U of California P, 1981).

13. Samuel Daniel, Epistle prefaced to *The Vision of the Twelve Goddesses*, I. 269, in *The Complete Works in Verse and Prose of Samuel Daniel*, ed. Alexander B. Grosart, 5 vols. (New York: Russell and Russell, 1963; first publ. 1885), 3: 196.

14. Andrew Gurr, *Playgoing in Shakespeare's London* (Cambridge: Cambridge UP, 1987), 93.

15. *The New Arden Hamlet*, ed. Harold Jenkins (London: Methuen, 1982), note to 3.2.1–35 (Longer Note, pp. 498–99).

16. [Thomas Nashe], *An Almond for a Parrat* ([London]: n.p., 1590), sig. A1; *The Works of Thomas Nashe*, ed. Ronald B. McKerrow (London: Sidgwick and Jackson, 1910), 3:341.

17. On Will Kemp's career as clown, see David Wiles, *Shakespeare's Clown: Actor and Text in the Elizabethan Playhouse* (Cambridge: Cambridge UP, 1987); and Max W. Thomas, "*Kemps Nine Dais Wonder*: Dancing Carnival Into Market," *PMLA* 107 (1992): 511–23. For representative jigs and discussion of Kemp's relation to the jig, see Charles Read Baskervill, *The Elizabethan Jig and Related Song Drama* (Chicago: U of Chicago P, 1929).

18. On *locus* and *platea*, I am indebted to Robert Weimann, who describes the theatrical *platea* as an "extension of the acting area" by a nonrepresentational, "unlocalized 'place,'" while the *locus* is a more restricted area that can "delimit a more or less fixed and focused scenic unit," whether it be a tent, throne, scaffold, table, or home. See Weimann, *Shakespeare and the Popular Tradition in the Theater: Studies in the Social Dimension of Dramatic Form and Function*

(Baltimore: Johns Hopkins UP, 1978), 74, 79. Kemp's practice appears to have had significant precedent in the medieval and early Tudor theater, where a Vice character might run through and around the audience, talking to spectators and including them in the playworld even as he separated himself from it. In *The Antipodes* (1638), Richard Brome has characters recall Kemp and Tarlton in an argument about theatrical decorum:

> LETOY: But you, sir, are incorrigible, and
>   Take license to yourself to add unto
>   Your parts your own free fancy, and sometimes
>   To alter or diminish what the writer
>   With care and skill compos'd; and when you are
>   To speak to your coactors in the scene,
>   You hold interlocutions with the audients—
> BYPLAY: That is a way, my lord, has bin allow'd
>   On elder stages to move mirth and laughter.
> LETOY: Yes, in the days of Tarlton and Kemp,
>   Before the stage was purg'd from barbarism,
>   And brought to the perfection it now shines with.
>   Then fools and jesters spent their wits, because
>   The poets were wise enough to save their own
>   For profitabler uses.   (2.2.39–53)

To Letoy, Byplay's "elder stages" immediately suggests Tarlton and Kemp, actors he associates with misspent wits and such theatrical barbarism as holding "interlocutions with the audients." Thus Hamlet's clowns who "will themselves laugh to set on some quantity of barren spectators to laugh too, though in the mean time some necessary question of the play be then to be consider'd." Brome from *The Antipodes*, ed. Ann Haaker (Lincoln: U of Nebraska P, 1966).

19.   When Prospero speaks of "the trumpery in my house" (4.1.186), it is defined shortly in a stage direction: "*Enter* ARIEL, *loaden with glistering apparel, etc. ...*." Prospero's "house" is thus like a playhouse in containing the "trumpery" and "glistering apparel"—i.e. costumes—central to the business of playing in early modern London. Indeed it is difficult to exaggerate the importance of apparel to the theatrical industry then. As the research of Ann Rosalind Jones and Peter Stallybrass demonstrates, the theaters of Renaissance London served as something like extensions of the urban clothing industry. It was hard for plays not to acknowledge that. Thus, for example, when in *The Changeling* Isabella asks Lollio for the key to his "wardrobe" to apparel herself as a madwoman—which she does in a brief interval—she could have received the actual key to the playhouse's wardrobe (where a madwomen's costume would be found), her project temporarily blurring the boundaries between madhouse and theater (cf. 4.3.49–102). In much the same way, Prospero manages his house's wardrobe, the "glistering apparel, etc." with which he tantalizes Caliban, Trinculo, and Stephano identical to the playhouse's wardrobe. See Ann Rosalind Jones and Peter Stallybrass, *Worn Worlds* (tentative title), forthcoming.

20.   Robert Nares, *A Glossary or Collection of Words, Phrases, Names, and Allusions to Customs, Proverbs, Etc. Which Have Been Thought to Require Illus-*

tration in the Works of English Authors, Particularly Shakespeare and His Contemporaries, 2 vols. (London: Gibbings and Company, 1901), vol. 1 s.v. "Haydigyes."

21. Will Kemp, *Kemp's nine days' wonder. Performed in a dance from London to Norwich* (London: N. Ling, 1600), reprinted in Edward Arber, ed., *Social England Illustrated: A Collection of XVIIth Century Tracts*, An English Garner (Westminster: Archibald Constable, 1903), 141, 143, 144, 147, 150.

22. See C. L. Barber, *Shakespeare's Festive Comedy: A Study of Dramatic Form and Its Relation to Social Custom* (Princeton: Princeton UP, 1959) and François Laroque, *Shakespeare's Festive World: Seasonal Entertainment and the Professional Stage*, trans. Janet Lloyd, European Studies in English Literature (Cambridge: Cambridge UP, 1991).

23. On Kemp in *Romeo and Juliet*, see Wiles, *Shakespeare's Clown*, 83–94.

24. William Empson, "*Honest* in *Othello*," chap. 11 of *The Structure of Complex Words* (Cambridge: Harvard UP, 1989; first publ. 1951), 218.

Nova Reperta. Engraving by Theodre Galles after a drawing by Jan van der Straet, c. 1580. Used by permission of the Folger Shakespeare Library.

Revisiting *The Tempest**

ARTHUR F. KINNEY

I

The most significant criticism of Tudor and Stuart literary texts in recent years
has returned these texts to the cultural moment that first produced them.
Explicitly or not, such literary criticism has contributed to a deepening understanding of historical consciousness in the period. "Considering literary texts
not as autonomous utterances out of history, but as illustrations of a Renaissance culture whose forms of representation are conditioned by the social,
political world they participate in," Thomas Healy observes, "has prompted
readings of texts which seek to restore their former agencies and original discursive energies."[1] While he goes on to ask how we might best gain access to
such a culture—a highly rhetorical one that privileged feigning—the general
practice has been to follow the "interpretive theory of culture" of Clifford
Geertz and his principle of "thick description" as practiced by Stephen Greenblatt, Louis Adrian Montrose, and Steven Mullaney among others—that is, in
the words of Geertz, "the study of culture [in which] the signifiers are not
symptoms or clusters of symptoms, but symbolic acts or clusters of symbolic
acts." For Geertz, all possible observations of a culture are "inscriptions" of it,
and his practice is one of "setting down the meaning particular social actions
have for the actors whose actions they are, and stating, as explicitly as we can
manage, what the knowledge thus attained demonstrates about the society in
which it is found."[2]

Such a semiotic practice of reading literary texts, customs, and actions as
cultural documents, as signs of a cultural moment, is for me even more firmly

*Reprinted from *Modern Philology* 95.2 (1995): 161–177. Copyright 1995 by The
University of Chicago. Reprinted with permission of the University of Chicago Press
and Arthur Kinney.

rooted in the theory of the *Annales* school represented in the work of Marc Bloch.[3] The powerfully influential argument of that school, that history must extend beyond conventional archival resources to include all kinds of evidence, so that even extra-verbal or nonverbal pieces of evidence such as a landscape are "read" as texts, has helped immensely in providing a fuller sense of history. The method supplies multiple viewpoints, often irreconcilable, which locate facets of a past moment or period that both extend and enrich our knowledge of it. While Bloch argues that all knowledge is indirect and must necessarily operate to reconstruct rather than to recover or reidentify the past, his further insistence that understanding the past always means interrogating the past has been especially useful. Bloch thus proposes a field theory of examination by which any single work or object under scrutiny is always seen in the wider context of which it is, and has always necessarily been, a part.

What we have long called literary texts, therefore, both register and interrogate the ideas and values of a culture at the same time they intervene in that culture and help constitute it. Some examples will show what I have in mind. When Sidney's Euarchus, at the close of the comprehensive fiction of *Arcadia*, finds himself unable to accommodate the guilt of his son because the laws of justice do not admit exceptions, the author makes a powerful comment favoring the newer courts of equity and an equally powerful questioning of the courts of common law, dependent wholly on precedent, under Elizabeth I. The fiction does not stop being a fiction, nor the romance a romance, but at the same time it interrogates the Tudor court system and interrupts the smugness with which other writers praised it in both London and the provinces. When Iago in *Othello* is able to challenge the self-confident judgment of his general by showing in the person of the drunken Cassio that Othello chose an inferior man as his lieutenant, that Othello's autocratic wisdom can be called to account and found lacking, Shakespeare not only draws directly on the military manuals of his day; he also demonstrates the inherent limitations of a military conditioning and mind-set given to absolute commands and irrevocable decisions that can be fallible—and he gestures even more dramatically toward the clear and present dangers of James VI, who displays an equally stubborn self-confidence in writing and publishing his political doctrine of enlightened absolutism. When, in "The Collar" the poet George Herbert, self-exiled to the small village parish of Bemerton in distant Wales, writes "I struck the board, and cry'd, No more / I will abroad," he is not merely announcing a frustration with the Christian faith or exemplifying the Christian state of near despair, he is also demonstrating through the textual register of meditative poetry how the Protestant who is neither Genevan nor papist can yearn for more than the Erastian provisos of the Church or England. He is talking about the plight of the religious in a nation which charts contradictory and unsettled religious paths.

Social and economic conditions also help us to resituate texts in their cultural moment. *All's Well That Ends Well* is a play that has long troubled me—not because it is a problem play in its admixture of realism and folktale, as Anne Barton and others have regarded it since W. W. Lawrence first made the case[4]—but because the play offers such strong resolutions based on strained premises. The king rewarding a commoner by approving marriage with nobility, for instance, is reminiscent of Thomas Dekker's improbable conclusion to *The Shoemaker's Holiday*. On this point Sheldon P. Zitner has helpfully noted that Shakespeare's play was written (and first performed) at the height of controversy over the Court of Wards, which enabled the Crown to profit from the persons and inherited property of minors by selling—or, for a fee, allowing its nobility to sell—the guardianship of orphans. Helena is such a ward, in effect surrendered by the Countess of Rossillion to the King as a chattel whose perquisite it is to assign control of her for profit; Bertram, on the other hand, is equally without control of his own property because his father had the bad fortune to die before his son came of age.[5] *All's Well*, then, starts with two recently orphaned youth of different genders whose actions put a hierarchical and relatively closed society to the test. The play is about what these orphans do. It is also, from this perspective, about what they can do: court service and military service for him; nursing and the convent for her. From another perspective, the play conducts a rigorous examination of rank and gender in late Tudor England (as well as France, where the action reputedly takes place).

In a different way, *The Merry Wives of Windsor* intervenes in its cultural moment, I think it is no accident that this play is set uniquely in Shakespeare's contemporary England because it means to question economic conditions there. Windsor, the play's sole location, was then a royal borough, but it was also a village devastated (as were other parts of the country) by four years of bad harvests between 1593 and 1597: by unusual dearth, poverty, starvation, and death. In this context the gluttonous Falstaff serves as the perfect ironic sign. As in the history plays, he is "out at heels" (1.3.31), while the merchants of the play, the Pages and the Fords, stuff themselves at feast after feast, *The Merry Wives* is a play about the haves and the have-nots, about the deepening economic divide in the late "golden years" of Elizabeth I. This play, too, functions as commentary, entering into the culture for its material, returning that material to the culture as farce. But why farce? Perhaps by way of analogy to the invention during the Great Depression in the 1930s of screwball comedies in Hollywood, musical comedies on Broadway, and the new game of Monopoly—to relieve economic distress by making light of it.[6]

But if texts can be seen as events,[7] events can also serve as texts. Essex's London revolt on February 8, 1601, is a textual event because it can be read as an act of political belief, interrogating Tudor justice and leadership, just as much as can John Hayward's account of the reign of Henry IV, which aligns Henry with Essex. Both were read as such in their own time, although only one of them is verbal. Both are signs of and in a particular historical consciousness. Both function semiotically, as "documents."

These and other instances have led me to formulate four working premises or axioms—starting places for examining texts and signs which may be subject to change, addition, or suspension but which nevertheless remain good heuristic points of departure:

1. No text is ever entirely unmarked by its time and place.
2. Every text has some intention; even when the intention is misconceived, unrealized, or misunderstood, no text is innocent of purpose or reception.
3. Every text potentially has multiple interpreters and multiple occasions through which it is interpreted or conveyed.
4. No text is completely unequivocal or conclusive.

The limitation when working with a past time such as the early modern period is that the only cultural signs are those preserved in the written or pictorial records available to us: even our knowledge of the event of Essex's rebellion relies on extant verbal documents. Such documents may be as formal as court proceedings or as informal as gossip recorded in letters or diaries, but they survive as potential objects of our knowledge because they are in written or printed form. In the absence of other means of knowledge they have served to privilege writing; and historically this has in turn served to privilege literature. But the uniqueness of written transmission does not make literature autonomous. In fact, it need not even cause us to categorize verbal texts as exclusively verbal, for such preserved records may also indicate sights and sounds that are equally important for reconstructing a cultural moment and a literary text within that moment. Shakespeare's *The Tempest* is a particularly significant case in point.

II

For the past decade, Shakespeare's works have been a chief site for the cultural examination of English literary texts, and *The Tempest* has been one of the foremost among them. The play is read as recording and interrogating several concerns of early Stuart England: absolutist rule, white magic, discovery of the New World, colonialism, imperialism, racism. In 1975 Geoffrey Bullough isolated twelve texts as "narrative and dramatic sources" of the play; in 1977, in a work dedicated to Bullough, Kenneth Muir confirmed these and added a few of his own.[8] Both emphasized three printed pamphlets of voyages to the New World and one manuscript account not published until 1625, all of them concerned with an expedition shipwrecked in the Bermudas which may account for Shakespeare's reference to "the still-vex'd Bermoothes" (*Tempest*

1.2.229). These four texts are *A True and Sincere Declaration of the purpose and ends of the Plantation begun in Virginia*, "set forth by the authority of the Governors and councillors" (1609), *A Discovery of the Bermudas, otherwise called the Ile of Divels, by Sir Thomas Gates, Sir George Sommers and Captayne Newport, with divers others*, attributed to Silvester Jourdain (1610), *A true Declaration of the estate of the Colony of Virginia, with a confutation of such scandalous reports as have tended to the disgrace of so worthy an enterprise* (1610), and a long letter to an "excellent lady" sent from Virginia on July 15, 1610, by William Strachey, Gates's secretary at Jamestown, eventually published as *A True Repertory of the Wracke and Redemption of Sir Thomas Gales, Knight; upon, and from the Ilands of the Bermudas: his coming to Virginia, and the estate of that Colonie, there, and after, under the government of the Lord La Warre*.[9] Muir largely dismisses these pamphlets as necessary sources, since the details they recount are generic to voyages and reflect common knowledge as well as common sense.[10] But Bullough uses the pamphlets to argue for dating Shakespeare's play in 1611. He especially emphasizes Strachey's letter. "After describing in detail the shipwreck," Bullough notes, "this letter gave a vivid account of the indiscipline, mutiny, and perils from savage Indians suffered by the colonists from June 1609 to July 1610.[11]

How Shakespeare could have seen this letter, which circulated at court in one or more manuscript copies at the time, is unclear: there is not a shred of evidence, in fact, that the playwright, not privy to the court himself, ever did see it. Bullough himself is conscious of this and hastens to defend his claim: "He must have known several members of the Council besides the Earls of Southampton and Pembroke, e.g., Sir Dudley Digges and Christopher Brooke, and perhaps Sir Henry Neville. Moreover he would know prominent investors such as William Leveson, who had been appointed in 1607 to raise money for the Company, and Sir Henry Rainsford of Clifford Chambers, two miles from Stratford, who, with Shakespeare, was mentioned in the will of John Combes in 1613. Any of these may have let him read a copy of Strachey's narrative."[12] The circumstantial argument is tenuous; it may also be moot. Greenblatt notes in summary that "the narrative materials that passed from Strachey to Shakespeare, from the Virginia Company to the King's Men: a violent tempest, a providential shipwreck on a strange island, a crisis in authority provoked by both danger and excess, a fear of lower-class disorder and upper-class ambition, a triumphant affirmation of absolute control linked to the manipulation of anxiety and to a departure from the island" were all less central to the play than other concerns. "The swerve away from these materials," Greenblatt continues, "is as apparent as their presence: the island is not in America but in the Mediterranean; it is not uninhabited—Ariel and Caliban (and, for that matter, Sycorax) were present before the arrival of Prospero and Miranda; none of the figures are in any sense colonists; the departure is for home rather than a colony and entails not an unequivocal heightening of authority but a partial diminution, signaled in Prospero's abjuration of magic." He adds that while Strachey's narrative moves toward martial law, Shakespeare's play moves toward forgiveness, toward marriage rather than punishment.[13] These are telling points of difference, yet Greenblatt himself is unwilling to surrender entirely the printed cultural document which has also universally been declared the primary basis of Shakespeare's play.

> The play seems to act out a fantasy of mind control, to celebrate absolute patriarchal rule, to push to an extreme the dream of order, epic achievement, and ideological justification implicit in Strachey's text. The lower-class resistance Strachey chronicles becomes in Shakespeare the drunken rebellion of Stephano and Trinculo, the butler and jester who, suddenly finding themselves freed from their masters, are drawn to a poor man's fantasy of mastery: "the King and all our company else being drown'd, we will inherit here" (2.2.174–75). Similarly, the upper-class resistance of Henry Paine is transformed into the murderous treachery of Sebastian, in whom the shipwreck arouses dreams of an escape from subordination to his older brother, the king of Naples, just as Antonio had escaped subordination to his older brother, Prospero.[14]

Moreover, "By invoking fratricidal rivalry here Shakespeare is not only linking the Strachey materials to his own long-standing theatrical preoccupations but also supplementing the contractual authority of a governor like Sir Thomas Gates with the familial and hence culturally sanctified authority of the eldest son."[15]

Despite the rich suggestiveness of these speculations, they do not address the question of Shakespeare's access to such a manuscript nor do they address in any conclusive way Muir's overall objection. The treachery of explorers in the New World, both old and young, both to their leaders and to the natives they discovered in their voyages to new lands, was commonplace. The discussion in and about the Exchange and Inns of Court in London, in streets and in pubs, would have given Shakespeare access to reports and gossip about New World voyaging. The chief problem regarding the Strachey manuscript is the way it has served to block further investigation, offering enough so that critics of early Stuart culture have not bothered to consider either an earlier printed pamphlet about another expedition that was available both to Shakespeare and to the members of his audiences, or certain related cultural phenomena—in this instance daily sights in London—that must have influenced both playwright and playgoers. What I have in mind are "Tahánedo, a Sagamo or Commander," "Amoret," "Skicowáros" and an unnamed male, both "Maneddo Gentlemen," and Sassacomoit, a servant"—five Native Americans brought from the New World to London in 1605 to be put on show as booty of a successful voyage.[16] The natives' daily presence in London must have had at least as much effect on Shakespeare and on the conceptualization of *The*

Tempest as any written pamphlets—live "texts" that could serve the playwright as "sources" in the very cultural moment he was writing his play.

Considering the vastly different cultural interpretations that have been given to Caliban in *The Tempest*—a noble savage, an unregenerate son of a witch—how were natives who have been captured and brought to England viewed in the early 1600s? There is no sure way of telling, and unanimity is unlikely in any case. But some indication may be found in the only extant account of their very existence: *A True Relation of the most prosperous voyage made this present yeere 1605, by Captaine George Waymouth, in the Discovery of the land of Virginia: Where he discovered 60 miles up a most excellent River: together with a most fertile land, Written by James Rosier, a Gentleman employed in the voyage.* This text was in circulation half a dozen years before the putative date of *The Tempest*, although Robert Cecil, earl of Salisbury, in collusion with Sir Thomas Smith, Sir Walter Cope, the East Indian and Levant Company merchant, and others, tried to suppress it because the work recounted the spoils of New England instead of Virginia where they had all directed their own investments.

Rosier's work begins, like *The Tempest*, with a battering storm followed by a providential land at "five fathoms" (cf. Ariel's song at 1.2.398): "We all with great joy praised God for his unspeakable goodnesse, who had from so apparent danger delivered us, & directed us upon this day into so secure an Harbour: in remembrance whereof we named it *Pentecost-harbor*, we arriving there that day out of our last Harbor in *England*, from whence we set saile upon Easterday" (sig. Blv; p. 262). Rosier describes the island as "woody, growen with Firre, Birch, Oke, and Beech, as farr as we saw along the shore; and so likely to be within" (sig. B1; p. 259) and then erupts in sheerjoy with a catalog of berries, bushes, trees, and wildlife (sig. B2v; pp. 265–66; sig. E3v-E4; pp. 304–7). But much of his attention is also directed to the "savages." While this term was by then commonplace—Shakespeare uses it in *The Tempest* (2.2.58) while Rosier employs it throughout his text and marginalia—the first occurrence of the word, in Rosier's preface, is already ominous. Rosier notes that those aboard the *Archangell* "could not allure our Captaine or any speciall man of our Company to combine with them for their direction, nor obtaine their purpose, in conveying away our Salvages, which was busily in practice" (sig. A2v; p.262).

Natives of the New World never appear in William Strachey's private account, but they are at the center of Rosier's more public one. Those on the *Archangell* at first find the natives "all very civill and merrie: shewing tokens of much thankefulnesse, for those things we gave them. We found them then (as after) a people of exceeding good invention, quicke understanding and readie capacitie" (sig. B3v; p.269). "They had been fishing and fowling," we are told, and when "we were ready to come away, they shewed us great cups made very wittily of barke, in form almost square, full of a red berry about the bignesse of a bullis [small round object, *OED* substantive 2], which they did eat, and gave us by handfuls" (sig. C3; p.280). Rosier expands on a report by Owen Griffin about the natives' manner

> and (as I may terme them) the ceremonies of their idolatry: which they per-
> forme thus. One among them (the eldest of the Company, as he judged)
> riseth right up, the other sitting still, and looking about, suddenly cried with
> a loud voice, Baugh, Waugh: then the women fall downe, and lie upon the
> ground, and the men all together answering the same, fall a stamping round
> about the fire with both feet, as hard as they can, making the ground shake,
> with sundry outcries, and change of voice and sound. Many take the fire-
> sticks and thrust them into the earth, and then rest awhile: of a sudden begin-
> ning as before, they continue so stamping, till the yonger sort fetched from
> the shore many stones, of which every man tooke one, and first beat upon
> them with their fire sticks, then with the stones beat the earth with all their
> strength. And in this manner (as he reported) they continued above two
> hours. (Sig. C2v; p.278)

These New World natives are, then, spectacular and Other, erotic, passionate, perhaps intractable: "One of them ware a kinde of Coronet about his head, made very cunningly, of a substance like stiffe haire coloured red, broad, and more than a handfull in depth, which we imagined to be some ensigne of his superioritie: for he so much esteemed it as he would not for any thing exchange the same" (sig. D1v; p.287). But Rosier's attempt to make the natives objects of knowledge does not at any point dismiss their strangeness: "they paint their bodies with blacke, their faces, some with red, some with blacke, and some with blew"; "they suffer no haire to grow on their faces, but on their head very long and very blacke" (sig. B3v; pp. 268–69). Quite liter-ally, these persons are, as Prospero calls Caliban, "thing[s] of darkness" (5.1.275).

At perhaps the crucial juncture of Rosier's account, he notes that the offi-cers of the *Archangell* gain the upper hand over the natives by tricking them with ostensible magic: "Our Captaine shewed them a strange thing which they wondered at. His sword and mine having beene touched with the Loadstone (magnet), [he] tooke up a knife, and held it fast when they plucked it away, made the knife turne, being laid on a blocke, and touching it with his sword, made that take up a needle, wherat they much marvelled. This we did to cause them to imagine some great power in us; and for that to oue [awe] and fear us" (sig. C1; p. 274). The explorers then bind the natives with stronger ties of ami-cability by giving them novelties and teaching them their uses:

> Our Captaine bestowed a shirt upon him, whom we thought to be their
> chiefe, who seemed never to have seene any before; we gave him a brooch
> to hang about his necke, a great knife, and lesser knives to the two other, and

to every one of them a combe and glasse, the use whereof we shewed them: whereat they laughed and tooke gladly; we victualled them, and gave them *aqua vitae*, which they tasted, but would by no meanes drinke; our beveridge they liked well, we gave them Sugar Candy, which after they had tasted they liked and desired more, and raisons which were given them; and some of every thing they would reserve to carry to their company. (Sig. B4v; p. 272)

But such actions incrementally corrupt the white men, who sense how readily they have come by their high regard. Rosier's straightforward narrative shows how easy it was for the explorers to begin exploiting the natives.

The next morning very early, came one Canoa abord us againe with three Salvages, whom we easily then enticed into our ship, and under the decke: where we gave them porke, fish, bread and pease, all which they did eat: and this I noted, they would eat nothing raw, either fish or flesh. They marvelled much and much looked upon the making of our canne and kettle, so they did at a head-peece and at our guns, of which they are most fearefull, and would fall flat downe at the report of them. At their departure I signed unto them, that if they would bring me such skins as they ware I would give them knives, and such things as I saw they most liked, which the chiefe of them promised to do by that time the Sunne should be beyond the middest of the firmament; this I did to bring them to an understanding of exchange, and that they might conceive the intent of our comming to them to be for no other end. (Sigs. B3v-B4; pp. 270)

Such ostensible "exchange" is followed by deception and betrayal, as the natives turn against those they had quickly accepted as superiors and the explorers react in turn: "We began to joyne them in the ranke of other Salvages, who have beene by travellers in most discoveries found very trecherous: never attempting mischiefe, untill by some remisnesse, fit opportunity affordeth them certaine ability to execute the same. Wherefore after good advice taken, we determined so soone as we could to take some of them, least (being suspitious we had discovered their plots) they should absent themselves from us" (sig. C4; p. 283). The tale darkens further as Rosier moves from capture to enslavement:

We manned the light horseman with 7 or 8 men, one standing before carried our box of Marchandise, as we were woont when I went to traffique with them, and a platter of pease, which meat they loved: but before we were landed, one of them (being too suspitiously fearefull of his owne good) withdrew himselfe into the wood. The other two met us on the shore side, to receive the pease, with whom we went up the Cliffe to their fire and sate downe with them, and whiles we were discussing how to catch the third man who was gone, I opened the box, and shewed them trifles to exchange, thinking thereby to have banisht feare from the other, and drawen him to returne: but when we could not, we used little delay, but suddenly laid hands upon

them. And it was as much as five or sixe of us could doe to get them into the
light horseman. For they were strong and so naked as our best hold was by
their long haire on their heads: and we would have beene very loath to have
done them any hurt, which of necessity we had beene constrained to have
done if we had attempted them in a multitude, which we must and would,
rather than have wanted them, being a matter of great importance for the full
accomplement of our voyage. (Sig. C4v; p. 284)

This entrapment constitutes the explorers' clear and historic measure of success: "Thus we shipped five Salvages, two Canoas, with all their bowes and
arrowes" back to England (sig. C4v; p. 285). The shipment is the resounding
triumph of their voyage. Naming the native captives in this report, then, is not
merely a matter of record but of high achievement—proof of a dangerous and
exotic voyage and a sign of material success. The natives have become captives and turned into live booty. However Shakespeare and his fellow Lon-
doners thought of these five Indians in 1611, they were presented in 1605 as
dark, savage, alien goods on display as a living wonder-box. The precise location of their capture is never given—nor is the location of Prospero's and Caliban's "uninhabited island" (editor's stage direction, p.1611) because it has
been the site of a slaving raid. By 1611, both Tahánedo and Caliban were func-
tioning as cultural texts, and Prospero's actions in Shakespeare's play could,
and for some would, have been construed by reference to the actions of those
aboard the *Archangell* six years earlier.

III

J.G.A. Pocock has written that "a text can and must be seen as both an action
and an event."[17] As I began by noting, events are likewise texts, cultural signs.
But if we are to restore past historical consciousness as much as possible, it
will be well not only to read cultural signs but to hear them too. Hearing is also
especially relevant for understanding *The Tempest*, although again we need
extant writings to tell us how. Marc Bloch cautions, however, that "even those
texts or archaeological documents which seem the clearest and the most
accommodating will speak only when they are properly questioned."[18] In continuing to question *The Tempest*, many twentieth-century readers sense within
it an earlier form that remains in the play as a trace of something else. The
notion of a trace is applicable here.[19] As Derrida's forebear, Emmanuel Levinas, has written in his essay on "Le trace," it interchanges foreground and
background to bring half-hidden markings to light: "La trace n'est pas un
signe comme un autre. Mais elle joue aussi le rôle du signe. Elle peut être prise
pour un signe. Le détective examine comme signe révélateur tout ce qui mar-
que sur les lieux du crime, l'oeuvre volontaire ou involontaire du criminel; le
chasseur marche sur la trace du gibier, laquelle reflète l'activité et la marche
de la bête qu'il veut atteindre; l'historien découvre, à partir des vestiges

qu'avait laissés leur existence, les civilisations anciennes comme horizons de notre monde."[20] In *The Tempest* what is brought to light are the markings of allegory. The sense of discovery is so common that Bullough comments on it at some length: "The whole piece is indeed so permeated with Christian feeling that it has been interpreted as a Mystery play in which Prospero, if not the Deity, is 'the hierophant or initiating priest' in a right of purification which the Court party must willynilly undergo."[21] There is indeed something archetypal about *The Tempest*—in my earliest teaching days, I used to begin classes on the play by asking how Shakespeare could hope to make a drama out of a situation in which the protagonist was all good and always in complete control. That is of course an oversimplification, but the sense of symbolism in the storm, the father-governor, and the good and bad servants keeps driving us toward a dual registration of the play as both universal and particular. However, if we bear sounds in mind as important dimensions of texts in a cultural moment, we may recall that *The Tempest* in its initial outlines comes remarkably close to one of the most popular tropes and oral narratives in Shakespeare's day, found in the story of Jonah.

Henry Smith's *First Sermon on the punishment of "Jonah,"* preached initially in 1592, was reprinted often in Shakespeare's day—in 1602, 1605, 1607, twice in 1609, and many times subsequently. Smith was the preacher at St. Clement Danes, a London parish especially popular with Elizabeth's Privy Council (and a benefice partly in the giving of Burghley, until his death in 1598). Smith was also called by Thomas Nashe "silver tongu'd" Smith, "whose well tun'd stile hath made [Poetry's] death the generall teares of the Muses." Nashe further salutes Smith as a model for poets: "Queintlie couldst thou devise heavenly Ditties to *Apolloes* Lute, and teach stately verse to trip it as smoothly as if *Ovid* and those had but one soule. Hence alone did it proceed, that thou wert such a plausible pulpit man, that before thou entredst into the rough waies of Theologie, thou refinedst, preparedst, and purifidest thy minde with sweet Poetrie."[22]

Smith's sermon on Jonah is full of experiential specificity: "suddenly the tempest rushes upon them before they are aware of it, and tumbles them up and down, and suddenly all is like to be undone."[23] The oral narrative from the pulpit resonates closely with the oral performance of Shakespeare's play. "The ship was faire and goodly, so strong that it might have encountred with instruments of warre, and so sure made, that it might have endured great tempests, and made maine voyages. Yet now with one tempest, and at one voyage, it was so deformed, so weakened, in such a taking, that it was like to bee shivered in pieces."[24] Smith's account gains momentum and force as Shakespeare's play does by enacting a scene that is at once both conceptualized—abstracted into virtual allegory[25]—and at the same time perceived in vivid detail. The preacher dilates upon the emotionalism of the scene he has evoked: "Mariners living in the Sea, almost as fishes, having the waters as their necessarie element, are commonly men voyde of feare, venturous, and contemners of danger. Yet now seeing the tempest so vehement on a sudden, that their goodly and tall ship was tost almost to a cocke-boat, and crackt so, that it was like to be torn all to pieces, and thereby were fully perswaded it was no common nor ordinary storme, but a revenging tempest, for some extraordinary cause, sent out upon them by some great power provoked."[26] The point is not just that Smith's power of delivery produces a cultural similarity between sermon and play, but that few playgoers in Shakespeare's time might see a play beginning with a sudden storm without recalling, if only half-consciously, the archetypal storm they heard about in their parish churches year after year. (The second, third, and fourth chapters of Jonah were the Old Testament lessons for morning and evening prayer on September 17.)[27] In sensing such textual traces, Greenblatt writes, "we can ask how collective beliefs and experiences were shaped, moved from one medium to another, concentrated in manageable aesthetic form, offered for consumption."[28] As Prospero's behavior in 1611 could be placed alongside that of the crew of the *Archangell*, so the crew of the ship in the first scene of *The Tempest*, and Prospero aboard the cockboat with Miranda as recounted in act 1, scene 2, could be collocated with Jonah: suddenly caught in life's storm, thrown on naked human resources, subjected to severe trial, and yearning for some kind of providence.

Moreover, in the connotative richness of his sermon's narrative, Henry Smith constructs, as Shakespeare will in his play, a storm which is instructive both as instance and as type in delineating the range of human reactions under duress:

> In the time of necessitie every one doth flye for helpe and ease unto that which most feedeth his owne humour, or best pleaseth him, that wherein he reposeth most confidence, perswading themselves of sufficient reliefe. . . hoping by those to feele reliefe. In sicknesse we cry, Come, Phisicke, helpe me: in heavinesse we call, Come musicke, cheare me: In warre we sound, Come, souldiers, succour me: in quarrels we say, Come, Law, defend me: evermore leaving the Creator, which is all godlinesse, and powerfull in himselfe, running to the creatures, which have no goodnesse nor power, save that they receive from him: neither by their goodnesse, can doe us good, but by his blessings.[29]

Alonso's caution, Gonzalo's hope, the irritation of Sebastian, and the self-indulgence of Antonio all have their counterparts here, while the Boatswain's impossible command in *The Tempest*—"Lay her ahold, ahold! Set her two courses. Off to sea again! Lay her off!" (1.1.49–50)—is echoed in Smith's sermon: "The meanes which the Mariners use to save themselves, are divers. First, they cry to their gods, then when that appeased not the tempest, they cast out their wares."[30]

Sermons, then, are part of the cultural moment of *The Tempest* together with accounts of voyages to the New World and the sight of American natives on display. Malone noted that the author of *A true Declaration of the estate of the Colony in Virginia* (1610) made the specific connection with Jonah, even if later editors failed to take up Malone's lead.[31] According to the author of *A true Declaration*, on July 24, 1609,

> there arose such a storme, as if *Jonas* had been flying unto *Tarshish*: the heavens were obscured, and made an Egyptian night of three daies perpetuall horror; the women lamented, the hearts of the passengers failed: the experience of the sea Captaines was amased: the skill of the marriners was confounded: the Ship most violently leaked, and though two thousand tunne of water by pumping from Tuesday noone till Fryday noon was discharged, notwithstanding the Ship was halfe filled with water, and those which laboured to keepe others from drowning were halfe drowned themselves in labouring.
>
> But God that heard *Jonas* crying out of the belly of hell, he pittied the distresses of his servants: For behold, in the last period of necessitie, *Sir George Summers* descryed land, which was by so much the more joyfull, by how much their danger was despairefull.[32]

Even if Shakespeare did not specifically intend *The Tempest* to call up scripture or sermon, the English *mentalité* at his cultural moment would not have been likely to have forgotten them. Communal memories, awakened by sight and sound, would pull a performance of *The Tempest* toward allegory as well as toward New World voyages—and toward New World voyages as allegorical. "The historian's reconstitution of the context that makes the text, as action and event, intelligible now becomes a matter of reconstituting the languages in which certain illocutions . . . were carried out," Pocock writes, "and of discerning what the individual text, author, or performance did with the opportunities offered and the constraints imposed by the languages available to it."[33] As Brutus observes in Shakespeare's, *Julius Caesar*, "the eye sees not itself / But by reflection, by some other things" (1.2.52–53). *The Tempest* was not unmarked by its time and place.

IV

"It would be sheer fantasy," Bloch warns, "to imagine that for each historical problem," such as understanding the cultural moment of *The Tempest*, "there is a unique type of document with a specific sort of use. On the contrary, the deeper the research, the more the light of the evidence must converge from sources of many different kinds."[34] For Derrida, elaborating on Saussurean linguistics, speech is present, obvious, and a site of ideal meaning, while writing is absent (i.e., the author is not among us writing as we read in the way that the speaker speaks while we listen) and so is merely notional and less reliable.[35] But even when speech necessarily comes to us by way of written documents, these can on occasion lead us past the written texts of a cultural moment to the sights and sounds that accompany those texts. When that happens, as with the references to captured natives in Rosier's pamphlet or the reference to the story of Jonah in the anonymous voyage pamphlet of 1610 that might have been occasioned by a sermon as much as by a page of scripture, we feel ourselves that much closer to past meaning because of the intensity of the interplay of various signs in a single work like *The Tempest*. We are not often so lucky. Even when we feel we are, we have no certain way of knowing exactly how a literary text was received. We know more only about the range of potential meanings in play at a given time. We know a text better by knowing more that the text may have signified, more of its compoundings of signs. But our readings and rereadings of signs will always remain partial and contingent.

Every text potentially has multiple interpreters and multiple occasions through which it is interpreted or conveyed; no text is completely unequivocal or conclusive. "Texts have readers and outlive their authors. The author, in creating the text, creates the matrix in which others will read and respond to it. Readers ... are like the actors as well as the critics in [a] dramaturgical analogy," Pocock asserts; "in fact, it seems important at this moment to call the reader an actor in the sense that he is one in a historical process. No text is ever read exactly as its author intended it should be read; there is a sense in which the reader re-enacts the text, and this never happens twice in exactly the same way."[36] Crucial cultural signs at the moment of a text's origination may not be crucial cultural signs at a later moment of reading. But that likelihood should not prevent us from searching out the signs in force at the cultural moment when the text under examination was first conceived and produced. Howard Felperin contends that a cultural moment is "laden with the traces of earlier and the latencies of subsequent moments,"[37] but we shall never register the traces or the latencies until we have first attended closely to what we can recover of the originary moment itself.

NOTES

I am grateful to Janel Mueller for her many suggestions in preparing this essay for publication.

1. Thomas Healy, *New Latitudes: Theory and English Renaissance Literature* (London, 1992), p. 60.
2. Clifford Geertz, *The Interpretation of Cultures* (New York, 1977), pp. 26–27.
3. Marc Bloch, *The Historian's Craft*, trans. Peter Putnam (New York, 1953).
4. Anne Barton, introduction to *All's Well That Ends Well*, in *The Riverside Shakespeare* (Boston, s1974), 502. William Witherle Lawrence, *Shakespeare's*

Problem Comedies, 2nd ed. (New York, 1959), 1–77. All quotations from Shakespeare's plays are taken from the *Riverside* text.

5. Sheldon P. Zitner, *All's Well That Ends Well*, Twayne's New Critical Introductions to Shakespeare (Boston, 1989), 42–46.

6. I develop the argument in greater detail in "Textual Signs in *The Merry Wives of Windsor*," *Yearbook of English Studies* 23 (1993): 206–34.

7. The phrase is J. G. A. Pocock's in "Texts as Events: Reflections on the History of Political Thought," in *Politics as Discourse: The Literature and History of Seventeenth-Century England*, ed. Kevin Sharpe and Steven N. Zwicker (Berkely and Los Angeles, 1987), 21.

8. Geoffrey Bullough, ed. *Narrative and Dramatic Sources of Shakespeare* (London, 1975), 8:275–339; Kenneth Muir, *The Sources of Shakespeare's Plays* (London, 1977), 278–83.

9. Bullough, 8:238–39.

10. Muir, 280.

11. Bullough, 8:239.

12. Ibid.

13. Stephen Greenblatt, *Shakespearean Negotiations: The Circulation of Social Energy in Renaissance England* (Berkeley and Los Angeles, 1988), 154–55.

14. Ibid., 155

15. Ibid., 156

16. James Rosier, *A True Relation of the most prosperous voyage made this present yeere 1605, by Captaine George Waymouth, in the Discovery of the land of Virginia; Where he discovered 60 miles up a most excellent River: together with a most fertile land* (London, 1605), sig. E4; also in David B. Quinn and Alison M. Quinn, *The English New England Voyages, 1602–1608*, Hakluyt Society, 2d ser., no. 161 (London, 1983), 309. Subsequent references will be to both texts and will hereafter appear in the text. Here and below I modernize i/j and u/v and silently emend contractions in the old-spelling text.

17. Pocock (n. 7 above), 23.

18. Bloch (n.3 above), 64.

19. Jacques Derrida, *Speech and Phenomena*, trans. David B. Allison (Evanston, Illinois, 1973), 156–57.

20. "The trace is not a typical sign, but it may play the role of a sign. It may be taken for a sign. The detective examines everything that marks the scene of the crime as a revealing sign, the intentional or unintentional work of the criminal; the hunter follows the trace of the game, which reflects the activity and the tread of the animal he seeks; the historian discovers ancient civlizations, beginning with the vestiges left by their existence, as horizons to our world." Emmanuel Levinas, "Le trace," in *Humanisme de l'autre Homme*, trans. Peter Sokolowski (Montpellier, 1972), 66.

21. Bullough (n.8 above), 8: 273.

22. Thomas Nashe, *Pierce Penilesse His Supplication to the Devill* (London, 1592), sig. D3v.

23. Henry Smith, *The First Sermon on the punishment of "Jonah"* (London, 1605), sig. A3. Further citations are to this later text.

24. Ibid., sig. A3v.
25. So too Anne Barton: "There has been a persistent tendency to regard the play as allegorical," to "feel that the heart of its mystery can be plucked out by means of some superimposed system of ideas" (introduction to the New Penguin text of *The Tempest* [Harmondsworth, 1968], 21).
26. Smith, sigs. A3v-A4.
27. John E. Booty, ed. *The Book of Common Prayer 1559: The Elizabethan Prayer Book*, Folger Documents of Tudor and Stuart Civilization, no. 22 (Charlottesville, Va., 1976), 44.
28. Greenblatt (n. 13 above), 5.
29. Smith, sigs. A4v-A5.
30. Ibid., sig. A4.
31. Edmond Malone, *The Plays and Poems of William Shakespeare* (London, 1821), 15:411; he makes no comment on this, however, being interested in the voyage pamphlet only as it gives a date for the voyage and for Shakespeare's play.
32. Reprinted in Bullough (n. 8 above), 8:295.
33. Pocock (n. 7 above), 26.
34. Bloch (n. 3 above), 67.
35. As summarized by Ross C. Murfin in "What is Deconstruction?" in *William Shakespeare: "Hamlet,"* ed. Susanne L. Wofford (Boston, 1994), 285.
36. Pocock, 29.
37. Howard Felperin, " 'Cultural Poetics' versus 'Cultural Materialism': The Two New Historicisms in Renaissance Studies," in *Uses of History: Marxism, Postmodernism and the Renaissance*, ed. Francis Barker, Peter Hulme, and Margaret Iversen, Essex Symposia (Manchester, 1991), 86.

Fantasy and History in *The Tempest**

RICHARD P. WHEELER

Prospero's tense account to Miranda of his brother's past treachery and of his own expulsion, with her, from Milan, is history in the making—a rendering of the past by one who has a compelling interest in telling it as he does, as if recounting its only possible truth. It is not difficult to imagine alternative versions, which would instead emphasize Prospero's responsibility for the events culminating in his overthrow. I am less concerned with how Prospero remembers his past, however, than with how the play remembers its past, with how *The Tempest* looks back on, and takes its place within, Shakespearean history. I am concerned with how *The Tempest* recalls and retells some motifs central to the development of Shakespeare's drama, with how it acts upon a history that is internal to that body of work.

I

Hans Loewald writes: "In the process of individuation, the human being becomes historical."[1] Loewald's characteristic concerns in his *Psychoanalysis and the History of the Individual* are with the ways in which our respective individualities emerge from and perpetuate a past that is alive in our present and indispensable to our future. The three chapters in Loewald's short volume were first given as the Freud Lectures at Yale University, where Loewald was clinical professor emeritus of psychiatry. These chapters, grounded in his life's work as a practicing analyst and as a psychoanalytic theorist of exceptional sophistication, reflect the depth and complexity of that work in ways that far exceed the reach of the short commentary that follows. But I have used

*Originally published in *The Tempest,* edited by Nigel Wood, for the Theory in Practice Series (Buckingham and Philadelphia: Open University Press, 1995), 128–160, 179–180. Reprinted by permission of Open University Press and Richard P. Wheeler.

Loewald's little book as the theoretical text to accompany my commentary on *The Tempest* because of what I find to be his apt and eloquent emphasis on a historical dimension fundamental to psychoanalytic inquiry since Freud started tracking down links between the symptoms of his earliest adult patients and events that had occurred early in their childhoods. Loewald's chapters are designed to identify what psychoanalysis shares with the disciplines of the humanities: "It is the scope of psychoanalysis to consider human nature in the fullness of the individual's concrete existence and covering the full range of human potentialities, with special attention given—for a variety of reasons—to its historicity.[2]

The part of individual history that psychoanalysis deals with most distinctively is infantile and childhood history—the development of the individual subject as separate from maternal environment, the history of the formation of the unconscious, the sequence of psychosexual developmental stages culminating in the Oedipus complex and its dissolution, and the development within that subject of id, ego and superego from an undifferentiated matrix. Tracing the deep psychological structure of a human subject or the work of a writer is to recover the durable and dynamic outcome of that childhood history. To identify the individual's historicity is to recover what can be inferred about how an individual has emerged from a past shaped by the interrelations of the individual's constitutional or genetic endowment, the social world in which the individual has matured, and what psychoanalysis speculates about unconscious mental processes.

In this project, all recovery is necessarily inferential, speculative, interpretative. The nature/nurture relationship—with which *The Tempest* is itself quite preoccupied—has been a subject of fierce and unresolved dispute in our own century as well as in Shakespeare's. Even if we had a complete history of every familial and social interaction Shakespeare experienced in growing up, and knew as much as could be known about qualities associated with his family (and, in fact, we know relatively little along either of these lines), we could not produce a factually verifiable account of the effect of his infantile and childhood experience on the shape of his later development. Reaching to the actually lived past of Shakespeare the person is not my goal in this essay, nor is it ordinarily the goal of psychoanalytically informed criticism. The crucial past in Shakespeare is what is carried forward from play to play and reconstructed throughout his career as a dramatist. The psychoanalytic understanding of human development can help identify and illuminate psychological patterns that emerge in such repetitions and reconstructions.

Loewald is sensitive to how that past shapes the individual, and to how the individual shapes a future through a confrontation with the past:

> The past comprises the inherited, innate potential of our genes, the historical, cultural, moral tradition transmitted to us by our elders, and finally that

primordial form of mentation, called unconscious or id, and the "contents"
of our lives that are experienced in this primordial form at the earliest level.
The past is to be acquired, appropriated, made ours in the creative development of the future.[3]

The past, in psychoanalytic thought, is never left behind. Highly sophisticated
forms of thinking emerge from what Loewald calls the "primordial form of
mentation" associated with the unconscious, but they do not replace the
unconscious. According to Loewald, "In its fundamental meaning, unconscious is the name for a mode of experiencing or mentation that continually,
throughout life, constitutes the active base and source of more differentiated
and more complexly organized modes of mentation."[4]

Loewald's statement of the enduring coexistence and interaction of
unconscious and "more complexly organized modes of mentation" is a characteristic claim for the psychoanalytic model of infantile and later human
development. Psychoanalysis posits a series of phases of infantile development, out of which a mature social identity ultimately emerges, but the experience of those early phases remains active in the psyche. The past, as it exists
for psychoanalysis, is not something that is left behind, but that endures as "an
earlier, archaic, form or level of mentation, an undifferentiated form or experiencing, that characterizes early developmental stages but is operative as well
at chronologically later stages."[5]

The psychoanalytic theory of development from the psyche of the newborn baby to the psyche of adulthood is complex and incomplete. But the
process just enumerated is basic to many aspects of it. The individual gradually emerges as a separate being from an undifferentiated matrix of experience
fusing infant and maternal care-giver. In the "primordial infant-mother psychic unit," Loewald writes, the mother functions "as a living mirror in which
the infant gradually begins to recognize, to know himself, by being recognized
by the mother."[6] But the achievement of separation through self-recognition,
upon which all subsequent development of the individual is based, is also an
estrangement, a loss of a primary unity with the world. The wish to be
absorbed back into that primordial unity, and, alternatively, the fear that this
wish is dangerous and will lead to a destructive loss of self, remains in the psyche through life. Similarly, in later phases of development, as a complex inner
self is constructed from identifications with crucial others in the child's world,
a higher level of organization is achieved, which enables the self to function
as an individual in a complex social world. As Loewald observes:

> But this internal other is only the end product of a complex differentiating—
> from another viewpoint, self-alienating—process that takes its start in the
> primary unity of the infant-mother psychic relationship. This development
> constitutes the individuation of the individual.[7]

In psychoanalytic thought, the initial, tentative emergence of the individual as separate from a maternal care-giver involves an estrangement from a primary oneness with the world. The later emergence of the fully differentiated psyche rests on an estrangement from what has become that individual's primary desire—for the mother. To this latter estrangement Freud gave the name "repression."[8] He saw in repression the constitutive gesture of the unconscious as a mental realm unaccessible to consciousness, and hence of ordinary human, Oedipal subjectivity. In repression, the boundary hardens between a crucial arena of desire and aggression in the dynamic unconscious and what is available to the self as conscious thought. The differentiated psyche is formed by its alienation from the desire that has been at the center of its developing existence and is now relegated to the unconscious. But this unconscious remains the "enduring origin and source for those more developed processes. What is repressed is drawn back into the archaic sphere of mentation, whence it stems."[9] And this archaic sphere continues to exert its force over the whole psyche.

The model of development so constructed is not a linear progression through time: "Human time consists in an interpenetration and reciprocal relatedness of past, present, and future."[10] Repetition is as basic to this model as is change. "Individual development" could be described as an ascending spiral in which the same basic themes are re-experienced and enacted on different levels of mentation and action. The transference relationship at the heart of psychoanalysis brings expectations initially structured by infantile and childhood experience into the analysand's ongoing relationship to the analyst, submerging the present in the patterned desires, fears, and frustrations of the past.

But if repetition is basic to the process of development as conceived by psychoanalysis, not all repetition is the same. "Repetition may be a reiteration of the same, an automatic, driven reenactment of early relationships. This is neurotic or pathological transference," the usurpation of present and future possibilities by the imposition of past patterns of relating. "But repetition also may be a re-creation, an imaginative reorganization and elaboration of the early, life-giving love experiences—troublesome, frustrating, and full of conflict as most of them have been."[11] Such repetition, Loewald writes, "reveals transference in its nonpathological meaning, as the dynamic of psychological growth and development."[12]

The development of Shakespeare's art is repetitive in this latter sense. There is nothing like a clear, linear progression from one work to another or from early work to late. As in the development of the human psyche, nothing is ever just left behind in Shakespeare's art. From the *Comedy of Errors* and the early history plays to *The Tempest* and beyond, characteristic themes, conflicts, relationships, configurations of desire and frustration and fear, are repeated over and over again. But nothing is ever just repeated either. Instead we can watch his art finding new possibilities in old configurations, and renewing the basis on which the old configurations exist. If the Sonnets poet frets over making "old offenses of affections new" (Sonnet 110, l.4), the drama is always making new explorations of affections old. *The Tempest*, a very late play, apparently written with a keen self-consciousness of coming near the end of a long and extraordinary career, is, for all its brevity, remarkably comprehensive in its reworking of major Shakespearean preoccupations. I hope the pages that follow can suggest how psychoanalytic thought can shed light on some of them.

II

The story Prospero tells Miranda about their past, whatever its claim to historical veracity, contains a simple and important truth at the heart of his post-Milan life. Once when he gave his brother his trust he lost his inherited political power; now that he has found another source of power he will trust no one. Prospero's power over the action of *The Tempest* is unparalleled in Shakespeare's drama—control by physical coercion over the worker Caliban; control by contractual agreement backed by physical threat over Ariel; control through Ariel over the men who took away his dukedom and over all the other visitors Prospero brings to his island; control over every condition of his daughter's courtship by and marriage to Ferdinand.

As Prospero tells of Antonio's treachery, a rather startling metaphor stands out. Antonio transformed the loyalties of the Milanese subjects, turning their hearts where he pleased, creating a situation in which, Prospero says, "now he was / The ivy which had hid my princely trunk, / And sucked my verdure out on't" (1.2.85–7). Antonio was the parasitical ivy wrapped around and sucking the living substance out of Prospero the ducal tree.

Perhaps the vine/tree metaphor seems startling here because it links two brothers in a figure often gendered female and male. In benign forms, the vine is a grapevine associated with fruitfulness and nurture. An apparent biblical source—"Thy wife shall be as a fruitful vine by the sides of thy house," (Psalms 128:3)—links wife/vine/fruitfulness, though without situating the husband as tree. In proverbial uses, vine and the tree unite in harmony: "The Vine and Elme, converse well together," or "As we may see of the Vine, who imbraceth the Elme, ioying and reioycing much at his presence."[13] In Ovid, the female vine and the male tree are joined to mutual benefit in a story used in an attempt to seduce Pomona, a garden-tending nymph who has spurned many suitors. Pointing to an elm supporting vines loaded with grapes, the satyr Vertumnus (disguised as an old woman promoting his own cause) observes that if the vine did not grow round it the beautiful tree would be barren of fruit, and that if "the vyne which ronnes upon the Elme had nat / The tree too leane untoo, it should upon the ground ly flat."[14] Here form, strength and uprightness gendered male and fruitfulness gendered female combine in an image of two joined in one to mutual benefit and to the benefit of others. In Prospero's image, the male ivy hides the male tree and drains its strength to the detriment of a dukedom thus bent "To most ignoble stooping" (1.2.116).

Shakespeare uses the vine/tree metaphor in two earlier comedies in which magic is a preoccupation. In *Comedy of Errors*, benign and parasitical forms indicate alternative fates for the man Adriana thinks is her husband.

> Thou art an elm, my husband, I a vine,
> Whose weakness, married to thy stronger state,
> Makes me with thy strength to communicate.
> If aught possess thee from me, it is dross,
> Usurping ivy, briar, or idle moss,
> Who, all for want of pruning, with intrusion
> Infect thy sap, and live on thy confusion. (2.2.165–72)

Adriana, as a vine who shares in and is strengthened by her husband's strength, does not offer her own fruitfulness in the metaphor, but neither does her sharing of the husband's strength diminish its source. She is pleading her need, flatteringly, not her bounty. The invasive ivy (or briar or moss) alternative—the other woman Adriana suspects—is parasitical growth out of control, which contaminates the man/tree's strength and thrives on the destruction resulting from her "intrusion." The ivy/sap/intrusion link here closely parallels the ivy/verdure/extrusion link in *The Tempest*; the breakdown of the parallel—female ivy that invasively corrupts the manly substance rather than sucks it out—adds to the interest. "Usurping ivy" certainly would seem to connect with the usurpation of Prospero's place and power by his ivy-like brother. But the female ivy Adriana refers to suggests a sexual threat to her husband. Is there any relation here to Prospero's metaphorical rendering of his brother's past crime?

Titania speaks the most eloquent and moving instance of the ivy/tree metaphor in *A Midsummer Night's Dream*:

> Sleep thou, and I will wind thee in my arms.
> . . .
> So doth the woodbine the sweet honeysuckle
> Gently entwist; the female ivy so
> Enrings the barky fingers of the elm.
> O, how I love thee! How I dote on thee! (4.1.37–42)

Here what is expressed is not the woman's bounty nor her need but her satisfaction. Enchanted Titania finds the fulfillment of her desire in her embrace of ass-headed Bottom.

Although Bottom is powerless to escape Titania's attentions—"Out of this wood do not desire to go: / Thou shalt remain here, whether thou wilt or no"

(3.1.126–7)—her power over him hardly seems to be the contaminating power Adriana imagines for "usurping ivy," much less the eviscerating power Prospero claims his brother exercised over him. And as the object of her desire, Bottom does not seem to figure male strength either as complemented or diminished by female ivy. As with an infant, Bottom's dependence creates a situation in which he seems to be magically empowered; he will come to experience omnipotence of mind, a magical responsiveness of the world to wish, defined for him by Titania's bounty:

> I'll give thee fairies to attend on thee,
> And they shall fetch thee jewels from the deep,
> And sing, while thou on pressèd flowers dost sleep;
> And I will purge thy mortal grossness so
> That thou shalt like an airy spirit go. (3.1.131–5)

For Bottom the demands of maintaining a masculine identity in opposition to the otherness of female sexuality—the demands that structure Oberon's world—are suspended. Without ever ceasing to be "bully Bottom," the center of his experience is "translated," back into the realm of infantile at-oneness with comfort, pleasure, fantasy, and conflict-free sensuality. The sight of the sleeping pair appears pitiful and hateful to Oberon, but Bottom awakens to recall "a most rare vision," a "dream, past the wit of man to say what dream it was," indeed, a dream that "shall be called 'Bottom's Dream' because it hath no bottom" (4.1.200–9).

Bottom's dream can point us back to *The Tempest*, but not directly to Prospero's curious use of the ivy/elm figure. Titania promises to purge Bottom's "mortal grossness," letting him "like an airy spirit go," but the figure in *The Tempest* who recalls Bottom's experience is not the airy spirit Ariel but the unpurged monster Caliban. As with Bottom, Caliban's monstrousness is clearly connected to sexuality and taboo. But whereas Bottom is for a brief time transported into a magical realm defined in part by a temporary suspension of taboo, for Caliban, a past, failed effort to break taboo has radically and permanently altered the world he inhabits. Bottom, ass-headed only for the night he spends in Titania's arms, regains his non-monster status as soon as Oberon reclaims his sexual partner. Caliban's irredeemable monstrousness, "Which any print of goodness wilt not take" (1.2.351), is represented most vividly by his early effort to rape Miranda. Bottom's night of pleasure is licensed by Oberon, who uses the occasion to recover his status as Titania's lover. Caliban has failed to overcome the taboo on Miranda's sexuality enforced by her father, who is also subject to it.

Caliban's account of his island's magical bounty, however, provides a curious parallel to the enchanting presence Bottom recalls. "Be not afeard," Caliban comforts the frightened Stephano and Trinculo:

> the isle is full of noises,
> Sounds, and sweet airs, that give delight and hurt not.
> Sometimes a thousand twangling instruments
> Will hum about mine ears; and sometime voices,
> That, if I then had waked after long sleep,
> Will make me sleep again, and then in dreaming
> The clouds methought would open and show riches
> Ready to drop upon me, that when I waked
> I cried to dream again. (3.2.133–41)

Caliban, too, has had a most rare vision, one of sublime, passive fulfillment—though with Caliban it seems to be fulfillment always just out of reach, something lost to the new order Prospero has brought to the island, particularly since the failed rape of Miranda. Bottom awakens to recall, as if in a dream, a world in which wish and reality corresponded, where one's complete dependence on the other was experienced as magical omnipotence. His emergence from this dreamlike world is experienced as a gain—it has given him something he can bring into the world he re-enters upon awakening, his characteristic zest for life renewed and enriched. For Caliban, by contrast, the sounds and sweet airs, the twangling instruments, the lulling voices, the riches poised to drop from the clouds of his dream, all are experienced as utterly alien to his everyday life of subjection.

The pleasures Caliban knows through a dreamlike rapport with the island's mysterious musical and sensual abundance have no place in his present reality. Something of the tenderness of the experience he describes to Stephano and Trinculo seems to have had a place in social reality in the distant past of his earliest relationship to Prospero:

> When thou cam'st first,
> Thou strok'st me and made much of me; wouldst give me
> Water with berries in't, and teach me how
> To name the bigger light and how the less,
> That burn by day and night; and then I loved thee,
> And showed thee all the qualities o' th' isle,
> The fresh springs, brine pits, barren place and fertile— (1.2.332–8)

Something of this readiness for adoring submission emerges again in Caliban's response to Stephano and the fantasy he brings of a future released from subjection to Prospero. But in his ongoing reality, there is no place for the responsiveness he brings to the island's bounty, or which that bounty elicits in him, Bottom wakes to bring a sense of dreamlike wonder back into his world, but Caliban cries to dream again.

I have moved from Prospero's ivy/elm metaphor describing his brother's treachery to Titania's use of that metaphor to describe her embrace of Bottom, then moved from Bottom's recollection of that embrace as a dream back to *The Tempest* and Caliban's experience of dreamlike riches. But whereas the two moments from *A Midsummer Night's Dream* provide two vantage points on the same blissful encounter, the two instances from *The Tempest* are quite remote from one another: Prospero tensely reconstructing the past treachery of his brother; Caliban, his slave, poignantly describing the near escape into dreamlike bliss the island can provide for him with its music. Can the connections to and within *A Midsummer Night's Dream* I have been trying to make illuminate the relationship between these two moments in *The Tempest*?

The psychological connection that has presented itself so far sees Bottom's account of his dream and Caliban's of his dreamlike relation to the island's musical abundance as fantasies deriving from early infantile relations to a nurturing Other, relations that provide the field upon which later fantasies are articulated. The early nurturing environment, if it is sufficient to ensure the infant's survival, will countenance the emergence of polarized fantasies of omnipotence and of total helplessness; of fusion with a benign, nurturant world and of annihilation by a hostile, rejecting world; of good objects and of bad objects located indeterminately inside and outside of a subjectivity still establishing its boundaries; of being loved unconditionally, and returning it in bliss, and of being hated without limit, and of returning that in rage. Introjection and projection—taking bits of the world in and making them parts of one's experience of one's person and taking parts of one's person and casting them into a world of not-self—are dominant psychic mechanisms, shaping a sense of one's person along the coordinates of need, satisfaction/frustration, pleasure/unpleasure, security/distress, bliss/rage.

Bottom's and Caliban's lyrical dreamlike riches share a base in the sensual and nurturant qualities of this level of psychic experience. Prospero's image of the ivy that hid his princely trunk and sucked out his vital spirit suggests a base in the negative register of early infantile experience. If we look just at the action components of the metaphor—the ivy embraces the elm, hiding it, and sucks the verdure from it—the connections come into focus. Holding and sucking, the principal actions conveyed in Prospero's metaphor, are basic to the formative beginnings of an individual. D. W. Winnicott gives the name "holding phase" to the very earliest stage of infantile existence: the physical experience of being held is central to and prototypical for the infant's relations to an environment that attends to all its needs.[15] Freud calls "sucking at his mother's breast, or at substitutes for it," the "child's first and most vital activity."[16] In the action of sucking, sexual pleasure originates and is split off from need satisfaction: when the sucking that seeks to satisfy the infant's hunger produces pleasurable sensations desirable in their own right, "the need for repeating the sexual satisfaction now becomes detached from the need for taking nourishment."[17] With the activity of sucking, the infant is initiated into human sexuality. As it negotiates experience within what Winnicott calls the "holding environment," the infant "comes to have an inside and an outside, and a body-scheme."[18]

Psychic maneuvers that characterize fantasies and dreams account for the transformations necessary to get from the infantile situation to Prospero's metaphor. Whereas the holding environment locates the infant in a world in which the subject can begin to know itself through the attention the world returns, Prospero speaks of the ivy that "hid" him (or at least hid that part of him designated by "princely trunk") from the world. The holding is malevolent rather than facilitating—a withholding. Its action is generated by projection and reversal: the sucking fundamental to the infant's hold on life becomes the action of the ivy that "sucked my verdure out." Angry, destructive feelings, associated with frustrations of sucking and feeding, are projected into a fantasized attack by the other.

In Prospero's metaphor for Antonio's ill-doing, two kinds of threat coalesce, mingling two kinds of relation (brother to brother, infant to mother) and two kinds of past (the fictionalized recollection from what the play ascribes to Prospero's young manhood and an infantile past lent to Prospero by his creator). That we can think about the maternal threat being submerged in the sibling threat seems richly suggestive in thinking about this play in which the role of women is so generally suppressed or restricted and in which the only strongly evoked maternal presence is the dead but sinister Sycorax, Caliban's mother and Prospero's predecessor. But now it is less important to pursue a subordinating structure than to note that the two threats point to a single infantile prototype: a male child for whom an apparently exclusive claim on the love of his mother is disrupted, not by a father, but by the arrival of a younger brother and by what appears to be the withdrawal of the mother's attention away from him into her preoccupation with the newborn son. Not surprisingly, Shakespeare's drama never represents this situation directly—that is, in the experience of very young children. But the basic structure—a male's love for a female is disrupted by a second male—is pervasive and powerful.

Oberon is in a situation like this when Titania's devotion to the Indian boy disrupts his sexual bond to her. Oberon disposes of his problem by passing on his situation to the Indian boy, whose claim on Titania's love is displaced by Bottom's, who can then be displaced by Oberon. The task is easy enough for Oberon, supernaturally secure in his own exotic manhood, and with a strong prior sexual bond to Titania to renew. The disruption of Prospero's bond to Miranda by the appearance of a young suitor is of a different sort. *The Tempest* must dramatize, not the comic renewal of a sexual bond that has been interrupted, but a father's relinquishing to another, younger man, the daughter upon whom his life has been centered ever since his exile to the island, and whose entry into adult sexuality must be her exit from his world.

As with *King Lear*, the jealous intensity of a father's investment in his

Painted for the Boydell Gallery, c. 1789; engraved in 1802 by the Reverend Matthew William Peters. Used by permission of the Folger Shakespeare Library.

daughter shapes the bond the younger man will interrupt. Like Lear, Prospero has gone to elaborate lengths to control the conditions of the marriage. Lear, however, tries to use the ritual division of his kingdom to ensure that Cordelia will go on loving her father all, even after her dynastic marriage to another man about to be ritualistically chosen by him; her refusal to cooperate in his plan sets in motion the play's tragic action. Prospero arranges to bring Ferdinand to his island as his chosen husband for Miranda, and he oversees a courtship between them that follows exactly his plan for it; their complicity and his willingness or capacity to make a gift of his daughter to the younger man make possible the play's comic outcome. But what enables Prospero to do what Lear could not? Or, what enables Shakespeare to move from the destructive exploration of Lear's love for Cordelia to the comic outcome of Prospero's love for Miranda?

There are certainly signs that Prospero is not wholly free of what drives Lear to act so tyrannically at the prospect of giving up Cordelia. Though he assures the play's audience that he could not be more pleased to welcome Ferdinand into the family, Prospero renders the young man powerless, threatens him with violence, mocks him in his apparent loss of a father, enslaves and imprisons him, and finally, when making a gift of his daughter, puts a curse on their relationship should they have sex before he binds them in marriage. And Shakespeare seems to want to make things as easy as possible for Prospero, on this count at least: Ferdinand is clearly a right-thinking young man, susceptible to the pieties Prospero enforces, chaste and worshipful in his love for Miranda, and appropriately awed by her magician father. But if one assumes the action of *The Tempest* opens on to the destructive potentiality realized in *King Lear*, it is not yet clear how these measures can protect the movement towards marriage from comparable violence.

Caliban's function as a nasty double to Ferdinand provides one way of defusing the anxieties in the marital situation: it lets Prospero disown and repudiate his own incestuous longing for Miranda and lets him expend his rage against a potential usurper on a vilified embodiment of brute sexuality. I think even more important, however, are the ways in which the play provides multiple situations shaped by the structure that organizes the comic movement toward marriage. Usurpation, of course, is everywhere in *The Tempest*: Antonio's past treachery when he stole Milan from Prospero; Caliban's conviction that Prospero has robbed him of an island properly his by inheritance from his mother; Prospero's charge that Ferdinand usurps his father's place as king of Naples; the plot to kill Alonso and make Sebastian king of Naples; the plot to murder Prospero, which would give Stephano both the island and Miranda. The two I want to focus on, and which I think are most crucial to the action, concern Prospero's charges against his brother and Caliban's experience of losing the island's bounty—Prospero's ivy/elm metaphor and Caliban's "cried to dream again" situation.

Although Prospero condenses fantasies of maternal threat and sibling threat into a single metaphor, the action of the play for the most part separates them out again—into Antonio's treachery, which points back especially to the extensive sibling violence of the very early histories, and into the evil legacy of Sycorax, the mother as powerful witch and Satan's partner in sex, heir to Joan de Pucelle, Queen Margaret, and Lady Macbeth. Here separation serves a double function of isolation: by keeping the threat posed by Antonio's betrayal separate from that posed by Sycorax's legacy of malevolent female power and debased sexuality, and by keeping both separate from the romance of Ferdinand and Miranda, it protects the marriage plot from the explosive violence engendered by the actions of *Othello* or *Antony and Cleopatra* or *The Winter's Tale*, where brothers or friends come to be seen as usurping enemies and beloved women are repudiated as whores.

I think, however, that the play's most complex, cruel and tender development of a pervasive Shakespearean structure of usurpation and betrayal is in the presentation of Caliban. Caliban's experience of betrayal closely parallels Prospero's story of an inherited claim usurped by someone he trusted and treated generously: "This island's mine by Sycorax my mother, / Which thou tak'st from me" (1.2.331–2). Caliban's relation to the island's bounty has been interrupted by the usurper Prospero. But Caliban's story of his past introduces a period between Prospero's arrival and Caliban's effort to rape Miranda in which the intruder Prospero has been the object of his love. In this interim period, the fantasy of maternal bounty is located in the relationship to the intruder, who stroked Caliban, made much of him, taught him how to read and how to name his world. Indeed, Caliban's story of trust and reciprocity recalls the infantile roots common to his situation and Prospero's more directly than anything Prospero says.

The generosity of Caliban's initial response to Prospero dramatizes a procedure, which Anna Freud called altruistic surrender, that compensates with exaggerated tenderness for resentment toward a rival for parental love; the subject seeks his own fulfillment in his service to another; the usurper is embraced and adored.[19] Altruistic surrender is built deeply into the extravagant generosity and adoration that Shakespeare the poet lavishes on the fair friend of the Sonnets, and into the poet's inclination towards extreme and sometimes almost savage self-effacement when that seems the only way to sustain his love. Caliban keeps the impulse towards adoration and generosity alive in *The Tempest*, not only through his recollection of his once worshipful regard for Prospero, but in his readiness to bring adoration and allegiance to Stephano: "Hast thou not dropped from heaven?" "I do adore thee." "I'll kiss thy foot. I'll swear myself thy subject" (2.2.131, 134, 146). But where the Sonnets poet debases himself to celebrate the glory of the friend, "Myself corrupting, salving thy amiss" (Sonnet 35, l.7), the play debases Caliban, makes a monster of him.

On this island where Prospero subordinates everything to his power, and trusts no one, attitudes of trust and worshipful regard are given extensive thematic development. Gonzalo's fantasy of a sovereignless utopia on the island assumes that trust can replace power as society's basic mode of relating. Ferdinand believes Miranda must be the goddess the island's spirits attend, and he quickly devotes himself to a worshipful love for the sake of which he is happy enough to endure enslavement and imprisonment by Prospero. Miranda thinks Ferdinand must be "A thing divine" (1.2.419); at the end, she sees her famous "brave new world" in the tarnished old order Prospero has reconstituted on the island. In these instances, Prospero's hard-nosed distrust is played against forms of sentimentality or *naïveté* that manage to ennoble, even while identifying the limits of, the characters who express them. Prospero's relationship to the debased Caliban is more complex. Caliban's pathetic tendency to enslave himself in the service of self-liberation is played against Prospero's wise but tough mastery. But Caliban's openness to, and need for, trust, joy and self-surrender can be set against Prospero's willed estrangement from that part of a human life brought into existence through the nurture of a trusted Other. Slave Caliban dreams about riches ready to drop upon him; master Prospero dreams about an "insubstantial pageant faded" (4.1.155), a world that recedes into dreamlike emptiness, and about death. Caliban embodies not only the lust and crude violence, but also the access to trust and spontaneity Prospero has repudiated in himself.

Having waded far enough into the troubled waters of authorial allegory to identify Caliban partially with the impulse toward adoration and subjection in the *Sonnets*, I find it tempting to situate Caliban's powerful lyricism against the aggressive theatricality by which Prospero manipulates the action of the play as if it were his play to write. I believe it makes sense to think of the astonishing, distancing control Shakespeare achieves through the drama as crucial to protecting his temperament from the potentiality for adoring self-surrender that many of the sonnets embody. Prospero uses his magic art to manifest that kind of dramatic control from within his position as character/on-stage director; he controls Caliban, and distances himself from him, with particular brutality.

I think, however, the play makes this distinction only to collapse it in the end. If Prospero in some fashion represents Shakespeare's power as dramatist, Caliban represents an impulse as basic to his theatrical art as Prospero's executive power. Where Prospero accomplishes sharply defined social and political purposes in the drama he stages through his magic, Caliban seeks his fulfillment in showing his world to others and sharing it with them. "I loved thee, / And showed thee all the qualities o' th' isle" (1.2.336–7), he reminds Prospero. "I'll show thee every fertile inch o' th' island," he assures Stephano: "I'll show thee the best springs"; "Show thee a jay's nest"; "Wilt thou go with me?" (2.2.142, 154, 163, 166). Caliban, in short, seeks himself in the pleasure he gives others; gives fundamentally by showing and surrendering to others the world he has a special claim to; and takes pleasure for himself in a kind of worshipful abjection that accompanies the giving: "I'll kiss thy foot" (2.2.146). It is an impulse built into Shakespeare's relation to the theater. As the character Prospero dissolves into the actor who speaks the Epilogue, begging forgiveness and indulgence, it is the impulse that needs to find its recognition and reward in the audience's applause, "or else my project fails, / Which was to please" (Epilogue, 5.1.330–1).

W. B. Yeats once described his "fancy that there is some one myth for every man, which, if we but knew it, would make us understand all he did and thought."[20] Yeats's notion is an extreme version of the sameness and difference issues raised in the first section of this essay: it makes everything each of us does into a variant or elaboration of a core theme. Indeed, Norman Holland has put Yeats's formulation to very interesting psychoanalytic use in developing his own claim that a core identity or identity theme, developed in an infant's early relations to a maternal provider, acts as a kind of master key to any individual's thought and behavior.[21] I do not wish to make a claim for the comprehensive interpretative power of a single myth or theme in the manner or either Yeats or Holland. But I think that Yeats's formulation of a unifying myth that controls variation in Shakespeare points to a pattern that links up suggestively with patterns I have been discussing in moving from *A Midsummer Night's Dream* to *The Tempest*.

Yeats wrote: "Shakespeare's myth, it may be, describes a wise man who was blind from very wisdom, and an empty man who thrust him from his place, and saw all that could be seen from very emptiness."[22] Yeats sees this myth being worked out in the succession of Hamlet, "who saw too great issues everywhere to play the trivial game of life," by the soldier Fortinbras. But his chief instance, in this essay prompted by his having just viewed six of the English history plays acted "in their right order,"[23] is "in the story of Richard II, that unripened Hamlet, and of Henry V, that ripened Fortinbras." Yeats's clear sympathies are with the otherworldly Richard II, whom he situates on one side of this opposition, and not with the all-too-worldly figure who occupies the pragmatic side:

> instead of that lyricism which rose out of Richard's mind like the jet of a fountain to fall again where it had risen, instead of that fantasy too enfolded in its own sincerity to make any thought the hour had need of, Shakespeare has given [Henry V] a resounding rhetoric that moves men as a leading article does to-day.[24]

Yeats's curious celebration of Richard the poet-king as "lovable and full of capricious fancy"[25] but blinded by an excess of wisdom, along with his strong distaste for Henry V as a heartless and ultimately inconsequential politician, sentimentalizes the English history plays. It also introduces an evaluatory register into the myth Yeats associates with Shakespeare that greatly diminishes its interpretative power. If we pull that evaluative register out, the opposition between Richard and Henry V looks rather like the opposition between Caliban's lyricism and Prospero's aggressive theatricality, mentioned earlier.

I do not wish to claim that Caliban is a "wise man who was blind from very wisdom"—although a powerful trend within criticism of *The Tempest* has long been occupied with a recognition that there is something in Caliban's way of relating to the world that is both precious and incompatible with the sort of order Prospero brings to the island, variants of the mix of attitudes built into the Renaissance notion of the noble savage.[26] Nor do I wish to argue exactly that Prospero, who "thrust [Caliban] from his place" on the island, is "an empty man, and saw all that could be seen from very emptiness." I do, however, find Yeats's use of the idea of emptiness here quite resonant, especially so since he makes it central to Shakespeare's own vantage point on human life: "He meditated as Solomon, not as Bentham meditated, upon blind ambitions, untoward accidents, and capricious passions, and the world was almost as empty in his eyes as it must be in the eyes of God."[27]

To formulate his Shakespearean myth in terms of an opposition between Richard II and Henry V, Yeats, of course, elides two crucial figures. Richard II is not thrust from his position by Henry V, but by Henry Bullingbrook, who thus becomes Henry IV. In order for his son Hal to become Henry V, the figure who must be thrust aside is Falstaff. If the figures missing from Yeats's account are restored, this opposition is worked out doubly in the movement from *Richard II* to *Henry V*: Richard II/Bullingbrook-Henry IV and Falstaff/Prince Hal-Henry V. In both cases, the dominating figure is the one with the superior power to manipulate history theatrically. Richard II is, of course, theatrical to the point of histrionics, but it is Bullingbrook who has the controlling theatrical imagination, who uses theatricality, not for expressive, but for political purposes. And although nobody loves play-acting more than Falstaff, it is Prince Hal who uses theater for effective political purposes, who makes Falstaff an actor in the political scenario he orchestrates throughout both parts of *Henry IV* to validate his power when he becomes King Henry V.

Both Richard II and Falstaff, like Caliban, are subdued by superior masters of theater. Do they have anything else in common? I think what they share is a psychological heritage I tried to associate with Bottom and Caliban, a psychological rootedness in themes characteristic of very early phases of infantile development. These connections can be clarified by returning briefly to Bottom and Caliban.

Bottom, too, wants to be an actor; he, too, is manipulated by a man of superior theatrical power when Oberon casts him in the role of Titania's beloved; he, too, will be thrust from his place in Titania's arms after he has served the theatrical effect Oberon seeks by making the Queen of Fairies fall in love with an ass. Bottom's extraordinary good fortune is to inhabit an unusually benign version of this situation. It is as if Bottom recovers in Titania's doting, nurturant love a symbolic replication of the infantile past that would account for the buoyant narcissism of his grown-up character, whereas Caliban can know those nurturant riches only in the longing created by their

failure to survive the realm of dream. Bottom's ready self-love is complemented and completed in Titania's adoration of him; Caliban's need to know
himself through his surrender of self to a worshipped other who will accept
his service reflects his situation in a world where he can only know his place
through the hatred and contempt of others. Only in Bottom's hunger for play-
acting do we get any hint of the neediness that will drive Caliban to seek
recognition through a new and adored master in Stephano. But if bully Bottom is ultimately empowered by his experience, others who share his slot in
the opposition I am tracing are not.

Bottom's robust egotism is completed through his inadvertent stumbling
into the magical world of Titania; Richard's grandiose but brittle egotism is
grounded on a magical identification of his person with a mystical conception
of kingly omnipotence. It is an identification in which even Richard can never
quite believe, except in so far as he can play the role of omnipotent king before
an audience eager to validate his illusion. Because he has no identity apart
from this identification, he seeks out those who will sustain his illusion with
flattery. When the inevitable crisis approaches, he swings wildly back and
forth between assertions of himself as the invulnerable because "anointed
king" (*Richard II*, 3.2.55) and approaches to what finally is completed in his
knowledge of himself as "nothing" (5.5.38) when the grandiose illusion has
been shattered by Bullingbrook. What reaches from one extreme to the other
is Richard's language, which he uses for purposes quite different from those
of any other character in *Richard II*. The "lyricism" that Yeats associates with
Richard springs from his use of language, not to negotiate a world, but to constitute a self, alternatively through illusions of omnipotence and through a
kind of masochistic cherishing of every nuance of his psychic distress.

Richard's necessary failure to merge with an ideal of kingly omnipotence
engages the same level of psychic development as is invoked by the happy fantasy Bottom enacts in *A Midsummer Night's Dream*. Bottom's rough and
ready narcissism rests on a deep trust of self and world that enables him both
to inhabit the seeming omnipotence of his position within Titania's dream-
world and to sustain himself when the dream is over. Richard's inability to
know himself apart from his identification with his dream of kingly omnipotence represents a failure to carry a securely internalized sense of trust into and
through the individuation process.

"I have long dreamt of such a kind of man," says the newly crowned
Henry V to Falstaff, "So surfeit-swelled, so old and so profane, / But being
awaked, I do despise my dream" (*2 Henry IV* 5.5.45–7). But the prince has
been dreaming with his eyes open, always shaping the dream to his own
shrewdly conceived and theatrically executed political purpose. That is what
he does best. It is Falstaff who has been blinded to reality by his own dream
of the prince as king and himself as the king's beloved favorite. Like Caliban,
who welcomed the exiled Prospero to his world and "showed [him] all the

qualities o' th' isle" (*Tempest* 1.2.337), Falstaff has welcomed the self-exiled prince to his tavern world and shared it with him. "When thou cam'st first, / Thou strok'st me and made much of me," Caliban reminds Prospero, "and then I loved thee" (1.2.332–3, 336). The wonderfully childlike situation evoked here by Caliban's recollection of Prospero's arrival on the island could hardly be more different from the sophisticated and sometimes rather savage give and take that has long marked the curious bond of Falstaff and Hal. But different as their relationship has been, Hal has, in his own way, made much of Falstaff as well, and Falstaff has, in his own way, responded with love: "My king, my Jove, I speak to thee, my heart" (*2 Henry IV* 5.5.42).

Like Richard and Falstaff, Caliban plays a part in a script controlled by another, but he brings to that part a spontaneous expressiveness he shares with no one else in *The Tempest*. Characters who open themselves most fully to those inner dimensions of psychic experience often speak the most widely and vividly expressive poetry in the plays, the poetry that conveys the texture of joy or agony, of rage or bliss, of a self fulfilled or left desolate. They also make themselves vulnerable to those who distance themselves from, or carefully mediate their relationship to, the force of such inner impulses.

Such a distancing process is exactly what Prospero narrates to Miranda as his past history at the opening of *The Tempest*. For him it is a movement from trust through betrayed trust to the assertion of power and control. Prospero, overthrown by his brother when he was himself lost in his imaginative engagement with magic, "transported / And rapt in secret studies" (1.2.76–7), his library a "dukedom large enough" (1.2.110), has made himself over as a figure of power. His power is that of a dramatist who has waited for years for those characters to arrive whom he needs to act his script.

One Shakespearean genealogy for Prospero would emerge from the theatrical manipulators of those figures I have tried to link to the lyrical impulse manifest in Caliban: Oberon in *A Midsummer Night's Dream*, Bullingbrook and Henry V in the history plays. It would be a group that emphasizes, whether for good or for ill, the effective integration of psychic components in selves geared towards accommodation of, and action taken to, shape social reality. Instead I would like to look briefly at a group of speeches, spread out over a wide range of Shakespeare's work, including a speech by Prospero, in which the immediacy of social accommodation and mastery recede behind the trope of life as a dream, or as theater, or as both. In these speeches, theatricality does not represent manipulative mastery and dream does not represent longing or desire.

"All the world's a stage," says Jaques in *As You Like It*, "And all the men and women merely players" (2.7.139–40). "Thou hast nor youth, nor age," Duke Vincentio counsels Claudio in *Measure for Measure*, "But as it were an after-dinner's sleep / Dreaming on both" (3.1.32–4). "Life's but a walking shadow," Macbeth says to no one in particular, "a poor player / That struts and frets his hour upon the stage, / And then is heard no more" (5.5.24–6). Prospero explains to Ferdinand, after the wedding masque is interrupted by his recollection of Caliban's conspiracy:

> Our revels now are ended. These our actors,
> As I foretold you, were all spirits, and
> Are melted into air, into thin air,
> And, like the baseless fabric of this vision,
> The cloud-capped towers, the gorgeous palaces,
> The solemn temples, the great globe itself,
> Yea, all which it inherit, shall dissolve,
> And, like this insubstantial pageant faded,
> Leave not a rack behind. We are such stuff
> As dreams are made on, and our little life
> Is rounded with a sleep. (4.1.148–58)

These speeches do not demonstrate theatrical control over an action, but something of how the world looks from the vantage point of Shakespearean drama when it is fully theatricalized. Each is spoken by a character who has rigorously distanced himself in one way or another from direct engagement in human intimacy and from direct responsiveness to powerful inner feelings. Of course, each of these speeches plays a complex dramatic function in the action to which it belongs. What is important to note here, however, is that all these very different characters, in their very different dramatic situations—in a comedy, a problem comedy, a tragedy and a romance—are making the same kind of point: they see life as merely theater, as no more substantial than a dream.

Jaques, the melancholy satirist who covets the fool's role; Duke Vincentio, the disguised ruler who has stepped out of his political role and is playing at being priest; the murderous tyrant Macbeth, who has cut all close ties to the living and has "almost forgot the taste of fears" (5.5.9); and Prospero, who has just married off his daughter—all become, in these speeches, poets of desolation. These are not versions of the "empty man" Yeats believed Fortinbras and Henry V to be, but their haunting expressions of a fundamental emptiness in human life recalls Yeats's claim that "the world was almost as empty in [Shakespeare's] eyes as it must be in the eyes of God."[28]

The emptiness evoked in Jaques's summary of the seven ages of man lies at the center of his melancholy; it reflects the distance imposed between himself and the world by his satiric spirit. Duke Vincentio's "absolute for death" speech expresses the emptiness of a character whose most compelling motive for action is to distance himself from what makes the other characters of *Measure for Measure* human, vulnerable, and flawed. Macbeth's "walking shadow" is split off from the futile hysterics of his engagement with the enemy; the remote and hollow theatricality of his meditative voice and the desperate violence of his actions present themselves as the double legacy of the disintegration of his merger with Lady Macbeth.

What about Prospero? What can account for the sudden retreat from the immediacy of action in this character who has controlled, with astonishing precision, the minute-by-minute activities of every other notable character in the play?

Prospero's great speech emerges from the only moment in the play when he is not actively controlling the lives of all the other characters in it. He speaks it when he has been startled to realize that, having allowed himself to become absorbed in the wedding masque, he has forgotten to attend to "that foul conspiracy / Of the beast Caliban and his confederates / Against his life" (4.1.139–41). He offers the speech to Ferdinand, who with Miranda has been startled by his agitation as reassurance:

FERDINAND	This is strange. Your father's in some passion
	That works him strongly.
MIRANDA	Never till this day
	Saw I him touched with anger, so distempered.
PROSPERO	You do look, my son, in a moved sort,
	As if you were dismayed. Be cheerful, sir;
	Our revels now are ended. . . . (4.1.143–8)

After he has brought his vision of life as the stuff dreams are made on to completion, Prospero himself comments on his "distempered" state:

> Sir, I am vexed.
> Bear with my weakness, my old brain is troubled.
> Be not disturbed with my infirmity.

Gently and humbly, he offers Miranda and Ferdinand the use of his cell for rest:

> If you be pleased, retire into my cell,
> And there repose.

But he still feels the aftermath of his strange agitation:

> A turn or two I'll walk
> To still my beating mind. (4.1. 158–63)

This lingering distractedness that completes Prospero's speech presents yet a new voice. He has himself demanded rapt attentiveness of Miranda and Ferdinand at the beginning of the masque: "No tongue! All eyes! Be silent!" (4.1.59). The only other interruption of the masque comes when Ferdinand questions him about the nature of the actors: "May I be bold / To think these spirits?" (4.1.119–20). Prospero explains: "Spirits, which by mine art / I have from their confines called to enact / My present fancies" (4.1.120–2). After Ferdinand rejoices at the paradisal prospect of spending his life where "So rare a wondered father" (4.1.123) resides, Prospero again calls for silent attentiveness, this time with just a touch of anxiety that something could go wrong:

> Sweet, now, silence!
> Juno and Ceres whisper seriously.
> There's something else to do. Hush, and be mute,
> Or else our spell is marred. (4.1.124–27)

Then, within the masque, Iris summons "temperate nymphs . . . to celebrate / A contract of true love" and "sunburned sickle-men" to join them "in a graceful dance" (4.1.132–3; 134; 138 s.d.). A particularly elaborate stage direction describes what happens then:

> *Enter certain Reapers, properly habited. They join with the nymphs in a graceful dance, towards the end whereof Prospero starts suddenly and speaks, after which, to a strange hollow and confused noise, they heavily vanish.*

What precipitates the rapid decay of the dance is Prospero's sudden recollection: "I had forgot that foul conspiracy / Of the beast Caliban . . ." (4.1.139–40). When Miranda and Ferdinand are alarmed by Prospero's agitation, he tries to calm them with the eloquent nihilism of "Our revels now are ended." Then immediately we hear this master of energy and execution sounding old, out of control, weak and infirm—"vexed" and "troubled."

Critics have understandably found it difficult to understand either why Prospero should be so agitated by the thought of Caliban and company,[29] since Ariel clearly has those pathetic conspirators under firm control, or exactly why the serene nihilism of this speech should be designed to bring cheer to the newly-wed couple. But perhaps the nature of the recollection that has broken Prospero's absorption in the masque is less significant than the uniqueness of Prospero's discovery that he has indeed been so absorbed, that for the first time in the play he has forgotten to attend to his plans. Or perhaps Caliban springs to mind here for some other reason than the danger he and his fellows pose to Prospero's life. And perhaps the purposes the speech accomplishes for its speaker are more prominent than its intended effect on Prospero's immediate audience.

The interrupted masque culminates the marriage plot, which drives the overall action of the play. Miranda has arrived at sexual maturity on an island in which the only two-legged males are her father and Caliban. Neither is an appropriate mate. Caliban has earlier posed a sexual threat to Miranda. As Prospero puts it: "thou didst seek to violate / The honor of my child" (1.2.347–8). Caliban is hardly repentant about this thwarted transgression:

> O ho, O ho! Would't had been done!
> Thou didst prevent me—I had peopled else
> This isle with Calibans. (1.2.349–51)

In his hopeful new servitude, Caliban concedes Miranda to Stephano: "she will become thy bed, I warrant, / And bring thee forth brave brood" (3.2.102–3). But Caliban remains powerfully associated in Prospero's mind with the sexual threat to Miranda. This threat has defined the social structure of the island ever since it was made. Expelled from Prospero's cell and "confined into this rock" (1.2.360), Caliban's enslavement dates from and perpetually punishes his aborted rape of Miranda.

Prospero replaces Caliban, a "thing most brutish" who tried to rape Miranda, with Ferdinand, a "thing divine" (1.2.356, 419) who sees Miranda as the goddess of the island. Caliban's degraded sexuality gives way to the idealized and idealizing Ferdinand, all by Prospero's careful design. The psychoanalytic allegory that is being worked out here looks something like this: Prospero's repressed sexual desire for his daughter is purged by his projection of it onto the loathsome Caliban; Ferdinand, ritualistically identified with Caliban by being temporarily imprisoned and enslaved as Prospero's log-carrier, is both punished in advance for the sexuality he brings to Miranda and ritualistically purged of the identification with Caliban's degraded sexuality when he has, with appropriate humility, "strangely stood the test" (4.1.7); Prospero maintains his control over Miranda's sexuality with his management of the steps leading to a marriage in which he gives her to the young suitor.[30]

The processes of control by splitting off and projection at work here are characteristic of Prospero, and they are turned towards what is, for him, the central issue in the play and in his life—the sexual maturation of Miranda and the impossible situation this creates for the two of them on the island. But these defensive processes cannot simply erase the deep connections that underlie them, nor can they undo what the passage of time has done to bring Miranda into young womanhood. Prospero sees the circumstances that allow him to bring the Italian ship to the island as depending on an "accident most strange," "bountiful Fortune" and a "most auspicious star" (1.2.178, 182). But the deeper necessity for the events of the play is Miranda's maturation. Prospero dramatizes the urgencies of this most time-conscious play in terms of his astrological art, but the clock that ultimately drives the play is a natural one, the biological clock in Miranda's body. And if Ferdinand is going to be the solution to the problem, he must, for all the idealizing that is going on, be a sexual solution; he must enact a desire that corresponds to the repressed desire in Prospero, earlier played out in degraded form in Caliban's attempt to rape Miranda.

Prior to the masque, Prospero is still struggling to control the conflicts deriving from his recognition of the need to marry Miranda to an appropriate mate and his repressed desire to keep his daughter for himself. He controls entirely the circumstances of the marriage, offering Miranda as "a third of mine own life," "my rich gift," "my gift," "my daughter," possessing her in his language even while making her Ferdinand's "own acquisition / Worthily purchased" (4.1.3, 8, 13–14). Should Ferdinand "break her virgin-knot" (4.1.15) prior to the ceremony Prospero has arranged, however, the marriage will be destroyed by the father's curse:

> barren hate,
> Sour-eyed disdain, and discord shall bestrew
> The union of your bed with weeds so loathly
> That you shall hate it both. (4.1.19–22)

Ferdinand provides the appropriate reassurance that nothing can convert "Mine honour into lust" (4.1.28), and, when warned again a few moments later about "th' fire i' th' blood," insists that "The white cold virgin snow upon my heart / Abates the ardour of my liver" (4.1.53, 55–6).

The marriage masque is itself constructed to dramatize an idealized image of marriage as a perfect harmony that somehow elides the sexual dimension.[31] The famous exclusion of Venus and Cupid from the ceremony explicitly averts "Some wanton charm" (4.1.95), but the effect is to exclude sexuality altogether, which can only, in Prospero's controlling imagination, be imaged as degraded.

What is presented, in Ferdinand's language, as "a most majestic vision, and / Harmonious charmingly," does, as Prospero says, "enact / My present fancies" (4.1.118–19, 121–2). This majestic vision, however, expresses only part of Prospero's present fancies, the idealized part, whereby he can keep at a distance the repressed desires for Miranda that form the unconscious dimension of his fancies. When the "graceful dance" of the reapers and nymphs is violently interrupted, when Prospero "starts suddenly and speaks" about "that foul conspiracy / Of the beast Caliban and his confederates / Against my life" (4.1.139–41), and the dancers, "to a strange hollow and confused noise, . . . heavily vanish" (4.1.138 s.d.), what is dramatized is the disruptive convergence of what Prospero has worked so hard to keep separate. Prospero's sudden memory of Caliban's plot against his life represents the intrusion of Prospero's own repressed desires into the idealizing process of the marriage masque.

The masque itself provides the verbal cue for Prospero's response. After "certain nymphs" have entered, Iris calls forth their dancing partners, rustic field-workers:

> You sunburned sickle-men, of August weary,
> Come hither from the furrow and be merry;
> Make holiday; your rye-straw hats put on,
> And these fresh nymphs encounter every one
> In country footing. (4.1. 134–8)

Iris calls for a rustic dance, described as "graceful" in the subsequent stage direction. But the language calling for that action provides the link to the underside of Prospero's imagination: "encounter . . . / In country footing" gives us a remarkably dense, redundant, sexual pun, recalling some of the most famous punning moments in Shakespeare.

One is Hamlet's bawdy exchange with Ophelia prior to the play within the play about "country matters" (3.2.108). In Partridge's reckoning, "country matters" here means "matters concerned with *cu*t*; the first pronouncing-element of country is **coun**."[32] "Coun" or "count," of course, is given its most notorious independent exercise in *Henry V*, with the English lesson Princess Katherine gets from Alice her gentlewoman:

> KATHERINE   Comment appelez-vous les pieds et la robe?
> ALICE   *De foot*, madame, et *de cown*.
> KATHERINE   *De foot* et de *cown*? O Seigneur Dieu! Ils sont les mots de son
>   mauvais, corruptible, gros, et impudique, et non pour les dames
>   d'honneur d'user. . . . Foh! *De foot* et *de Cown*!
> (Henry V, 3.4.44–51)

Here "foot" for French "foutre"—"to copulate with"[33]—is added to the pun on "count."

As it is, indeed, in *The Tempest*. For all the effort to dissociate sexuality from the marriage masque, Iris's instructions to the reapers—"these fresh nymphs en*count*er every one / In *count*ry *foot*ing"—release into the masque the debased sexuality associated with Prospero's repressed desire, and with Caliban. Caliban here represents the return of the repressed for Prospero, and the intractable permanence of the repressed as well, its resistance to the demands of civilized morality:

> A devil, a born devil, on whose nature
> Nurture can never stick; on whom my pains,
> Humanely taken, all, all lost, quite lost. (4.1.188–90)

"The minute of their plot / Is almost come" (4.1.141–2), Prospero says in his distraction. What I am trying to argue is that the intrusion of the Caliban plot to murder Prospero into the dance that culminates the marriage masque of Ferdinand and Miranda makes a kind of deep psychological sense. It is not, I believe, the threat to Prospero's life that is at issue here, but the threat to his psychic equilibrium posed by his repressed incestuous desires. In surrendering himself to the progress of the masque, in letting himself become absorbed into a process that does "enact / My present fancies," Prospero loses conscious control over the direction in which his "fancies" lead him. The "*count*ry *foot*ing" of the reapers and the nymphs comes to represent for him the repressed sexual dimension of his longing for his daughter, and the violent dissolution of the dance breaks the hold of the masque turned to nightmare. Prospero's understanding of the interruption as his sudden memory of Caliban's plot both disguises the threat and identifies it, since it is Caliban as a representation of his own repressed sexuality that figures unconsciously into the memory.

The exquisite poetry of "Our revels now are ended" expresses Prospero's full recoil from his dangerous absorption in his "present fancies." The masque has drawn him into a process that, for the first time in the play, eludes his control, draws him into a closeness with deeply repressed dimensions of himself—not only his desire for Miranda but his very capacity to give himself over to an experience that follows a logic deeper than his conscious manipulations. The psychological result, as he recovers himself, and before he turns to the business of resuming control over the action, is a movement in the opposite direction from control. After the marriage masque has drawn him too deeply into its symbolic action, Prospero retreats to a vantage point where nobody is in control and where it does not much matter.

Prospero's lyrical vision of the world as "insubstantial pageant" in some respects recalls Caliban's account of his dream of imminent riches that are all but his, but that waking deprives him of. "I am full of pleasure" (3.2.114), Caliban says, when he thinks all will work out with Stephano. It is a momentary perception, ill grounded, but its expression catches the whole orientation of Caliban's character. This orientation is most fully expressed in his account of the "Sounds, and sweet airs, that give delight and hurt not" (3.2.135), of the clouds he thinks will "open and show riches / Ready to drop upon me" (3.2.139–40)—the experience to which he gives himself in his dreams, and for which, upon awakening, he cries to dream again.

My notion here is that Prospero's marriage masque captures him in something of the same way that Caliban is captured by his dream of imminent but elusive riches. It is the closest this power-dominated man comes to a point where it would make sense for him to say, with Caliban, "I am full of pleasure." In his absorption in the masque, which represents his "present fancies," that pleasure proves to be disruptive. Suddenly vulnerable to a threat from within himself, Prospero for the first time finds himself in a situation where he cannot address his crisis by magically manipulating the external world. He cannot act on, cannot even acknowledge directly, the sexual component of his need for Miranda—though he will, later, in a famous and problematic statement, say of Caliban: "this thing of darkness I / Acknowledge mine" (4.1.275–6). And he cannot stop the socially inflected but ultimately natural clock that has brought Miranda to sexual maturation and that demands that he surrender her to another. In short, Prospero, the master manipulator, the nearly omnipotent controller of the action of this play, finds himself in a position beyond the limits of his control, a position of helplessness before his own need and before developments in his world that will not yield to his magic.

Prospero's immediate response is not to cry to dream again. Nor is it to reassert the sort of control that has been crucial to his life on the island. Instead, Prospero retreats to a vantage point from which neither the nature of his feelings nor the control he exercises over his world matters. Where Caliban, in his dream, envisions a world heavy with riches ready to drop upon him, Prospero envisions a receding world, of no more substance or consequence than "this insubstantial pageant faded," dissolving, without a trace, into nothingness. His life, those of his daughter, her suitor, the usurping visitors to the island on whom he still seems to plan vengeance—a little world of people about whom Prospero has made the finest distinctions, ranging from his precious daughter to his pernicious brother, from the venerable Gonzalo to the despised Caliban—all are simply "such stuff / As dreams are made on." Their lives, all lives, add up to a "little life / . . . rounded with a sleep" (4.1.155–8).

When Prospero the master of magical power confronts his own helplessness in the face of a situation beyond the limits of his control, he retreats to a vantage point in which action no longer matters, where the precise distinctions and discriminations and the minute-by-minute timing that have characterized his relation to the world are dissolved in the blank emptiness of eternity. On the one hand, this vision of all of life as an insubstantial pageant faded is the extreme form of theatricality as a defense, Prospero's version of Macbeth's poor player who struts and frets his hour upon the stage, and then is heard no more. But the tone or feeling of the speech could hardly be more different from that of Macbeth's. Prospero describes an emptiness as radical as Macbeth's, an emptiness that suggests Yeats's notion of Shakespeare meditating on a world "almost as empty in his eyes as it must be in the eyes of God." But Prospero's speech conveys something very different from the embittered desolation of Macbeth. It is offered to comfort Miranda and Ferdinand; and it seems to bring comfort to Prospero, to break the agitation of his thought of Caliban.

Part of Prospero's comfort, of course, derives simply from the distancing this vantage point provides, the relief of watching his inner conflict and the vexations of managing his world recede into oblivion. But the comfort provided seems to be more richly textured than the comfort of the world's absence. And Prospero's speech, unlike Macbeth's, seems shielded from the perception of life's emptiness as a source of despair, or of terror.

It is harder to point to what there is in the language of this speech that accounts for this more positive sense of comfort and reassurance. But I think important keys are in the lines that bring Prospero's vision of the world's emptiness to a culmination:

> We are such stuff
> As dreams are made on, and our little life
> Is rounded with a sleep.

It seems to me that there may be some sense in which "stuff" brings as much substantiality to "dreams" as "dreams" brings ephemerality to "stuff." There is, moreover, a kind of gentleness about this utterance, a tenderness even, quite uncharacteristic of Prospero elsewhere in the play. But I think more important is what happens in the last clause.

The plain sense of the passage is that human lives emerge out of a dark, sleeplike void and pass back into it at death and that these brief lives are of small matter in this everlasting movement from nothing to nothing. But "our" in "our little life" seems to play against the sense of dispossession that the speech has turned on. The word "little" does not suggest paltriness or insignificance here so much as the vulnerability of tininess. I associate "little life" here with infancy, a little living person. The phrase "little life . . . / . . . rounded with a sleep" seems to present a kind of holding, almost a caressing image, the little life held by the sleep, or held in ways that facilitate sleep, protecting it from the hurly-burly of the larger world. And "rounded" here seems to me to convey something of the same tenderness that we can find in this account from *A Midsummer Night's Dream*: "For she his hairy temples then had rounded / With coronet of fresh and fragrant flowers" (4.1.48–9), describing Titania's tender and protective dotage over Bottom.

In short, the speech has submerged within it the tender infant-mother paradigm I earlier associated with Bottom's fulfillment through Titania. In this phase of Shakespeare's development, I think it suggests a point of connection to the two romances from which it most differs: to the promise for renewed life associated with Marina's infancy in *Pericles* and Perdita's in *The Winter's Tale*. Within *The Tempest*, it points back to the nostalgic evocations of Miranda's infancy, both to her distant memory, "rather like a dream than an assurance / That my remembrance warrants" (1.2.45–6), of being attended by feminine presences in Milan, and to Prospero's memory of the courage he gathered from Miranda's infantile presence on the "rotten carcase of a butt" (1.2.146) that brought them to the island in their exile: "O, a cherubin / Thou wast that did preserve me" (1.2.152–3).

Within the play, it also reaches out to Caliban's dream of maternal riches about to drop upon him. If Caliban's sexuality unconsciously represents to Prospero his repressed incestuous longing for Miranda, Caliban's psychological orientation toward a nurturant, giving world represents for Prospero a comparably repressed wish to turn oneself over in trust to a world understood as the heritage of the infantile world of oneness with maternal bounty. Forgoing this wish has defined Prospero's post-Milan world of magic, power, mastery. Obliquely, but poignantly, following his recognition of his helplessness before his own desires and developments in his world, and in the course of an imaginative vision of universal emptiness, Prospero touches base with that wish. It is, I think, an important moment for him, one that contributes crucially to the gestures that culminate his role in the play: his surrender of his magical power, his foregoing of his plan for vengeance, his final, formal release of Miranda to Ferdinand, his acknowledgement of Caliban, and his readiness to prepare himself for death in Milan, "where / Every third thought shall be my grave" (5.1.310–11) and where his own little life will be rounded with a sleep.

III

There is something perhaps disingenuous, even perverse, about including "history" in the title of this essay, since I have almost completely ignored those historical and political lines of inquiry that have dominated critical discussions of *The Tempest* in recent years. My purpose has been to emphasize a different sort of history, what Loewald calls the historicity of the individual. A fuller reading of the play would be responsive both to how the play is situated within its historical moment and to how it is situated in what is distinctive to Shakespeare's psychological development.

Many recent readings have rigorously emphasized the importance of the play's relation to the colonialist enterprise. In response to such readings, Meredith Skura has pointed to ways of integrating psychological and historical concerns in discussions of *The Tempest*. Skura writes:

> Shakespeare's assimilation of elements from historical colonialist discourse was neither entirely isolated from other uses or innocent of their effects.

But she goes on to say:

> Nonetheless, the colonialism in his play is linked not only to Shakespeare's indirect participation in an ideology of political exploitation and erasure but also to his direct participation in the psychological after-effects of having experienced the exploitation and erasure inevitable in being a child in an adult's world.[34]

Skura's essay is an impressive effort, not just to resituate psychological considerations in a critical discourse that has come to be dominated by political considerations, but also to show how psychological and political considerations can complement each other.

Clearly the dominant political and ideological currents of a historical moment do not make everyone just like everyone else who inhabits that moment. They do not even make all members of one class or another just like everyone else who belongs to that class. They do not make all residents of the same region just like everyone else in that region. And they do not make all members of the same family just like everyone else in that family. Of course, all these considerations are crucial—historically shaped ideologies, class structure, regional difference, familial characteristics, all, obviously, shape people in both enabling and limiting ways. But if such considerations do not make virtually identical all members of the category they comprise, then something else belongs in the discussion as well.

The Elizabethan/Jacobean stage belongs to history. All who participated in the shaping of what was distinctive to it were shaped by its historical moment. But what the dramatists shared because of belonging to the same age cannot account for what differentiates one dramatist from another, cannot account for what is distinctive to the work of Shakespeare, or Marlowe, or Jonson, or Marston, or any of the many individualized styles that came into focus through the theaters common to them.

Nor does the enormous historical divide that separates us from Shakespeare put his works out of our reach, make their concerns seem alien to us. Accounting for this is a serious critical problem, of course. The ahistorical explanation for this phenomenon is that Shakespeare's work provides us with a supreme representation of universal human nature, transcending history. Older historical accounts saw our affinity to Shakespeare as largely illusory, based on an illegitimate appropriation that so blurred difference into identity that the Shakespeare we read or view and think we understand has little to do with what Shakespeare wrote, what he meant to his age.

Raymond Williams efficiently sketches the development and the effective critical bankruptcy of both of these kinds of explanations in the Afterword to *Political Shakespeare*. Williams sees the "most practical and effective new direction . . . in analysis of the historically based conventions of language and representation: the plays themselves as socially and materially produced, within discoverable conditions; indeed the texts themselves as history."[35] Other critics have turned to analysis of how history itself has mediated the relationship of succeeding generations of readers to Shakespeare's work, as in Greenblatt's understanding of how "collective enterprises, including the educational system in which this study is implicated, have focused more on the text than the playhouse."[36] Both critics are concerned to place Shakespeare's work historically, Williams in the "multivocal" and "inherently interactive" development of dramatic form in Renaissance England,[37] Greenblatt in the institutional shift from a particular, historically situated theater to texts that can be "endlessly reproduced, circulated, exchanged, exported to other times and places."[38]

I turned to Hans Loewald at the beginning of this essay because his little book provides a compelling statement of the historicity that is built into individual development. We are separated from Shakespeare by massive historical differences. Historically based criticism can show us what Shakespeare has in common with his own age and how that historical commonality is alien to ours. Loewald and psychoanalysis can provide some ways to approach both what, on the one hand, is distinctive to Shakespeare within his own age and what, on the other hand, can bridge the gap between his historical moment and ours.

Psychoanalysis does this because it focuses on what the individual brings to the encounter with history, out of which the subject is constituted. We do not share with Shakespeare the historical moment that produced the Globe Theater and the beginnings of a British colonialist venture that would affect the entire world. The particularities of that moment belong to history—they are not reproducible, and we cannot fully inhabit them, however powerful our historical imaginations. But like Shakespeare, we do lead lives that began in a situation of total infantile helplessness and dependence, lives that were given distinctive form as our unfolding capacities for human development encountered first the familial world and then the broader social world we were born into. And like Shakespeare, we go on re-encountering, renegotiating, and re-forming that formative past for as long as we live. Our history may separate us from Shakespeare, but what Loewald calls our individual historicity is crucial to what makes his work matter to us as something more than the representation of a lost historical moment. As we refine the historicist project of placing Shakespeare in his historical moment as distinct from our own, it seems to me important as well to develop a critical vantage point that does not sever all connections between the life Shakespeare led, the lives his works dramatize, and the lives we continue to lead in the historical moment and the particularized familial circumstances that have shaped us.

NOTES

All quotations from *The Tempest* are from the Oxford University Press edition, ed. Stephen Orgel (1987).

1. Hans Loewald, *Psychoanalysis and the History of the Individual* (New Haven, Connecticut, 1978), 29.
2. Loewald, 6.
3. Loewald, 24–5.
4. Loewald, 30.
5. Loewald, 12.
6. Loewald, 13.
7. Loewald, 14.
8. For an account of the uses to which Freud put the term "repression" see Laplanche and Pontalis, *The Language of Psychoanalysis*, trans. Donald Nicholson-Smith (New York: Norton, 1973), 390–4. Freud uses the term to designate both a specific, albeit prototypical, defensive maneuver and the larger domain of the defenses generally. I am using the term here in its narrower range, which Laplanche and Pontalis specify as follows:

   > Strictly speaking, an operation whereby the subject attempts to repel, or to confine to the unconscious, representations (thoughts, images, memories) which are bound to an instinct. Repression occurs when to satisfy an instinct—though likely to be pleasurable in itself—would incur the risk of provoking unpleasure because of other requirements ... It may be looked upon as a universal mental process in so far as it lies at the root of the constitution of the unconscious as a domain separate from the rest of the psyche. (390)

9. Loewald, 18.
10. Loewald, 23.

11. Loewald, 48.

12. Loewald, 49.

13. M. P. Tilley, *A Dictionary of Proverbs in England in the Sixteenth and Seventeenth Century* (Ann Arbor, Michigan, 1950), 5:61.

14. Ovid, *Shakespeare's Ovid, Being Arthur Golding's Translation of the Metamorphoses*, ed. W. H. D. Rouse (Carbondale, Illinois: Southern Illinois UP, 1961), 183.

15. D. W. Winnicott, *The Maturational Processes and the Facilitating Environment* (London, 1965), 44–50.

16. Sigmund Freud, *The Standard Edition of the Complete Psychological Works*, ed. J. Strachey, 24 Vols (London, 1953–74), 7:181.

17. Freud, 7:182.

18. Winnicott, 45. Drive-centered theories and object-relations theories of psychoanalysis have their respective points of departure in this situation—the emergence of infantile sexuality within the nurturant environment that provides both the first objects of desire and the object relation in which the infant's primary sense of being in the world is anchored.

19. Anna Freud, *The Ego and the Mechanisms of Defense*, rev. ed. (New York, 1966), 123–34.

20. W. B. Yeats, "At Stratford-on-Avon," *Essays and Introductions* (London, 1961), 107.

21. See Norman Holland's chapter on the poet H. D., called "A Maker's Mind," in his *Poems in Persons: An Introduction to the Psychoanalysis of Literature* (New York, 1973), 5–59.

22. Yeats, 107.

23. Yeats, 97.

24. Yeats, 108.

25. Yeats, 105.

26. Recent readings of the play as either a complicit celebration of or a subversive indictment of the colonialist enterprise complicate and extend that trend. When Caliban complains to Prospero that his "profit" from learning the Europeans' language is "I know how to curse" (1.2.362–63), Greenblatt writes: "Ugly, rude, savage, Caliban nevertheless achieves for an instant absolute if intolerably bitter moral victory" (*Learning to Curse: Essays in Early Modern Culture*, [New York, 1990], 25.) For Paul Brown, even the dream that seems to give Caliban something he "may use to resist, if only in dream, the repressive reality which hails him as villain," is ultimately the expression of desire generated by and within colonialism: "the colonialist project's investment in the process of euphemisation of what are really powerful relations here has produced a utopian moment where powerlessness represents *a desire for powerlessness*" ("'This thing of darkness I acknowledge mine': *The Tempest* and the Discourse of Colonialism," *Political Shakespeare: New Essays in Cultural Materialism*, eds. Jonathan Dollimore and Alan Sinfield [Manchester, 1985], 65, 66.)

27. Yeats, 106–7.

28. Yeats, 107.

29. Meredith Skura, however, points tellingly to several situations in Shakespeare's earlier drama that provide parallels to this moment when the exiled, manipulative, paternalistic duke erupts in anger in response to a figure who embodies qualities he has repudiated in himself: Antonio to Shylock in *The Merchant of Venice*; Duke Senior to Jaques in his satiric mood ("thou thyself hast been a libertine") in *As You Like It*; Duke Vincentio to Lucio in *Measure for Measure*; the newly crowned Henry V to Falstaff in *2 Henry IV* (60–65). See Meredith Skura, "Discourse and the Individual: the Case of Colonialism in *The Tempest*," *Shakespeare Quarterly* 40 (1989): 42–69.

30. The psychoanalytic components of this narrative have been distributed variously in different psychoanalytic accounts, but they have been in place since, "Otto Rank [in *Das Inzest-Motiv in Dichtung und Sage* (1912)] set out the basic insight" (Norman Holland, *Psychoanalysis and Shakespeare* [New York, 1966], 269).

31. Prospero's pageant presents a mythic utopian vision which Skura compares to Gonzalo's "more socialized" utopia and to Caliban's dream: all three "recreate a union with a bounteous Mother Nature. And like every child's utopia, each is a fragile creation, easily destroyed by the rage and violence that constitute its defining alternative—a dystopia of murderous vengeance; the interruption of Prospero's pageant is only the last in a series of such interruptions" (68).

32. Eric Partridge, *Shakespeare's Bawdy*, 2nd ed.(London, 1968), 87.

33. Partridge, 108.

34. Skura, 69.

35. Raymond Williams, afterword, *Political Shakespeare: New Essays in Cultural Materialism*, eds. Jonathan Dollimore and Alan Sinfield (Manchester, 1985), 239.

36. Stephen Greenblatt, *Shakespearean Negotiations: The Circulation of Social Energy in Renaissance England* (Berkeley: U of California P, 1988), 160.

37. Williams, 238.

38. Greenblatt, *Shakespearean*, 160.

PART III

Performances of *The Tempest*

The Tempest at Covent-Garden*

WILLIAM HAZLITT

As we returned some evenings ago from seeing the *Tempest* at Covent-Garden, we almost came to the resolution of never going to another representation of a play of Shakespear's as long as we lived; and we certainly did come to this determination, that we never would go *by choice*. To call it a representation, is indeed an abuse of language: it is a travestie, caricature, any thing you please, but a representation. Even those daubs of pictures, formerly exhibited under the title of the Shakespear Gallery, had a less evident tendency to disturb and distort all the previous notions we had imbibed from reading Shakespeare. In the first place, it was thought fit and necessary, in order to gratify the sound sense, the steady, sober judgment, and natural unsophisticated feelings of Englishmen a hundred years ago, to modernize the original play, and to disfigure its simple and beautiful structure, by loading it with the common-place, clap-trap sentiments, artificial contrasts of situations and character, and all the heavy tinsel and affected formality which Dryden had borrowed from the French school. And be it observed, further, that these same anomalous, unmeaning, vulgar, and ridiculous additions, are all that *take* in the present farcical representation of the *Tempest*. The beautiful, the exquisitely beautiful descriptions in Shakespear, the still more refined, and more affecting sentiments, are not only not applauded as they ought to be (what fine murmur of applause should do them justice?)—they are not understood, nor are they even heard. The lips of the actors are seen to move, but the sounds they utter exciting no corresponding emotions in the breast, are no more distinguished than the repetition of so many cabalistical words. The ears of the audience are not prepared to drink in the music of the poet; or grant that they were, the bitter-

---

* First printed in *The Examiner* 23 July 1815, reprinted in *A View of the English Stage*, collected in Vol. 5 *The Complete Works of William Hazlitt*, ed., P. P. Howe, after the edition of A. R. Waller and Arnold Glover (New York: AMS Press, Inc., 1967), 234–237.

ness of disappointment would only succeed to the stupor of indifference.

Shakespear has given to Prospero, Ariel, and the other characters in this play, language such as wizards and spirits, "the gay creatures of the element," might want to express their thoughts and purposes, and this language is here put into the mouth of Messrs. Young, Abbott, and Emery, and of Misses Matthews, Bristow, and Booth. "'Tis much." Mr. Young is in general what is called a respectable actor. Now, as this is a phrase which does not seem to be very clearly understood by those who most frequently use it, we shall take this opportunity to define it. A respectable actor then, is one who seldom gratifies, and who seldom offends us; who never disappoints us, because we do not expect any thing from him, and who takes care never to rouse our dormant admiration by any unlooked-for strokes of excellence. In short, an actor of this class (not to speak it profanely) is a mere machine, who walks and speaks his part; who, having a tolerable voice, face, and figure, reposes entirely and with a prepossessing self-complacency on these natural advantages: who never risks a failure, because he never makes an effort; who keeps on the safe side of custom and decorum, without attempting improper liberties with his art; and who has not genius or spirit enough to do either well or ill. A respectable actor is on the stage, much what a pretty woman is in private life, who trusts to her outward attractions, and does not commit her taste or understanding, by hazardous attempts to shine in conversation. So we have generals, who leave every thing to be done by their men; patriots, whose reputation depends on their estates; and authors, who live on the stock of ideas they have in common with their readers.

Such is the best account we can give of the class of actors to which Mr. Young belongs, and of which he forms a principal ornament. As long as he contents himself to play indifferent characters, we shall say nothing: but whenever he plays Shakespear, we must be excused if we take unequal revenge for the martyrdom which our feelings suffer. His Prospero was good for nothing; and consequently, was indescribably bad. It was grave without solemnity, stately without dignity, pompous without being impressive, and totally destitute of the wild, mysterious, preternatural character of the original. Prospero, as depicted by Mr. Young, did not appear the potent wizard brooding in gloomy abstraction over the secrets of his art, and around whom spirits and airy shapes throng numberless "at his bidding"; but seemed himself an automaton, stupidly prompted by others: his lips moved up and down as if pulled by wires, not governed by the deep and varied impulses of passion; and his painted face, and snowy hair and beard, reminded us of the masks for the representation of Pantaloon. In a word, Mr. Young did not personate Prospero, but a pedagogue teaching his scholars how to recite the part, and not teaching them well.

One of the actors who assisted this sacrifice of poetical genius, Emery, we think as highly as any one can do: he is indeed, in his way, the most perfect actor on the stage. His representations of common rustic life have an absolute identity with the thing represented. But the power of his mind is evidently that of imitation, not that of creation. He has nothing romantic, grotesque, or imaginary about him. Every thing in his hands takes a local and habitual shape. Now, Caliban is a mere creation; one of the wildest and most abstracted of all Shakespear's characters, whose deformity is only redeemed by the power and truth of the imagination displayed in it. It is the essence of grossness, but there is not the smallest vulgarity in it. Shakespear has described the brutal mind of this man-monster in contact with the pure and original forms of nature; the character grows out of the soil where it is rooted uncontrouled, uncouth, and wild, uncramped by any of the meannesses of custom. It is quite remote from any thing provincial; from the manners or dialect of any county in England. Mr. Emery had nothing of Caliban but his gaberdine, which did not become him. (We liked Mr. Grimaldi's Orson much better, which we saw afterwards in the pantomime.) Shakespear has, by a process of imagination usual with him, drawn off from Caliban the elements of every thing etherial and refined, to compound them into the unearthly mould of Ariel. Nothing was ever more finely conceived than this contrast between the material and the spiritual, the gross and the delicate. Miss Matthews played and sung Ariel. She is to be sure a very "tricksy spirit": and all that we can say in her praise is, that she is a better representative of the sylph-like form of the character, than the light and portable Mrs. Bland, who used formerly to play it. She certainly does not sing the songs so well. We do not however wish to hear them sung, though never so well; no music can add any thing to their magical effect.—The words of Shakespear would be sweet, even "after the songs of Apollo!"

Shakespeare, Illustrated
Charles Kean's 1857 Production of *The Tempest**

MARY M. NILAN

In our century *The Tempest* has assumed a special prominence, many modern critics contending that through this work Shakespeare presented mankind with a "new vision" or at least with the playwright's "final vision" of the world. E. M. W. Tillyard suggests that the play embodies the theme of "regeneration" in which "Ferdinand and Miranda sustain Prospero in representing a new order of things that has evolved out of destruction."[1] For Mark Van Doren, the play is an attempt "to fix a vision...Shakespeare is telling us for the last time about the world. . . . *The Tempest* does bind up in final form a host of themes with which the author has been concerned."[2] And G. Wilson Knight observes that the play "repeats, as it were, in miniature, the separate themes of Shakespeare's greater Plays. . . . It yet distils the poetic essence of the whole Shakespearian universe."[3]

In the first half of the nineteenth century, however, *The Tempest* was not accorded such a significant role in the Shakespearean repertoire; it was considered by most literary critics of the period as a more or less delightful romantic fantasy and little more. It was for Samuel Taylor Coleridge, "a specimen of the purely romantic drama";[4] for William Hazlitt, a "fantastic creation" where "the real characters and events partake of the wildness of a dream";[5] for Thomas Campbell, "a comparatively grave counterpart to *A Midsummer Night's Dream*. . .for its gayety is only less abandoned and frolicsome."[6]

Why this disparity in views from one century to the next? The answer may be at least partially discovered through a study of nineteenth-century stage presentations of *The Tempest*. Professional Shakespearean productions have tended to influence contemporary concepts about the significance of

*Originally published in the *Shakespeare Quarterly* 26 (1975): 196–204. Reprinted by permission of *Shakespeare Quarterly*.

individual characters and about the overall meaning of any given drama. For example, Hazlitt, writing in 1820, noted with regard to *The Merchant of Venice*:

> When we first went to see Mr. Kean in Shylock, we expected to see, what we had been used to see. . . . We were disappointed because we had taken our idea from other actors, not from the play. . . . But so rooted was our habitual impression of the part from seeing it caricatured in the representation, that it was only from a careful perusal of the play itself that we saw our error.[7]

Hazlitt was certainly not the only critic influenced by theatrical representations rather than the literary text. As Charles Shattuck comments in his introduction to *The Shakespeare Promptbooks*:

> It does not matter very much, practically, whether the original author of the play was Francis Bacon or Edward de Vere; it has often mattered greatly that the "effective" authors have been . . . all the Garricks and Guthries whose stage imagery has spread upon the plays the form and pressure of their separate generations.[8]

Thus what the critic as well as the general public has at times accepted as "Shakespeare's intention," has only been what a leading producer believed that intention to be.

With this in mind, it is interesting to analyze one major production of *The Tempest* in the mid-nineteenth century, one which was really the culmination of a long-established trend toward emphasizing the purely theatrical aspect of the work while deemphasizing the text itself. Early in the nineteenth century, Coleridge had commented on this tendency in *Tempest* productions:

> Although the illusion may be assisted by the effect on the senses of the complicated machinery and decorations of modern times, yet this sort of assistance is dangerous. For the principal and only genuine excitement ought to come from within,—from the moved and sympathetic imagination; whereas, where so much is addressed to the mere external senses of seeing and hearing, the spiritual vision is apt to languish, and the attraction from without will withdraw the mind from the proper and only legitimate interest which is intended to spring from within.[9]

Coleridge notwithstanding, the trend toward theatrical emphasis continued, reaching a peak with Charles Kean's staging of the piece.

By 1857 Kean was already noted as a Shakespearean producer who spared no effort or expense and insisted on historical accuracy in costumes, properties, and decorations. In preparing *The Tempest* for its 1 July opening at the Princess Theatre, however, he apparently felt himself free from the confines of any specific historical period and at liberty to exercise his unrestrained imagination. John William Cole, the producer's contemporary biographer, probably summed up the concept which guided Kean when, in *Bell's Weekly Messenger* of 4 July 1857, he said:

> In a fanciful creation, such as *The Tempest*, in which the exhaustless genius
> of the poet has soared beyond existing worlds and imagined new ones, no
> boundaries are defined and no restrictions are imposed. In transferring this
> majestic drama to the stage, an outline is sketched by the original inspiration,
> the details of which may be filled up according to the extent, comprehension
> and understanding of kindred tastes.[10]

The critic for the *Morning Chronicle*, writing 3 July 1857, defended this concept:

> No objections can possibly be raised to the employment of the utmost extent
> of scenic efforts or artistic accompaniments in the representation of those
> fairy productions of the genius of Shakespeare. A world of dreams, of fairies,
> of haunted woods, and enchanted caves has to be made visible to the spec-
> tator, and the play of human passions is subordinate.

Assuming that Shakespeare sketched only an "outline" and that the producer was to fill the void, Kean spared no effort or expense in meeting the challenge of making visible to the spectator the "world of dreams, of fairies, of haunted woods, and enchanted caves."

Kean's opening shipwreck scene followed the example of Samuel Phelps' 1847 rendition in making use of a large practical ship on a truck; Kean far out-did the earlier producer, however, by employing various special lighting effects in order to pinpoint specific pictures in the overall darkness of the scene.[11] Thus the audience was left with the memory of a series of vivid tableaux within the total moving picture. The scene was pictured in detail by the reviewer for the *Era* of 5 July 1857:

> The whole available space of the stage is devoted to a representation of the
> ocean lashed into boiling fury by the howling tempest, while filling up the
> center is the royal galley, with lamps suspended round her poop, dashed
> hither and thither by the waves off a lee shore. . . . To the utter helplessness
> of the ship is added the wild half-smothered shrieks of the sailors as they are,
> from time to time, revealed by the fitful lightning in groups or seen in the
> lurid beams from the poop lamps. Ariel flits among the frantic mariners as
> with flashing axe they hew the mast. Ariel is seen darting into the cabin, sur-
> rounded by white globules of ethereal fire contrasting admirably with the
> mortal red of the lamps and the clear blue of the levin. The wild plunges of
> the ship. . .the boom of the falling masts, and the sharp crack as she splits and
> rends on the rocks, forms a picture of grand and startling illusion.

This opening sequence became an "act" in itself or, as the playbill termed it, a "prologue" to the play.[12] At the close of the scene the curtain fell and the orchestra played the overture.

The curtain then rose to reveal the mist of the storm gradually dispersing and the sun slowly ascending. Prospero was seen "superintending the effect of his art" from the pinnacle of a rock which jutted out over the sea. Miranda stood beside him as she begged her father to "allay" the waters; in response to his daughter's request, the magician stretched forth his hands and the waves began to recede from the shoreline, revealing the "yellow sands." By the time the dialogue of the scene between father and daughter was concluded, the waves were hushed, the tide had receded, and a glorious flood of sunlight poured over the sands.

For Ariel's first entrance, Kean made use of William Macready's "business" in which a "ball of fire" was hurled from the flies above into an open stage trap below. The trap, in Kean's production, was masked from the audience's view by a scenic bush, and thus, after his fiery entrance, the sprite appeared to rise up from this bush. At the close of his scene with Prospero, Ariel suddenly disappeared and was then seen "rising from the sea at the back of the stage on the back of a dolphin." As the spirit bade adieu to his master, the dolphin appeared to "sink" beneath the receding "waves." In the final scene of the act, Ariel was seen making a skimming flight across the beach, beckoning towards Ferdinand, while the stage became filled with the sounds of an invisible chorus singing the airs which Shakespeare had assigned to the sprite alone. Throughout the play many scenes were permeated with music from an invisible orchestra as well as from a chorus, so that the island was indeed "full of sweet airs"; Ariel was relieved from singing any solos, a duty "too material," Kean felt, for the airy spirit.[13]

Act II, when compared with the parade of spectacles in the prologue and Act I, was relatively simple. The scenes, of course, offered no real opportunity for elaboration, but there was a new scenic display: "a view of the interior of the island with basaltic columns of rock piled on each other in fantastic forms" against a background of sea and high white-capped mountains. In this setting both scenes of the second act were played. In the first, Ariel actually floated above the nobles playing on a lyre, so that "a general drowsiness seems to pervade all on stage." After Ariel wakened the group, they left the stage, and Caliban, Trinculo, and Stephano arrived to provide some comedy. While there were no memorable theatrical innovations here, Kean may well have desired his audience to have a momentary respite between the breathtaking effects that had preceded and those still to come in the ensuing acts.

For the banquet scene Kean was apparently guided by the theme of "metamorphosis." As the comic conspirators left the stage and the shipwrecked nobles arrived, the scenery itself seemed to become animate. The set, consisting of two bare trees and a number of barren rocks, had remained constant throughout an abbreviated version of Act III, but now, in the words of the *Daily Telegraph* (2 July 1857):

> Gradually the effect of fertilization grows upon the spectator. Little by little, the solid rocks give place to blooming herbiage and the leafless trunks of trees burst into foliage and blossom. Slowly, and by degrees, the evidence of luxuriant vegetation arises on every side while at length, from the land dividing, a river flows forth through the scene and fountains of clear crystal-like water spring up from where formerly all was dry and inanimate.

In the fertile landscape naiads arrived to dance on the surface of the undulating waters. Satyrs and wood nymphs who had, in the words of Kean's playbill "taken the place of the ludicrous and unmeaning monsters hitherto presented," came on stage laden with baskets of fruits and flowers. Then in the words of the *Times* (3 July 1857):

> The old fashion of making a table arise from a trap is abolished, and the Nymphs, who carry baskets of fruit on their heads, bring them together, so that they themselves form the banquet table, the illusion being perfected by the festoons of flowers [deposited in a ring by the satyrs] that conceal their figures while they crouch beneath the load of conglomerated dainties.

Once the banquet circle was formed, Ariel as "the harpy," was hoisted up in the center in a basket of fruit. From this position, to the accompanying roll of thunder, he pronounced his dire prediction and, as thunder crashed, the stage darkened. The harpy and festive baskets disappeared through a trap; as the lights returned, the nymphs and satyrs scattered about the stage so that the banquet table actually appeared to "break up" before the eyes of the astonished nobles. The scene then concluded with what the *Morning Advertiser* (2 July 1857) described as "a dance of fauns and satyrs that realizes all Theocritus could suggest or Poussin paint."

Just as the banquet scene represents the focal point for Act III, the masque does the same for Act IV. Phelps had set the precedent for treating this sequence in the manner of a court pageant, and Kean continued and elaborated on this idea. The act opened with a view of the interior of Prospero's cave; gradually the back wall dissolved, revealing a view of clouds and the heavens. Iris opened Kean's masque by appearing stage right, riding on a cloud drawn by doves who were driven by Cupid. The second vision, which appeared stage left, depicted a far-off view of Eleusis, the shrine of Ceres, surrounded by nodding cornfields and prolific gardens, and attended by the goddess herself, who was surrounded by all the attributes of peace and plenty. The final climactic vision, completing the triptych effect, took place center stage: Juno appeared suspended high up in her chariot with, in the words of the *Era* (5 July 1857), "her peacock steeds half lost in rosy-lighted clouds, while arching round her head, hang the circling Graces in robes of ruby, sapphire and changing opal." Directly over Juno's head, Hymen appeared; below her, on stage level, seven water nymphs were seen sporting in a crystal clear pool, and rainbow arches encircled the completed vision.

After Juno and Ceres had ended their song (the only air not reinforced by a chorus), the vision dissolved through enveloping clouds and the rocky wall of Prospero's cave was seen again. As the vision disappeared, rolling thunder was heard and continued in the background until the act ended with the routing of the comic conspirators in an anti-masque. Kean had announced in his playbill that "to preserve the mythological tone throughout, the principal demons and goblins commanded to torture the brute Caliban and his drunken associates, Trinculo and Stephano, at the close of the fourth act, are copied from Furies depicted on Etruscan vases." These were supervised by Ariel, "flying on a Bat's back and setting them on."

Shakespeare had provided no indication of a spectacle with which to close Act V; Kean, however, began his presentation with a scenic prologue and apparently felt that, in order to maintain the self-imposed framework, there should be a fitting scenic epilogue. He therefore devised a series of tableaux within a total moving picture with which to close the production. According to the directions:

> Clouds rise and fall. Night descends. The Spirits, released by Prospero, take their flight from the island into the air. An invisible Chorus of Spirits sings "Where the Bee Sucks." Clouds close in on the Spirits and rise again, discovering a ship in a calm, prepared to convey the King and his companions back to Naples. The epilogue is spoken by Prospero from the deck of the vessel. The ship gradually sails off. The island recedes from sight and Ariel remains alone in mid-air, hovering over the sea, watching the departure of his late master. A distant Chorus of Spirits is heard singing, "Merrily, Merrily."

Thus Kean's *Tempest* ended with a spectacular finale, far more elaborate than that conceived by any previous producer.[14] In earlier presentations the Neapolitan fleet usually had been simply "seen in the distance"; in Kean's version, however, an actual ship appeared on stage to carry off Prospero at the conclusion of Shakespeare's epilogue. Ariel was thus left alone, both literally and figuratively "in the limelight."

Despite the fact that the play was, in Kean's words, "an imaginative drama," the producer's penchant for historical accuracy evidenced itself at several points. The ship, for example, was an exact replica of an Italian one of circa 1294–1330 with the insignia for the kingdom of Naples painted on her sails.[15] The tempest, the movement of ship and crew during the storm, was made as life-like as possible. Even Ariel's initial meteoric appearance was, in the words of the playbill, "in accordance with an ancient omen of a tempest." Moreover, since Shakespeare stipulated no precise time for his action, Kean supplied an historical context: "I have taken the liberty of selecting the thirteenth century as a date."[16] The producer's costume books reveal that pictures of Italian noblemen from this century served as models for the dress of Prospero and the shipwrecked courtiers, while sketches of mythological figures on

Greek vases inspired the costumes for the goddesses, harpy, satyrs, naiads, and wood nymphs. Miranda and Ariel's attire resembled that of the nymphs.

Kean's revival, more than any previous one which actually used Shakespeare's text, emphasized theatrical elements, including scenery, properties, costumes, invisible music, and other aural effects.[17] According to the *Morning Post* (2 July 1857) on opening night Kean made the following appeal to his audience:

> The kind indulgence of the public is requested should any lengthened delay take place between the acts during the first representation of *The Tempest*. This appeal is made with great confidence, when it is stated that the scenic appliances of the play are of a more extensive and complicated nature than ever yet been attempted in any theatre in Europe, requiring the aid of above 140 operatives nightly, who (unseen by the audience) are engaged in working the machinery, and in carrying out the various effects.

It was well that Kean made such a special plea, because the *Morning Advertiser* (2 July 1857) noted that the opening-night audience, arriving at 8:00 P.M., was not to leave the theater until nearly 1:00 A.M., after a total of some five hours. One week later, on 8 July 1857, the *Morning Post* reported that "this magnificent play is now shortened a full hour, by the rapidity with which practice has brought the working of the machinery."

Although the finished production ran four hours, prior to opening night Kean found it necessary to prune much of Shakespeare's text in order to allow sufficient time for his various theatrical displays.[18] While he omitted no scene, he did make liberal cuts within scenes and within speeches. All dialogue was deleted in I.i and the exposition sequence of I.ii was pared down to the barest essentials. The first meeting between Miranda and Ferdinand was condensed. The two scenes of Act II were combined into one with about two-thirds of the dialogue among the nobles deleted (II.i), although the subplot comedy sequence (II.ii) was left intact. Each subsequent act then focused on a particular spectacle: Act III, on the elaborate banquet scene; Act IV, on the masque; Act V, on the scenic epilogue. Dialogue not connected directly with the focal sequence of the particular act was condensed in order to save time for the major displays. Still the playbill boasted that Shakespeare's "original text" had been preserved with the proper sequence of scenes and with "only occasional" cuts.

While most critics praised the entire production, most echoed the sentiments of the *Saturday Review* critic (4 July 1857), who commented with reference to the acting that "there is not much room for it," and the *Globe* critic (2 July 1857), who contended that "the acting, with such illustrations, is secondary." But apparently in the eyes of most reviewers, excitement over Kean's theatrical displays far outweighed any sense of loss regarding the poetry or the opportunities for acting. The presentation was accorded unanimous raves by the critics, only one periodical, the *Saturday Review* (4 July 1857), offering any reservations, and these expressed only after many paragraphs of praise for the various displays:

> There is no attempt made by Mr. Kean to draw the attention of the audience from what is seen to what is said. Their eyes, not their ears are consulted. . . .
> As a series of spectacles illustrating a drama of Shakespeare, it is in every way to be praised and admired. Still, no beauty of scenery, and no success in contrivance and decorations can entirely content us.

But that is the central question: If Shakespeare had had all the resources of mid-nineteenth century stagecraft available to him, would he have wished *The Tempest* to be so produced? Although the playwright did have all the resources devised for court masques at his command, there is no indication in the Folio text that the original production made more than an occasional use of the theatrical devices available. Certainly Shakespeare intended to appeal to the ear at least as much as to the eye; it is obvious that the playwright expected the spoken word to be given an emphasis equal to or surpassing that of the theatrical display, else he would not have endowed *The Tempest* with some of his most beautiful poetry nor used this drama as the vehicle to convey what some modern critics have termed his "new vision" or his "final vision" of the world.

While he was Charles Dickens' houseguest in England, Hans Christian Andersen attended Kean's *Tempest*. Although his commentary on the presentation in the Danish daily, *Berlingske Tidende* (a series printed from 24 January through 2 February 1860), indicates his obvious fascination with the spectacles and particularly with investigating the specific techniques used to create them, he concludes:

> Everything was afforded that machinery and stage direction can provide, and yet after seeing it, one felt overwhelmed, tired, and empty. Shakespeare was lost in visual pleasure: the exciting poetry was petrified by illustrations; the living word had evaporated. No one tasted the spiritual banquet—it was forgotten for the golden platter on which it was served. . . . A work of Shakespeare performed between three simple screens is for me a greater enjoyment than here where it disappeared beneath the gorgeous trappings.[19]

Almost as if in response to this kind of commentary, the *Art-Journal* for 16 August 1857 attempted to reply to any would-be critics of Kean's highly theatrical production:

> We must offer a few words of comment on a question which has been raised as to the propriety of this large amount of illustration applied to the works of the dramatic poet in general and Shakespeare in particular. The objection proceeds on an intimation that the poetry of the scene painter is substituted for the poetry of the poet; and that he who undertakes to illustrate Shakespeare assumes to supplant him. Without insisting on the not very flattering

want of faith in Shakespeare on the part of the objector himself, when he hints at the possibility of the mechanist thus putting out the poet, we confess that we do not see how he is able to maintain his argument, unless he forbids the use of scenic illusion altogether. What the manager does in this respect constitutes the exact difference between stage representation and closet reading; if he may assist the illusion of his text at all by material realization of the times and places, why may he not do so on a sufficient scale? Where will the objector divide the principle, or draw the line of its application?

Almost twenty years earlier, when discussing Macready's presentation of *The Tempest*, the critic for *John Bull* (21 October 1838) had discussed the very problem which the *Art-Journal* now raised and had concluded at that time that a producer was not wrong in making use of theatrical devices to assist the illusion of the play, as long as these remained "subservient to the spirit of the scene."[20]

By this criterion Kean's elaborate spectacle would have had to be condemned, for he made an assault on the auditor's senses but apparently not on his mind. The 1857 reviewers, almost to a man, bemoaned the fact that the beauty of the production was "fleeting" and, once withdrawn from the boards, would be lost for all time. The *Morning Post* for 3 July echoed the feelings of the other papers when it stated: "The only regret is what [sic] we may safely affirm that it will never again be equalled on the stage in our time." Commentators described various displays in detail yet quoted no memorable lines. Apparently Kean had not hinged his theatrical delights on the sound framework of Shakespeare's poetic thought. Theatricality had not assisted the dramatic illusion but had instead supplanted it, so that, in the words of the *Saturday Review*, the production became "a series of spectacles illustrating a drama of Shakespeare." The opening shipwreck sequence became something Shakespeare had never intended, a separate prologue piece. To complete the framework, Kean then created a scenic epilogue so spectacular in its effect that it obscured the textual epilogue Shakespeare had written. Furthermore the presentation imparted a feeling that Ariel, rather than Prospero, was the central figure of the drama, as the *Times* (3 July 1857) noted: "As Ariel is the ever-prominent personage throughout the action, so does he remain sole occupant of the stage at the end of the play." Indeed Ariel was both literally and figuratively in the limelight, and much of the presentation focused on the effects of his magic-making.

In the final analysis, of course, the audience was treated to a fairy tale, viewed through the larger-than-life illustrations of a childhood imagination—a wonderful piece of art in itself, but hardly what Shakespeare had intended. Yet, while the production may not have remained subservient to the spirit of its author, Kean's version was extremely popular in its day, holding the boards for a total of eighty-eight performances, a lengthy run for any production in that period and more than half again the number accorded Macready's very successful revival twenty years earlier. There was not to be another major professional presentation in England until that of Herbert Beerbohm Tree at the turn of the century. In the meantime, for those who had missed Kean's staging, the printed acting edition of the 1857 version was available.[21]

Charles Kean must certainly be listed (to quote Shattuck) as one of those "effective authors" who shaped the concept of Shakespeare in their era.[22] It must also be repeated, however, that this highly theatrical rendition of the play was simply the culmination at mid-century of an already well-established trend towards "theatricalizing" presentations of *The Tempest*. The influence of such productions on nineteenth-century readers and critics should be obvious.

NOTES

1. E. M. W. Tillyard, *Shakespeare's Last Plays* (London: Chatto and Windus, 1938), 49–58.
2. Mark Van Doren, *Shakespeare* (New York: Doubleday, 1939), 178–85.
3. G. Wilson Knight, *The Shakespearian Tempest*, 3rd ed. (London: Methuen, 1964), 247.
4. Samuel Taylor Coleridge, *Shakespearian Criticism*, ed. Thomas Middleton Raysor, 2nd ed. (New York: Dutton, 1960), 1:118.
5. William Hazlitt, *The Characters of Shakespeare's Plays* (London, 1817), 116.
6. Thomas Campbell, *Dramatic Works of Shakespeare* (London, 1838), 87.
7. Hazlitt, 276–77.
8. Charles Shattuck, *The Shakespeare Promptbooks* (Urbana: U of Illinois P, 1965), 1. (In his descriptive catalogue Shattuck assigns a number to each of the primary source materials he lists as available to the researcher. Where applicable, these numbers will be cited.)
9. Coleridge, 1:118.
10. All reviews quoted are from the "London Scrapbooks—Princess Theater" (3 vols.), in the collection of the Folger Shakespeare Library.
11. The details of this production can be ascertained from a study of the promptbooks at the Folger. Except when specifically attributed to another source, information concerning Kean's staging is taken from the "souvenir promptbook" (Shattuck 19) which was compiled in 1859 by the prompter, T. W. Edmonds and includes 14 small watercolor rendering of the settings to guide the scene painters, Mr. Grieve and Mr. Telbin. The Folger also possesses the "rehearsal workbook" as well as a "cuebook for *Richard II* and *The Tempest*" (Shattuck 21, 22) both by George Ellis, the stage manager. (For a more detailed account of this and other source material see Shattuck 453–54.)
12. Playbill for 1 July 1857 in "*The Tempest* Scrapbook," in the Theatre Collection of the New York City Public Library.
13. See John William Cole, *The Life and Theatrical Times of Charles Kean* (London, 1859), 2:220.
14. The history of earler productions is recounted in my unpublished doctoral dissertation, "*The Tempest*: A Question of Theatricality" (Northwestern University, 1967).

15. Watercolor sketches, with some notations by the Hamilton Smiths, for the vessel as well as costumes, are found in "The Kean Costume Books" (Shattuck 25, 26), at the Folger.

16. From the playbill.

17. There were, of course, adaptations based on Shakespeare's play including the comedy of John Dryden and William Davenant in 1667, and the later Shadwell operatic version of 1674, as well as various other operatic alterations in the eighteenth century.

18. It should be noted that Kean did rely on Shakespeare's original text and that, despite very liberal "cuts," the version presented was uncontaminated by the Davenant-Dryden comedy or by the Shadwell opera.

19. Commentary quoted (in his own translation) by Frederick J. Marker, in "The First Night of Charles Kean's *The Tempest*—from the Notebook of Hans Christian Andersen," *Theater News* 25 (1970): 23.

20. Review quoted in George C. D. Odell, *Shakespeare from Betterton to Irving* (New York: Scribner, 1920), 2:218–19.

21. *Shakespeare's Play of The Tempest, arranged for representation at the Princess Theatre, with historical and explanatory notes by Charles Kean, as first produced on ... 1 July 1857 ...* (London: J. K. Champman & Co., n.d.).

22. Shattuck, *The Shakespeare Promptbooks*, 1.

The Tempest at the Turn of the Century
Cross-Currents in Production[*]

MARY M. NILAN

The history of *The Tempest* on the English-speaking stage from the Restoration era through the mid nineteenth century is mainly a story of high theatrical adaptations and alterations or of spectacular "illustrations" of Shakespeare's play.[1] While, by the close of the nineteenth century, Shakespeare's original text was the basis of presentations, many minor producers were still imitating the theatrical innovations of Samuel Phelps's 1847 revival and major ones, such as Augustin Daly and Herbert Beerbohm Tree, were attempting to surpass the lavish illustrations of Charles Kean's 1857 extravaganza.[2]

But, at the same time, a new trend was evident, one which conflicted with the highly theatrical theory of staging and indicated a new direction for *Tempest* revivals in the twentieth century. For, at the turn of the century, some professional producers were intentionally attempting to pare down the traditionally super-imposed spectacles rather than condensing the text to make room for them, and others, because of financial limitations, chose to present a simpler theatrical version rather than none at all. A study of this era is then particularly interesting because two conflicting theories of *Tempest* staging were being tested, providing reviewers and critics with an opportunity for comparison.

I

In America by the end of the nineteenth century, *The Tempest* was no longer a play for the audiences of the Eastern metropolises alone. On 23 June 1889, it was presented by Mr. McVicker at his theater in Chicago. *The Chicago Times*

*Originally published in *Shakespeare Survey* 25 (1972): 113–123. Copyright Cambridge University Press 1972. Reprinted with the permission.

reported that the play had "never been tried in this country west of New York."[3] According to the same paper, while McVicker did present the original Shakespearian text, he did some "re-arranging":

> The order of the scenes at the opening is reversed and the whole is condensed into four acts, with "cutting," of course, distributed throughout, but nothing material is omitted and nothing is added but music and bits of dances, if they can be said to be additions.

The "additions" included, in the words of the *Chicago News*, "music that is ascribed to the version of Davenant and Dryden." The paper did not specify exactly how much was added, but according to the *Chicago Evening Journal* "the singing is done by Ariel and the Philharmonic and Schumann Lady Quartettes, the latter being invisible to the audience."

Although in the McVicker production I, i followed I, ii, and there was some added music from the Restoration version, the beginning of a new trend or a new philosophy in staging may be detected in that six Chicago reviewers concurred with the observation of the *Chicago Tribune*: "More pretentious and sensuous spectacles have been offered; but here, not only the eye was flattered but the imagination was stimulated by the poetry which swept all realms of thought, from fairyland to high philosophy." And the *Chicago Inter-Ocean* reported: "The stage pictures. . .are pleasing without attracting attention, to the sacrifice of the ideals of the poet." Apparently the theatricality of McVicker's production did not obscure Shakespeare's text.

The producer relied on two spectacles. The first which caused comment among the reviewers was the storm scene, transposed to the close of act I. As described by the *Chicago Inter-Ocean* it appears to have been as elaborate as Kean's rendition of 1857:

> The swift-passing clouds, penetrated ever and anon by vivid flashes of lightning, the beating waves, ominous in the darkness, and the huge ship that comes plunging into view, its decks crowded with people, and is finally driven upon the rocks as a lightning stroke shivers its mast, makes a remarkably realistic picture.

The second major visual display occurs in the masque where, according to the *Chicago Globe*, "the cars of Juno and Ceres, drawn respectively by the sacred peacock, and glittering butterflies, enter amid filmy clouds and, in a forest scene, mermaids float dreamily through running waters." The masque then focusses on a series of dances. The one which excited the most admiration was executed, according to the same reviewer, by "a throng of brightly costumed children and girls." The goddesses leave their cars and "dance in company with the sprites" and Ariel then executes "a pleasing dance solo."

Apparently, however, the storm scene and the masque were the only extravaganzas in the show. While the reviewers praised the various scenes of "caves and landscapes," no other elaborate scenic displays are mentioned. Moreover, according to the *Chicago News*, instead of presenting a series of separate production numbers, McVicker attempted to merge one scene into the next by the skillful use of stage lighting. He also attempted to merge one act into the next by using a series of special "act curtains," each depicting a scene from the play which blended with the previous one. The main curtain was never used "to break the illusion" and the time between each act was "only a short space."

Since McVicker's production featured a storm sequence as elaborate in its own way as Kean's and a masque with numerous scenic delights, a large corps of dancing girls and children, and an invisible chorus composed of the Philharmonic and Schumann Ladies Quartettes, it is likely that the Chicago producer could have rivaled Kean's lavish presentation spectacle for spectacle. It is significant, however, that with the exception of two major displays the American producer chose not to do so, but instead devoted his attention to merging smoothly scenes and acts, letting Shakespeare's poetry speak for itself without being smothered by the numerous theatrical distractions prevalent in most productions of the period.

II

Two years later, Frank Benson's troupe, which had been playing in the English provinces, was performing at the Stratford Memorial Theater. In the summer of 1891 Benson offered *The Tempest* at the Stratford Festival. He portrayed Caliban and made a starring role of the part. His conception of the monster was based on Daniel Wilson's *Caliban: the Missing Link* (1873). Here it was asserted that Shakespeare had imaginatively created in Caliban, the creature which fills a gap between the highest ape and the lowest savage:

> There was obviously something marine or fishlike in the aspect of the island monster. "In the dim obscurity of the past," says Darwin, "we can see that the early progenitor of all the vertebrates must have been an acquatic animal". . .In Caliban there was undesignedly embodied, seemingly, an ideal of the latest stages of such an evolution. (p. 73).

Following this suggestion, Benson played Caliban on all fours with costume and makeup suggestive of an ape.[4] He would scurry up a corrugated palm trunk, hang from a branch head-downward and then swing through the branches of a tree. He always entered with a large and very real fish clenched between his jaws.

Because of his limited budget, Benson attempted to give a somewhat simpler theatrical version of *The Tempest*. In some ways, however, he did try to imitate the lavish stagings of Phelps and Kean. Since he could not hope to match the magnificent storm and shipwreck prologue of his predecessors, he simply cut the scene. The play commences then with Miranda and Prospero discovered "on a sea-marge, sterile and rocky hard." The main setting depicts the luxury of a tropical island with rocky ledges surrounding a gorge of fern and palm. The "yellow sands" are reminiscent of Kean's production as is the masque with its "rainbow arch, Juno descending through the clouds in a shaft of light in a peacock-drawn car, and the naiads floating in a lily-pond below." For the finale Benson again imitated Kean by showing a tableau of Ariel and attendant spirits in flight; however, he was not able to follow his predecessor in presenting a practical ship to bear Prospero away from the island. But Benson did add some innovations of his own including a number of lavish ballets and an elaborate entrance for Ferdinand who comes on stage "drawn by a silver thread, held by two tiny Cupids whose costumes" are "chiefly wings."[5] This somewhat simpler theatrical revival of *The Tempest* met with success and was to be repeated in ensuing years at Stratford as well as the Lyceum Theater.

III

Despite the fact that McVicker had made some attempt to simplify theatricality in his presentation, the idea seemed to persist in America that, as the theater critic for the *New World* (7 April 1897) suggested: "*The Tempest* is by no means a comedy that could be presented with curtains for scenery and imagination for effects." Writing on the same date, William H. Fleming contended in the *Looker-On*: "From the nature of the play, it is not possible to give a presentation of it which is very powerful and dramatic. It appeals not so much to the thoughts and emotions of the spectator as to his aesthetic nature."

Assuming apparently that the play would not appeal to "the thoughts and emotions of the spectator," Augustin Daly felt free to cut liberally Shakespeare's text and this he did for his New York revival which opened on 6 April 1897. On 7 April the *New York Herald* observed that "of the 2,064 lines. . .surely 1,000 are missing, too great a condensation." A study of Daly's production prompt-book confirms the estimate.[6] For example, in act IV, which coincided with act V in Shakespeare's printed text, 156 out of 318 lines are omitted. Daly not only made numerous cuts in the text but he also transposed speeches freely. Daly's act III is a peculiar mélange which Marvin Felheim, in *The Theatre of Augustin Daly*,[7] constructs from the Shakespearian text as follows:

III, iii
IV, i, 164–92
III, ii, 48–73
IV, i, 194–5, 221–35
III, ii, 76–132
IV, i, 1–59, 118–24, 146–57 (p. 265).

According to the prompt-book, during the masque Prospero is directed to "recite slowly" the speech beginning "Our revels now are ended," as a sort of background to the vision itself. Besides obscuring the speech, the direction also seems pointless as the "revels" are beginning, not ending.

Rather than magical effects, the production emphasizes songs, dances, and striking stage pictures; each act ends with a climactic tableau, featuring song and dance. For example, act I closes with the entrance of Ferdinand and the directions read:

> Ariel, floating in the air, attended by Nymphs and Spirits, playing and singing "Full Fathom Five." Other spirits enter and dance round Ferdinand as if to distract him from Miranda. Ariel sings "Come Unto These Yellow Sands" as the act ends.

Act II concludes with the second scene between Miranda and Ferdinand and, at the close, Ariel arrives to sing "Where the bee sucks" (transposed from act V) and attendant spirits dance again. Act III closes with the spectacle of the masque which follows the now traditional concept of a triptych of goddesses, surrounded by a rainbow arch. And, reminiscent of Kean, act IV terminates with a scenic epilogue:

> Ariel appears in the air at the back of the stage. The walls of the Cave dissolve. The sea appears beyond, and a ship approaches the shore—Prospero's Spirits guiding the ship (as the curtain falls) singing "Merily, Merrily."

Daly added more music to *The Tempest*. Ariel renders "Oh, bid thy faithful Ariel fly" and Miranda and Ferdinand are given a duet at the close of act II. While the producer used the compositions of both Arne and Purcell to accompany the airs, he also used an additional score, Taubert's "Tempest," written for the Munich Court Theater. A musical background is provided for each scene. As Felheim concluded: "Music and scenery together apparently seemed to Daly the quintessence of poetic drama" (p. 265).

The critic for the *New York Herald* objected to this emphasis on theatricality, stressing that in *The Tempest* the text was more important than any scenic or pantomimic representation:

> The ship scene as Shakespeare wrote it, word for word, properly acted, and without a rag of scenery, would be a thousand times more impressive and more stimulating to the imagination in a theatre than the finest scenic representation of a wreck, as would the beautiful "cloud-capp'd towers" speech, a bit of poet's frenzy, which is torn out of its proper place and recited slowly as the accompaniment to an actual vision of gorgeous palaces and solemn temples on a "back cloth."

Essentially, then, the *New York Herald* critic was contesting the *New York World*'s contention that "*The Tempest* is by no means a comedy that could be presented with curtains for scenery and imagination for effects."

IV

While the *New York Herald* reviewer might be in the minority in America, the concept which he espoused was being tried out, and defended by at least one notable critic in England. In the same year that Daly's elaborate production held the boards in New York, William Poel's semi-professional London group, the Elizabethan Stage Society, was presenting *The Tempest* without any elaborate scenery on a stage re-created to resemble the Society's conception of the original Elizabethan one. It will be recalled that in Chicago, almost ten years earlier, McVicker had concentrated on devices for merging one scene into another and one act into another. In 1897 Poel's group overcame the problem by eliminating scene shifts altogether.[8] Moreover, the large and often augmented orchestra, which had been an accepted part of professional productions, was omitted. Instead of elaborate music scored for wood-wind and percussion, Mr. Dolmetsch's background music made use of simple instruments of pipe and tabor. The only element in the production which might be termed "elaborate" was the costuming, an area in which the Society had made a reputation for itself. But essentially Poel intended that the audience listen to Shakespeare's verbal imagery and then create for itself the magical effects and the vision of Prospero's island.

This concept was applauded by one of the more notable reviewers of the day. In his capacity as theater critic for the *Saturday Review*, George Bernard Shaw discussed the production of 13 November 1897.[9] Approving the basic philosophy behind the Society's presentation, Shaw compared it to the kind of production accorded the play for the last fifty years in both England and America:

> The poetry of *The Tempest* is so magical that it would make the scenery of modern theatre ridiculous. The methods of the Elizabethan Stage Society. . .leave to the poet, the work of conjuring up the isle "full of noises, sounds and sweet airs." And I do not see how this plan can be beaten. If Sir Henry Irving were to put the play on at the Lyceum next season. . .what could he do but multiply the expenditure enormously, and spoil the illusion? He would give us the screaming violin instead of the harmonious viol. . .an expensive and absurd stage ship; and some windless, airless, changeless, soundless, electric-lit, wooden-floored mockeries of the haunts of Ariel. They would cost more but would they be an improvement on the Mansion House arrangement?

Despite the absence of the scene changes, the production was not taken at the rapid-fire pace which typifies most revivals done "in the manner of the Elizabethan stage" in our day. The costumes were somewhat restrictive, allowing for interesting stage pictures but not for freedom of movement. On this point Shaw observed:

> The whole performance had to be taken in a somewhat low key and slow tempo, with a minimum of movement. If any attempt had been made at the impetuosity and liveliness for which the English experts of the sixteenth-century were famous throughout Europe, it would not only have failed, but prevented the performers from attaining what they did attain.

But despite the shortcomings Poel's revival was a landmark, hearlding a new era for future productions of *The Tempest*.

V

The Elizabethan Stage Society's revival did not immediately influence the style of *Tempest* presentations in the next decade. Benson's simplified imitation of earlier lavish revivals was repeated at Stratford in the same year as Poel's production and it was to be revived at the Lyceum in 1900 and again at the Memorial Theater in 1904, 1908, and 1911.

In 1903 the western half of America was treated to a touring production of *The Tempest*. Originating at the Columbia Theater in San Francisco, the revival by Frederick Warde (who played Prospero) and Louis James (who played Caliban as a "missing link") visited, among other theaters, the McVicker's in Chicago and English's in Indianapolis. Ignoring all the obvious hazards of touring a highly technical production, the Warde-James presentation came complete with a realistic storm and shipwreck sequence and a bag of elaborate "supernatural" stage tricks. The *San Francisco Chronicle* for 27 January 1903 exclaimed: "Why there have been so few attempts to stage it stands explained when one sees how much of scenic and other effects it needs!" From the *Indianapolis Journal* for 11 April 1903 we learn that "in places the text of Shakespeare had been departed from so as to allow the interpolation of long songs or ballet measures and much identical music." One of these interpolated songs, rendered by Ferdinand, consisted of words from one of Shakespeare's sonnets set to "suitable music." (The precise sonnet is not mentioned.)

Now, however, theater critics were becoming more outspoken in questioning the value of such a highly theatrical *Tempest*. Thus, when the tour reached Chicago, reviewers had an opportunity to compare the elaborate Warde-James revival with McVicker's comparatively simple one fourteen years earlier. On this point the *Chicago Tribune* (23 March 1903) commented: "The production here in 1889 by the late J. H. McVicker had about it more of the atmosphere of poetry and fantasy than does the present one." One specific difference which the *Tribune* noted was the fact that McVicker had employed a series of gauze drops while Warde-James relied on heavy, painted flats. But more significantly, some reviewers questioned the philosophy behind the touring revival. Should Shakespeare's poetry be lost amidst theatrical displays? *The Chicago Daily News* critic echoed the thoughts of his colleagues when, on 23 March 1903, he observed:

> Disillusionment is perhaps the inevitable result of a stage presentation of *The Tempest* and a real lover of the poetic fairy fantasy must forgo the sight of his favorite fairies embodied in the flesh, if he would retain the elusive delight of their being which the lines of Shakespeare conjure up. This is true even with all the elaboration of scenic investiture which characterizes the production at McVickers.

Indeed it would seem that "scenic investiture" had not aided the illusion but had created "disillusionment."

VI

In the same year that the Warde-James tour was performing *The Tempest* in America, a London revival by J. H. Leigh at the small Royal Court Theater ran for between seventy and eighty performances—certainly an excellent record at that time for a Shakespearian production at a minor theater where the actors were not well known. The question naturally arises: What was it that attracted the audiences? It was undoubtedly a combination of the good acting of the performers and, even more, the simplicity of the presentation. There was no attempt to imitate the lavish extravaganzas of the major theaters; while some semblance of settings and theatrical additions were employed, these were held to a minimum. For this reason, as the critic of the *Illustrated Sporting and Dramatic News* (5 December 1903) observed, Shakespeare's poetry was projected with unusual clarity:

> The fact that although the scenery and accessories were sympathetic, they were neither costly nor overwhelming, was an important feature of the production. I could not help asking myself why my attention had been engaged by interest in the poetry of the play and whether half-hours of elaborate sets and gorgeous processions, with which it seems at present the fashion to adorn the bard—or subordinate him—are really and truly after all worth five minutes of actual Shakespearean acting.

VII

Sir Henry Irving, who managed the Lyceum from 1878 until 1901, never produced *The Tempest* although he allowed Frank R. Benson to stage his version there in 1900. But a year after the elaborate Warde-James tour in America and the relatively simple Royal Court Theater presentation, Herbert Beerbohm

Tree added *The Tempest* to his repertoire of Shakespearian revivals at His Majesty's Theater, London. Staged first on 14 September 1904 with William Haviland as Prospero, Tree himself as Caliban, his daughter Viola Tree as Ariel, and Louis Calvert as Stephano, the production became a staple at His Majesty's and was revived there in succeeding seasons from 1904/5 through 1907/8.

Tree used Shakespeare's text but made some changes. He transposed the second Caliban-Trinculo-Stephano scene (III, ii), placing it between the banquet scene (III, iii) and the masque (IV, i).[10] He cut Shakespeare's epilogue and concluded the play instead with Prospero's speech beginning "Ye elves of hills, brooks, standing lakes, and groves" (V, i, 33–57). While there were a number of deletions throughout the text, the principal ones occur in act V; the act was reduced to about one-half its former length.

By 1904 stage mechanism had progressed to such a point that the prompt-book for Tree's production speaks of almost all scene changes being of a 1 1/2-minute interval. (In the mid nineteenth century, if we are to judge from William Burton's 1854 prompt-book, 4- to 8-minute waits were common.[11]) Tree did not, however, use the additional time to retain more of Shakespeare's dialogue but instead inserted additional pieces of "business."

Where his predecessors had concentrated on devising spectacles and effects to be achieved through scenery and machinery, he concentrated on creating pantomimes to interpret Shakespeare's text and to enlarge on the Folio stage directions. In an apology attached to the souvenir program for the fiftieth representation of his *Tempest* revival, he attempted to justify all his pantomimic innovations as merely an elaboration of Shakespeare's implicit or explicit directions: "What in this production was not actually contained in the letter of Shakespeare's text, sprang from the spirit which animated it."[12] Moreover, he assumed that such pantomimes were a part of the original presentation and that, had Shakespare had turn-of-the-century stagecraft at his command, the playwright would have made ample use of it to achieve effects similar to Tree's own: "Of all Shakespeare's works *The Tempest* is probably the one which most demands the aids of modern stagecraft."

As has been noted, there was a growing feeling among critics against "scenic Shakespeare" and it is significant of course that Tree's innovations involved business rather than scenery. While he had as many individual settings (twelve) as Kean had had fifty years earlier, still, with the exception of the opening shipwreck sequence, there was a decided difference about the type of setting employed. The turn-of-the-century producer relied on small set-pieces such as rocks and water rows working in combination with gauze drops and subtle changes in color and intensity of stage lighting. Kean had relied chiefly on heavy painted scenery, using gauze and special lighting only for certain specific magical effects. Tree's prompt-book, on the other hand, shows more concern for "light changes" that "scene changes." For example, near the close of act I, by changing the dominant lighting from amber to purple he was able to change the yellow sands into "a misty vision," described as "the light that never was on land or sea."

Tree may have sensed the direction modern stagecraft would take with emphasis on lighting rather than scenery in presentations of poetic drama in general and Shakespearian drama in particular. In his book of memoirs, *Thoughts and Afterthoughts* (1913), he noted under "Afterthought" regarding *The Tempest*: "The art of stage presentations has progressed—and I think rightly progressed—in the direction of greater simplicity of treatment. This progress is chiefly due to the increased facilities for economy in the lighting of scenery. Suggestion is often stronger than actuality where purely fantastic and imaginative works are concerned" (p. 224). But in 1904 Tree's three-act version of *The Tempest* was anything but "simple" or purely "suggestive."

Act I opens with the inevitable storm and shipwreck sequence done in a manner to rival Kean's realistic illustration, but there is one interesting innovation: four small boys dressed as mariners are on the replica of the Neapolitan vessel; they pretend to speak the lines of the scene which are, in reality, spoken by offstage actors. Thus, gauged in relation to the size of its mariners, the vessel appears to be full scale. Apparently Tree was striving for as much realism as possible here. The same is true of the exposition sequence which takes place in Prospero's cell. The setting is fitted out with books, which the magician is reading at the opening; a couch, upon which Miranda sleeps in the course of the scene; and a table, on which Ariel perches for part of the dialogue with Prospero.

Suddenly, prior to the entrance of Caliban, a far more imaginative and fanciful picture is presented, one of Tree's many added pantomimes:

> As Ariel exits from Prospero's cell, there is a blackout. The curtain and gauze comes down. "Come Unto These Yellow Sands" is sung by the offstage chorus. As the chorus starts, the curtain goes up in the dark and lights gradually come up to purple, disclosing Nymphs playing on the waters and on the sands. Four Nymphs on wires are behind the first water row. On the last lines of the song, lights gradually check down. Nymphs go off slowly behind rocks R and L and lights gradually come up amber, revealing the yellow sands.

Now with his magic wand Prospero strikes the forbidding rock inhabited by Caliban; it opens disclosing the monster, who "crawls out with a fish in his mouth." His dress consists of fur and sea-weed and around his neck he wears a string of pearls, shells, amber, and coral. Dropping the fish, he announces: "I must eat my dinner." As he proceeds to search the beach for more shells to add to his necklace, Prospero exits. Caliban, left alone, starts after his master in a threatening manner but is stopped by the strains of prelude music; he listens, looks up and attempts to dance before finally exiting over some rocks. (Throughout the production Tree insisted on Caliban's quick responsiveness to the "sounds and sweet airs" of the island.) Another pantomime then follows in which six nymphs assist Ariel in a dressing routine. Properties for the sequence are a shell, comb, headdress, necklace and cloak. Once the sprite is attired, the nymphs, with Ariel between them, "form a circle centre, dancing." They are interrupted by a note in the orchestra. "The Prelude to 'Yellow Sands' is sung offstage and they steal away by various exits." Ariel, singing the Shakespearian air, disappears only to reappear a moment later, waving Ferdinand on. Nymphs are directed to peep at him "over the rocks and in the waves." Ariel toys with a large sea-shell while singing "Full fathom five."

The stage is set for the meeting between the Prince and Miranda. Tree added more physical business between the two lovers than had any previous producer. At the close of their first scene, "they advance slowly toward each other in the wonderment of first love." During the course of Prospero's long aside, "Ferdinand touches Miranda and kneels at her feet"; Miranda presents the Prince with a shell which she finds on the shore. The scene closes with some pantomimic business in which Caliban enters carrying wood and regarding the lovers with hatred. As the monster raises a log to strike the Prince, he is charmed by Prospero and skulks back to his rock. Since Ferdinand is the last to leave the stage, the act ends with a tableau of Caliban "crouching in his cell and looking at Ferdinand" as the Prince looks offstage after Miranda.

Act II begins with the first scene involving the shipwrecked nobles, but prior to the scene there is another pantomime in which Ariel is discovered in a bower made by surrounding trees "from which wild honeysuckle stands in profusion." The sprite sings "Where the bee sucks" and the song is echoed by a chorus of children offstage. Lowered to the stage, Ariel sings the refrain and then dances before exiting. The nobles arrive and the scene proper begins. Ariel, hidden behind a gauze set-piece, suddenly is revealed to waken the sleeping courtiers. There is a pantomime here too: at the end of the song, Antonio and Sebastian make a sudden rush at Alonso and Gonzalo; Antonio is above Alonso, with sword drawn, and Sebastian is above Gonzalo, with a dagger; the music swells and stops dead. After the nobles retire, Ariel is taken up in the swing and from the honeysuckle bower sings a chorus of "Merrily, merrily."

Caliban, Stephano, and Trinculo appear for their first scene together. This is followed by the second sequence between Miranda and Ferdinand. Again there is more physical business as, at the close: "The lovers kiss for the first time. They walk slowly up and look out at the sea. A silence falls. The lights begin to fade. Miranda's head falls on Ferdinand's shoulder and sweet music is heard as the scene fades out." The act concludes with the banquet scene. The "strange shapes" are dispensed with and a pantomime involving tumbling acrobats is substituted. To the sound of thunder the table rises through a stage trap and the lights are brought up to reveal the banquet. Two boys enter and, presenting a spoon and fork to each of the principals, invite them to eat. They then exit by tumbling offstage to the accompaniment of rolling thunder. There is a blackout and a crash of thunder. During the brief distraction, "Ariel is helped up on the table by the principals and then switches on the lights in headdress." The nobles kneel around the table and are directed to stab at the harpy but Ariel "laughs and it is re-echoed off-stage by children." The speech ended, there is another blackout during which Ariel leaves and the table sinks.

Act III opens with the second Caliban-Trinculo-Stephano scene (Shakespeare's III, ii). At the beginning "Caliban is discovered seated on the shore listening to sweet music in the air, weaving a wreath of flowers wherewith to crown his new-found master. Placing the wreath on his head, he looks at his reflection in the pool." There are numerous pieces of business to indicate Caliban's admiration for Stephano. He presents his master with garland, strokes, pats and fans him. Throughout the episode the "invisible" Ariel flits about the stage with a long lily which is used to tickle the other three participants in the scene; they, thinking it is a fly, attempt to catch it. At the end "Ariel leads them about like a will-o'-the-wisp, then flies above them, still playing in the air." Caliban listens to the music and attempts to dance and sing; Stephano and Trinculo "watch him with curiosity."

The masque follows as the second scene of act III. The three goddesses each appear in turn in a spectacle reminiscent of Kean's presentation. Juno and Ceres sing and then disappear in a blackout. In the darkness Iris takes up a position on a platform in the center and naiads take up their positions behind water rows. As blue lights come up gradually Ferdinand starts to speak but Prospero silences him and, according to the cue, "when the blues are full up, the Nymphs are seen playing in the water." Obedient to Iris's command, the naiads leave the water and come to dance on the land. A pantomimic ballet follows, so involved that Tree explained it in his souvenir program:

> The sudden appearance of the boy Cupid interrupts their revels—the Naiads modestly immerse themselves in the water. Cupid, ever a matchmaker, brings in his train of sunburnt sicklemen who, leaving their lonely furrow, are enjoined by Iris to make holiday with the nymphs "in country footing." The reapers attempt to embrace the nymphs but their advances are repulsed, the maidens pointing to their ringless wedding-fingers, it being illegal (in fairyland) to exchange kisses without a marriage certificate. Thus rebuffed, the reapers continue their dance alone. Suddenly Cupid re-appears on the scene and shoots a dart in the heart of each coy maiden—at once they relent; they sue to the reapers, but the reapers are now obdurate. They laugh, the maidens weep. Cupid now shoots an arrow into the heart of each of the reapers, who seeing their little friends weep, now sue to them pointing to their wedding-fingers. Cupid re-appears and an impromptu wedding is arranged. To the wedding song of "Honour, riches, marriage blessings," the nymphs assume the marriage veils which they gather from the mist of the

lake, and having received a ring and a blessing at the hands of Rev. Master Cupid, they dance off in quest of everlasting happiness.

The ballet finished, Prospero delivers his speech beginning "our revels now have ended."

The time has come for Prospero to punish Caliban and his associates, and again there is a special pantomime for this anti-masque. The conspirators are seen creeping stealthily into the monstrous cave of Prospero. Suddenly Ariel enters clashing cymbals and dashes across the stage; there is an accompanying crash of thunder and then darkness. When the blue lights return the three discover themselves in a cave filled with strange and monstrous animals. The directions, at the beginning of Tree's III, iii, continue:

> Caliban, in pantomime, shows a way of escape and all three make for it, holding on to each others' coat tails. Just as they reach the entrance, a horrible thing appears with a long neck and bows to them in silence. The three back off in terror and are met by three other animals. They cross from R to L and are met by two more who drive them upstage where they are met by a six-legged horse and more animals. At this moment, a wild yell is heard and noames enter from all sides, some down over the rocks. Illuminated heads appear and disappear quickly on the back cloth and on rock pieces. Acrobats enter quickly from behind rock row and climb a tree from behind so that when Caliban, Stephano and Trinculo climb it, the acrobats come tumbling to the ground. Caliban, Stephano and Trinculo then rush downstage where four goblins drop in front of them from an overhanging bridge. The three attempt to battle with them and the curtain descends.

In Tree's words "the comic Inferno dissolves and we are once again in Prospero's cave."

The final scene is a highly condensed version of Shakespeare's act V. The ship sails away, carrying Prospero and the others as the nymphs sing a reprise of "Come unto these yellow sands" and the "homing-song" of the sailors is heard in the distance. Creeping from his cave, Caliban watches the departing ship. Ariel appears singing a reprise of "Where the bee sucks." "Taking flight at the words 'merrily, merrily,' the sprite's voice rises higher and higher until it merges into the song of the lark—Ariel is now free as a bird." At the end the curtain rises for a final tableau showing Caliban stretching out his arms towards the departing ship in mute despair. "The night falls and Caliban is left on the lonely rock. He is king once more." Thus Tree's version concludes with Caliban both literally as well as figuratively "in the limelight."

London critics now had an opportunity to contrast this elaborate revival with Benson's simpler one and with Poel's even more simple version. The critic of the *Daily Chronicle* (15 September 1904) yearned for less ornate music, such as that used by Poel: "Roze's or Sullivan's music would have been well replaced by a note or two of Purcell's simple old 'Come unto these yellow sands' for which one listened in vain." Regarding Tree's realistic shipwreck sequence, the same reviewer contended that it "failed to prove even so appealing as the device resorted to by the Elizabethan Stage Society who. . .allowed their mariners to pretend to be wrecked on a simple balcony above the stage—with a result that was curiously effective." Contrasting Tree's revival with Benson's, the critic remarked: "It is to be doubted if the spirit of the production was anything like as true to the play as was Mr. Benson's far less splendid effort at the Lyceum."

The London *Times* (15 September 1904) compared the presentation with the original Jacobean one, and Tree's again came off second best for the reviewer emphasized that Shakespeare had achieved his effects by words, not illustration:

> Above all Prospero is a man of words. Ariel is a sprite of words. And Caliban is a monster of words. Shakespeare got his atmosphere mainly through the utterances of his personages. They made their set speeches, and sang their songs, and the imagination of the audience had to do the rest. This cannot be so today. It is the manager and his stage managers who had to do the rest. And the "rest" is now the chief part. All the sensorial elements of drama become prominent and all the words take second place. . . The atmosphere of enchantment has no longer to be suggested; it has to be realized.

The most pronounced indictment, however, was published in *Blackwood's Magazine* for October 1904. This particular criticism elicited Tree's "Personal Explanation," first published in the souvenir program of the fiftieth representation of the play and later reprinted in *Thoughts and Afterthoughts* (pp. 211–24). The *Blackwood* critic was disturbed by the use of an ornate musical background rendered by a full orchestra: "As the cast always speaks to musical accompaniment, generally slow, it is surprising that they make a single speech intelligible." And, more than this, the reviewer observed:

> Tree has so betricked and bemused the author's text that, were it not for the purple patches which now and then silence the orchestra, hidden beneath a mass of vegetables, you would not have the smallest suspicion that you are assisting at a performance of Shakespeare's comedy. . . . Shakespeare's plays afford no decent opportunity for elaborate scenery. Shakespeare has kept his hold upon the world's admiration by the splendour and beauty of his poetry which require no embellishment . . . Imagination and fancy cannot be expressed by the stage carpenter.

The *Blackwood* critic thus joined his colleagues on The *Times* and the *London Chronicle* in condemning Tree's version and in yearning for less highly theatrical revivals of *The Tempest*, ones which would free Shakespeare's poetry.

Tree's production can be viewed not only in chronological terms as a turn-of-the-century revival but also, in terms of stage history, it can be seen as the turning point for a new era. Apparently Tree at least had intimations that twentieth-century producers would move in the direction of substituting business for machinery and would emphasize lighting rather than settings in Shakespearian productions. But his presentation also climaxed an era which emphasized spectacles and magical effects over the text. Tree, like major producers before him, offered the spectator a series of illustrations, pantomimic or scenic, accompanied by a full orchestrational and choral background. However, in 1897, Poel had demonstrated that simple music and simple staging could be more effective, if not most effective, where this play was concerned; Tree's lavish revival of 1904 thus inspired many critics to address themselves to this problem of simplicity versus elaborateness with respect to theatricality and *The Tempest*. By the turn of the century most critics had almost completely abandoned the position of their mid-century colleagues as they hailed the producers of less highly theatrical revivals as the true "innovators," concurring that simplicity was a virtue devoutly to be wished. And this consensus was to influence the staging of *Tempest* revivals in the first half of the twentieth century.[13]

NOTES

1. There were of course exceptions, notably David Garrick's 1757 revival of Shakespeare's text whch deemphasized theatricality.
2. The history of earlier as well as later productions is recounted in my unpublished doctoral dissertation, *"The Tempest*: A Question of Theatricality" (Evanston, Illinois, 1967).
3. Unless otherwise specified all theatrical reviews in this study are from *"The Tempest* Scrapbook: Clipping, 1777–1936," in possession of the Theater Collection of the New York Public Library. Reviews of McVicker's production are all for 24 June 1889.
4. Except when otherwise specified information on Benson's production is taken from J. C. Trewin, *Benson and the Bensonians* (London, 1960), pp. 71–4.
5. See Lady Constance Benson, *Mainly Players* (London, 1926), p. 94.
6. Unless otherwise specified citations concerning Daly's production are from the 1897 prompt-book (Shattuck, 33) in possession of the Theater Collection of the New York Public Library. For a more detailed account of this and other source material, see Charles H. Shattuck's descriptive catalogue, *The Shakespeare Promptbooks* (Urbana, Illinois, 1965), pp. 453–4. (Shattuck assigns a number to the listed source material and, when applicable, these numbers are cited in this study.)
7. Cambridge, Mass., 1956.
8. See Robert Speaight, *William Poel and the Elizabethan Revival* (London, 1943), pp. 89–92.
9. Reprint of this review available in *Shaw on Shakespeare*, ed., Edwin Wilson (New York, 1961), pp. 191–3.

10. Citations concerning Tree's production are from a transcription of the final prompt-book by Fred Grove, in possession of Folger Shakespeare Library (Shattuck, 39).

11. Burton's 1854 prompt-book in possession of Folger Shakespeare Library (Shattuck, 15).

12. "*The Tempest*: Souvenir Programme," in possession of the Theater Collection of the New York Public Library.

13. Since 1945 a number of professional productions of the play have been presented in England, the United States and Canada. While at this time it is impossible to determine with any historical perspective the relative importance of these revivals, a certain trend can be seen insofar as the majority of revivals tended to return to the concept of emphasizing aural and visual potentialities. While *The Tempest* has continued to be performed on the platform stage suggested by Poel and popularized in the early years of this century; nevertheless, more magical effects, more combinations of music and various sounds, and more scenic displays have been added.

Peter Brook's *Tempest* *

MARGARET CROYDEN

Peter Brook's "experiment," as it became known, was originally launched by Jean-Louis Barrault in Paris in May, 1968, under the auspices of the Théâtre des Nations, and later performed in London. Barrault had invited Brook and the Royal Shakespeare Company to organize a company of international artists-actors, directors, scenic designers (including Joe Chaikin, Victor Garcia, and Geoffrey Reeves)—to examine and experiment with some fundamental questions in form: what is theatre, what is a play, what is the relationship of the actor to audience, and what are the conditions which serve all of them best? As a frame of reference for this research, Brook decided to work on ideas from *The Tempest*. The play appealed to Brook because, according to him, it had always appeared on the stage as something sentimental and pallid. Among other things, he wanted to "see whether *The Tempest* could help the actors find the power and violence that *is* in the play; whether they could find new ways of performing all the other elements which were normally presented in a very artificial way. . .and whether the actors could extend their range of work by using a play that demanded this extension."[1] But most important, Brook hoped that by commingling foreign artists, he could achieve a synthesis of style relevant to our times, which could obviate the conventional passivity of bourgeois audiences.

The experiment was performed in the Round House in London, formerly a 19th-century station house for the end-of-the-line trains, and currently a center for Arnold Wesker's working class theatre group. The Round House is a circular building with an enormous round dome; one has to climb a steep flight of old wooden stairs to reach its entrance. Inside, the place is equipped with dressing rooms, rehearsal rooms, and offices. The "theatre" appears to be a

*Originally published in *TDR* (*Tulane Drama Review*) 13.3 (1969): 125–128. © 1969 *TDR*. Reprinted with the permission of *TDR*.

huge gymnasium; no stage, but enormously high ceilings, from which Brook had hung a circus-like white canvas tent. The only other "scenery": a number of low Japanese-type wooden platforms of various dimensions, jutting out into the open space. Stationed right, left, and diagonally are several giant mobile pipe scaffoldings with wooden planks, on which actors and spectators sit. At various moments, these scaffoldings, complete with passengers, are "rolled" or "flown" into the open playing area. Otherwise, the audience sits on three sides: on boxes, benches, stools, and folding chairs; five musicians (drums and percussion) sit parallel to the platforms. Most of the time the lights remain on—at full blast and very white.

Spectators can sit anywhere, and many choose the scaffolding—especially the highest planks. Before the performance, people mill around the arena: actors and audience are indistinguishable. But soon the actors vocalize, dance, play ball, do handstands, turn cartwheels, and limber up.

Finally a group appears in the center of the open space: they arrange themselves in pairs, stand perfectly still for a moment, and then begin the "mirror" exercise. This is combined with a low hum that grows louder and louder as the audience becomes quieter and quieter; we know the play is about to begin. Suddenly the actors "break the mirror," and run onto the platform. What follows is not a literal interpretation of Shakespeare's play but abstractions, essences, and possible contradictions embedded in the text. The plot is shattered, condensed, deverbalized; time is discontinuous, shifting. Action merges into collage, though some moments are framed, then, as in a film, dissolve and fade out.

The actors wear work clothes. Ariel, played by a Japanese actor, wears his native kimono; Prospero, played by an English actor, wears a white Karate suit. Both are thereby set apart.

Having broken the ritual of the mirror, the actors face the audience and display archetypal masks (made with their facial muscles) and correlative physicalizations. Accompanying these are animal sounds, grunts, moans, howls, whispers, intonations, and gibberish—attempts to find a correspondence between the facial, the physical, and the vocal. The "masks" are those of the people aboard the ship, just prior to the tempest; they mean to be essentially social as well as archetypal. (According to one actor, the masks were derived from a study of the seven deadly sins. Later, someone suggested the actors study the seven deadly virtues so that they could assume a mask-on-top-of-a-mask, as people do in life. The difficulty of creating contradictory masks is obvious: there was so much distortion that no mask was really clearly delineated.) While part of the group plays the passengers, others play the ship itself; the remaining enact the altercation between Prospero and his brother. Meanwhile, Ariel has been evoking the storm: he uses the sleeves of his kimono as wings with which he calls forth the spirits; his voice (a combination of Japanese and non-verbal sounds) and powerful Noh foot movements evoke the wind, rain, and thunder. As the storm increases, the shipwrecked crew moan: "Lost, all is lost," counterposed to the sounds of those in lifeboats, the crash of the ship as it sinks (the percussion instruments help), and the rest of the cast (a chorus) who echo key words. Meanwhile, Miranda and Prospero converse: she intones the Shakespeare lines—using no end stops. As she speaks, she jumps, runs, skips, climbs the scaffolds, and once appears on the runway on top of the tent about 60 feet up. The Shakespearean lines are delivered ametrically, the object being to imagize or abstract the driving force *beyond* the symbolic word—gesture and sound are central.

The crew lands on the island half-dead and half-blind. Miranda and Ferdinand meet, fall in love; as innocents, they touch, look (part of the mirror exercise), and make love in the rocking position. This is homosexually mimicked and mocked by Caliban and Ariel; other members of the cast in turn mirror Ariel and Caliban. The possibility that Ferdinand and Miranda themselves embody monster characteristics appears to be the implication here. (The "mirror" exercise is essential to the meaning of the performance: every image used in the production is either contradicted, counterposed, or mocked by the "mirror.")

The awakening of the near-dead crew is a fascinating sequence. They stir blindly. As if in "The Garden of Delights," they touch, smell, look, feel, and copulate—to the echoes of "brave new world" and "how beauteous is man." The islanders revel in sensuality, a primitive microcosm. But soon the forces of darkness are unleashed upon the "good"—Caliban is born. He and his mother Sycorax represent those evil and violent forces that rise from man himself regardless of his environment. The monster-mother is portrayed by an enormous woman able to expand her face and body to still larger proportions—a fantastic emblem of the grotesque. Running to the top of the platform, she stands there, like a female King Kong, her legs spread. Suddenly, she gives a horrendous yell, and Caliban, with black sweater over his head, emerges from between her legs: Evil is born.

Prospero tries to contain Caliban by teaching him the meaning of "I," "you," "food," "love," "master," "slave"—the last two words unleashing Caliban's apparent rebelliousness and innate brutality. Helped by the percussion instruments and the "flying" scaffoldings, he escapes Prospero, climbs the scaffolds, jumps to the platforms, rapes Miranda, and tyrannizes the whole island, only to be captured and imprisoned in the "caves" (openings between the platforms). The percussion accompanied by atonal music, begins again. Ariel moans, "Ah, ah, brave new world"; the chorus moans (or mocks), "how beauteous is man." Caliban escapes; the takeover of the island begins.

The islanders become monsters; the slave, Caliban, is now monster-master; he and his mother dominate the scene, enacting a wild orgy, mirrored by the company's fast and fluid sexual configurations. Caliban, large and fat, but somehow acrobatic, stands on his head, legs spread; Sycorax (also large and fat) stands behind him, her mouth on his genitals. Then they reverse positions. The others follow suit: fellatio, cunnilingus, and other variations of anal and oral intercourse convey a monster-sexuality, a Dantesque phantasmagoria: the "Garden of Delights" has been transformed into the "Garden of Hell." The entire cast forms a giant pyramid on the scaffoldings: Caliban on top, Sycorax on the bottom, holding Ariel prisoner. "This thing of darkness I do acknowledge mine" is the leitmotif echoed by the group as they prepare to kill Prospero.

Prospero is pursued and captured. He is wheeled in on a table, and then thrown to the floor. Now the group seems a pyramid of dogs: they are on top of him, they bite him, suck him, and chew him. The leading image is homosexual rape, Caliban and Prospero locked in each other's arms. All at once, there are loud obscene sounds—gulping, swallowing, choking, defecating, and farting. For a moment, everything is post-coitally still: the "dogs" lie spent at Prospero's stomach and genitals.

The tension is broken by Ariel's arrival; he brings ribbons, costumes, gay clothing—material things—to bribe the dog-pack. The group breaks into game improvisations, and the scene dissolves into Miranda's and Ferdinand's marriage ceremony, performed in Hebrew-Hippie-Japanese rites. On some nights, the rites are discarded for the Hokey-Pokey dance. The wedding over, Prospero says: "I forgot the plot." Each actor stops where he is, thinks a moment, then someone begins the lines from the epilogue: "And my ending is despair"; another picks up, "Unless it be relieved by prayer"; a third, "Which pierces so, that it assaults / Mercy itself and frees its faults." The verse is spoken in various rhythms, inflections, intonations, and phrasings—all of which mix until the sounds fade out, leaving the audience in stillness. Only the echoes of "... ending ... despair ... relieved ... by prayer ..." are heard in the distance. The lights do not go off, there is no curtain, the empty space remains quite empty ...

NOTES

1. From my interview with Brook in London, June 1968.

The Tempest
(National Theatre at the Old Vic on 5 March 1974)

PETER ANSORGE

> The Tempest by William Shakespeare. Presented by the National Theatre at
> the Old Vic on 5 March 1974. Directed by Peter Hall, designed by John
> Bury, lighting by John Bury and Leonard Tucker, music by Gryphon, move-
> ment by Claude Chagrin.
>
> Alonso, Joseph O'Connor; Sebastian, William Squire; Prospero, John
> Gielgud; Antonio, Cyril Cusak; Ferdinand, Rupert Frazer; Gonzalo, David
> Markham; Adrian, Peter Rocca; Francisco, Christopher Guard; Caliban,
> Denis Quilley; Trinculo, Julian Orchard; Stephano, Arthur Lowe; Master of
> Ship, Alex McCrindle; Boatswain, James Mellor; Miranda, Jenny Agutter;
> Ariel, Michael Feast; Iris, Julie Covington; Juno, Dana Gillespie.

The Tempest is Peter Hall's first production of a Shakespeare play since Macbeth, with Paul Scofield, in 1967. And it's being widely suggested that Hall's
intermediary flirtation with the world of opera has weakened his hold on the
kind of stage realism pioneered by the RSC in such productions as The Wars
of the Roses and Hamlet. Certainly the basic conception of his opening production at the National would seem, at first sight, to refer more closely to
Hall's recent staging of an intimate opera like Cavalli's La Calisto than to the
harsh political world, shaped from wood and steel, created for the RSC cycle
of History plays in 1964. In fact John Bury's raked settings for this Tempest
have been deliberately conceived as a means of conjuring up a dazzling series
of images drawn from the dream-life of the English renaisance. There's a
quicksilver Ariel, who descends from a bone-like trapeze to ensnare the island
visitors in a court of monsters who might have been kidnapped from a
Hieronymus Bosch canvas: a gaudily baroque Iris, who gazes at the lavish fer-

*Originally published in Plays and Players 21.7 (1974): 34–35. Reprinted with the
permission of Plays and Players (Mineco Designs Ltd.).

tility rite taking place beneath her brilliant rainbow in the sky: a Caliban conceived as a Mohican-like dweller in the New World; plus a group of extravagantly wealthy statesmen who fall into the hands of a powerful magician. Such stuff, indeed, as Prospero's dreams are made on.

Yet it would be false to assume, as several reviewers have, that Peter Hall has staged *The Tempest* as a mere "insubstantial pageant"—an extravagant product of the National's special effects department. In my view the production is soundly based upon the kinds of skills, and insights into a Shakespeare text, that we have come to associate with the name of Peter Hall. For, unlike a Peter Brook or Jonathan Miller, who will transform an entire play to suit a particular period or point of view, Hall's presentations have always tended to express Shakespeare's essential ambiguity. As Pinter's most consistent interpreter, Hall is not inclined to pull a play in any one direction. I stress the point in order to explain why several of Hall's most legendary Shakespearean productions to date (especially the David Warner *Hamlet*) have met with a surprisingly negative response from the first night critics and audiences. During *The Tempest*, for instance, I was struck (unlike almost every other reviewer) by Hall's subtle explication of the political issues at stake in the play.

John Bury's interlocking designs enabled the scenes to follow on from each other with remarkable efficiency, clarity and speed. Thus Caliban's first thoughts of rebellion, provoked by the dubious Trinculo and Stephano, were immediately succeeded by a scene in which young Ferdinand contemplates the pleasures of losing his freedom for Miranda's occasional company. Denis Quilley's powerful cries of emancipation ("Freedom, high-day *freedom!*") are finely counterpointed with Ferdinand's delight in his new-found condition of slavery. It brings that favourite Shakespearean debate of order versus revolt, liberty opposed to discipline, into the centre of the production. It's a conflict which John Gielgud's Prospero seems unable to resolve (he is, ambiguously, imprisoning and liberating the rest of the characters throughout the evening). At the centre of the brilliant masque, which he presents for Miranda and Ferdinand, there is a harmonious vision of order—but controlled by a Juno who closely resembles the dead Queen Elizabeth, suggesting a measure of nostalgia in Prospero's hierarchical dreaming. This ambiguity spreads to the final scene and the famous act of forgiveness. After circling his enemies rather suspiciously, Prospero finally grants them redemption—but he noticeably fails to greet his brother Antonio. In the final moment, the two brothers confront each other in silence dressed in darkly rich, identical costumes—clearly their conflict remains unresolved. And, in the epilogue, Gielgud's Prospero, in pained eloquence, begs the audience "to set me *free.*" Far from presenting Prospero as a weaver of empty spells and pointless spectacles, it seems to me that this reading of *The Tempest* (it was Hall, after all, who directed Tippett's *The Knot Garden*, based on the play) presents the magician as an explorer of the possibilities and limits of art—the fact that the imagination of order is by no means a reflection of its actual presence in life.

Gielgud has been fortunate in the choice of his Ariel—the executor of Prospero's art. Michael Feast's Ariel is a truly Protean achievement, a being fully versed in the pagan renaissance mysteries. Whether descending as a white Cupid from the heavens, or garbed as a Botticelli-like androgyne, addressing Ferdinand in a perfect counter-tenor, or inciting the clowns to further idiocies as a haunted jester—this Ariel never resembles the faceless ethereal spirit of conventional productions. His arrival on the mysterious banquet table is powerfully grotesque—a gnashing, bird-like instrument of Prospero's imagined revenge. Feast's final departure at the end of the play is stunning—a swift, sudden withdrawal of his powers, marking the running down of Prospero's own tempestuous mind.

Both Arthur Lowe's Stephano and Julian Orchard's Trinculo make imaginative, music-hall sense of the comedy—including a measure of naturalism in their performances in order to remind us of the darker implications of their deeds. In particular, Lowe threatens to turn into a mini-Macbeth at the prospect of becoming the ruler of the island. The Lords, a livelier crew than some of the reviewers have implied, are led by Cyril Cusak's Antonio, who bears all the cynical distinguishing marks of the kind of Shakespearean politician defined so expertly during Hall's regime at the RSC. Apart from Julie Covington and Dana Gillespie's singing of the blank verse as Iris and Juno, the rest of the performances reveal less self-confidence. Both Jenny Agutter's Miranda and Rupert Frazer's Ferdinand are awkward, clumsily glamorous emblems of sweetness and light—most of their energies went into a mastering of the iambics rather than an exploration of the characters. It's a pity that Denis Quilley's full-blooded redskin wasn't allowed to develop the political consciousness he was so excitingly gaining during the middle acts. Perhaps a closer reading of Leslie Fiedler's study of Caliban as Red Indian in *The Return of the Vanishing American* might have brought this interpretation to a more satisfactory conclusion.

Interestingly, Peter Hall is also out to make a specific, if controversial, historical statement about the staging of *The Tempest*—namely, that Prospero's magic was conceived by Shakespeare as a response to the theatrical innovations of its own day, the movement towards indoor productions. Artificial moons, storms and masques (as explored in *The Tempest*) had become a practical proposition for producers and playwrights. Hence the (to me) rather intimate, touching and romantic effect of John Bury's designs for the National production—a tribute to the birth of the proscenium arch and the discovery of stage perspective. Peter Hall has begun his reign at the National in a suitably magnificent manner.

Prospero, or the Director*
Giorgio Strehler's *The Tempest*

JAN KOTT

Right in front of the foot-lights stands "invisible" Prospero, back to the audience, watching the magic table covered by the enormous wings of Ariel-Harpia. While a terrified Alonso and the would-be regicides leave in panic, Ariel appears on stage. In his hand he is holding Harpia's apparel. He cocks his head, drops a curtsy, smiles, awaiting praise. "Bravely . . . hast thou perform'd my Ariel," Prospero cries from the audience. At the final rehearsal before opening night, Giorgio Strehler repeated that scene seven times. He pushed Prospero aside; none of his gestures seemed to him sufficiently expressive. Twice Strehler ran to congratulate Ariel and shake hands with him. The entire episode was only to elaborate a single line of Shakespeare's text. On that night before the opening I saw two *Tempests*, one on the stage, where Prospero puts all the wonders and all the terrors of his theatrical magic into motion, and the other in the audience, where the last theater duke of Piccolò Teatro di Milano usurped the part of Prospero. Strehler directed that *Tempest* with his back to the stage and to his actors; in the enormous, still empty theater he was playing a magus to his first audience: his fellow-critics and a handful of friends. "*Impossibile*," he was shouting, "if I manage to show half of *The Tempest* it will be a *miracolo*." But which half? Prospero's magic or the failure of it? The vanity and the power of an almighty director able to will the elements to obey him, or a bitter renunciation of an Art capable of recreating all of the world's history but having no power to change it?

*This translation appeared in an earlier version as "Prospero or the Director: Giogio Strehler's *The Tempest* (Piccolo Teatro di Milano)," trans., Barbara Krzywicka in *Theater* 10.2 (1979): 117–122. The revised version reprinted here at the author's request appears in *The Bottom Translation: Marlowe and Shakespeare and the Carnival Tradition*, trans. by Daniela Miedzyrzecka and Lillian Vallee (Evanston: Northwestern UP, 1987), 133–141. Copyright held by Jan Kott. Reprinted with the permission of Jan Kott and Northwestern University Press.

The frontispiece to Rowe's edition of Shakespeare's *Tempest* (1709) shows a three-masted frigate, its sails folded, being struck by huge waves. Zigzags of lightning shoot across a sky covered with dark clouds. Over the ship, whose stern is plunging into the sea, floats a tiny figure with open wings, holding a torch. Ariel was carried above the sinking ship as a ballerina hanging from a wire. After the Restoration and up until mid-eighteenth century, *The Tempest* was staged as opera-ballet. Prospero's island, where the drama of the Old and the New World is played out, became a fairy-land. In Dryden's and Kemble's adaptations the tragic themes of *The Tempest* were already lost: but for the first time there was discovered and presented a magic fairy-land which Shakespeare could not produce either in the empty "O" of the "Globe" or even on the courtly stage at Blackfriars. There are two theaters in *The Tempest*, the old theater of emblems and the new stage of illusion which Inigo Jones carried over from Italian pastoralle to the Stuart masque. *The Tempest* is the most Italian of all Shakespeare's plays, not only in plot, in the names of its characters, in the Milan and the Naples which he evokes. *The Tempest* is Italian in its amazing evocation of *The Aeneid*. But the most Italian aspect of *The Tempest* is its theatrical fabric, from Ariel's recitativo, Stephano's and Trinculo's *lazzi*, repeated after the *dell'arte* scenarios, to the Roman goddesses to the betrothal Masque. Giorgio Strehler had decided to bring the English *Tempest* back to its Italian lineage: Prospero was to return to Milan for the second time.

In the prologue, a huge transparent canvas drops down and billows out. A frigate with open sails is visible through the cloth. Sailors climb up the lines trying to save their lives. The mast breaks. The deck collapses into the waves. It was the most spectacular theatrical storm I have ever seen. But theatrical inventions are almost always the repetition of tradition. Strehler's spectacular storm was performed almost precisely in accordance with a well-known recipe which had been described in a mid-sixteenth-century treatise on theater. The orchestra pit was divided into three corridors with its floor shaped into mounds and hollows. "Operators" hidden inside the corridors walked up and down the mounds and hollows, pulling behind them wide blue ribbons which rose and fell like waves of a stormy sea. The Baroque *macchina* was moved by human hands. Strehler's first plan was to make the "machine" visible. Later he decided not to show it. Only at rehearsal—and this was one of the most beautiful "theatrical moments"—did I see for a fleeting instant the boys and girls carrying the blue sea on their raised arms.

The director of *The Tempest* did not disclose his art, yet he did not conceal his power. When in the second scene the frightened Miranda rushes in, crying over the drowning people, Prospero gathers her to himself, putting his left arm around her. In his right hand he holds a rod with which he slowly calms the waves. Prospero's staff, the wand of Mercury, was changed to an opera conductor's baton; the book of magic spells from the Renaissance library is a director's copy from the theater library.

The stage is an island, and the island is a stage. Prospero's island is a platform built of wooden boards nailed together, surrounded on two sides by the sea. Luciano Damiani's scenography is astonishing in its simplicity, consisting of a few elements, all of them rich as theatrical emblems. The wooden deck which, when cut in half and placed at a slant, becomes "another place" on the island, is at the same time a raft on the sea and a platform of a popular theater stage. In the center it is covered with sand. The magic circle is the zodiac outlined in the sand. Prospero, in a white outfit, apparently made of sailcloth, has an embroidered kerchief thrown over his shoulders. As soon as the magic incantation is over, the father and daughter shall fold it into eighths, just like the sheets hurriedly taken out of the house, which Goneril and Regan also folded into eighths and threw into baskets in Strehler's *Re Lear*. The raft-stage is also a props room. Miranda will lift the wooden lid and she will place the magic cloth in the chest hidden inside the platform. Prospero will take Ariel's costumes out of another chest inside the island-props room.

Ariel is lowered by the cable down from the opera stage "heavens." He falls in the sand, turns over on his back, rolls on the ground. Then he floats up again, glides through the air like a circus acrobat and disappears; only his legs, rapidly walking through the air, can be seen under the upper frame of the proscenium. He comes down again to sit on Prospero's shoulders. Ariel is not a spirit: in Prospero's theater "actors . . . were all spirits." Ariel's "substance"—and here is one of the discoveries of the Milan *Tempest*—is his theatrical body. Ariel's "humanness" is his theatrical profession. In a white tunic and white, flowing trousers, neither boyish nor girlish, having only a theatrical gender, Ariel is a Pierrot out of Watteau imprisoned on Prospero's island. Giulia Lazzarini has Pierrot's sad, sometimes ironical little face powdered with flour.

Ariel is obedient; he will play any role and is proud of his skill and his travesties. But at the same time he is scared to death of his acting. He yearns for freedom, and when Strehler-Prospero delays the moment of his liberation, he tugs at the theatrical cable to which he is tied as to a chain. The prop suddenly becomes a metaphor and a sign. In this surprising theatrical psychomachy, a master-slave bond is converted into a director-actor relationship. Strehler is, furthermore, a prisoner of his imagination, of this theater and of all the plays he has ever directed. In his *Tempest* Ariel is sometimes transformed into the Fool from his *Re Lear*. In Strehler's production the Fool and Cordelia were played by the same actress. The Ariel of his *Tempest* is a "theatrical" daughter of Prospero. He has more affection for Ariel than for Miranda. I do not blame him.

The theatrical interpretation of the text is a discovery of the proper signs. The sign of the magic stroke was always for me the sword suspended in the air. Strehler interpreted the text better: "If you could hurt, / Your swords are now too massy for your strengths, / And will not be uplifted." When Ferdinand swings the sword at Prospero, Ariel pushes it down to the ground with one little finger and buries its blade in the sand. Shakespeare's Ariel lulls the new arrivals to sleep with his singing, as Orpheus lulled Charon to sleep in Monteverdi's opera. For Strehler, the singing was not enough; he tried to give it a visibility. His Ariel lulls the castaways to sleep by throwing the sand in turn into the eyes of Gonzalo, Alonso, and his court. And there are other theatrical inventions. Ariel is first transformed into a "nymph o' th' sea." I had never before quite understood the purpose of this disguise, since Ariel was to be "invisible." Strehler's Ariel-Nymph reels Ferdinand in on a fishing rod from the depths of the orchestra pit.

An opening in the center of the platform island, covered with a wooden lid, makes up Caliban's cave. Before letting Caliban out of the cave, Prospero takes off his wide leather belt. The belt is a sign of the power of a planter in colonies of the New World. Slowly a pair of black hands rise out of the cave and take hold of the frame at the opening. With difficulty Caliban pulls himself up onto the platform-island. There is a strap around his hips, his hair has fallen over his eyes. He is a black slave who might, except for his fear of the leather belt, attack his master. Yet when Miranda steps out from behind Prospero, suddenly the face of Caliban changes. For an instant he is a desperately sad, almost timid boy. He has brushed his disheveled hair back from his face: against the background of a glowing horizon, on the bright, sand-covered island, he is a beautiful black youth.

There is one other brief moment in the Milan *Tempest* when a lyrical flow of poetry engulfs the stage and suddenly seems to permeate the figure of Caliban. Shakespeare gave Caliban a staggering line: "The Isle is full of noises." Ariel's music in the Milan *Tempest* is played on medieval instruments. Caliban hears the music and he hears Ariel's song. In the scene with the drunkards he will suddenly repeat Ariel's song. These are the only two instances in the play in which Shakespeare's Caliban—awakening from his dreams only to dream again, the "noble savage" of the Renaissance philosophers and the rebellious slave of *The Tempest*'s colonial metaphor—has not been trivialized.

Summoned forth in *The Tempest* are all the types of theaters that Shakespeare knew, from the Plautine comedy about two slaves—the clever and the lazy—to the baroque illusionary stage of the myth enacted. But they are never resuscitated for the sake of show. They are repeated like a counterpoint in music, once in a lyrical key and later in buffo. In two scenes with the buffoons, "this thing of darkness," born by a witch from the devil, is transformed into a comical monster from *lazzi* of *dell'arte*. But even in this grotesque transformation, the themes of tragedy return: Caliban swears upon a bottle of sack to be the true subject of a drunken butler, and kisses a bottle as though it were the Bible. Shakespeare is never afraid of a great parable. On the island of the New World, two drunkards and a slave from the plantation set out to kill a tryant. In this violent dramaturgy, the *dell'arte* scenario suddenly becomes a political tragicomedy. On the desert island, the drunken feast of rebellion is in progress.

Traditionally, Caliban has almost always had a kind of proto-human, animal-fish appearance. Strehler places across his shoulders the skin of a sea reptile with stuffed skull and fins. That totem-skin is to be a remnant of the times when Caliban was the king of the island or a tribal chief. Strehler unfortunately succumbed to the temptation of primitivism or "strangeness" in a quasi-"anthropological" and now-fashionable version. For this Caliban he added to the Shakespeare text, or rather "staged-in," some African or Voodoo rituals and made him hop around in a ceremonial war dance. This artistically wrong stylization contradicts the Renaissance vision.

Trinculo is the Neapolitan Pulcinella, Stephano the Capitano from *dell'arte*. In Milan's *Tempest*, the *lazzi* grow into a long and wearying intermedium of a dumb savage and two drunkards of whom Ariel, transformed suddenly into a clown, makes fun. In the Shakespearean *Tempest*, Caliban's rebellion was not foreseen and is the most awesome failure of Prospero's education. Prospero never sent Ariel to accompany the drunken lazzi. The "tricks" of Ariel playing on a tabor and pipe are merely the music which unsettles and warns. Shakespeare's Prospero is a director of limited resources who never abuses his power. Ariel is used by him for most important tasks. Strehler is a director who never has enough of the feast of the spectacle.

When the magic table disappears, Ariel—the she-bat with claws and enormous black wings—glides in and out of the ceiling of the stage. Tall waves are again beating against the platform-stage. The table vanishes, covered by wings. In the shimmer of stroboscopic lights, against the background of a large, billowing canvas, the black she-bat castigates Alonso and two sinners for crimes committed and predicts their doom.

But although Prospero praises Ariel for his recitation, the prediction is drowned by loud thunder. In this spectacular show, Strehler again departed from the classical images of the baroque theater, where Virgilian myths, antique icons, and the symbolic banquet reappeared. The wonders and the awe of that theater were both antique and Christian. Shakespeare's Harpia utters a Virgilian prophecy from the *Aeneid*. The table with food and drink is a Renaissance banquet as well as a Last Supper from which the Sinners were banished. It should have pitchers with water and wine and large loaves of bread on it. Shakespeare's usurpers go through the torture of hunger and thirst on the desert island.

The three men of sin give up their splendid garments as they escape in panic. Alonso will lose his crown. Ariel will pick up these Milanese riches and put them in the prop-room inside the island-platform. He will take them back when Caliban and the two drunken jesters return to carry out their attempt on Prospero's life. Pulcinella-Trinculo will throw the royal robe over his shoulders. Capitano-Stephano will put on the crown. Strehler wanted to repeat in buffo the symbols of usurpation and regicide. But in Shakespeare's histories, or even his comedies, a royal crown has never rested on the head of a clown. In the Shakespearean scenario, only glistening rags were hung out on the line by Ariel. When the water-drenched drunkards throw themselves on these, Caliban understands he is dealing with fools. He knows that Prospero's power is in the Book. But the book of Prospero is the director's script. For Strehler the operatic score is more important than a royal crown.

Strehler's Prospero does not want to part from his conductor's stick. In Shakespeare's *Tempest* Prospero drowns the book in the depths of the sea and breaks his staff in half after uttering Medea's terrible vows, as a prelude to the final scene of mercy. In the Milan *Tempest*, Prospero breaks his conductor's stick in half and tosses his operatic score into the orchestra pit at the very end of the drama.

Ariel's last service is to bring Prospero the insignia of the Duke of Milan, hidden away on the island during twelve years: a coat, a hat, and a rapier. In *The Tempest* of my imagination, the only thing left of the last dukedom is rags, eaten away by the sea water, while the rapier is brown with rust. In these rags the real Duke of Milan should stand before the usurpers wearing a cloth of gold and ermine, untouched by the ocean waves. Strehler's solutions are traditional, but, as in his entire interpretation and treatment of act 5, it is not a return to the Renaissance rigors or even to the baroque vision, but to a melodramatic, tame, and shallow nineteenth-century Shakespeare.

In this four-hour play, Strehler omitted the most cruel scene of the entire drama, where the actors playing Roman goddesses in a vision of the Golden Age and Lost Paradise turn into terrible shades of hunting dogs. At the finale of Strehler's *Tempest*, the buffoon Trinculo will sit at the feet of the King of Naples, while the repentant Caliban, watched by all the scoundrels who had been pardoned in the "brave new world," will return to his dark cave in the island.

Shakespeare's *Tempest* reverts to its beginning, so that everything can begin once more. It is a return to the time twelve years before the overture of the play, when Prospero, the Lord's anointed, was exiled from his dukedom and landed on a desert island where the rightful ruler, the Lord's non-anointed, was Caliban. Of all the possible endings in *The Tempest*, Caliban's return to his rock-prison seems the most false and revolting. When Prospero and the new comers from the Old World leave the island, Caliban should remain alone on the stage: deceived twice, he is richer in experience only.

In the last scene of the play, before the epilogue, Prospero frees Ariel from the wire-chain, but he is not departing to the cold freedom far away from the world of mortals. The free Ariel crosses over the ramp and walks among the audience. When in the epilogue Prospero steps downstage, Ariel returns to sit at his feet. In the profound reading of *The Tempest*, life and theater, two spectacles and two illusions, send back their reflections, like two mirrors. The opposition of theater and life was replaced by Strehler with the unity of the stage and the audience. Shakespeare's Prospero in the epilogue walks down to the audience not only to ask for the applause but to pray for absolution, mercy, and release from the theater. He returns not to the people, not to the audience, but—to the seclusion of Milan—where one-third of his thoughts shall be devoted to death. Strehler's Prospero returns to a Milan which is the house of illusion and glory.

This surprising, disturbing, yet touching identification of the director with the character of the drama, of Strehler with Prospero, is the source of all the revelations and enchantments of the Milan *Tempest*, as well as all its limitations. Shakespeare's Prospero knows that when he dims the lights the actors will vanish into thin air like spirits and the Paradise Regained will change into a wooden platform, but Prospero-Strehler also knows that when he puts the lights on, the wooden platform will be transformed again into the golden sand from which Miranda and Ferdinand shall gaze at the rising sun.

These two theatrical visions have two different messages: the reduction of the golden age to an empty platform lays bare the illusion of the theater and the illusion of the myth; the transformation of the wooden platform into a Paradise Lost is an affirmation of the theater, which recreates myths. Prospero-Strehler breaks his magic wand and throws it to the bottom of the sea, knowing that in an instant the stage manager in the orchestra pit will hand him a new conductor's stick. The Milan version of *The Tempest*, despite its beauty, has almost nothing of the Shakespearean bitterness and renunciation.

Translated by Barbara Krzywicka

NOTE

Strehler's *Tempest* was performed for the first time in Milan on June 28, 1978. Since that first performance Strehler has modified his staging at least twice. In the last version, at the ending, the whole structure collapsed into a spectacular nothingness and from this nothingness once again emerged the stage. In Strehler's world and ethos, the stage could perish only for a short instant.

A Brave New *Tempest*[*]

LOIS POTTER

The Tempest, as directed by Sanford Robbins for the Professional Theater Training Program at the University of Delaware in December 1991, was as much a brave new world for me as for Miranda. New because it made me feel that I was seeing the play for the first time. Brave, in Miranda's sense of the word, because it was stunning to look at; brave, also, in that it dared to take a positive view of a play that most recent productions have treated rather bleakly. Stephen Orgel's admirable introduction to his Oxford edition of the play (1987) claims that the theater is still dominated by the "traditional sentimental" productions—that is, those that present Prospero as a basically "good" magician and the play's final reconciliation as a genuinely happy ending.[1] This may be true; nevertheless, among the genuinely interesting versions of the play that I can recall from some thirty years of theatergoing, only two seemed to me to take this view. The first was Ron Daniels's for the Royal Shakespeare Company (1982–83) with Derek Jacobi as a saddened but apparently hopeful Prospero; the other was Peter Brook's at the Bouffes-du-Nord in Paris (1990–91), where the tall African Prospero (Sotigui Kouyaté) hummed gently to himself as he placed his magic stones in a circle, never doubting his ability to change the universe by sheer mental power. Apart from these, the productions that were for me most memorable have emphasized not Prospero's forgiveness but his aged bitterness (John Gielgud, directed by Peter Hall in 1973), his tyrannical colonialism (Graham Crowden and Max von Sydow in the two London productions by Jonathan Miller in 1970 and 1988), the deeply sinful nature of his dabbling in magic (Michael Bryant at the National Theatre, directed by Peter Hall, 1989), or his comical human falli-

*Originally printed in *Shakespeare Quarterly* 43.4 (1992): 450–455. Reprinted with permission of *Shakespeare Quarterly* and Lois Potter.

bility (John Wood, directed by Nicholas Hytner, 1990). Some directors have even treated the whole play as a compensatory revenge fantasy: Prospero has been an exiled ruler forever brooding on his wrongs and imagining ways of returning to his lost kingdom (Bill Wallis in Michael Bogdanov's productions at Leicester in 1976 and London in 1979) or a director forcing actors to improvise in accord with his changing moods (Timothy Wright in Declan Donnelan's, Cheek by Jowl production in 1988).

Of course, the productions I have been describing were British; it is possible that the "traditional sentimental" reading still *is* the norm in the United States and that the ex-colony and its ex-colonizer are destined forever to be polarized like characters in a Henry James novel, the one exclaiming, "O brave new world!" while the other replies, indulgently or bitterly, " 'Tis new to thee." But it has been a long time since the United States could be described as innocent, and I suspect that the pessimistic interpretations of *The Tempest* have another cause—or rather, two causes. The first is a distrust of any unproblematically presented authority figure. The second is the longstanding dominance in Western theater of an acting tradition that happens to be particularly unsuited to this play. Prospero is a magician, and his role depends not merely on what he says but on the effectiveness of his "art" as displayed in performance. The kind of director who wants to do a play like *The Tempest* is not always the kind who wants to create spectacular stage illusions. To underplay the magic, or make it look intentionally or unintentionally phony, has obvious consequences for our reaction to Prospero and Ariel, the sources of that magic. Even in productions that take a basically sympathetic attitude to Prospero, the most effective scenes are likely to be those that can be played with the greatest psychological realism, such as the one between Antonio and Sebastian in 2.1. Irony, allusiveness, and subtlety can be given full scope here, making us realize how much we miss them in the rest of the play. Or these qualities can be imported into other parts of the play, either by blurring the moral distinctions between characters or by undercutting their spiritual dimension through emphasis on physical mannerisms and detail. For instance, one of the most characteristic touches in John Wood's interpretation of Prospero came in the final scene when, putting on his Milianese garments, he ruefully discovered that he had gained weight since he last wore them twelve years ago. I found this irrelevance endearing rather than objectionable, having come to believe that a "traditional" reading of the play was bound to be empty and boring.

The peculiar quality of the Sanford Robbins production at the University of Delaware resulted in part from the nature of the group that performed it. As someone whose theatergoing experience has taken place largely in England, I have been surprised to find how much of the best theatrical work in the U.S. is done in university settings. Delaware's Professional Theater Training Program (PTTP) admits only one intake of students (some of them already professional actors) every three years. Plays in the first two years are double-, sometimes triple-cast, so as to give the actors the widest possible range of experience, and it is only in the final year of the course that audiences see the actors and the productions at their most mature stage of development. Meanwhile, of course, the students' several-year commitment to the program develops not only an exceptionally high degree of technical skill but a collective ethos quite different from that of even the most harmonious professional company. The youthfulness of the actors and their temporary freedom from the harshly competitive world of professional theater combine to make them accept the program's classical acting style, which subordinates the individual personality to what Samuel Johnson called "just representations of general nature." Asked in separate interviews what was the most difficult thing about playing the roles of Prospero, Ariel, and Caliban, the three actors each replied with some version of "Keeping myself out of the part."[2]

A corollary of this approach is a distrust of subtext. The PTTP is anti-Method; productions normally move quickly, and actors play the lines rather than the spaces between them. Until I saw their work, I had not realized how comparatively slowly most serious Shakespearean scenes are played in British productions, how important the Pinteresque pause tends to be, how much I normally expect to be told by bits of business rather than by what characters say. One reason for this is that British directors are less likely than American ones to alter the words of the text, probably because they would be detected more easily by the A-level students who make up a good part of their audience. Paradoxically, this respect for the text means that British directors will often deal with speeches that are either verbally or ideologically difficult by using nonverbal signals to clarify or subvert the apparent meaning. American directors prefer to cut or modernize. Thus in the PTTP *Tempest*, Robbins changed "want" to "lack" in the Epilogue, even though it broke the rhyme scheme, because he was anxious to avoid any ambiguity about Prospero's willingness to do without "spirits to enforce, art to enchant"; since an African-American actor was playing Caliban, he also made Prospero refer to Caliban's "vile stock" rather than his "race." Like most directors everywhere, he also made cuts to the text, each of which, of course, represented an interpretative decision. It seemed to me nevertheless that his production kept faith with all the words to which he had committed the actors. There was no unimportant line, no verbal wallpaper.

More important than all this, and harder to explain, was the production's willingness to face the risks inherent in any attempt to make us believe in Prospero's magic and the ends to which it is used. This does not mean that the play was softened or overidealized. The bawdy possibilities in Stephano and Trinculo—as, for example, Stephano's song about Kate—were fully developed. As Gonzalo made plans for his ideal commonwealth, Antonio and Sebastian, in the background, were sharpening their weapons. On the other hand, there was no attempt to introduce the kind of complexity that depends on creating vices or weaknesses without the support of the text. Ferdinand and Miranda were played as wide-eyed, open, and innocent; Gonzalo was gentle and humorous, not a bore. Stephano and Trinculo gradually became more quarrelsome, even dangerous, as power and alcohol went to their heads (Stephano drew a knife as they approached Prospero's cell), but their white Pierrot costumes kept them firmly within the comic genre to which they returned in the final scene. Ambiguity and complexity were located not in the personalities of the characters but, in issues raised by the play.

The sense of evil was essential, however, precisely because it was going to be transcended. All disturbing elements were firmly controlled by Prospero's magic, often symbolized by Ariel's presence onstage. Leslie Bisco's original score for the play made the isle full of noises from the beginning, when invisible choral music preceded the outbreak of the storm. Lighting changes and music occurred not only in the set pieces but also during many of Prospero's asides and at moments like Ferdinand and Miranda's exchange of vows in 3.1, suffusing the whole play with a sense of strangeness. The magic effects were unusually impressive, but, despite their beauty, they were produced by very simple means, and the staging emphasized their theatrical nature. The set was essentially a sketch of an Elizabethan stage, with upper level and curtained recess. At the beginning the curtain was looped up to form a sail, and Prospero, on the upper level with the traditional book and staff of the stage magican, was seen making the gesture that set the storm in motion. On the stage below, in flashes of lightning, the shipboard characters, in a circle, spoke their lines while straining against a rope; at the end of the play, many of them would find themselves in the same circle but no longer imprisoned. As the scene ended, the sail whipped back and became a curtain variously demarcating the entrance to Prospero's cell and other "discoveries"; Ariel manipulated it during the masque to reveal Iris (above) and Juno (below), and it parted in the final scene to reveal Ferdinand and Miranda at chess. The "strange shapes" of 3.3 were amorphous beings in sacks. The "quaint device" that enabled the banquet to vanish instantly was achieved by having Ariel himself crouch under what appeared to be a banquet table covered with a cloth; he had only to rise, flinging his cloak and arms backward, to become a winged harpy.

This interdependence of staging and individual performance was most striking in the case of Prospero. Doug Zschiegner's tall, Nordic, slightly graying magician—just old enough to have a fifteen-year-old daughter—was the embodiment of the skill and control that informed the entire production. His frequent demands for Miranda's attention were played not as evidence that she was bored by his narrative (she clearly was not) but as his way of underlining the most important facts in it. At this stage, Prospero was still able to analyze his own story, recognizing as he spoke that he himself had "awaked an evil nature" in his brother. The following scenes with Ariel and Caliban were also a reliving of earlier experiences: he turned his staff into the imprisoning pine in which Ariel had been living until his release; the half-naked Caliban made several dashes at Miranda, only to be jerked into agonizing contortions by another gesture of the staff. Prospero's revenge plot was calm and rational nearly all the time, but the dangerous nature of his delight in it came to the surface on several occasions. At the end of the harpy scene, the cutting of the last lines of his last speech gave him an almost gloatingly triumphant exit on "and in these fits I leave them" rather than the softer reference to Ferdinand and Miranda; later (in 4.1), with a similar glee, he looked forward to plaguing Caliban's cohorts "even to roaring." Miranda herself refers to her father as "touched with anger" and "distempered," but she also says that she has never seen him like this before. What the production set out to trace was the movement from this aberrant anger not merely to the norm but to something that went beyond it.

This process of change was indicated less in Prospero's own behavior than in the whole experience of the play, particularly the masque in Act 4. This was by far the best realization I have seen of an episode that nearly always disappoints in the theater. Though shortened and slightly adapted, it was relatively "authentic in its use of recitative, its processional element, its sudden transformations, and its stress on the themes or wedding and fertility. Juno made her entrance accompanied by two small children carrying flowers for Ferdinand and Miranda; when she called for the entry of the nymphs and reapers, wedding bells rang out, a maypole descended from above, and with amazing rapidity the stage was filled with song and dance. When Prospero ordered the dancers to vanish, they and the maypole disappeared as suddenly as they had come. The famous lines on the illusory and transient nature of all worldly things seemed an inevitable response to the brevity and beauty of what we had seen. Though Prospero went on to brood in soliloquy over his failure with Caliban, the play was now permeated with a sense of the smallness of human affairs *sub specie aeternitatis* that prepared the way for the abandonment of vengeance at the beginning of Act 5.

As in many productions, this moment was clearly signposted as a turning point, with a pause before and after Ariel's very slow "Mine would, sir, were I human." Prospero's subsequent explanation of his decision—

> Though with their high wrongs I am struck to th' quick,
> Yet with my nobler reason 'gainst my fury
> Do I take part. The rarer action is
> In virtue than in vengeance

—is precisely the kind of speech that an actor committed to psychological realism finds hard to play without hinting at some motive outside the speaker's knowledge: smugness or still-unconquered fury. The controlled and classical style of Zschiegner's performance made it possible to accept that a rational and virtuous character might be aware of his own decision to behave virtuously without being smug about it and might describe, rather than act out, the pain that had been transcended by this decision.

The classical style worked, if anything, still better for the characters most remote human realism, Ariel and Caliban, without endowing any of them with what is usually called "personality." Since it was obviously impossible for any actor to be as fast as Ariel is supposed to be, Lorenzo Gonzalez-Fontes behaved as if in a different time scheme from everyone else, moving very slowly, with the sinuous grace of an underwater swimmer. The uncanny sense of a creature from another element was accentuated by his androgynous appearance—shaven head, greenish skin, transparent filaments on arms and legs—and by the music that usually accompanied his entrances. He sang countertenor and spoke in a slow, high-pitched voice, except in reproving the "three men of sin," when he took on the voice of Prospero. Without any obvious expression, he nevertheless registered total absorption in the characters that his invisibility enabled him to overhear; his was the kind of love that Simone Weil defined as "paying attention to people." As the actor pointed out in discussion later, Ariel himself learned something in the course of the play: that Caliban is sensitive to the island's music, though without knowing that Ariel is the source of it.

To take an uncomplicatedly pro-Caliban stance from the beginning would have been to forgo the possibility of making the play as much a spiritual journey for him as for Prospero. Thus this character was at first a frightening spectacle, half-amimal with tufts of hair sprouting from his skin, roaring and racing about the stage in impotent fury. From this point the actor (Steve Harris) developed the role with considerable subtlety. On his second entrance he responded with fear rather than defiance to the thunder that he took to be yet more of Prospero's magic directed specifically against him. The contrast with Trinculo's totally pragmatic reaction to the same thunder was, of course, initially funny, as was Caliban's reverence for Stephano and his bottle. But audience laughter at the deep solemnity with which he kissed Stephano's foot soon died in embarrassment, as this laughter found its echo in the inane yelps from Trinculo and Stephano themselves. "Be my god!" was a moving line, in spite of the absurdity of his mistake, because the production was far more sympathetic with the desire to worship than with the desire to ridicule. In later scenes Caliban's increasing awareness of the inferiority of his new masters led to a growth in his dignity. In the final scene he at first seemed ready to return to his original relationship of terrified hatred toward Prospero, flinching when Prospero, on "This thing of darkness I / Acknowledge mine," knelt beside him and touched him gently. In his next lines Prospero firmly told him to go tidy up the cave—but he also put him, for the first time, in charge of someone else, and emphasized that there were conditions on which he might "look / To have my pardon": the word "pardon" was strongly stressed. As Caliban gradually took in what this might mean, he rose, for the first time in the play, to his full stature. He had, after all, learned that he was dealing with human beings rather than with irrational forces and had begun to see that he had some control over his relationship with them. Robbins hinted at the possibility that Prospero's acknowledgement of the larger view of life might transform not only him but others as well.

The greatest problem in this interpretation is of course the absence of any indication of repentance in Antonio and Sebastian in their last scene. However, Robbins had worked with the excellent actor who played Antonio (Lee Ernst) to create a figure desperately in need of change. Even the wit of his first scene seemed to well up from depths of unexplained rage and bitterness, or from that guilt which Gonzalo describes as "Like poison given to work a great time after." His and Sebastian's cynical lines in the final scene were played as a half-hearted and unsuccessful attempt to recapture their earlier tone. Locked in his private egotism, Antonio remained isolated, staring tremulously out front, as the rest of the cast went upstage into Prospero's cell. Prospero's "Please you draw near" became an invitation directed specifically to him, Antonio turned, started to walk past Prospero toward the cell, stopped, removed his ducal chain of office and placed it around Prospero's neck, turned away again—then, suddenly, threw himself on Prospero's breast. As they embraced, there was no doubt that Prospero had finally accomplished everything he had set out to do. After Antonio's exit, he proceeded to abandon his magic in a particularly spectacular way, first throwing down his book (which exploded, scattering its pages), then breaking his staff and handing the two pieces to Ariel and Caliban, who appeared on opposite sides of the upper level. As they disappeared, he began his Epilogue, which concluded with the reappearance of the dancers from the masque; the curtain call was taken in a context of festive dance and song.

Showing Antonio's repentance required more obvious "pointing" than was given to earlier episodes; this was also the production decision that could most easily be accused of sentimentality. The character's silence at the end of the play, like Isabella's when the Duke makes his semi-proposal at the end of *Measure for Measure*, can of course be taken to signify stubborn resentment, and this is how it has been taken in much important *Tempest* criticism during the last two decades. But it is only the naturalistic emphasis on the subtext that allows silence, in performance, to speak as loudly as words. If we restore the emphasis to the words themselves, we have to admit that, while neither character says yes, it is also true that neither says no: the overwhelming emphasis of the spoken dialogue is on forgiveness. More important than any rationalization, however, is the fact that the interpretation worked theatrically; that is, it created in the audience an almost frightening sense that, after all, it might be possible to believe in "a better world than this." I suddenly glimpsed something of what tragicomedy might have meant when it burst onto the European stage in the late sixteenth century—not the sentimental drama of wish-fulfillment that it sometimes seems to us but an attempt to bring a classical kind of drama within the range of contemporary audience experience and beliefs. One might describe this dramaturgy as post-Classicism. The cynical productions I referred to earlier can be seen, equally, as the rejection of conventional interpretations by a post-Christian society. But it seems to me debatable whether such productions any longer speak for their society, in the United States at least. What we have seen in recent years are the attempt to unite the capitalist emphasis on freedom with the socialist desire for social justice; the capacity for forgiveness shown by some of the hostages released from years of solitude and suffering; the general disgust with political and personal corruption; and the passionate public desire for an authority figure able to combine political astuteness with personal integrity. These expressed aspirations toward transcendence are unlikely to be fulfilled, any more than previous ones have been, but they have a real existence, and it is too easy to explain them away by positing a universal subtext of exploitation and greed. The great achievement of the *Tempest* production was that it not only spoke to such aspirations but found a production style in which to express them. Classical acting in this form, means setting a high valuation on control in speech and action rather than devaluing them because what lies behind them is, inevitably, inferior to the ideal. It also means seeking the highest rather than the lowest common denominator with its audience. If the young graduates of the PTTP succeed in steering American theater in a new direction, the recognized resemblance between politicians and actors, instead of being a source of cynicism, may become a means of rehabilitating both professions.

NOTES

1. Stephen Orgel, Introduction. *The Tempest* (Oxford and New York: Oxford UP, 1987), 87.
2. References to the views of actors and director of *The Tempest* are based on interviews that I conducted shortly after the production, videotaped for local circulation.

The Tempest in Bali*

DAVID GEORGE

PRELUDE

The Tempest had long fascinated me intellectually for its rich vein of philosophical polarity, its multi-layered metatheatricality. It needed to be explored
and tested in performance. But the very opening lines were already daunting:

On a ship at sea. A storm with thunder and lightning.

The undulating strips of green and blue cloth, the smart lighting and
sound effects which normally resolve the problem were never very satisfactory and ultimately counter-productive, for in the very next scene we learn that
this storm was caused by Prospero whose "magical power" is therefore
exposed already as mere stage manipulation. G. Wilson Knight has called
Ariel "Prospero's stage manager." The Indonesian shadow play offered a
potential solution to this opening scene, for an Indonesian dalang is credited
with the sort of magical power over the elements ascribed to Prospero: once
Prospero becomes a dalang, Ariel becomes light, Caliban matter, the Pros-
pero/Antonio rivalry the Pandawa/Kurawa rivalry . . . for two years we chased
the analogies and the parallels.

The Murdoch Performing Group first presented *The Tempest in Bali* to a
Western Australian audience, and in doing so trod the classical intercultural
path, for both those who doubt the ethics of the whole venture and those who
are its enthusiastic advocates assume that the audience for which such experiments are undertaken is never of the culture from which the borrowings have
been made. Craig, Grotowski, Schechner, Brook et al. have borrowed Asian

*David George, "*The Tempest in Bali*," published in the *Performing Arts Journal*
33/34, vol. 11.3 (1989): 84–107. Copyright 1989, *Performing Arts Journal*. Reprinted
with permission.

performance techniques for the sake of Western audiences, to the extent that interculturalism in the theatre is assumed always to mean drawing on one culture's traditions in order to present a new version of a play to the audience of another culture. Brook's now seminal *Mahabharata* used Indian performance conventions for a Western audience just as Indian, Japanese, Chinese, and Indonesian dramatists and directors have used Western performance conventions to revitalize their theatres and shock their audiences. Always the intended audience has been other than the one from which critics such as Gautam Dasgupta and Rustom Bharucha have questioned.[1] The questions remain pointed: can a Western performer so casually pick up performance techniques which take "the natives" years to master? Can these be read "correctly" or even usefully by a Western audience? If not, is this not mere exoticism, archaeologism, or cultural rape? Though Balinese theatre was originally used to revive a Shakespearean play for a Western audience, that was but a prelude: the ultimate goal was reached when the producton was taken "back" to Bali—a quite different matter, for instead of those performances saying: "look how another culture might present our plays," the offer now became: "look what we have learned from you and have made of it." We took a new step which made this production fundamentally different from other experiments, in what could be a productive way.

From the beginning our ambition was not to learn and use the shadow play or wayang wong in any "authentic" manner. What could be the point in that? We cannot be as good as them at it and must be different. Rather our approach was to be inspired by the other and then to tap that inspiration, not to reproduce and copy but to adapt and develop. The Balinese were presented with a shadow play which sought in no way to be authentic; it was meant to be experimental (the screen made of painted silks not plain canvas, hung in a cyclindrical tube, not flat; our "Arjuna" did not attempt to copy a wayang dancer but devised his own movement patterns from simulating marionette movements in a human—and very Western—body, and so forth). Consequently, the otherwise damning charges—of inauthenticity, failure to master the conventions, illiterate audience, etc.—no longer apply. Instead, with a mixture of arrogance and humility, we set out to play new variations on the conventions and then present them to their source for adjudication.

In other words, and summarizing what is *strategically* different here: instead of ransacking Asian theatre for clues, formulae, tricks and aides to revive our own waning powers, the inspiration of an Asian culture was used creatively to deconstruct a Western classic and then offered to the source culture for feedback. Instead of one—classical—*technique* being adopted and reproduced more or less correctly in order to revive another—classical—text, both text and technique were simultaneously and mutually challenged. And the judges were not a Western audience exposed at best to an exercise in exotic reading, but an Asian audience invited to witness a creative adaptation of their own classical heritage, along with an introduction to ours.

It is the audience which is always the ultimate test and therefore must be the key focus of our inquiry into the whole intercultural experiment. Our "two audience" format enabled us to test not only whether their signs and icons can blend with ours (Arjuna/Ferdinand, Sycorax/Rangda), enrich ours (Prospero/dalang/Betara Guru), deconstruct ours (Caliban the world turtle), or revitalize them, but also whether ours can then be read by another culture in culturally accessible, non-verbal modes. It also enabled us to test the extent to which Western bodies can be molded into Asian postures, and the extent to which emotional expression, body language, kinesics, and proxemics are transculturally readable. Lastly, it enabled us not only to test whether Asian sights and sounds could revitalize a Western literary classic but also whether, conversely, that literature could be subliminally understood as meaningful by an audience when supported by images from their own cultural heritage. What was involved in such an adaptation, what occurred when we took it back to Bali: they are the substance of what follows.

THE TEMPEST IN BALI: AN ADAPTATION

> *. . . new created*
> *The creatures that were mine, I say—or changed 'em,*
> *Or else new-formed 'em . . .*

That this experiment of the Murdock Performing Group should have focused on what is now called "East-West Fusion" is explained by our geographical position: separated by two thousand kilometers of treeless desert (The "Nullabor") from the rest of Australia, we have to turn elsewhere to alleviate our sense of isolation. To the West the Indian Ocean, to the North Indonesia: Perth is closer to Jakarta than to Sydney. Many would prefer it if our geographical neighbor were culturally more European but, by default, it is to a land of the Gamelan that we naturally look. It is a land with which we have had stormy relationships, for it is at once feared for its size, condemned for its betrayal of our democratic wishes, criticized for its intolerance of our journalists' interference, accused for its violations of our codes of diplomatic behavior and, at the same time, embraced as a venue for sunny holidays on a shoestring budget.

That combination of intolerance and condescension characterizes also the still widespread feeling most Americans have towards our own—now indigenous—Asians whom we still tend to treat as a source of cheap, exotic food and casual labor. The Murdoch Performing Group is currently a company of thirteen different ethnic backgrounds, but it remains a fact that Australia as a whole is still struggling somewhat reluctantly out of its white-only past towards a new multi-cultural society. More and more Australians do now accept, albeit grudgingly, that our future lies in Asia, an Asia we don't (but now know we need to) understand. The effort is for us to make, because most of our neighbors have abandoned us as an irrelevance. The task is both international and national, for Australia is committed to becoming a multi-cultural society and does need to reassure its neighbors that they are respected: hence there is more than academic interest in intercultural experiments which offer themselves as one potent means to those intercultural ends.

We in the theatre have, however, a second "intercultural" mission, for we are a house divided not just ethnically but also between theory and practice, between academic study and professional craft, and it is a gulf quite as wide and contentious as the other. The ultimate test of both "bridging" experiments is the audience. There are "big theories" to consider here: definitions of performance as audience-oriented behaviour, the complementary realization that drama theory in both the West and Asia has always been teleological, a "speculation on spectators."

But one does not need those big theories to realize that the crucial problem of interculturalism is the simple question: can the audience read what we are writing? This problem appears to question the very possibility of East-West Fusion and, even more generally, any profound Western comprehension of Asian theatre as such—until one realizes that the same problem applies historically within any single culture as between cultures. For if it is true that there are problems confronting any Westerner hoping to appreciate Noh or Raslila or Topeng as well as their native audiences, then there are equal problems in any *contemporary* Westerner appreciating "their own" Shakespeare or Ibsen or the Greeks.

All plays are written for particular audiences and therefore to be performed in particular cultural contexts. If there is a limit to the extent to which we can possibly jettison or bracket our own cultural and ideological baggage (all the assumptions, attitudes, prejudices, and beliefs which education in our own culture has caused us to accept as somehow "natural"), if there is a limit to how far we can re-program our minds to think in culturally different terms, then there is an equal limit to the extent to which we can somehow purge our minds of all the accumulated cultural conditioning which separates us just as much from "our own" cultural heritage as from any other culture. We can no more *be* an Elizabethan actor of a Shakespeare original than we can become a Japanese spectator of a Noh play.

The Tempest was written at a time when the "New World" had recently been discovered, when the Pope had divided it between Spain and Portugal; the age of Hieronymus Bosch, More's *Utopia*, Sidney's *Arcadia*, Calderon's *Life is a Dream*. "Radical" contemporary critics like to castigate Shakespeare and this play for its imperialistic arrogance, its contemptuous treatment of Caliban, a symbol to them of "natural man" and colonial slave. This is problematic already because Caliban's mother, Sycorax, had already usurped the island from Ariel; so who's colonizing whom? Such a "radical" reading is an attempt to make the play contemporary but it appears unable to do anything with Prospero and his magic. Prospero-the-magician can mean as little to us today as a dalang in Indonesia, and the question is whether some such other, contemporary culture can restore to us what our own cultural history has taken away.

We undertook the adaptation in the belief that this question was worth answering.

We began with the opening storm scene recast as a shadow play: Prospero toys with his enemies, manipulating the puppets much as Prospero manipulates everyone in the Shakespearean text. In Indonesia, it is believed that a shadow play can arouse natural forces, influence the natural world, and so the storm spreads from the screen to the world outside. Why is he doing it? In the play his motives are complex (revenge, dynastic succession) but one is to bring young Ferdinand to his island as a potential mate for his daughter: at the same time we undertook what became a fascinating exercise in finding Indonesian equivalents for each of the characters.

Arjuna early emerged as a natural fit for Ferdinand and that first recourse to the *Mahabharata* then supplied us with equivalents for the others (Prospero an amalgam of Yudistira, Abijasa, and Betara Guru; Miranda Titisari and Dewi Partawati;[2] Alonzo: Suyudana; Gonzalo: Durna. . . .) At first this search for iconographic equivalence was an indulgence, for there was very little likelihood that any Western spectator would be able to read the puppets' shapes and color codes.

Later, that identification became one of the things we felt we could place our hopes on for Balinese comprehension of our play. But it was not easy, since what we were looking for were transcultural character archetypes, and they do not exist. Heroic qualities are very relative to cultural ideals (Arjuna, for example, is usually danced by a woman, since he combines strength and male sexuality with grace; Prospero's vitriolic passion is incompatible with Indonesian ideals of wisdom). Bharucha and Dasgupta have, rightly, criticized those who see interculturalism as a method to uncover some elusive cultural "universals": our project recognized early on that what one finds are differences. "Difference" is, however, now sanctified by post-structuralism as a creative method, one which can challenge and inspire, not alienate and repel.

The second scene of *The Tempest* is as daunting as the first but for a different reason: Prospero's lengthy exposition to Miranda of their pre-history goes on forever: we resolved this problem (and at the same time motivated her distraction in the text) by supplementing his narrative with mime, the figures he refers to danced by giant, pin-spotted human puppets. These were modeled on Wayang Golek, three-dimensional wooden puppets. Their iconography is the same as the shadow puppets which necessitated not only making huge masks for them but also employing now an Indonesian dance teacher to train Western bodies (the "problem of the hips")—it turns out that bodies are as culturally molded as minds. We are not used to squatting and hence our pelvic regions are more solid and less flexible than required for Javanese dance. On the other hand, the inevitable angularity of our actor's movements did enhance their puppet-like quality.

Ariel then appears in our production only as light and a voice-over. In Australia we could use an elaborate "chaser" and "gobos"; in Bali we had to use a simpler system and translate all his words into Indonesian to provide the audience with some verbal access to the story, and locate magical power firmly in their culture.

If Ariel is light, Caliban must be matter. His costume preoccupied us for months. Conceptualized as matter, as earth, we would have liked to have him cover the whole stage, or rather all that part of it outside and around the small circle of protected space—the "island"—which Prospero has carved out. Inspired by such diverse elements as Dasamuka, Bedawang, the Goa Gajah cave, and the Balinese meru, Caliban eventually became a gigantic black blob of formless matter inside which he scuttled and slithered around the stage, emerging alternately in one of three masks: one made by Wayan Wedja out of parasitic wood which we had previously used for Lear because it was full of gnarled pain and grief, another Fool's mask, also used in Lear, and the third a single-eyed, phallic Shiva.

Prospero brings Ferdinand and Miranda together: to point the meaning, Ferdinand was brought on by Prospero manipulating a Wayang Golek Arjuna puppet. The actor had to match the puppet movements exactly until Prospero hands the puppet to his daughter to control, to educate, to tame. In the Shakespearean text, the education of Ferdinand takes the form of hauling heavy logs; in our version, these logs became the wood out of which the puppets are carved and the lontars on which shadow play scripts are written, so that his education now became initiation into the secrets of being a dalang. For he and Miranda are not only to marry but to replace Prospero at the end as a composite male-female dalang to face the "brave new world" of the epilogue. In the process of his education, our Ferdinand traced a fascinating path: we have reason to believe that, historically, Indonesian dance evolved from shadow puppets through marionette play until humans at first imitated puppet movements and then evolved into more graceful human dance. Our Arjuna-Ferdinand followed this historical line, being "born" in the opening scene as a shadow puppet, then incarnated and incarcerated in the body of a Wayang Golek which Prospero manipulates to control a human Golek, then handing him over to his daughter until he is humanized by her influence. A play of dynastic revenge is thus transformed into a play about the reconciliation of opposites: male/female, power/knoweldge, nature/art.

But our adaptation did not merely consist in finding iconographic equivalents and exploiting Indonesian theatrical conventions and techniques to create a sensual experience: from the beginning, the purpose of the exercise was deeper, philosophical. The really interesting analogy concerns the "magic" for in Shakespeare's time alchemy would have provided a Western philosophical background to the play,[3] and alchemy was similarly concerned with power, with control of natural forces and, above all, with the reconciliation of opposites. In Shakespeare's time, such a "mysticism" would have been at least credible; today it is either fanciful, historical, or needs a contemporary equivalent to be revitalized. In the text, this power of Prospero is pointed as being "theatrical": he controls and manipulates through illusion. In Indonesia the dalang—a wise man who is magically powerful and a theatre "director"— offers the perfect equivalent and so the exercise became an investigation of the degree to which alchemical polarity and Balinese cosmology meet, overlap, and divide. That exceeds the scope of this paper but does point to the conclusion of the original adaptation: the play "worked" in Australia but only in the sense that it suggested how it made sense in a neighboring culture. The most enthusiastic spectators were Indonesian scholars. And it was they who first suggested: you should take it up there, show it to them, they'll understand it . . .

A DIRECTOR'S LOG

Friday, November 20, 1987

Here in this island we arrived . . .

Thirty-two students and professional actors, muscians, and a television documentary crew flew into Bali. Everyone was looking a bit anxious—the sheer audacity of going to one of the world's capitals of dance drama and presenting them with our responses to their inspiration was beginning to sink in. The most anxious people were the television crew: they had been given a verbal go-ahead to film the production but nothing in writing: "Jakarta is still discussing the case." Jakarta had a problem. They had banned all Australian media after an article in the *Sydney Morning Herald* comparing Indonesia to the Phillipines: the Indonesian government doesn't want to hear about "people power" and the fall of corrupt governments with strong military links. But they weren't going to ban a multi-cultural television crew filming a Shakespeare play in Bali, just as they weren't going to give official permission to an Australian film crew to enter. We were all in no-man's land.

Both my co-director, Serge Tampalini, and I had been on earlier exploratory trips to Bali. We had made contact with I Gusti Agung Supartha, the head of the Arts Centre, a prince and foremost Balinese choreographer.

He was waiting at the airport with garlands of marigolds and frangipani. It was already raining.

Though it was dusk we wanted to show the company the stages. We had been offered two—one indoors, lit by neon: it looked as dingy-dismal as when I'd seen it before.

The outdoor (Kechak) stage was dark, unlit, but sitting there in the warm milky heat, it was the place we had come to perform in. Pak Kirana, the factotum Supartha had assigned to us, expressed his doubts about the possibility of performing outside in the monsoon season. "We haven't come here without believing in our luck." We sat and soaked in the atmosphere; Pak Kirana took Dede aside (Dede Sujatna plays Ariel, speaking his lines in Indonesian); he also choreographed the dance movements and will now begin his job as interpreter. Pak Kirana explained to him about the Pawang, a holy man: he can stop the rain for you, but he costs 70,000 Rupiah ($65). "Does he give guarantees?" "You can ask him yourself." I somehow already liked the idea of employing someone to mediate to stop a real tempest destroying the "tempest" we had come to raise. We will talk with this man.

Saturday, November 21

Where can this music be? I' the air or the earth?

I made a phone call to ASTI next door, was lucky, contacted I Made Bandem, the head, an international scholar—the first Balinese to write on Balinese dance and drama and get a Ph. D. Yes, they had a Javanese gamelan: could we come on Monday? Could we come over and just see it today? I had asked him to write the preface to a book I had been commissioned to write on Balinese ritual dance drama. It would be nice to talk about that too.

Pak Kirana lead us like geese through the rice paddy to ASTI; the television crew filmed the Australians encountering "their" gamelan—a classical set, not one they were used to. Was it free to use? I Made Bandem looks at the two teachers: "You could do without it?" Yes, it is free for our use. We organized a lorry then and there, paying an exorbitant fee but we wanted to have a breakthrough today and one gamelan is better than none. That evening, after many excuses for their unfamiliarity with the instruments, they played for us. We sat and smiled; it sounded so good; they were playing the same sequences but on different keys. We thought it sounded like it was meant to sound in our heads.

Meanwhile, Pak Kirana had alerted the Pawang; some of the actors scoffed but the romanticism of it appealed (and I had used bomohs in Malaysia with great success—and failure: they had helped us adopt our daughter by giving me a magic perfume to wave under the judge's nose but they had been unable to stop me being refused tenure for being "a secret admirer of things Chinese").

Pawang Giweng is a small, compact man with a serious-cheerful face (shades of a monk) and eyes that flicker and search for ways to respond in words. "What sort of guarantee can he give?" He can only humbly ask for the gods to spare our theatre space from rain while we perform. No guarantees from gods here either. But tomorrow, there is a big public performance—a Dramagong—in the large open air theatre and he has been employed by the Arts Centre to work his magic. We could go tomorrow and watch him perform and decide for ourselves. Done.

We went back to the open-air Kechak stage, an island on an island, a fusion of nature and art stuck in the center of one of the ugliest cities on earth, which is, however, also capital of one of the world's symbols of beauty. And one of those things happened which renews faith: Serge and I both sat and looked at the space and, though we didn't speak, we both realized that the set we had brought with us was mistaken. But it had been designed for a stage in our heads—a vision; now the physical space rejected it as an intrusion.

The problems were trivial; the only important one was that we would have to give up using a real motorbike for the clowns' entrance: they mime it so much better. The space was beginning to speak back to us and the dialogue was commencing. And we needed that: we had rehearsed vigorously and thoroughly before leaving, but we needed the injection of creative danger, the acceptance that we are here to improvise in response to what this place says to us.

Sunday, November 22

> *Be not afeard; the isle is full of noises,*
> *Sounds and sweet airs that give delight and hurt not.*
> *Sometimes a thousand twangling instruments*
> *Will hum about mine ears; and sometimes voices ...*

It's one of my favorite speeches and moments in the play: Caliban's poignant evocation of the dreams he has when the music of the island lulls him to sleep:

> *... in dreaming,*
> *The clouds methought would open and show riches*
> *Ready to drop upon me, that, when I waked,*
> *I cried to dream again.*

I always thought it a shock even in such an ambiguous play as this to put such lyricism into the mouth of a monster, especially after the clowns have reduced him to malevolent brutish evil.

We had pointed the scene by permitting our Caliban to strip back the masks he has been wearing until then and show his face underneath. It was a moment I had always waited for—so did Darrel, the actor, but for a different reason: he hated the costume for its heat, its lack of air, its weight, its oppressive stinking burden. At Sunday's rehearsal he finally collapsed under it and nearly passed out. Many people had, however, commented on how wantonly wasteful we were to put him in a mask at all, for the man has a face of great dynamic plasticity and was now desperate to be allowed to make it work as well as three masks. . . All right: we'll hang the whole huge cloak as a cave towards the rear of the set in the bushes: you'll still begin talking through the masks but then you can emerge in just a pair of black cotton britches and knee pads. Nothing else. Darrel is from Sri Lanka and has rich light brown skin and green eyes in a face full of bones and sinews he knows how to use. He understands the problem and the challenge: if the audience, for one instant, identifies you with a brown man enslaved and persecuted by this bunch of white imposters, we'll have to make a quick exit from Bali.

People had already begun to gather informally during rehearsals: suddenly I recognized someone I hadn't seen for eight years when he'd turned up in Australia as the last survivor of a *Commedia dell'Arte* group which had left Italy to wander East looking for the secret of universal comedy. Here he is, eight years later, on a motorbike. I knew he lived near by, knew he'd married a Balinese girl, had a son, taught at ASTI, performed whenever he could with Balinese companies as a clown. *Ciao, come sta. . . ?*

He is also very aware of the politics of the whole arts scene and warns that we must tread carefully: have you seen so-and-so, talked to so-and-so, have you offered a donation to ASTI for the gamelan, have you invited so-and-so, consulted so-and-so, got the support and sponsorship of . . .? I didn't really listen too carefully then; on that Sunday it all seemed to be running along so smoothly that I was quite unprepared for the intercultural shock which he was warning me about. Because "interculturalism" at this level is not just about artistic fusion and compromise and interaction: it is also about politics and economics and therefore, about power.

Pino advises us in favor of using the pawang and we go to see him, in a little compact house with a crowing cockerel, turtle doves in bamboo wooden cages, a sunlight porch on which he agrees to sit and be filmed for multicultural television. He then invites us into the back room, where he has his altar: tangled drawings, leaves, flowers, bits of cloth, candles; he goes into a light trance, chants, invokes, and suddenly reaches back and whips a flower from behind his ear and throws it at the altar, rapidly sprinkling holy water after it, then sits, meditating. . . Is that it? Yes. He is at pains to show us his receipt for this job: 100,000 Rupiah; he does not want us to think he is cheating us as foreigners or that this is something about which one can bargain. If we want him we must say, now . . . well, tomorrow morning at the latest.

That night, six thousand people turned up to see a Dramagong in the big open air theatre and it didn't rain until half an hour after it finished. Peter— our Prospero—said he could feel the humidity drain out of the air from about 6:30 that evening. He asked to be allowed to rehearse at less than full volume that night and the next day had lost his voice, and hence his ability to raise the opening tempest.

We had lights for the first time that night, not a dimmer board but a panel

with six on-off switches. They fused: the third time they did, the two Balinese
electricians ran away. They said they had heard laughter from the bushes at the
rear of the stage, then a female voice saying that these foreigners were dese-
crating a sacred space and that they, the electricians, should not be working for
us. They asked for a special ceremony of propitiation to be performed for
20,000 Rupiah. Every day from then on there were flower offerings on the
steps and in the centre of the stage.

The lights still fused, but the electricians fixed them. We had a company
meeting and voted in favor of employing the pawang.

Monday, November 23

> *This island's mine by Sycorax my mother,*
> *Which thou tak'st from me. When thou cam'st first,*
> *Thou strok'st me, and made much of me . . .*

This day was reserved for the official meeting with Supartha. We had not seen
him all weekend but had prepared ourselves for an occasion by bringing a gift:
a digeridoo. Peter had got one from an Aboriginal musician-friend and learned
how to blow a few sounds out of it. We were looking forward with some eager
anticipation to presenting it to him. SBS would be there, filming it and, in any
case, there was much to arrange—Supartha's Legong dance for the climax of
the production, much help with lights, a sound system, additional musical
instruments, shadow puppets.

We all went in: handshakes; Serge presented the digeridoo; Peter played
it, Ugo filmed it; Supartha gave a speech back and presented us with three cas-
settes of his music. We discussed the problem of using a Balinese dalang's
invocation at the very opening of the play. We had thought that it would help,
but Dede had already been warned not to use it, for it is magical and Supartha
agrees: there are some things foreigners may know but that Balinese should
not be able to understand. Then he dropped his bombshell: no official government permit has been received: he had warned us.

Time to think fast: the Australian Ambassador had announced his intention of coming to the show and inviting the Governor of Bali. I had stalled but
now saw that we would need such assistance. Two hours of phone calls to
Jakarta confirmed that there was a permit. By then, however, Supartha had
made other arrangements for his company to perform on Friday. "Maybe one
performance of such a play would be enough, perhaps Saturday would be a
good day: many of the students have examinations now and there would not
be a good audience for four days' worth. And have you consulted 'my'
pawang? He is very good: we always use him, so you should employ him."

We parted: there was a note from Steve and Daniel. They were stuck at
Customs—a bad scene. Come to the airport.

Dark glasses, trim moustache, big scowl, big desk, gold braided hat in plastic bag in one corner and a row of sporting trophies in the bookcase. No, the Customs Inspector does not speak English: he interrogates Ramles, a man we know who gets us cars and tickets and things. He is from Sumatra and the Government Inspector doesn't like him and is insulting to him, contemptuous, but we need him to translate. I stumble through lines about cultural exchange, government-to-government . . . He holds up his hand: I have been tricking you, I speak excellent English, I was educated in Washington . . . We discuss the excellence of his English and how to define his particular accent. I may phone the consulate to ask if they will act as guarantor. Their line doesn't answer. We must put up a guarantee. How much? 680,000 Rupiah. When do we get it back? He smiles: when all the papers have been properly signed in all the different offices and the set is on the plane back to Australia, then you get it back.

Tuesday, November 24

> *I' the commonwealth I would by contraries*
> *execute all things . . .*

I wake with Rangda in my head and a strange peace to know that this whole island operates from a deep awareness of pain, despair, self-obliteration as the necessary complement of creative exuberance.

The whole day is taken up by diplomatic maneuvers and rebuilding the set out of rattan and bamboo. The actors are left to their own resources, but there is already a buoyant mood, as if everyone had decided to take both personal responsibility for their own performance, and a general responsibility for the show. Jeremy (Ferdinand) and I had had a session in which we talked about "Pokok," a Balinese aesthetic and dance concept which means that an actor learns how to find a gesture, a pose, a position, a spot, what Brecht would call a *Gestus*: an iconographic concentration and expression of character which then becomes the "trunk" or "root" out of which everything else grows.

The clowns, however, are low. Having decided to omit all the scenes with Alonzo and company from the Balinese production in order to keep it down to the hour's running time we had been advised would be the norm, we had rewritten the clowns completely to supply them with the menace the play needs. Rewritten as an Australian Ocker tourist in Kuta Beach and an American filmaker, they had stolen the show from Prospero and his family in the Australian performances, and Prospero's voice was not getting any better in spite of the dosage of warm ginger tea. But the clowns just weren't firing here: they have realized what they are imitating and satirizing, beginning to understand the satirical (even political) role they are playing in recognizing openly the combined ridiculousness and real threat of Aussie tourists, of television culture. Suddenly it just wasn't funny to them anymore.

Wednesday, November 25

... Trinculo, the King and all our company else being drowned,
we will inherit here.

We began with a "re-motivation session." In performance every actor stops, starts, stands, points, faces, and walks according to a blocking plan. But before a performance, they need to re-motivate, convert all that into psychological motivations and needs and therefore a session where they walk, individually, through their whole part, asking every time why here, why there, why start, stop, stand, point, face, and give not a blocking reason but a psychological reason.

As *Commedia dell'Arte* derivatives, the clowns' original dialogue would certainly have been improvised, topicalized, and so we had no compunction about rewriting their scenes, and much creative fun in doing so. The trick was to leave all of Caliban's speeches as they are but rewrite the clown's lines around them to give a quite different meaning. In our version, Caliban becomes a symbol of Bali's exploitation by tourism on the one hand, and the new "world culture" of television on the other, with the additional element that this filmmaker was once an anthropologist, enabling us to make fun of earlier "imperialistic" exploitations of the island's culture. His plot is that he has come to make a Spielberg-type sci-fi film about a local magician who, through meditation, has lured a space ship to the island (the "tube"); the other clown's plot is that she is there as a tourist, wandering around zonked on juice and mushrooms. Both, in other words, have plots which parody the main plot, and more: we were aware from the beginning that in satirizing our compatriots we were also implicitly satirizing our own presence.

The clowns went through their part episode by episode, stopping at the end of each segment. Pino and I discuss, propose, and then do workshop variations with them, all the time seeking to provide them with hooks, with sure-fire hooks they can throw at the audience and be sure to connect. It means expanding gestures, holding poses, exaggerating mime, working with big faces, tongues, bottoms, hips. As their bodies tire, their spirits rise: by the end of the session they are exhausted but buoyant. There is not more than thirty seconds ever when they haven't got a hook to throw at the audience, knowing that the audience is there to fish.

SBS films the workshop and it will make a good little tape in its own right, a genuine contribution to Theatre Anthropology.

The actors are called for at 6:00 p.m. and all are on time; by 8:00 Supartha is still rehearsing his dancers and musicians—in effect still teaching them their moves! It is not the Legong we had asked for; rather a folk dance he has choreographed especially for us. As they learn their parts, it becomes clear that this dance, to be performed at the wedding of Ferdinand and

Miranda, has borrowed a number of gestures from them and incorporated them into the choreography.

Supartha has called Jakarta: the Ambassador cannot change the Friday date. Supartha is upset; I am polite but point out that it is his party and the Governor is his special guest. "I have advised them to invite you too—as my guest. We will pay the pawang for Friday; will you pay the pawang for Saturday?" Saturday was his idea. Yes, also shadow puppets, Golek stands, electricians, lamps, a Lesung: suddenly everything is available. It is now Supartha who has a problem: he is double-booked for Friday, having accepted the other engagement that Monday morning when he had all but washed his hands of us.

I realized then the difference between the way I am playing his game and he is. To him this performance was not the result of two years' intensive effort and hence winning this round has less significance for him. Or had, until now, when his own Governor was to be his guest and he the guest of his own Governor's host's guest. He had no real choice but to lose, but losing and winning are transient to him, like theatre. The tangible tokens of winning the power game—money, status, possessions—are like a play script, and a box of costumes or a video-tape, mere outward signs, inadequate tokens of the real thing, not, like a performance, given over entirely to time.

After an hour Supartha returns, in full Balinese prince outfit: his Joget troupe is performing at a FIAT convention and we are invited to witness it. We go over to the open-air theatre, climb up to the top of the masonry and look down—on fifteen exquisite girls dancing a Joget to an audience of overfed car salesmen. How old are they: the girls are aged between fifteen and eighteen: "my little eroticism," he whispers. They peel off into the audience, each takes a pot-bellied car salesman in an ill-fitting sarong and dances with him. It is both grotesque, ugly, and a terrible way to poke fun at the invaders. Supartha smiles and tells me his plans to make the village of Tabanan a major tourist center.

Thursday, November 26

> *If I have too austerely punished you,*
> *Your compensation makes amends ...*

The show that evening was one of the performances we dreamed of and still do. The set required the whole afternoon to brace but it was ready to hang the silks at 7:30. The goddesses rose out of a chaos of mythical fairytale creatures, up into the white light of the tube. The frangipani tree threw shadows on the other side: it was wreathed in Ariel lights which flickered also on the temple gateway at the rear. The tree was also hung with woven Penjer, threaded with frangipani flowers and marigolds. In front of the tube were rich batiks and then the magic circle of woven mats delimited by a ring of threaded marigolds. Jody and her team of Balinese kids had worked on it the whole afternoon. More frangipani flowers were scattered over Prospero's territory. Caliban's masks and costume, hung from bamboo poles, completed the other side of the set.

The play opens with a Prelude: Miranda is born inside the tube as Dede speaks the cosmic storm scene from a traditional Wayang Kulit play and Caliban activates his masks before he enters, slithering across the stage as Miranda emerges rubbing her eyes. They dance the first act of creative polarity. Prospero then begins the Shakespearean storm, performing it as a shadow play, ending with conjuring up Arjuna in a shadow puppet body. The romance is there but it is the clowns and Caliban who steal the show: when Darrel appears, the kids in the audiences shriek. It is, after all, just as well he is not performing in costume not only for his health but for the kids too, because they are genuinely terrified of this monster and love when the clowns enter and poke fun at him. The gamelan weaves and knits the scenes together, playing character-themes and mood-themes, the whole performance a sensuous blend of Shakespere for the ear, and Indonesian inspired and impoverished movements, costumes, masks for the eye. The fusion is often such that one forgets it had to be adapted at all.

The censor is there: the permit specifies that the play must be seen by the censor. But though we are advised by Pino to literally sit at his feet and respectfully ask for his criticisms, we just don't believe he's going to cancel it the day before the Governor comes. So we simply smile and say: anything you think is offensive and he smiles back and says no, and laughs. But there is not much time for discussion because the drizzle has begun, half an hour after we came down. The audience breaks away: about one hundred and fifty people that night, of which perhaps twenty are Australian and other tourists, the rest Balinese and we realize that we have actually done it.

Friday, November 27

> *There be some sports are painful, and their labour*
> *Delight in them sets off; some kinds of baseness*
> *Are nobly undergone; and most poor matters*
> *Point to rich ends ...*

The only real excitement was whether the Governor would like the clowns (and the Ambassador because the joke was on him, but he was watching the Governor), and whether he would be offended by Caliban turning his bum on him (suddenly I noticed—dear God, let Darrel be wearing red underpants because he's split the black trousers and there is something red peeking out when he turns his bottom on the Governor ... Irene does a quick repair job behind the bushes where Caliban lives). The Governor laughs at the clowns; afterwards he says: "It is the first time Westerners have come here and made fun of themselves for our entertainment." He likes the fact that some of us realize how ridiculous we are in their country and then went and shook hands with everyone, favoring the clowns and Caliban. The Ambassador beamed and patted everyone on the head and talked about a new era in Bali-Western Australian relations, where was Murdoch, and yes of course, he'd pay the electricity bill and thank you for a most entertaining... I am not going to give some big speech now about cultural exchange and intercultural activities as diplomatic tools or political priorities. There were people there that night who saw an aspect of the West they did not know even existed, who learned that not all Westerners are Kuta tourists or nosy journalists, but that there are Westerners who study Indonesian culture and are inspired by it and seek a creative dialogue with it.

"The first time Westerners had made fun of themselves for our enterainment": I'll sleep on that.

Saturday, November 28

> *... For I must*
> *Bestow upon the eyes of this young couple*
> *Some vanity of mine art. It is my promise,*
> *And they expect it from me.*

The performance that night was relaxed, joyful, technically excellent: some of Jeremy's work has spread to Lisa and the love scene actually comes off this time. The clowns are improvising, confident now of their part. When Cary turns up for the dress call, he is mobbed by Balinese kids who mimic his walk, his gestures; when they see Darrel, they run away, yelling out "brown monster, brown monster!" Some of them have seen the show three times and know when to go and get a drink, when to come back for the next clown scene. The scenes have great tension now because Darrel is determined not to let the clowns get the better of him, to retain his fearful malevolence throughout their ridiculous antics. He actually nearly missed the show: he and Peter had left the hotel at 6:30 and it was pouring rain, such a deluge that they knew we would not be able to perform that night. Within half a kilometer of the stage, the rain suddenly stopped and so it remained that night: a ring of thunder clouds and rain.

When we stripped the Ariel lights off the tree, we discovered that four of them had been stolen—souvenirs or talismans ...

Indonesian television is there: they want to film the whole show and show it on nationwide television. An audience of 100 million! The company agrees to the show. An extra performance on Monday night.

Sunday, November 29

> *... We are such stuff*
> *As dreams are made on ...*

We were due in Tabanan—Supartha's village, formerly the home of Mario, perhaps Bali's most famous dancer. The truck was late but apart from that everything went smoothly: the gamelan and actors clambered in the back of the truck with props, instruments for a mad ride to the village. This is the Balinese way to travel to a village show but our actors had to duck their heads to avoid having them chopped off by overhanging branches.

Supartha shows us round his village: it dates back, like his family, to Majapahit, the Golden Age of Bali Java culture. His ancestors are rulers, artists, dancers, again that mixture of powers. The highlight is his own Pura Dalem—Temple of Death: there is a special shrine to Taksu, the spirit of inspiration, genius. He tells us how, before a major performance, he sits and meditates in the garden underneath this particular shrine.

Four hundred villagers line the roadside, welcoming us. There is the stage we will perform on tonight: a large stone square island surrounded by a moat full of flowering lotuses.

We spent the day workshopping with Balinese dancers and musicians, in the process exposing our clumsy Western bodies. It begins to rain, the sky full of threatening storm clouds. Supartha is responsible for employing his own pawang today: he excuses himself and leaves. We go off to Tanah Lot, one of the two great sea temples in Bali: it is here I always wanted to perform *The Tempest* because it is a small island off the coast dominated by a temple. Maybe, in twenty years time, it will be performed here with giant marionettes in a *son et lumière* production.

When we return to the village, the whole stage is sopping wet; dark clouds hang in the sky. There are only two alternatives: the old cock fighting arena, covered, but dingy and with the stench of death in it, and the rehearsal space: small, cramped, lit by neons. We discuss the problem with Supartha: his mouth says that he has confidence in his pawang but his eyes say otherwise. We discuss the pros and cons, vote and come to a rational, democratic decision: the only place to perform is in the small rehearsal room. The crowd, however—four hundred of them—is gathering around the outside stage: have we really come here to be rational, sensible, practical? Someone says: "Isn't it better to change a bad decision than persist with a mistaken choice?" I have never overruled the company before but now I do. Interculturation is also about how companies are run, and perhaps this power-thing has gone to my head too: we are performing outside.

Within half an hour the gamelan has been set up, the screen rigged between the temple gates, the stage covered in marigolds and frangipanis.

Supartha gives a short speech and then, miraculously, the moon breaks through and the performance begins. And it is the one we have come here to perform: a magical mystery blending East and West. All round towering coconut palms rise into the now moon-drenched air. The lotuses in the moat open and in the inner circle Ferdinand and Miranda dance their love duet on a carpet of frangipani flowers.

And then it is over.

Surpartha asks if we are pleased and then says: "You must understand, both you and I must wear two hats. Today I could be an artist, work with you as an artist; tomorrow I must become Director of the Art Center again and you director of your people." He sighs, and we embrace farewell, there are tears in his eyes.

Our revels now are ended...

We performed for Indonesian television: I have not seen their version and I'm not sure I want to but it is not everyday that a small company is offered the opportunity to perform in front of 100 million people.

There remained the last financial haggling sessions, the last diplomatic dances, the last hassles with Customs and airlines, the last speeches, the last farewells. I went to Candidasa for two days rest, rented a little Balinese hut on the edge of the sea and sat, exhausted, looking out over a lake of flowering lotuses: the classical tropical idyll, as corny as the lines I endlessly repeat from Prospero:

> ... *We are such stuff*
> *As dreams are made on, and our little life*
> *Is rounded with a sleep.*

(Stop Press: the latest issue of the *Bali Newspaper* reports that, on February 14, 1988, *Macbeth* was put on by a Balinese company in the middle of the rice fields in Bona Kelod, Gianyar ...)

NOTES

The Murdoch Performing Group was founded in 1976, an ad hoc company of varying size and composition dedicated to testing out theoretical problems through experimental praxis. Among its "intercultural" experiments have been *Lear—the Monologue* and *Mishima: Confessions of a Mask* (both inspired by Noh), *Saint Genet*, inspired by Japanese concepts of "bana" and Indian concepts of "bhangi"; radio adaptations of Chinese, Japanese, Indonesian, and Indian classical and modern dramas, and a "Taoist" Brecht revue.

1. Bharucha, Rustom. "Peter Brook's *Mahabharata*: A View from India." *Theater* 19.2 (Spring, 1988): 6–20. See Gautam Dasgupta, "Peter Brook's Orientalism," *Performing Arts Journal* 10.3 (1987): 9–16. Also Rustom Bharucha, "A Colli-

sion of Cultures: Some Western Interpretations of the Indian Theatre," *Asian Theatre Journal* 1.1 (Spring, 1984): 1–20.

2. One Balinese lakon is as follows: "Dewi Partawati, a princess, dreams of Arjuna, tells her father about it and her desire to marry him. Her father was Partakusuma, king of the ghosts of Java. He summoned Arjuna and, when Arjuna expressed reluctance to marry the girl, cast a spell on him to make him fall asleep, and transported him to Java. When he woke, he was so taken with the princess' beauty that he agreed to marry her. After the wedding, Partakusuma conferred the island on Arjuna, killed himself and was reincarnated in Arjuna...."

3. On alchemy in Shakespeare's time, see Frances Yates, *Shakespeare's Last Plays* (London, 1975).

Tampering with *The Tempest**

VIRGINIA MASON VAUGHAN AND ALDEN T. VAUGHAN

Adaptations of *The Tempest* are almost as old as the play itself. In the 1670s, John Dryden and William Davenant's *Enchanted Island* took immense liberties with Shakespeare's script, as did, in the same decade, Thomas Shadwell's operatic version and Thomas Duffett's *Mock Tempest*. A trend was thus launched that has persisted through the centuries and has included philosophical, poetic, filmic, and theatrical adaptations. Many of those *Tempest* offshoots veer radically away from the First Folio's text by altering the plot and cast of characters and by adding music, broad humor, explicit sexuality, and lavish staging. Even if purists were appalled, the general public seemed to enjoy such tamperings in the seventeenth century and still does today. The specifics, of course, have changed appreciably in response to audience tastes and theatre technology.

Shakespeare's enduring impact on popular culture was apparent last fall in New York City when aficionados could witness three wildly different adaptations of *The Tempest*. Using disparate media and geared to diverse audiences, Bob Carlton's *Return to the Forbidden Planet*, Peter Greenaway's *Prospero's Books*, and Aimé Césaire's *A Tempest* demonstrated how varied late twentieth-century adaptations of *The Tempest* can be. Considered together, they also indicate that, while the colonial theme so prominent in *Tempest* interpretations during the 1960s and 70s still lingers, Shakespeare's most spectacular play is now more often the inspiration for visual display and fantasy than for political didacticism.

Of the three productions, *Return to the Forbidden Planet* is furthest from Shakespeare's original. In London, this science fiction rock musical won the

*Originally published in the *Shakespeare Bulletin : A Journal of Performance Criticism and Scholarship* 10.1 (Winter, 1992): 16–17. Reprinted with the permission of the *Shakespeare Bulletin*.

1990 Olivier Award for best musical and earned a cult following among nostalgic baby boomers who grew up with the rock-and-roll of the fifties and sixties. At New York City's Variety Arts Theatre, the audience seemed somewhat bemused but equally enthusiastic. Classic rock-and-roll punctuates the script; scarcely any of the show's music is original. The plot, loosely adapted from the 1956 science-fiction film, *Forbidden Planet* (based on *The Tempest*), requires no knowledge of Shakespeare's drama or of the film, though familiarity with both makes the experience more "intertextually" humorous. Prospero the mad scientist and his daughter Miranda have been marooned on a distant planet and are now visited by a space ship, commanded by Captain Tempest and crew. Ariel is the super-intelligent robot (highly mobile on roller skates), while Caliban appears as the evil Id inside Dr. Prospero and, concurrently, the lustier side of Cookie, the space ship's cook who pines for Miranda. This monster, generated by Prospero's desire for revenge against his wife, who set him adrift in space twelve years earlier, and by Cookie's anger at losing Miranda to the handsome Captain Tempest, threatens to destroy the spaceship. At the finale, the participants are, predictably reconciled and begin their return to earth.

What holds *Return to the Forbidden Planet* together is its flamboyant use of stage technology—lights, video, amplifiers, sound effects, smoke screens, and costume—and its reliance on talented, versatile musicians who render the score's rock music with high-decibel gusto. The pleasure of the performance is enhanced by three kinds of recognition: (1) seeing how familiar rock-and-roll classics can fit aptly and comically into the wacky plot; (2) discovering the resonance of fractured Shakespearean quotations from all over the canon; and (3), for sci-fi fans, recognizing time-worn technological conventions within this uncharacteristic format.

The music creates its own intertextual jokes. When the space ship hits an asteroid storm (the tempest in this extravaganza), the crew bursts into "Great Balls of Fire." As Miranda and Captain Tempest approach each other for the first time, the cast slips into a version of the Beach Boys' "Good Vibrations." Commanded by her father not to go near Captain Tempest, Miranda plaintively sings, "Why Must I Be A Teenager in Love?" And Prospero's estranged wife (who quips about "the Id that marches") is named "G-L-O-R-I-A, Gloria." After the spaceship successfully escapes the forbidden planet to the tune of "Wipe-out," Prospero sings "The Monster Mash," with the audience joining in. These musical extravaganzas are skillfully performed on electric guitars, drums, trombones, saxophones, and synthesizers, the musicians demonstrating incredible versatility as they move from one instrument to the other, singing all the while.

The fractured Shakespearean quotations seemed largely lost on the New York audience, but, for those who recognize them, their whimsy enriches the show. For example, when Captain Tempest arrives on the forbidden planet, he asks, "What planet, friend, is this?" The Navigation Officer replies, "D'Illyria, Captain." When the Captain first sees Miranda, he exclaims, "But soft. What light from yonder air-lock breaks?" Cookie, who also falls in love with Miranda at first sight, exclaims in Lucentio's lines, "Comrade, I burn, I pine, I perish, comrade, / If I achieve not this young modest girl." Miranda's love for Captain Tempest makes her rebel against her father, who asks, in the words of King Lear,

> But goes thy heart with this?
> MIR. Aye, my good lord.
> PRO. So young and so untender.
> MIR. So young, my lord, and true.
> PRO. Let it be so, thy truth then be thy dower.

And so it goes.

Equally delightful are the technological wonders of the Chorus narrated from a large video screen, the lights pulsating to the music's rhythms, the smoke, the robot's acrobatics, and the sudden appearance of the monster's tentacles from various spots in the ceiling.

Return to the Forbidden Planet is, in sum, a rock musical enriched by Shakespearean allusions, by a 1950s film, and by 1990s technology. Though some will be dismayed that Shakespeare should be culled for corny jokes and raucous songs, that he can be lampooned as the epitome of high culture in a popular farce is another sign of his staying power. This son of boundless travesty has been integral to the popular theatre since the early nineteenth century; it confirms Shakespeare's cultural versatility and persistence.

Peter Greenaway's film, *Prospero's Books*, is another spectacle that self-consciously appropriates Shakespeare's *Tempest*, but the intended audience is avant-garde screen buffs. Starring Sir John Gielgud in what may be his last feature role, *Prospero's Books* is a self-indulgent fantasy by both director and actor that allows Gielgud to play all the parts with Bottom-like enthusiasm and to recast the script with more concern for Gielgud's finale than Shakespeare's text. Thus, in *Prospero's Books*, Shakespeare's play becomes the magician's fantasy, a fiction he makes up and records word by word in seventeenth-century calligraphy as he sits among his books. Gielgud mouths the lines he assigns to each character—Ariel, Caliban, Ferdinand, Alonso, even Miranda. He controls all the actions and all the texts. As he composes, scene by scene, the camera samples the books from his library, displaying Greenaway's own masque of occult Renaissance lore and lavish artistic display. The visual impact of scenes reminiscent of Breughel, Rembrandt, Van Eyck, and Holbein among others, is too rich and exhausting to be absorbed at one sitting.

As the film progresses, the viewer (perhaps) becomes accustomed to Greenaway's obsession with frontal nudity and the numerous naked figures of Prospero's island come to seem natural in contrast to the absurdly dressed

Europeans who appear in three-foot wide ruffs and six-inch-high chopins. More unsettling and less useful is the strain of sadomasochism that runs through the film. For example, the camera becomes a voyeur, taking us to Claribel's wedding bed, where her genitals run with blood; in another shot, Prospero's medical books open to bloody organs and actual dissections of the human body. The eye is bombarded in this film with a wide array of violent and sexual images, many of them apparently gratuitous. Nothing links them to the rest of the montage to provide coherence or thematic integrity.

In this cinematic adaptation, Prospero's books are, at the end, literally drowned in a reflecting pool. Released from the magus' art, the characters can at last speak for themselves and complete Prospero's script. Prospero, in turn, can return to Milan, and—in a more serious intertextual joke than those of *Return to the Forbidden Planet*—*The Tempest* is at long last incorporated into the empty opening leaves of the First Folio.

In contrast to *Return to the Forbidden Planet*, where the audience need have no familiarity with Shakespeare's play, Greenaway's film would be meaningless to the uninitiated. Even to the experienced Shakespearean who appreciates Gielgud's resonance in Prospero's familiar lines, Greenaway's visual banquet is elusive, its meaning opaque, and its purpose confused. In this film, Shakespeare is exploited in an effort to create self-conscious "high art," an effort that largely fails.

The closest recent adaptation to Shakespeare's original is also the simplest. On a comparatively bare stage in the intimate Ubu Repertory Theatre, Aimé Césaire's *A Tempest*—like Shakespeare's *The Tempest*—relies on language for its impact. Its intentionally brief run featured an unpretentious, straightforward rendition of Césaire's 1969 play, translated from French into English by Richard Miller. Punctuated by Caribbean calypso music and African chants, the text's matter-of-fact prose conveyed Césaire's dry humor, a subtle irony that was especially apparant to those in the audience who knew Shakespeare's poetic version. Though Cesaire's idiom is contemporary, the sense is often the same as that of the dramatist's 1623 text. The Boatswain, for example, cries in Shakespeare, "What care these roarers for the name of king?"; in Césaire, he shouts, "Shove it! If you want to save your skins, you'd better get back down to those first-class cabins of yours."[1]

When first published in 1969, *Une Tempête* reflected the profound anticolonialist sentiments of its era. The current production's all-black cast highlights the conflict between white Europeans and black natives by using partial white masks (except Caliban). As the play opens, the actors are choosing from a variety of masks, each adopting his or her role to fit the selected prop. Ariel is listed in the cast of characters as "a mulatto slave" in contrast to Caliban's role as "a black slave." The setting is in the Caribbean (Césaire is from Martinique), and the discourse is dominated by questions about hegemony and racial politics.

Ariel longs for his freedom as much as Caliban does and is visibly shaken at the suffering he has inflicted on the ship's occupants. Prospero responds, "Oh, so you're upset, are you! It's always like that with intelectuals!"[2] Ariel dreams of a peaceful world where he, Caliban, and Prospero can build a new society:

> I've often had this wonderful dream that one day Prospero, you and I, we would all three set out, like brothers, to build a great world, each one contributing his own special thing: patience, vitality, love, will-power too, and rigor, not to mention the dreams without which mankind would smother to death.[3]

Caliban responds that Prospero is not "the collaborative type"; Prospero is the master, a man who seeks power and revels in its use.

Césaire's Caliban is angry, intent on getting his freedom even if that requires violence. After he consorts with the drunks Stephano and Trinculo, who think he is a "Nindian," Caliban realizes "What an idiot I am! How could I ever have thought I could create the Revolution with swollen guts and fat faces."[4] He determines to fight Prospero to the death, alone.

Prospero, by contrast, tries to reconcile Caliban, claiming that "in spite of everything I'm fond of you" and that "It's odd. . . . No matter what you do, you won't succeed in making me believe that I'm a tyrannt."[5] Rather, Prospero sees himself as the enlightened ruler, working to make everything right. But in this play, where Gonzalo's "guano" is Antonio's "birdshit," no one sees himself or his fellows clearly. Earlier, Prospero insisted that the Neapolitans must cede to his will:

> They wrong me by not eating. They must be made to eat out of my hand like chicks. That is a sign of submission I insist they give me. . . . That is how power is measured. I am Power.[6]

In short, Césaire's Prospero is self-deceived, and his attitude toward Caliban is consistently rooted in subconscious bad faith.

Despite Césaire's modernization of characters and language, his basic story line is Shakespeare's. The shipwrecked survivors come ashore; Ferdinand and Miranda meet and fall in love; Alonso is beset with repentance and guilt; Antonio and Sebastian's attempted coup fails; Stephano discovers Caliban and Trinculo under the gaberdine. But there are important variations. The wedding masque, for example, is not interrupted by Prospero's remembrance of Caliban's plot but by Eshu, an indigenous phallic god who "can whip you with his dick." Moreover, within Césaire's text lie post-colonialist assumptions about native culture, especially that, in Caliban's words, "I respect the earth, because I know that it is alive," whereas the Europeans think the earth is dead and "tread upon it with the steps of a conqueror."[7]

The post-colonialist theme climaxes this play, for, unlike Shakespeare's Prospero, Césaire's does not leave the island. He stays with Caliban and gradually rots away, while the fecund nature he had sought to conquer and control reasserts itself. He stays, as Caliban charges, because he's "just an old colonial addict." He can't give up the power voluntarily so it must be stripped from him gradually. As the play concludes, we see him losing his control and feel sure Caliban will overwhelm him eventually.

None of Césaire's wry humor or political edge was lost in the Ubu Repertory Company's rendition, the premiere in the United States of this play. The text was uniformly well-acted, from Arthur French's stern Prospero to Sharon McGruder's pert Miranda, to Leon Addison's gleefully devilish Caliban and Clebert Ford's pompous Gonzalo. The calypso songs seemed natural and spontaneous in the Caribbean setting. The costumes and sparse trees-and-rocks scenery were understated, allowing the audience to concentrate on the dialogue. Consequently, despite its overt political purpose, Césaire's *A Tempest* seemed the most true in spirit of these three adaptations to Shakespeare's original play. *The Tempest*, for all its spectacle, is rich in language and complex in ideas. Césaire chose to focus on only one of those ideas—the colonial motif—but he does so intelligently and tolerantly, rarely with anger.

For Shakespeare, spectacle was another means of probing life's complexities, not an end in itself. We suspect if he had been reincarnated in New York in late 1991, he would have loved the energy of *Return to the Forbidden Planet*, marvelled at Greenaway's visual imagery, and felt most at home at Césaire's *A Tempest*.

NOTES

1. Aimé Cesaire, *A Tempest*, trans., Richard Miller (New York: Ubu Repertory Theater Publications, 1986), 5.
2. Césaire, 12.
3. Césaire, 26.
4. Césaire, 63.
5. Césaire, 70.
6. Césaire, 32.
7. Césaire, 15.

Shakespeare at the Guthrie
The Tempest Through a Glass, Darkly[*]

RANDALL LOUIS ANDERSON

The Tempest. *Presented at the Guthrie Theater, Minneapolis, Minnesota, 13 October—17 November 1991. Director, Jennifer Tipton; Set and Costumes, John Conklin; Lighting, Scott Zielinski; Sound Environment, Hans Peter Kuhn; Dramaturg, Michael Lupu.* CAST: *Alonso, Peter Thoemke; Antonio, Stephen Yoakam; Ariel, Kristin Flanders; Caliban, Christopher Bayes; Ferdinand, Shawn Hamilton; Gonzalo, Richard Ooms; Miranda, Jennifer Campbell; Prospero, Richard S. Iglewski; Sebastian, Stephen Pelinski; Stephano, John Bottoms; Trinculo, Richard Grusin.*

> I'll tell you all my ideas about Looking-glass House. First, there's the room you can see through the glass. . . . [T]he books are something like our books, only the words go the wrong way: I know *that*, because I've held up one of our books to the glass, and then they hold up one in the other room.
> —Lewis Carroll, *Through the Looking-Glass*

> Now, Ariel, I am that I am, your late and lonely master,
> Who knows now what magic is: the power to enchant
> That comes from disillusion.
>
> —W. H. Auden, "The Sea and the Mirror"

Highly acclaimed as a lighting designer, Jennifer Tipton made her directorial debut with a challenging, provocative interpretation of *The Tempest* at the Guthrie Theater. *The Tempest* (previously staged at the Guthrie in 1970 and 1981) now joins *Hamlet* (1963, 1978, and 1988) as the only play to be reprised more than once among the Guthrie's twenty-nine Shakespeare

*Originally printed in the *Shakespeare Quarterly* 44.1 (1993): 87–92. Reprinted by permission of *Shakespeare Quarterly*.

productions. While I did not see its predecessors, this *Tempest* likely proved a radical departure from them, as well as a new experience for readers of the play. (One comment I overheard during the intermission neatly summed up the audience's general attitude: "I need to read the play again to see how I've missed all that's going on here.") Tipton knows, better than most, the power of illumination—not only to facilitate reflection but also to promote obfuscation; by selective illumination of the text, she provided a *Tempest* in *chiaroscuro*, its darkness grimly overwhelming the traditional assumptions and generic expectations one brings to the play.

Tipton is a close but, at times, an overtly programmatic reader. In particular, the generalizations expressed in her program notes became overwrought and attenuated on the stage:

> This play is about mirrors and shadows—about itself reflected brightly and darkly [cf. Sonnet 43]. *Each person represented is found within another or has characteristics deeply buried in the dark side of the other.* It is only when we face the mirror and are able to see our own shadows within and without that we can indeed become "all of us, ourselves / When no man was his own." [italics mine]

I suspect that Tipton's diction is pointed—that her attention to "shadows" is meant to invoke the rich multiplicity of meaning the word had to Elizabethan ears, signifying delusions as well as reflections, specters as well as actors. Her vision of *The Tempest* seemed to encompass, most of all, the phantasmagoric shadows that fall, to borrow from T.S. Eliot's echo of *Julius Caesar*, "Between the idea / And the reality / Between the motion / And the act" ("The Hollow Men")—the shadows of desperation and despondency that disconnect humanity from itself. Elsewhere in her program notes Tipton asserts that *The Tempest* "is an ecstatic expression of despair," which makes her earlier quotation of Gonzalo's discovery—how they found themselves "When no man was his own"—all the more troubling; in this context his commentary on self-awareness was not a celebration but a challenge. The questions that Tipton's reading raised with some urgency are not unrelated to Alice's familiar remarks on the optics of Looking-glass House: is our confidence in the source of the reflection—the play's normative interpretation as a tragicomic exploration of violence (natural and unnatural) and vengeance, its tragic potential defused by forgiveness, grace, and penitence—actually a manifestation of our own myopic self-delusions? Do we fulfill our wishes for a happy ending by imposing our expectations of romance upon a text that cannot support them? Or, ultimately, are all readings of the play merely illusory inversions of other possible readings of the play (dependent only upon which side of the mirror you happen to lose yourself)? This *Tempest* certainly encouraged the audience to reexamine its self-satisfied, secure notions of the play, but did not offer much firm, dry land upon which to stake any claim of determinacy.

*

The Tempest is a play that lends itself to the breaking down of conventional boundaries between reality and theatrical illusion and to the celebration of the invigorating potential of the imagination. To these ends Scott Zielinski's cold white light spilled over into the first half-dozen rows of the theater, physically incorporating the audience into the play and affirming, in turn, that the play invades the psychic space of the audience. John Conklin's set served at once as web and rock: freshly varnished planks of the stage accommodated twisted ship's rigging (into which was woven a neon lightning bolt that disappeared through a fire-scarred hole), a monstrous boulder, and incongruous seawrack (two rusty oil barrels), while a distorted steel beam hung precariously overhead, dangling a light fixture, a hinged panel of planks, holding a single chair and displaying a thread of white neon, abutted the rear of the stage. Most prominently, a large circular looking-glass was embedded down stage right, serving as both a reflective and transparent surface. All costumes but Miranda's (and those of the sundry strange shapes) were dark—primarily black or gray (the characters literally clothed in the shadows under which they labored)—and of a futuristic cut, not so much suggesting the timeless accessibility of the play as embedding it outside of any temporal experience.

In the opening scene Tipton exaggerated the fact that *The Tempest* is perhaps Shakespeare's most obtrusively self-conscious artifact: the mariners and the court party paraded onstage, scripts in hand, and took seats in straight-backed chairs (standing in turn when stiffly declaiming "the mischance of the hour"). In one of many alterations to the Folio stage directions, Prospero, Miranda, Ariel, and Caliban were installed upstage in 1.1, further blurring the line between imagination and meteorological reality. The storm itself was suggested only by Hans Peter Kuhn's sound environment, which welcomed the arriving audience into the arena with soothing sounds of the sea but which, two minutes before the house lights went down, changed to rising, raging surf. The audience learned immediately whose will was being done at sea: Ariel drove two rocks together to silence the storm and free the confusion aboard ship. The spirit then mingled among the travellers, enjoying their dismay and finally ripping the script from the boatswain's hands when he cried "Lay her a-hold." This last gesture of Ariel's was a deft touch: not only did it suggest the futility of trying to navigate against Prospero's (Shakespeare's?) plans, but it also symbolically destabilized the denotative, expository function of language at the precise moment that the text switches from prose to blank verse.

The interaction of Prospero with Miranda, Ariel, and Caliban in 1.2 deserves detailed commentary. Tipton did not represent Prospero as an evil colonial imperialist but, rather, emphasized his self-absorption and his disjunction from the natural world (i.e., Nature, on the island; politics, his *natural* office, in Milan), thereby manifesting his malevolence in his Art. By all indications the price paid for the bettering of one's mind is not enviable;

Richard S. Iglewski presented Prospero as a bilious practitioner of a magic not altogether white, not altogether benign. In 1.2 Iglewski functioned largely as puppeteer, asserting his mastery over Miranda and Ariel through gestures meant to have magical efficacy: he controlled his daughter with a combination of nervous twitch and hypnotist's sleight-of-hand; he drew Ariel against his chest (as if he were a magnet) and closed his arms around her when he threatened, "I will rend an oak / And peg thee in his knotty entrails." These movements seemed all the more insidious when set beside the power of Prospero's rhetoric, which seems sufficient to control Miranda and Ariel; here he added an unsettling physical component to his domination of them.

Prospero's early exchanges with Caliban were, by contrast, wholly reliant upon linguistic superiority and the psychological power of invective. It was painfully clear that Prospero was baiting Caliban to furnish diversion for himself and Miranda: to provoke response he derisively sang out Caliban's name and then addressed him much as one would a dog ("Thou earth, thou! *speak*"). The discrepancy between Prospero's answer, "There's other business for thee," to Caliban's "There's wood enough within," and his later sending him off to "Fetch us in fuel" is not immediately obvious; Iglewski, brilliant as *provocateur*, drove home the emptiness of Prospero's goading demands. Christopher Bayes's sympathetic Caliban—a dread-locked Caucasian in tortoise-shell glasses—was not so much ignoble savage as he was, by Prospero's standards, learning-impaired (and Prospero seemed guilty of the fault that if you persistently tell a student he or she is worthless, eventually that student begins to believe it). Caliban's inability to "know [his] own meaning" in the same terms that "good natures" (i.e., Miranda and Prospero) putatively know theirs—through language and, by extension, through Art—was employed here to reveal that his subjugation is intellectual and psychological much more than it is physical. While Caliban's sloth at first raised the magician's ire only mildly, Iglewski's wrath exploded when Caliban had the presumption to answer Prospero's vituperation with his own: he got Prospero's full attention by appropriating the mode of discourse that the magician jealously guarded. Indeed, his evaluation of Miranda and Prospero's tutelage—"You taught me language; and my profit on 't / Is, I know how to curse"—seemed here the feeble, painful taunt of a disaffected schoolboy. Similarly, his sexual interest in Miranda seemed at least as much a misguided plea for attention as instinctive passion. To intensify the depiction of Caliban's inferiority complex, Jennifer Campbell, in her confrontation with Caliban, put a particularly abusive edge to her otherwise meek, ingenuous Miranda. Throughout her "Abhorrèd slave" speech she pursued Caliban around the stage, striking him while he cowered and self-consciously covered his mouth with his hand. Tipton's most ingenious, original maneuver—and the maneuver with the most far-reaching implications—came with Prospero's dismissal of Caliban in 1.2: a deep, courtly bow from Caliban was not enough—the magician proffered his shoe to be licked when commanding "So, slave; hence." Not only does this action make sense (for how else would Caliban know boot-kissing is a sign of subservience to Stephano in 2.2?), but it also brutally highlighted Tipton's reading of the island's environment in which superiority is based on language and intellect.

Prospero remained a manipulator of language throughout this production—of his own incantatory language of course but, more significantly, also of the language of others. There was the growing sense that, on his island, the magician was the creator of all speech acts (and, thereby, creator of all the conspiracies he will show virtue in forgiving). Prospero's control was clear in several instances: Ferdinand spoke in unison with him when he warned, "I can here disarm thee with this stick / And make thy weapon drop"; Sebastian first delivered "It is a sleepy language" as if he were a 78 record played at 45 rpm, only to repeat the line at normal speed; each time that Ariel gave Caliban the lie in 3.2, Trinculo's mouth, as if involuntarily, formed the words that implicated him; throughout the "three men of sin" speech, Prospero knelt before the looking-glass (as if before an altar) and mouthed the entire passage in unison with Ariel; after Prospero exited in 3.3 and Ariel took his place before the mirror, Antonio and Sebastian struck out again at the shadowy "ministers of Fate"—gestures that were, significantly, also in the direction of Alonso's turned back—and spat out a few syllables of backward nonsense.

If we needed more explicit evidence of Prospero's control of the thoughts that grow on his island, it was furnished by his unexpected presence in 2.1; he patrolled the stage, magic book in hand, during the dialogue between Antonio and Sebastian. The value of the book was ambiguous: did Prospero need it to elicit, or to protect himself from, the thoughts of the conspirators? In the following scene Prospero carried the same magic book during the overtures between Ferdinand and Miranda, thus strongly reminding us that this was a book referred to for compelling and conjuring, rather than for remedies. We could work backward to the same conclusion by noting that the only scenes where Tipton kept Prospero offstage were 2.2 and 3.2—the scenes with Caliban, Stephano, and Trinculo. The only thoughts that seemed spontaneous—without Prospero's direct influence—in the entire play were those of these three as they planned their conspiracy. The attempted usurpation by Stephano would seem the kind of unwanted distraction that merited a convenient magical remedy, and when the time for such a remedy came in 4.1, Prospero's curses seemed extemporaneous rather than carefully studied.

In the sense that Prospero was represented as controlling the language and thoughts on his island, Tipton's thesis that the magician had some of his own "characteristics deeply buried in the dark side" of the accidental tourists held true. Her formula broke down, though, when one probed the production for signs of the new self-awareness suggested by Gonzalo. Many scenes were carefully choreographed around the mirror, but by play's end I was not convinced that any of the characters had any more profound, searching analysis of the reflections they encountered than did Lewis Carroll's Alice. At times, in fact, the mirror intruded on the play without any satisfactory resolution, as a few examples will make clear: Miranda turned to the mirror when admitting that Caliban is "a villain . . . I do not love to look on"; as Caliban exited and Ferdinand entered in 1.2, they opposed each other in the mirror; Antonio stared at his own reflection when proclaiming "I am more serious than my custom"; Antonio used the mirror to admire how well his princely garments sat while Sebastian assured him "Thy case . . . shall be my precedent." Each of these examples is contradicted by the character's behavior—Miranda herself treated Caliban villainously in 1.2; Ferdinand never quite seemed in control of the ardor of his liver; Antonio showed no contrition or remorse; Sebastian only grew increasingly officious—in short, the characters' reflections did not change the nature of the characters reflected. In two instances (both in the love scene in 3.1) the mirror seemed judiciously employed: Ferdinand and Miranda opposed each other throughout much of the "Admir'd Miranda" passage, joining sides when Ferdinand concluded "O you! / So perfect and so peerless, are created / Of every creature's best," and, a few lines later, Miranda stood alone before the mirror as she urged herself to banish "bashful cunning" and declare her feelings for Ferdinand.

An unfortunate casualty of Tipton's mirroring agenda was Kristin Flanders's Ariel, who, when "invisible," functioned predominantly as a reflection made manifest; attired in a shiny, black, and otherwise nondescript costume, she served as an unattached, roving shadow, draping herself in a veil for her visitation of Ferdinand in 1.2 and wearing a cloak and a ruffled collar during 2.1 (a preview of the cloaks and collars worn by the court party in 5.1). In 3.2 Ariel was a shadow in the more conventional sense: she crouched between Stephano's knees while he sat, standing when he did to walk before him in tight rank. This obtrusive costuming and direction had a lasting (and undesirable) effect, making the character seem to obey not Prospero's commands but Jennifer Tipton's. By extension, Ariel's interaction with Prospero and her interventions on his behalf appeared contrived and predetermined. The sense of disconnectedness was uncomfortably evident when Ariel asked "Do you love me, master? no?" Both the question and Prospero's answer seemed perfunctory, and there was little display of the affection possible to find between the two. Nonetheless, there was, in Act 5, one touching moment between Ariel and Prospero: helping to attire him in his robes of state, Ariel held Prospero's magic staff while Prospero put on his rapier; when he reached out for the staff he had so recently renounced, Ariel held it back (a gesture that prompted Prospero's "Why, that's my dainty Ariel"). I only wish that Kristin Flanders had been given more opportunity to display her own sense of the character instead of being subsumed in the director's concept.

Although Tipton exploited the possibilities of Prospero's magic book, she showed less confidence in treating the two supernatural spectacles in *The Tempest*. The harpy scene was visually incoherent: four figures, draped in white and wearing gas masks beneath white gauze, ushered in the banquet. Antonio and Sebastian rushed to break bread with Alonso, but when they split the loaf, it poured out a nest of rubber snakes and then disappeared down the center-stage hole in a burst of flash powder. (One night a woman sitting next to me nearly wrenched my arm off when she saw the snakes.) Ariel's harpy was clad in black and wore black rubber contamination gloves; a light was mounted around her waist and directed up at her face. Trinculo's observation that "misery acquaints a man with strange bed-fellows" was unexpectedly played out during this cheap magic-show: Sebastian cowered behind Gonzalo, and Antonio behind (the invisible) Prospero.

Tipton's strangest turn was her replacement of the masque in 4.1 with five sonnets spoken in turn by Prospero ("So oft have I invoked thee for my muse," Sonnet 78), Miranda ("As an unperfect actor on the stage," Sonnet 23), Ferdinand ("Mine eye and heart are at a mortal war," Sonnet 46), and Ariel ("When most I wink, then do mine eyes best see" and "Music to hear, why hearst thou music sadly?" Sonnets 43 and 8). This explosion of lyricism seemed prompted by four enigmatic, gauze-wrapped figures—masquers *sans* masque—who silently circled the stage with various illuminated polyhedrons in hand. Tipton explained this choice to me by saying that she found the sonnets "a succinct expression of a theater art." While sonnets *are* a mode of great self-dramatization, I would argue that, in this context, extracts from Shakespeare's sequence hardly conveyed the same metadramatical force as Prospero's masque as it appears in the Folio text. Further, given the intentions of the lighting design, it seemed especially contradictory to eliminate this moment of communion when the theater's performers and patrons are meant to be part of the same audience. Tipton's excision of the masque also betrayed her reluctance to sanction the movement from chaos to order—a reluctance to turn the tragic potential to happy ends. Indeed, without the antidote of a balancing theatrical display, the antimasque—the conspiracy, or its symbolic equivalent, the storm—was never satisfactorily contravened, leaving the harmonious resolution of the plot seriously in doubt.

Sonnet 78 was to me a particularly troublesome addition to the play. Directed at Miranda, the closing couplet ("thou art all my art") was not suggestive of anything positive: either Prospero here effectively pre-empted his later renunciation of magic (thus undercutting the sincerity of his forgiveness, since he presumably chose to abjure his staff and book as a symbol of his mercy toward the court party), or he revealed an unadmirable pride in the calculated control of his daughter's life and her sexuality. (There was an earlier indication of this: when his success was clear toward the end of the love scene in 3.1, he closed his magic book and clutched it to his chest.) In another production the viewer might not have faced these unattractive alternatives, but by this point in the production, Prospero's grimness had been so explicitly established that one could not hear the sonnet in any other way. I suspect it took Richard Iglewski a great deal of effort to embody Tipton's dark vision of Prospero. He was still trying to find his character when I attended a preview, but by the second time I saw this production, Iglewski exhibited an impressive, passionate understanding of the magician's featured dark side. When, for example, he proclaimed, "We are such stuff / As dreams are made on," it was with a quality of deep disgust that was not self-referential; the lives manipulated by Prospero's phantasms were "little" not in the sense that they were mortal but in the sense that they were petty. Equally unnerving was his response to the reminder of Caliban's insurrection, a reminder that drove Iglewski into such a frenzy that he nearly foamed at the mouth in anticipation of his enemies' arrival.

The discomfiting effect of the first four acts precluded the possibility of redemptive closure. Contrary to Portia's dictum, in this case the quality of mercy *was* strained, and Antonio and Sebastian responded to Prospero's offer in kind—conditionally. After the remission of his dukedom, Antonio petulantly turned his back to the court party, reacting only to mock Gonzalo's blessing of Ferdinand and Miranda with the same throaty, sneering laugh he and Sebastian directed at the old counsellor throughout 2.1. Gonzalo's remarks abruptly lost their risibility for Antonio when Gonzalo pointed to the quest for "all of us ourselves." Antonio's silence was ominous: I got the very real sense that we were looking at the once and future usurping Duke of Milan, for Antonio remained at the end as dangerous to the state as Prospero was unconvincing in his forgiveness. In spite of the boatswain's report—aided by Ariel's prompting with the script—that their ship (a wooden model carried by the shipmaster) was seaworthy, I left the theater feeling that the "three glasses" past merely filled the eye of an uncontrollable teleological and ontological storm that would never dissipate.

*

Jennifer Tipton's open challenge to audience complacency left the most abiding impression on me: as the program notes advertise, both the island and the stage of her *Tempest* were designed to encourage us (characters and audience alike) to get "so lost in the mystery of otherness that we find ourselves anew." But if the audience, as addressed in the Epilogue, is indeed the true creator and manipulator of *The Tempest*—if the audience is meant to assume the imaginative consciousness of the playwright—then I found myself unable to liberate *this* Prospero from the many hard questions that incarcerated him in my mind. Instead I brooded over a play that was no longer as comfortably accessible to me as it had been when I entered the theater, and the magician's *mal d'esprit* strained my willingness to indulge not only him but, eventually,

Tipton's whole interpretive strategy. The effect of this unwillingness could have been subtly instructive, making us ask how we might accord the presence of Shakespeare's great self-constituting work of the imagination even after it had begged for its release. The play did not, however, conclude with Prospero's last lines. Instead, after the Epilogue and after some nervous, tentative applause, Caliban took centerstage and, surveying the audience, removed, cleaned, and replaced his glasses (better to see either the island that reverts to him or, perhaps, those who were greater sots than he for applauding this wholly reproachable Prospero). We had been thrust into a position where we could not unquestioningly listen to the pleas of Prospero's Epilogue and were prepared to carry our unease with us, but Caliban's prolonged closing gesture seemed to question the audience's capacity to render critical judgment. Inevitably the subjective reconciliation of playgoing, rather than the objective reconciliation within the play itself, furnished the intellectual exercise of this production. For my part, unfortunately, I could not apprehend this interpretation of the play as occurring (to use the parlance of one strain of literary theory) in my own disengaged consciousness. In the end the ideas of this *Tempest* were too ambitious for its own good. While I admired Jennifer Tipton's courageous originality, that originality necessarily set itself against the constraints of genre, and thus functioned at the expense, rather than to the profit, of the text.

Tempest in a Smokepot*

ROBERT BRUSTEIN

George C. Wolfe's dynamic production of *The Tempest*, which played last season in the Central Park and has now moved to the Broadhurst, proves once again that Joe Papp's latest successor is a brilliant showman. There is hardly a moment in this New York Shakespeare production that is not alive with dazzling and spectacular effects. Bunraku puppets, Indonesian shadow play, Caribbean carnivals, Macy's Day floats, Asian stiltwalkers, death masks, stick dancing, magical transformations effected through a haze of smokepots. Don't look to spend any quiet time here. The stage is in constant motion. This may be the busiest *Tempest* in history.

It has the advantage of a confident central performance by Patrick Stewart in the role of Prospero, the wronged Duke of Melon (this actor's way of pronouncing "Milan"). Best known to American audiences as Jean-Luc Picard in *Star Trek: The Next Generation*, Stewart comes to the part with considerable stage experience, particularly in England (perhaps this explains why his bio is seven times the length of any other actor's). Although Stewart is clearly better trained for Shakespeare than William Shatner or Leonard Nimoy, his star presence nevertheless tilts the production. It's hard to believe that this cool self-possessed Englishman could be father to Carrie Preston's hyperactive Miranda or brother to Nestor Serrano's hot-blooded Antonio. Stewart represents a calm island of RSC acting in a confused sea of American multiculturalism. Usually, two worlds are represented in *The Tempest*; here I counted at least eight.

Alas, none of them is very deeply probed. Aside from Serrano's Antonio, a darkly brooding misanthrope with considerable emotional resources, few of the other characters display an internal life. Even Stewart left me relatively

*Originally published in *The New Republic*, December 4, 1995. Reprinted by permission of *The New Republic*, (c) 1995, The New Republic, Inc.

unmoved, though he certainly enjoys moments of transcendence, particularly during his renunciation speech, spoken with great suffering at the pace of snails making love. I would guess that Wolfe lavished more time on devising theatrical effects than on deepening character or clarifying action. This is understandable, given his need to hold a distracted spectator's attention in big spaces like the noisy Delacorte and the cavernous Broadhurst. But I left the theater thinking that, rather than being a transplant, this *Tempest* truly belonged on Broadway, in company with such other stage spectaculars as *Phantom of the Opera* and *Sunset Boulevard*.

In the tradition of current historical revisionism, Wolfe has interpreted the play as a critique of European imperialism. Not only Caliban but also Ariel behave with overt hostily toward their slaveholding colonial master. Because these black islanders treat Prospero more like a malignant Simon Legree than a benign Robinson Crusoe, lines like "So, slave, hence!" and "this thing of darkness I acknowledge mine" ring with new racial meaning. Something is gained in this interpretation. Something is also lost. Played by Aunjanue Ellis in what looks like a decaying Balmain gown, Ariel always seems to be scowling and threatening other characters when she is not hopping, dancing and twirling as if auditioning for Merce Cunningham.

As for Caliban, Wolfe's casting and directing of Teagle F. Bougere in the role strikes me as a major miscalculation. His head shaven and painted red (he looks like he's wearing a colorful bathing cap), Bougere is a slender actor with a winning quality, given to broad smiles, worldly winks and graceful bows. He'd make a fine Puck. I'd even like to see him play Ariel. But a smiling, worldly, winning graceful Caliban? In his effort to redeem the natives, Wolfe seriously underplays Caliban's brutal, lecherous quality. This "monster," after all, represents man in a state of nature (his very name is an anagram for "cannibal"). Wolfe also chooses to gloss over the fact that, rather than being allies, Caliban and Ariel fear and loathe each other, and that he almost raped Miranda.

And what a Miranda! Behaving as if she trained for the part by flipping between network sit-coms, Carrie Preston indulges in such goofy glandular mannerisms she manages to persuade us that the girl is not only ignorant but simpleminded. Preston is mismatched with Paul Whitthorne's lyrical Ferdinand, Trinculo and Stefano are simply tiresome vaudevillians. And the courtiers, with the exception of Serrano and MacIntyre Dixon's gentle Gonzalo, seem to be as stranded in their characters as in the Bermoothes.

What I did admire were the elements of physical production: Riccardo Hernandez's setting—a circular ramp, miraculously covered with sand after the opening storm at sea; Paul Gallo's shafts of pinpoint lighting; the thunderous sound design of Dan Moses Schreier. Barbara Pollitt's mask and puppet designs; Hope Clarke's lively choreography; and the usually unendurable masque of Juno, Ceres and Iris (played on stilts). All of Wolfe's design collaborators, in fact, have united to provide a visual and aural feast. And the epilogue constitutes a breath taking piece of stagecraft, as Prospero with no art left to enchant, speaks his lines in front of a disappearing set, revealing a naked stage wall illuminated by bare stage lights. But because of Wolfe's emphasis on racial divisions, a play about forgiveness is not sufficiently allowed to enjoy its reconciliations. Near the end of the show, Antonio refuses Prospero's hand, and Caliban almost clubs him. Shakespeare's isle "is full of noises / Sounds and sweet airs that give delight and hurt not." Wolfe's enchanted island is certainly full of delight. But, lacking sufficient human dimenson, it offers not much depth or warmth. (N.B. It behooves me to mention that my own company is performing *The Tempest* this fall.)

Listening for the Playwright's Voice
The Tempest, 4.1.139–5.1.132

ROBERT HAPGOOD

In a passage of 160 lines toward the end of *The Tempest*, Prospero experiences two quite different revelations, expressed in his "our revels now are ended" and "the rarer action is in virtue" speeches. This essay seeks to chart the processes by which he, and indeed the whole play, arrives at these moments and moves from the one to the other. By doing so I hope to make out the dramatic values latent in the passage, plus the distinctive features of style by which these values are rendered.

Examination of these matters can help to make more audible the playwright's implied voice guiding its interpretation. For although *The Tempest* is open to many interpretations, it is not so open as to be subject to just any interpretation. It is an oversimplification to claim as does Stephen Orgel in his edition that "all interpretations are essentially arbitrary, and Shakespearian texts are by nature open, offering the director or critic only a range of possibilities."[1] "Essentially arbitrary"? Partial, yes; but an interpretation becomes "arbitrary" only to the extent that it fails to heed the playwright's guidance. In *The Tempest*, this guidance is complex and supple, both subtle and challengingly bold. Certainly the playwright offers "a range of possibilities." They are so numerous as to seem infinite. Yet plenitude is not infinitude. The playwright does not offer "*only* a range of possibilities." The large degree of freedom he offers his interpreters, on-stage and off, is placed within limits and emphases that are indicated in his text.

These limits and emphases are variously defined, according to the dramatic element concerned. As discussed in my *Shakespeare the Theatre-Poet*, the playwright's guidance is most evident and definite in the play's action—in what the characters do.[2] There is no doubt about the importance of this passage, for it includes decisive developments that bring all the strands of his plot to their penultimate phases, awaiting only their completion in the finale. Their momentum is powerfully propelled by such traditional dramatic intensifiers as surprise (at Prospero's interruption of his masque), suspense (as to how far he will go in his retaliation against his enemies), and sudden reversal (as his fury turns to self-restraint). Yet these intense moments do not preclude philosophical reflection (4.1.148–58; 5.1.20–32), elaborated narration (4.1.169–84; 5.1.8–17), or bawdy word-play (4.1.235–9). The characteristic rhythm of action in this passage is of a spurt of hurried activity followed by a leisurely glide or pause.

Large patterns in stage movement and dialog are the next most reliable sources of authorial guidance. Choreographically, the play begins with two groupings: the mainlanders on the ship and the islanders. At Prospero's command the mainlanders are then "dispersed" (1.2.220): Ferdinand is at first alone; Stephano and Trinculo make a second group; Alonso and the other lords a third; and the mariners a fourth. These groupings remain identifiable throughout the play, but with significant subdivisions, defections, and combinations. Antonio and Sebastian make a twosome separate from the other lords. Rebelling against Prospero, Caliban joins Stephano and Trinculo. In the finale dispersal gives way to convergence as Prospero brings all the characters together outside his cell, with only self-isolated Antonio and Sebastian holding back from the general spirit of reconciliation. In the passage to be analyzed, this coming together has already begun. In their previous scene together (3.1) Ferdinand and Miranda privately plighted their troth: he gave her his hand and she gave him hers (89–90); at the beginning of 4.1, Prospero is added to the new alignment as he formally gives his daughter as a gift to Ferdinand's hand (5–14). Although physically Caliban is driven off with the others at the end of the scene, his disillusionment with Stephano here begins his eventual return to Prospero.

In its dialog *The Tempest* like each of Shakespeare's other plays develops a distinctive complex of themes. His perennial concern with illusion and reality is manifested in many aspects—magical shows, dreams, liquor, symbolic clothing, memory, romantic love—with a fascination for the strange and wonderful that exceeds even that of *A Midsummer Night's Dream*. Art in general receives special emphasis, whether in magic, books and education (the "liberal arts"—1.2.73), dance, and music (an exceptional number of songs contrasts with an exceptional amount of loud noise). Nature is as always an important theme, distinguished here by its emphasis on the elements of air, earth, fire, and water and its subjectivity: to Adrian the island air "breathes upon us here most sweetly," and to Gonzalo the "lush and lusty" grass is strikingly green; to Antonio and Sebastian the air seems "perfumed by a fen" and the ground "tawny" (2.1.46–53). Time and timing are even more than customarily important ("now" recurs frequently); the influence of Fortune and providence is lightly suggested. In the realm of public conduct, politics is as usual a central focus, involving issues of tyranny, rebellion, usurpation, made unique by the play's awareness of the differing ways of the mainland court as compared with those of the sea and the isle. In personal conduct, instances recur of anger and pity, suffering and joy, the noble and the vile or monstrous, chastity and lust, reason and madness or drunkenness, dominance and subservience, loss and recovery, confinement and release or freedom, constancy and change. Instances of all these motifs are to be found in the passage under consideration; such thematic concentration is one reason it stands out. In particular, each of Prospero's speeches of revelation takes part in a motif extensively developed in the dialog, concerning respectively the changeableness of existence and the importance of human fellow-feeling. Remarkably, both of these motifs have hitherto been largely delineated by other characters: Prospero's revelations do not derive from an extended progression in his own thought; instead they advance a general process of discovery being worked out by the play as a whole.

As usual in Shakespeare the dialog of *The Tempest* is distinguished by certain iterative modes of speech. The play is full of fierce maledictions, of curses and caustic insults; where Caliban is concerned, even Miranda joins in the vituperation (1.2.350–61). In contrast, the pleas for mercy and expressions of affection, comfort, and cheer stand out. Among these the two revelations are given the special emphasis that comes from repetition. Prospero's "revels now are ended" speech reassuring Ferdinand about the departure of the spirit-actors chimes with Caliban's earlier reassurance to the bewildered Stephano and Trinculo that "the isle is full of noises" (3.2.133–41) while in the face of Prospero's fury Ariel's intercession on behalf of Gonzalo and the others chimes with Miranda's earlier pleas to Prospero for pity toward the ship-wrecked victims of the tempest he has fomented: in both cases he assures the compassionate pleaders of his own compassion.

These then are the large features of *The Tempest* in which the playwright's voice is most clearly audible. They provide guidelines for understanding the aspects of the play that are most open to interpretation: characterization, individual line-readings, and overall meaning. Where characterization is concerned, for example, the plot-structure helps to confirm the centrality of Prospero throughout, even though, apart from the second and last scenes, Prospero does not speak a great many lines. For in this passage, as elsewhere, it is he who with the aid of Ariel is the key figure in all the plot-strands and holds them together.

I. THE ROLE OF PROSPERO

Something about Prospero has polarized his interpreters, inclining them either to glorify or vilify him. Is it because he is so emphatically an Authority Figure in his own eyes? In his dukedom he was like King Lear in assuming that his absolute sovereignty would prevail even though he did not exercise it; on the isle, he has no doubt that he is rightly the "lord" of it (1.2.457; 5.1.162); in his family he is lovingly patriarchal. To Dowden and his many followers, he was seen as a philosopher king, benign and serene, uniting wisdom with power, a view its later critics have found "sentimental."[3] More recently what was earlier regarded as authoritative about Prospero has come to be seen as merely authoritarian, and he has been transformed into a cruel tyrant, often with colonialist overtones, self-serving and irascible, a view that has been termed "cynical."[4] At various points Prospero may answer each description; the last scene best supports the former view; the second scene, the latter. Considered as a whole, however, Prospero seems to me better understood as a human being as complex in his strengths and weaknesses as a Shakespearian tragic hero, one whose attitudes are capable of significant change and whose responses to changing circumstances can be volatile, even mercurial. That at any rate is the Prospero who will figure in my detailed analysis.

Prospero is prescient (1.2.180) but not omniscient and certainly not omnipotent. It is true that with the aid of his magic he can halt the actions of his adversaries, torment their bodies and minds, and influence the inner lives of those who are susceptible. Yet unlike Oberon in *A Midsummer Night's Dream* with his love-potions he cannot finally control the fundamental attitudes of others, cannot compel those who resist his influence to submit to it willingly. For this reason he cannot be sure how his efforts will turn out. When he reviews the course of his project at the beginning of the last act—"My charms crack not, my spirits obey" (2)—one hears a note of self-congratulation or relief. Perhaps things have not always gone so well! As with Hamlet and his "mousetrap," there is an element of ad hoc improvisation in all the shows he and Ariel put on.

There is much that is sympathetic about Prospero and his situation. He and his daughter have been grievously wronged by his "extirpation" (1.2.125) from his dukedom. Ultimately, his efforts in the play serve to further the return of legitimate rule and the consummation of young love. By nature he is exceedingly trusting, as is evident in his initial relations with Antonio (1.2.68–70) and Caliban (1.2.345–7). When that trust is abused, however, he like Timon and King Lear retaliates fiercely.

Chiefly it is in the nature and degree of that ferocity that the playwright provides the most options for interpretation. Against his enemies, is Prospero seeking just retribution or revenge? Will he go too far in his retaliation? As the storm and the harpy scenes confirm, he is prepared to drive his mainland adversaries into madness and to suggest that they take their own lives. (It is Gonzalo who seeks to prevent their doing so—3.3.106–9). Is he prepared himself to take their lives? That remains an open question until the last act. Caliban too he has at times driven into madness (2.2.13–14); he takes sadistic pleasure in the pain he inflicts on him. Even with those closest to him Prospero can be harsh. When Ariel at first resists a brief extension of his (perhaps over-generously) shortened term of service, the severity of Prospero's threats seems excessive. When Miranda intercedes on Ferdinand's behalf, he demeaningly rebukes her insubordination: "My foot my tutor?" It represents a significant step in self-awareness when at the beginning of 4.1 he fears that he may have gone too far in the "austerity" of his testing of Ferdinand.

In addition to a propensity to over-react, Prospero must also come to terms with something reclusive in his nature, a tendency to withdraw from direct contact with others in order to pursue his studies and fancies. Before his exile, as he himself explains, this tendency led to his disengagement from active rule. One of his most admirable qualities is his ability to acknowledge how this disengagement contributed to the corruption of his brother and his own downfall. On the island, however, he seems to have learned the error of his earlier ways: the second scene shows him actively asserting his authority with Ariel and Caliban. Harsh as his methods are, they work. He understands his island subjects well enough to use the threat of confinement and promise of freedom to bring Ariel back into line while resorting to threats of physical punishment to enforce his control of Caliban.[5] Later he will correctly appraise Stephano and Trinculo as "thieves" at heart rather than serious assassins, dupes who can be easily distracted by the trumpery clothes.

The most sympathetic way of regarding Prospero's severities is to see them as the excesses of one to whom face-to-face assertion of authority does not come naturally, who in forcing himself to this assertion overdoes it. The second scene shows him beginning to overcome another aspect of his reclusiveness, his resistance to self-disclosure. Whereas he had before postponed Miranda's inquiries (1.2.34–7), he now holds forth at length about who they both are, how they came to be on the island, and why he raised the tempest. Note that he has doffed his "magic garment" while making these disclosures. Through most of the rest of the play, however, Prospero holds back from direct confrontation with the mainlanders, retreating into his roles as pretended domestic tyrant (with Ferdinand) and (with Alonzo and his shipwrecked companions) as magician, more a detached supervisor than a direct participant. Prospero is least involved in the Caliban/Stephano/Trinculo encounters. He never observes them until their assassination plot comes to a head; it marks the beginning of a significant change when he directly participates in pursuing them. Only in the last act will he present himself in his own person, with repeated promises to discourse at length upon "the story of his life." When the play ends, however, these remain promises.

With the audience, too, Prospero is reticent. As usual in Shakespeare, his motives are only partially revealed. It is clear from the outset that he wants Ferdinand and Miranda to get together; his purposes and methods in that respect are explicitly set forth throughout. But his political purposes are not clear, perhaps even to himself, until the finale. Only then, in hindsight, does one see that Prospero's successes have come from winning over Alonso to give him back his dukedom and to bless the match of Ferdinand and Miranda.

Are his motives disinterested or merely self-serving? The playwright gives little guidance in this respect. The harpy's speech that Prospero has instructed
Ariel to deliver does suggest a concern for the redemption of the wrong-doers,
advising them to escape perdition by means of "heart's sorrow, / And a clear
life ensuing" (3.3.81–2). But elsewhere the playwright leaves this an open
question.

That the Prospero we meet at the beginning of the play is deeply flawed
is thus clear. Yet by the end of the play, his conduct has changed for the better.
His improvement is not complete (it rarely is in Shakespeare) and subject to
relapse yet moving in the direction of self-restraint and open interaction with
others.

II. ACT 4, SCENE 1, LINE 139 TO ACT 5, SCENE 1, LINE 6

Let us look closely now at the first part of the passage under analysis. Why is
Prospero so very upset when he breaks off the masque? Partly he is angry at
"that foul conspiracy / Of the beast Caliban and his confederates / Against my
life." Fear of awakening his anger had been enough to keep Ariel from reminding him of the threat (167–9). Partly he is angry at himself for being forgetful
(his first words are "I had forgot. . ."), the only instance, in a potentially dangerous situation, in which his constant concern for precise timing had failed
him. It may well be too that his anger against himself is heightened by his realization that he has, as before, let himself become "transported / And rapt"
(1.2.76–7) to the neglect of practical matters. Just before he has seemed much
caught up in his "present fancies": he hushes the others: "be mute / Or else our
spell is marred (4.1.126–7). But if this point is too strongly made in performance (if, for example, Prospero shakes his head as if coming to after total
entrancement in his own production) it may overly anticipate his realization,
shortly to come, of the danger of losing himself in an imagined world. The
playwright's voice seems to advise a strategic reticence, delaying full revelation. For in order to have full dramatic value, Prospero's anger must be surprising and puzzling to the audience as well as "strange" to Ferdinand and out
of character to Miranda. Certainly, commentators who have mixed his anger
at Caliban's threat with frustration and regret over his failure with his former
protégé would steal the thunder of another moment shortly to come
(4.1.188–90). The playwright has delineated a step-by-step progression that
cannot be leap-frogged without loss.

Ferdinand and Miranda express their concern (is she altogether surprised
at his outburst of temper or trying to explain it away?—compare 1.2.497–9),
giving Prospero a little time to regain his composure. For he must then change
gears for his "revels now are ended" speech. Although it is usually treated as
a set-piece, the playwright makes it clear that it should be addressed in the first
instance to Ferdinand, being framed by references to "sir" (147, 158). Why to

Ferdinand? He is concerned that his "son" (the first time he has referred to him thus) looks in "a moved sort." It seems not to have occurred to him that Ferdinand's "dismay" was occasioned by his own "passion." Prospero attributes Ferdinand's reactions to the ending of the revels and recurs (149) to their earlier exchange:

> FERDINAND   This is a most majestic vision, and
>   Harmonious charmingly. May I be bold
>   To think these spirits?
> PROSPERO   Spirits, which by mine art
>   I have from their confines called to enact
>   My present fancies.
> FERDINAND   Let me live here ever.
>   So rare a wondered father and a wife
>   Makes this place paradise.   (4.1.117–124)

The shared lines in the quoted passage and the overlapping use of the word "spirits" suggest a continuity of thought between the two, a shared engagement with the spirit-world. In general, the Neapolitans are notably suggestible, whether for ill or for good. Although Alonso, Sebastian, and Stephano are all susceptible to influences toward usurping power, the initiatives come from Antonio and Caliban, who are quite prepared to kill to gain it. On the positive side, Ferdinand, like his father, is very responsive to Prospero's influences. In particular, Ferdinand as here is drawn to the spirit-world and is now able to recognize spirits when he sees them (earlier he had not been able to tell Miranda from an island goddess). Prospero may thus see in Ferdinand a kindred soul, someone who like himself feels the paradisiacal lure of virtual reality and is thus a suitable person with whom to share his thoughts about the spirit-actors.

In general the revels speech marks a turning point in the developing relationship between Prospero and Ferdinand. Prospero has often been taken to task for an excessive concern for premarital chastity. Yet Ferdinand himself makes that a primary consideration; when he first encounters Miranda, he tells her:

>   O, if a virgin,
>   And your affection not gone forth, I'll make you
>   The Queen of Naples.   (1.2.447–9)

Does not Prospero have reason to mistrust the son of his enemy, who has had wide acquaintance with women (3.1.39–46)? Has not Miranda already broken two of her father's precepts (3.1.35–6, 57–8)? Since the two lovers are so much in each other's power, they may already be giving physical expression to their love. Such instances seem the likely occasion for Prospero's repeated warnings earlier in this scene to be "more abstemious" (4.1.53).

Indeed, Prospero might arguably be found to be once again too trusting. In 3.1 Ferdinand might well be thought to protest too much in his flowery declarations of sincerity, especially in contrast with Miranda's simple directness; it is she who takes the lead in talk of marriage (83–9). Yet Prospero professes satisfaction with the course of their courtship (74–6). In 4.1 he finds Ferdinand's reassurances "fairly spoke," although their gist is that he will exercise self-restraint now simply because he doesn't want to take the edge off his wedding night (23–31). In the finale when he is playing at chess with Miranda, the fact that he appears to have been cheating may forecast things to come.

But to Prospero whatever lingering mistrust he may have harbored toward Ferdinand is progressively removed in the course of 4.1. His confidence no doubt strengthened by the fact that Ferdinand for the first time refers to Prospero as "father" and Miranda as "wife," Prospero will make a remarkable act of trust at 161–2 when he invites the couple, unsupervised, "to retire into my cell / And there repose."

Although Prospero plainly addresses the first lines of his speech to Ferdinand, by 150 he appears to modulate into a new key, as though like Macbeth he is "rapt" and carried away by his own line of thought. The ambiguities of 152–4 reflect the very blurring of planes of reality that he is describing (are the "cloud-capped towers" scenery or real? is the "great globe" the Globe Theater or the world?). There is often something self-generating about Prospero's thoughts and feelings. Here his awareness of the evanescence of the pageant extends to the real external world in all its glory and from there to a realization that humans too are no less so. As one thought leads to another, Prospero seems himself to be entering new and troubling realms. His observation that "We are such stuff as dreams are made on" may signal the beginning of his return to his immediate situation, with "we" applying to Ferdinand, himself, and Miranda; however, it seems more likely that he is still transported in his vision, with "we" meaning humanity generally since it is "our little life" rather than "lives" that is rounded with a sleep.

We have not heard such thoughts from Prospero before, or indeed from any other character, although they push to new extremes the play's general preoccupation with transformation, especially the blending of one plane of existence with another.[6] In a sense it is surprising that Prospero should be the bearer of this revelation. Nowhere previously has he used such imaginative language. And he is the one character who is familiar with both the mainland and the isle and thus not subject to the confusions that beset the encounters between mainlanders and islanders. He is also the character most adept at moving between the worlds of mortals and spirits. Perhaps his revelation is to be understood as an intimation of esoteric truths of the sort vouchsafed only to masters of a calling.

However that may be, Prospero is deeply troubled by his visionary discoveries, terming his raptness a "weakness" and "infirmity." When he says that he is "vexed," it is not anger or irritation so much as perturbance, as with "the fierce vexation of a dream" (*A Midsummer Night's Dream* 4.1.69). He feels the need to "still my beating mind": "A turn or two I'll walk." Still concerned, Ferdinand and Miranda say "We wish your peace" (their first "we"). Is "I thank thee" addressed to them, as some have thought?[7] If so it will require a very rapid change of mood in which he calls for Ariel immediately. If the whole speech is addressed to Ariel, as the Folio punctuation suggests ("Come with a thought; I thank thee, Ariell: come"), Prospero can walk "a turn or two" before beginning his next project. Note that, as if feeling the need for an ally, he tells Ariel that "*we* must prepare to meet with Caliban" (165).

Ariel, who has had time during the "revels" speech to change out of his Ceres costume, follows his master's lead in speaking of that "beast Caliban" as less than human; but as usual in Shakespeare this is a resemblance with a difference: Ariel more gently likens the conspirators to colts and calves. When he reports that the three "lifted up their noses / As they smelt music" he simultaneously puts an emphasis on both hearing and smelling that pervades this episode: the playwright leaves no doubt that Caliban and his associates are loud and smelly. Prospero then ratchets his disgust a level further, from the bestial to the infernal:

> A devil, a born devil, on whose nature
> Nurture can never stick; on whom my pains,
> Humanely taken, all, all lost, quite lost;
> And as with age his body uglier grows,
> So his mind cankers. I will plague them all,
> Even to roaring.   (188–192)

With his usual keen eye for finely graduated emotional progressions, Shakespeare has shown Prospero's anger proceeding from controlled indignation in 1.2 (more restrained with Ariel than with Caliban), through simulated severity with Ferdinand, to fierce denunciation in 3.3 ("some of you there present / Are worse than devils" [35–6]) and hand-rubbing satisfaction ("these, mine enemies, are all knit up / In their distractions" [89–90]). Here Prospero's propensity for demonizing his adversaries goes even further and releases a determination to "plague them all, / Even to roaring" that threatens to get out of control. Within the passage itself one can observe the self-generating quality in Prospero's nature pushing to this extreme. The playwright also adds nuance to Prospero's mounting anger by mixing in a large helping of self-pity in his lament that his "pains, / Humanely taken" should be "all, all lost, quite lost." Shortly, the lugubriousness of his lament will be comically echoed in Stephano's lament over the "infinite loss" (209) of the wine bottles in the stinking pool.

Ironically, Prospero's despair over Caliban's ineducability is premature. In another finely modulated progression, the playwright precisely marks Caliban's growing independence of Trinculo and even Stephano. At the end of 3.2, where the three last appeared, Caliban took the lead, albeit at Stephano's command to do so. In 4.1, although still verbally deferential to "King" Stephano ("Prithee, my king, be quiet" [214]), he shows a strength of purpose and self-control notably lacking in the other two.

Caliban is as concerned as Prospero about timing, worrying that the assassins "shall lose our time" (248). In other places too his language echoes that of Prospero. Like a deft courtier he assures Stephano after their wade through the filthy pool that "the prize I'll bring thee to / Shall hoodwink this mischance" (204–5), recalling Prospero's reassurance to Ferdinand at the beginning of the scene (1–2). His mention that Prospero's torments could turn them into "strange stuff" (234) is reminiscent of Prospero's observation that "we are such stuff / As dreams are made on" (155–6). These verbal affinities between the two may forecast their final reconciliation.

Here Caliban mostly rebukes Trinculo. But at one point his words may apply to Stephano as well: "What do you mean / To dote thus on such luggage? Let't alone / And do the murder first" (230–1). The ambiguity allows the actor of Caliban to fine tune the degree of his independence at this point. At most, of course, his enlightenment is less than complete: his growing maturity is after all in the service of an assassination attempt. He briefly obeys Stephano's order to be quiet and, although he refuses to take the clothing from the tree, he at Stephano's command bears the clothing that the other two pile upon him as they all head off to the wine-butt.

The fact that Prospero pursues them even though the would-be assassins have abandoned their attempt helps to emphasize that his anger has reached a new level. Descending himself to the bestial, abandoning all the restraints of reason, he not only sicks the spirit hounds on them (two are aptly named "Fury" and "Tyrant") but dwells in detail on the convulsions and cramps to be inflicted by his goblins and gloats that "At this hour / Lies at my mercy all mine enemies." "Mercy" seems to be the last thing he has in mind.

Thus 4.1 pushes to ultimates the two propensities in Prospero that the last act will bring him to overcome and abandon: his attachment to his fantasy world of magic and his drive toward vindictive retaliation. Each verges on a form of madness. His intimation of the evanescence of existence perturbs his "beating mind"; his fury (an extreme form of anger in Shakespeare) at Caliban causes him to abandon all the restraints of reason. Yet although he pulls back from these extremes, it seems that there was something corrective about his brushes with madness; Alonso too passes through madness to the realization of the error of his previous ways.

Here as elsewhere Shakespeare takes pains not only to calibrate the progressive increase of passion but also to show its gradual subsidence. In Prospero's fury he had directed Ariel to "go" immediately to deliver his charge to the goblins. But by the last three lines of the scene, his fury has begun to abate. He looks forward to the end of their joint labors, promises Ariel freedom, and quite gently says to him: "For a little / Follow, and do me service." Shortly he will describe a comparable loss of rationality and its gradual return (5.1.58), a process he seems to know first-hand.

It is contrary to Elizabethan stage convention for a character to leave the stage at the end of one scene and return to it at the beginning of the next. Almost certainly Prospero's exit and immediate re-entrance here reflects a pause between acts.[8] For a time lapse is needed for Prospero to change costume, as indicated by the Folio stage direction: "Prospero (in his Magicke robes) and Ariel." Ariel will have needed time to check on the Neapolitan court group on which he immediately reports; futhermore, we learn later that he has carried out his master's charge to the goblins (Stephano says, "O touch me not; I am not Stephano but a cramp" [5. 1.286]), and this act break appears to be the only time that he might have done so. Prospero's opening lines also seem to presuppose that time has passed, as he reviews the course of his project and checks the time to see if he is on schedule. The sense that time has elapsed is especially important because it allows further opportunity for Prospero to cool off from the peak of his fury in the previous scene. He is thus in a more receptive mood for his second revelation, as with Ariel's help he comes to realize that "the rarer action is / In virtue than in vengeance" and to break his charms.

In one sense the two revelations are parallel. It may help Prospero to part with the magical control he has over his enemies to have realized that his fantasy-living can lead to a disturbing awareness of the evanescence of all existence including his own. In another sense the revelations are apparently at odds since if life is but a dream as discovered in the first revelation why engage in its conduct with the moral earnestness that characterizes the second? However that may be, as the play unfolds it becomes evident that both revelations contribute to the encompassing theme of human fellow-feeling. Since magic gets in the way of direct human interaction while anger substitutes hatred for empathy, Prospero's disenchantment with the spirit world and his moderation of his anger allow him to enhance his feelings of kinship with his own kind.

III. THE THEME OF HUMAN FELLOW-FEELING

Although Prospero's change of heart is a discovery for him, the importance of human fellow-feeling is by no means something new in the play as a whole. It pervades the work throughout. Since the theme is so central yet has not received much comment, I should like to explore its ramifications in some detail.

The two chief exemplars of fellow-feeling are Gonzalo and Miranda. Both are so sensitive to the suffering of others that they often weep and repeatedly intercede in behalf of the sufferers. To other characters, with some justice, both seem overly hopeful and naive, she in her youth, he in his age; yet, the playwright grants them valid intuitions: Miranda surmises that the wrecked ship had "some noble creature in her" (1.2.7); Gonzalo that the Boatswain will not drown (he thinks him "born to be hanged") and that the spirits (including Ariel) have manners "more gentle-kind than of / Our human generation" (3.3.32–3). Gonzalo's principal concern is for Alonso, seeking in 2.1 to comfort him in his despair over the supposed loss of his son and to shield him from the ill-timed recriminations by his brother; in 3.3 he acts to prevent his king from drowning himself. Miranda's principal concern is for Ferdinand. In 1.2 she tries to comfort him (496), repeatedly tries to intercede in his behalf with her father ("Sir, have pity" [475]) and in 3.1 tries to help him carry logs.

Typically of *The Tempest*, the love relationship between Miranda and Ferdinand puts a special emphasis on the humanity of the lovers. At first he mistakes her for a goddess as she mistakes him for a spirit. But after her father advises Miranda that Ferdinand "eats and sleeps, and hath such senses / As we have—such" (413–4), she declares that she has "no ambition / To see a goodlier man" (483–4); she advises her wondering admirer that she is "certainly a maid." In 3.1 they declare themselves in each other's service; weeping for joy as well as pity, she tells her "good friend" (51) that "To be your fellow / You may deny me, but I'll be your servant / Whether you will or no" (84–6).

In the imagined world of the play's dialog, sympathetic feelings are not confined to humans. Prospero recalls how, cast off in their leaky boat, he and his infant daughter sighed to the winds "whose pity, sighing back again, / Did us but loving wrong" (1.2.150–1); he reminds Ariel of the torments that Sycorax had inflicted: "Thy groans / Did make wolves howl, and penetrate the breasts / Of ever-angry bears" (1.2.287–9). Miranda imagines that when the log Ferdinand is hauling burns "'Twill weep for having wearied you" (3.1.18–19). At the end Ferdinand says: "Though the seas threaten, they are merciful" (5.1.178). Thus in the face of mankind's inhumanity, nature's sympathy for human suffering matches the tender-heartedness of Ariel, "which art but air" (5.1.21).

In the past Gonzalo's sympathies extended to Prospero and his infant daughter. Prospero gratefully remembers how "out of his charity" (1.2.162) he had provided food, water, clothing, and Prospero's beloved books. Prospero also gratefully recalls the encouragement he received from Miranda's infant smiles; for her part she weeps as she hears his account of their sufferings and regrets the trouble she must have caused him. Her love for him and his for her (he tells her "I have done nothing but in care of thee / Of thee, my dear one, thee, my daughter" [1.2. 16–17]; he later calls her his "loved darling" [3.3.93]) has been made especially strong by their isolation on the island (1.2.171–4). Their closeness is part of *The Tempest*'s strong emphasis on the love of parents and children. Alonso and Ferdinand too are first shown searching for each other and grieving at their supposed loss.

Since Prospero has no peer as a friend, he has often been thought to be a lonely and isolated figure. Yet in addition to Gonzalo and Miranda his Milanese subjects loved him dearly (1.2.141), and on the isle he has the companionship of his tricksy spirit Ariel, who asks "Do you love me, master? No?," to which he replies: "Dearly, my delicate Ariel" (4.1.48–9). Before their estrangement, he loved his brother Antonio, next to Miranda, best of all the world (1.2.68–9). It is the lack of brotherly feeling on Antonio's part that especially torments Prospero (1.2.67–8, 117).

Commentators have often taken Prospero to task for extending forgiveness to Antonio at the end, even though Antonio has not expressed the penitence which Prospero at first stipulated as a condition for his forgiveness. Certainly his attitudes toward his brother are far from unwavering. Yet Prospero may be understood as a developing character registering inner conflict. It may be his growing sense of charity that prompts him to leave behind his initial stipulation of penitence (in Christianity it is up to God to insist on penitence). Furthermore, he is certainly not blindly over-trusting, as before. Even in extending forgiveness he adds "unnatural though thou art."

Indeed, other commentators have questioned whether Prospero's forgiveness was truly heartfelt. Should he have tempered his condemnation with acknowledgment of his own inadvertent contribution to his brother's corruption? Yet Prospero's final and unqualified condemnation does not come until Antonio has started to make an attempt on Alonso's life and in 3.3 has resisted the same promptings that brought Alonso to see the error of his own ways. Nevertheless, Prospero does not lose sight of the fact that his perfidious "brother mine" is of his own "flesh and blood" (5.1.73–4). This acknowledgement comes while Antonio is still under Prospero's spell. When the charm has been lifted from Antonio, Prospero has discased his magic robes and donned his ducal attire, and nothing stands between a direct confrontation between the two brothers, Prospero's inner turmoil is evident. Antonio having failed voluntarily to join Alonso in resigning the dukedom and asking pardon for his wrongs, Prospero "requires" his dukedom of his brother. He cannot restrain his abhorrence:

> Most wicked sir, whom to call brother
> Would even infect my mouth, I do forgive
> Thy rankest fault—all of them . . .   (5.1.130–2)

His words reflect the high value he places on brotherhood; yet his vehemence seems to deny his own brotherhood toward Antonio—a relapse from the sense of kinship he had acknowledged earlier. In the same breath with forgiving Antonio his rankest fault, he clearly is not forgetting it, or all his other faults. Like that of other major Shakespearian characters, Prospero's progress toward enlightenment is neither total nor unwavering.

As for Antonio's feelings, although earlier Alonso refers to Antonio as "brother" (3.3.51) and Sebastian calls him "dear friend" (2.1.288), the nearest he himself comes to expressing regard for anyone is when he calls Sebastian "worthy" and "noble"—and those are clearly terms of calculated flattery. Indeed he prides himself on his rise above his former "fellows" (2.1.278–9). For his part Sebastian promises to "love" Antonio when the latter has killed his brother (2.2.292). His deficiencies in family feeling are further emphasized at the end, where his response to the miraculous return and marriage of his nephew (developments that undo his hopes for the crown) would be totally out of character unless spoken with bitter irony: "A most high miracle" (5.1.176). Speaking of the young couple, Alonso's line may well be addressed to silent Sebastian: "Let grief and sorrow still embrace his heart / That doth not wish you joy" (214–15).

When Prospero grants Ariel his freedom and betrothes Miranda to Ferdinand, he is losing the kind of companionship that sustained his time on the island. As keenly as he feels the loss of his daughter (145–8), he is reconciled to it and through the "soft grace" of patience professes himself "content" (142–4); Ariel he will "miss" (95), yet his last words to him are "Be free, and fare thou well" (318). At the same time he has found a larger sociability. He embraces Gonzalo (earlier he had joined Gonzalo's sorrow for the enchanted sufferers: "Mine eyes, ev'n sociable to the show of thine, / Fall fellowly drops" (63–4). Especially Prospero's sense of family enlarges to include not only Ferdinand (who speaks of him as a "second father") but Alonso, whom he heartily welcomes even before the King has asked his pardon. At their embrace Alonso is relieved to confirm that the Duke's pulse beats "as of flesh and blood" (113–14). In turn Alonso feels that Miranda is "my child" and that he is her "second father." When he starts to ask her forgiveness, Prospero intercedes: "There, sir, stop. / Let us not burden our remembrances with / A heaviness that is gone" (197–9). When Gonzalo asks the blessing of the gods on the young couple, Alonso says amen (204) and takes their hands (213).

By the end of the play Prospero's embrace extends to all. In the last words of the play proper, he invites Alonso and the others: "Please you, draw near." His enhanced sense of human fellow-feeling lies behind the humble prayer to the audience that concludes the Epilogue: "As you from crimes would pardoned be, / Let your indulgence set me free."

As Shakespeare often does, in the Stephano/Trinculo/Caliban plot-strand he holds up a comic, distorting mirror to many aspects of the treatment of human fellowship in the rest of the play. Stephano's presumed assumption of power involves him in many such reflections. In response to Caliban's worship of him as the man in the moon, Stephano begins—like Antonio (1.2.102–3) and Sebastian (2.1.292)—to think of himself as to the manner born. How immediately this takes place depends on the interpretation of Stephano's line: "Fellow Trinculo, we'll fill him [the bottle] by and by again" (2.2.170). Does "fellow" mean "inferior" or "equal"? Is "we" royal or plural? If the first option, Stephano has already assumed his new status. At any rate, by 3.2 Stephano is so much the ruler that he stands up for his "servant monster" against Trinculo's provocation: "The poor monster's my subject, and he shall not suffer indignity" (3.2.34–5). Later, anticipating Prospero, he warns Trinculo that in his anger he may "turn my mercy out o' doors" (69) and in his fury beats him. By 3.2.105 Stephano has elevated himself to King and offers to make his two companions viceroys; he tells Trinculo: "Give me thy hand. I am sorry I beat thee" (109). But then, anticipating Prospero's provisional reconciliation with Antonio, he adds: "But while thou lov'st keep a good tongue in thy head."

Unlike Miranda and Ariel who seek mercy for others, Stephano is like the shipwreck victims (1.1.60) in begging for "Mercy, mercy!" for himself (2.2.92) when he is confronted by the four-legged monster; and when he, along with Trinculo, and Caliban, hears the mysterious tabor and pipe he beseeches "Mercy upon us!" while Trinculo pleads "forgive me my sins!" (3.2.128–30). Such self-centeredness was made explicit by the Boatswain in the first scene; when Gonzalo, mindful of the king's presence on the ship, told him to "remember who thou hast aboard," his reply was: "None that I more love than myself" (1.1.20). In contrast, when Stephano enters in the last scene, he declares: "Every man shift for all the rest, and let no man take care for himself." Dazed and drunken, he may well have meant to say "Every man shift for himself and let no man take care for the rest." In any case, he has stumbled into a fine summary of the spirit of fellowship that inspires the finale. He and Trinculo again take their place as members of the true King's company when Prospero advises Alonso that "two of these fellows you / Must know and own" (274–5), just as he himself acknowledges that "thing of darkness" Caliban as his. Both rulers accept their subordinates as such by giving orders that are obeyed (291–8).

IV. ACT 5, SCENE 1, LINES 6–32

The play's extensive concern with human fellow-feeling supports the importance that performers and critics have attached to this passage. Ariel's response to Prospero's "How fares the King and the followers?" is artfully phrased to sway his sympathies. By repeated use of the word "you" Ariel emphasizes that Prospero is wholly responsible for their initial and continued confinement and charmed distraction: "They cannot budge until your release." He emphasizes the idea of brotherhood, referring to Sebastian and Antonio as the King's "brother and yours." He saves until last the exemplary image of "Him that you termed, sir, the good old Lord Gonzalo" so "Brimful of sorrow and dismay" that "His tears runs down his beard like winter's drops / From eaves of reeds." Only then, perhaps cued by signs of a softening in Prospero's manner does he venture: "if you now beheld them, your affections / Would become tender."

Then comes the crucial turning-point:

PROSPERO   Dost thou think so, spirit?
ARIEL   Mine would, sir, were I human.
PROSPERO   And mine shall.

Prospero's first response is another of those points that allow an actor to fine-tune his interpretation. Is Prospero immediately touched by Ariel's appeal, making his monosyllabic half-line a half-step toward the indubitable change in his next half-line? In that case he might accentuate "thou." Or, a more volatile Prospero might accentuate "think" in his first response, with a note of asperity in his voice at Ariel's impertinence in telling him what he would feel?—an irritation that is assuaged when Ariel, using yet another of his deferential "sirs," declares "Mine would, sir, were I human." "And mine shall" settles the matter, although still in the future tense.

The fellow-feeling at the heart of Prospero's reversal is made explicit in his next lines:

Hast thou, which art but air, a touch, a feeling
Of their afflictions, and shall not myself,
One of their kind, that relish all as sharply
Passion as they, be kindlier moved than thou art?

The play on "kind" sums up the idea of kindliness inspired by a sense of human kinship. If these lines are simply addressed to Ariel, they can seem to show merely an attitude of emulation, a determination to be holier than thou. His phrasing keeps a distance between "myself" and the others (referred to as "they" and "their"); he might have said "one of the same kind." But if Prospero is also addressing the lines to himself, they can be read as self-exhortation. It is true that he says "kindlier" rather than "as kindly," suggesting competition. Yet shouldn't a human be moved more than a spirit? especially since Ariel does not say that he is moved but only that he would be if he had human feelings? The Folio punctuation places a comma after "sharply," widening the range of shared feeling.

Shakespeare likes to present moments of psychological stress with great concentration. Changes that novelists would spread over time and a chapter the playwright may cover in a line or two. Yet although he may condense, he rarely elides: each stage is gone through. So here the movement from intention to decision is clearly marked by the change from future tense ("Shall not myself") to present:

> Though with their high wrong I am struck to th' quick,
> Yet with my nobler reason 'gainst my fury
> Do I take part. The rarer action is
> In virtue than in vengeance.

The first phase of his decision is to exercise restraint, to side with his reason in its struggle with his fury. It's true that his drive for retaliation against the high wrongs done him has already been partially satisfied by the afflictions he has already visited upon his wrongers. Yet he might well have gone on to take the lives of those who had been prepared to take his.

The passage just quoted is much illuminated by its source in Montaigne.[9] In it he observes that it is a "rare action" for someone naturally mild and good not to retaliate against injury; but it is much more admirable and virtuous when someone "stung to the quick with any wrong or offence received, should arm himself with reason against this furiously-blind desire of revenge," a mastery achieved only "after a great conflict" within himself. Much of the drama in the rest of the last act comes from the "great conflict," in Prospero between virtue and vengeance. Editors have often glossed "virtue" as "forgiveness," but this is to leave out some intermediate steps that the playwright specifies. At this point, Prospero's change of heart is conditional on the penitence of the wrongdoers. Not until 78 does he speak of "forgiveness" for his brother with no mention of penitence. Here Prospero does proceed from theory to practice, directing Ariel to release the prisoners from his spell: "My chains I'll break, their senses I'll restore, / And they shall be themselves." Again his change is partial and for the future: he seems to have in mind only the spell he has cast upon Alonso and his associates. Not until the end of his next long speech does he renounce magic altogether, resolving to break and bury his staff and drown his book. Even then, however, he still uses the future tense.

As here, significant change in Shakespeare is usually partial and wavering. Yet by the end of the passage under analysis, the critical turning point has been passed.

V. THE VOICE OF THE PLAYWRIGHT

If one steps back from the analysis of particular portions of the passage and looks at it as a whole, what is revealed about the playwright's general concerns? Continuity and integration are clearly primary. As his plot-strands approach their climaxes, he takes care to sustain clear lines of development. As we have seen these developments are propelled at key points by surprise, suspense, and reversal; yet, they proceed through precisely graduated phases, as with Caliban's growing independence from his confederates. Or take

Shakespeare's careful preparation for Prospero's renunciation of magic. First Prospero interrupts the betrothal ritual (it is the first spell we have seen him break; here it is impulsive, later it will be deliberate), then he discovers the disturbing apercus that the end of the revels lead him to, then for the first time since the second scene he recurs to his promise to relinquish his control over Ariel on completion of the project, then he renounces the vindictive retaliation which magical powers would have made possible. Only then does he resolve to break his charms over his enemies.

The playwright is also much concerned to integrate these progressions. How skillfully he modulates from the betrothal ceremony into the Caliban episode and from that into his dealings with Alonso and company! He makes an especially neat suture between Prospero's anger at Caliban and his associates and at Alonso and his. In his last lines in 3.3 Prospero had gloated that Alonso and his other enemies "are all knit up / In their distractions. They now are in my power" (89–90). In 4.1 his anger against Caliban becomes even more intense, and in his last speech in the scene his fury extends to Alonso in words that recall his earlier gloating: "At this hour / Lies at my mercy all mine enemies" (263–4). It is this heightened anger that he will need to restrain toward Alonso in 5.1.

As storyteller Shakespeare thus lays down a solid superstructure. Yet within it he also allows himself a large measure of freedom from literal-mindedness. As we have seen, when it suits his purposes he can expand the ordinary passage of time to allow Prospero to expatiate on the evanescence of existence or condense its pace to intensify his reversal from vengeance to virtue. As with Ariel's synesthesia (he reports that Stephano and his companions "smelt music" [178]), his imagination can dissolve ordinary barriers. So at the end of Act 4, Prospero's enemies coalesce, while he himself seems almost to share a common identity with Ferdinand in their involvement with the spirit world. In the kaleidoscope of verbal associations that Shakespeare spins in this passage, affinities are even suggested between Prospero and Stephano and Caliban. In both of his revelations Prospero seems to be not only speaking for himself but giving voice to perspectives discovered by the whole play.

In taking these liberties Shakespeare seems confident that he can take his audience with him. He does not hesitate to call for subtly mixed responses. For example, he has often previously presented Gonzalo as being at once admirable and silly. Here Shakespeare does not hold back from that combination at a most crucial spot, Ariel's account of Gonzalo's sorrow: "His tears run down his beard like winter's drops / From eaves of reeds." The sympathetic understanding that prompts his tears is exemplary, indeed it is an example that Prospero will soon follow. This is the primary effect. Yet the image of a beard not merely soaked with tears but dripping them has a hint of the ludicrous about it. Shakespeare trusts his audience to credit this vividly rendered nuance without cancelling the primary effect.

In its accommodation of a free play of imagination within firm guidelines, Shakespeare's own practice thus corresponds to the combination of freedom and responsiveness to guidance that he invites in his interpreters.

NOTES

1. Stephen Orgel, introduction, *The Tempest*, ed., Stephen Orgel (Oxford: Oxford UP, 1987), 12. All line references are to this edition.
2. Robert Hapgood, *Shakespeare the Theatre-Poet* (Oxford: Clarendon P, 1990), 61–95.
3. Edward Dowden, *Shakspere—His Mind and Art* (London, 1875), ch. 8. Harry Berger, Jr., "Miraculous Harp: A Reading of Shakespeare's *Tempest*," *Shakespeare Studies* 5 (1970): 253–283.
4. Lois Potter, "A Brave New *Tempest*," *Shakespeare Quarterly* 43 (1992), 450–455.
5. Paul Cantor, "Prospero's Republic: The Politics of *The Tempest*" in John A. Alvis and Thomas G. West, eds., *Shakespeare as Political Thinker* (Durham, NC: Carolina Academic P, 1981), 239–255.
6. Reuben A. Brower, "The Mirror of Analogy: *The Tempest*," in Brower and Richard Poirier, eds., *The Fields of Light: An Experiment in Critical Reading* (New York: Oxford UP, 1951), 95–122.
7. Frank Kermode, ed. *The Tempest* (London: Methuen, 1976), p. 105 n.164.
8. Peter Holland, "The Shapeliness of *The Tempest*," *Essays in Criticism* 45 (1995): 208–227.
9. Eleanor Prosser, "Shakespeare, Montaigne, and the Rarer Action," *Shakespeare Studies* 1 (1965): 261–264.

Detail from Sebastião Lopes' *Map of Brazil*, 1565. Photograph courtesy of the Edward E. Ayer Collection, The Newberry Library. Used by permission of The Newberry Library.

438

Alien Habitats in *The Tempest*

GERALDO U. DE SOUSA

This essay will focus on notions of place, home, and habitat in *The Tempest*; therefore, I will start with definitions. "Habitat," from the third person singular, present tense of Latin *habitare*, literally meaning "it inhabits," was originally a term used in books of flora and fauna written in Latin to designate the natural place of growth or occurrence of a species, especially where the species finds the food, water, and shelter that it requires.[1] "Habitat" conjures up images of the complex ecological relations of all living organisms to their physical surroundings, habits, and modes of life. Underscoring the experiential and cultural nature of our engagement with the physical environment, Douglas Pocock writes that "place relates to an area which is bounded and has distinctive internal structure, to which meaning is attributed and which evokes an affective response."[2] "Home" is a specific kind of place; it suggests both the house or dwelling in which one habitually lives or regards as one's proper abode and a place, region, state, or country to which one properly belongs and in which one's affections center or where one finds rest, refuge, or satisfaction.[3] "Home" evokes "the remembered field of familiar experience" and "the loci of memorable personal events."[4] The English Franciscan scholastic philosopher Roger Bacon (c. 1214–1294?), known as the Admirable Doctor, underscored the importance of place in our lives when he wrote that "place is the beginning of our existence."[5]

In *The Tempest*, the characters enter a world that the First Folio describes simply as "The Scene, an un-inhabited Island."[6] Adrian views the island as "Uninhabitable and almost inaccessible" (2.1.38); Ariel indicates that this is a place "Where man doth not inhabit" (3.3.57); and Prospero, in the epilogue, refers to "this bare island" (8).[7] John Block Friedman suggests that ancient, medieval, and early modern writers imagined the far corners of the known world as "uninhabitable" places, which were not necessarily empty of life; rather, such places "were considered to be likely and appropriately habitats for monstrous races."[8] I believe, however, that in *The Tempest* the term means something else. Obviously, Prospero's "uninhabited Island" is neither devoid of life nor uninhabitable, except perhaps in the imagination of the play's characters. Although the island, as a habitat, does sustain human life, none of the characters, with the exception of Caliban, wants to claim this place as their home. Even for Caliban, who proclaims that "This island's mine by Sycorax my mother" (1.2.332), the island seems at times like home, at times like an alien place. I will, therefore, refer to the island as an "alien habitat," to suggest both ecology and culture. As an ecological entity, the island sustains human life; as a cultural construct, it represents the opposite of home. Flung upon this alien habitat, the characters must confront a profound sense of not belonging, of inhabiting a place that they cannot and will not call home. I submit that in this alien habitat, they must revisit and re-imagine the very notion of home.

Like *The Winter's Tale*, which gives landlocked Bohemia a sea coast, *The Tempest* defies cartographical logic. Like *Pericles* and *The Winter's Tale*, *The Tempest* is set in the Mediterranean region, the customary backdrop of Hellenistic romance; but unlike those other plays, its action also seems to be simultaneously set in the New World. Further, the play curiously lies at the intersection of history and romance, something which Charles Frey describes as a "peculiar merger."[9] The play was written in late 1610 or 1611; and its first recorded court performance took place on 1 November 1611. *The Tempest* represents the culmination of the romance genre to which Shakespeare turned at the end of his career, but it also evokes the growing national interest in the colonial enterprise in Virginia in particular and in the New World in general, as well as in domestic environmental issues, especially widespread deforestation in England and shortages of wood both for fuel and for building material. The play's setting and issues resonate on multiple levels. History, ecology, and romance converge in the play's exploration of our relationship to place.

I. HISTORICAL AND ECOLOGICAL CONTEXTS

The ancient geographer Strabo argued that our knowledge of the environment comes from the "experience" of habitation, "the evidence of our senses," and acts of geographical exploration.[10] Strabo believed that sometimes it is not possible for us to rely on the evidence of our senses, the experience of habitation, or acts of geographical exploration. When confronted with *terra incognita*, we must seek knowledge elsewhere: "And wherever we have not been able to learn by evidence of our senses, there reason points the way."[11] From Strabo's remarks, John L. Allen concludes: "Imagination, then, must be viewed as critical for the processes of geographical exploration by which unknown lands are brought within the horizons of human experience."[12] Our senses, logic, and our imagination thus supplement each other in the exploration of our physical surroundings.

In a study of Gonzalo Fernández de Oviedo's illustrations of the New World, Kathleen Myers raises a fascinating question about how a European traveler can describe "a world in which European words and analogues are inadequate to convey its essence."[13] She examines a tradition of visual epistemology and the rising emphasis on empiricism in the Renaissance, through which "a new relationship emerged between vision and the apprehension of knowledge."[14] She adds, "To state it another way, the reliance during the Renaissance on the sense of sight led increasingly to the need for scientists, historians, and artists to experience through observation their subject of inquiry in order to establish their own authority to represent the subject."[15] According to Myers, Oviedo employed verbal and visual methods of representation in an attempt to bridge the reality of what he observed and the formulas of geographical representation inherited from old authorities, thus becoming "both *the* author and *the* authority on America."[16]

Shakespeare's sources for *The Tempest* express less certainty about authoritative geographical representation; and, in fact, they suggest that our senses, imagination, or habits of living and thinking may run counter to the empirical impulse. In his essay, "Of the Caniballes," which provides material for Gonzalo's utopian plantation, Montaigne records an interview with a Frenchman, a long-time resident of Brazil, and with Brazilian natives whom he met in France. Montaigne values the "most sincere Reporter" who relies on first-hand observation, but he realizes that much travel writing consists of nothing but fantasy. In unmistakable terms, he calls for a change:

> We had need of Topographers to make us particular narrations of the places they have beene in. . . . I would have everie man write what he knowes, and no more: not only in that, but in all other subjects. For one may have particular knowledge of the nature of one river, and experience of the qualitie of one fountaine, that in other things knowes no more than another man: who nevethelesse to publish this little scantling, will undertake to write of all the Physickes. From which vice proceed divers great inconveniences.[17]

The imagination, rather than empirical knowledge, fills the lacunae in our knowledge of remote regions of the world.

The Bermuda pamphlets underscore the unreliability of reporting. Silvester Jourdain speaks of the commonly accepted view of the Bermuda islands:

> For the islands of the Bermudas, as every man knoweth that hath heard or read of them, were never inhabited by any Christian or heathen people but ever esteemed and reputed a most prodigious and enchanted place, affording nothing but gusts, storms, and foul weather, which made every navigator and

mariner to avoid them as Scylla and Charybdis, or as they would shun the Devil himself; and no man was ever heard to make for the place but as, against their wills, they have by storms and dangerousness of the rocks, lying seven leagues unto the sea, suffered shipwreck.[18]

Sir Thomas Gates and the other Virginia colonists shipwrecked on the island in 1609, however, prove the region to be not the Devil's Island but a lush tropical paradise: "Yet did we find there the air so temperate and the country so abundantly fruitful of all fit necessaries for the sustentation, and preservation of man's life."[19] Thus, he concludes, "Wherefore my opinion sincerely of this island is that whereas it hath been and is still accounted the most dangerous, infortunate, and most forlorn place of the world, it is in truth the richest, healthfullest, and pleasing land (the quantity and bigness thereof considered) and merely natural, as ever man set foot upon."[20] Thus, Jourdain affirms that Bermuda is a natural, not a supernatural place.

Likewise, William Strachy, in his "A True Reportory of the Wracke," contrasts the violent effects of a hurricane to the actual peaceful atmosphere of Bermuda. He writes that, "like an hell of darkenesse turned blacke upon us," the hurricane of 1609 brought out the horrors of death at sea:

> For indeede death is accompanied at no time, nor place with circumstances every way so uncapable of particularities of goodnesse and inward comforts, as at Sea. For it is most true, there ariseth commonly no such unmercifull tempest, compound of so many contrary and divers Nations, but that it worketh upon the whole frame of the body, and most loathsomely affecteth all the powers thereof: and the manner of the sicknesse it laies upon the body, being so unsufferable, gives not the minde any free and quiet time.[21]

The "restlesse tumult" of the tempest was so furious that the colonists' imagination could not conceive of any greater violence: "fury added to fury, and one storme urging a second more outragious then the former."[22] The crew and passengers alike could find no words of comfort for one another because, as Strachy writes, "our clamors dround in the windes, and the windes in thunder. Prayers might well be in the heart and lips, but drowned in the outcries of the Officers: nothing heard that could give comfort, nothing seene that might incourage hope."[23] Strachy recognized that the Atlantic hurricanes had given the Bermuda islands their reputation: "because they be so terrible to all that ever touched on them, and such tempests thunders, and other feareful objects are seene and heard about them, that they be called commonly, The Devils Ilands, and are feared and avoyded of all sea travellers alive, above any other place in the world."[24]

Yet even amidst so much peril, all of the colonists miraculously survive the hurricane. Strachy sets out to challenge other voyagers' reports:

> And hereby also, I hope to deliver the world from a foule and general errour:
> it being counted of most, that they can be no habitation for Men, but rather
> given over to Devils and wicked Spirits; whereas indeed wee find them now
> by experience, to bee as habitable and commodious as most Countries of the
> same climate and situation: insomuch as if the entrance into them were as
> easie as the place it selfe is contenting, it had long ere this beene inhabited,
> as well as other Ilands.[25]

On this island, the stranded colonists discover wild hogs, edible fruit and
plants, and water. They also discover abundant timber, from which they are
able to build two small ships which will carry them to Virginia nearly a year
later. Strachy indicates that we should draw the following lesson from this
experience: "Thus shall we make it appeare, That Truth is the daughter of
Time, and that men ought not to deny every thing which is not subject to their
own sense."[26] The experience of habitation and geographical exploration
forces us to discern the truth behind the illusion of our senses or of unreliable
reports. In these documents, Bermuda undergoes a transformation from a
supernatural forlorn, desperate, and uninhabitable place to a natural, fertile,
habitable geographical location.

From an ecological perspective, these colonists, especially those who had
never been to the New World, must have been astonished by the luxuriant veg-
etation of Bermuda. They left England amidst a national debate about how
humans can exploit and destroy natural resources, which brought on severe
shortages of firewood and timber in the early seventeenth century for the construction, cabinet making, and shipbuilding industries. The rapid growth of the
iron, glass, and other industries led to unprecedented demand on the English
forests and the depletion of the woodlands. As the historian John Perlin puts
it, this "resulted in more destruction and waste of woodlands than in any preceding period."[27]

Many foresaw this ecological disaster, although few tried to do anything
about it. In his *Description of England* (1577; 1587), Harrison speaks of a
time when England was "well replenished with great woods & groves"; he
adds, however, that at the present time, there is much scarcity of wood: "a man
shall oft ride ten or twentie miles" and find few trees or none at all, "except it
be neere unto townes, gentlemens houses, & villages, where the inhabitants
have planted a few elmes, okes, hasels or ashes, about their dwellings, for their
defense from the rough winds, and keeping of the stormie weather from
annoiance of the same."[28] William Harrison astutely points out the possible
causes of the scarcity of wood in England:

> This scarcity at the first grew (as it is thought) either by the industrie of man,
> for maintenance of tillage (as we understand the life to be doone of late by
> the Spaniards in the west Indies, where they fired whole woods of verie great

compasse, therby to come by ground whereon to sow their graines,) or else
through the covetousnesse of such, as, in preferring of pasture for their
sheepe and greater cattell, doo make small account of firebote and timber.[29]

Such nefarious practices as burning tracts of forest to clear the land for pas-
tures or tillage have brought on shortages of timber and firewood. Harrison
realizes that England still has forests, but the decay of the woodlands is apparent when compared to what England used to have: "Although I must needs
confesse that there is good store of great wood or timber here and there, even
now in some places of England, yet in our daies it is far unlike to that plentie,
which our ancestors have seene heretofore."[30]

Three decades later the situation became even worse. The policy makers
of Stuart England tried to focus the attention of the country on the problems
brought on by widespread deforestation. Addressing Parliament at Whitehall
on 21 March 1609/10, King James urged passage of a "new Statute for preservation of woods." He argued that "The maintenance of woods is a thing so
necessary for this Kingdom, as it cannot stand, nor be a Kingdom without
it."[31] James viewed deforestation as a threat to the personal comfort and survival of every Englishman, to national security, and to royal recreation. A
shortage of cooking and heating fuel jeopardized everyone's life: "for neither
can the people live in these colde Countries, if they want fire altogether, nor
yet can you dresse your meate without it; and I thinke you will ill live like the
Cannibals upon raw flesh: for the education of this people is farre from that."[32]
He argued that "the decay of woods will necessarily bring the decay of Shipping, which both is the security of this Kingdome."[33] Likewise, "by the decay
of Shipping," he told Parliament, "will you loose both all your forraine commodities that are fit for this contrey, and the venting of our owne, which is the
losse of Trade, that is a maine pillar of this Kingdome." Finally, James suggested that deforestation could wipe out wildlife and deprive the king and
nobility of their favorite recreation: "And as for Pleasure yee know my delight
in Hunting and Hawking, and many of your selves are of the same mind." In
conclusion, he strongly admonished Parliament: "Ye have reason therefore to
provide a good Law upon this subject."[34] James foresaw an ecological
calamity. Devoid of its natural resources, England could not sustain an
advanced civilization; his subjects would revert to barbarians, trade would
end, national security would be compromised, and the king and the nobility
would be deprived of their favorite pastime.

The two most vocal critics of widespread deforestation were someone
known only by the initials R. Ch. and Arthur Standish, a pioneer ecologist who
devoted four years of his life visiting various parts of Britain and studying
British agriculture. R. Ch. published a treatise entitled *An olde thrift newly
revived* in which he remarks on widespread deforestation and shortage of
wood, and sounds a serious note of alarm:

> For if Coale should faile (as it is too apparant it beginneth to grow deere and
> scarce, and in many places there is none to be had) how then should we doe
> for this materiall of fuell? for doe we thinke that wood alone can beare the
> brunt to satisfie every mans chimney? assuredly now, except it were more
> plentifull. Then must there needs be some speedy means used for prevention
> of felling whole woods of timber, and grubbing up of Copies at pleasure to
> convert them into pasture, arrable, or meadow grounds, else in short time,
> this waste and scarcitie will grow to a consummation of the whole.[35]

Standish was much impressed by the rapid deforestation of the country, a phenomenon particularly noticeable in living memory.[36] He published and repub-
lished treatises on the subject between 1611 and 1616. Standish dedicated his
1611 treatise, *The Commons Complaints*, to King James:

> Wee doe in all humblenesse complaine unto your Majesty of the generall
> destruction and waste of wood, made within this your Kingdome, more within
> twenty or thirty last yeares, then in any hundred yeares before. Little respect
> is taken but by your Majestie, for the posterity and prosperity of your King-
> dom; too many destroyers, but few or none at all doth plant or preserve: by rea-
> son thereof there is not Tymber left in this Kingdome at this instant onely to
> repaire the buildings thereof another age, much lesse to build withall.[37]

He emphasizes how essential wood is to the kingdom, arguing that without
firewood, "mans life cannot be perserved" because wood is essential in the
manufacture of bricks, tiles, iron, lead, and glass for "the building of habitations"; in providing materials for shipbuilding and navigation, for "bruing and
keeping of drinke, and all other necessaries for housekeeping."[38] He indicates
that shortage of wood would have a disastrous effect upon the entire economy,
so much so that he concludes: "so it may be conceived, no wood no Kingdome."[39]

After making dire predictions, Standish presents a plan, which I will consider later, to replenish the despoiled forests by a national effort to plant trees.
King James must have read Standish's treatise because when Standish reissues
a revised edition of *The Commons Complaint* in 1612, it comes with the impri-
matur of the King:

> Whereas Arthur Standish Gentleman hath taken much paines, and beene at
> great charges in compositing and publishing a Booke, some projects for the
> increasing of woods; the decay whereof in this Realme is universally com-
> plained of; And therefore we would be glad that by invention might further
> the restoring thereof; wee have therefore been pleased to give allowance to
> his Booke, and to Printing thereof.[40]

Through the printed word, Standish thus establishes a dialogue with his
king about the ability of humans to destroy the environment as well as to
rebuild it in some fashion. Both king and subject confront an environmental

disaster and paint a vivid picture of home turned into a wasteland that cannot sustain civilization.

But deforestation was also beginning to affect the New World. In 1504 an armada of six ships under the command of Gonçalo Coelho set sail for South America. An account of this expedition, entitled *Lettera di Amerigo Vespucci delle isole nuovamente trovate in quattro suoi viaggi*, also known as "Letter to Soderini," appeared in 1505 or 1506.[41] Sailing south along the Brazilian coast, Vespucci erected a fort and established a *feitoria*, the first permanent trading post in Brazil, for the purposes of logging and exporting brazilwood. Vespucci left twenty-four men at the Cabo Frio *feitoria* to supervise the logging operations.[42] The logging activities at the *Feitoria* at Cabo Frio were impressive indeed. The log-book of the *Bretoa*, records in 1511 that this fortified large-bellied ship stayed at the *Feitoria* for one month and two days, loading a cargo of 5,008 brazilwood logs, in addition to "thirty-five slaves, jaguariticas (a kind of small, spotted leopard), some parrots and long-tailed monkeys of the species *Midas ursulus*."[43] The brazilwood, from which a red dye was extracted for use in the textile industry, became such an important commodity in Europe that it led to the change of the name of the newly-discovered Portuguese America from "Land of the Holy Cross" to "the Land of brazilwood."

Lopo Homem's map of Brazil of 1519, now in the Bibliotèque Nationale, offers the first pictorial representation of the beginning of the logging industry.[44] Indians bearing European axes cut down trees, while others gather the logs presumably for export to Europe. Like Lopo Homem's, Sebastião Lopes' map of Brazil in a manuscript atlas on paper (1565), now at the Newberry Library, depicts an Indian holding a European metal ax, cutting down trees. Here we observe a desolate scene. Two large trees dominate the illustration under one of which sit a mother and her child, whom she seems to be breast-feeding. Upstanding next to her is a man, holding an axe. The landscape looks barren. The stumps of five trees dominate the foreground. No other trees can be seen, except four on top of a hill in the distant horizon. This map provides evidence of widespread deforestation of certain areas of Brazil to make way for new waves of colonists, a problem that persists in the Amazon region to this day.

A passage from Harrison, which I quoted earlier, points out that the Spaniards set fire to the West Indies forests in order to clear the land for plantations. Sir Francis Drake offers testimony to similar fires in the Atlantic Forest of Brazil. In 1577–80, Sir Francis Drake undertook a voyage of exploration to retrace in part the route of the voyage of circumnavigation of the globe, begun by Magellan, in 1519. Having safely crossed the Atlantic, Drake's fleet caught sight of the Brazilian coast on 5 April 1578. Drake was astonished by what he saw: "Great and huge fires made by them in sundry places" and incredible dust storms and thick smoke, which in fact impeded navigation.[45] Drake attributes the fires and dust storms to rituals performed by devil worshippers; but in all likelihood, they were Brazilian natives and Portuguese colonists clearing the forests to make way for the plantations. In fact, the first phase of Portuguese colonization of Brazil had begun several decades earlier with logging of Brazil-wood, the first viable commodity to be exported from Portuguese America.

The historical and ecological contexts of *The Tempest* explore the dynamics of human interaction with the physical environment both in England and in the New World. Although Bermuda had been imagined as a god-forsaken, desolate, wind-swept desert inhabited by devils, the English colonists discovered a tropical paradise. Despite evidence of reckless exploitation of natural resources in the West Indies and in South America, the New World must have seemed as a promised land of endless natural resources. In England, the situation seemed to be the reverse. The colonists had left what many, including King James, thought was a nation dangerously depleted of its forests. Without this vital natural resource, England could turn into a desolate barren island peopled with cannibals; whereas, the New World, perceived as the land of cannibals would have to become home. This, I propose, becomes one of Shakespeare's central concerns in *The Tempest*. This play centers on notions of home and alien habitat as human constructs and on the power of the imagination and will to represent, shape, and transform the physical environment. In this play, Prospero dedicates several years of his life to assembling the pieces of his shattered world.

II. PROSPERO'S ISLAND

Prospero's island is a curious place. It seems to be a "real" place and an imaginary one, where natural and supernatural phenomena often cannot be separated. The experience of human habitation shows that the ecology of the island can meet basic needs and support some economic activity. Household chores must be carried out, and the necessities of life cannot be dispensed with. Prospero employs his slaves, Caliban, Ariel, and later Ferdinand, in various activities. Caliban, basically a household slave, attends to everyday chores: "But as 'tis, / We cannot miss him: he does make our fire, / Fetch in our wood, and serves in offices / That profit us" (1.2.310–313). The stage direction in Act II, scene ii indicates: "Enter Caliban with a burden of wood." Caliban fetches firewood and water and gathers edible fruit, roots, and plants. Prospero also refers to Ariel as his "slave" (1.2.270; 344), whom he employs in staging a storm and theatrical spectacles such as the banquet and the masque of the goddesses, and in a variety of other tasks at the bottom of the sea, which may imply pearl diving, and "in the veins of th'earth" (1.2.255), which may suggest mining activity. Ferdinand, however, is employed as a lumberjack. The stage direction in Act III, scene 1 reads: "Enter Ferdinand (bearing a Log)." Ferdinand explains his menial and painful labor: "I must remove / Some thousands of these logs and pile them up, / Upon a sore injunction" (3.1.9–11). When Miranda offers to "bear your logs the while," Ferdinand, flush with romantic enthusiasm, naturally refuses: "I had rather crack my sinews, break my back / Than you should such dishonor undergo / While I sit lazy by (3.1.26–28). Still later, he refers to his "wooden slavery" as a "patient log-man" (3.1.62; 67). Again, Ferdinand's temporary employment suggests large scale economic activities, as if Prospero's island were a *feitoria* presumably dedicated to logging and the export of timber.

But *The Tempest* also represents this island as a harsh environment, whose natural resourses are either depleted or hard to find. Trinculo, for example, finds neither "bush nor shrub to bear off any weather at all" (2.2.18–19), and Prospero intimates to Ferdinand that the island has nothing to offer but "sea water" and inedible or non-nourishing food: "fresh-brook mussels, withered roots, and husks" (1.2.463–64). Caliban realizes that his main asset is, in fact, his knowledge of the sparse resources of the island. When Prospero and Miranda arrived. Caliban showed them "all the qualities o'th' isle, / The fresh springs, brine-pits, barren place and fertile" (1.2.337–38) After meeting Stephano and Trinculo, Caliban once again offers to serve as their guide: "I'll show thee every fertile inch o'th' island" (2.2.144). Yet a little later, he offers his services: "I'll show thee the best springs; I'll pluck thee berries; / I'll fish for thee, and get thee wood enough" (2.2.156–157). He promises to show Stephano the treasures of the island: crabs, pignuts, jay's nest, the "nimble marmoset," "clust'ring filberts," and "young scamels" (2.2.163–168). Ironically, Caliban hopes never again to make "dams for fish," to fetch wood, or to "wash dish" (2.2.175–180). Without a guide, one may find it difficult to survive in this alien world.

Culturally and psychologically, the island also disorients the mind, and the characters discover that their senses prove unable to convey the essence of the island, which refuses to become anything but an alien habitat, *terra incognita*, an unchartered territory. This is particularly startling if we take into account that Prospero and Miranda have lived on the island for twelve years, and before them the place was occupied by the Algerian exile Sycorax and later her young son Caliban. The island has no name. As Paul Shepard observes in *Man in the Landscape*, "an environment without place names is fearful"; and "landscapes without place names are disorienting."[46] Prospero recognizes the importance of naming, because, according to Caliban, he sought to teach Caliban "how / To name the bigger light, and how the less" (1.2.333–34); yet he lives in an island without place names. Unlike him, Sir Thomas Gates and his fellow colonists in 1609 carefully surveyed the natural resources of Bermuda and named various locations. For example, the bay where they landed was named Gates's Bay after Sir Thomas Gates, the appointed governor of the Virginia colony. In *The Tempest*, the absence of place names forces the island dwellers, Ariel, Caliban, and Prospero, to use circumlocutions to identify specific places.

Although Ariel can name such places as Algiers, Naples, Milan, the Mediterranean sea, and Bermuda, he lacks names for places on the island. When reporting his creation of the storm and shipwreck of the first scene, Ariel tells Prospero that he left the king's ship safely in harbor "in the deep nook where once / Thou call'dst me up at midnight to fetch dew / From the still-vexed Bermoothes" (1.2.227–29). For Ariel, other places are equally vague: he lures Ferdinand to the "yellow sands" (1.2.375) and Trinculo, Stephano, and Caliban through "Toothed briers, sharp furzes, pricking goss, and thorns" to a cesspool or oxidation pond: "At last I left them / I'th'filthy mantled pool beyond your cell, / There dancing up to th'chins, that the foul lake / O'erstunk their feet" (4.1.180; 181–84). Prospero's cell becomes the main point of reference. Like Ariel, Prospero refers to specific geographical locations such as Milan, Naples, and Algiers; but about the island, he is vague.

Caliban, who has lived on the island all of his life, knows no place names, either. As I have indicated above, he knows how to find the island's resources, and yet he seems disoriented in this environment, seemingly unable to understand his sensory experiences. He says that Prospero's spirits pinch him, frighten him with "urchin-shows," lead him "like a firebrand, in the dark / Out of my way (2.2.1–6). At other times, he finds the fauna of the island disturbing. He says that apes "mow and chatter" and then bite him; hedgehogs "mount / Their pricks at my footfall"; and adders wrap themselves around his body and "with cloven tongues / Do hiss me into madness" (2.2.9–14). Later he explains to Trinculo and Stephano that he is enchanted by the beautiful noises, sounds, voices, and sweet airs "that delight and hurt not"; and then he adds, as if in a dream, "The clouds methought would open and show riches / Ready to drop upon me, that, when I waked / I cried to dream again" (3.2.138–140).

Dispersed around the island, the new European arrivals find it difficult to orient themselves. Like Caliban, Ferdinand seems particularly attuned to sounds and noises, but unable to determine the source of the music. Mesmerized, though disoriented, he follows the music in the air, unaware of any landmarks. For both Ferdinand and Caliban, the environment seems familiar and strange. Ferdinand states that "Sitting on a bank / Weeping again the King, my father's wrack," he heard music, which "crept by me upon the waters" (1.2.390–393). So he has followed the tune, not knowing where it will take him. Immediately after catching his first glimpse of Miranda, he notes that she speaks his language in such a beautiful way (1.2.429–431). Sounds lead to a glorious vision: "My spirits, as in a dream, are all bound up" (1.2.486); in her presence, he discovers "Space enough" for his contentment and happiness, seemingly indifferent to his new surroundings.

Other members of the royal party respond to the island in contradictory ways. As the royal ship approaches the island, the characters begin to feel the chaos into which they are being thrust. The storm, which we learn later was created by Prospero's magic, disorients the voyagers and threatens to erase markers of rank. Gonzalo yearns for the return of hierarchy and a system of justice, which would ensure the punishment of the insolent Boatswain. As the ship seems about to sink, Gonzalo bids farewell to the life he is leaving behind, and hopes for the best. His wish is about to be granted.

Adrian, Gonzalo, Sebastian, and Antonio cannot agree about the nature of the island. Adrian remarks on the contradictory nature of their perception: the island seems to be a "desert"; yet it is "of subtle, tender and delicate temperance (2.1.42–43). He praises the pleasant odors; whereas Sebastian and Antonio smell something rotten in the air. Gonzalo remarks that the grass looks green, but Antonio thinks that "the ground indeed is tawny" (2.1.53). They cannot even agree on whether their garments are stained with salt water or are "now as fresh as when we put them on first in Afric" (2.1.66–67). As Antonio and Sebastian are about to kill Alonso and Gonzalo, Gonzalo wakes up and reports that he heard a strange humming in his ear; whereas Sebastian reports hearing "a hollow burst of bellowing / Like bulls, or rather lions" (2.1.305–306). Inebriated, Trinculo and Stephano wander through the island, hearing its sounds. Stephano says that his "cellar is in a rock by th'seaside, where my wine is hid" and seems to know his way around the island (2.2.130–31); later, however, he, Trinculo, and Caliban in an inebriated state get lost and wander through the landscape until they come to rest in the cesspool outside Prospero's cell. Even the ever sensible Gonzalo admits that he is lost: "My old bones ache: here's a maze trod indeed / Through forthrights and meanders" (3.3.2–3). Ariel casts spells on members of the royal party and guides them, as prisoners of their senses, to "the line grove which weather-fends" Prospero's cell (5.1.10). But even after "their rising senses / Begin to chase the ignorant fumes that mantle / Their clearer reasons" (5.1.64–68), they remain confused. In fact Gonzalo responds to the strange events, "Whether this be / Or be not, I'll not swear" (5.1.122–23). Thus, as Prospero suggests, everyone has been "justled" from his senses (5.1.158). This is one of the markers of the island's strangeness, what Prospero describes as "some subtleties o' th' isle, that will not let you / Believe things certain" (5.1.124–25).

Even Prospero's daughter, Miranda, straddles illusion and reality. In Act I, scene ii, she correctly supposes that magic created the storm; yet she erroneously concludes: "Poor souls, they perished!" (9). Her sense of sight proves unreliable here as she cannot discern illusion from reality, although later sight connects her to Ferdinand. She notices Ferdinand's good looks and "brave form": "I might call him / A thing divine; for nothing natural / I ever saw so noble" (1.2.418–20). Throughout the first half of Act I, scene ii, Prospero doubts her ability to listen attentively, as he repeats several times the question, "Dost thou attend me?" (1.2.78).

Thus the characters cannot trust their perceptions of the island. This alien habitat seems to have few trees and yet yields thousands of logs; it has a scarcity of food and fresh water, and yet it sustains human life. It seems to be a wasteland, and yet has great natural resources. Empirical observation proves impossible because human senses cannot discern illusion from reality, magic from nature. The environment of the island is, in some ways, like the forest in *A Midsummer Night's Dream* where, as Demetrius underscores, the characters question whether they are awake or in a dream: "Are you sure / That we are awake?" (4.1.191-92).[47] Neither island nor the forest offers fixity; yet the stay on the island functions as a crucial stage in the characters' journey.

III. PROSPERO'S HOUSE

When he instructs Stephano to kill Prospero and burn the books, Caliban makes a curious statement about Prospero's belongings: "He has brave utensils (for so he calls them) / Which, when he has a house, he'll deck withal" (3.2.93–94). Caliban does not identify or list Prospero's "utensils"; it is, therefore, difficult to determine what objects Prospero must be collecting. Caliban is, however, an astute observer of Prospero's character. Although Prospero has no house, he is busily preparing himself for one. In fact, one could view the action of *The Tempest* as Prospero's attempts to extricate himself from the alien island of his exile and to regain his lost home in Italy. In this regard, the island becomes a way station, where Prospero keeps his material possessions and acquires new ones, gathers his memories and his family, assembles his enemies and friends, and envisions his and Miranda's return to their homeland.

In his stunning film *Prospero's Books* (Miramax, 1991), Peter Greenaway captures well this function of the island. Prospero, played by John Gielgud, surrounds himself with representations of home: rich clothing, abundant food, great halls of a palace, a library, a lavishly furnished throne room. A multitude of disrobed spirits replaces his Milanese courtiers, who attend to the court's business. Eventually, Prospero also brings to the island the royal family of Naples and the Neapolitan court, made up of king, crown prince, councillors, and hangers-on. Flashbacks reenact the birth of Miranda and Prospero's escape from Milan and thus function as an imaginary extension of the island. Greenaway's Prospero surrounds himself with memories of home, possessions, family members, friends, and enemies. He seems to possess an imagination dominated by what Lisa Jardine refers to as the Renaissance's "conspicuous consumption" and "unabashed enthusiasm for belongings."[48] I believe, however, that the material possessions form but one sign of Prospero's obsession with home.

In Shakespeare's play, Prospero's escape from Milan reveals a concern for material possessions. Prospero and Miranda are hurried out of the city in the middle of the night in a bark, which transports them to a "rotten carcass of a butt" (1.2.145), which was not rigged and had neither "tackle, sail, nor mast" (1.2.146–47), something that not even rats would call home. However ill equipped, the boat was loaded with water, food, goods, material possessions, and mementos of home:

> Some food we had, and some fresh water, that
> A noble Neapolitan, Gonzalo,
> Out of his charity, who being then appointed
> Master of this design, did give us, with
> Rich garments, linens, stuffs, and necessaries
> Which since have steaded much. So, of his gentleness,
> Knowing I loved my books, he furnished me
> From mine own library with volumes that
> I prize above my dukedom.   (1.2.159–168)

The food and water aid in the outcasts' survival at sea and later on the island. The rich garments, linens, stuffs and necessaries will help Prospero and Miranda maintain a semblance of their former state. The books link Prospero to his library and cultural heritage.

I suggest that these possessions have the opposite effect of what we might expect. Although they make life in an alien environment more comfortable, they also serve to maintain a bond to his former life. In fact, one can read Act I, scene ii as Prospero's attempt to help Miranda to sever her ties to the island and to reestablish a connection to Europe. To do so Prospero reintroduces Miranda to her home, family, and heritage. His narrative rests on a foundation of memories: "Canst thou remember / A time before we came unto this cell?" (1.2.38–39), and he adds, "By any other house or person?" (1.2.42). In vague memories, she nevertheless remembers the faces of servants, although not her mother: " 'Tis far off / And rather like a dream than an assurance / That my remembrance warrants. Had I not four or five women once that tended me?" (1.2.44–47). Prospero shapes a narrative, which begins with the library, where he pursues his studies in "the liberal arts" and isolates himself from the responsibilities of government, delegating the business of the state to his brother, Antonio, who takes possession and control of the rest of the house and manages Prospero's household as if it were his own. Antonio learns "how to grant suits, / How to deny them, who t'advance, and who / To trash for over-topping" (1.2.79–82). Through this narrative, Miranda learns about her father's life and former position, her mother, her uncle Antonio, her servants, and the circumstances of her father's banishment. Thus, Prospero guides Miranda to the beginning of her existence, to the place of her origins.

For a long time, Prospero has, in some ways, been making plans for

Miranda to assume her dynastic role as a European princess. After his narration of his brother's betrayal, Prospero points out to Miranda: "Have I, thy schoolmaster, made thee more profit / Than other princess can, that have more time / For vainer hours, and tutors not so careful" (1.2.172–74). Her home schooling will be crucial to Prospero's plan to marry his daughter to Ferdinand and make her queen of Naples. This alliance will help defeat Antonio's dynastic aspirations.[49] One could further argue that by a process of recollection of events of twelve years before, Prospero defamiliarizes the island for Miranda and redefines it as not home, although it may be the only home that she can remember.

Prospero also assembles a European court on the island. Interestingly, two centuries after the play was composed, history would repeat Prospero's feat. To enforce a continental blockade against England, Napoleon ordered the invasion of Portugal in 1807. To escape from the invading troops, the Portuguese royal family and the court decided to take sanctuary in the Portuguese colony of Brazil.[50] Escorted by four British warships, an armada consisting of the flagship *Príncipe Real*, sixteen Portuguese warships, and thirty merchant vessels set sail for the New World on 29 November 1807. Jam-packed aboard the vessels were some 10–15,000 people: Queen Dona Maria I, who was mentally ill; Prince Dom João, Regent of the Kingdom of Portugal; his wife Dona Carlota Joaquina, daughter of Carlos IV of Spain; the nine-year-old Crown Prince Dom Pedro, the future Emperor of Brazil and King of Portugal, and his younger brother Dom Miguel; as well as "the members of the council of state, ministers and advisers, justices of the High Court, officials of the Treasury, the upper echelons of the army and navy, the church hierarchy, members of the aristocracy, functionaries, professionals and businessmen, several hundred courtiers, servants and hangers-on, a marine brigade of 1,600 and miscellaneous citizens who managed by various means to secure passage."[51] The ships also transported a priceless cargo: the royal treasury, government files and other important documents, a printing press, and libraries, especially the Royal Library of Ajuda, with rarest medieval and Renaissance documents and books and several incunabula. In fact, holdings of the Royal Library of Ajuda would stay in Brazil to form the core of the Biblioteca Nacional of Brazil in Rio de Janeiro.[52] The fleet reached Bahia on 22 January 1808 and Rio de Janeiro on 7 March. The roles of colonial power and colony would be reversed: the colony became the capital of the Portuguese empire. As Bethel points out, this was the first time that a reigning European monarch had set foot in the New World.[53] Interestingly, the independence of Brazil would emerge out of this accident of history, for the crown prince Dom Pedro would proclaim Brazil's independence in 1822 and plant a long-lasting European monarchy in the New World.

Prospero, however, wishes to do differently. He assembles what seems like an entire European court, but not to establish a new kingdom in the New World; rather, he brings together presumably everyone who will be a part of his daughter's future life as Queen of Naples and Duchess of Milan. Through various characters, *The Tempest* presents competing versions of home, exemplified by Caliban and his confederates, Antonio and Sebastian, Alonso, and Gonzalo. Through these, Prospero hopes to forge a new home for himself and his daughter.

But in forging a home for Miranda, Prospero must also discover what home represents for each one of the characters, especially after they barely escape from drowning. Prospero finds in Alonso a poignant reminder of himself. Unwittingly, Gonzalo reminds Alonso of Claribel's wedding to the king of Tunis. Alonso regrets his decision because as a result of this his son is now lost: "Would I had never / Married my daughter there! for, coming thence, / My son is lost; and, in my rate, she too, / Who is so far from Italy removed / I ne'er again shall see her" (2.1.103–107). These references open a window into courtly intrigue and conflicting interests in Alonso's household in Naples. Sebastian recriminates his brother for the political and dynastic miscalculation:

> Sir, you may thank yourself for this great loss,
> That would not bless our Europe with your daughter,
> But rather loose her to an African,
> Where she, at least, is banished from your eye
> Who hath cause to wet the grief on't.   (2.1.120–24).

Unrelenting, Sebastian states that several persons begged Alonso not to send Claribel to Africa: "You were kneeled to and importuned otherwise / By all of us; and the fair soul herself / Weighed, between loathness and obedience, at / Which end o' th' beam should bow" (2.1.124–127). By tormenting Alonso about Claribel's suffering and misfortunes, Sebastian reminds us that Alonso has shattered whatever home he had, losing his daughter and his son and heir.

Antonio and Sebastian consider the island to be no-man's land, a perfect place for acts of villainy and ironically for their own political and dynastic machinations. Taking advantage of their travelling companions, who have fallen into a narcoleptic state, Antonio and Sebastian proceed to assert their own vision of home. Antonio tempts Sebastian to kill Alonso and take advantage of the opportunity that has arisen as a result of Alonso's mistakes and of the storm. Antonio sees a world of possibilities:

>   What might,
> Worthy Sebastian—O, what might?—No more!
> And yet methinks I see it in thy face,
> What thou shouldst be. Th' occasion speaks thee, and
> My strong imagination sees a crown
> Dropping upon thy head.   (2.1.198–203)

Not altogether sure whether he is asleep or awake, Sebastian listens to Antonio's proposal: the impossibility that Ferdinand is "undrowned" (231); the fact that Claribel is now queen of Tunis, "she that dwells / Ten leagues beyond man's life" (240–41); the great distance between Naples and Tunis. "'twixt which regions / There is some space (250–51); and Alonso's incompetence as a ruler, "there be that can rule Naples / As well as he that sleeps" (2.1.256–57). Sebastian agrees:

> As thou got'st Milan,
> I'll come by Naples. Draw thy sword. One stroke
> Shall free thee from the tribute which thou payest,
> And I the King shall love thee.   (2.1.284–288).

Antonio stands to gain much. His newly forged alliance with Sebastian will free him from the tribute that he has committed Milan to pay to Naples in order to rid himself of Prospero.

Alonso, Sebastian, and Antonio destroy rather than build. It seems appropriate that Prospero gives them a double vision of home, represented by the banquet and the appearance of the harpy. The banquet might be seen as the very emblem of a European court: all the trappings of royal hospitality and the sumptuousness of a privileged form of life. The stage direction reads: "Solemn and strange music; and Prospero on the top (invisible). Enter several strange Shapes, bringing in a banquet; and dance about it with gentle actions of salutations; and, inviting the King &c. to eat, they depart" (3.3). Alonso praises the harmony of the occasion and the "kind keepers" who have provided the feast. Sebastian vows not to dismiss the existence of unicorns and the phoenix anymore; Antonio renews his faith in travellers' tales. Even good Gonzalo wonders how people at home will react to his report: "If in Naples / I should report this now, would they believe me / If I should say I saw such islanders?" (3.3.27–29). The banquet symbolizes the good life, which they value much.

Yet this is nothing but an insubstantial pageant. As the royals approach to feast themselves at the table, the banquet vanishes; and a harpy appears to point out the crimes that all three—Alonso, Antonio, and Sebastian—have committed or would commit. The harpy utters words of condemnation, and reminds them that "From Milan [they] did supplant good Prospero; / Exposed unto the sea, which hath requit it, / Him and his innocent child" (3.3.70–72). The island becomes a place of damnation; nature itself has risen to torment them. The stage direction indicates that the harpy vanishes, and the shapes appear to "dance with mocks and mows," with grimaces and gestures. Through this, Prospero concludes: "And these, mine enemies, are all knit up / In their distractions; they now are in my pow'r" (3.3.88–92). Indeed, they become so desperate that they exit as if seeking their own deaths. From this, we can see that the home that these three men would build has been shattered; it is but an illusion. They have discovered the hell of their conscience.

In some ways, the life that these characters have would resemble Caliban's own pursuits. Caliban makes a double attempt to build a home on the island. At first, Prospero apparently treated Caliban as the son he did not have: "I have used thee / (Filth as thou art) with humane care, and lodged thee / In mine own cell till thou didst seek to violate / The honor of my child" (1.2.345–48). Caliban gloats about what he would have done: "O ho, O ho! Would't had been done! / Thou didst prevent me; I had peopled else / This isle with Calibans" (1.2.349–51). Miranda herself shows nothing but revulsion to his plans; she refers to him as an "abhorred slave" and "savage." When Stephano and Trinculo appear, he joins forces with them. Emboldened by wine, the three set out to kill Prospero, rape Miranda, and reconquer the island. All of this ironically parallels in part Antonio and Sebastian's plot against Alonso. The three are defeated not by the alcohol that they have consumed but by Prospero's rich garments, which Trinculo and Stephano try to steal.

Gonzalo also offers a view of an ideal home that he would like to build upon the island. In a passage derived from Montaigne, he imagines the island as a utopian paradise:

> I' th' commonwealth I would by contraries
> Execute all things; for no kind of traffic
> Would I admit; no name of magistrate;
> Letters should not be known; riches, poverty,
> And use of service, none; contract, succession,
> Bourn, bound of land, tilth, vineyard, none;
> No use of metal, corn, or wine, or oil;
> No occupation; all men idle, all;
> And women too, but innocent and pure;
> No sovereignty. (2.1.143–152).

Gonzalo would impose a European system of government, a monarchy, over which he wants to reign, but avoiding all the shortcomings of home. He proposes to eliminate trade and to create an economy without commodities. No one would work for anyone else, for "All things in common nature should produce / Without sweat or endeavor" (2.1.155–56). He would banish European technology and anything that could be used for acts of violence, such as sword, pike, knife, gun, or "engine" (2.1.156–160). Gonzalo envisions a return to the golden age. Little does he know that before long, Antonio and Sebastian will attempt to kill Alonso and in fact take Gonzalo's life, as well. The serpent has crept into Gonzalo's utopian garden, long before he has the opportunity to direct its colonization.

Thus *The Tempest* asks us to focus on the visions of home that several of the characters have to offer. Alonso confronts the effects of his destructive acts; Antonio and Sebastian, and Caliban and his confederates want to build a life through acts of violence and murder; and Gonzalo hopes to erect the foundation of a new world, one that seems in some ways the opposite of the life he has known. But Prospero has his own vision of what home should be like, and he proceeds to investigate its possibilities.

To celebrate the betrothal of Ferdinand and Miranda in Act IV, Prospero stages a masque, a mythological spectacle about Greco-Roman goddesses and fertility. Iris speaks of rich grasslands and meadows covered with wheat, rye, barley, and other crops (60 ff.); and Ceres refers to her woodlands: "My bosky acres and my unshrubbed down, / Rich scarf to my proud earth" (4.1.81–82). Ceres' final words promise abundant harvest: "Scarcity and want shall shun you, / Ceres' blessing so is on you" (4.1.116–17). Ferdinand is truly impressed with his father-in-law: "Let me live here ever! / So rare a wond'red father and a wise [wife] / Makes this place Paradise" (4.1.122–24). Iris summons the Naiades to "this green land" in order to help celebrate "a contract of true love" (4.1.130; 133).

Through the marriage of his daughter, Prospero forges a dynastic alliance with Alonso, ensures his daughter's future as queen of Naples, and regains his position as duke of Milan. In addition, he also offers Miranda and Ferdinand a vision of a new kingdom, where farming does not lead to shortages of wood; the forests and groves still provide abundant firewood and timber. Interestingly, Arthur Standish also offered a similar vision through which he hoped to guide his king and his fellow countrymen out of the woes brought on by deforestation. In his books, Standish offers simple, practical solutions: that farmers should plant their hedges with trees to be "topped and lopped for firewood"; that for every acre of arable land at least four trees be planted and preserved for timber; that those who own woodlands be enjoined "to plant and preserve so many trees and so much wood, as hereafter they shall fell or waste"; that all tenants be encouraged to do the same; that landowners enclose so many acres and take appropriate measures to protect saplings from damage caused by cattle and sheep.[54] When he issues his *New Directions of the Experience Authorized by the Kings most excellent Majesty* in 1616, Standish enumerates in his dedication to King James the benefits to be accrued from his reforestation guidelines: "By which Plantation, these subsequent goods usually follow: Timber restored, fire-wood at reasonable rate valewed, Iron-workes, and Glasse-houses in few yeares provided, and Most, not altogether unprofitable, plenteously affoorded."[55]

As an insubstantial pageant, the masque of the goddesses melts into thin air, but it provides Ferdinand and Miranda with a dream to strive for. That dream involves for Miranda a discovery of her home and homeland and the potential that it has. At the sight of her father-in-law and the Neapolitan court over which one day she will preside, she exclaims "O, wonder / How many goodly creatures are there here! / How beauteous mankind is! 0 brave new world / That has such people in't" (5.1.181–84). Gonzalo sums up the experience of the play: "Was Milan thrust from Milan that his issue / Should become kings of Naples? O, rejoice / Beyond a common joy, and set it down / With gold on lasting pillars" (5.1.205–208). Thus, *The Tempest* presents characters estranged from their environment and examines how we perceive, respond to, or live in an alien world, a place to which we do not belong. From this alien habitat, we try to reassemble the pieces of our lost or shattered home. Like Standish, Prospero reaffirms a vision of place as the beginning of our existence, a return to our cultural and ecological roots.

NOTES

1. Paraphrased from the OED definition.
2. Douglas C. D. Pocock, "Introduction: Imaginative Literature and the Geographer," *Humanistic Geography and Literature: Essays on the Experience of Place*, ed., Douglas C. D. Pocock (London: Croom Helm; Totowa, New Jersey: Barnes & Noble Books, 1981), 17.
3. This statement paraphrases and combines several OED definitions.
4. David E. Sopher, "The Landscape of Home: Myth, Experience, Social Meaning," in *The Interpretation of Ordinary Landscapes: Geographical Essays*, ed., D. W. Meinig (Oxford and New York: Oxford UP, 1979), 136.
5. Roger Bacon, *The Opus Majus of Roger Bacon*, trans., Robert Belle Burke (New York: Russell & Russell, 1962), 1:159.
6. William Shakespeare, *The Norton Facsimile The First Folio of Shakespeare*, ed., Charlton Hinman (New York: W. W. Norton, 1968), 37.
7. William Shakespeare, *The Tempest*, ed., Northrop Frye (New York: Penguin, 1981). All quotations from the play will be from this edition.
8. John Block Friedman, *The Monstrous Races in Medieval Art and Thought* (Cambridge, Massachussetts: Harvard UP, 1981), 36.
9. Charles Frey, "*The Tempest* and the New World," *Shakespeare Quarterly* 30 (1979): 41. In "Voyage to Tunis: New History and the Old World of *The Tempest*," *ELH* 64 (1997): 333–357, Richard Wilson argues that "the New Historicist success in relocating *The Tempest* in Virginia has transported it too far from Virgil, and the Old World of Aeneas where its fiction is set, between Tunis and Naples" (333). He sets out to emphasize the Mediterranean, not the New World setting of the play.
10. Strabo, *The Geography of Strabo*, trans., Horace Leonard Jones (Cambridge: Harvard UP; London: William Heinemann, 1917), 1:1.8.
11. Strabo 1:1.8.
12. John L. Allen, "Lands of Myth, Waters of Wonder: The Place of the Imagination in the History of Geographical Exploration," in *Geographies of the Mind: Essays in Historical Geosophy*, eds., David Lowenthal and Martyn J. Bowden (Oxford and New York: Oxford UP, 1976), 43.
13. Kathleen A. Myers, "The Representation of New World Phenomena: Visual Epistemology and Gonzalo Fernández de Oviedo's Illustrations," in *Early Images of the Americas: Transfer and Invention*, eds., Jerry M. Williams and Robert E. Lewis (Tucson: U of Arizona P, 1993), 188.
14. Myers, 191–92.

15. Myers, 192.
16. Myers, 206.
17. Michel de Montaigne, *The Essays of Montaigne*, trans., John Florio (London, 1603; rpt. London: David Nutt, 1892), 220–21.
18. Silvester Jourdain, "A Discovery of the Bermudas, Otherwise called the Isle of Devils" (London, 1610), in *A Voyage to Virginia in 1609: Two Narratives*, ed., Louis B. Wright (Charlottesville: UP of Virginia, 1964), 108. In his *Annales* (London, 1615), John Stow reports that the Bermuda islands were "supposed to be inchanted, and inhabited with witches, and devills, which grew by reason of accustomed monstrous Thunder, storme, and tempest, neere unto those Ilands also for that whole coast is so wonderous daungerous, or Rockes, that few can approach them, but with unspeakeable hazard of shippe wrack" (944).
19. Jourdain, 108.
20. Jourdain, 109.
21. William Strachy, "A True Reportory of the Wracke, and redemption of Sir Thomas Gates Knight," in Samuel Purchas, *Hakluytus Posthumus or Purchas His Pilgrimes* (Glasgow: James MacLehose and Sons, 1906), 6.
22. Strachy, 7.
23. Strachy, 7.
24. Strachy, 13.
25. Strachy, 14.
26. Strachy, 14.
27. John Perlin, *A Forest Journey: The Role of Wood in the Development of Civilization* (New York: W. W. Norton, 1989), 177.
28. William Harrison, *Harrison's Description of England*, ed., Fredrick J. Furnivall (London: New Shakespeare Society, 1877), 336–37. Joannes Boemus, in *The manners, lawes, and customes of all nations*, trans., Edward Aston (London, 1610), speaks of plentiful woodlands in the England of the past: "Thick woods served them [the British people] in steed of cities, wherein they builded them cabbines and cottages, harboring themselves and their cattaile under one roofe" (386–87).
29. Harrison, 336–37.
30. Harrison, 337.
31. James I, King of England, *The Political Works of James I*, ed., Charles Howard McIlwain (Cambridge: Harvard UP, 1918), 323.
32. James I, King of England, 323.
33. James I, King of England, 323.
34. James I, King of England, 324.
35. R. Ch., *An olde thrift newly revived, wherein is declared the manner of planting, preserving, and husbanding yong trees of divers kinds for Timber and Fuell* (London, 1612), sig. A3v-A4.
36. Arthur Standish, *Common Complaints* (London, 1611), sig. B2.
37. Arthur Standish, *The Commons Complaints* (London, 1611), sig. C1. This is quoted from the Huntington Library's copy of STC 21772, which seems to be a revised and cleaner version of a copy owned by the British Library.
38. Standish, *Commons Complaints*, sig. C1.

39. Standish, *Commons Complaints*, sig. C1v.

40. Arthur Standish, *The Commons Complaint* (London, 1612). I have consulted the Folger Library copy of STC 23203.

41. For an account of this expedition, see Max Justo Guedes, "Portugal-Brazil: The Encounter Between Two Worlds," in *Portugal-Brazil The Age of Atlantic Discoveries*, eds., Max Justo Guedes and Gerald Lombardi (Lisbon: Bertrand Editora; Milan: Franco Maria Ricci; New York: Brazilian Cultural Foundation, 1990), 167–68.

42. Thomas More, in *Utopia* (1516, translated into English by Ralph Robinson in 1550), portrays an imaginary Portuguese scholar by the name of Raphael Hythlodaeus, who presumably had been left at the *Feitoria* by Amerigo Vespucci: "[Raphael] joined Amerigo Vespucci and was his constant companion in the last three of those four voyages which are now universally read of, but on the final voyage he did not return with him. He importuned and even wrested from Amerigo permission to be one of the twenty-four who at the farthest point of the last voyage were left behind in the fort" [Thomas More, *Utopia*, ed., Edward Surtz (New Haven and London: Yale UP, 1964), 12–13.] Shakespeare may have been acquainted with More's universally acclaimed work, especially considering his interest in More's life: Shakespeare participated in the revision of the play *Sir Thomas More* around 1603–4 and wrote a scene for the play. See Walter Cohen, "Sir Thomas More: Passages Attributed to Shakespeare," in *Norton Shakespeare*, ed., Stephen Greenblatt et al., (New York: W. W. Norton, 1997), 2011–2014. Strachy also records, on a much smaller scale, logging activities in Bermuda, especially for obtaining the wood necessary to build the ships that would transport the colonists on to Virginia.

43. Guedes, 168.

44. Guedes, 167.

45. Sir Francis Drake, *The World Encompassed, Collated with an Unpublished Manuscript of Francis Fletcher* (London: Hakluyt Society, 1854), 34. It is interesting to compare this passage to one in the romance, *The Mirrour of Knighthood*, translated by R. Parry in c. 1586. Aboard a ship, the Knight of the Sun and his crew run into a great storm: "they tumbled and tossed with that tempest all that day and the night following, without any semblaunce of calmenesse" [*The Mirrour of Knighthood*, trans., R. Parry (1586?) in *Narrative and Dramatic Sources of Shakespeare*, ed., Geoffrey Bullough (London: Routledge & Kegan Paul; New York: Columbia UP, 1975), 8:304.] The crew discovers a certain island far off, "and out of the middest thereof they might perceive ascend up into the aire at times great flames and sparkes of fire, with a terrible darke and thicke smoake, as though they hadde beene burning of some drie things" (304). This, they discover, was the Island of the Devil or "solitaire Iland," a place formally ruled by Artimaga, a woman "so abhominable and evill, that never the like was seene nor heard of amongst women." When she was fifteen years old, Artimaga "had talke and conversation with him [the Devil], as though he had bene hir husband" (304). From here, Shakespeare may have derived materials for Prospero's narrative of Sycorax's story.

46. Paul Shepard, *Man in the Landscape: A Historic View of the Esthetics of Nature* (College Station: Texas A&M UP, 1991), 41, 43.

47. William Shakespeare, *A Midsummer Night's Dream*, ed., Madeleine Doran (New York: Penguin, 1987).

48. Lisa Jardine, *Worldly Goods: A New History of the Renaissance* (New York and London: Doubleday, 1996), 15.

49. I have discussed this point and examined the gender implications of Prospero's struggle with Antonio in "*The Tempest*, Comedy, and the Space of the Other," in *Acting Funny: Comic Theory and Practice in Shakespeare*, ed., Frances Teague (Rutherford: Farleigh Dickinson UP, 1994), 52–71. See also Chapter 6 of my book, *Shakespeare's Cross-cultural Encounters* (London: Macmillan P; New York: St. Martin's, 1999).

50. For accounts of the events, see Mary Wilhelmine Williams, *Dom Pedro the Magnanimous: Second Emperor of Brazil* (Chapel Hill: U of North Carolina P, 1937), 4–6; and Leslie Bethell, ed., *Brazil Empire and Republic, 1822–1930* (New York and Cambridge: Cambridge UP, 1989), 1–21.

51. Bethell, 15.

52. Bethell, 16.

53. Bethell, 16.

54. Standish, *Commons Complaints* (1611), sig. B2. I am here quoting from the British Library copy. The Huntington copy waters down this passage: "and further, that all such persons as have at this instant their grounds furnished with wood in such sort as is required, might be also injoyned to continue the same, and to preserve so many Timber trees, and so many for fire wood, as hereafter they may fell or waste" (sig. C2).

55. Arthur Standish, *New Directions of Experience Authorized by the Kings most excellent Majesty, as may appear for the increasing of Timber and Fire-wood* (London, 1616), sig. A3.

Title page of Lewis Robert's *The Marchant's Mapp of Commerce*, 1638. Used by permission of the Folger Shakespeare Library.

Peopling, Profiting, and Pleasure in *The Tempest*

Barbara Ann Sebek

He that loveth pleasure shall be a poor man. (Proverbs 21:17)

The mistress which I serve quickens what's dead
And makes my labors pleasures. (Ferdinand, 3.1.6–7)

What is a gentleman but his pleasure? (Viscount Edward Conway)

I am full of pleasure. (Caliban, 3.2.118)[1]

Like a number of "economic" texts in the early modern period, *The Tempest* registers and participates in wider cultural efforts to understand the place of pleasure in a proto-capitalist "world system" of commodity exchange.[2] I juxtapose the quotations in my epigraph in order to foreground the threat of illicit, pleasurable exchanges across the boundaries of class and culture at issue in Shakespeare's play, as it dances round the dangerous possibilities that crop up when pleasure and labor coincide. Viscount Conway considers a man's experience of pleasure the sole constituent of class identity. A number of texts similarly link pleasure to gentility, presenting pleasure and profit as an either/or configuration. The title page of Lewis Robert's global commercial atlas *The Merchant's Mappe of Commerce* (1638) announces, for example, that his book is necessary "for all Gentlmen & others that travell abroad for delight & plesure, and for all marchants or their factors that Excercise the Arte of Marchandizeinge in any Parte of the habitable world."[3] Here, Roberts produces class identifications akin to those of Viscount Conway, regarding the pleasure-seeking traveller primarily as a member of the gentility. In Henry Peacham's chapter on travel in *The Compleat Gentleman* (1622), the gentleman must choose between pleasure or profit as the motive for travel: "if you intend to travell you must first propound unto yourself the end . . . which either is pleasure or profit."[4] Considered alongside Roberts' *The Merchant's Mappe of Commerce* and Arthur Golding's translation of Seneca's *De Beneficiis* (1578), Shakespeare's play reveals how pleasure can become a problem when social and commercial relations are played out in a remote locale, dependent on the exploitation of a native population and native resources (otherwise known as "the colonial situation").[5] The play reveals how pleasure can confound what commercial cosmographer Roberts approvingly calls "the Motive Profit." It likewise reveals how injunctions against material pleasure in the Senecan economy of the "benefit" pave the way for profit-driven commodity exchange, even though those who transact in benefits are enjoined to "tread profit underfoot."[6]

It is a truism in postmodern criticism that class, race and other categories of identity are not states of being, but rather are constructed positions or ideologically produced relations, structures that must be continually re-articulated. Setting its action in a remote setting, beyond the pale of European "civilization," *The Tempest* explores what happens in a context largely devoid of ordinary markers of class difference.[7] Witness, for example, the chaos of the opening scene in which the Boatswain talks back to his superiors, accusing them of "mar[ring] our labor" (1.1.13), ordering them below deck. Consider the fact that Miranda, according to Prospero, is "ignorant of what thou art, naught knowing / Of whence I am" (1.2.18–19). Hear, as well Ferdinand's conditional assertion to Miranda that "I am the best of them that speak this speech, / Were I but where 'tis spoken" (1.2.433–34). If a gentleman is nothing but his pleasure, and if Caliban is indeed "full of pleasure," how are Ferdinand and Caliban to be differentiated, especially given that they do not find themselves where the language of pleasure-seeking gentlemen is spoken? The question is especially charged since both Caliban and Ferdinand (each in his own way) are laborers for love.[8] Questions of labor, pleasure, and profit cluster around Miranda, an erotic property construed as a specifically aristocratic affair, the "acquisition / worthily purchased" (4.1.13–14) by the pleasurefully laboring Ferdinand. If Miranda has "no ambitions to see a goodlier man" (1.2.486–87) than one of the first on whom she opens her fringed curtains, what is to prevent any day-laborer from laying claim to her as erotic property? And, potentially even more disconcerting, what is to prevent her from desiring and peopling with one of *them*?

One way of exploring the relations between traders (or would-be traders), laborers (or would-be laborers) and the conceptual status of the goods in which they trade (or over which they labor), is invited by the following little ditty, in which tobacco is accorded powers like those of Miranda, the "mistress . . . which quickens what's dead":[9]

> Tobacco, tobacco, sing sweetly for tobacco!
> Tobacco is like love, oh love it;
> For you see, I will prove it.

> Love maketh lean the fat men's tumour,
> So doth tobacco.
> Love still dries up the wanton humour,
> So doth tobacco.
> Love makes men sail from shore to shore,
> So doth tobacco.
> 'Tis fond love often makes men poor,
> So doth tobacco.[10]

As a sought-after commodity, tobacco profits those who travel for and trade in it, but indulging in the desire for it depletes and impoverishes its consumers, including the traveller/trader who procures it from distant lands. If the trader's focus turns to the pleasures tobacco provides rather than its exchange value, consumer desire confounds the profit motive. It is those compelled by "the motive profit" to travel and trade in foreign lands whom Lewis Roberts enjoins to read and thereby "profit" from his voluminous commercial atlas and commodity catalogue, *The Merchant's Mappe*. In a universalizing claim like John Wheeler's notion that "all the world choppeth and changeth, runneth and raveth after Marts, Markets and Merchandising," Roberts says that trade is driven by "the natural inclination of Mankind to enrich themselves."[11] But what is the enterprising merchant to do when that "natural inclination" butts up against the desire to smoke the goods (or sleep with the goods) instead of profiting from them—when use-value wins out over exchange-value? Indeed, with its extensive lists of the commodities to be procured from across the globe, Roberts' *Mappe* might function for its readers not only as a guide for locating profit-providing tradables, but as a kind of Sears Catalogue, producing consumer desires.

By intoning that tobacco, like love, "makes men sail from shore to shore," the tobacco song suggests not only how the commodity is a desired thing, but also how the drive for profit from commodity exchange is like erotic desire. Moreover, the song insists on the lovable potential of things: the confounding of the separation between things and persons in commodity exchange.[12] In a profit-driven commodity culture, the potential for one's relations with persons to approximate one's relations with things becomes more salient; the conceptual status of "that most precious category of goods," the "supreme gift"—women—becomes particularly problematic.[13] A key distinction that *The Tempest* draws is that between profit-receiving aristocrats and profit-providing laborers. Though it risks mapping later structures back onto an earlier period, we can read Caliban as a prototype of exploited labor-power, and Prospero as a capitalist. Miranda becomes a figure for the ambiguous status of goods and persons in capitalism: she is that which is labored for and that which is exchanged between men. Yet in positioning her in these ways, the play groups her with laborers like Caliban and the sunburned sicklemen in the masque of Ceres, a grouping made more possible by the intimacies and isolation of the colonial situation. So the play gives us a glimpse of counter-balanced threats: of cross-cultural peopling, of the blurring of the line between laboring servants and aristocratic bosses, of pleasurable transactions that do not turn a profit, and of taking too much pleasure in the goods.

The Tempest helps us see how the tangle of "economic" and "erotic" motives is particularly dense in a dynastic sex/gender system that is inter-twined with capitalist forms of profit. The conceptualization of an aristocratic woman such as Miranda as an exchanged object rather than as a transactor herself threatens to collapse class difference, since it potentially makes her an erotic property for men other than aristocrats and princely heirs. Prospero manages this threat by heightening the similarity between laborer and legitimate aristocratic suitor in order to then differentiate them. By insisting on the pleasure that Ferdinand takes in log-bearing, the play tries to ensure that Miranda can be objectified as an erotic property (an "acquisition worthily purchased" and Prospero's "gift") without lumping her with that other category of goods, the laborer. This ideological process is not ultimately successful, however, since Miranda defies simple categorization. Although the normative construction of "woman" in the early modern period's legal, economic, and political discourses was premised on the idea of women as property, we are dealing with a historical moment in which competing symbolic and material economies were available, ones that construed "property" of different sorts.[14] We must particularize and historicize the way goods are construed in the period's available economic discourses in order to see how Miranda is not objectified in any simple or straightforward sense—how, in fact, this elusive contradictory property is required to be an active, desiring subject. By doing so, we can complicate an idea all too often taken as a given—that women function as mere "objects" of exchange between men.

*   *   *

Just as Miranda cannot be objectified in a simple way, Caliban is not "othered" in any simple way; he is subsumed into the "master category of the 'other'" but simultaneously "seems to exist at the site of a conflict of discourses."[15] By focusing specifically on Caliban as a servant, Fran Dolan helps show how the threat of Caliban consists of his familiarity, the fact that he "is not 'other' enough."[16] Indeed, when Miranda expresses pleasure in Ferdinand, Prospero likens him to Caliban: "to the most of men this is a Caliban" (1.2.484). Moreover, Prospero reassures Miranda that Ferdinand is indeed human, one of us, by pointing to the very features by which *Caliban* might be likened to us: "it eats and sleeps and hath such senses / As we have such (1.2.416–17).

John Dryden, in his adaptation of *The Tempest*, bypasses the way that Shakespeare's play suggests an identity between Ferdinand and Caliban; instead, Dryden gives Ferdinand the pseudo-rival Hippolito, a European who grew up on the island and who has been prevented by Prospero from seeing women before the action of the play begins.[17] By making Hippolito rather than Caliban Ferdinand's rival, Dryden's plot displaces the threat of cross-cultural sex onto the "lowlife" plot, giving us Caliban's sister Sycorax who has sexual and dynastic designs on Trincalo: "Thou shalt get me twenty Sycoraxes, and I'le get thee twenty Calibans" (3.2.41–42). This plot structure defuses the threats of sexual commerce that crosses lines of culture and class. Instead of the marital alliance between Alonso's daughter Claribel and the African Tunis—the transglobal trade that serves as the pre-dramatic catalyst bringing the Europeans to Prospero's island in Shakespeare's play—Dryden's Italians have been on a military expedition, driving the Moors of Spain from Portugal:

ANT.	Indeed we first broke truce with Heav'n:
	You to the waves an Infant Prince expos'd,
	And on the waves have lost an only Son;
	I did usurp my Brother's fertile lands, and now
	Am cast upon this desert Isle.
GONZ.	These, Sir, 'tis true, were crimes of a black Dye,
	But both of you have made amends to Heav'n,
	By your late Voyage into Portugal,
	Where, in defence of Christianity,
	Your valour has repuls'd the Moors of Spain. (2.1.21–30)

In the early seventeenth century, southern Spain was experiencing a regional economic crisis, one that both precipitated and was intensified by the expulsion of Moors who went on to "people" and "profit" the region they settled in Northern Africa. The years 1609–1614 witnessed the expulsion of 250,000 unconverted Moslems from the region. The expulsion—an effort, it has been argued, to scapegoat the Moors for the region's economic woes—had the effect of compounding these problems, weakening southern Spanish agriculture and halting rent payments to overlords, who then could not repay their mortgages. By the mid-seventeenth century Spanish wool exports begin losing to English competition. According to King Philip IV's confessor in 1633:

> It is a very short time ago since the moriscos were expelled, an action which did such harm to these kingdoms that it would be a good idea to have them back again if they could be persuaded to accept our holy faith.[18]

The Moors could not be so persuaded, however, having settled across Northern Africa. Their beneficial impact on the region where they settled is later characterized by Lewis Roberts in the *Merchant's Mappe*:

> This kingdom is much bettered and inriched by the labour of those Moores which by thousands were banished from Spain, who have here built many Cities, and Temples, according to their superstitious use, planted Vines, Oranges, Lemons, etc and thereby have both much peopled and profited this whole countrye.[19]

Following the list of fertile fruit trees, this alliterative, euphonious, even euphuistic conjoining of "peopling" and "profiting" forges a discursive link that calls up the various forms of exchange, as well as the labor, on which a flourishing economy depends. The political and military threats to Christian Europe that accompany such an economy are alluded to in an even earlier period in Marlowe's *Tamburlaine*. Usumcasane brags that if the Moorish king Bajazeth were to "bring millions infinite of men / *Unpeopling* Western Africa" (3.3.33–34), the Moorish threat would be crushed by the mighty Tamburlaine.[20]

Like Roberts's account of the Moorish influence in Barbary, Shakespeare's *Tempest* suggests links between peopling and profiting, links that are disturbingly located in the figure of Caliban, the "villain," according to Miranda, "I do not love to look on." Her proximity to the unlovable object of sight must be tolerated, since, as Prospero replies: "But, as 'tis, / We cannot miss him. He does make our fire, / Fetch in our wood, and serves in offices / That profit us" (1.2.312–316). Prospero's reply puns on "villain," indicating its sense as a laborer as well as a generally nasty fellow.[21] Unlike the Spanish who expelled the Moors and then suffered economically for so doing, Prospero keeps the "other" around to be profited from. The "profit" that the villein Caliban provides causes the toleration of the threat of illicit, unprofitable "peopling" that he poses. As Caliban says of his attempted rape of Miranda: "Would it had been done! / Thou didst prevent me; I had peopled else / This isle with Calibans" (1.2.353–54). As in Roberts's and Marlowe's accounts of provinces "peopled" with Moors, anxiety over the notion of Moors "peopling" lurks behind Caliban's desire to "people" the island where Prospero currently holds sway.

The attempted rape to which Caliban refers can be understood, as Kim Hall argues, as an attack on "a cultural integrity that must be protected from encroachment by outsiders."[22] This is one of the very threats that the expulsion of the Moors from Spain arguably aimed to eliminate, but the effect of their expulsion was to deplete the economy in Spain and to "people" and "profit" the "whole country" where they settled. Caliban's assault on Miranda can likewise be seen as a result of the engendering of desire across the line dividing ruler from laborer in the colonial situation. The proximity of the European masters and their profit-providing laborers opens the possibility for unruly desires that exceed the aims of a system of trade premised on procuring, and profiting from, commodities from distant locales. In addition to an allegory of the threat of cross-cultural sexual commerce, the Miranda-Caliban plot can read as an allegory for the interested construction of difference that is specifically a matter of class. Aristocratic Miranda is to be among those profiting from, not coupling with, the natives. The Caliban-Miranda plot invokes and manages the threat of sexual and social commerce between the labor pool and those whom they profit.

By being opposed to Caliban's effort to violate aristocratic, maiden honor, peopling the island with Calibans, the dramatization of Ferdinand's labors for Miranda furthers the construction of class difference. Although a number of feminist critics have considered how *The Tempest* constructs both affinities and distinctions between Caliban and Ferdinand vis-a-vis Miranda,[23] none attends fully to the extent to which Ferdinand's *pleasure* in labor helps draw that distinction. The scene in which Caliban plots with Trinculo and Stephano to overthrow Prospero opens with Caliban carrying in a "burden of wood." The very next scene opens with Ferdinand "bearing a log" and concludes with the two young lovers exchanging marriage vows without paternal consent. This parallel stage business of log-bearing underscores potential parallels between Caliban and Ferdinand, both of whom desire Miranda, and both of whose desires need to be tamed and controlled by Prospero. But the similarity ends there, since, for Ferdinand, labor is pleasurable whereas for Caliban it is painful and enforced. Caliban's wood-bearing tasks are punishment for acting on desire for Miranda whereas Ferdinand's are chivalric sport, insistently differentiated from the profit-providing "offices" in which Caliban serves. For Ferdinand, labor *is* pleasure; desire for Miranda, Ferdinand says, "makes my labors pleasures" (3.1.7); "for your sake / Am I this patient log-man" (66–67). Indeed, in the soliloquy which opens 3.1, the log-carrying Ferdinand self-consciously en-nobles himself in pursuing "this my mean task." The speech is full of knotty aphorisms about labor and pleasure that distinguish the "base," "mean task" and "poor matter" from the noble pursuit of them, and from their "rich ends" (3.1.1–15), i.e., the noble goal of acquiring aristocratic Miranda. Miranda herself, according to Ferdinand, says that "such baseness / Had never like executor" (12–13). In order to obscure the parallel between Ferdinand and Caliban, then, the play turns Ferdinand into a version of "delicate" Ariel" (4.1.49), one whose "industrious" service (4.1.22) to Prospero entails pleasure—in contradistinction to Caliban for whom enforced labor is punishment.[24] Prospero's role as senex—imposing tasks on Ferdinand "lest too light winning / Make the prize light" (1.2.455–56)—serves to reinforce likenesses (both carry logs, seek Miranda, take pleasure in her company, submit to Prospero) in order to differentiate the function that labor serves for the aristocratic suitor versus the laboring villein.[25]

Although Miranda is positioned as the prize, the goods to be won, she is herself a desiring, speaking transactor: she reveals her name in the same breath that she indicates that doing so is proscribed ("O my father, / I have broke your hest to say so" [3.1.36]), and she speaks just as she violates paternal regulation ("but I prattle something too wildly, and my father's precepts / I therein do forget" [57–59]). Miranda even goes as far as offering herself to Ferdinand:

> [I] dare not offer
> What I desire to give, and much less take
> What I shall die to want.
>
>
>   Hence, bashful cunning,
> And prompt me, plain and holy innocence!
> I am your wife, if you will marry me;
> If not, I'll die your maid. To be your fellow
> You may deny me, but I'll be your servant
> Whether you will or no.   (3.1.77–79, 81–86)

Since Miranda has already given herself away before Prospero hands her over to Ferdinand, the very explicitness of the play's staging of the "worthy gift" and "acquisition" of Miranda as goods in 4.1 unsettles the "traffic in women" paradigm, a paradigm that even a recent reading as nuanced and persuasive as that of Jyotsna Singh basically rehearses.[26] Of course, Prospero does control the courtship in ways that Miranda does not realize. But as Richard Wheeler points out, Prospero is at his most powerless when he oversees the masque celebrating the marital union.[27] Moreover, as far as Miranda is aware, she is indeed rebelling against paternal authority when she gives herself away before gaining Prospero's consent. We might then read her as a figure for the subject in ideology, since she does not recognize the degree to which her longing and pleasure are being manufactured and channeled into a profitable enterprise.

While the play presents the spectacle of Caliban's laboring body as that which profits Prospero and Miranda, Miranda herself wants to get in on the game: "If you'll sit down, / I'll bear your logs the while. Pray, give me that. / I'll carry it to the pile" (3.1.22–24). Perhaps an even more unsettling offer than giving herself to Ferdinand in marriage is this offer to perform his labor. She resists being positioned as the prize that is labored for. This move—like her willful insistence on being Ferdinand's servant "whether he will or no"—aligns her with the labor pool, and the whole point of Prospero's "project," as well as the project of the play, is to keep her away from them. So the individual character Miranda is indeed arguably contained by patriarchal—and proto-capitalist—authority, but her offer to perform labor introduces conceptual slippage that threatens the logic of a commodity economy.

Prospero tries to re-assert his control over Miranda's circulation, ceremoniously handing her over to Ferdinand; but his very efforts to regulate pleasure are troubled by his unfailing focus *on* that pleasure:

> . . . as my gift and thine own acquisition
> Worthily purchased, take my daughter. But
> If thou dost break her virgin-knot before
> All sanctimonious ceremonies may

> With full and holy rite be ministered,
> No sweet aspersion shall the heavens let fall
> To make this contract grow; but barren hate,
> Sour-eyed disdain, and discord shall bestrew
> The union of your bed with weeds so loathly
> That you shall hate it both. (4.1.13–22)

The conditional nature of the gift points to Prospero's effort to regulate desire for that which is being given—to contain sexual pleasure ceremoniously. The condition is articulated here in the form of a curse, an utterance which links Prospero to the play's most salient exemplar of cursing, Caliban: "you taught me language and my profit on't / Is I know how to curse" (1.2.366–67). Unlike Lear, who curses his daughter with infertility—"into her womb convey sterility; dry up in her the organs of increase" (1.4.277–73)—Prospero's condition/curse centers not on the *issue*, but on Miranda and Ferdinand's *pleasure* in the "union of your bed": "Barren hate / Sour-eyed disdain, and discord shall bestrew / The union of your bed with weeds so loathly / That you shall hate it both" (4.1.13–22). In imposing the log-bearing tasks, and in ceremoniously giving away the gift of Miranda, Prospero dramatizes the effort to exercise control over the daughter's sexuality by insisting on her chastity. Such control of female sexuality ensures control over bloodlines, the transfer of wealth, and the forging of desired political alliances.[28] But there is more going on here: Ferdinand's *enjoyment of* and *pleasure in* the "acquisition" is what Prospero is depicted as trying so laboriously to control. So while we do indeed see the paternal regulation of female sexuality, Prospero's enforcement of pleasurable labors serves to *produce* desire for this particular merchandise. And, as Prospero's "both" in the condition that "you shall hate it both" (22) reveals, the prize itself might take pleasure in the union.

Even as Prospero tries to negate the pleasure that the "prize" herself takes in the union, he points to its possibility. In fact, Miranda *must* take pleasure in Ferdinand in order for Prospero's "project" to succeed. The "loathly" weeds with which Prospero curses the pre-marital union recalls the "loathness" which Sebastian claims Claribel, the play's other new bride, felt toward the King of Tunis. According to Sebastian, the "fair soul herself / Weighed between loathness" at the match and "obedience" to her father (2.1.130–132). Claribel's obedience to paternal control enables the transglobal political alliance, but only after her purported "loathness"—her lack of pleasure in the union—threatened to undermine it.[29] Unlike Alonso, who forced his daughter into an undesired match, Prospero instead *produces*, while also overseeing, his daughter's desires. Even as it "objectifies" Miranda, then, Prospero's project points to the necessity of construing aristocratic daughters as active, desiring subjects.

*   *   *

As social relations themselves are increasingly understood as relations of exchange, and as labor is increasingly commodified, a transactional understanding of social life gains ground in the early modern period. Sandra Fischer, surveying the sixteenth-century's socioeconomic changes, argues that English culture witnesses a new preoccupation with the "economics" inhering in all domains of human life: "Love, courtship, friendship, marriage, sex, propagation, child-rearing, inheritance, celebration, and stewardship all become economic relationships."[30] Although contemporary understandings of "economics" were strongly intertwined with matters of moral and personal conduct, this is the historical moment when "the profit motive"—rather than the sin of avarice—is being invented in preliminary form.

Given the potentially conflicting ways that pleasure and profit function in a commodity economy, however, we have seen how the profit motive is not a simple and straightforward one. For Lewis Roberts, the "motive Profit" laudably spurs on the community of merchant adventurers he constructs. For Golding's Seneca, on the other hand, profit must be relinquished in favor of forging social relations between transactors. Arthur Golding's translation of Seneca's *De Beneficiis* exemplifies the popular appeal to an idealized gift economy as commodity exchange cast an increasingly wider net. Golding's Seneca is a manual for good giving which insistently distinguishes "benefiting"—the "doing, receiving, and requiting of good turns" (title page)—from merchandizing, or ordinary bargains and loans. "It is a vile Usury to keep a reckoning of benefits, as of expenses." Those who wish to bestow a good turn "must tread profit underfoot." One must seek bonds with co-transactors rather than desire the materials in which one transacts.[31]

This Senecan contrast between benefits and ordinary transactions is compatible with the fundamental distinctions between "gift" and "commodity" as theorized by anthropologists. According to Christopher Gregory, the fundamental contrast between the "gift economy" and "commodity exchange" is that, in gift exchange, transactors are in a state of "reciprocal dependence" while those in commodity exchange are in a state of "reciprocal independence"; the exchange of gifts creates "personal relations between people," while commodity exchange creates "objective relations between things." Because commodities are alienable—sharply distinguished from the person who owns them and hence transferable to others—their exchange constitutes a "price-forming process" rather than the formation of personal or social bonds. Because transactors in commodity exchange are mutually independent, once their transaction is finalized, each is free to sell, trade or use the obtained commodity. Those who engage in a gift transaction, on the other hand, are bound perpetually in a network of giving, receiving, and requiting gifts. These bonds and obligations are the basis of social organization in a culture based on gift exchange. Desire for profit, which derives from the exchange-value of the object of exchange, marks commodity exchange, while a desire for gift-debtors, not profit, motivates the exchange of gifts. According to Gregory, "What a gift transactor desires is the personal relationships that the exchange of gifts creates, and not the things themselves."[32] Since both Ferdinand and Caliban quite pointedly desire the "thing" herself, she slips into a different register; she cannot be said to function as a "mere gift" between father and (would-be) son-in-law.

Despite its strict distinction between benefits and ordinary transactions, however, *De Beneficiis*'s very insistence on treading profit underfoot mystifies material value in a way that ultimately ends up serving the "motive Profit" fueling commodity exchange. Within the economy of the benefit, itself distinguished from ordinary transactions, Seneca draws a careful distinction between the "matter of the benefit"—the thing exchanged, the "thing that is seen," whether a material object or a favor—and the "benefit itself"—the idealized bond between transactors:

> These things [money, offices] are badges of benefits, but not the benefits themselves. The benefit itselfe may be carried in heart, but it cannot be touched with hand. There is great difference between the matter of a benefit, and the benefit itself. Therefore, neither Gold, nor Silver, nor any of the things that we receive of our neighbours, is a benefit: but the good will of the giver. . . . The thing that is seen is not a benefit, but the sign and token of a benefit.[33]

The locus of value in this system lies *in the fact of* the properly motivated transaction and in the transaction's intended effects, not in the object given.[34] Although exchange in the material domain has to happen in order to manifest the immaterial bond between transactors, the Senecan economy negates the value of the material object of exchange, of the "thing that is seen."[35]

Abstention from pleasure in the "thing that is seen" or "touched with hand" actually helps pave the way for a system of exchange premised on exchange-value, on profiting from the sale of the stuff instead of consuming it (or having sex with it). If the mere "badge" being procured from distant locales becomes desirable and is consumed, the effect is to tread profit underfoot, (and not necessarily with the effect of forging bonds of good will between transactors). Ultimately, the Beneficiian dictate to tread profit underfoot—to seek an exchange of good will and not material advantage—ends up serving the interests of commodity exchange, since it cultivates a kind of disciplined abstention from partaking of the pleasures of transacted goods. In effect, then, this effort to mystify use-value, to efface the potential for pleasure in the tangible, visible, possessible objects, serves to contend with the ways in which peopling and profiting under capitalism are premised on, borne out of, or rely on both the continual reproduction *and* the regulation of pleasure/desire—those very contradictory operations at work in Prospero's orchestration of Miranda's courtship. Despite its seeming opposition to commodity exchange, the economy of the benefit paves the way for procuring and profiting from products from transglobal locales.

In addition to theorizing the relational nature of gifts and commodities in the early modern period, I also hope to have complicated what is all too often taken as a given—that women function as mere "objects" of exchange between men, and that women and/or women's sexuality are commodified. The pervasiveness of the assumption is evidenced even in quite sophisticated criticism that aligns itself with feminist concerns. Theodora Jankowski, for example, equates the centrality of the marriage paradigm in the construction of early modern women's subjectivity with the perception of "the woman" as "a piece of property to be exchanged between two men." This formulation fails to acknowledge how the early modern period construed properties of very different sorts. Douglas Bruster similarly reiterates the notion that women were often "portrayed as commodities" and that "wives are frequently considered and treated as objects."[36] Without theorizing the commodity, asserting that women are "commodified" potentially re-inscribes their objectification. Of course, women can be and often are "objectified" in both the gift and commodity schemes, but they are in different and sometimes contradictory ways, and hence with different effects. If we attend to the different and particular forms that exchange (of women or anything) could take, we will better understand these different ways women could be objectified. Potentially, then, we can understand the different ways women could be transactors or could resist, forms of resistance that we will not attend to unless we particularize—and historicize—the forms that exchange could take. Attending to heretofore neglected kinds of resistance is what my reading of Miranda has aimed to achieve.

Plays in which female characters try to transact actively in social and sexual exchange intensify cultural questions about relations of exchange, pointing to the greatest reason why women's position in the symbolic economies of gift and commodity is so slippery—they are not only a contradictory kind of property, but are also potential subjects and active transactors. Once a woman is desired physically, as a material "thing that is seen," she slips into a different register than a mere exchange-value, and can try to resist or refuse her suitor, or, as in the situation dramatized between Miranda and Ferdinand, she can offer to carry logs in her pursuit of him.

Prospero's effort to limit Miranda as an active, desiring subject potentially unsettles the effort to keep the classes separate, since it recalls the threat of her sexual transaction with other commodified figures—indeed it positions her in the same category/position as such figures—a threat that had been expunged with the brutal enslavement of Caliban. By insisting too strongly on Miranda's status as that which is transacted between Prospero and Ferdinand, the play re-introduces the connection between aristocratic women and laborers. The same might be said of Miranda's offer to help Ferdinand in his log-bearing labors. The appearance of the swarthy, sweaty sicklemen at Ceres' masque might be similarly understood. Summoned to dance and celebrate the union of Miranda and Ferdinand, the joining of the "sunburned sicklemen" in "country footing" with the nymphs discomfits Prospero and reminds him of Caliban's "foul conspiracy." Although the eroticized dance of the masque celebrates licit sexuality in the marital union, the bawdy punning in "country footing" suggests that the conspiracy Prospero recalls so angrily includes the illicit sullying of Miranda's maidenly honor.[37] Stripping aristocratic women of subjectivity in sexual/marital transactions, the play suggests, makes them structurally akin to the laboring classes. To insist too fully on Miranda's status as "acquisition" or "gift" is to emphasize the likeness between her and the likes of Caliban and the sicklemen whose labor is commodified, to raise the specter of her unprofitable peopling with them. Moreover, Prospero's giving of the gift "worthily purchased" by Ferdinand parodies the Levi-Straussean exchange of women between men. Prospero's diction confounds the insistent separation between ordinary merchandise and benefits; viewing the exchange of women paradigm through the Senecan lens, we see how Miranda is not the "mere badge" of the bond between Ferdinand and Prospero. As one who "quickens what's dead," she engages Ferdinand's desire. And, as Prospero himself both orchestrates and begrudgingly acknowledges, Miranda herself is an active, desiring subject.

NOTES

1. All references to Shakespeare are from *The Complete Works of Shakespeare*, fourth edition, ed. David Bevington (New York: HarperCollins, 1992). Edward Conway is quoted in Robert Matz "Sidney's Defence of Poesie: The Politics of Pleasure," *English Literary Renaissance* 25:2 (Spring 1995): 135. I extend thanks to the Colorado State University English Department faculty colloquium for providing a supportive venue for the earliest incarnation of these ideas. A draft of this essay was circulated in the seminar on early modern economies at the Shakespeare Association of America, Washington, DC, March 1997. I am particularly grateful to Ann Christensen, Patrick Murphy, and Chip Rhodes for indispensable feedback on earlier drafts.
2. On a "world system" of exchange, see Eric Wolf's use of Immanuel Wallerstein in *Europe and the People Without History* (Berkeley: U of California P, 1982).
3. Lewis Roberts,*The Merchants Mappe of Commerce* (London, 1638). Roberts, born in 1596, sought service with the East India company in 1617, was employed by it and the Levant Company, and later became a director of both. On the expansion of London overseas trade and the rise of the East India-Levant Combine, see Robert Brenner, *Merchants and Revolution: Commercial Change, Political Conflict, and London's Overseas Traders, 1550–1653* (Princeton, 1993). The *Dictionary of National Biography* calls *The Merchant's Mappe* "one of the earliest systematic treatises on its subject in English. The first

edition appeared in 1638 (STC 21094) followed by four others, in 1677, 1690, 1700 and 1719. A facsimile reprint of the original edition is available in *The English Experience* series. A very short excerpt of the work appears in *Seventeenth-Century Economic Documents*, Joan Thirsk and J. P. Cooper, eds., (Oxford: Clarendon Press, 1972), 491–94. I discuss the *Mappe* and the ideological and cultural work that it performs at more length in "'Strange Outlandish Wealth': Transglobal Commerce in *The Merchant's Mappe of Commerce* and *The Fair Maid of the West, Parts I and II*," in Virginia Mason Vaughan and John Gillies, eds., *Playing the Globe: Genre and Geography in Renaissance Drama*, (Fairleigh Dickinson, 1999).

4. Henry Peacham, *The Compleat Gentleman* (London 1622), reprinted in *The English Experience* 59 (New York: Da Capo, 1968), sig. Dd.

5. Although I'm not entirely at ease with the spatial metaphor implicit in "alongside," I prefer it to troubling over the temporal relations between *Merchant's Mappe*, *De Beneficiis*, and Shakespeare's play. I think of these various texts as neighbors, participants in a more generalized discourse of social and sexual commerce. Leah Marcus's account of what distinguishes the "new philology" from New Critical and poststructural notions of the text is helpful here, and is compatible with how I construe the relation of *The Tempest* to other texts treated in this essay: the new philology, Marcus contends, insists upon "a wider historical and cultural matrix as constitutive, an integral part of [a playtext's] network," *Unediting the Renaissance: Shakespeare, Marlowe, Milton* (New York: Routledge, 1996), 23.

    The most influential colonialist readings are Paul Brown, "'This Thing of Darkness I Acknowledge Mine': *The Tempest* and the Discourses of Colonialism," in *Political Shakespeare*, Dollimore and Sinfield, eds., (Manchester, 1985) and Francis Barker and Peter Hulme, "Nymphs and Reapers Heavily Vanish: The Discursive Con-texts of *The Tempest*" in John Drakakis, ed., *Alternative Shakespeares* (New York: Routledge, 1985).

    The first three books of Seneca's *De Beneficiis* were translated into English by Nicholas Hayward, *The Line of Liberalitie Dulie Directinge the Wel Bestowing of Benefits* (1569; STC 12939). Seneca's work was also translated by Thomas Lodge in 1613, enlarged in a second edition in 1620 (STC 22213, 22214). The text I am using is *The woorke of the excellent Philosopher Lucius Annaeus Seneca concerning Benefyting, that is too say the dooing, receyving, and requyting of good Turnes*, translated out of Latin by Arthur Golding (London: John Day, 1578; facsimile reprint *The English Experience*, 694 [Amsterdam: Walter J. Johnson, 1974]).

6. *The Merchant's Mappe*, sig. Bl; *De Beneficiis*, sig. M2V

7. Stephen Greenblatt's discussion of the collapse of the distinction between those who labor and those who rule is compatible with the ideological operations in the play that I am unpacking. See his "Martial Law in the Land of Cockaigne" in *Shakespearean Negotiations* (Berkeley: U California P, 1988).

8. Laboring, of course, is in early modern England a—if not *the*—key differentiator between man and man: pre- and post-lapsarian man, and gentleman and villain. On these distinctions and the role of laboring in constructing them, see Greenblatt, 149 and Thomas Cartelli, "Jack Cade in the Garden: Class Con-

sciousness and Class Conflict in *2 Henry VI*" in Richard Burt and John Michael
Archer, eds., *Enclosure Acts: Sexuality, Property, and Culture in Early Modern
England* (Ithaca: Cornell UP, 1994). The play's attention to physical markers of
difference is of course hugely important, but I am bracketing it from my discussion. See Kim Hall, *Things of Darkness: Economies of Race and Gender in
Early Modern England* (Ithaca: Cornell UP, 1995). Leah Marcus also attends to
the question of race and physical difference.

9. The use of the relative pronoun "which" to refer to persons as well as things was
    more common in the sixteenth century. Ferdinand's use of it here is still note-
    worthy, especially if we consider Caliban's following address to Prospero: "For
    I am all the subjects that you have, / Which first was mine own king" (1.2.344).
    For a twentieth-century reader, Caliban's claim of sovereignty over self bristles
    against the use of the relative pronoun "which" instead of "who."

10. The song is included in *Musical Humours* (1605) and is quoted in James Bruce
    Ross and Mary Martin McLaughlin, eds., *The Portable Renaissance Reader*
    (New York: Viking Penguin, 1968). On the popularization of tobacco and the
    meanings attached to it—both its material and ideal import—see Jeffrey Knapp,
    "Elizabethan Tobacco" in Greenblatt, ed., *New World Encounters* (Berkeley: U
    of California P, 1993), 273–312. Tobacco, of course, is a good imported from
    America, which is only one of the colonial contexts that reverberates through
    The Tempest. As recent work on the play attests, multiple contexts are crucially
    part of its participation in colonialist discourse. See especially Barbara Fuchs,
    "Conquering Islands: Contextualizing *The Tempest*" *Shakespeare Quarterly*
    48:1 (Spring 1997): 45–62 and Richard Wilson, "Voyage to Tunis: New History
    and the Old World of *The Tempest*," *ELH* 64 (1997): 332–357.

11. John Wheeler, *A Treatise of Commerce* (Middelburgh, 1601; facsimile rpt., ed.,
    George Burton Hotchkiss [New York: New York UP, 1931]), sig. B2. *Merchant's
    Mappe*, sig. B6.

12. This is what Marx calls commodity fetishism. See "The Fetishism of Com-
    modities and the Secret Thereof" in *Capital* Volume I, (New York: Modern
    Library, 1906), 81–86. In "The Problem of the Fetish, I" *Res* 9 (Spring 1985):
    5–17, William Pietz argues that the notion of the fetish emerged in the intercul-
    tural exchange space of the West African coast in the sixteenth century. This
    space functioned to transvalue objects between Christian feudal, African lin-
    eage, and merchant capitalistic social systems. Pietz argues, "the fetish could
    originate only in conjunction with the emergent articulation of the ideology of
    the commodity form that defined itself within and against the social values and
    religious ideologies of two radically different types of noncapitalist society, as
    they encountered each other in an ongoing cross-cultural situation" (7).

    Marcel Mauss discusses older notions of the relationship between res and
    personae. "Things are a part of the family: the Roman *familia* comprises res as
    well as the personae" (48). Mauss sees the conceptual separation between per-
    sons and things as a crucial turning point in human history in how people think
    about and carry out exchange. Tracing the etymology of "res," Mauss speculates
    that it originally meant "a thing which one gives and which gives pleasure"
    (119), which is interesting in light of the difficulties that will arise in Seneca
    over the value of "the thing that is seen" and in light of the tensions caused by

women's physical desirability in idealized gift relations between men. Mauss insists that "the res *cannot originally have been the brute and tangible thing, the simple and passive object of transaction that it has become*" (my emphasis, 48). See Mauss, *The Gift: Forms and Functions of Exchance in Archaic Societies*, trans., Ian Cunnison (Glencoe, IL: The Free Press, 1954).

13. Claude Levi-Strauss, *The Elementary Structures of Kinship*, trans., Bell et al. (Boston: Beacon Press, 1969), 61–65. Levi-Strauss extends Mauss's analysis in *The Gift* to include women, regarding their exchange as the founding structure of culture. I have benefited from Nancy Hartsock's work theorizing the link between the erotic and the economic in *Money, Sex, and Power: Toward a Feminist Historical Materialism* (New York: Longman, 1983).

14. Peter Stallybrass, "Patriarchal Territories: The Body Enclosed," in *Rewriting the Renaissance: The Discourses of Sexual Difference in Early Modern Europe*, eds., Margaret Ferguson, Maureen Quilligan, and Nancy J. Vickers (Chicago: U of Chicago P, 1986), 127.

15. Howard Felperin, "Political Criticism at the Crossroads: The Utopian Historicism of *The Tempest*" in Nigel Wood, ed., *The Tempest* (Philadelphia: Open University Press, 1995), 49.

16. Frances Dolan, *Dangerous Familiars: Representations of Domestic Crime in England: 1550–1750* (Ithaca: Cornell UP, 1984), 67. On the complex history of Caliban's otherness, see Alden T. Vaughan and Virginia Mason Vaughan, *Shakespeare's Caliban: A Cultural History* (Cambridge: Cambridge UP, 1991).

17. John Dryden and William Davenant, *The Tempest, or the Enchanted Island*, in Vol. 10 *The Works of John Dryden* (U California P, 1970). Taken with Miranda's sister Dorinda when he first discovers her, Hippolito is soon delighted to discover that "There are more fair Women / Besides that I love" (3.6.49–50), and he determines to have all of them. When Ferdinand dutifully informs him that he "cannot love two women, both at once" (69), Hippolito refuses to accept the doctrine of private property: "Sure 'tis my duty to love all who do resemble / Her whom I've already seen. I'le have as many as I can / That are so good, and Angel-like, as she I love. / And will have yours" (70–73). Hippolito cannot conceive that Ferdinand should "desire but one" since it would mean "He would be poor in love" while Hippolito would "be rich" by loving many women (96–97). I am very grateful to Patrick Murphy for calling my attention to Dryden's adaptation.

18. Quoted in John Elliott, *Imperial Spain, 1469–1716* (New York: Meridian Press, 1963), 304. Thanks to Edward Shannon Tenace for calling this material to my attention. On the effects of the expulsion see Eric Wolf, *Europe and the People Without History*, 113.

19. *The Merchant's Mappe*, sig G4^v.

20. Christopher Marlowe, *Tamburlaine the Great, Part I*, in Vol. 1 *Drama of the English Renaissance*, eds., Russell Fraser and Norman Rabkin (New York: Macmillan, 1976), my emphasis. Barbara Fuchs, "Conquering Islands," 54. Discussing the connection of Ireland, America as colonial sites, Fuchs explains that the English efforts in Ireland were compared to the Spanish expulsion of the Moors from Grenada, 51–54. Fuchs demonstrates that signs of anxiety over Islamic expansion in the Mediterranean "abound in the play."

21. Paul Brown notes the double meaning of "villain" as well, "This Thing of Darkness," 65.
22. Kim Hall, *Things of Darkness*, 125–26.
23. Jyotsna Singh, "Caliban versus Miranda: Race and Gender Conflicts in Postcolonial Rewritings of *The Tempest*" in *Feminist Readings of Early Modern Culture: Emerging Subjects*, eds., Valerie Traub, M. Lindsay Kaplan, and Dympna Callaghan (Cambridge: Cambridge UP, 1996), 197. Kim Hall, *Things of Darkness*, 148. Marjorie Raley, "Claribel's Husband," in Joyce Greene MacDonald, ed., *Race, Ethnicity, and Power in the Renaissance* (Madison: Fairleigh Dickinson UP, 1997), 99–100. See Leah Marcus's account of the way in which the "blew" eyes of Sycorax and the magical charms of Prospero "eerily reverberate with their supposed moral opposites" in *Unediting the Renaissance*, 15–16. On the resonances between Caliban and Prospero, see Richard Wheeler, "Fantasy and History in *The Tempest*" in *The Tempest*, ed., Nigel Wood (Open University Press, 1995), 151–153, and David Sundelson, "So Rare a Wonder'd Father: Prospero's *Tempest*" in *Representing Shakespeare*, eds. Murray Schwartz and Coppélia Kahn (Baltimore: Johns Hopkins UP, 1980), 41.
24. According to the OED, the oldest sense of "delicate"—a repeated epithet for Ariel—is "the quality of being addicted to pleasure." It might be Prospero's fantasy that Ariel takes pleasure in serving him. Terry Eagleton calls Ariel a "closet aesthete who would rather sport than labour" in *William Shakespeare* (New York: Basil Blackwell, 1986), 95.
25. Mercantile capitalist and aristocratic economic interests often overlap in early modern England. My argument anticipates capitalist productive relations that emerge fully later.
26. Although offering brief cautions, Singh basically accepts that Miranda's status is simply that of gift ("Caliban versus Miranda," 198–99). The phrase "traffic in women" comes from the widely influential explanation of the paradigm by Gayle Rubin, "The Traffic in Women: Notes on the 'Political Economy' of Sex" in *Toward an Anthropology of Women* ed., Rayna Reiter (New York: Monthly Review Press, 1975), 157–210.
27. Wheeler says that this moment "is the closest this power-dominated man comes to a point where it would make sense for him to say, with Caliban, 'I am full of pleasure.' In his absorption in the masque . . . that pleasure proves to be disruptive. Prospero, the master manipulator, the nearly omnipotent controller of the action of this play, finds himself in a position beyond the limits of his control," ("Fantasy and History," 151). For additional views of Prospero's power as limited, see Nigel Wood's "Introduction" to *The Tempest*: "The closer we look the less convinced we are that Prospero's patriarchal hold is omnipotent" (27). Singh argues that Prospero controls the feelings of Miranda and Ferdinand "as he feels his power slipping" (197). Dolan argues that the energy of the scene derives from our sense that "Prospero is not completely in control and that the outcome is not wholly predictable" (61).
28. In the case of Miranda specifically, see Singh, 197 and Hall, 148.
29. The Claribel-Tunis marriage suggests that alliances across cultural or "racial" lines do not necessarily undermine the interests of global exchange and its patriarchal control, despite how Sebastian berates Alonso for forging a transglobal,

cross-cultural alliance. "Sir you may thank yourself for this great loss, / That would not bless our Europe with your daughter, / But rather loose her to an African" (2.1.124–27). Fuchs points to the outrageousness of this European-African alliance given Islamic power in the Mediterranean at the time of the play (58). I agree with Singh that Claribel haunts the play's "happy ending" because the possibility of miscegenation is not dispelled (201–02); but Claribel's lack of pleasure in the union is perhaps a more primary threat. Marjorie Raley offers a compelling reading of the Claribel-Tunis trade in "Claribel's Husband." For a slightly different but provocative view, see Fuchs.

30. *Econolingua: A Glossary of Coins and Economic Language in Renaissance Drama* (Newark: U of Delaware P, 1985), 28. According to Fischer, economy "operated almost exclusively in Aristotle's sense of household management. The Church fathers and the Schoolmen had modified Aristotle's legacy only slightly, in turn bequeathing to the Renaissance a system of economic ethics that worked handily under feudalism, when most economies were linked to the land, to subsistence production, and to personal and traditionally-sanctioned exchanges of goods. In fact, economy was a branch of religious morality, based on Biblical texts and classical teaching" (14). Tawney points out that "When the sixteenth century opens, not only political but social theory is saturated with doctrines drawn from the sphere of ethics and religion, and economic phenomena are expressed in terms of personal conduct" (15). Economic activity was viewed as "one among other kinds of moral conduct" (20). See *Religion and the Rise of Capitalism* (Harcourt, Brace & World, 1926; rpt. New York: Mentor Books, 1947), 15.

31. *De Beneficiis*, sigs. A2v, M2v.

32. Christopher Gregory, *Gifts and Commodities* (London. Academic Press, 1982), 12, 8, 19. Gregory combines the theoretical work of political economy, primarily Marx's theories of commodity exchange, and a range of twentieth century anthropologists, most notably Marcel Mauss's *The Gift*. Rather than classifying qualities that inhere in objects, then, the categories gift and commodity conceptualize relations between transactors, the motives of those who engage in exchange, or the *systems* of exchange by which a particular culture operates.

33. *De Beneficiis*, sigs. Bi-Bii.

34. This emptying of the benefit's material value in Seneca counters the great range and intensity of values and powers that inhere in the gift-object in Marcel Mauss's "classic" account of the gift economy; see, for example, *The Gift*, 21–45.

35. Seneca's creation and hierarchizing of dualisms (benefits over and against merchandise; the immaterial bond between transactors over and against the matter of benefit) might be compared to the series of oppositions which, Jean-Joseph Goux claims, become dominant over social life with the "victory" of a monetary economy over the "natural economy" in seventh-century Greece:

> From this point on, major oppositions reign over social life, structuring the exchange relations in which subjects are involved and which constitute them: the determinant subordination of a working class to a propertied class; the subordination of commodities (of products) to money (becoming capital); the subordination of the female sex to the male sex (in the sense of gendered individuals but also in

> the symbolic sense of genital organs in imaginary and signifying functions . . . ; the subordination of mother to father (in social role and in the signifying function). . . . Finally, translated into the domain of philosophical conceptualization, this system of antagonisms means the dominion gained by the category of mind over the category of matter.

By linking the subordination of female to male to the subordination of matter to mind, Goux helps us see the implications of Seneca's effort to efface the material domain as a locus of value for the question of women's position and women's value. See *Symbolic Economies After Marx and Freud*, trans., Jennifer Curtiss Gage (Ithaca: Cornell UP, 1990), 90.

36. Theodora Jankowski, *Women in Power in the Early Modern Drama* (Urbana: U of Illinois P, 1992), 24. Douglas Bruster, *Drama and Market in the Age of Shakespeare* (Cambridge: Cambridge UP, 1992), 42–43. Figuring women of any rank as objects strips them of active pleasure-taking in husbands; this violates the need to procreate, since Renaissance medical discourses believed that female orgasm was necessary for conception. To say "women" are "commodified" ignores that aristocratic women are not the only women. The laboring poor are commodified materially as well as discursively.

37. See Wheeler, "Fantasy and History," 150–51.

Print History of *The Tempest* in Early America, 1623–1787

CHRISTOPHER D. FELKER

> *An affectation of displaying ones gifts before Throngs, is*
> *too often an abominably proud Fishing for popular*
> *Applause; but my work in the Pulpitt, must bee, rather to*
> *acquit myself well, in the Discharge of the Duties incum-*
> *bent on mee there, before the All-Seeing Eye of that*
> *Majestie, who to mee, shall be Theatre enough.*
>
> COTTON MATHER, 1685

Every student of American literature has encountered the premise that the fundamental experience of North American settlers with a new land was a radical, generative and altogether exceptional intersection of older "civilizing" tendencies and raw, newly-discovered "natural" contexts. This informing narrative was crystallized in Leo Marx's seminal chapter in *The Machine in the Garden* which treats Shakespeare's *Tempest* as a prelude to much of the American literature of the nineteenth-century. "The topography of *The Tempest*," Marx suggested, "anticipates the moral geography of the American imagination. What is most prophetic about the play, finally, is the singular degree of plausibility that it attaches to the notion of a pastoral retreat. By making the hope so believable, Shakespeare lends singular force to its denial. *The Tempest* may be read as a prologue to American literature."[1] Marx's thesis about *The Tempest* continued a tradition of intellectual history started by F.O. Matthessien and Perry Miller that conflated certain ideological presumptions about the founding generation with notions of justice, enlightened government, and a deep appreciation for the pastoral basis of life exemplified by nineteenth-century America in places like the Ohio frontier and Concord Massachusetts. Andrew Jackson's transcendental, democratic maxims and Mark Twain's story of one boy's journey down the Mississippi River further refined and intensified the American reception of Shakespeare's themes and plays. The pernicious assumptions of the nineteenth-century (which was in large measure marked by an attempt to "elevate" American letters to the standards imposed by English and Continental artistic achievement) were part of a general process to correct the supposed "cultural drift" of America from its roots in the Old World.

Some of the attempts to hold Shakespeare as a particularly luminous standard for America ignore two truths about books and their influence in early America: (1) Most claims regarding the significance of one particular work or the output of a writer serve larger ideological (and potentially) political ends. Viewed from the standpoint of an even moderate historical perspective such claims (for instance, the "best" fashions or movies in any given year) seem preposterous, misguided and ultimately curiously overstated. Recently, Hugh Armory, a professional librarian and book scholar, echoed this point by writing "the history of reading labors under an unfortunate difficulty: books are a sufficient but not a necessary cause of their interpretation. The history of reading is thus a series of farcical misunderstandings."[2] (2) If a book has the license to stand in for a consensual political, social or legal position, it does so not because it expresses the "reality" of the given position but instead, effectively masks the work's relationship to market forces, institutional practices and beliefs and the ability of individual entrepreneurs to leverage their efforts in collaborative associations. In other words, *The Tempest* became important in its relationship to pastoralism and transcendentalism because those promoting (editing, publishing, teaching) such a reading were, in fact, establishing their own intellectual paradigms for reasons with which we are all familiar: success at publishing for the undergraduate and graduate market, acceptance of one's ideas among colleagues and the establishment of a coherent "story" linking together disparate experiences in different time frames.

I

The purpose of this essay is to focus on a period in American colonial history when *The Tempest*, which found some of its source material in early seventeenth-century writing about America, was strangely absent from American letters. I want to study the vacuous and minimal response accorded to *The Tempest* in the American colonies (after the text's initial use of colonial materials had faded from view) in order to counterbalance what have been primarily rhetorical and ideological arguments made to support Shakespeare's "original" contributions to the subsequent flowering of American literature in the nineteenth century. Although some of Shakespeare's plays were performed in the colonies, the theatrical history of *The Tempest* during the colonial period is fairly sparse.[3] In fact the printed history of the play is recorded in a fragmentary historical record. Therefore, I have presented this study of *The Tempest*'s absence in the printed archive in a series of discontinuous parts: an examination of Cotton

Mather's description of American natives on Martha's Vineyard and his Sermon on a storm of 1722/23, which uses Montaigne's "Of Cannibals"; an analysis of the library catalogs at Harvard and the College of William and Mary; a brief treatment of *The Tempest* among American Revolutionaries; and a discussion of the bibliomania in Philadelphia which contributed to the local conditions for the emergence of The Shakespeare Society of Philadelphia in 1852. This scattered record constitutes the physical conditions of the reception, production, and transmission of Shakespeare's work in the colonial era. And based on this knowledge, whenever *The Tempest* figures in the cultural debates in America prior to 1788, it is better interpreted (in the major chord of history in the colonies) as providential history and not, as Leo Marx and other idealist critics have read it, as a pastoral commentary on the New World. This pastoral tradition was invented in the nineteenth century for purposes that ran counter to the experience of many early colonists. The general elevation of Shakespeare by nineteenth-century critics was a retroactive phenomenon super-imposed upon the experience of North American settlers in an effort to create a common Anglo-American tradition which might serve to compensate for an American culture perceived as distant, different, and culturally adrift.

It might be helpful to review the circumstantial case linking Shakespeare's play with the New World. Shakespeare had Europe primarily in mind since the play is set on an island in the Mediterranean, somewhere between Naples and Tunis. This conceit goes farther back than Shakespeare's time of course; the Arabic Text *Island of Animals* written in the 12th century uses a similar setting to examine the interrelationship of a "natural" population in contact with a superior, literate race. This discussion, about the relative superiority of men over animals, has the animals cast as slaves and the representatives of mankind claiming their innate superiority by reason of their literacy and cognitive abilities. Like Prospero, the dialogue is mediated by a magician/spirit figure, the Djinn whose resolution of the conflict depends on a literal reading of a passage in the Koran.[4] The formula, of a superior intelligence, mandating the existence of a natural, untamed world has a parallel some seven hundred years before Shakespeare's own time.

As Charles Frey has indicated, there are several moments in the text that lend credence to the idea that the New World is Shakespeare's subtext: Ariel speaks of fetching magic dew from the "still-vex'd Bermoothes."[5] Caliban says that Prospero's art is powerful enough to control the god worshipped by Caliban and his mother, Setebos.[6] Some readers believe that Shakespeare found the name of Caliban's mother in Richard Eden's sixteenth-century account of Magellan's experiences among the Patagonian natives "who cryed upon their great devil Setebos to help them."[7] Trinculo mentions the English willingness to pay a fee "to see a dead Indian."[8] Finally, Miranda exclaims upon seeing the courtiers "O brave new world / That has such people in 't."[9] Edward Malone was one of the first nineteenth-century editors of Shakespeare to discuss connections between the events in the play and the storm and ship-wreck encountered by Sir Thomas Gates and other Jamestown colonists. These materials have always been considered important linkages in what is a prototypically English myth passed from Strachey to Shakespeare, from the Virginia Company to the King's Men. However, there are materials in the play that contradict this tradition: the island is not located in America but in the Mediterranean; it is not uninhabited; none of the figures are in any obvious sense colonists; the departure is for home rather than for a colony, and the end result for Prospero is not an unequivocal increase in his authority, "but rather a partial diminution, signaled in Prospero's abjuration of magic."[10] Therefore, the parallels in the text with colonial America are also sources of vexing dis-junctures.

There are several moments in John Smith's *The Generall Historie of Virginia* that remind some readers of Shakespeare's *Tempest*.[11] In his work on Shakespeare's narrative and dramatic sources Geoffrey Bullough suggested that Smith's *True Relation*, published in 1608, may have contributed to Shake-speare's knowledge of the foolish settlers who confused talc for gold. How-ever, Bullough dismissed Morton Luce's suggestion that "the relations between Miranda and Ferdinand were affected by the story of how Pocahon-tas later saved Smith from death when he was Powhatan's prisoner and about to be killed." Noting that the *Generall Historie* was not printed before 1624, Bullough thought "To identify Miranda with Pocahontas is a tempting fancy which must be sternly repressed."[12] Although Bullough's opinion has remained highly influential, many readers have been reluctant to let the asso-ciation rest. Recently Jeffrey Richards has suggested that during the Jacobean period the world had become "a nearly inescapable stage" which produced several different kinds of response from those Puritans who desired to destroy the theater altogether and from writers like Burton whose analysis of social theatricality led to his "retreat into a personal theater of philosophy." Accord-ing to Richards, John Smith chose a path different from "the ideological nar-rowness of the Puritans and the effete histrionics of the Anglican elite." Instead, Richards thinks Smith made himself both "the central actor in a land free of playhouses,"[13] and a writer who simultaneously functioned as both an actor and an author:

> Smith the writer creates a character something like that of a politically savvy Prospero; throughout the Virginia narratives, the adventurer appears to manipulate events, turning adversity into opportunities for displaying his prowess. If Virginia is a brave new world, then it requires new tactics from a brave man to tame it. The Captain Smith of the histories—with the 'non-pareil," Pocahontas, as his savage Ariel—often finds his suggestions ignored or ridiculed (in which case, trouble soon follows) and himself more sinned against than sinning, but he never wavers or gives himself over to despair and cynicism as a more thoughtful, less active man might.[14]

According to Richards, Smith used "something like" Shakespeare's characters to find homologies within his own situation while differentiating himself
from Prospero's putative failures of contemplation which led to Antonio's
usurpation of Milan. Yet, Richards does not explore the next step: namely, that
John Smith may have been familiar with Shakespeare's *Tempest*. Smith had
returned to England by 1611 (when the play was performed at Whitehall), and
he was still in England in 1613 (when there was another performance for the
marriage of Princess Elizabeth to the Elector Palatine). Moreover, since the
First Folio was published in 1623, Smith may have read *The Tempest* while he
was revising his narrative about Pocahantas.[15] Perhaps familiar with the manner in which Virginia had been recently represented in masques at court,[16]
Smith describes a strange encounter with native Americans, which many have
found similar to the masque of Ceres. Upon the arrival of Christopher Newport, Smith is sent to appease Powhatan by arranging a festive coronation. At
Werowocomoco he describes a "Virginia Maske" bearing a relation to the
English court traditions:

> 30 young women came naked out of the woods (only covered behind and
> before with a few greene leaves) their bodies al painted, some white, some
> red, some black, some partie colour, but every one different.[17]

In his Virginia narrative, Smith brings forward dramatic elements—the sudden arrival of supply vessels, the interventions of Pocahontas (Ariel?) and a
timely frightening of savages. Smith uses his compass, "that Globe-like Jew-
ell" to explain "the roundnesse of the earth, and skies, the sphaere of the
Sunne, Monne, and Starres, and how the Sunne did chase the night round the
world continually; the greatness of the Land and Sea, the diversitie of nations,
the variety of complexions, and how we [the English] were to them Antipodes,
and many other such matters."[18] These moments in Smith's narrative seem to
bear a passing relation to Shakespeare's play; however, when we consider the
chronology of the writing, it appears that *The Tempest* and related materials
such as Chapman's Virginian masque, performed at court on the same occasion as *The Tempest*, were suggestions or anterior texts for Smith's writing and
not the reverse. Therefore, the text of *A Generall Historie* does not lend itself
to the detailed and sweeping conclusions of Sidney Lee, Morton Luce and
Charles Mills Gayley who posit a continuous tradition of Shakespeare's influence upon America. For instance, Gayley writes, that Shakespeare "believed
in the right of the individual to liberty, property and the pursuit of happiness;
in equality before the law; and in law 'all binding, keeping form and due proportion;' in even-handed justice; in duty to the common order in society and
state; in fraternity of effort and patriotic allegiance."[19] Instead, once we see
that John Smith may have used Shakespearean materials and other masques
appropriated by performances at the English court, the absence of Shakespeare's *Tempest* in the emergent colonies makes it difficult to accept Leo

Marx's idea of a continuous tradition. Before the nineteenth century could appropriate Shakespeare in this fictitious manner, the Shakespeare who befriended American colonists had to be forgotten, and a different Shakespearean America had to be invented.

Michael Dobson finds evidence for "an American nationalist and republican prejudice against Shakespeare" in two poems written by Peter Markoe in 1787 and 1788, as well as some evidence in the *Freeman's Journal* of Philadelphia in 1784 for a "debate over the propriety of staging Shakespeare in postwar America."[20] Dobson also points out that George Washington cited Prospero's revels speech in a private letter to Henry Laurens in 1778, and he saw an operatic performance of the Dryden adaptation in Philadelphia while framing the constitution in 1787. In the first instance, according to Dobson, General Washington identified with Caliban; in the second Dobson suggests something had changed "to allow this entertainment, hitherto virtually synonymous with British power in the New World. . .to be regarded as a suitable diversion for the Father of the American Republic."[21] One year earlier Thomas Jefferson used a few lines from the same speech in his *Thoughts on English Prosody* as an example of how foreigners may miss the rules of accent imperfectly represented by scansion.[22] Both Jefferson and Adams visited Stratford in 1786. Jefferson recorded the price of admission in his journal; Adams was disappointed: "There is nothing preserved of the great genius which is worth knowing; nothing which might inform us what education, what company, what accident turned his mind to letters and to drama."[23] Dobson suggests that Michael Bristol overlooks the "deeply vested national interest which conditions Adam's representation of Stratford as 'vitiated' and 'parochial.'"[24] And Dobson thinks Michael Bristol mistaken in his "lament" that the "Shakespearizing" of America defeated its revolutionary ideals because "no innocently egalitarian, pre-Shakespearean America seems to have existed." "By the time of the drafting of the Constitution," Dobson argues, "it appears. . .the United States, claiming Shakespeare's magic book as its right, was already committed to the role of Prospero."[25] I want to challenge this contention by saying that Americans generally distanced themselves from Shakespeare and from things "English" in order to create an American identity defined apart from European standards.

II. NOR'EASTERN GALES: COTTON MATHER AND PROVIDENTIAL HISTORY

In seventeenth-century New England, Cotton Mather was the preeminent public intellectual. Prior to the Revolution, Mather's *Magnalia Christi Americana* provided the basis for an exemplaristic and decisive proto-nationalistic impulse *away* from that of the mother country; Mather's preface to the work reads, "I WRITE the WONDERS of the CHRISTIAN RELIGION, flying from the deprivations of Europe, to the American Strand."[26] During the formation of the early Republic, Mather's text functioned as the incubator for several classic American texts, many of which Leo Marx had in mind when he wrote *The Machine in the Garden*. It is these texts that served to declare America's "independence" from the literatures of other nations, even though, paradoxically, the main thrust of the American Renaissance was to correct for America's cultural drift away from Europe by reconstituting the styles, tastes and audiences for European literature. How wonderful it would be if we could trace a knowledge of *The Tempest* somewhere through the four hundred and forty-four extant publications we have by Mather's own hand. Were such a connection made, it would lend an unprecedented amount of authority that the original vision of the American experiment was, in fact, percolated with the Elizabethan concern for liberty, expansion and general respect for the English colonial mission. In fact, many critics have assumed such a background, overly optimistic in their appraisal of the role played by English dramatic literature on shaping the minds or experiences of visitors and citizens of the colonies.

It is striking that Cotton Mather, a man whose literary output was prodigious, who was a quick and avid reader (according to some accounts endowed with a photographic memory), who held a library in his early ministry of over a thousand volumes (augmented by gifts and purchases of English books over his lifetime until it was, without doubt, the largest library in the American colonies), does not once mention *The Tempest* or William Shakespeare. Such omissions cannot be the work of judicious editing after the fact, but instead illustrate that, one hundred and eighteen years after the performance of the play in London, the work had no effect on the mind of Cotton Mather.

Not until the work of Mather Brown (1761–1831) did Shakespeare have any measurable influence on a member of the Mather family. Brown, the portrait painter whose career was assisted by the family friend Benjamin Franklin, is famous for his paintings (created in London) of Thomas Jefferson and John Adams.[27] Brown's illustrations were well represented in John Bell's twenty-one volumes of *The Dramatick Writings of Will. Shakspere* (1785–87). A remarkable publishing event in England, Bell's edition was patronized by the Prince of Wales and the Duke of York with extensive commentary of Samuel Johnson and George Stevens. Mather Brown's interest in illustrating Bell's edition of Shakespeare is an excellent early example of the methods used by other American artists (in many modes) to correct the perceived "drift" of American tastes away from the cosmopolitan centers of Europe. Typically, such efforts were recognized and refined in the popular press, anticipating the sophistication of nineteenth and twentieth-century markets. In the *New York Packet*, Brown's work received deserving praise, "We are told that our countryman, Brown, has drawn most of the principal performers on the stage, in the best scenes in Shakespear—Engravings from all of which have been taken for Bell's edition of that work. He has, we are also told, in his room in London, pictures of near one hundred Americans, who are universally known."[28] It is important to recall however, that Brown spent fifty years of his life in London and therefore, his involvement in Shakespeare's work more reflects a rising English consciousness of the writer's importance to English literary history.

If Cotton Mather was aware of Shakespeare's play, it was a private and unrecorded knowledge. Nevertheless, Mather was captivated by many of the same themes that Shakespeare is said to have had in mind for *The Tempest*. In fact Mather knew that his father and grandfather had long accustomed to seeing themselves at the center of a New England polity not unlike that described by Prospero's island. The Mather clan had, over the course of a hundred years maintained a web of influence over Connecticut by "keeping up a large correspondence with ministers starved for news and ideas and by entertaining visitors when they came in from the provinces."[29] In this way, the Mather's own personal dramas were seen to have significance largely because the stage for most of New England's cultural and economic activity was considered to be the same small area in which they had settled. Some of these thoughts are recorded in two extraordinary documents, the Appendix to the sixth chapter of the sixth book of *Magnalia Christi Americana* titled "The Triumphs of Grace" and the classic jeremiad *The Voice of God in a Tempest: A Sermon Preached at the Time of the Late Storm*, February 24, 1722/23. Both of these texts deserve close consideration because they demonstrate that the Puritan vision was affective as well as rational and that, while there is no evidence that Shakespeare's version of the English enterprise played more than a subconscious role, the apprehensions of those in Mather's generation were more closely focused on salient issues that made knowledge of one Elizabethan play irrelevant.

The Puritan scholar studied all history as an exhibition of divine wisdom, and frequently discovered in the accounts of Christian and heathen experience, firm evidence that God's plan was meticulously unfolding. To those promoting the New England commonwealths, this plan, observable in the past, was seen as a dramatic prologue. In the Puritan mind, there was no place for true contingency, fortune or accident either in the past or in the events that were to come. This was especially so in national affairs, the predestined impulse of history determined the rise of empires, the timing of revolutions and the predominant institutions. Operating under the provisions of the Covenant of Grace with God, the archive of history was seen as being organized in an elaborate pattern, presenting surface variety, but underneath maintaining a steady, ordered and continuous line of reasoning that exemplified God's logical designs for the world. In this conception, the unknown (or rumored) past and the portions of the future that lay under shadows of fear and uncertainty, were in fact manageable because the leading Puritan texts and scripture permitted the confidence that a plan was indeed at work. The prophesy of Scripture was invaluable because, as Nicholas Noyes informs, "*Prophesie* is *Historie antedated*; and *Historie* is *Postdated Prophesie*: the same thing is told in both"; therefore, the chief task for the Puritan writer was the determination of position along the time line suggested by God, "near what Joynt in that Line of Time, we are now arriv'd."[30] For Mather, some evidence of his nearness to an auspicious joint in the divine timeline was observable on the island of Martha's Vineyard. He writes

> It is not among the English only, but among the Indians also, that our glorious Lord Jesus Christ hath been glorify'd in "doing of wonders."[31]

Mather's interest in this island demonstrates a strategy he employed in the second half of *Magnalia*, to portray the design of New England's divine mission as an ethnographic excursion. Mather generally looks to classical sources to ground his assertions, naming Aquinas, the Koran and Aristotle in his prologue to the account of six incidents among the Indians; but I suspect he borrows freely from Montaigne as well, especially that section of "Of Cannibals" that records conversations with a traveler. Mather offers the suggestion that "some of the Americans may be the posterity of those Canaanites, who after the wars of Canaan, set up their pillars in Africa, with that inscription, "We are those that fled from the face of Joshua the robber!'" in order to make the following point: "How far our sovereign and gracious God may in an extraordinary manner discover of himself unto some among the poor Pagans that have not enjoy'd the preaching of the gospel, who can particularly determine?"[32] In Montaigne, there is this passage:

> Men of intelligence notice more things and view them more carefully, but they comment on them; and to establish and substantiate their interpretation, they cannot refrain from altering the facts a little. . . . We need either a very truthful man, or one so ignorant that he has no material with which to construct false theories and make them credible; a man wedded to no idea.[33]

In Shakespeare's *Tempest*, the man of intelligence—Prospero, does the observing that is shared by Caliban; in Mather, it is John Eliot (or himself) who sees and interprets the experiences shared by Japhet, a child of Pammehanuit (an "Indian of prime quality") converted to the ministry by the English settlers on the island; and finally, in Montaigne, it is the sailor's account of life in Brazil that forms the basis of his objective and inductive account of society in the New World. For Mather, the conceit of the Christian philosopher is crucial to the overall design of *Magnalia*. After all, each of these writers was interested in utopian formulations and, in the case of Mather and Montaigne, it is essential that the writer be able to stand away from previous ideas and assume the perspective of the "new scientist" liberated from scholastic custom (though remaining reverent) but squarely immersed in empirical particulars, and the natural state or anomie of the New World populations. The notion of Antipodes is the preliminary moment that is most crucial to Mather's sense of the English colonial project. In Book I he writes the repetitive formula that is echoed in Book VI:

> I can contentedly allow that America was altogether unknown to the penmen of the Holy Scriptures.... I can assert the existence of the American Antipodes: and I can report unto the European churches great occurrences among these Americans; ... it is a fable, and *nulla ratione credendum*.... for we may count America to have been concealed, while mankind in the other hemisphere had lost all acquaintance of it, if we may conclude it had any from the words of Diodorus Siculus, that Phonecians were, by great storms, driven on the coast of Africa, *far westward*, ... *for many days together*, and at last fell in with an island of prodigious magnitude; or from the words of Plato, that beyond the pillars of Hercules there was an island in the Atlantick Ocean, ... *larger than Africa and Asia put together.*[34]

Mather relates six moments in the lives of the praying Indians of Martha's Vineyard: 1) the revelation of God to Japhet, whose mother, fearing his demise from illness prayed to God for his health. When his strength returned, Japhet's mother caused her son "to dedicate this child unto the service of that God who had preserv'd his life"; 2) a miracle cure of an Indian whose withered arm was restored to a healthy condition; 3) the "resurrection" of William Lay, a converted Indian near death who was raised by Japhet to live for another year and a half and the rescue (as if repeating Moses deliverance of the Israelites through the Red Sea) of Abel Aosoowe whose canoe was trapped in ice several miles offshore. Aosoowe prayed and God opened up a channel "just at the head end of their canoo" as they moved to the shore, the "ice closing still together again just as the canoo had passed it"; 4) the punishment of a man resistant to conversion by the burning of his house and the death of this three children in the blaze; 5) the discovery, exposure, repentance and execution of the murderer Pamahtuk who killed a squaw in 1668 to conceal the existence of an illegitimate child; and 6) the reversal of witchcrafts evident in Indian "powaws" by the "correction" of the behaviors of three notorious "wizards," one adept at ferreting out stolen goods, one whose botched assassination of another Indian resulted in the slaying of his own brother and, the conversion of one expert in using snakes to torment his victims.[35]

Mather's island was a place of confusion and disorder and chaotic organization, especially when compared with the holy civilization imagined (and half-erected) on the mainland in Boston. As Mather's inordinate attention to the Indian powwows throughout the chapter illustrate, the wilderness was also a place of many positive evils, with land not hedged in and deprived of both spiritual and physical light. The Christian souls visiting the island must make its way through such an island on the way to spiritual salvation. In his 1672 election sermon, Eye-Salve, Thomas Shepard exclaimed that in churches, schools and commonwealth God "hath granted to us light and salvation," but that the wilderness was clearly the place of Satan, the master of chaos (3–6). Not insignificantly, with Indian presence acutely felt off shore to the East and along the western and southern frontiers of the Massachusetts colony, Mather's description of Boston itself as an island stronghold has a certain figurative (if not geographic) precision. In a sermon delivered in 1722/23, he would capitalize on this notion comparing the English in Boston to the Assyrian Christians.

Mather's *The Voice of God in a Tempest: A Sermon Preached at the Time of the Late Storm*, February 24, 1722/23 provides a better approximation of what constitutes the major chord of colonial American history, a providential basis for managing the commingling of civilization and the natural potential of the Americas. On February 24, 1722/23 a violent storm coming up in the night, Cotton Mather rose in the morning to "entertain his auditory with a discourse which in the time and the heighth of such a storm would not be unseasonable. . . . when such as could hear the sermon went home at noon they found that god had in a suprising and uncommon manner had poured the waters of the sea on the earth and the tide having risen considerably higher than we have ever known in our memory the damage which the city suffered was incredible ; how manner thousands of pounds it cannot be easily computed."[36] Based on the account of this storm, Benjamin Franklin expanded on Mather's scientific insights, looking for a characteristically rational accounting of the nature and importance of the tempest Mather described.[37] The tempest theme reemerges in both Franklin and Mather precisely because it forms one of the most persuasive discursive contexts for the early experience of the colonies. Essential to that context is the critical examination of a new Dominion acquired with a title of Divine Right. "The Epitaph which is to be written on the Ship, the Warff, the Goods that are lost in the Storm! Lord, Thou dids't it! O Pious Loser {Gaining in Piety!} This will be enough to quiet thee."[38] As Franklin, and his fellow patriots would later proselytize, the assumption of divine rights require a sound, detached and scientific basis.[39] In Shakespeare's polity, this is a concern as well.

The Tempest embodies several models of human association, each clearly intended as a gloss on the others. They are as follows: first, the situation on board ship. Secondly, the traditional polity of Milan under Prospero, which we only hear about, but which is largely recapitulated, conspiracy and all, in the marooned Neapolitan court. Thirdly, the polity of the island, with Prospero as supreme authority over all, both the original inhabitants and the castaways. Fourthly, the comic polity of Stephano, the nominal sovereign over Trinculo and Caliban. Lastly—and least—the Saturnian commonwealth (an alternative vision of the state of nature) borrowed by Gonzalo from Montaigne and by

Montaigne largely from Ovid. The premise of a storm respecting no geographic boundaries constitutes a persuasive argument for federalism, is implicated in all three writers. Madison, borrowing from Montesquieu, recognized after the revolution that factions will lose their force if the size of the government or design were large enough to prevent excesses by any one individual at the pinnacle of an hierarchy. A passage in Mather's sermon illustrates this point: "Whatever may be the energy of Evil Spirits, in any of our Storms, as well as in Jobs, and whatever the Prince of the power of the Air, may be able to do in Violent Agitations of the Air, 'tis all by the Divine Permission."[40] Later, Mather's interest in the civic reform of Boston's citizens will take on larger significance in the drafting of the Constitution, "There is a *Repentance*, which thou knowest not, O Man, that thy *Tempestuous Adversity* should scourage thee to? Find out what is to be *Reformed*, and let it be amended; Find out what is to be *performed*, and let it be practiced. . . . Behold a just and a wise and a *Faithful* GOD, Operating in all that is done unto you, stop not at *Second Cause* . . . BELIEVE Gracious designs of GOD, in all that is done unto you."[41] Amendment and practice is the very core of Mather's message.

Mather's sermon is written as an exceedingly refined jeremiad: the church-state was to be a model of Reformed Christianity and the threat of God's punishment was meant to be a celebration of that potential. "Piety requires that the voice of god in such things have a due notice taken of it: and the maxims and lessons of piety agreeable of such occasions be published that they may be lodged in some few hands where they may not be unacceptable or unprofitable."[42] Mather draws an instructive parallel between New England Christians and the Assyrian Christians who, according to tradition were converted by St. Thomas and maintained their faith after the Moslem invasion of the Middle East by occupying a wilderness area in North Kurdistan where they were able to maintain a high degree of autonomy.

As is the case in *Magnalia*, Mather depends on multiple origin and excessive probabilities to conflate disparate experience: "The Old Geographers, express a Desultory Levity, and strangely contradict themselves as well as one another, in assigning the *Place* of it [the New World]."[43] In Mather's text "THERE were *Terrible Things* a coming upon the greatest City then in the World. The Fate of *Ninive* is here foretold, which was in a most astonishing manner fulfilled in the days of King *Josiah* by *Nabopollasar* & *Aslyages* uniting their Forces that utterly destroyed that Renowned City. It was once called, *A City of God*; it may be for the special *Care* that GOD had of it."[44] Even at this early stage, it is clear that Mather's Tempest is to serve a parallel, though more highly focused purpose than that of Shakespeare's play. *The Tempest* is a fable about human association where individuals thrive in relation to a providential pattern which both embraces their experience and informs their understanding of the world.

In Mather's case, this significance falls from heaven as rain: "THIS therefore is the DOCTRINE of GOD that shall *distil* as the gentle *Rain* upon you, while the *stormy Wind & Tempest*."[45] As was the case in Mather's earlier consideration of the mainland and the islands in Massachusetts Bay, the populace of the colony is divided between the civilized elect and the barbarous, partially redeemed savage. In the sermon, the "Sea-faring Bretheren" are the object of God's (Prospero's) work. In a telling image, God is transfigured into the Renaissance Prospero-type, "The Glorious GOD is to be Adored, as the *Author* of the *Storms* that beat upon us; Even that Glorious GOD who has gathered the *Wind in his Fist*, and who has *bound the Waters as in a Garment*."[46] As minions locked into a corrupt and isolated form of government, the sailors are among the most exposed in God's Commonwealth, "It is extremely probable, that in such an Hour as this, we may have some of our *Sea-faring Bretheren* on the Coast, whose Hazard may be much greater than ours."[47] The warning is expressed in a passage from the Gospel of Matthew, "*Behold, There arose a great Tempest in the Sea, in so much as the Ship was covered with the Waves.*"[48] Mather continues "Since I have spoken a Good Word for the *Sea-faring* People, I hope they will hear me speaking to them. . . That you would so behave your selves at all *other Times*, that you may with Courage look up to Heaven when *Storms* do oblige you to it. . . If in *Fair Weather* there is nothing to be heard aboard, but the Language of Fiends, nothing but *Swearing*, and *Cursing*, and *Obscene Talk*, and the reviling and slandering of *Good Men*, in *Bad Weather* only you betake your selves to *Prayers*."[49] Mather's catalog of inequities is not meant to merely chasten, it also produces an unshakable optimism that the brand of Christianity he promotes can redeem the worst example. This devotional use of grief was preparation for one's own place in heaven.[50]

Among Mather's auditors, it would have been clear that despite God's terrible destructive potential, God's admonitions are primarily meant to be corrective. "For a *Storm* is the *Work* of that GOD, who *flies upon the Wings of the Wind*. If a *Storm* rise, we are to consider, That it is GOD who rises it. . . . For in a Storm, there is a Work, wherein GOD enjoins us to pay Homage unto Him, who is now giving a Shock unto us. When a *Storm* comes, we are to consider that there are *Good Things, which the Lord our GOD now requires of us*."[51] Puritans did not seek out affliction, but when the opportunity arose to consider its effects, ministers such as Mather zealously recorded the instances of God's mercies as a way of illustrating the larger promise awaiting the pious Christian.[52]

> If the Great GOD be slow to Anger, we must know 'tis not for want of *Great Power* to Revenge Himself upon the Wicked. The Assyrians were not presently destroyed upon the Prediction of what was to come upon them. No, *Ninive* continued a Hundred Years after this. . . . The Memorable and Unparallel'd *November-Storm* which fill'd the English World, with Horror near

Twenty Years ago was but a very little to what the Omnipotent GOD *can do*, He shall *come*, and it shall *be very Tempestuous round about Him*.[53]

This Christian dualism (Christ *agonistes* and Christ glorified) has a long tradition and is perhaps the most commonplace trope in Christian homiletics. Even more than we observed in Mather's chapter in *Magnalia*, the storm in this sermon expresses a confidence in God's original design. "The Glorious GOD is to be acknowledged as the Orderer of all the Storms that incommode us."[54] In choosing the introductory passage from the sixth chapter of *Micah*, "The Voice of God Crieth to the City," Mather means to evoke a chain of prophesy from the eighth-century before the fall of Samaria to the condition of Boston in 1722/23, taking into account the differing ethnographic perspectives on a common problem.

> All of our *Storms* are of a Higher Original, *O Magtan, O Manichee*, Dream not of an Evil God, who in spite of the Good One, may bring the *Storms* upon thee. With an Eye doubtless to such Fools once abounding in *Persia, Our Good* GOD says, *I create Darkness, I create Evil, I the Lord do all of these things* (Isaiah, XLV, 7) The Afflictions, which we know will abide us, have that Resemblance; *A Tempest in the Day of the Whirlwind* (Amos, I, 14). We meet with Humbling Things, *wherein we go down the Wind*. We meet with articles of *Adversity*, wherein it may be said, *The Winds are Contrary*.[55]

Mather, aware no doubt of his listener's faith and experience, drives home the promise of millenialism suggesting the echo of John Winthrop, that Boston might be at the center of a cosmic convergence. The impact of his words was meant to reiterate the fusion of secular and sacred history and to suggest moral obedience and civic virtue.[56]

For the Puritans of New England, the loss of social cohesion resulting from displaced and disorganized populations, the breakdown in traditional housekeeping roles and increasing numbers was transformed into an opportunity to form new social covenants.[57] Those opportunities would become ever more numerous throughout the eighteenth century, and Mather's sermon, with its depiction of an idealized reality besieged, is a finely-tuned response. By the conclusion of the sermon, Mather has offered his listeners valuable, if politically-inflected, advice concerning their spiritual destiny. An imperiled people, Mather suggests, can interpret the violence of *The Tempest* in order to better understand the promise of their individual and collective salvation. In this new utopia, the macrocosmic body of the world reflects microcosmic changes in the body of the state punctuated by supposedly "natural" portents and outbreaks of the supernatural will of the creator. The monarchical model, explored in Shakespeare's *Richard II* and *The Tempest* dependent on cure, balance and restoration is supplanted by a utopian vision founded on number, timetable and discipline. In such a schematic, Caliban, because he adopts the trappings of an outmoded monarchy suffers terribly as do Mather's "Sea-faring Brethren" whose fixation within a contained world ruled by a master-captain will be among the first lost in *The Tempest*-tossed sea. If we properly understand the explicit typology in Mather's sermon, we can see that Mather's tempest translates secular history, whether of individuals or of communities, into spiritual biography.[58]

III. SHAKESPEARE AT HARVARD AND THE COLLEGE OF WILLIAM & MARY

The situation in Cambridge and Williamsburg before 1788 was poor for the reception and transmission of Shakespeare's plays. Shakespearean performances were not plentiful, but Colly Cibber's adaptation of *Richard III* which had opened New York City's theatrical season in 1750, also opened the first theatrical season in Williamsburg, Virginia in 1751.[59]

Harvard College was never merely a theological seminary. From its foundations, it was expected that arts, sciences, and good literature be taught and that "the education was suitable for general purposes or for professional training in law or medicine."[60] However, the original Harvard commencement program, *New Englands First Fruits*, made it clear that the chief function of learning was to assist theology, that piety was not to be divorced from intellect and that reason and religion were joined in an indissoluble unity. If Shakespeare lived at the end of an era about to begin tremendous advances in speculative philosophy and new scientific thinking, the American colonies experienced a stunted intellectual life that, even at the close of the seventeenth-century, was poorly institutionalized. The first catalog for Harvard College, prepared for English benefactors by Thomas Hollis and Daniel Neal (1723), does not list a copy of *The Tempest*. Its stated purpose was "[that?] they may know what books you have and it is now a likely time to be supplied with many that you may want." The second catalog (1773) does record a volume of Shakespeare, published in London, by J. Tonson, 1734.[61] This Harvard catalog was the first American library catalog purporting to address an undergraduate audience, in response to new directions in the curriculum and governance of the college. Because thirty nine years passed between date of publication and the date of the catalog, it is difficult to say exactly when the first edition of *The Tempest* was made available to Harvard undergraduates.

If Shakespeare's *Tempest* was read, discussed or even known at all by many William & Mary undergraduates, it would have been a wondrous thing, since we could then say with some certainty that Shakespeare's play influenced the founding generation. According to Rhys Issacs, degree courses were rarely undertaken, "since the college's most important function was as a provincial center where young gentlemen from the various parts of Virginia could simultaneously acquire higher accomplishments, knowledge of government affairs, and acquaintance with one another."[62] The college started to educate large numbers of students beginning in the 1720s. About fifteen students matriculated at the college each year in the 1750s and 1760s, and this number increased to about twenty a year in the 1770s. Most classes at William and Mary included representatives from the significant tidewater families like the Burwells, Byrds and Carters.[63]

It is doubtful that the plays of Shakespeare were discussed or debated in Cheasapeake venues. The preponderance of evidence, anecdotal as well as biographical, suggests that by the time William & Mary was founded, colonial sentiments ran deep against English culture. Franklin noted that the Reverend Commissary Blair, who began the project for a College in the colony of Virginia, solicited Queen Mary (in the absence of William) who instructed King William's Attorney-General Seymour to be given a charter and two thousand pounds. Blair, on his arrival at Seymour's chambers, was told that the Attorney-General opposed the grant on the basis that England was engaged in an expensive war, that the money was wanted for better purposes, and that "he did not see the least Occasion for a College in Virginia." Reminded that the purpose of the College was to educate and qualify young men to be ministers who were much in demand in the colony, and as such the People of Virginia had souls to be saved as much as the people of England; "Souls!" said Seymour, "damn your souls. Make Tobacco!"[64]

Only half-jokingly did Benjamin Franklin write in *Remarks Concerning the Savages of North America* that, after the Treaty of Lancaster in 1774, the Iroquois representatives respectfully declined an offer to have members of the Six Nations educated at William and Mary. According to Franklin, the Iroquois speaker declined, remarking "We are convinced that you mean to do us good by your proposal.... But you who are wise must know that different Nations have different Conceptions of things; and you will not take it amiss, if our Ideas of this Kind of Education happen not to be the same with yours." Although it is unclear William & Mary contributed enormously to the education of the Virginia gentry, the Iroquois rationalized that "Several of our Young People were formerly brought up at the Colleges of the Northern Provinces (Dartmouth); they were instructed in all your Sciences; but when they came back to us, they were bad Runners, ignorant of every means of living in the Woods, unable to bear either Cold or Hunger, knew neither how to build a Cabin, take a Deer, or kill an Enemy, spoke our language imperfectly; were therefore neither fit for Hunters, Warriors, or Counselors; they were good for nothing."[65] Nonetheless, the offer made to the Iroquois was genuine, and at the time, it suggested that the College presented the best of Anglo-American opportunity.

What the Iroquois were rejecting was the notion, expected of Virginia gentility, that "liberality" was a quality that defined a man. For the colonial planter, this term was a part of the *translatio imperii*; it denoted freedom from material necessity; it meant freedom from servile subjection; it evoked calculations of self-interest; and, most importantly, it denoted the freedom to elevate the mind by application to the authoritative books that contained the higher learning.[66] It remains a subject of considerable doubt, how (or if) Shakespeare's *Tempest* was a part of this calculus; but we do know that by the nineteenth-century, a careful study of the Shakespearean classics would become a cornerstone of the "liberal arts."

IV. HOMESICK EXILES: *THE TEMPEST* AMONG THE AMERICAN REVOLUTIONARIES

Writing to John Adams from Monticello in 1814, Thomas Jefferson worried that "our post-revolutionary youth" were finding that "the information of books is no longer necessary; and all knolege [sic] which is not innate, is in contempt, or neglect at least."[67] At Monticello books filled every available wall space of his wing, they pushed out into floor space, and overflowed into other quarters. After selling that incomparable collection to help with his debts, he set out to build another library to rival it. Jefferson's classification of the 6,700 books he sold to the Library of Congress (books that became the core of the library after the British destroyed the original collection in the War of 1812) illustrate that he had a voracious appetite for practical information and, less often, for pleasure reading. Jefferson's catalog arranged the books by subject categories that were part of an overall classification system adapted from Francis Bacon's *Advancement of Learning*. Bacon had organized all knowledge into three categories: memory, reason and imagination. Jefferson renamed these: history, philosophy and fine arts. Shakespeare's writing clearly had a place within Jefferson's categories; yet, his dramatic works are rarely mentioned, and *The Tempest* is quoted briefly, as we have seen, as an example of verse in his *Thoughts on English Prosody*.

In a plan of study sent to Bernard Moore (and at least two others), Jefferson suggested one "Read the best of the poets, epic, didactic, dramatic, pastoral, lyric &c. But among these Shakespeare must be singled out by one who wishes to learn the full powers of the English language. Of him we must advise as Horace did of the Grecian models, 'vos exemplaria Graeca Nocturna versate manu, diversate diurna.' "[68] Since Jefferson rarely mentions Shakespeare, it appears his advice about the English dramatist was a rather static example. In 1771 Jefferson suggested to Robert Skipwith a list of books essential for a gentleman's library. This list included an edition of Capell's Shakespeare, suggesting that "the nature of the human mind evinces that the entertainments of fiction are useful as well as pleasant."[69] In *Notes on the State of Virginia*, Jefferson laments "America has not yet produced one good poet. When we shall have existed as a people as long as the Greeks did before they produced a Homer, the Romans a Virgil, the French a Racine and Voltaire, the

English a Shakespeare and Milton, should this reproach be still true, we will enquire from what unfriendly causes it has proceeded." But Jefferson is quick to point to Washington and Franklin as being among the great lights of American culture, claiming in the same passage that Great-Britain, owing to its population has produced no more than three persons of equal genius.[70]

Both Thomas Jefferson and John Adams shared an ambivalence to English standards.[71] Even in such native-born examples of genius, Jefferson and Washington could be counted on to display contradictory conclusions.[72] The discourses generated in the British Isles were sufficient to maintain a high interest in the play: issues of absolutism, property, rebellion and subjection central to *The Tempest* were never mistaken by Shakespeare's original audiences as anything other than English concerns.[73] Much of the play's content would have celebrated the perspective of a viewer in the metropole, London, and the distant shores of America, if considered at all, would be the "boundary" marker of English tastes. It is not without irony that the few dramatic plays of this period of American history are rich with images of the provincial "bumpkin" whose common-sense is often awkwardly balanced against an ironic exterior poise of aristocratic taste. It is not that the central issues of *The Tempest* were completely unknown in the colonies, but the intricate social dynamics which were presumed to infect English culture were thought to be deflected by America's "openness" and, in the eyes of some, the "empty" natural and cultural space.

Of all the literary or artistic activities in America following the Revolution, the theater was the least well-developed and the most controversial. In 1774, the Continental Congress included theater in activities banned by the Continental Association. It also passed legislation calling for the non-importation, non-consumption and non-exportation of dramatic material. Such views lead to the dismantling of the single acting troupe in the colonies before the Revolution, the London Company of Comedians (later renamed the American Company of Comedians). Late in 1785, some of this company returned, determined to provide the latest London productions with a semblance of professionalism. In many proposed venues the Company met with petitions against drama, rioting, insults and intense anti-theatrical legislation. These facts, combined with the popular belief, espoused by Benjamin Franklin, that the "Arts delight to travel Westward" demonstrate an important point about the reception of Shakespeare and that is, Shakespeare's initial reception was squarely within the confines of *translatio studii* or *translatio imperii*, the belief that civilization and culture inevitably originated in classical Greece and Rome, emerged during the Renaissance, and reappeared in Enlightenment thought. This tradition explains in large measure why early Americans appreciated Shakespeare's *Julius Caesar* since it seemed to demonstrate many political themes between the American Republic and the classical traditions of Rome. Such a belief accorded with many popular notions about America's exceptionalism, since it was assumed that America would "inherit" the mantle of greatness from the Old World.[74]

The dominant strain in American cultural history has been to witness the Puritan migration as a sacred origin; the telos was the Revolution. Essential to the success of the American revolution was the usurpation of an American identity imbued with exclusive meaning. Elsewhere during the same period of the late 18th and early 19th centuries, Enlightenment rhetoric proved to be a major obstacle: for Robespierre in France, for Hidalgo in Mexico. For to be an American did not mean (as is commonly mistaken) to be of the people, but rather to be a representative as Cotton Mather intended, of a limitless mission, preordained to an orderly succession towards nationhood.[75]

Few Americans were able to afford new and important books. English subscription lists confirm this fact, containing most frequently the names of noblemen, merchants, clergymen and professionals.[76] English books typically found their way to the American colonies within a year or two of publication, sometimes books were present in the colonies before they were known in the rural countryside of Great Britain. The principal port of entry for English books was Philadelphia because, during the eighteenth-century, it was the third city of the empire (after Edinburgh and London). Booksellers, usually the active printer-publisher of the city, secured books in a variety of ways: from correspondents and colleagues, imported shipments (either bought outright or held on consignment) or, for the very few, direct orders from London booksellers or their European agents.

Economic exigencies and trade relations both were reflected in the finished literary products brought to America. Throughout the eighteenth-century, English novels reprinted in America were reduced in bulk; they were issued in one volume if the original had appeared in two; American editions were often abridged. In the 1760s Shakespeare was advertised by all the major booksellers. From the scattered documentary evidence, we know that John Witherspoon, president of the College of New Jersey (later Princeton) bought a copy of Shakespeare's works in 1772; Charles Thomson, schoolmaster, merchant and secretary of the Continental Congress had a copy in 1760. John Penn, in 1786, was in possession of a Shakespeare Folio, perhaps an inheritance from his father or grandfather.[77]

American publishers were little concerned about literary integrity, but nevertheless their choices—reductions in size, the addition of explanatory footnotes to define archaic English words in Shakespeare, ridding books of tedious introductions—initially favoring the balance-sheet also were thought to be supporting American tastes and proclivities. Thus, the first locally-produced volume of Shakespeare's plays exemplified these peculiar circumstances.

The first locally-produced volume of Shakespeare was *The Plays of William Shakespeare. In Seventeen Volumes* published in Philadelphia by

C. & A. Conrad & Co; Conrad, Lucas & Co. Baltimore; Somervell and Conrad, Petersburg; and Bonsal, Conrad & Co. Norfolk, 1809. As a product of a jointly published imprint, this family-based combination mitigated concerns about dealing with strangers and ensured the investment and distribution in both the north and south was managed under the scrutiny of family members and their partners. As with many joint publications, no printer was named in the imprint.[78] In 1820, McCarty and Davis decided to have the complete dramatic works of Shakespeare stereotyped. Stereotyping involved the casting of metal plates from molds taken from set type. These plates could be used over and over again and then easily stored. Because it could make the publisher's business more efficient, stereotyping had obvious attractions. When a publisher invested the capital and effort of stereotyping a work, it was unlikely that another publisher would be willing to repeat the effort.

As with any early technology, the initial stereotyping of the Shakespeare works did not proceed smoothly.[79] In 1823, McCarty and Davis printed the first volumes from their shop in Philadelphia and, later that year entered a risk-sharing agreement with Carey and Lea to co-publish the work. After the first printing, subsequent printings using sold or rented plates were made in New York and Hartford. The large two octavo volumes set the standard for how Shakespeare's plays would be published in America throughout the nineteenth century.

It is no accident that, however limited the libraries and booksellers of the eighteenth-century were, in the comparatively new republic, the existence of colonial presses made Philadelphia a center for Shakespeariana in the nineteenth. It is somewhat singular that Philadelphia should have produced no less than two Shakespeare societies that have made a permanent record in print, of their proceedings.

The Shakespeare Society of Philadelphia (1852) was founded by Horace Howard Furness. In 1866 the society published "Notes on the Study of the *Tempest*"; the Minutes of the Shakespeare Society of Philadelphia for 1864–65 show that there were 60 copies printed of "The Notes" consisting chiefly of textual emendations, all possible sources of information ransacked for material, and an exhaustive bibliography. The "Notes" is the only publication of any Shakespeare Society in America that is of lasting value. This society, from its origin, mixed dinners with art, and according to some sources, it took special pride in bills of fare, that "form an interesting series, and display great ingenuity, even though, as has sometimes been the case, the dishes are made to conform to the quotations, rather than the quotations to the dishes." Later, in January 1875, the organization published articles on Caliban, in a small eight page paper called the "Literary Gem," published by the Crescent Literary Society. Two pages were set aside for the use of the Shakespeare Society of Philadelphia. In addition a series of notes on *The Tempest* was begun. With its sixth issue, the paper was discontinued, and thus ended the first attempt at a Shakespeare Society of Philadelphia journal.[80] A second fraternity, a club of young men in Philadelphia, who styled themselves the New Philadelphia Shakespeare Society was remarkably successful for the first year, but in the second, when more ambitious plans were proposed, it had dissolved almost before the members were aware of it.

IV. CONCLUSION

Shakespeare was championed, published, popularized, taught and performed in America (as was the case in England as well) long after the Revolutionary War. The late-blooming nature of Shakespeare's status is readily apparent in the designs of William Slade, the first director of the Folger Library, who in 1931 wrote of an extraordinary cartography:

> [A] line drawn from the site of the Folger Shakespeare Memorial through the Capital building and extended onward, will all but touch the monument to Washington and the memorial to Lincoln—the two Americans whose light also spreads across the world. The amount of deviation of the extended line will, in fact, be only great enough to indicate the alteration from the older order which finds its summation in the name of Washington, for more than half his lifetime an English subject, albeit an English colonial, and which agains finds its summation in the name of Lincoln.[81]

The principal lens through which Shakespeare has been viewed in America, reflects the rhetorical and cultural assumptions of the Transcendentalists, especially Emerson (in Bristol's case) and Thoreau (in Marx's case). One principal legacy of the Concord Idealists was to manufacture a civil faith that the disparate ends of democracy and inheritance could be managed. But along the margins of that ideology, in the literature of Melville,[82] Hawthorne and Poe for instance, the scene is different: the islands of *The Tempest* and the cultural/social isolation of America yield a twisted geometry.[83]

In the second chapter of *The Machine in the Garden*, Leo Marx makes a case for the centrality of a pastoral tradition in American culture. He looks to Shakespeare's *Tempest* for the best example among many of an English proclivity towards the pastoral mode. As Marx says, "Prospero's situation. . .is one of which American experience affords a singularly vivid instance: an unspoiled landscape suddenly invaded by advance parties of a dynamic, literate, and purposeful civilization. *It would be difficult to imagine a more dramatic coming together of civilization and nature.*"[84] However, the reception of English works was undeniably more complex, private and ambivalent than Marx's thesis suggests. Where the play was noticed at all, it was so because it illustrated providential history. In reviewing Shakespeare's conception of Prospero's island, Marx himself suggests a providential character to a New Eden. Marx's garden is dualistic—in one version, man tends a bountiful garden synergistically expressing his intellectual superiority and nature's creative impulses; the second version reflects a wilderness that threatens to overcome man's capacities for disciplined control.

Leo Marx was not the first to recognize the connection between a pastoral, idealized "island" such as America and the colonial expansionism of (principally) European powers. In fact, from many traditions touched by English colonialism (the Sandwich Islands, Australia, New Zealand, South Africa) the idea of a Prospero myth, whereby enlightened (albeit ambiguously motivated) individuals encounter and organize the sometimes strange (often horrifying) worlds, is commonplace. Leo Marx and Cotton Mather both wrote sermons worth hearing, but, in fact, the audience is what matters most.

NOTES

1. Leo Marx, *The Machine in the Garden: Technology and the Pastoral Ideal in America* (New York: Oxford University P, 1964), 72.
2. Hugh Amory, Review of *A Colonial Woman's Bookshelf* by Kevin J,. Hayes (Knoxville: U of Tennessee P, 1996), *New England Quarterly* (September 1997): 510.
3. For performances of Shakespeare in early America consult: Charles H. Shattuck, *Shakespeare on the American Stage:From the Hallams to Edwin Booth* (Washington D.C.: The Folger Shakespeare Library, 1976); Gary A. Richardson, *American Drama From the Colonial Period through World War I: A Critical History* (New York: Twayne, 1993); Don B. Wilmeth and Christopher Bigsby, eds., *The Cambridge History of American Theatre: Volume One: Beginnings to 1870* (Cambridge: Cambridge UP, 1998); Hugh F. Rankin, *The Theater in Colonial America* (Chapel Hill: U of North Carolina P, 1965).
4. In Peter Greenaway's screenplay to *Prospero's Books* two of the twenty four volumes Prospero has in his possession are *A Book of Mythologies* and *A Bestiary of Past, Present and Future Animals. The Book of Mythologies* is a compendium, in text and illustration, of mythologies with all their variants and alternative tellings; cycle after cycle of interconnecting tales of gods and men from all the known world, from the icy North to the deserts of Africa, with explanatory readings and symbolic interpretations. With this book as a concordance, Prospero can collect together, if he so wishes, all those gods and men who have achieved fame or infamy through water, or through fire, through decit, in association with horses or trees or pigs or swans or mirrors, pride, envy or stick insects.
5. *The Tempest*, ed., Stephen Orgel (Oxford UP, 1981), 1.2.229.
6. *Tmp.* 1.2.375; 5.1.261.
7. Richard Eden, *Decades of the New World* (London, 1555), 219 and *History of Trauayle* (London 1577), 434.
8. *Tmp.* 2.2.33.
9. *Tmp.* 5.1.182–83. Charles Frey, "The Tempest and the New World," *Shakespeare Quarterly* 30 (1979): 29–41.

10. Stephen Greenblatt, *Shakespearean Negotiations* (Berkeley: U of California P, 1988), 154.

11. What many have assumed was English "first contact" at Jamestown, was at best, "second contact" with altered outcomes, perhaps ones more suitable for literature. Clearly the best approaches to Shakespeare's *Tempest* have been preoccupied with sources, but Smith's version is not in fact the first or even the most meaningful. Those looking for correlations between Shakespeare's sources might look at the connection between Spanish texts pertaining to Ajacán and already postulated sources such as Bartolomé de Las Casas, *The Spanish Colonie*; Richard Hakluyt, *A Notable Historie containing foure voyages . . . unto Florida* (1587) and Robert Harcourt, *Relation of a Voyage to Guiana* (1613).

12. Geoffrey Bullough, ed. *Narrative and Dramatic Sources of Shakespeare: Volume 8 Romances*: Cymbeline, Winter's Tale, The Tempest. (London: Routledge & Kegan Paul; New York: Columbia UP, 1975), 241.

13. Jeffrey Richards, "Prospero in Virginia: The Example of Captain John Smith," Chapter 4, *Theater Enough: American Culture and the Metaphor of the World Stage, 1607–1789* (Durham NC: Duke UP, 1991), 85.

14. Richards, 90.

15. For a recent study of Smith's possible motives for specific revisons of the Pocahantas story in 1624 see Mary C. Fuller, *Voyages in Print: English Travel to America, 1576–1624* (Cambridge: Cambridge UP, 1995), 103–134.

16. For a reading of *The Tempest* as a parody of Chapman's *Memorable Masque*, which was self-consciously about Virginia (although it drew upon adventures in Guiana as well, consult: John Gillies, "Shakespeare's Virginian Masque," *ELH* 53.4 (1986): 673–707.

17. John Smith, *The Complete Works of Captain John Smith*, ed., Philip L. Barbour, 3 Vols, (Chapel Hill: U of North Carolina P, 1986), 1:235–36. Richards, 93.

18. Smith, 2:147.

19. Charles Mills Gayley, *Shakespeare and the Founders of Liberty in America* (New York: Macmillan, 1917), 161. Arthur Kinney notes, Gayley's entire thesis rests on a very suspicious notion that Strachey had access to an unpublished letter giving vivid details of indiscipline, mutiny and travails of the Jamestown colonists from June 1609 to July 1610: "How Shakespeare could have seen this letter, which circulated at court in one or more manuscript copies at the time, is unclear: there is not a shred of evidence, in fact that the playwright, not privy to the court himself, ever did see it." Arthur Kinney, "Revisiting *The Tempest*," *Modern Philology* (1995): 166.

20. Michael Dobson, "Fairly Brave New World: Shakespeare, the American Colonies, and the American Revolution," *Renaissance Drama* 23 (1992): 199.

21. Dobson, 197.

22. Thomas Jefferson, *Writings* (New York: Library of America, 1984), 611.

23. Quoted in Michael D. Bristol, *Shakespeare's America, America's Shakespeare* (New York: Routledge, 1990), 53.

24. Dobson, 199.

25. Dobson, 203.

26. Cotton Mather, *Magnalia Christi Americana; or The Ecclesiastical History of New England*, 2 Vols. (1852, rpt in New York: Russell and Russell, 1967), 1:25.

Cotton Mather exploited public drama in his stage-managed performance at the Boston Town-House on the April 18, 1689, where he delivered the twelve articles contained in the *Declarations* from the gallery. See Christopher Felker, *Reinventing Cotton Mather in the American Renaissance* (Boston: Northeastern UP, 1994), 40–48 and Kenneth Silverman, *The Life and Times of Cotton Mather* (New York: Harper & Row, 1984), 70–71.

27. Copies of these paintings hung at Monticello and Adams' house. Jefferson's copy (of Adams' portrait) was sold at a Boston auction in 1833; it was bought by George Francis Parkman who later bequeathed it to the Boston Athanaeum where it hangs in the Trusetees Room. The original Brown portraits of both presidents are lost.

28. *New York Packet* 2 November 1786.

29. Stephen Foster, *The Long Argument: English Puritanism and the Shaping of New England Culture, 1570–1700* (Chapel Hill: U of North Carolina P, 1991), 270.

30. Quoted in Perry Miller, *The New England Mind: The Seventeenth-Century* (Cambridge: Harvard University Press, 1939), 464.

31. Mather, *Magnalia*, 2: 440.

32. Mather, *Magnalia*, 2: 440.

33. Montaigne, *Montaigne's Essays in Three Books* (London: B. and B. Barker, 1743), 2:108.

34. Mather, *Magnalia*, 1: 41.

35. Mather, *Magnalia*, 2: 440–446.

36. Cotton Mather, *The Voice of God in a Tempest: A Sermon Preached at the Time of the Late Storm; wherein many and heavy and unknown losses were suffered at Boston, (and parts adjacent,)* [Evans microform no. 2461], February 24, 1722/23, (Boston: Printed by S. Kneeland), 1.

37. Benjamin Franklin, *Writings* (New York: The Library of America, 1987), 287.

38. Mather, *Voice*, 8.

39. See R. A. D. Grant, "Providence, Authority, and the Moral Life in *The Tempest*," *Shakespeare Studies* 16 (1983): 235–263.

40. Mather, *Voice*, 6.

41. Mather, *Voice*, 12–14.

42. Mather, *Voice*, 1.

43. Mather, *Voice*, 1.

44. Mather, *Voice*, 2.

45. Mather, *Voice*, 3.

46. Mather, *Voice*, 5.

47. Mather, *Voice*, 8.

48. Matt., Chapter 8.24.

49. Mather, *Voice*, 9.

50. Charles Hambrick-Stowe, *The Practice of Piety: Puritan Devotional Disciplines in Seventeenth-Century New England* (Chapel Hill: U of North Carolina P, 1982), 229.

51. Mather, *Voice*, 4–5.

52. Interestingly, in relation to the crises felt by the pious Puritan and the wrath of a vengeful, but desirous father and son, Leverenz sees Shakespeare's *Hamlet* as

most nearly approximating the language of feeling denoted in these passages and countless others drawn from the canon of Puritan texts. David Leverenz, *The Language of Puritan Feeling: An Exploration in Literature, Psychology and Social History* (New Brunswick: Rutgers UP, 1980), 103–105.

53. Mather, *Voice*, 7–8.

54. Mather, *Voice*, 10.

55. Mather, *Voice*, 10–11.

56. Mather, *Voice*, 16–19.

57. For Puritan utopias see James Holstun, *A Rational Millennium: Puritan Utopias of Seventeenth-century England and America* (New York: Oxford UP, 1987), 34–91.

58. For typology see Sacvan Bercovitch, *The Puritan Origins of the American Self* (New Haven: Yale UP, 1975), 35–40.

59. Rankin, 32, and Gary Taylor, *Reinventing Shakespeare: A Cultural History from the Restoration to the Present* (New York: Weidenfeld & Nicolson, 1989), 196.

60. Perry Miller, *New England Mind: The Seventeenth Century* (Cambridge: Harvard UP, 1939), 75–76.

61. *Catalogus Librorum in Bibliotheca Cantabrigiensi Selectus, Frequentiorem in Usum Harvardinatum, Qui Gradu Baccalaurei in Artibus Nondum Sunt Donati* (Cambridge, Mass., 1773).

62. Rhys Issacs, *The Transformation of Virginia, 1740–1790* (Chapel Hill: Published for the Institute of Early American History and Culture, Williamsburg, VA by U of North Carolina P, 1982), 130.

63. Allan Kulikoff, *Tobacco and Slaves: The Development of the Southern Colonies in the Chesapeake, 1680–1800* (Chapel Hill: U of North Carolina P, 1986), 277–78.

64. Franklin, 1096.

65. Franklin, 970.

66. See Issac, 131–138.

67. Jefferson, 1342–1343.

68. Jefferson, 1560.

69. Jefferson, 741, 743.

70. Jefferson, 190–191.

71. Dobson 198–99; Bristol, 51–59.

72. A prime example is the widely varying responses to the poetic talents and work of Phillis Wheatley, who dedicated some of her poems written in a Miltonic strain to George Washington (who praised her) but who was also criticized by Thomas Jefferson (probably on racial grounds). See Christopher Felker, " 'The Tongues of the learned are insufficient': Phillis Wheatley, Publishing Objectives and Personal Liberty," in *Texts and Textuality: Textual Instability, Theory and Interpretation*, ed., Philip Cohen (Wellesley Studies in Critical Theory, Literary History, and Culture; New York: Garland, 1997), 81–120.

73. See Alden T. Vaughn and Virginia Mason Vaughan, *Shakespeare's Caliban: A Cultural History* (New York: Cambridge UP, 1991), 52; Jeffrey Knapp, *An Empire Nowhere: England, America and Literature from* Utopia *to* The Tempest (Berkeley: U of California P, 1992), 222–223, 232; and Arthur Kinney.

74. See Robert E. Shalhope, *The Roots of Democracy: American Thought & Culture 1760–1800* (Boston: G.K. Hall, 1990), 53—54; 76 -81.

75. See Sacvan Bercovitch, *The Rites of Assent: Transformation in the Symbolic Construction of America* (New York: Routledge, 1993), 29–67.

76. See W.A. Speck, "Politicians, Peers and Publication Subscription 1700–1750," in *Books and Their Readers in Eighteenth-Century England*, ed., Isabel Rivers (Leicester: 1982), 47–68.

77. So little is known about woman's reading activities, that it is hard to ascertain if (or when) Shakespeare was experienced principally as a text and not as a performance by women. Interestingly, Kevin Hayes has found that in 1766, Margaret Rees inherited her husband's share in the Hatboro (PA) Union Library and that, in 1766 she borrowed Lady Montagu's Letters . . . written during Her travels in Europe, Asia and Africa and the seventh volume of Lewis Theobald's edition of Shakespeare (13). Such a connection is tantalizing, because it suggests that women often read travel literature and, as we know from many nineteenth-century women writers, such as Harriett Beecher Stowe in *The Minister's Wooing* and Edith Wharton, knowledge of such travel literature was often combined with dramatic performances meant to illustrate a growing sense of female empowerment. *The Minister's Wooing* in fact demonstrated a possible allusiveness between *The Tempest* and feminine influence. In Stowe's novel, Prospero's "secret studies" and Aaron Burr's treasonous geopolitical madness are definite parallels. We know, for instance that Stowe's novel is heavily informed by Cotton Mather's sources and that, in the novel the customs of different climes and countries are usefully combined in an effort to appeal to her largely feminine readership, as in this line from the novel: "{Mary, the Puritan Exemplar} wonders at the mobile, many-sided existance of warmer races, whose versatility of emotion on the surface is not incompatible with the most intense persistency lower down."

See Christopher P. Wilson, "Tempests and Teapots: Harriet Beecher Stowe's *The Minister's Wooing*," *New England Quarterly* 58.4 (1985): 554–577; 564–569; Richard D. Brown, *Knowledge Is Power: The Diffusion of Information in Early America, 1700—1865* (New York: Oxford UP, 1989), 189–193; and Christopher D. Felker, *Reinventing Cotton Mather in the American Renaissance* (Boston: Northeastern University Press, 1994), 157–179. For an excellent discussion on the link between Winthrop's notion of marriage as "a great creative allegory," *The Tempest* and Henry James's *The Portrait of Lady*, consult Douglas Anderson, *A House Undivided: Domesticity and Community in American Literature* (New York: Cambridge UP, 1990), 162–166.

78. See Rosalind Remer, *Printers and Men of Capital: Philadelphia Book Publishers in the New Republic* (Philadelphia: U of Pennsylvania P, 1995), 90–99.

79. Remer, 97–98.

80. See JVL, "Shakespeare Societies of America: Their Methods and Work," *Shakespeariana* Vol. 2, 1885 (rpt. NYAMS Press, 1965); "Shakespeare Societies," 484, 485.

81. William Slade, "The Significance of the Folger Shakespeare Memorial: An Essay Towards an Interpretation,' *Henry Clay Folger* (New Haven: privately

printed, 1931), 41–42. Quoted in Michael D. Bristol, *Shakespeare's America, America's Shakespeare* (London and New York: Routledge, 1990), 76.

82. Melville's experiments in fiction are compelling because they have a resonance with recent theoretical debates about the possibility of colonialism and capitalism working at two conflictual levels. Homi K. Bhabha has emphasized the extent to which these two levels fused and were, in operation inseparable; he has shown how colonial discourse operated not only as an instrumental construction of knowledge but also according to the ambivalent protocols of fantasy and desire. It is also interesting to note, as has David Reynolds, that "despite his well-known admiration for Shakespeare" Melville utilized Shakespearean devices in only one novel, *Moby-Dick*, "and even there modernized these devices by using bombastic rhetoric, black humor, and gory adventure derived largely from his own popular culture . . . Melville, while drawn to the art of Shakespearian truth telling, recognized the need to add American embellishments to a writer who was widely regarded as too staid by the mass of Americans." See David Reynolds, *Beneath the American Renaissance* (Cambridge: Harvard UP, 1988), 475–76.

83. Melville's sustained focus in his trip to Hermoupolis/Syra in 1856 and, a year earlier in the publication of *Benito Cereno*, was the framing of cultural drift in terms of "customary relationships." That the words "custom" and "customer" stem from Melville's ethno-historical preoccupations illumines the images of commerce and American-European exchange pervading *Benito Cereno*. In both the Greek visitation and the text of *Benito Cereno*, Melville exploits the full range of semantic and historical possibility inherent in "customary exchanges," and the convergence of the social, commercial, and aesthetic aspect of these exchanges create some of the more dynamic and revealing tensions underlying the development of a national, and potentially subversive, literature.

84. Marx, 35–36, emphasis added.

"Their senses I'll restore"
Montaigne and *The Tempest* Reconsidered

ALAN DE GOOYER

If it is true that any addition to knowledge adds to our sorrow, we might feel some slight trepidation if we recall that both Montaigne's essays and the plot of *The Tempest* are set in motion by the withdrawal from public life to the shelter of the study. At the beginning of both works the pursuit of knowledge is presented as a real, if not an already realized, peril, and despite their honorable intentions, neither Montaigne nor Prospero are granted the benefits of new learning–at least in the manner they had anticipated. As a matter of fact, in different ways but with unusually similar results, their withdrawal from the world to the privacy of the study provokes some form of insurrection and anarchy. Montaigne makes his famous mid-life retreat into his tower with the hope of achieving a sort of spiritual convalescence: "It seemed to me then," he says

> that the greatest favour I could do for my mind was to leave it in total idleness, caring for itself, concerned only with itself, calmly thinking of itself. I hoped it could do that more easily from then on, since with the passage of time it had grown mature and put on weight.[1]

But it was not to be. Though he had anticipated a quiet, re-creative idleness that would help him collect and restore his sagging spirits, instead he finds himself betrayed by an unruly imagination which

> bolted off like a runaway horse, taking far more trouble over itself than it ever did over anyone else; it gives birth to so many chimeras and fantastic monstrosities, one after another, without order or fitness. . . .[2]

It was no easy matter, it seems, settling his spirit into some mode of rewarding felicity, and rather than providing a contemplative oasis, his quiet was vexed with a disordered excess of imagination which soon began to alienate him from himself and from those around him. Rapt in mystifying fits of speculation and imagination, he turns melancholic, a condition he describes as "most inimical to [his] natural complexion"[3] (II.8.433)–and soon he becomes, to use one of our own accurately ambiguous idioms, beside himself.

Montaigne's antidote for this agitated self-distraction was to write essays. They became for him an instrument of self-recovery, a way of controlling rebellious thoughts by directing his thought upon itself. In fact, he admits that he began his *Essais* in order to tame his imagination's rebellious progeny: "to contemplate at my ease their oddness and their strangeness," he writes, "I began to keep a record of them, hoping in time to make my mind ashamed of itself."[4] Thus Montaigne began writing his essays hoping to create a space of relative comfort and sanity to calm his mutinous imagination, to discover an island of security where he could compose (if not control) the waywardness of his mind by forcing it to consider itself. Shame was to be the expedient. Simultaneously composing and maintaining a critical self-presence, he hopes to ease his mind by essaying, to discipline his fancy's roving—if, that is, his literary self-presentation will sufficiently chide his imagination into submission. The project of the *Essais* is fundamentally redemptive: through an effort to assay his own thoughts and test them against the thoughts of others, he will be able to re-appropriate the self he had lost in reverie and melancholy; he will be able to fix his straying mind and his skittish emotions through the discipline of writing. Through writing, in other words, he will become his own again. It is a familiar story of loss and recovery.

The Tempest, too, is a story of selfish abdication gone awry. In surprising ways, the odd story of Prospero's *otium* presents a kind of allegorized narrative of Montaigne's self-exile, loss of control, and eventual recovery through the timely application of his art. The whole play is of course set in motion by Prospero's retreat to his study, a decision for which he offers relatively slim justification. Recounting the events that led up to his banishment, he informs his daughter—rather moodily—how he had retired to enjoy the felicities of leisured study. For the sake of the "liberal arts" he puts off the burden of government—"thus neglecting worldly ends, all dedicated / To closeness and the bettering of [his] mind" (1.2.89–90)—and cast his civic obligations as Duke of Milan upon his brother.[5] But cloistered away in rapt self-concern he eventually becomes "transported," until by degrees he "grew stranger to [his] state" (1.2.76). This statement, as so much in the play, is hard to pin down— we can understand it to mean that he had fallen out of touch with his subjects, or that he had grown alienated from himself. The reward for Prospero's retreat into his book-lined study is also a loss of selfhood; he is cut off from his past, cast adrift—with the difference, of course, that in Prospero's case the threats are not internal but external, that the rebellion is not found in his own imagination so much as it is realized (all too literally) in his brother's murderous ambition and heartless plotting. Expelled from his dukedom and cast out upon the sea by his fratricidal brother, Prospero is set down "by providence divine" (1.2.159) upon Ariel and Caliban's wondrous isle. He responds with passing bouts of melancholy—"Me, poor man, my library was dukedom large enough" (1.2.109–110)—and (even) twelve years after washing ashore he can barely contain his anger and regret at his expulsion from his reclusive studies. While cloaked in his magician's robes, he sets his old friends and enemies down on (what is now) his island and "transports" them with "chimeras and fantastic monstrosities" that undermine their reason until they are beside themselves in ecstasies of grief, ambition, drunkenness, or wonder. With the help of his salvaged books, Prospero recovers at least a partial sovereignty over the conspirators that have plagued him. But he puts aside his magic, forgoes his revenge, and allows the gathered company to regain their lost senses and (to paraphrase Gonzalo) to become again themselves when no man was his own (5.1.212). At least some will have been chastened by a sense of shame, will cast-off the delusions conceived in their exile, and will promise to seek grace thereafter. And Prospero is no longer stranger to his state.

Montaigne uses the essay to hold the mirror up to his own folly, and with an intent not so different, Prospero performs his magic so that the shipwrecked might see their own folly. As unlike as the two works are in form and performance, they both arrive at a similar conclusion: after an initial spell of exile (or self-exile) both Montaigne and (some of) the characters in *The Tempest* achieve a renewed sense of self-understanding whereby they are able to "enjoy their being as they ought." And, in both works, this new understanding depends upon a complicated sense of the "kindness" of all humans, and a sadly tempered recognition of human frailty that entreats us to give up any pretensions we may have of escaping ourselves, our weaknesses, our places. And in their different ways, they both end on a note of renunciation. Neither conclusion is unambiguous, of course, nor should we assume that these verdicts necessarily represent a "last word" of any kind; but both the *Essais* and *The Tempest* end with the clear suggestion that we "come to our senses"—in other words, they ultimately enjoin us to quit chasing the untenable and unattainable in either philosophy or in the world, to amend our desires and our behavior with human limitations in mind, and, in the last instance, to put aside wonder and return to reality. "We are never 'at home': we are always outside ourselves," writes Montaigne, "Fear, desire, hope, impel us towards the future; they rob us of feelings and concern for what now is, in order to spend time over what will be—even when we ourselves shall be no more."[6]

These similarities are drawn rather casually, I admit, and are open to qualification—particularly this last (as yet) unexamined correspondence. Certainly, there is a great distinction to be made between essaying one's own thoughts and using one's powers to fool and to assay those in one's power; and one, of course, is an historical figure and the other a dramatic creation. And yet, the two works seem to present, roughly, a paradigm of self-exile involving some kind of "transport" or ecstasy, a subsequent rebellion and loss, and eventually a chastened recovery that is achieved through the practice of their respective arts. And the odd similarity of beginnings and endings points to a paradoxical connection between what may be Shakespeare's most self-consciously theatrical play, in the sense that it constantly questions the powers of illusion, and the essay—arguably, the least theatrical of genres. The one is propelled by Prospero's use of manipulative theatrics, devised to direct events more or less deliberately toward the reformation of his adversaries and restoration his dukedom; the other is propelled—as the work of most essayists—by a movement that is "essentially reflective" and that is "designed to give the impression of a mind thinking on a subject with no predetermined goal or formulaic conclusion toward which it need aim."[7] In form, method, and purpose, then, the two works would seem to have little in common. But this has not lessened the sense that the two texts are somehow connected, and connected by more than a couple of verbal appropriations on Shakespeare's part. The verbal echoes are there, of course. Florio's translation of the *Essais* has been persistently mined for parallels, so much so that Francis Yates remarked over sixty years ago that study of the influence of Florio's *Montaigne* upon Shakespeare had already panned out—"This is a question which has been exhaustively studied."[8] But comparisons have continued nonetheless, shifting gradually to questions about how Shakespeare employed the *Essais* rather than what exactly he borrowed. In the past few years, for instance, there has been exaggerated focus on Shakespeare's familiar borrowing from "Of the Cannibals," usually with the revisionist goal of illustrating European exploitation of New World inhabitants and propounding on his (and Prospero's) complicity. Such conclusions have been effectively challenged as ahistorical and reductive, though (at least in America) they have nearly acquired the status of orthodoxy–despite the fact that Shakespeare's intentions concerning the passage from "Of the Cannibals" have been terribly hard to pin down.[9] Is he mocking Montaigne by giving his ideas to Gonzalo? or mocking Gonzalo with Montaigne's ideas? or is Shakespeare perhaps promoting a political agenda? It is unlikely these questions will ever be resolved, and we probably are well-advised to accept Stephen Orgel's conclusion concerning Shakespeare's use of this particular essay: "as he so often does, [he] dramatizes both sides of the debate, and in the process renders a resolution to it impossible. . . . Shakespeare has taken everything from Montaigne except the point."[10] The other generally accepted borrowing, one much less equivocal in its handling, is from the essay "Of Cruelty." The borrowed passage comes at the play's turning point, at the moment when Prospero accepts that "the rarer action is / In virtue than in vengeance" (5.1.28–9) and gives over his opportunity for revenge; and here, Shakespeare seems to take up Montaigne's opinion without question, simply paraphrasing the passage, putting it in the mouth of the protagonist, and following it with actions that seem to confirm its truth.[11] (Oddly, this acknowledged borrowing has received far less attention, for reasons that probably have to do with the fact that the passage is ethical rather than political in nature.) And finally, Gail Kern Paster has attempted to explain, fairly convincingly I think, the curious passage in *The Tempest* on "widow Dido" through the lens of the *Essais*.[12] There are many other echoes of Montaigne, less audible and certainly less lucid, and that rarely go beyond a noted semblance of vocabulary.[13] Nevertheless, as Paster remarks, "only in *The Tempest* are echoes from Montaigne so clear as to be unmistakable. While writing this play, if not while writing any other, Shakespeare seems to have had Florio's translation at his elbow."[14]

I do not intend to go over these particular borrowings again. Rather, I would ask whether or not we can identify possible connections beyond the mere borrowing of phrase and content. Can we find areas of common concern? or associations of ideas that take us beyond the devoted straining of ears for verbal echoes? It is unlikely that larger connections between the essay and *The Tempest* are to be found in particular examples of generic inclusion, or even modal extension, so it is difficult to see how the essay works its way into *The Tempest* on a formal level: the form of the essay—to the extent that it actually has a form—does not become part of the play's style or structure.[15] And, admittedly, almost any other type of proposed connection other than verbal borrowing or generic development will probably remain (merely) annotative, or be so loose as to become plainly speculative. This can be helpful, no doubt. Criticism almost always vacillates between these two poles—and what critic can do without annotation or speculation?—and such procedures are certainly defensible if and when they complicate our sense of the play's meanings. But connections other than verifiable borrowings are difficult to confirm, and when suggested they are always in danger of falling prey to charges of vagueness, of relying on some misty notion of *zeitgeist* or some thinly attenuated claim that cultural negotiations are (secretly) at work. Against such criticisms there is little to be said, except that if we relate the two works in order to complicate and deepen our sense of the play, or as a way to nudge us out of the rut of the familiar transcendental and revisionist readings, we have done the play some service. One such attempt can be found in a recent essay by Arthur Kirsch, who argues that:

> In the absence of a narrative source, Shakespeare's organization of the action, as well as Prospero's, seems unusually informed by the kind of working out of ideas that suggests the tenor of Montaigne's thinking: interrogative rather than programmatic; anti-sentimental but humane; tragicomic (a quite familiar Renaissance genre) rather than only tragic or comic, incorporating adversities rather than italicizing them as subversive ironies. The particular constellation of ideas in the play, moreover—forgiveness, compassion, imagination—is habitual in Montaigne.[16]

With considerable success, Kirsch goes on to consider *The Tempest* in terms of this trinity of humanistic values as understood by Montaigne. The risks still remain: by identifying a "constellation of ideas" we are irrevocably pointed toward the sighting of thematic correspondences, in such a way that we end up simply noticing common ideas held in common. And likewise, in identifying the "tenor of Montaigne's thinking," as difficult as that is, we may arrive at connections that depend more upon tone or perspective than they do upon any clearly shared ideas. But Kirsch points us in the right direction, I think, and his approach complicates our understanding of the play and even helps dislodge some of the too familiar readings (though this of course depends on the critic's temperament, on the willingness of the reader to withhold judgment, to measure his or her responses with a note of sympathy, and to allow for openness and inclusiveness—in other words, to respond the play as the essayist responds to the world, with a sense of contingency, inclusiveness, and ironic acceptance). With these reservations in mind I would like to look at two aspects of the play that, I think, can be related to Montaigne and the essay, both of which might help us develop a more sympathetic, or at least a different, response to the play: the first is rather general and has to do with the interrogative nature of both *The Tempest* and the genre of the essay, and the second with the play's implicit condemnation of various forms of ecstasy or prolonged fits of "wonder," and, as I have hinted, its implicit call for the characters to come to their senses. This latter aspect is directly related to the conclusion of Montaigne's *Essais*.

In many ways, the background against which I write is the tendency over last two decades to question (negatively) *The Tempest*'s participation in an emerging colonialism, to suspect the motives of Prospero and the inconclusiveness of the play's ending, and in general to turn what were once considered virtues into ideologies or pathologies. This has no doubt been a useful corrective to idealist readings that see Prospero as a beneficent conjurer who redeems the sins of all. But, while we have looked for cracks in which to drive our wedges, we have often overlooked the fact that the play sends back its own set of questions. In fact, *The Tempest* is burdened with questions, so much so that questioning becomes one of its primary means of development. There is hardly an event or encounter in the play that does not provoke some form of bewildered inquiry. This particular aspect of the play can be related to the essay and the essayist's tendency to raise and respond to questions: the motive of Montaigne, after all, was to "assay" experience and ideas with the aim of increasing one's critical self-awareness. In other words, he developed the essay as an important tool of apprehension and revaluation that provided an open, deliberative response to changing circumstances. It is a curious coincidence, certainly, that the essay was first put to use (at least in England) at about the same time as the country's drama reached its height—a coincidence understandable in part because the essay allowed writers to respond to social upheaval by trying out different ways of knowing and trying on different ways of self-knowing. The interrogative bias of the essay is relevant to *The Tempest* in that the play is constantly testing its characters with extraordinarily new experiences, choices, and opportunities. The marvels confronting the sea-swallowed travelers once they have miraculously washed ashore, the obstacles placed before the young lovers, the occasions for murderous insurrection, the vanishing banquets and the judging harpy, the invitation to revenge that Prospero considers, even something so shallow as the offer of oblivion in Stephano's butt of sack—all of these, and more, force the marooned characters to face up to questions about who they are and what they know.

That is to say, the play asks of its characters and through its characters a number of fundamental ethical and epistemological questions. They begin at once, during the crisis of the opening storm. Threatened with a watery death, the seafarers are abruptly challenged with the kind of life and death question that is usually reserved for the philosopher in his study meditating on life's end—"What must our mouths be cold?" (1.1.52). Of course, we soon learn that their plight is of Prospero's manufacture, that the travelers' time has not yet come, and that they may yet die a dry death; but the play raises other questions just as quickly—out of the opening tumult we hear a number of interrogative cries: "What Cheer?"; "Where's the master?"; "What cares these roarers for the name of king?" (1.1.2,9,16–17). Though less apocalyptic than the fearful shouts of drowning men, these passing questions can take on heightened thematic, even philosophic, significance if seen in retrospect: with deceptive ease Shakespeare raises in the first scene the fundamental issues of temperament, authority, and political power that haunt the play. There are also less direct methods of inserting questions of course. Sometimes the questions are merely implied or insinuated, as are those suggested in the troubling ambiguities that end the play—for instance, what are we to make of Caliban's future? How are we to understand Antonio's reticence during the final scene? But in many cases, the questions are generated directly out of the characters' troubled apprehensions. To give but one example, Stephano, when he confronts the tormented Caliban bellowing in the mud, cannot fathom what he sees or what he should do. His response to the mysterious creature is, naturally, one of blinking incomprehension. It is fitting that he should ask, "What's the matter? Have we devils here?" (2.2.56).

Even in incomprehension Stephano has spoken truer than he purposed. On a very basic level his question points to a shared dilemma, echoed throughout the play, as to whether or not the characters can recognize the matters that concern others. Can they understand the feelings—or the matters—that motivate each other? Stephano also asks, rather unwittingly, what exactly it is that makes a human being? Who and what are we? Is Caliban one of us? Or, for that matter, is Antonio, when he refuses to acknowledge Prospero's invitation to forgiveness? Though both are central to the play, these two recalcitrants refuse to belong gratefully to the restored community at the play's end. What is it that isolates them and makes them so unregenerate? How, then, are matters resolved? or are they? All of these questions (many of them quite familiar, of course) shade so imperceptibly into one another that it might help to try and make a few distinctions. To begin, *The Tempest* persistently questions whether or not we can share and understand others' feelings and motivations. For instance, the guileless Miranda seems perpetually at a loss, wondering frequently whether her emotions are at all reflected in the hearts of others. In what must be one of the most uncalculated of loving overtures, one in which almost all forms of cautious courtship are absent, she asks Ferdinand, simply, "Do you love me?" (3.1.67). When after a bit of posturing admiration he says yes, she artlessly responds, "My husband then?" (3.1.88). Free from any hint of coquetry, Miranda has so little context within which to place any of her new experiences that she cannot be expected to comprehend—or suspect—much of anything so suddenly thrown at her. She gets right at the heart of the matter, though, and this is part of her charm. But even where experience suggests she might be able to understand others' feelings she often remains baffled. Her father's motives and emotions are a recurrent mystery to her—his irritability during his early narrative, for instance, or the anger he expresses toward Ferdinand and his occasions of annoyed despondency: they provoke her naive puzzlement. And a similar sense of bewilderment is common in other less sympathetic characters as well. Much later, for instance Alonso asks with revived compassion whether Prospero has suffered a grief similar to his own: "You the like loss?" (5.1.144). Ostensibly, he is asking about Prospero's misfortunes (particularly, his ironic statement that he has lost his daughter), but it also reveals in Alonso a surprised recognition that others' feelings may be as real as his own.

Though the play ultimately calls for an awakened recognition of others' passions and sorrows, it still leaves unanswered the problem of the other characters' potential for good or evil. Mysteries surrounding the iniquity of others, no matter how near in relation, present dilemmas that almost invariably propel *The Tempest*'s plot forward. As we have already noted, suspicion is caught sleeping at the doors of Prospero's study, and he is soon violently thrust out. Yet throughout the play he remains puzzled and angered by the mystery of Antonio's perfidy, for it still wakes in him the bitter memories of what he once was and what he has suffered. And it is this sense of unfathomed iniquity that provides the motive for his displays of power and, insofar as it remains unexplained, is the source of the play's equivocal conclusion. In fact, an air of moral inscrutability infects all levels of the play: Miranda misjudges—or more likely does not recognize—Caliban's lust for her; Ferdinand misunderstands Prospero's intentions as evil when he is falsely accused of usurping his father's dukedom; Alonso sleeps unsuspecting while Antonio and Sebastian plot his murder; even Caliban misinterprets the purpose of Stephano and Trinculo when they cease to be assassins and become playactors instead, prancing about in stolen garments—"Let it alone, thou fool" carps Caliban, "it is but trash" (4.1.223). This last is an instance of evil gone off track, and elsewhere it is clear that even among the allied conspirators there are uncertainties about commitments. They are thus continually testing their associates' willingness to sin. Caliban avidly questions Stephano and Trinculo concerning their determination to drive a nail into Prospero's skull—"Dost thou like the plot, Trinculo?"... "Wilt thou destroy him then?" (3.2.108,112). And a few scenes earlier, Antonio, his head shaking in mock wonder, openly ponders the wondrous possibilities should Alonso's throat be slit–and he goads Sebastian with sinister hypocrisy: "What might, / Worthy Sebastian, O what might—?" (2.1.202–3). The riddle of their villainy, it seems, can only be solved with more questioning.

These types of questions are meant to incite the imagination to evil even as they attempt to feel their fellows out; they are, in other words, the kind of questions meant to press unwelcome choices upon reluctant confederates, to solicit others so one is not forced to be mutinous alone. Such solicitations inevitably force those asked to examine what they are and what they would be; they compel the characters queried to a fundamental—if inevitably hasty— self-evaluation. This can and occasionally does work for good in the play. Questions that solicit actions can excite characters to act with charity as easily as malevolence, depending of course on who is questioned. This is clearly the case as the play begins its final act and the "project gather[s] to a head." Here, Ariel implicitly questions Prospero about his potential for compassion:

ARIEL   Your charm so strongly works 'em
                    That if you now beheld them, your affections
                    Would become tender.
PROSPERO   Dost thou think so, spirit?
ARIEL   Mine would, sir, were I human.
PROSPERO   And mine shall.
                    Hath thou, which art but air, a touch, a feeling
                    Of their afflictions, and shall not myself,
                    One of their kind, that relish all as sharply
                    Passion as they, be kindlier moved than thou art? (5.1.17–24)

Ariel has gathered together the spell-bound victims of Prospero's magic, and he holds them up—the good and the bad, the distracted and the sorrowful—as a motley portrait of humanity for Prospero to reflect upon. Ariel expects him to be sympathetically moved by their afflictions, to relish their passions and recognize that he is in some sense "kindly." In this Ariel touches upon another means by which to solicit Prospero's good-will to his enemies: though Prospero has from the beginning offered assurances that his intentions toward this spell-bound assembly are estimable, he is here expected to acknowledge their shared humanity.[17]

It is a simple and at least here an effective argument. But are we "kindly" in the fullest sense of the term? Is it true that, as Montaigne claims, "Every man bears the whole Form of the human condition"?[18] As a fundamental premise this is one of the most important statements in the *Essais*: it places his self-reflections at the nexus of private and public so that they become more than merely exercises in idle narcissism or private therapy. The fact that Montaigne sees himself in others, and expects others to see themselves in him, allows him to be both skeptical of others' aspirations and yet comprehensive in his understanding– it means, basically, that no one in their basic humanity is either more and less than he is. But *The Tempest* questions even this. On both the moral and the physical level the play confronts its characters with forms that seem to be other than human, forms that literally bear the stamp of conditions well above or beneath "common humanity." Ariel, who takes all kinds of shapes, none of them human, seems to look upon the play's exiled humanity from a perspective that none of them can share. Ariel's may be a privileged view, and yet the play's optimistic conclusion (insofar as it is optimistic) seems to depend upon his belief that, though some may seem different or be guiltier, at least the nature of our affections should be tendered commonly. After all, implies Ariel, our being is common. But the question of humankind's common form never quite goes away. It is raised on a comic level earlier in the play when Stephano initially encounters Caliban—he reacts quite naturally with amazed disbelief: "Have we devils here? Do you put tricks upon's with savages and men of Ind? Ha?" (2.2.56–57). And surely, coming upon such a strange fish as Caliban might naturally puzzle the beached butler and his fellow jester, Trinculo, just as he still puzzles us; but even the Caliban, when he first sees Trinculo, mistakes him for another of Prospero's spirits sent to plague him. Caliban can easily be forgiven this particular misperception—he after all has little to compare them with outside of Prospero, Miranda, and of course, Sycorax. But the play also seems to stress that encounters between fellow humans are just as oddly perplexing, and again, the question is the same: how much do others really share the same form? No one seems to be taken on first encounter for what he or she is. When Miranda first opens the "fringéd curtains" of her eyes and sees Ferdinand, her response is delighted wonder—"What is't?—a spirit? (1.2.408, 410). And at first, with equal wonder, Ferdinand assumes she is a goddess. As does Alonso at the end of the play, despite that fact that he has been slowly dragged back to his senses by Prospero: "Is she the goddess that hath severed us, / And brought us thus together?" (5.1.187–88). Ferdinand answers quite plainly, "Sir, she is mortal" (5.1.189).

Still, this simple fact that we are all mere mortals seems yet another mystery. Though finally all the charmed company gradually come to recognize each other as human, this apparently simple fact is something that must be constantly re-cognized. Early in the play, for instance, Prospero must inform Miranda when she first sees the entranced Ferdinand that he is not a spirit—

"No, wench, it eats and sleeps, and hath such sense as we have–such" (1.2.413–14). Even the jaundiced Caliban feels the need to remind his accomplices and himself that Prospero is but mortal: "Remember / First to possess his books; for without them / He's but a sot, as I am, nor hath not / One spirit to command" (3.2.890–90). But if Prospero is at bottom merely a man, and (from Caliban's perspective) merely a sottish one at that, so too is the malformed Caliban human, and though he remains a "thing of darkness" (5.1.275), he is finally recognized by Prospero as one of us. If we do share the same form, then, as the play ultimately grants that we do, why must this be learned and learned again? One reason may simply be that so much happens so fast to so many of the characters that they can no longer trust their senses. From the beginning, all the characters (with the usual exception of Prospero) have had to confront the unexpected and the inexplicable. Such confrontations are a constant part of their experience on the island, and they unavoidably raise the question as to how much of their experience they really do understand. How much can they? In his opening exposition, for example, Prospero draws attention to the murkiness of our remembered origins: "Canst thou remember," Prospero asks Miranda, "a time before we came unto this cell?. . . .What seest thou else / In the dark backward and abyss of time?" (1.2.38–9, 49–50). Our endings appear just as dark, as the revels end and the pageant fades away. But if our lives are rounded with sleep, there is also much in between that seems to produce the sleep of reason, whether it comes out of traumatic loss, out of the disorienting encounters with the unfamiliar, or out of the kind of visions created by Ariel.

Between the beginning and ending of the play, behind the entirety of experience for the whole troop of castaways, lie mysteries that they cannot begin to fathom–despite all their questions. In fact, most of the shipwrecked characters comprehend their experiences on the island as outright wonders, and the usual effect on them is one of open-mouthed bafflement. For years Miranda has been left in the dark as to the reasons for her existence on the island, and when told her response is one of awed surprise (from which Prospero must repeatedly recall her with his brusque demands for attention). Other characters, as we have seen, are often astonished or even stupefied when they first encounter the island's other inhabitants or witness its apparitions. Throughout, the well-meaning Gonzalo expresses the company's sense of wonder with near choric regularity. As witness to the Ariel's banquet, for instance, he ponders its enchanting effect—"If in Naples / I should report this now, would they believe me?" (3.3.27–28); after the banquet vanishes he wonders at Alonso's state of mind—"I' th' name of something holy, sir, why stand you / In this strange stare?" (3.3.94–95); and at the end of the play he offers his astonished summary of the play's action in the form of a wide-eyed question—"Was Milan thrust from Milan that his issue / Should become kings of Naples?" (5.1.25–26). Yet if Gonzalo often seems to be the spokesman for the mystified band of mariners, something similar could be said of Caliban, the island's one native, who periodically speaks for the island's subtleties:

> Be not afeard, the isle is full of noises,
> Sounds, and sweet airs, that give delight and hurt not.
> Sometimes a thousand twangling instruments
> Will hum about mine ears; and sometime voices,
> That if I then had waked after long sleep,
> Will make me sleep again, and then in dreaming
> The clouds methought would open and show riches
> Ready to drop upon me, that when I waked
> I cried to dream again.   (3.2.133–41)

But if so much of their experience seems dream-like, their questioning of that experience tends to lead them back to themselves and their lack of understanding. How are they to confront the new? the mysterious? If, when they are about to be sea-swallowed, the prospect of immediate death has not turned the travelers into embryonic philosophers, their miraculous survival ought at the very least to make them consider the feeble nature of their existence. After all, as Hans Blumenberg has said, "Shipwreck, as seen by the survivor, is the figure of an initial philosophical experience."[19] That is, shipwreck, as an ordeal of isolation and loss, invites—and even forces—its survivors to cast off their old sense of self and think on what they had been and will be; it should make them wonder at their own mortal existence. This is perhaps the largest question the play asks: what are we to do when everything is lost? How do we get it back given the chance? With magic? through vengeance? or perhaps we let it go by forgiving or by seeking grace?[20] Of course, providing the shipwrecked with such a compelling motive for self-reflection is all Prospero's doing: it is he who has violently forced the travelers to suffer the existential privations of shipwreck, the loss of place, family, and wealth. Though the island provides temporary sanctuary for the stranded passengers, Prospero continues to assay all the characters by fabricating experiences that will disturb even the most cynical out of their complacency: the separated parties know nothing of each other, each group is forced to undergo the intense stimulation (and often frustration) of their apprehension, and to varying degrees they are made to suffer dynamic emotional changes. None of Prospero's actions has gone without criticism of course, but nevertheless we should remember that Prospero sets up the island to serve as a testing ground to question the character of his enemies, to give them the chance to remember and repeat their past mistakes, or to start over, to contemplate their past so that they might see their own actions as they would see another's. Whether we see Prospero's provocations as inviting reflection, or merely baiting a trap, may be a matter of our (chosen) perspective as audience, but the shipwrecked are nevertheless free to respond to the island's invitation to philosophic self-reflection.

Ideally, their suffering would challenge each one of them to abate their too strong desires and elicit remorse for their past transgressions.[21] But they often act otherwise, they allow their imaginations to revert to fantastical (and yet predictable) "chimeras" of monarchical power and colonial rule, or to descend into suicidal grief or out-and-out drunkenness. Too often the shipwrecked simply confirm their weaknesses, miserably failing Prospero's trial of their character: Antonio and Sebastian mock Gonzalo's vision of utopia with cynical ferocity and revert to their old ways—fratricide and usurpation; Stephano and Trinculo join with Caliban and plot murder to establish their tinhorn monarchy; Alonso, faced with his son's death, would lie mudded with him on the ocean's bottom. But Prospero's illusions do transform those who will let them: Alonso must experience what it is like to suffer as Prospero has done—he loses his kingdom and undergoes an attempt on his life; Ferdinand submits willingly (after an aborted show of resistance) to the trial of his love, recognizing in Miranda a perfection that answers all his past amorous disappointments. The point is that the stimulus of Prospero's magic forces each of the castaways to answer questions about themselves and their past. His victims may take advantage of their exile to look at themselves, to rein in their imaginations, to value rightly, and possibly to shame themselves into a greater critical self-awareness. If, that is, they can use their exile, not to let their imaginations run wild, but (as Montaigne had done) to scrutinize their past and present lives with their own philosophic gaze.

It is perhaps unnecessary to say that Prospero's subjects don't often succeed. And it is partly his fault. In presenting the shipwrecked with so many unfathomable experiences Prospero often (quite deliberately) pushes them over the edge. Cut off, exiled, overwhelmed with experiences they cannot comprehend and questions they cannot answer, at some point they almost all fall into a state of benumbed amazement. This raises another, equally significant tendency of *The Tempest* that deserves attention here, one that is also related to the paradigm of loss and recovery with which Montaigne describes his essays.[22] Instead of inciting the shipwrecked to sober philosophic reflection, their experience tends to throw them instead into some form of ecstasy or *véhémentes agitations*. All of Prospero's orchestrated illusions—however we may end up judging their motive and purpose—primarily serve to temporarily intensify the bewilderment of their audience. From the opening storm until he wakes them from their charmed stupor, the characters subjected to Prospero's power usually react to their experience on the island with unwitting astonishment, or madness, or become confounded by extremes of grief, ambition, drunkenness. Overcome, stupefied even, their loss of self-awareness must be countered, and it falls upon Prospero to bring back each castaway to his senses. Having abused their powers of perception, Prospero must call his victims back to what is resolutely human, temperate, and conditional, from

experiences that have been—for many of the characters much of the time—
dream-like in their insubstantiality.

> They being penitent,
> The sole drift of my purpose doth extend
> Not a frown further. Go, release them, Ariel.
> My charms I'll break, their senses I'll restore,
> And they shall be themselves.   (5.1.28–32)

Gradually, the survivors of the shipwreck are forced to return from their
trances, to come to their senses, even if only for the play's momentary and
incomplete resolution.

So however much *The Tempest* keeps us wondering, it does not keep us
in a state of wonder or ecstasy. This is evident, for instance, in Shakespeare's
presentation of the courtship of Ferdinand and Miranda. We witness the convention, familiar from Shakespeare's romances, of love at first sight, and when
it arouses Prospero's (feigned) disapproval we can foresee *in potentia* the tale
of young love forbidden, of the lovers' self-exile and self-estrangement and all
the attending follies. But in *The Tempest* the potential madness of the lovers is
overseen (quite literally in 3.1) by Prospero, whose soul actually "prompts"
their love, and who from the beginning steers them from the dangers of
romantic and sexual abandon. He simply insists that Ferdinand's intentions be
made clear, and his desires tested and tempered "lest too light winning / Make
the prize light" (1.2.407–8). Despite the psychological spin we may be
tempted to put upon Prospero's moderating influence—or we might say, his
fearful prudery—he is at least in the green world with them making sure that
the course of their love runs smoothly and chastely. Never will he let them lose
themselves in embraces that enkindle sexual rapture, for this is exactly the
kind of self-loss that Montaigne rejects (especially in his essay "On Cruelty"):
too ecstatic, warns Montaigne, is the sexual ardor which "transports us outside
ourselves" and "enraptures us in voluptuousness," and he rejects such ecstasy
on the basis of his own experience.[23]

The love of Ferdinand and Miranda, then, is an example of a potentially
dangerous ecstasy successfully contained—no doubt because of Prospero's
surveillance, and perhaps because the romance is overcast by reminders of
Caliban's attempted rape and the specter of (what is believed to be) a father's
recent death. Almost invariably in this play, instances of wonder, confusion,
or ecstasy, are presented so as to arouse suspicion. And here we can again see
Montaigne squarely in the background. M. A. Screech has argued in *Montaigne and Melancholy* that Montaigne comes to question all the various
forms of ecstasy—whether they be madness, melancholy, sexual passion,
drunkenness, or ambition—and concluded that they are nothing but seductive
illusions:

> Increasingly Montaigne saw [these ecstasies] as a desire to escape not sim-
> ply from "the body" but from *l'homme*, from "Man" as such. Any sugges-
> tion of spiritual possession—including *enthousiasme* and Montaigne's
> pejorative *daemoneries*–also entail a theory of ecstasy. When the soul is
> deeply disturbed. . .the ecstasy concerned was classed as a form of admira-
> tion (amazement)—a common yet often vitally important variety of trance
> or ecstatic confusion. All of these states overlapped various forms of mad-
> ness caused by the maladjustment of soul and body: common terms for them
> are *folie, resverie, fureur*, and *manie*.[24]

The arguments of Montaigne's essays are predictably unsystematic, but ultimately he rejects any form of ecstasy as making us not more but less than
human; for, he concludes, to live wholly our minds cannot be estranged from
our bodies, or our spirit from our senses, for such exaltations of the soul
merely represent disruptive energies that throw our fragile equilibrium out of
balance. But what he describes as "amazement" or "ecstatic confusion" is a
state that almost all the characters in *The Tempest* are subjected to. It can and
often does come upon them suddenly. When we first see Ferdinand and
Alonso, for instance, they are beside themselves with grief over their perceived loses. Montaigne, almost predictably, offers a comment on this form of
ecstasy:

> The force of extreme sadness inevitably stuns the whole of our soul, imped-
> ing her freedom of action. It happens to us when we are suddenly struck with
> alarm by some really bad news: we are enraptured, seized, paralysed in all
> our movements in such a way that, afterwards, when the soul lets herself go
> with tears and lamentations, she seems to have struggled loose, disentangled
> herself and become free to range about as she wishes.[25]

Ferdinand, when we first see him is numbed by grief, sitting in the familiar
pose of the melancholic with his arms folded in a "sad knot" (1.2.224). In particular, though, Montaigne's remarks describe the dumbfounded state in
which we see Alonso, who, believing that he has just lost his son in the shipwreck, remains morose and inconsolable, gravely unresponsive to the bland-
ishments of Gonzalo or the mockery of Antonio and Sebastian and eventually
oblivious to everything but his own suicidal despair.[26]

As the play winds to a close, of course, Alonso recovers his senses, or as
Gonzalo smilingly put it, he (like his companions) has recovered himself "when
no man was his own" (5.1.213). But for each to become again his own, to
become again a sensible and self-possessed being, he must have been in some
sense lost to himself or—to use another current idiom—he must have been "out
of his mind." It is surprising how frequent this kind of self-estrangement occurs
in the play. Alonso's grief is but one kind of ecstasy, for in fact any desire or
experience which exalts or abstracts the mind in an intense, distracting ecstasy
can make any one of the characters "vehement" (that is, literally, "deprived of

mind"). We have already noted that an exalted desire for learning sets both *The Tempest* and the *Essais* in motion–for both Prospero and Montaigne had sought to escape their conditions, and found themselves transported–in the literal as well as the figurative sense of the term. Prospero, we recall, lost his dukedom while "transported / And rapt in secret studies" (1.2.73–6), and he ultimately drowns his books; Montaigne, when he would be bettering his mind, suffered a profound sense of self-estrangement caused by the agitation of his roving imagination, and he soberly concludes that "we must not let our edge be blunted by the pleasure we take in books: it is the same pleasure as destroys the manager of estates, the miser, the voluptuary, and the man of ambition."[27] Evidently, the longing of the learned for yet more learning is just another form of ecstasy. This reminds us, I think, that in a sense theirs was a longing not wholly different from the ambitions of Antonio and Sebastian, who in their lust for power and place also desired to exalt themselves above their condition. While others drift off to sleep, both consipirators appear rapt in some strange dream of selfish possibility:

ANTONIO   My strong imagination sees a crown
              Dropping upon thy head.
SEBASTIAN   What? Art thou waking?
ANTONIO   Do you not hear me speak?
SEBASTIAN   I do, and surely
              It is a sleepy language, and thou speak'st
              Out of thy sleep. What is it thou didst say?
              This is a strange repose, to be asleep
              With eyes wide open—standing, speaking, moving,
              And yet so fast asleep.   (2.1.206–213)

Antonio answers this incomprehension by connecting Sebastian's strange state with his political fortunes—"Thou let'st thy fortune sleep" (2.1.214). This is a sly segue, no doubt, as it leads to Antonio's suggestion that they slay the others in their sleep and assume power. Yet it also suggests a subtle connection between their odd state of waking sleep, of semi-consicousness and self-absence, and their murderous ambition. Their reigning desires emanate from a dream-like state, though it seems clear that, were these two more responsibly self-possessed, they would not be attempting to possess what is not theirs. In other words, if they were good subjects, they would have subjected themselves to attentive and wakeful self-scrutiny which would have brought them back to their senses, and also made them easier to keep in order. Self-control would work then in the service of political control–this is now a familiar argument of which we have become rightly suspicious. But the play nevertheless insists that it is a dangerous mixture, this blend of political ambition and agitated imagination, and the dangers are reflected elsewhere in the play—when, for instance, it connects ambition with the crudest form of ecstasy: drunkenness. The comic inebriation of Stephano and Trinculo and Caliban helps them concoct the same exultant ambitions—they too would be kings—but like the usurping Duke and his accomplice they are carried away in just another ecstatic fantasy. Perhaps the surest condemnation comes as we watch Caliban's guzzling of sack increase his admiration for Stephano. "Other vices harm our intellect" Montaigne says in clear disgust, "this one over-throws it; and it stuns the body."[28]

Love, grief, ambition, drunkenness, even vengeance—all of these are types of ecstasy that threaten to take the characters from themselves, to make them unresponsive to the claims of reason and responsibility. In fact, Mon-taigne says later (in the same essay on drunkenness) that it "is right to call *folly* any leap—however praiseworthy it might be—which goes beyond our reason and our discourse. All the more so in that wisdom is a controlled handling of our soul, carried out, on our soul's responsibility, with measure and propor-tion."[29] Montaigne is not absolute; he hints, slightly, that there may be some benefit to remaining open to ecstasy—and it is, for example, a necessary pre-requisite of transformation familiar in Shakespeare's early comedies, praise-worthy in that it signals the renewing love of the young. And openness to wonder is certainly a positive good in *The Tempest*. Ferdinand and Caliban benefit from their receptivity to the wonders of the island, but it is especially important to Alonso for whom it becomes a necessary purgatory that helps him recognize his sin and become again himself. All those that the play rewards in some way suffer from a loss of self, all are taken over at one point or another by "extravagant chimeras," the ability to wonder at the island's wonders is something that helps distinguish the good characters from the bad, or at least those open to regeneration from whose who are not–as Antonio is not. And though in some way at some point in the play everybody gets carried away, they are never quite out of Prospero's (or at least Ariel's) sight. He is always exerting a directing power that, whatever we may think of it, prevents the actions from descending into fatal trespass or anarchy: Ferdinand's pas-sions are watched over; Antonio's second attempted murder is prevented; Alonso, suicidal, mudded deep in grief, is lifted out of his agony by Ariel. And, of course, Caliban and his cohorts have their enterprise interrupted. But however much Prospero's magic induces such wonders, whether he does it for his own revenge, as part of a selfish theatrical display, or perhaps to secure his dynastic ambitions, or to move the shipwrecked to charity, the play at last works to waken the shipwrecked from their various states of wonder. The rev-els must end; the characters, harrowed by their experience, must return to their senses and their world.[30] Their home is elsewhere, and their exile must end. "Abandoning your life for a dream," says Montaigne, "is to value it for exactly what it is worth."[31]

Whether alone in the study or after enduring the existential privations of shipwreck, each of the ecstatics must be brought back to reality, and the soul's temporary exaltations re-subjected to (in Montaigne's words) "the common mould and humane model."[32] As we have seen, this return to self's beginnings is a particular concern of Montaigne's, who, in order to control the "chimeras and fantastic monstrosities" of his roving imagination had turned to writing to subject them to the controled handling of his soul. Through the mediation of his essays he was able to perform "that exercise of thought on itself that reactivates what it knows, calls to mind a principle, a rule, or an example, reflects on them, assimilates them, and in this manner prepares itself for reality."[33] Preparation for reality is Montaigne's objective, and for him reality means, simply, becoming more oneself. This is, in many ways, the one great discovery of the *Essais*, and it is stated most emphatically in his famous conclusion:

> *It is an absolute perfection, and as it were divine for a man to know how to enjoy his being loyally.* We seeke for other conditions because we understand not the use of ours: and goe out of our selves, forsomuch as we know not what abiding there is. *Wee may long enough get upon stilts, for be wee upon them, yet must we goe with our owne legges. And sit we upon the highest throne of the World, yet sit we upon our owne taile.* The best and most commendable lives, and best pleasing men are (in my conceit) those which with order are fitted, and with *decorum* are ranged to the common mould and humane model: but without wonder or extravagancy.[34]

I have used Florio's translation here because it seems best to convey his distrust of any kind of ecstatic self-exile that may tempt the individual with what may seem a better condition. Through his writing Montaigne tries to resign himself to reality, knowing that he can only find an abiding with himself when it is understood that his condition is common, limited, and human, when he ceases to wonder and comes down to earth. And this seems to me, also, the sentiment with which *The Tempest* ends. Prospero is still mounted on stilts at the beginning of the last act, and though his exile is nearly over, he remains wrapped in his magic robes with his powers yet intact; he has been and still is the comfortable spectator at a tragicomedy he has directed. Up to this point he has used his powers to mystify, to charm, and to imprison his enemies in wonder—so that (he would claim) he can help them recognize their sins and show remorse. Now, with Ariel's help, he draws a magic circle, but just before he herds all his amazed enemies in, he renounces his magic, he breaks his staff and drowns his books. While they still "stand charmed" Prospero enters the circle and addresses each of them in an act of private atonement. And then, in a further gesture of submission to the "common mould" of humanity, he disrobes, transforming himself at once from the Piconian magus to (only another) injured man. At precisely the moment he is in danger of remaining a "wonder" to them all by manifesting his imagined revenge and thereby the bonds that tie them together, Prospero steps down. As the conspirators slowly wake from their trances, their senses are still "jostled"—

> All torment, trouble, wonder, and amazement
> Inhabits here. Some heavenly power guide us
> Out of this fearful country! (5.1.158, 104–6)

But it is no heavenly power that answers his plea, but only the "wrongéd Duke of Milan" lately divested of his magic. He has one more trick to play—he gives Alonso back his drowned son—but this requires no magic, and as soon as the rest of the company is gathered and acknowledged he invites them to his poor cell so he can "deliver all" with the story of his exile and abandoned sorcery. Prospero puts an end to the drama with the promise of a story, one that will answer the company's questions and temper their wonder with understanding.[35]

In each instance, it seems, Prospero's final actions work to relieve the island's inhabitants of any transport or ecstasy that might still carry them away. He would bring them all back to themselves and back to each other, not in a way that fancifully reclaims a lost state of sinlessness, but in a way, I think, that would admit guilt and affliction and yet would also deny cynicism its advantage and innocence its simplicity. Shakespeare is careful not to make Prospero's renunciation or reconciliation easy or naive—the story he tells his newly delivered companions, for example, must include the story of their crimes. When he responds to his daughter's vision of the brave new world facing her with his muttered irony—"'Tis new to thee"—it is, I think, tinged with the melancholy that has shadowed him in the last scenes of the play. From up on his stilts he had looked down upon too much to be sentimental; he has witnessed again the unregenerate exploits of Caliban, Trinculo, Stephano, and worse, those of Sebastian and Antonio. Though he has to swallow hard, he manages to embrace all of them at the end of the play, even the reticent Antonio, and having made the choice to forgive rather than to avenge, he can no longer set himself apart and above his victims like so many other Jacobean avengers. He must arrange his life to fit along with the "common mould" of others with as much decorum as his virtue can summon, and without resort to either "wonder or extravagancy." It is not an easy task for Prospero, to come down to the level of others and simply go upon his own legs again, and it requires on his part an irony that is charitable and inclusive rather than cynical or dismissive. To deny that he does embrace them is to refuse him the merits of his struggle, but to deny that he does so with a bitter ambivalence is to refuse to credit him with a sense of reality. A transcendent reading which would like to see everything resolved through Prospero's gracious mercy, would be just as insufficient as a too skeptical reading that finds all motivations self-serving and hypocritical.

But that Prospero does humble himself before his enemies, despite his grievous reservations, suggests that he has made a crucial choice to forgive his enemies rather than merely grant them mercy. And this choice rests upon what I think is an important distinction which again shows his desire to forgo wonders and abide unassumingly with the "humane model." He could have remained the magician and made an imperious public show of his mercy, for mercy requires the power to control, to punish, and even kill, as well as an audience to behold its munificence. Mercy depends upon authority and status, upon setting oneself above others to make them witness one's power with appreciative wonder. Forgiveness, on the other hand, is something privately felt, and it requires that one see one's self as a thing of darkness implicated in sin and bound with all to a common ending in the grave. Insofar as we see Prospero's forgiveness as tied to the difficult acceptance of his own mortal condition, we can perhaps see Shakespeare giving dramatic substance to another important theme of Montaigne's. Of course this may simply be a matter of perspective, of spotting a constellation of ideas in one and projecting it on another. But it seems relevant. For, to give one last instance, they both recognize at the end that old age will yet reduce all of us to the "common mould," that it will bring us painfully back to our senses, that it will check our mad ambitions, our desires, our flights of wonder at brave new worlds encountered; age will, as they are both sadly aware, mortify us with our most human limitation. And they both beg for its indulgence—"Old age," Montaigne sighs, "has some slight need of being treated more tenderly. Let us commend it to that tutelary god of health–and, yes, of wisdom merry and companionable."[36] And though he is less light-hearted, Prospero echoes this tender solicitation for the sympathetic handling of old age. As he parts the curtains and steps before the audience, undisguised, without "spirits to enforce" or the "art to enchant" (5.1.332), with only faint strength and with every third thought now devoted to the grave, Prospero humbles himself again, becoming just another old actor begging our forgiveness. Now that he shares a condition as common as ours, he will include us in his plea for forgivness—"As you from crimes would pardoned be / Let your indulgence set me free" (5.1.337–8). For after all, we in the audience we need pardoning as well: we have, from the groundlings on up, abandoned ourselves to the lurid ecstasies of the theater and we must sooner or later come back to our senses.

NOTES

1. Michel Montaigne, "Of Idleness," *The Complete Essays*, trans. M.A. Screech (London: Allen Lane, The Penguin Press, 1991), 31.
2. Montaigne, "Of Idleness" 31.
3. Montaigne, "On the Affection of Fathers for Their Children," 433.
4. Montaigne, "Of Idleness" 31.

5. *The Tempest*, ed. Stephen Orgel (Oxford: Oxford UP, 1987), 1.2.89–90. Further citations will use this edition and be included in the text.

6. Montaigne, "Our emotions get carried away beyond us," 11.

7. Ted-Larry Pebworth, "Not Being, But Passing: Defining the Early English Essay" *Studies in the Literary Imagination* 10 (1977): 18.

8. Francis Yates, *John Florio: The Life of an Italian in Shakespeare's England* (Cambridge University Press, 1934; rpt. New York: Octagon Books, 1968), 242.

9. For a convincing rebuttal to criticism that would turn *The Tempest* into colonialist propaganda see Meredith Anne Skura, "Discourse and the Individual: The Case of Colonialism in *The Tempest*," *Shakespeare Quarterly* 40 (1989) 42–69.

10. Orgel, Introduction, 35–36.

11. Eleanor Prosser, "Shakespeare, Montaigne, and the 'Rarer Action,'" *Shakespeare Studies* 1 (1965): 251–64.

12. Gail Kern Paster, "Montaigne, Dido, And *The Tempest*: "How Came That Widow In?," *Shakespeare Quarterly* 35 (Spring 1984): 91–94.

13. To Alice Harmon these fairly remote verbal parallels are not an acceptable basis for comparison; see "How Great Was Shakespeare's Debt to Montaigne?" *PMLA* 57 (1942): 88–100.

14. See Paster, 92: "the documented fact of borrowing here leads one to harbor the following suspicion: that if Shakespeare consulted two essays of Montaigne not particularly close to one another in the collection during his work on *The Tempest*, he may well have consulted others. Or, others may have provided indirect influence in his shaping of the play. In other words, despite the understandable reluctance of scholars to credit parallels between Shakespeare and Montaigne based only on a general congruence of ideas, we can entertain the possibility of such indirect influence in *The Tempest*. . ."

15. For a discussion of these kinds of generic modulation see Alastair Fowler, *Kinds of Literature: An Introduction to Genre and Genre Theory* (Cambridge, Mass.: Harvard U P, 1982), 106–11; 191–212.

16. Arthur Kirsch, "Montaigne and *The Tempest*," *Cultural Exchange between European Nations during the Renaissance* (Uppsala, 1994): 112. Focusing on the less commented on borrowing from Montaigne—from his essay "Of Cruelty"—he goes on to argue convincingly that these qualities mentioned in his last sentence are central to *The Tempest*.

17. See Kirsch, 117.

18. "On repenting," 908. On Montaigne's belief in the correspondence between particular example and the general form, for example, see Screech 104–106: "Montaigne is not a 'particular'—an individual man—because of his body alone. He is this particular *man*—one-soul-in-one-body: that is, he is one particular case of the form of the species Man imposed upon matter" (105).

19. Hans Blumenberg, *Shipwreck with Spectator: Paradigm of a Metaphor for Existence*, trans. Steven Rendall (Cambridge, Mass. and London: The MIT Press, 1997), 12.

20. For Montaigne the loss of belongings, friends, family, and life is a condition for which we should be continually preparing: "Let us bring our thoughts and

reflections back to ourselves and to our own well-being. Preparing securely for our own withdrawal is no light matter: it gives us enough trouble without introducing other concerns. Since God grants us leave to make things ready for our departure, let us prepare for it; let us pack up our bags and take leave of our company in good time; let us disentangle ourselves from those violent traps which pledge us to other things and which distance us from our selves. We must unknot those bonds and, from this day forth, love this or that but marry nothing but ourselves" ("Of Solitude" 271).

21. See, for instance, Alvin Kernan's comments on how the characters act out a range of responses to the new world: *Shakespeare, the King's Playwright: Theater in the Stuart Court, 1603–1613* (New Haven and London: Yale UP, 1995), 158–59.

22. I should make it clear that I am not trying to equate the essayist and the magician: certainly, there is a great distinction to be made between essaying one's own thoughts and using one's powers to test others, and I do not wish to downplay the presumption of power behind Prospero's magic that galls so many of the play's recent critics. My point is rather that, by looking at different aspects of the play, we may be able to see it as providing experiential rather than propositional knowledge.

23. See M. A. Screech, *Montaigne and Melancholy: The Wisdom of the Essays* (Duckworth, 1983), 71.

24. Screech, *Montaigne and Melancholy*, 12.

25. "On Sadness," 8.

26. Screech remarks that, "Astonishment, too, was associated with melancholy. Since *estonnement* is an ecstasy, it is not explained simply in terms of the soul's being stunned within the body but as the soul's striving to leave its body behind. Some men and women ecstatics are 'beside themselves' or 'outside themselves' for joy or fear or wonder. When they recover they are said to be 'given back to themselves' or to 'come back to themselves" (33).

27. Montaigne, "On Solitude" 275.

28. "On drunkenness," 382.

29. "On drunkenness," 390.

30. See Peter G. Platt, *Reason Diminished: Shakespeare and the Marvelous* (Lincoln: U of Nebraska P, 1997), 169–87. Platt points out how "through a series of spectacles and their interruptions. . . Shakespeare attempts to address the problems that the marvelous raises. . .without allowing himself or his audience to become lost in wonder" (183). Platt's argument is similar to mine though I wish to put it in the particular context of Montaigne's *Essays*.

31. "On diversion," 945.

32. "On experience," 1269.

33. Michel Foucault, "Self Writing,"*Ethics: Subjectivity and Truth*, ed. Paul Rabinow, trans. Robert Hurley and others (New York: The New Press, 1997), 209. Foucault is commenting on Epictetus, but his remarks seem just as applicable to Montaigne.

34. "Of experience," *The Essayes of Michael Lord of Montaigne*, trans. John Florio, 6 vols.(London: Dent, 1897), 6:314–15.

35. Prospero has also used a story to dispelled Miranda's wonder early in the play. In the second scene Prospero calms Miranda's fright at the opening storm: "Be collected. / No more amazement, Tell your piteous heart / There's no harm done" (1.2.13–15). Miranda helps him remove his magic garments, and he again reassures her: "So. / Lie there, my art.—Wipe thou thine eyes; have comfort. . . . Sit down, For thou must now farther" (1.2.23–4, 32–3). Snapping at her to attend his narrative may be his way of making sure she is not lost in wonder.

36. "On Experience," 1269.

Drama's "Inward Pinches"
The Tempest

JAMES STEPHENS

Readers and spectators often describe *The Tempest* as a mystical drama and yet it is not exactly that. It does express in clear, lovely language, a perception that words will not do the job for us, if we are genuinely seeking some path to an enduring truth. Language is merely "the eye of the needle" (as actor Michael Pennington describes it in a Films for the Humanities videotape called "Passion and Coolness"). As we age, as our experience accumulates, as we gradually take in a lifetime of living, we find that we cannot utter what we know. The sensation of being tongue-tied, after many years of confident talking and writing, struck Shakespeare as it does us all, but he was a dramatist and knew his way out. In his final plays, all of them full of his most glorious language, he dramatizes his last vision, which is simply that "the cloud of unknowing" is our heritage and words alone will not dispel the mist. They tend, in fact, to make the weather worse and the confusion more irritating. Mystics have always made this point, but perhaps Shakespeare makes it more powerfully by dramatizing it for the stage.

Here, I will argue the point by examining *The Tempest* as a staged effort to say what cannot be said. Certainly, we can draw conclusions about "the final vision" and "the last words," and so on. But they always sound trite, even trivial, as I know from many times drawing such conclusions in class after class. What we actually have in the play is a series of spectacles, all profound, none interpretable, despite the words. Most of the characters, including the wise guru, Prospero, acknowledge as much. The argument is organized here under simple, but intricate rubrics: nature, love, providence, art, the great mysteries of human experience. Though many do not accept the truth claims of love and providence, who can deny the reality and force of nature? And what of art? In his Epilogue, the artist asks us to take him with us on our life's journeys and we have done so. But what do we have with us? I agree with Philip

Edwards, who said years ago that we must aim to see "more of" rather than "more in" this extraordinary play.[1]

In the most artificial stage setting possible, it opens with a ship, full of dignitaries, in a terrible storm. The ship's passengers include mainly politicians and their servants, returning from the arranged marriage in Tunis of Claribel, King Alonso of Naples's daughter. The remarkable attitude of the nobles is that the Master and the Boatswain should be able to control the storm in consideration of "whom thou hast aboard," which, of course, is absurd, since "What cares these roarers for the name of king?" (1.1.16ff.). The command to "use your authority" (23), addressed to Gonzalo, is similarly preposterous, since Gonzalo has no authority against nature. It is amusing that the characters pray and cry mercy here against all evidence of their certain annihilation.

Yet, this "direful spectacle" (1.2.26) is entirely a product of Prospero's art and no one in the play is annihilated, only pinched. Miranda's "very virtue of compassion" (27) has, he says, touched her so to the soul that she waylays perdition and pinches us all. It is difficult to comprehend her mystic power, yet she has it in trumps. As Prospero further explains, she dozes, yet gets the part where her father's brother proves evil. Though a child, who knows nothing of civilization, she seems to take in fully the ensuing dialogue about how her uncle "new created" people, trashed some for "overtopping" and evolved into a "screen between the part he played / And him he played it for" (70–108). Miranda's natural compassion results in tears for all the suffering she has heard of, yet the real boon of nature was clearly the salvation of Prospero and Miranda by "the wind" which did them "loving wrong" by wafting them to the magic island which they have long inhabited. Miranda, whose name evolved from "miracle," also saved her father, as he says, by behaving as a "cherubin" with her smiles and "fortitude from heaven" (154), a touching point that all fathers of daughters understand. Thus, in the first two scenes, Shakespeare sets up the dialectic between nature and providence that will dominate the play. Though nature clearly has its powers to destroy and create, though providence (for the believer) can do both easily too, neither really has the upper hand, since this action is Prospero's creation and *of* his "art." Or is it?

Having met Caliban and Ariel at the end of act 1, scene 2, seeing plainly that one is nature and the other providence, we come to the meeting of Ferdinand and Miranda in the same lengthy scene. These youngsters are undoubtedly both nature and providence combined in a miraculous, if entirely natural, "coil." While Prospero refers to his shipwrecking power as a "coil" that would "infect reason" (207–8), he says the same of his power over the two lovers ("it works" [493]). Like the double helix, these two people combine and twist into a deep spiritual and physical relationship in act 2, scene 1. In their dialogue, they employ such words as "divine," "wonder," and "goddess," as Ariel and

Prospero urge them on. The huge mysteries of love, death, divinity, and salvation, play themselves out in this haunting scenario. There is a young man,
washed up on the beach, thinking of the loss of his father, of death and decay,
of mystery and music, until an incredible miracle appears before him. Obviously, this is no "mortal business," for just as Miranda thinks he might be a
"spirit," a thing divine," he sees her as a goddess and heavenly "instructor"
(407–26). Her very presence obliterates all the larger questions he had raised.
Enhancing the irony and reflexiveness of this scene is the stage direction
"Enter . . . Ariel invisible, playing and singing" (374). All Miranda can think
is that, if Ferdinand is evil, he is a temple wherein "Good things will strive to
dwell" (459). His response is simply that "My spirits, as in a dream, are all
bound up" (488). A "sea-change" of real proportion is taking place here. But
not even Prospero's words can suggest what it is. Only the music and the wonderfully metadramatic presence of "Ariel invisible" can even lend us a hint.
The very simple truth is that Ariel is not invisible to us and that Ferdinand and
Miranda are ordinary young people like those we see every day. And, of
course, that Caliban, the "hag-seed," "shalt be pinch'd / As thick as honey-
comb, each pinch more stinging / Than bees that made 'em" (328–30). These
physical pinches include urchin bites, cramps, side-stiches, and other products
of "his art" (373). What we have observed here is the spectacle of nearly
everyone in the cast of characters being quite unable to say what they think,
or to even know what they think.

But, then, we get to know the politicians, beings even more like ourselves,
though selfish and plotting! They are not certain that their salvation is the miracle that Gonzalo calls it. Perhaps they have been saved like creatures in a
Resurrection pageant, but they do not think so. It is just the "luck of the draw."
We are alive; let us scheme and plot against one another. The tension between
nature and providence is once again highlighted, as Gonzalo, an "old cock"
(30), winds his watch of words. One of those blessed people who find the good
in everything, Gonzalo is thought by his companions to "mistake the truth
totally" (58) and to be a purveyor of "impossible matter" (59). We can believe
that their clothes are miraculously fresh, because we know that Carthage *was*
the modern Tunis, as Gonzalo states as fact, only to be ridiculed. The politicians intensely dislike Gonzalo's tendency to "cram words" against the "stomach" of sense, yet he is right to suggest, as many Renaissance travellers did,
that the discovery of new worlds provides corrupt Europeans with a chance to
start all over again, as in Eden, "innocent and pure" (156). Many Americans
even today subscribe to Gonzalo's dream of this new world. Alonso, gravely
pinched by the loss of his son and the forced marriage of his daughter, is
beginning to melt, to acknowledge that he has not only a still-beating heart
but, in fact, "a heart." A truly defeated man, though, he says to Gonzalo that
"thou dost talk nothing to me" (172). Then, in just seconds, Ariel appears,
again "invisible," to oversee and direct the action, opposing as an artist should

the baser appetites and behavior of mortals. What can a spirit do against a power-driven man like Antonio, a person who asks where conscience lies and declares firmly that "I feel not / This deity in my bosom"(277–78)? When it is so easy to kill any number of Sir Prudences, to get the mobs to follow you, to take over a kingdom, and when "one stroke" can free you of servitude, one must not lose the name of action. Because this is a staged drama, as Shakespeare so often reminds us, Ariel intervenes with a *coup de theatre*. In this little pageant, there is talk of "angels," of awakening, and of a possible "miracle," the resurrection of Alonso's son. Much more remains to be done to convert these sinners, but it appears at this point that providence, thanks to art, is winning over human nature just now. But is it?

In true balletic fashion, the clowns enter as the politicians leave, and there ensues a farcical evocation of being hissed "into madness" (2.2.14) by nature itself. Caliban is all over pinch marks, caused by creatures quite like hedgehogs, apes, and adders. It is no wonder that he mistakes Trinculo for a God, as he must be a "spirit of his" (that is, Prospero's). Not surprisingly, they suspect him of being a devil. What follows is the hilarious scene where the drunken Stephano confuses Caliban and Trinculo, under a coat to avoid the impending storm, for a four-legged monster of the island. A neatly-stitched play, *The Tempest* weaves this action seamlessly into the larger fabric. Men of no great intelligence or capacity for wonder, all three mistake nature for providence. Clearly, four legs imply a monstrous devil, and fins are sinister. The immortalizing powers of alcohol are thought to convey the gift of language, to transform our natural eyesight into visionary insight, and to render us wondrous in many ways, even as our stomachs churn. How did we escape the certain death by shipwreck and live to tell the story? And to salvage a whole butt of liquor too? It is a miracle! We must "kiss the book" (not the Bible, but the bottle) several times. Caliban, in the meantime, and a bit drunk, concludes that Stephano and Trinculo are "brave" gods who bear "celestial liquor" (117). They must have "dropp'd from heaven" (137). Once again, after Miranda's dozing off, and the jokes about Gonzalo's verbosity, it is necessary to indict language as an obstructive and confusing skill of man alone. Caliban is instructed bluntly by Stephano to "lead the way without any more talking" (173–74). The "credulous monster" will show them the island's natural miracles (soil, crabapples, springs, bluejays and such), if they will be his god. Now it seems that nature is winning out over providence, since the amusing vulgarity and drunkenness of the three characters prevails. But is nature triumphant even here?

Act 3 of the play presents three mysterious scenes in which Prospero's art asserts itself fully. In scene 1, we wonder at the beauty and sacrifice which love entails; in scene 2, we marvel at the oafish Caliban's mingling of sexual desire, music, and mystery; in scene 3, we exult when Ariel brings out some much-used stage devices to teach the politicians about perdition and guilt. The dominant note in act 3 is mystery and the failure of human language to cope with it. Prospero the artist, a persona of the playwright Shakespeare, presides over this stage with the aid of his imagination, his stage manager, Ariel. Here he mingles the huge themes of human life—birth and death, sin and salvation, love and hate, mercy and justice, providence and nature—into a web of inexpressible clarity. Throughout act 3, Prospero and Ariel appear "unseen" and "invisible." There is music in the words and in the air. And nearly all the characters, as per Prospero's "project," experience a revelation of sorts. All three scenes conclude that there is still "much business appertaining" (Prospero, 3.1.96). The tasks are clearly named. We must put an end to the foul plot to murder Prospero. We must restore the politicians to "their proper selves" (3.3.60). Above all, we must ratify the union of Ferdinand and Miranda.

Act 3, scene 1, is a brief, sweet attempt by lovers to say what they mean. They know what they mean but cannot say it. It is apparent that Ferdinand does not mind moving logs around as Prospero demands, but he is unable to get much beyond cheap sentiment when it is required that he use words. She is "the top of admiration" (38) and "perfect and peerless" (47). And she, equally tongue-tied, speaks of how, knowing virtually no men at all, she lacks imagination to "form a shape, / Besides yourself, to like of" (56–57). Wisely admitting that she prattles wildly, she simply confronts him: "Do you love me?" (68), and, as expected, he prattles about how "beyond all limit" he does "love, honor, prize" her (70–71). Watching "unseen," Prospero can only see their love as a sign of "grace." Because they cannot say anything original is little reason to deny them their mystical powers. What else can lovers ever say, since their special grace lies in non-verbal communication?

As these characters leave the stage in joy, the clowns return in act 3, scene 2, with Caliban's tongue apparently "drown'd . . . in sack" (12–13). Though he does not stay silent for long, it is obvious that he has been "visited," conceivably only by the liquor. Perhaps Trinculo is more right than he knows when he speaks of how strange it is "that a monster should be such a natural" (32–33), with a pun (unintended no doubt) on "natural" as both normal and unspoiled by civilization, on the one hand, and idiotic, on the other. It is doubtful that he comprehends the truth that, by "civilized" standards, the two states of being are not incompatible. Ariel, yet again, enters "invisible" and tortures the three drunks, accusing them of lying and then playing on tabor and pipe the tune to a song whose refrain is "Thought is free." The clowns, mystified by the musical invasion, pray for mercy and give up all thoughts of authority. Caliban takes over with his splendid lines on mystery, music, and mysticism. This island has penetrated him, and, though he spends his life in fear of pinches, and in lust and cursing (hardly shocking), he recognizes beams of something other:

> Sometimes a thousand twangling instruments
> Will hum about mine ears; and sometime voices,
> That if I had then wak'd after long sleep,

> Will make me sleep again, and then in dreaming,
> The clouds methought would open, and show riches
> Ready to drop upon me, that when I wak'd
> I cried to dream again (137–43).

Returning to his fascination with sleep and awakening, with the dullness and the sharpness of our most rare visions, Shakespeare again allows a clown to express in his way the inexpressible. As the sound fades, the crew takes off to do their business (murder etc.) though, as Stephano says, it would be good if they could see "this taborer; he lays it on" (150–51). What he lays on is not entirely obvious, though a sense of propriety, sobriety, and common decency would not be off the track.

In act 3, scene 3, the action begins to rise and close as the politicians from Italy face the truth and drama's "inward pinch" starts to assume its reality. Each man is weary. Gonzalo requests patience as he declines to face the maze before him, and Alonso concurs, feeling exhausted and mocked by the sea, which he thinks has consumed his child. Since they are "oppress'd with travail" (15), they are open once again to conspiracy, and conspire is what Antonio and Sebastian do. And at just that moment, with two politicians lacking vigilance and two of them plotting as usual, mysterious, dramatic music arises and everything changes. In the most dramatic phantasm yet, Ariel presents *"several strange* SHAPES" to set up a banquet (common in Christian temptation scenarios); these ordinary human islanders (actors) stage a dumb show, full of dance and salutations, full of music, which reminds the audience of what they are witnessing. Such a "living drollery" (puppet show) can tell us nothing that we can ever put in words. What emerges is entirely a question of belief and who would believe them and their foolish story of a large banquet that appears and, just as simply, disappears? Alonso puts it succinctly:

> I cannot too much muse
> Such shapes, such gesture, and such sound expressing
> (Although they want the use of tongue) a kind
> Of excellent dumb discourse. (36–39)

Just before Christ delivers his Sermon of Parables, designed to further articulate the Mystery of the Kingdom of Heaven, he warns us about the words we use:

> And so I tell you this, that for every unfounded word men utter they will answer on Judgment Day, since it is by your words that you will be acquitted, and by your words condemned. (Matt.12:36–38).

Whether excellent or not, a "dumb discourse" is more than these compromised men can handle. What they seem to sense is that no word we use is exactly "founded" and that it would be best just to eat of the banquet, since at least we know "we have stomachs" (41). Well into his fifties, Shakespeare seems typically to think often of the stomach, but, fortunately, he thinks as well of how our "proper selves" lose authority with us over the years and of how nice it would be if grown men and women could experience a "sea-change" through drama. After a number of extravagant stage effects (quaint devices), Ariel delivers a simple sermon about sin, guilt, and the helplessness of man against the scheme of things. He tells them about nature and providence; your swords "may as well / Wound the loud winds, or with bemock'd at stabs / Kill the still-closing waters" [62–4]), as truck with me, he threatens. There is more: your hoped-for peace is doomed, because you tried to murder the god-like Prospero and his innocent child" (72); "Ling'ring perdition" (77) awaits pathetic old Alonso for causing his son's "death"; and nothing awaits you but "wraths to guard you" (79) and "heart's sorrow" (81) . This grim, dishonest curse is immediately followed by still another dramatic *coup* as the politicians, except Gonzalo, are truly mesmerized by the disappearance of their splendid banquet and the "mocks and mows" of the actors who remove it. Can there be a more vivid evocation of drama's "inward pinch" than the performance of these "meaner ministers" (actors), as they take away all signs of mystery and do it with mocking faces? Prospero, who comments in this scene about evil says again that evil confronted with grace (like that of Ariel's art) knits us all up in distraction. The long scene ends with the terrified, pinched language of mortal sinners. These men are desperate, pinched in spirit, in an ecstasy. What can save them? Drama. Perhaps.

All the action and thought in this play then dovetail in acts 4 and 5, which consist of one scene each. Highly theatrical and plainly anti-theatrical, both acts intensify the wonder and bemusement of characters and audience. When I posed the question "Or is it?" several times here, I meant to suggest that neither nature nor providence ever has the upper hand in *The Tempest*. Only art has ultimate power. I must now ask, or does it? Judging from Prospero's remarks in acts 4 and 5, what can we answer but "no"? Perhaps the impotence of art itself, or dramatic art anyway, is really the play's argument.

Many, many critics have noted what they describe as "a tragic and puzzling epilogue" expressing the end of humanism and the "bitter wisdom" that only despair can bring;[2] they have focussed on the failure and abandonment of art and the limits of the imagination, hope, redemption, and grace;[3] more recently they speak of Prospero's psychic makeup and his "fantasy of omnipotence"[4] and of such themes as European imperialism and the nobility of savages.[5] All this is interesting, but even more to the point are critics like Hallett Smith, who speak directly to the question of illusion and its "philosophic dimension,"[6] or Robert Egan, who stresses the audience's role in the dynamic of the play's production, "which "entails both an act of faith . . . and a confrontation with reality."[7] And, of course, there is G. Wilson Knight's famous declaration that, quite simply, *The Tempest* is "the most crystal act of mystic vision in all of literature."[8] An exceptional essay is by John Greenwood, who sharpens our vision of mannerism and the magical spells it generates; he especially enjoys the globe/Globe pun.[9] All things considered, however, we might agree with Henry James, who takes us "authorities" to task, for producing a "large body of comment and criticism" which presumptuously consists of "affirmed conclusions, complacencies of conviction, full apprehension of the meaning and triumphant pointings of the moral." It is not strange that James denounces "interpretive zeal" and then proceeds with zealous interpretation for several glittering pages.[10] Whether or not we glitter, most of us are compelled to comment.

And so, in act 4, the elegiac tone of *The Tempest* is profoundly enhanced by a ratification of Ferdinand and Miranda's mysterious bond. Prospero's gift of his daughter hurts him, but he believes that if the young man can avoid giving "dalliance / Too much the rein" (4.1.51–52), all will be well. Of interest in the early part of this scene is its emphasis on the uncertainty of words and what they really mean, if anything. Ferdinand has a certain kind of smile on his face that prompts a stern warning from Prospero about lust and the importance of "sanctimonious ceremonies" (15–17). The young man's responses to this paternal rigamarole are generic; my honor shall never melt into lust is just one of the absurd things he says. In conventional fashion, he complains about the length of the days, as if night were "kept chain'd below" (31). Prospero is not fooled, though he says he is. It is definitely time now for "no tongue" (59). It is essential to "be mute" (126) if we are to sustain the incandescent beauty of this charming pageant and ritual event in human experience.

Ariel is then called to stage a wedding masque, a "vanity" of Prospero's art, complete with "*Soft* music" and actors dressed as Iris, Ceres, and Juno. What they say amounts to mere words, almost nonsense, because that is the style of the masque, which focuses most sharply on music, costume, and dance, but the words themselves are splendid and the lines scan elegantly. These "goddesses" are but "tricks" or "corrolaries" of Prospero's art, but they seem to Ferdinand a "most majestic vision and / Harmonious charmingly" (118–19). Prospero must correct this youthful hallucination. The actors are spirits, yes, but not goddesses, just creatures I conjured for the occasion, just as any other artist might call in actors or models for a project. He asks Ferdinand to stop talking about Paradise and just watch the pageant. The fine presentation of dancers, costumed reapers and the nymphs posing as goddesses, is interrupted by hollow, confusing noises as Prospero recalls the clowns and their vile plot. He abruptly dismisses the actors and in a foul distemper, addresses the naive Ferdinand in one of Shakespeare's most celebrated speeches.

In context, it is a simple speech. Young people are often dismayed by reality, though dimly they acknowledge death, evil, and pointless disaster. Just a little bit of truth will do no harm to Ferdinand and Miranda, who, after all, are about to embark on a life of power and responsibility in the concrete world of Renaissance Italy. Fantasy and illusion have no place there. The truth is that no substantial products of the idealizing mind exist for long and that, in fact, in grim certainty nothing at all exists for long. After the party, "Our revels now are ended" (148), but it has been quite a spree. Now it is time to return to work, which, today, entails some business with three power-hungry, lascivious drunks. They must be pinched. It is just a fact that all those nymphs and reapers have "melted into air, into thin air" (150). Such things happen; actors go home after the show. Remember that the Globe signifies the essential truth about the globe itself:

> And like the baseless fabric of this vision
> The cloud-capped towers, the gorgeous palaces,
> The solemn temples, the great globe itself.
> Yea, all which it inherit, shall dissolve,
> And like this insubstantial pageant faded
> Leave not a rack behind (151–56).

Young people are not devastated by such frankness, and they know that Prosporo simply has a headache. It has been a long day. His mind is "beating" and he cannot resist his famous truism: "We are such stuff / As dreams are made on; and our little life / Is rounded with a sleep" (156–58). And yet, accept these verities as we must, we still have before us children, vocations, accomplishments, and joys. Ferdinand and Miranda say in unison simply that "We wish you peace" (164). They have been properly pinched, and it is good that they say no more. It is difficult to find despair or existential angst in this part of act 4 and impossible to uncover anything of the sort in the rest of the act.

For there, the drunken clowns are fooled by a simple costume shop into believing briefly that they can be anything they choose to be. Drunk, at a vintage clothing store, stinking all over of horse-piss (at least, Trinculo is), each oaf is ripe for pinching. For them the true "disgrace and dishonor" (209) lies in dropping your liquor bottle in a pool of urine, but for Prospero these animals require some serious moral lessons. It is encouraging that Caliban sees through Stephano and Trinculo; that they should be so entranced by more "trash" and "luggage" amazes him, when there is rape and murder to be performed. A small *coup* is required and so they are chased off the stage by dogs and hounds, driven on by Prospero and Ariel. Animals chasing animals. These clowns, like everyone else are "pinch-spotted" (279). It is now time for the grand finale, the Big Pinch.

At exactly the sixth hour, Prospero's project gathers to a head. He agrees immediately that no one who is human could avoid a feeling of tender affection for the politicians, who have been charmed and distracted, not just by his art but by their own guilt and loss. Gonzalo, undistracted, weeps tears "like winter's drops" (16) and this pinches Prospero: he relishes "all as sharply" (23) and is "strook to th' "quick" (25). Having achieved his goal and encouraged real penitence in his former enemies, he can easily declare that "The rarer action is / In virtue than in vengeance" (27–28), that "they shall be themselves" (32). On the other hand, the real "action" so far has been the aesthetic thrust of Prospero's powers. And now he promises to drown his "book." As he draws a charmed circle for the sinners to stand in, he acknowledges that his art is but "rough magic" yet "so potent" (50). The more potent "heavenly music" (52) of Ariel materializes at just this point to administer the "inward pinches" (77) required. Relying little on words here, Shakespeare establishes a tableau of frantic actors, a magical circle, and a "a solemn air." This majestic vision finesses all distinctions we might make between music, spectacle, and words. Though he talks briefly about morality and the inward pinches we all must suffer (not just Sebastian and Antonio), and though there is a round of mutual forgiveness and even affection, the real action lies in the spectacle of this final scene. That is the pinch.

Prospero discases himself like a caterpillar at last becoming a butterfly, and Ariel sings a haunting song about how merrily, merrily I shall live now (93). To live "on the bat's back" and "under the blossom" is to be truly liberated and to "drink the air" (102). Perhaps Prospero is an "enchanted trifle" (112), as Alonso suggests, but the "subtleties o' the' isle" will never allow any of us to "Believe things certain" (124, 125). Maybe the guru is a devil, and maybe he is a saint, but he is not above a silly word game with Alonso about the loss of a child (devilish of him), and not below bestowing forgiveness on all those who hurt him so badly (which is saintly). His last "production" is to pull a curtain, or to disclose, a very simple picture of Ferdinand and Miranda playing chess (a most symbolic game). Is it a simple snapshot or a "vision of the island" (176)? Is it a most high miracle" (177)? Can anything this ordinary amount to the meaning of it all? Is "Where the bee sucks, there suck I" (88) a mystical revelation, like the plum blossom in a Zen parable? Without answering any of these questions, we can, at least agree that act 5, scene 1 of *The Tempest* is about renewal and liberation.

Before the play ends completely, there must be some notes of irony and shifting points of view. We could agree with Miranda as she thrills at the "brave new world" she sees, or with Prosopero's simple " 'tis new to thee" (183–85). We could accept Ferdinand's concepts of a merciful sea (if we overlook the play's first scene) and a providence which bestows a second life (if we ignore the play's second scene). And then there is Alonso who thinks Miranda could be a goddess, or just a girl; yet either is miraculous.

But Prospero is entirely on the mark to say that we must not infest our minds with the "strangeness of this business" (247), which can only drive us mad. We must focus instead on the here and now, the "real," which is to say, the drunken clowns. Two of these fools, "reeling ripe" (279), belong to the politicians, but, as Prospero says of Caliban, "this thing of darkness I / Acknowlege mine" (275–76). Caliban is sure that he will be "pinch'd to death" (277), and Stephano and Trinculo fear similar physical abuse, but they are dismissed with hints of grace and a pardon. No more is said, except "draw near" (319), or enter my cell for further illumination.

All that clarity that Prospero promised will not come in words. Alonso is right to say that only an oracle can unsort so strange a maze (242–44), that "these are not natural events" (227), yet Prospero is a former artist, not an oracle. He admits that in his Epilogue. Since "my charms are all o'erthown," only the audience itself can pardon him, the deceiver, and set him free. It is we who cast the spell, and it is our option to indulge him through prayer and a piercing mercy that "frees all faults." All these words from an older actor, stripped of his cape and scepter, standing alone, remind us that there is nothing mystical about *The Tempest*, yet the play as a whole is an extraordinary act of "mystic vision." Instead of probing for meanings, we accept the truth that we are all pinched by paradox. And that, it seems, is the meaning.

NOTES

1. Philip Edwards, "Shakespeare's Romances: 1900–57," *Shakespeare Survey*, 11 (1958): 1–18, esp., pp. 11–12, 17–18.

2. Jan Kott, *Shakespeare Our Contemporary*, trans., Boleslaw Taborski (Garden City, New York: Doubleday, 1964), 165–68.

3. Howard Felperin, *Shakespearean Romance* (Princeton: Princeton UP, 1972), 246–283.

4. Coppélia Khan, "The Providential *Tempest* and the Shakespearean Family," *Representing Shakespeare: New Psychoanalytic Essays*, eds., Murray Schwartz and Coppélia Khan (Baltimore: Johns Hopkins UP, 1980), 217–43, esp., 236.

5. For example, see Stephen Greenblatt, Introduction [to *The Tempest*] in *The Norton Shakespeare*, eds., Stephen Greenblatt et al. (New York: Norton, 1997), 3051–52.

6. Hallet Smith, Introduction [to *The Tempest*] in *The Riverside Shakespeare* (Boston: Houghton Mifflin, 1974), 1607.

7. Robert Egan, *Drama Within Drama: Shakespeare's Sense of His Art* (New York: Columbia UP 1975), 118.

8. G. Wilson Knight, *The Crown of Life* (London: Oxford UP, 1947), 29.

9. John Greenwood, *Shifting Perspectives and the Stylish Style: Mannerism in Shakespeare and his Jacobean Contemporaries* (Toronto: Toronto UP, 1988), 150–84.

10. Henry James, "Introduction to *The Tempest*," in *Shakespeare: The Tempest*, ed., D.J. Palmer (London: Macmillan, rev. ed., 1991), 67, 68.

Modernist Versions of *The Tempest*
Auden, Woolf, Tippett

EDWARD O'SHEA

Every adaptation or recasting of a literary text is at least implicitly a reinterpretation or repositioning of that text in a new cultural formation. My example here will be primarily W.H. Auden's "Commentary" on *The Tempest*, *The Sea and the Mirror*, written between 1942 and 1944[1] and published in the volume *For the Time Being* (1944), and the cultural formation is what might be called "late Anglo-American Modernism." While I focus on Auden's work, I want also to show how the preoccupations of that work are more generalized in related Modernist works, and, therefore, I will look briefly at Virginia Woolf's *Between the Acts* (1941). Finally, to accentuate certain contrasts, I want to consider another recasting of *The Tempest* by a rough contemporary of Auden's and Woolf's—Michael Tippet, who also shared the same intellectual and social milieu but who composed a much different work at a much later date, an opera, *The Knot Garden*, first performed in 1970.

The question of adaptation is more complex than first appears because, while Auden (we would now say) writes as a late Modernist, the Shakespeare Auden reinscribed existed in a complex formation of historical/cultural associations, interpretative commentary, and performance history that cannot be excluded from discussion if we are to determine why Auden writes his "commentary" on the play as he does.[2]

My intent is to contextualize Auden's poem in the late period of Anglo-American Modernism and in developments in Shakespearean performance and criticism in the thirties and early forties but also in the social and political circumstances which are unavoidable in any discussion of a poet as topical as Auden. However, Auden himself makes this task more difficult because of his tendency to regularize his poetic history by printing poems without dates as in the Random House *Collected Longer Poems* (1969), a practice consistent with that of earlier editions, and by his (somewhat notorious) attempt to remove what he came to regard as embarrassing ideological statement from his work, a process fully documented by Randall Jarrell and Joseph Beach.[3]

Arguably, the cultural moment at which Auden composes *The Sea and the Mirror* coincides with the nadir of Modernist confidence: Yeats dies in 1939, Joyce and Woolf in 1941, and the period signals a distinct change of direction in Eliot's work. This is the period of "The Circus Animals Desertion" (1939) where Yeats resorts to ritualized repetition to galvanize his failed creative powers, of Woolf's meditation on the intractability of nature and audience in *Between the Acts* (1941), and of Eliot's lowered expectations for poetry as expressed in *Four Quartets*, especially "Little Gidding" (which first appeared in the *New English Weekly* in 1942). The great Modernist cultural centers of London, Paris, and Berlin and the artistic and intellectual communities they sustained are disrupted and dislocated. The sense of energy, brashness, and experimental exuberance that we associate with earlier Modernism is distinctively transformed into something more muted and lacking in confidence. *The Sea and the Mirror* documents a crucial moment in Auden's personal trajectory but also in the narrative of Anglo-American Modernism. In terms of Auden's own esthetic the poem represents a degree of retreat from his earlier work in respect to his claims for poetry effecting social change—a retreat underscored in "In Memory of W.B. Yeats": "For poetry makes nothing happen; it survives / In the valley of its making. . . ."[4] In the face of the crises of the thirties, the inexorable descent into the war, this is not surprising. Auden, like some of his contemporaries, reads *The Tempest* as a play about diminished expectations. Prospero's control is slipping. The poet recognizes the inadequacy of the metamorphosing powers of imagination. Something, in fact a great deal, lies outside of the abilities of the artist to transform it. As Auden summarized his new position in 1949: "We live in an age in which the artist neither can have such a unique heroic importance nor believes in the Art-God enough to desire it."[5]

In addition to his verse reworking of the play in *The Sea and the Mirror*, Auden also makes two prose references to *The Tempest*: first, in a lecture delivered in early 1949 and later published in the volume *The Enchafed Flood* (1950) and, second, in a 1954 essay, "Balaam and His Ass." The essay seems approximately consistent with the verdict of *The Sea and the Mirror* in its severity with Prospero and its elevation of Caliban:

> One must admire Prospero because of his talents and his strength; one cannot possibly like him. . . . One might excuse him if he included himself in his critical skepticism but he never does. . .we cannot help feeling that Prospero is largely responsible for his [Caliban's] corruption, and that, in the debate between them, Caliban has the best of the argument.[6]

While in his 1954 lecture Auden identified G. Wilson Knight's *The Shakespearean Tempest* (1932) as a formative influence on his own thinking about the play, especially in respect to the antithetical symbolic clusters represented by tempest-music,[7] Auden's *The Sea and the Mirror* is a strong, audacious misreading of Knight's criticism of the play as published in his "Myth and Miracle" in 1929. The relationship between Knight's essay (and for that matter Shakespeare's play) and Auden's poem is chiastic. While *The Sea and the Mirror* replaces Prospero's Epilogue with a brief Postscript spoken by Ariel to Caliban, it is Caliban's section which truly anchors the end of the poem. In contrast, Knight identifies what he calls "the Shakespearean progress," the movement from the problem plays through the tragedies and the late plays as paralleling the unfolding of *The Divine Comedy*: *Inferno*, *Purgatorio*, and *Paradiso*.[8] "The progress from spiritual pain and despairing thought through stoic acceptance to a serene and mystic joy is a universal rhythm of the spirit of man."[9] Now "serene and mystic joy" is not the mood of Auden's poem nor of the late Modernist works already enumerated. The trajectory rather moves from varying degrees of confidence in the artist's powers to a strong sense of limitation and closed possibility. Auden's Prospero concedes "But we have only to learn to sit still and give no orders."[10] Similarly, *Four Quartets* ends with the penitential "Little Gidding" which suggests a true reversal of Knight's description of Shakespeare's progress with patience and purgation replacing "mystic joy."

In addition to the chiastic reversals, Auden's formal disruptions of the play are also extended to genre. A number of commentators have underscored *The Tempest*'s semantic openness. As M. C. Bradbrook puts it, the play "permits an immense number of mythical, personal, and social extrapolations, and is accommodating to them all. . . . The play is among Shakespeare's shortest but it is his most elastic, most mutable composition."[11] Auden's adaptation obviously takes full advantage of the play's pliability in this respect. But Bradbrook also identifies the play as romance, claiming that while romance is "the least inherently dramatic of the forms that contributed to the Elizabethan stage, [it is] the most powerful in terms of group response and group affirmation."[12]

On the one hand, Auden in his poem intensifies the anti-dramatic tendency that Bradbrook associates with romance. As a "commentary," the "action" takes place after the play is completed; the characters do not engage in dialogue, in fact they do not interact at all. They are laconic, sometimes almost mute, at times speaking "sotto voce," and while the poem gestures towards the elements of drama as in the title of the third section, "Caliban to the Audience," there is the nagging question which Lucy McDiarmid has posed: "what audience? Shakespeare's? How would that be possible? Auden's? No live audience could tolerate the poem's difficulty; it's hard enough to understand on the printed page. . . ."[13] But it is in respect to Bradbrook's "group affirmation" that the poem is most uncongenial for romance. In the poem it is Miranda who in her short speech comes closest to articulating the position of romance: "So, to remember our changing garden, we / Are

linked as children in a circle dancing."[14] But disconcertingly, she seems immature and fixated at a narcissistic stage. Her relationship to Ferdinand is as her
own face reflected in a mirror: "My Dear One is mine as mirrors are lonely."
Her villanelle is also permeated with the language and imagery of the ballad,
the nursery rhyme and the fairy tale: "He kissed me awake and no one was
sorry."[15] The images of garden and dance in this context seem to associate
romance with infantile wish fulfillment. Significantly, and consistent with the
general pattern in Antonio's resistance to incorporation, Miranda's dancing
circle is mocked by his solipsistic dance of death in the section immediately
following hers: "The Only One, Creation's O / Dances for Death alone."[16]

If *The Sea and the Mirror* works to rewrite some contemporary criticism
of Shakespeare's play, it can also be understood in the context of some developments in performance practice. In *Reinventing Shakespeare*, Gary Taylor
describes a production of *Julius Caesar* at the Mercury Theater in New York
in 1937 directed by Orson Welles in which Caesar is explicitly compared to
Mussolini and his supporters to fascist brown-shirts.

> As an actor Orson Welles played Brutus, the enemy of political dictatorship;
> but as director of the production he played the part of artistic dictator. *Total
> theater*, not for the first time, bore an uncomfortable resemblance to its con-
> temporary, totalitarianism. Hitler the would-be scene designer appropriated
> not only Wagner's myths but also his music, his subordination of all arts to
> a single emotive purpose. . .[17]

The Sea and the Mirror, at least implicitly, rejects this emphasis on "total theater," on a unified effect, the play orchestrated as a score to develop a complete
homogeneous illusion. The disintegration of the plot of *The Tempest* in
Auden's poem is consistent with Modernism's devaluation of narrative in general, but it also underscores the inability of a single vision (Prospero's) to
encompass the disparate perspectives that are generated in Auden's poem.

The debate between a single vision versus multiple perspectives easily
modulates to others which are at play in Auden's poem, in similar Modernist
works, and indeed in the literary elite's understanding of Shakespeare's practice at this time: is art escape or exposure to reality, is it directed to the elite or
to the community, is the drama best expressed in "group theater" or in drawing room drama?[18] Ultimately these dichotomies are unresolved and insolu-
ble in the work of Auden and his contemporaries. Lucy McDiarmid has fully
documented these conflicting tendencies in Yeats, Eliot and Auden: the desire
for a "living voice," an easy interchange between artist and a generalized popular audience versus the artist as solitary producer of esoteric works.[19] Yeats's
efforts to develop a popular theater for Ireland, his early and late interest in
ballads and marching songs, his desire for "unity of culture" are well known
but equally discernible is his deep impatience with an uncomprehending middle class audience and his concomitant development of an aristocratic drama

modeled on the Noh which was more suitable for the drawing room than the Abbey. Even Auden, who temperamentally may be most attuned to this goal of rapprochement, has produced in *The Sea and the Mirror* a work that could, by its very character, never have a popular audience. While it is true that *The Sea and the Mirror* subverts the concept of a totalizing vision whether produced by the artist or kindred magicians, at the very time it is produced there are powerful esthetic and critical forces working to just the opposite effect. Perhaps not coincidentally, Taylor gives special prominence to Cleanth Brooks's famous essay on *Macbeth* published a year after Auden's poem. In his essay, which treats the play as a symbolist poem, Brooks deliberately detaches it from any historical context, resolves apparent imagistic disparities, and ignores the temporal dimension of the play, in effect treating it as the sculptural object implied by the title of the collection where the essay later appeared, *The Well Wrought Urn*.[20] Closer at hand, it was also at about this time, in making the volume called *Collected Poetry* (1945), that Auden was shaping his own work for presentation to a general audience, imposing on it a unified esthetic vision, and, if we are to accept Warren Beach's analysis, removing what he, Auden, regarded as embarrassing or outmoded political sentiments.

Auden's Caliban, not Prospero, reflects most cogently on these dichotomies. Auden's treatment of Caliban is consistent with developments at least since the Victorian period which served to detach characters from Shakespeare's plays and allow them to speak for themselves: Browning's "Caliban upon Setebos," Tennyson's "Mariana" and in the Modern period Eliot's "Marina" and "Coriolan."[21] (The unruly character rebelling against the designs of the artist is also familiar enough from works like Pirandello's *Six Characters in Search of an Author*.) Auden's decision to have Caliban speak in complex if inelegant prose has adequate foundation in Shakespeare's play where Caliban may speak in either prose or verse.[22] Another explanation may be M. Bakhtin's assertion that in a period when the novel is the dominant form, all other genres are brought into its orbit, are in effect novelized.[23] If, to specify further Bakhtin's assertion, at a time when the Modernist novel is dominant (arguably very much so in the early forties), it can be expected to exert a strong force on Auden's poem. This applies not only to the prose character of Auden's Caliban section, but to the fact that his section is inherently undramatic; if it is not quite speech, it is also not altogether "monologue interieur" either, but it is very much heterogeneous, a hybridization as much as Caliban himself.[24] It is routinely claimed that in *The Sea and the Mirror* Caliban's style is a parody of late Jamesian prose, but it is equally James Joycean. Caliban's floating, unanchored pronouns have precedent in Auden's earlier work, but they are also found in Molly Bloom's soliloquy. His "he" is sometimes Shakespeare, sometimes Prospero, but also sometimes Ariel and even Caliban himself. Caliban's own referents are equally protean: at times the

unruly boy, the undifferentiated id, lumpish prime matter intractable to appropriation by the imagination, even Auden himself. However, Auden's Caliban
while brash and by his own description, outre, is not in any sense without
insight and intelligence. We are reminded that Caliban's speeches in Shakespeare are not altogether degraded and have their own poetry.[25] A close
approximation to Caliban in other Modernist discourse is the "folk" and the
primitive as found in Yeats and Lawrence. Caliban represents, in one guise
"the wisdom of the body," expressed in "Crazy Jane Talks with the Bishop"
("a truth. . .Learned in bodily lowliness") or in Birkin's description of a piece
of African sculpture in *Women in Love*: "Pure culture in sensation, culture in
the physical consciousness, really ultimate *physical* consciousness, mindless,
utterly sensual."[26]

Caliban's discourse in Browning's "Caliban upon Setebos" works predominantly through analogy in a representation of a ruthless, even sadistic
food chain (Setebos is to the "Quiet," as Caliban is to Setebos, and as the animals of the island are to him). Auden's Caliban in contrast works primarily
through impersonation: he speaks to Shakespeare on behalf of an audience; he
speaks to the audience on the playwright's behalf; he addresses the would-be-
artist directly; he speaks to an undifferentiated popular audience on behalf of
himself *and* Ariel.

To the extent that *The Sea and the Mirror* shows Caliban and Ariel to be
mirror reversals of one another, insofar as the work shows that they require
each other in a mutual economy, Auden complicates the spirit/body
dichotomy often attributed to Ariel and Caliban. Antithesis becomes
reversibility: "the lover's nip and the grip of the torturer's tongs are all,—ask
Ariel,—variants of one common type, the bracket within which life and death
with such passionate gusto cohabitate, to be distinguished only by the plus or
minus sign that stands before them. . . ."[27]

The Sea and the Mirror then imagines another scenario for *The Tempest*
in which Ariel as muse after faithfully and profitably serving Prospero (represented at this moment in Auden's poem by the apprentice artist), refuses to be
dispatched and acts in the manner of an angry lover. Ariel's resistance now
elides into Caliban's, and Ariel becomes, by his own admission, "a gibbering,
fist-clenched creature with which you [Prospero] are all too unfamiliar."[28]

The Sea and the Mirror describes another kind of mutual economy in its
descriptions of idealized and realistic art. This complex interrelationship complicates the apparent opposition between esoteric and popular reflected in so
much of the literary and theatrical history of the period. As Auden writes in
The Dyer's Hand:

> We want a poem to be beautiful, that is to say, a verbal earthly paradise, a
> timeless world of pure play, which gives us delight precisely because of its
> contrast to our historical existence with all its insoluble problems and
> inescapable suffering; at the same time we want a poem to be true, that is to

say, to provide us with some kind of revelation about our life which will
show us what life is really like and free us from self-enchantment and deception, and a poet cannot bring us any truth without introducing into his poetry
the problematic, the painful, the disorderly, the ugly.[29]

This esthetic and moral dilemma is not unique to *The Sea and the Mirror*.
Instructively, the Scylla and Charybdis section of *Ulysses*, which perhaps not
coincidentally relies heavily on Shakespearean (pseudo) biography, posits a
similar dichotomy, an art for angels associated with A.E., or a purely physio-
logical art ("the honeymoon of the hand") represented by the scatological
Buck Mulligan. *The Sea and the Mirror* correlates these positions to social
class as it imagines the "plebs" asking Caliban-Ariel to release them, to
deliver them back to a world of childhood need gratification,[30] while those at
the "top of the ladder," ("exhausted lions of the season") request that Ariel-
Caliban bring them to the "Heaven of the Really General Case" which will
conveniently not touch their consciences.[31] In effect, both esthetic positions
lead to the same escapism.

While it can be truly argued that the competing claims for art as illusion-
building versus a reflection of a heterogeneous reality represent a perennial
esthetic debate (as in the Romantic distinction between primary and secondary imagination), there are good historical reasons why Auden's poem and
other Modernist works deliberately engage this aspect of *The Tempest* (as
Prospero's magic is to one degree or another resisted): the arrival of a "culture
of the masses" foregrounds the critical challenge for the Modernist writer of
finding a sympathetic and comprehending audience for other than "illusion
building." At the same time, the mid-century represents a particularly grim
version of the "nightmare of history" from which the Modernist writer, with
perhaps more reason than Stephen Dedalus, may be tempted to awake into
more entrancing labyrinths of his or her own design.

The Sea and the Mirror identifies the end of Shakespeare's play as a very
dangerous moment for Prospero, the other characters in the play, and indeed
for the audience, insofar as the action is complete and the participants are
poised to leave Prospero's charmed island with its "blessed climate" and
return to Milan. In a witty redaction of the classical theory of tragedy, the
poem describes how through Ariel's power on Prospero's island social barriers are leveled, time is suspended, space becomes benign and neutral, and disorder "made tidiable."[32] In the world of art, "the poisonous / Resentments
scuttle over your unrevolted feet, / And even the uncontrollable vertigo, /
Because it can scent no shame, is unobliged to strike."[33] While the poem (like
The Tempest) imagines a final and necessary "exhaustion of art," there is no
apotheosis. There is rather a movement to a penitential condition ("the
unbothered state" familiar, in different terms, from Eliot's late poetry) where
Auden's petitioner contemplates the "Wholly Other Life from which we are

separated by an essential emphatic gulf of which our contrived fissures of mirror and proscenium arch. . .are feebly figurative signs."[34] Thus the illusion of art weakly signifies a more perfect order of existence which can be given many names—utopia, a world of religious transcendence, a more perfect social order. But this order cannot be reached through merely human effort and, typically, Auden's fine evasion will not allow us to specify it completely.

While Virginia Woolf's *Between the Acts* (1941) makes no specific reference to *The Tempest*, it rehearses many of the most important issues of the play and of Auden's poem. It is a testimony to the potency of the particular Modernist formation that I am describing that many of same concerns expressed in *The Sea and the Mirror* return with some variation: reflection on the sources of creativity; the mimetic problem (the relation of art to nature); the potential intractability of subject matter; the role of the producer/director in establishing a "total theater"; and themes of popular versus elite art.

While there is no explicit reference to *The Tempest* in Woolf's last novel, her general impatience with Shakespeare's characters "cut out with a pair of scissors" and with his plots "which are just cracky things" is easy to document—as is her enthusiasm for the magnificence of his language.[35] Some of her reservations may stem from her experience of weak contemporary performances: *Orlando* describes what Woolf imagines to be an Elizabethan staging of *Othello*: "a black man was waving his arms and vociferating. There was a woman in white laid upon a bed. . . . the actors running up and down a pair of steps and sometimes tripping, and the crowd stamping their feet and whistling, or when they were bored, tossing a piece of orange peel on to the ice which a dog would scramble for."[36] Significantly, however, when she turns to *Between the Acts*, her own plot centers not on the composition of a painting (*To the Lighthouse*) as emblematic of artistic production but to an amateur performance of a pageant in the English countryside with all the embarrassments and flaws that implies. Woolf's move from the static object of a painting to the dynamic performance of the play is striking. While we usually imagine Woolf's compositional strategy as intensely personal and "closeted" (Lily Briscoe places her painting down flat so no one can see it), Woolf also can imagine a larger audience. As she writes to Ethel Smyth: "Do you I mean feel when you write that the curtain rises and the stage is lit?"[37] The political pressures of the late thirties have apparently led Woolf to appropriate a more social and public esthetic format than that of painting: the "play within the novel."

Miss La Trobe's pageant in Woolf's last novel enacts English history from Chaucer to the present through a series of shifting tableau. Despite its sweep and its ironic character, the pageant has masque-like elements: the scene, set in front of an historical, if undistinguished, English country house is decidedly pastoral—in fact when the creaky plot breaks down the cows and swallows fill in the silences. The actors are drawn from the locals, both high-born and lowborn.[38] The audience is incorporated into the performance in a variety of ways, most emphatically at the end of the play when the "players" flash mirrors at the spectators. The gramophone, hidden in the bushes, while it does not provide "strange music" punctuates, sometimes cacophonously and inappropriately, the performance. While it is not clear that Iris actually acts in the pageant, she at least serves as a stagehand.[39]

Woolf's use of the masque device in this novel at this date seems purposeful. The masque, historically, whatever its variants, and they are considerable, was used (as in Ben Jonson) as a means of celebrating and legitimizing the monarchy and as a way of constructing an idealized English identity.[40] While the historical circumstance intrudes only obliquely into the novel through newspaper stories of atrocities on the continent, references to refugees, the barracks room rape, and the formation of airplanes overhead, it is rather transparent that this way of life depicted in the pageant and represented by these people is fragile and vulnerable. If England is worth preserving, what is it essentially about this way of life that should be preserved? The answer is equivocal: there is enough triviality, sentimentality, and bathos (Miss Swithins) always to maintain an ironic sense, but surely the novel endorses some sense of the need to preserve what is best (though what this is remains elusive) in the English nation, threatened as it is by continental politics.

Central to the novel are questions of composition and inclusion, both social and esthetic. These questions are focused in the relationship between the author-producer, Miss La Trobe, and her rather fractious unruly audience, distracted so easily and always threatening to wander off in the intervals and not return. There are strong anti-masque elements in the pageant itself (the disordered state of the actors) and from the audience. The pageant is constantly in danger of short-circuiting, either through the ineptness of the actors, the ineffectualness of the dramatic machinery, or the inattention of the audience. If the masque elements prevail, the triumph is only transitory and accomplished only at a symbiotic moment when actors, audience, and the natural scene (the heavens "weep" empathically) achieve a brief epiphany quite familiar to Woolf's readers.[41]

But it is the character of Miss La Trobe which connects the novel most strongly to *The Tempest* and *The Sea and the Mirror*. The Epilogue to *The Tempest* establishes a relationship of dependency between the audience and Prospero/Shakespeare. Significantly, and consistent with its diminished sense of audience, in *The Sea and the Mirror* the Postscript is spoken by one character to another (Ariel to Caliban) rather than to the audience. Miss La Trobe, in contrast to the note of mutuality in Shakespeare's play, seeks control over the audience. In her attempt at "total theater" and in her need to conjure a complete illusion that will enforce her vision, at times she approximates the artist-as-totalizer, even the artist-as-fascist. More subtly, the novel through Miss La Trobe explores the rhythm of imposition and receptivity needed for creative work. As a writer, director, and producer who would impose her vision on an entire parish, Miss La Trobe represents a considerable departure from Lily Briscoe pursuing her moment of private vision in her painting. Miss La Trobe, in her personality and mannerisms, is closer to the stereotypical male, Giles Oliver, than to any other character. If Giles is associated with bloody shoes, *she* carries a riding whip: both are fascist props. Like Giles, "Bossy" acts decisively and impatiently: he "nicks" the lawn chair into position, she "nicks" the clasp on her phonograph box. In fact, in a passage in the early typescript, not retained in *Between the Acts*, Miss La Trobe admires Giles as a nordic type: "Blue eyes, straight nose, firm chin; the physical attribute of the savior were his."[42]

We have to admire Miss La Trobe's attempt to impart her vision of English history to her audience with the limited talent and material means she has available. But there is a fine line between "imparting" and "coercing," and she often crosses it. For her, art is assault. In Brechtian fashion, she would "imprint" her ideas on the audience,[43] she would "expose them," "douche them" with reality; she imagines them as animals slipping from her noose.[44] At other times, she considers herself abased, a slave to her audience. In fact, she is humbled repeatedly as the pageant breaks down, and she is saved only by the barnyard animals or the good spirits of the audience. In her worse moment, she imagines the perfect play written for *no* audience, but this would surely be "death, death, death," when not illusion but the audience fails.

In turning from action and imposition of will, Miss La Trobe finds some limited hope and continued creativity. She retreats to the pub, that "foul rag and bone shop of the heart," and as drink and sleep loosen her grip on the daylight world, primitive "words of one syllable" sink into the mud, the primeval but fecund "soup" from which all life has come, there to be fertilized and bubble up again, the beginnings of a new play. With Woolf's novel we have moved beyond a reprise of Shakespeare's *The Tempest* to a true intertextuality. In *Between the Acts*, Woolf is rehearsing elements essential to Modernism and to a Modernist understanding of the play by exploring the relationship of the artist as producer of illusion to the materials of that illusion and with her relationship to her audience, both incorporated and implied.

Sir Michael Tippett's three act opera, *The Knot Garden*, first performed in 1970, participates in the complex intertextuality that is typical of Modernist rewritings of *The Tempest*. The epigraph of the libretto is Parolles's statement from *All's Well That Ends Well*: "Simply the thing I am / Shall make me live" (4.3.333–34). The third act, a "Charade," is a reprise of *The Tempest* in which five of the major characters play themselves as well as characters from Shakespeare. Tippett himself has declared Shakespeare the major influence on his work, describing the playwright as "an enormous cauldron which we pour things into and take things out of."[45] Additionally, the very end of the opera is an explicit reference to the penultimate passage of *Between the Acts*, describing Giles's and Isa's "reconciliation":

> Left alone together for the first time that day, they were silent. Alone, enmity
> was bared; also love. Before they slept, they must fight; after they had
> fought, they would embrace. From that embrace another life might be born.
> But first they must fight, as the dog fights with the vixen, in the heart of dark-
> ness, in the fields of the night.[46]

Originally, Tippett had considered using this passage verbatim to close his
opera, but he immediately realized that it was too complex to be used
directly,[47] though some of Woolf's language survives in Tippett's text. Both
novel and opera describe a complex reversal of mirror and image: as the curtain descends on the world of illusion, it simultaneously rises to reveal a continuation of the lives of the main characters: Giles/Faber, Isa/ Thea.

Tippett, two years older than Auden, came from that same intellectual-
social milieu that produced the poet. Both Auden and Tippett were close
friends of Benjamin Britten. Yet, Tippett's longevity (he died in January 1998
at 93) brought him into another, more contemporary, cultural formation with
immediate repercussions for his version of *The Tempest*. One of Tippett's decisions was to cast Prospero as a psychiatrist, our modern magus (Tippett's
"Mangus") attempting to work his magic in a dysfunctional world of shifting
and broken relationships. Tippett's "retreat" from the political-historical plot
of *The Tempest* is explicit: he eschews altogether the political intrigue of
Milan concentrating on the personal relationships of Prospero, Miranda, Ariel,
and Caliban. He diffuses the character of Ferdinand by having him also serve
as the husband of another major character, Thea, who has no Shakespearean
analogue. He sees his opera as part of a theatrical tradition

> in which we withdraw from the political or the communal elements, which
> are so exemplified in stories like the *Iliad*, where the family is entangled in
> a whole set of historical and necessary wars and responsibilities, and find
> [themselves] in a dramatic set of situations which appear. . .to be solely per-
> sonal relations, which can be said to be a kind of dance or a kind of pattern,
> self-subsisting in itself.[48]

This then is Tippett's most emphatic departure from Shakespeare: he turns
what *The Tempest* depicts as a social/political disruption into an existential
breach or rather a set of alienations: Faber from Thea, Faber from Flora, Dove
from Mel. These in turn reconnect into new, even startling realignments. Shakespeare's play and the atemporal quality of romance, in a sense, give Tippett this
license to emphasize fluidity, metamorphosis and transformation both in terms
of personal relations (Faber can be Flora's stepfather but also, as Ferdinand, her
lover) and in setting (characters are whirled on and offstage as in a vortex).
Additionally, by eschewing Shakespeare's masque with its associations with
ceremony, panoply, and potential historical reference and by choosing instead

the "charade" for his explicitly Shakespearean third act, Tippett further reduces his venue to that of the parlor game turned combat, allowing the participants to explore alternative pairings and alliances. (Albee's *Who's Afraid of Virginia Woolf* has been cited as one of Tippett's sources for the opera.)

In *The Knot Garden* Flora/Miranda undergoes the most transformation at Tippett's hand. Initially frightened by her stepfather's real or imagined advances, her cries (in Act I) are not fully human, but are those of a frightened bird (which Tippett conveys by using Flora's voice abstractly as part of the complex instrumentation). Or she can only "hum," or later, when she first interrogates Dov and Mel, she speaks "with a tiny voice like a stage Alice."[49]

When Flora is again fleeing Faber in Act 2, scene 8, she encounters Dov who attempts to stabilize her frenetic condition through a kind of musical therapy. At Dov's instigation, Flora sings (in German) the first three lines of Schubert's "Die Liebe Farbe" from *Die Schöne Müllerin* which Dov translates (with a comment):

> "I will dress myself in green,
> In green weeping-willows:
> My love's so fond of green:"
> But that's a boy's song.[50]

To which Flora responds:

> Sometimes I dream I am a boy,
> Who dies for love.
> And then I am a girl again.
> Dov, you understand.[51]

The transformation is startling here as Flora's inchoate vocalizing is transformed into her lyrical rendering of Shubert's song of young love which her terror of her stepfather has not allowed her to experience before. Imagination (Flora's dream) allows her to transcend her wounds and to see possibilities where before she had before experienced only trauma.

Flora's escape is only complete in Act 3, scene 5 when Faber/Ferdinand and Flora/ Miranda play chess. In complicating Shakespeare by having one character play both Flora/Miranda's stepfather and lover, Tippett hints at an oedipal/incestuous relationship as the origin of Flora's neurosis. After overturning the chessboard, Flora declares: "Dov-Ariel lend me your wings. / I'm free: I'm free"[52] and as last described in Act 3, scene 9, she "departs alone, radiant, dancing."[53]

The relationship between Dov and Mel shows less clear development in the opera, though it does provide Tippett with an opportunity to establish another analogue for Ariel and Caliban (Dov-Ariel as musician, Mel-Caliban as librettist) and to suggest through the music-words tension yet another way to formulate a dichotomous relationship between Shakespeare's characters.

Tippett also engages the New World associations of *The Tempest* with a contemporary emphasis by casting Mel as a black from the South and through references to the civil-rights movement (a quotation of "We Shall Overcome"). The music of the opera borrows heavily from jazz and blues, and Mel, addressing Flora, celebrates the lushness of the Americas—blending Keats and Shakespeare (Ariel's "Come unto these yellow sands")[54] in a lyrical passage (or as close to one as Tippett permits):

> Come with me to the warm south
> Or the golden Californian west
> Come with me to the warm south
> Where the palm trees grow so mighty tall. . .[55]

As in Auden's *The Sea and the Mirror*, Mangus-Prospero's powers are shown to be inadequate. It is Dov, not Mangus, who provides the most effective therapy for Flora. But Thea is Mangus's most explicit detractor: "Scenes turn in the hand, / Beyond your book, / When played by persons."[56] "And what are you, Mangus? / Man of power / Or dabbler, pimp: voyeur?"[57] And in the Finale, Mangus, speaking Lear-like directly to the audience, admits as much: "Prospero's a fake, we all know that. . . . I'm just a foolish, fond old man. / Just like the rest of you. / Whistling to keep my pecker up."[58]

In the final scene, the Epilogue, Thea and Faber hold the stage alone, in what is only apparently a post-Shakespearean moment. The reference, as noted earlier, is explicitly related to the end of *Between the Acts*. Thea puts away her "seed packets" and Faber his "factory papers." The mise en scene becomes enlarged: the garden and workplace as solipsistic refuges are transformed to "The vast night [which] gives a huge dimension to the dark around them." As in Flora's "dream," the restorative powers of imagination are once again invoked:

| THEA | Memory recedes in the moment. |
| FABER | I am all imagination.[59] |

The precedent for Tippett may be the "rarer action" moment which begins Act 5 of *The Tempest*. Ariel, conventionally associated with imagination, reports to Prospero the condition of the prisoners:

> Your charms so strongly works em,
> That if you now beheld them, your affections
> Would become tender.[60]

To which Prospero responds: "And mine shall."[61] While this scene has generated intense discussion among Shakespeareans,[62] the intent for Tippett seems evident enough: memory ties us to the past, connecting us only to ancient wrongs. Imagination allows us to transcend those wounds, to forgive, and to see possibilities where before we had experienced only trauma. As for Flora romantic love, so for Faber and Thea desire makes this liberation possible. They intone together: "I encompass the vast night with an image of desire. . . . Our enmity's transcended in desire."[63] The implications are clear: this dysfunctional pair can recoup their marriage through a return to an earlier moment of sexual frankness before their relationship had become infected with pettiness and jealousy.

This movement at the end of *The Knot Garden* suggests a way of reading it that in fact establishes another synchronization with *The Tempest* and with at least a few of the Modernist recastings of the play. I would argue that *The Tempest* depends on a return to an earlier moment, if not precisely to origins, at least to Milan as the historical/political matrix of the play, in order to fully realize and to test the reconciliations of the island. At least some of the works under discussion follow this rhythm, this return to an earlier order of things as a necessity and a possible solution. What the Modernist works under discussion have in common is a sense of impasse or an experience of exhaustion perfectly comprehensible in terms of literary and political history (the exception would seem to be Tippett, but in some sense he is not "A Child of (his) Time" but a member of an older generation). The response to this impasse or exhaustion varies from artist to artist. Eliot and Auden seem to find one solution, penitential waiting, (because for Auden, at least, the world of boyhood is a magical state that cannot be reentered), while Yeats, Woolf, and Tippett appropriate another strategy, a return to origin. In "The Circus Animals' Desertion" Yeats tries to galvanize his imagination by a return to beginnings, the personal-historic and physical matrix, the "foul rag and bone shop of the heart." The Old Man in *Purgatory* returns to the moment of his conception in an attempt to neutralize the infection of miscegenation passed on through his father and mother. Miss La Trobe in the pub at the end of *Between the Acts* lapses into a kind of atavistic stupor (into the primordial "soup" of imagination) before beginning her next effort (a condition which is also alarmingly trance-like and death-like). The couples in Woolf and Tippett must renounce modern identities and habits and return to a primitive condition in an attempt to recoup a lost relationship.

In any case, with these Modernist recastings of *The Tempest* we are quite far from the *Paradiso* that G. Wilson Knight describes as being the last stage of "Shakespeare's Progress." We may be on the threshold, but further progress (as with Prospero's return to Milan) requires a problematic step backwards.

NOTES

1. Monroe K. Spears, *The Poetry of W.H. Auden* (New York: Oxford UP, 1968), 216.

2. This context is exhaustively described in chapter 5, "Good-bye to All That," in Gary Taylor, *Reinventing Shakespeare: A Cultural History, from the Restoration to the Present* (New York: Weidenfeld and Nicolson, 1989).

3. "This process of turning to the purposes of sound thinking and edification work that in 1945 seemed unsound or questionable in its original form is facilitated by the comparative inaccessibility of Auden's earlier publications to the general reader, the fact that in the earlier volumes most of the poems do not have titles, but are identifiable only by their opening lines, and the almost complete darkness in which the reader is left in the *Collected Poetry* as to the date and provenance of any particular poem and the context in which it was originally conceived." Joseph Warren Beach, *The Making of the Auden Canon* (Minneapolis: U of Minnesota P, 1957), 11.

4. W. H. Auden, *Collected Shorter Poems: 1927–1957* (New York: Random House, 1964), 142.

5. W. H. Auden, *The Enchafèd Flood* (New York: Vintage Books, 1967), 150.

6. W. H. Auden, *The Dyer's Hand and Other Essays* (New York: Vintage, 1968), 129.

7. Auden, *Enchafèd Flood*, 11.

8. G. Wilson Knight, "Myth and Miracle (1929)," rpt., *The Crown of Life: Essays in Interpretation of Shakespeare's Final Plays* (London: Methuen, 1948), 30.

9. Knight, 29.

10. W. H. Auden, "The Sea and the Mirror: A Commentary on Shakespeare's *The Tempest*," *Collected Longer Poems*, (New York: Random House, 1965), 204.

11. M. C. Bradbrook, "Romance, Farewell!: *The Tempest*." *English Literary Renaissance* 1.3 (1971): 245.

12. Bradbrook, 248.

13. Lucy McDiarmid, *Saving Civilization: Yeats, Eliot, and Auden Between the Wars* (New York: Cambridge UP, 1984), 88.

14. Auden, "Sea," 224.

15. Auden, "Sea," 223.

16. Auden, "Sea," 224.

17. Taylor, 271, emphasis added.

18. See Taylor, 249–50.

19. See McDiarmid, especially the chapter "The Living Voice in the Thirties."

20. See Taylor, 291.

21. See Taylor's discussion of Eliot, 284.

22. Jeanne Addison Roberts writes: "One of the most puzzling problems in *The Tempest* text is the difficulty of sorting out prose and verse. In I.i, eleven of the first seventy-nine lines are, rather inexplicably, in verse. The language of Caliban, though usually poetic, is often not blank verse which can be perfectly scanned" (225). For her speculation on the reasons for this, see "Ralph Crane and The Text of *The Tempest*," *Shakespeare Studies* 13 (1980): 213–33.

23. M. M. Bakhtin, "Epic and Novel" in *The Dialogic Imagination* (Austin: U of Texas P, 1981), 5–6.

24. For the protean historical depictions of Caliban, see Alden T. Vaughan and Virginia Mason Vaughan, *Shakespeare's Caliban: A Cultural History* (Cambridge: Cambridge UP, 1991).

25. Derek Traversi, *Shakespeare: The Last Phase* (New York: Harcourt-Brace, n.d. [c. l953]), 227.

26. D. H. Lawrence, *Women in Love* (London: Penguin Books, 1995), 79.

27. Auden, "Sea," 238.

28. Auden, "Sea," 237.

29. Auden, *The Dyer's Hand*, 338.

30. Auden, "Sea," 243.

31. Auden, "Sea," 245.

32. Auden, "Sea," 226–9.

33. Auden, "Sea," 205.

34. Auden, "Sea," 250.

35. Quentin Bell, *Virginia Woolf: A Biography* (New York: Harcourt Brace, 1972) 1:68–9.

36. Virginia Woolf, *Orlando. A Biography* (New York: Harvest Books, 1956), 56–57.

37. Virginia Woolf, *The Letters of Virginia Woolf, Vol. 6, 1936–1941*, eds., Nigel Nicholson and Joanne Trautmann (New York: Harcourt, Brace, l980), 367.

38. William Poel was known for using amateur actors in late-Victorian productions of Shakespeare. See Taylor, 267.

39. Virginia Woof, *Between the Acts* (London: Granada, l978), 23.

40. See especially David M. Bergeron, introduction, *Pageantry in the Shakespearean Theater*, ed., David M. Bergeron (Athens: U Georgia P, l985); Stephen Orgel, *The Illusion of Power* (Berkeley and Los Angeles: U of California P, 1975); and Jonathan Goldberg, *James I and the Politics of Literature: Jonson, Shakespeare, Donne and Their Contemporaries* (Baltimore: Johns Hopkins UP, 1983; reissued, Stanford: Stanford UP, 1989).

41. Stephen Orgel makes it clear that this epiphanic moment is entirely consistent with the effect of the masque: "Every masque concluded by merging spectator with masquer, in effect transforming the courtly audience into the idealized world of the poet's vision." See Stephen Orgel, introduction, *Ben Jonson: The Complete Masques*, (New Haven: Yale UP, l969), 2. In Woolf's novel, the players flash mirrors at the spectators to literally incorporate them into the production. For a discussion of the relationship between landscape, pageant, and power in certain Renaissance productions, see James Yoch, Jr., "Subjecting the Landscape in Pageants and Shakespearean Pastorals" in Bergeron, ed., *Pagentry*, l95–219. Yoch describes the unifying effect of Queen Elizabeth's presence at certain pageants and relates it to the "unifying image" that Prospero imparts to the scenery of *The Tempest* (196). This encourages me to read Miss La Trobe as a political as well as esthetic actor.

42. Virginia Woolf, *"Pointz Hall": The Earlier and Later Typescripts of* Between the Acts, ed., Mitchell A. Leaska (New York: John Jay Press, l982), 108.

43. Woolf, *Earlier and Later Typescripts*, 108.

44. Woolf, *Between the Acts*, 179–80.

45. Michael Tippett, quoted in Meirion Bowen, *Michael Tippett* (London: Robson Books, 1982), 71.

46. Woolf, *Between the Acts*, 158.

47. Eric Walter White, *Tippett and His Operas* (New York: Da Capo Press, 1982), 99.

48. Michael Tippett quoted in Richard Elfyn Jones, *The Early Operas of Michael Tippett* (Lewisten: Edward Mellen, 1996), 159. Jones's source is "Love in Opera," Four unpublished talks recorded for the CBC, (Schott & Co.:, ms., n.d.).

49. Michael Tippett, *The Knot Garden: An Opera in Three Acts, Libretto* (London: Schott, 1969), Act 1, Scene 9, page, 9. Further citations will refer to the act, scene, and page numbers.

50. Tippett, *Knot*, 2.9. pp.20–21.

51. Tippett, *Knot*, 2.9. p. 21. Flora's gender confusion may reflect Tippett's awareness that as Shakespeare's Miranda her part was played by a boy actor.

52. Tippett, *Knot*, 3.6. p. 26.

53. Tippett, *Knot*, 3.9. p. 31.

54. William Shakespeare, *The Tempest*, ed., Stephen Orgel (Oxford: Oxford UP, 1987). All further citations will be to this edition. *Tmp.*, 1.2.374–84.

55. Tippett, *Knot*, 2.9. p. 21.

56. Tippett, *Knot*, 3.3. p. 24.

57. Tippett, *Knot*, 3.5. p. 26.

58. Tippett, *Knot*, 3.9. p. 30.

59. Tippett, *Knot*, 3.10. p. 31.

60. *Tmp*. 5.1.17–19.

61. *Tmp*. 5.1.20.

62. For an example of the Modernist discussion of this problem, see E. M. W. Tillyard's response to Dover Wilson in *Shakespeare's Last Plays* (1938, rpt. New York: Barnes and Noble, n.d.): "when Dover Wilson would have this to represent Prospero's sudden conversion from a previously intended vengeance, I cannot follow him. It is true that Prospero shows a certain haste of temper up to that point of the play, and that he punishes Caliban and the two other conspirators against his life with some asperity; but his comments on them, after his supposed conversion, have for me the old ring. . ." (53). Tillyard's Prospero does not essentially change from the beginning of the play to the end, since the tragic pattern in Shakespeare's last plays has been left behind.

63. Tippett, *Knot*, 3.10. p. 31.

Seamus Power, J. Anthony Murphy, Derek Chapman, and Mike Finn in a scene for Island Theatre Company's production of *The Tempest* at Kilmainham Gaol, October 11–16, 1993; at the Dublin Theatre Festival. Photograph by Arthur Gough; used by permission of Terry Devlin for the Island Theatre Company.

The Tempest as Political Allegory

CLAUDIA W. HARRIS

From "An Open Letter to William Shakespeare, or, As I Don't Like It . . . "

> *I suppose that bit by bit I should have been preparing myself to realize that*
> The Tempest *was your gravest mistake. I, of course, had wrongly held that*
> *it was your finest play; I had imagined it to be a* Faust *in reverse, the last in*
> *your final cycle of plays about mercy and forgiveness, a play that is through-*
> *out its length a storm, reaching calm waters only in its final pages. I had felt*
> *that you were in your right mind when you made it hard, craggy and dra-*
> *matic. I felt that it was no accident that in the three plots you contrast a*
> *lonely, truth-seeking Prospero with lords crude and murderous, with greedy*
> *and darkly wicked clowns. And I felt that you had not suddenly forgotten*
> *about the rules of playwriting, such as the one of "making every character*
> *like someone-or-other in the audience," but you had deliberately put your*
> *greatest masterpiece a little farther away from us onto a higher level. Now,*
> *after reading all the notices, I find that* The Tempest *is your worst play—the*
> *very worst, this time—and I must apologize to you for failing to disguise its*
> *weakness more thoroughly.*
>
> —Peter Brook[1]

On 9 October 1969, the curtain call following a production of *The Tempest* changed the course of Dutch theatre. Shakespeare's play was being performed by Nederlandse Comedie, then Holland's leading theatre company. That October night following the competent but apparently uninspiring performance, tomato-wielding students of the Amsterdam drama academy rose up from the audience in the municipal theatre and pelted the actors taking their bows. Since Action Tomato, the name given this student protest over the lack of innovation, experimental has defined mainstream theatre in Holland. This symbolically bloody act started a revolution—established companies suddenly collapsed, repertory companies gradually disintegrated, actors even committed suicide—and Dutch theatre changed course to its present highly confrontive and often shocking style.[2] So, appropriate to one of the play's fundamental elements, that of first overturning and then reconstructing order, *The Tempest* helped inspire an uprising, a social drama, that then led to the experimental nature of contemporary Dutch theatre.

Whether or not the Dutch students' protest was consciously driven by which play was being performed, pure coincidence would, nonetheless, be impossible to argue persuasively. Growing chaos followed by a reordering of elements is a process inherent in any storm as well as being basic to the structure of any play, but this chaotic process is especially apparent in *The Tempest*. The student protest was a startling expression of life imitating art. The metatheatrical qualities inherent in *The Tempest* can heighten an appreciation for the intrinsic drama in life. Giorgio Strehler, in his inaugural production for the *Théâtre de l'Europe* in 1983, capitalized on this innate theatricality; Strehler presented Prospero as a director/magician whose theatrical artifice produced the events in *The Tempest*. When Prospero, standing in the auditorium, broke his staff at the conclusion of Strehler's production, the stage collapsed. Prospero's plea to release him as he was releasing the audience was also an invocation, a blessing on the audience since he was returning them to the world with heightened theatrical perceptions.[3]

Given the play's commentary on dramatic aspects to life, *The Tempest* often arouses strong reactions and lasting impressions—reason enough for any production's emphasis on social/political interpretations. Even anthropologist Victor Turner credits this play with inspiring his specific scholarly focus: "Perhaps if I had not had early exposure to theatre—my first clear memory of a performance was Sir Frank Benson's version of *The Tempest* when I was five years old—I would not have been alerted to the 'theatrical' potential of social life."[4] Recognizing the innate theatrical quality to life can make many experiences more understandable, and political action, in particular, can become more comprehensible when viewed as a theatrical performance.[5] But politics is not just *like* theatre, it *is* theatre. When a production is highly politicized, when the themes, actions, or characters of *The Tempest* take on metaphoric meaning related more to the producing culture than to Shakespeare's text, then that performance becomes a political allegory. This essay explores several productions of *The Tempest* which demonstrate a variety of social/political implications from mere happenstance to an embedded intention to change an audience's beliefs and behavior.

Proving Turner's assertion that "theatre is perhaps the most forceful, *active,* if you like, genre of cultural performance,"[6] Action Tomato dramatically eliminated the separation of the actors from the spectators and overturned expectations for appropriate audience behavior. This protest changed those audience members armed with tomatoes into the leading actors in a new drama. Refusing to permit Dutch theatre to continue along its traditional path, the students insisted, instead, on "immediate"[7] theatre which spoke to their own experiences. The students' social action was the most dramatic event that evening in 1969 and irrevocably altered the experimental dimension of their nation's theatre. That a production of Shakespeare so enraged these drama students is in no way surprising. "Deadly" Shakespeare, especially for a group of theatre artists, would be an even greater affront than bad Shaw or Brecht or Beckett. Director Peter Brook argues that Shakespeare's contradictions make his plays burn deeply, causing disturbing and unforgettable impressions through "an atonal screech of absolutely unsympathetic keys." Calling for a move back to the future, Brook says Shakespeare "contains Brecht [introspection] and Beckett [metaphysics], but goes beyond both. Our need in the post-Brecht theatre is to find a way forward, back to Shakespeare. . . Brecht and Beckett are both contained in Shakespeare unreconciled. We identify emotionally, subjectively—and yet at one and the same time we evaluate politically, objectively in relation to society."[8]

For thirteen years during the Great Cultural Revolution, China's stages were dark except for the eight approved "Revolutionary Model Plays." The ten years following, 1978 to 1988, is seen as a Shakespearean golden age in China. Shakespeare's plays were performed in large population centers and in remote areas: for instance, *The Tempest* was performed at the Shanghai Drama Institute, 5–15 January 1982; also in January 1982, the Tibetan Drama Troupe presented *Romeo and Juliet* on the highest stage in the world. Then on 10 April 1986, the Inaugural Chinese Shakespeare Festival began simultaneously in Beijing and Shanghai; twenty-three companies performed twenty-eight productions with over one-hundred performances for audiences of more than one hundred thousand.[9] That Shakespeare became the focus of a new cultural revolution should certainly not be surprising, nor should the extent of this Shakespearean renaissance. As Brook says, "everything remarkable in Brecht, Beckett, Artaud is in Shakespeare. For an idea to stick, it is not enough to state it: it must be burnt into our memories."[10] After years of "Model Plays" in China, here, at last, was Shakespeare, exposing the contradictory facets of humanity. Brook believes that "the strength and miracle of Shakespearean texts lie in the fact that they present man simultaneously in all his aspects."[11] China was looking for "a way forward, back to Shakespeare."

Action Tomato did not occur in a cultural vacuum in 1969. The protesting students from the Amsterdam drama academy not only understood thematic and metatheatrical aspects of *The Tempest* but were also fully aware of the sweeping changes taking place in the European theatrical climate. In this age of experiment, European theatre practice was naturally swept along, and these students had a clear sense of the *avant-guarde* possibilities of Shakespeare's text. David Williams explains that "1968 was a significant year in European theatre. It saw the publication in English of Grotowski's *Towards a Poor Theatre* and of Brook's *The Empty Space*, two of the seminal theoretical texts for modern theatre."[12] Brook had provided the vocabulary for the Dutch students' protest against what they deemed a "deadly" museum theatre; the immediacy they sought was impossible with too great a separation between the art they saw and the lives they were living. But more than that, intense theatre experiments had swirled around them for a decade, everywhere except in major Dutch companies.

The "immediate," experimental theatre Brook advocated required a "harrowing collective" improvisational process rather than a "polite" collaboration of theatre artists preplanned by the director.[13] During this decade, which began when Antonin Artaud's *The Theater and Its Double* was published in English in 1958, theatre practice throughout the world underwent a sea change. Brook, a major instigator of this storm, mounted his many experiments in Artaud's Theatre of Cruelty for the Royal Shakespeare Company at Stratford. Despite his interest in Artaud, however, Brook remains a committed interpreter of Shakespeare: "The 'cruelty' of Artaud could be considered an effort to recover, by other means, the variety of Shakespeare's expression, and our experiment. . . as the search for a theatrical language as flexible and penetrating as that of the Elizabethans."[14] *The Tempest*, which by its complex contradictory nature invites experimentation, was Brook's initial project upon severing his ties with the RSC in 1968 and gave him his "first taste of working with actors from many cultures."[15] Believing his two productions of *The Tempest* at Stratford (1957 and 1963) had not succeeded in reaching to the play's heart, Brook focused again on the play during his 1968 intercultural workshop in Paris.

Arguably one of the most experimental theatre directors of the century, Brook is eclectic, using whatever methods available to challenge texts, performers, and spectators. Although *The Tempest* contains all of Shakespeare's major themes, nonetheless, Brook thinks the play seems "pallid" in performance. For the workshop, he wanted to investigate the violence he believed inherent in the play. He planned to explore Shakespeare's sources for *The Tempest*, "particularly five *commedia dell'arte* scenarios . . . as well as some of the 'Autos sacrimentales' of Calderón."[16] Much like Shakespeare, Brook is a *bricoleur*—constructing new artistic meaning from creative recombination.[17] Richard Schechner lists many directors including Brook who "neither interpret old texts nor compose wholly new ones but practice a kind of theatrical *bricolage*, deconstructing/reconstructing texts and mises-en-scènes from a variety of sources, including the lives of the performers.[18] Turner describes experimental theatre as "performed" or "restored" experience, as that process where "meaning emerges through 'reliving' the original experience (often a social drama subjectively perceived), and is given an appropriate aesthetic form. This form then becomes a piece of communicable wisdom, assisting others. . .to understand better not only themselves but also the times and cultural conditions which compose their general 'experience' of reality."[19]

Experimental theatre is social drama's closest analogue. Particular genres, such as drama, Turner believes, become paradigms for political action, freezing the principals into a specific course: "A paradigm of this sort goes beyond the cognitive and even the moral to the existential domain; and in so doing becomes clothed with allusiveness, implications, and metaphor. . . . Paradigms of this type, cultural root paradigms, so to speak, reach down to irreducible life stances of individuals, passing beneath conscious prehension."[20] Performance can lead to the expression of deep, intercultural root paradigms. Sounding much like Turner, Brook describes in *The Shifting Point* how Shakespeare's plays inhabit this existential domain, how his work creates both identification and distance, how it is possible to be submerged in the illusion or remain outside it, how a primitive situation might agitate the subconscious while simultaneously the conscious mind can watch, comment, meditate: "Because deep roots are sunk beyond the everyday, poetic language and a ritualistic use of rhythm show us those aspects of life which are not visible on the surface. Nevertheless, with a break in rhythm, a sudden move toward prose, by slipping into dialect or an aside directed at the audience, Shakespeare also manages to remind us where we are, and thus bring us back to the solid and familiar world."[21] Shakespeare's work is a distillation of the dynamic process through which individuals experience these subtle intricacies in themselves and in others. Theatrical experience discloses that inner self which otherwise would remain obscured and is the center, the womb as Turner implies, where change gestates.

The Tempest provides an excellent example of this free movement Brook describes between inner and outer consciousness. The play openly acknowledges its multilayered artifice, of both tapping deeply into root metaphors—into themes of freedom, loyalty, and power—and yet simultaneously reminding artists and spectators they are participating in a performance. The pervasive metatheatrical quality mediates between the metaphoric implications of the play and the "solid and familiar world." This liquid aspect extends to the play's characters themselves. Brook says a Shakespearean character has the "complex consistency of one who is absorbed in his own fluid, interior life, yet at the same time presents a precise and recognizable outline."[22] The "incredible density and complexity" of Shakespeare's thirty-seven plays, Brook argues, mean that "any single word, line, character or event" calls up a multiplicity of interpretations, much like reality does. But, he says, every interpretation is subjective: "Each person, whether it's a scholar writing, an actor acting, a director directing or a designer designing, brings to it—and always has and always will—his subjectivity." Brook warns the play might be diminished if "any of the artists or scholars dealing with a play by Shakespeare allow their love and excitement and enthusiasm to blind them to the fact that their interpretation can never be complete."[23]

Of all Shakespeare's plays, Brook claims, "none is so baffling and elusive as *The Tempest*."[24] This opinion, no doubt, accounts for his turning to *The Tempest* four times so far—1957, 1963, 1968, and 1990. Brook believes the play must be taken as a whole if "a rewarding meaning" is to be found. After discounting the plot, writing, and "pot-pourri" of effects, Brook points to the play's paradoxical nature, "how it takes place on an island and not on an island, during a day and not during a day, with a tempest that sets off a series of events that are still within a tempest even when the storm is done, that the charming pastoral for children naturally encompasses rape, murder, conspiracy and violence." While unearthing Shakespeare's carefully buried themes, "we see that it is his complete final statement, and that it deals with the whole condition of man."[25] Whether or not *The Tempest* is Shakespeare's "complete final statement" might be disputed, but Brook is accurate in his description of the perplexity productions of the play present both artists and audiences. But nonetheless, Brook believes Shakespeare's plays contain the formula needed to decipher them; the total works are a "set of codes, and these codes, cipher for cipher, stir in us vibrations and impulses which we immediately try to make coherent. . . .Our present-day consciousness is our own aid [to understanding]. And this consciousness into which we plunge has of course its own dark forests, its own underground, its own stratosphere. The strange corners of Shakespeare's work that at first sight seem archaic or remote can, if we let them, awake secret zones in ourselves."[26] Perhaps more than any other Shakespearean play, *The Tempest* is saturated with "strange corners" which plunge participants into "secret zones."

The power and popularity of *The Tempest* rests in how well it invites exploration of "the whole condition of man," in how well it taps into intercultural root paradigms. Theatre, especially Shakespearean theatre, does not just mirror life but is an intensification of life. Richard Schechner explains that drama does not replicate all human action "but only the problematical, taboo, difficult, liminal and dangerous. . . . Drama arises where clarity of signal is needed most: it is where the risk is greatest and the stakes highest that communication needs the most careful management."[27] The insecurities and ambiguities of the theatre experience, especially an experimental performance, foster liminality; the experience itself is a rite of passage. And no Shakespearean play examines liminality better than *The Tempest*. Spectators are immediately apprised of Ariel's artifice in creating the storm, thrusting them over the threshold into a metatheatrical awareness. Then, in addition, by removing the barrier between artist and spectator, many directors, including Brook in his 1968 production, move the audience into a liminal state by placing them on the stage/island. All become initiates in a subverted, inverted world. *The Tempest* is in no way a simulation but is an exaggerated performance of those interactions, according to Schechner, which are most problematic to society. This is true of all Shakespearean theatre; his comedies, histories, and tragedies alike deal with what is taboo and dangerous. Shakespeare's plays, because of their universality and complexity, tap into deep root paradigms; but Shakespeare's tropes and themes also feed those ever-changing, evolving paradigms—reasons enough to account for *The Tempest*'s widespread and enduring appeal.

Theatre is a distinctive cultural product because it formally dramatizes much of what is true about a culture. As Turner explains: "Every type of cultural performance, including ritual, ceremony, carnival, theatre, and poetry, is explanation and explication of life itself."[28] But truth in art, as in life, is cumulative; once all the pictures are painted, all the stories are told, all the dramatic narratives are performed, a truer understanding of a culture is possible since metacommmentary has developed. Metacommentary is the play a group acts out about itself, thus interpreting experience through reenactment. Varying repeated productions of *The Tempest* play this cultural role. Although any art is an observable aspect of culture because it discloses truths about life, performance discloses life most completely.[29] Of course, the story will never be definitive; each era has both the impetus and the responsibility of reshaping and retelling its own story. And any one person's idiosyncratic view is less than the whole story. But because an artifact such as the script of a performance exists, the critic/artist can play the archaeologist's role and declare that therefore the culture revealed also exists. A script could include a director's notes, a production record, a theatre review. Script need not mean a written work but can also define a planned performance—even a performance as loosely organized as drama students on their way to the theatre stuffing their book bags with tomatoes.

Turner describes this process of playing with life and art to create meaning; the unconscious, uncontrollable forces tapped through drama become the compelling reasons for its existence: "The stage drama . . .is a metacommentary, explicit or implicit, witting or unwitting, on the major social dramas of its social context (wars, revolutions, scandals, institutional changes). . . . Life itself now becomes a mirror held up to art, and the living now *perform* their lives. . . neither mutual mirroring, life by art, art by life, is exact, for each is not a planar mirror but a matricial mirror; at each exchange something new is added, something old is lost or discarded." Turner argues that not only are aesthetic drama and social drama interrelated but that learning occurs "*not* through social drama, or stage drama (or its equivalent) *alone,* but in the circulatory or oscillatory process of their mutual and incessant modification."[30] Turner demonstrates here the relationship between social and aesthetic drama, and in so doing, describes the playwrighting process, especially when that writer is Shakespeare. But in addition, Turner is describing the experimental theatre process, particularly when the workshop director is Brook. This oscillating process is also what happens when there are multiple productions of the same play over time. Theatre history which develops from accumulated production records, theatre reviews, and critical analyses

becomes a part of this circulatory process, as well, through carefully docu-
menting a multiplicity of performances and their unending modifications.

The production history of *The Tempest* provides an apt example of the
type of complex mirroring Turner articulates. Each new performance of *The
Tempest* is a reinterpretation, adding to the understanding of the play and of
the particular culture which produced it as well as influencing future interpretations. This essay describes how repeated performances of *The Tempest* are
responsible for ever greater understanding and redefinition of both script and
culture. For example, Brook's third encounter with *The Tempest* was in 1968
when he used the play as raw material for a two-month intercultural workshop
in the Mobilier National, a furniture factory in south-west Paris. The 150-foot
long, 40-foot wide, 25-foot high exhibition hall in the factory approached
Brook's idea of an empty space. Jean-Louis Barrault, director of the *Théâtre
des Nations*, invited Brook to assemble an international group of artists in
Paris beginning May 1968. Brook employed nine English, five American, one
Japanese, and seven French actors in an effort to achieve some synthesis of
style and theme. Originally, Barrault and Brook had planned to develop a version of Genet's *The Balcony*, thinking it "offered a grotesque reflection of the
revolutionary turmoil of France at that time. This project was soon abandoned
in favour of Shakespeare's *Tempest*, a version of which was to be performed
before invited audiences for one week in July."[31] Brook regarded the play "as
rich material for exploration because each of the themes could be looked at
and opened up without the feeling of doing violence to a perfectly formed text.
Indeed the multiplicity of themes made it very inviting."[32]

But just days before rehearsals began, the Paris student revolt of 1968
erupted, complete with tear gas, burning cars, protest marches, and the
inevitable police lines. Despite the general call to strike, Brook continued the
government-funded workshop amid endless discussions and pauses to join the
marches in support. Brook focused the group on every minute aspect of *The
Tempest*, trying to prevent the pressing social action outside from overwhelming completely the aesthetic concerns of the project being explored
inside. Not wanting the performance to become a "living newspaper," Brook
worked to maintain the power of the complex modifying process Turner
describes—"art by life, life by art." In fact, one of Brook's experimental techniques which figured prominently in the subsequent performance is a mirroring exercise not unlike the matricial mirror Turner defines. For Brook, actors
"imitating each other's movements, provided an image of the ideal feedback
between performer and observer, where every action arouses a corresponding
reaction that in turn modifies the next action."[33] One month into the workshop,
however, funding for the project stopped when Barrault lost his position for
not denouncing the students who took over his theatre. The strike finally
brought the country to a halt, and all of Brook's non-French participants took
whatever military flights they could and reassembled in London. Brook

moved the workshop into the Round House—at that point another empty space, eighty feet in diameter.[34]

Brook's London Round-House version of *The Tempest* "retained less than 50 lines of the original and included characters Shakespeare never created."[35] The controversial hour-long "experiment" played five performances in July 1968 to invited audiences of approximately 500. According to Williams, "The fragmentation and distillation of the text led to accusation from certain RSC directors of 'raping' Shakespeare,"[36] in itself a violent image in keeping with Brook's goal of helping the actors concentrate "on the buried themes of social exploitation, violence, incest, sexuality and revolution that would turn it into a universal statement."[37] Irving Wardle in his *Times* review says that "what the Round House audience saw was a double experiment which investigated a number of general acting problems while seeking a new way of penetrating Shakespeare's text."[38] A white circus tent hung from the huge Round House dome; the performance under the tent incorporated mime, song, chant, with actors and spectators sharing movable scaffolding bathed in an unrelenting white light. The production was a demonstration of "immediate" theatre which Brook defines as an attempt to unite spectator with performer in a celebration of experience.[39] Margaret Croydon, emphasizing the performance's postmodern, experimental quality, describes it as "not a literal interpretation of Shakespeare's play but abstractions, essences, and possible contradictions embedded in the text. The plot is shattered, condensed, deverbalized; time is discontinuous, shifting."[40] Some Round-House performances shifted focus responding to unique audience reactions.

For both theatre artists and spectators, performance is a communal, collaborative experience; so audience response becomes a more influential factor than for other arts. And spectators, especially with Brook, are always potential actors in the drama. Susan Bennett says, "Not only has the innovative, if controversial, work of Peter Brook and later RSC directors at the RSC transgressed received assumptions about Shakespeare, but more generally there has been a determined attack on the expectations and tolerance of the mainstream, middle-class theatre audience."[41] True, Brook consciously designs his theatre experiments to overturn expectations, but then Brook is not aiming his work toward the sensibilities of a mainstream audience. And to insure that his work is available to all, Brook keeps ticket prices low and even gives free performances. Schechner questions the role of the audience: "Are they to watch from a distance and judge, as Brecht wanted his audiences to do? Or are they meant to be swept up into the performance, responding with such intensity—as at some of the churches I've attended in New York City— that during the peak of the service everyone, or nearly everyone, is performing? Between these extremes almost every other kind of audience deportment and participation can find its place."[42]

By opening up the performance to fuller audience collaboration, Brook

expects and gets a committed audience, at times as involved as the church performances Schechner notes. If Brook had completed his experiment with *The
Tempest* in the Mobilier National in Paris, his plans called for the audience to
move around in that large space, freely choosing which aspects and what order
of the performance to watch. Brook—with much the same impulse as Schechner, Turner, and Growtowski—is investigating the process of theatre itself. In
November 1970, Brook moved to Paris and organized The International Centre of Theatre Research (CIRT) "dedicated to an international investigation of
the nature of theatrical performance."[43] Contrary to what Brook refers to as
"fragmented theatre" where like-minded people of the same class, views, and
goals form companies, CIRT "brought together actors with nothing in common—no shared language, no shared signs, no common jokes."[44] Focussing
as Brook does on experimenting with intercultural performance, the initial
questions for his 1968 *Tempest* investigations continue to engage him: "What
is a theatre? What is a play? What is an actor? What is a spectator? What is the
relation between them all? What conditions serve this relationship best?"[45]

   Brook's 1990 encounter with *The Tempest—La Tempête*, a French version
of Shakespeare's text by Jean-Claude Carrière—addressed these same questions but culminated in a vastly different response to the text. Carrière's script,
although inventive, followed the Shakespearean text more closely than did
Brook's 1968 version. Brook's theatre experiments in Africa with CIRT, no
doubt, influenced his choices for the performance, including his casting of
African actor Sotigui Kouyate as Prospero. *La Tempête* was performed in the
clay-floored Parisian theatre the *Bouffes du Nord* where little has changed
since 1974 when Brook took over the dilapidated theatre. He does not want to
erase any of the hundred years of life that has passed through the theatre.[46] The
playing area for *La Tempête* was a large rectangle of sand which reached back
to the white backwall of the stage and forward to the spectators' cushions, thus
marking out a clear separation between performers and spectators. The innovative, and at times, minimalist production surprisingly used theatrical effects
such as lighting that Brook had not employed for two decades. Reviews were
mixed, but spectators caught the sense of celebration, according to Albert
Hunt and Geoffrey Reeves: "What the joy of the evening makes clear is that
Peter Brook at the Bouffes, has, over the years, created a space in which theatre magic can happen."[47]

   A comparison by Hunt and Reeves of Brook's 1968 and 1990 productions
of *The Tempest* demonstrates the oscillating, mirroring process Turner
describes: "Twenty-two years ago, Brook gave us a rough *Tempest* at the
Round House in which actors simulated a sexual orgy when Caliban's rebellious powers erupted against Miranda. But now Brook has told a BBC inter-
viewer on television that *The Tempest* speaks to us, in our present time, of
chastity and virginity." Apparently for Brook, there is nothing unusual in this
contradiction: "The metaphysical Brook has often said that Shakespeare is so

rich that his voice speaks of different visions to different ages. And the practical Brook has always had his finger on the pulse of his audience—in the sixties, sexual orgies were in; the eighties are reported to have rediscovered chaste virtues."[48] Rich texts like Shakespeare's open up theatrical possibilities for innovative artists like Brook. The theatrical medium coupled with profound themes fosters experimentation. *The Tempest*'s familiarity, its widespread popularity, has given the play the power of a cultural story. Then multiple performances uncover root paradigms, and this oscillating process also reveals inevitable cultural and transcultural transformations. The mythic stories a people tell themselves about themselves, these endlessly repeated narratives, divulge the embedded issues that concern society. *The Tempest* is a cultural story whose importance does not depend on its believability but on its multiplicity of possibilities, on its reflection of truths which can be endlessly recast. Each reinterpretation of the play adds layers of meaning, enriching both the text and the participants in any given performance.

Brook's evolving work with *The Tempest* demonstrates this capacity for reinvention, of the text as well as of the context. Any cultural story has the benefit of looking at the past in light of the present, any story told possesses this retrospective quality. But present issues can also temper how that past is represented; ultimately, any story gives shape to both past and present. Performance then provides both an artifact of culture and a major way cultural stories develop. Hugh D. Duncan states the obvious that "the canons of dramatic form used in Shakespeare's historical plays are not the same as the canons used in mounting a drama of hierarchy in the coronation of the Queen of England, or of the investiture into office of the President of the United States. Shakespeare was writing a play; the citizens in charge of the coronation, or the presidential inauguration, are upholding the majesty of a social office."[49] However, all of Shakespeare's plays, including *The Tempest*, can be seen as a commentary on the coronation of English monarchs, and the United States presidential inauguration comments on English coronations, as well. The line between the plays and the events is not clearcut; in fact, Shakespeare's plays may have done more to uphold the majesty of public office than either of the events. Turner says that "life, after all, is as much an imitation of art as the reverse."[50] When the political ends of the participants take over the aesthetic stage, the ensuing production will usually confront difficult issues and attempt to change attitudes and behavior. Art then becomes a political allegory with an understood metaphoric code. Politicized productions of *The Tempest*, under particular circumstances, have become just such an allegory, a distinctive type of cultural story where themes or actions or characters in the play metaphorically stand for specific political stances of the producing culture.

During the October 1993 Dublin Theatre Festival, the Island Theatre Company (ITC) performed *The Tempest* at Kilmainham Gaol[51] in Dublin, Ireland; while in England at Stratford during that same time period, the Royal

Shakespeare Company (RSC) was also performing *The Tempest*. Specific political intentions were evident in the staging of both the ITC and the RSC productions of the play, not only demonstrating the contradictory, paradoxical nature of Shakespeare's text but also highlighting the fine demarcation line between aesthetic and social drama. At both Kilmainham and Stratford, the play transformed into political allegory, as a way to reiterate and, therefore, reinforce the distinctive Irish and English cultural stories. These two fall 1993 productions are good examples of the mirroring process Turner outlines—"art by life, life by art"—and illustrate how art can unabashedly become politics. Comparing the Kilmainham and Stratford productions can underscore the differences in the cultural stories of the Irish and the English. During distinct actions or for certain clear-cut purposes, each production crossed over from the realm of aesthetic drama into the sphere of social/political drama. The Kilmainham *Tempest* focussed on Irish displacement and English colonization while the Stratford *Tempest* concentrated on English imperialism and class-based repression. These two productions reemphasize that what is called theatre and what is called politics are frequently indistinguishable on several dimensions; in fact, as this discussion demonstrates, the relationship could be described as an analogy—theatre is to politics as politics is to theatre.

Certainly, any performance at Kilmainham Goal would reveal in Ireland an overarching political dimension such as *The Tempest* did on 12 October 1993. ITC politicized *The Tempest* simply by using the large East wing in the notorious gaol now devoted to a museum commemorating the seemingly endless Irish-English conflict. This four-story room is ringed about with now-empty cells; the dungeon is the unseen fifth story. Despite the vast dimensions of the space, the room's political resonance leaves it far from empty. Caliban was more sinned against than the sinner in the Kilmainham production because, uncharacteristically, he was played by Brian Thunder, a striking blond young man with a tragic face, an Irish accent, and a tattered cloak of creamy Irish cable knit trailing after him. Prospero was played by an English-sounding Derek Chapman, barely five-feet tall, wearing a long silk red cloak trimmed with braid and alternately carrying as his magic wand a lighted neon tube or a six-foot metal carpenter's level, symbols of technological advancement and exacting judgment. A nearly taciturn Thunder towered over Chapman's strident Prospero. With this casting, his urge to people the island with Calibans took on new meaning. Other characters seemed brutish and mean-spirited compared to this Irish Caliban, forced by a demanding, cruel Prospero to content himself with the dungeon. This passionate *Tempest* was about displacement, about unfair colonization, about rising up against the oppressor.

In comparison, the RSC *Tempest* was performed precisely in Regency costumes; everything about the performance was beautifully coordinated but sparse—bare stage, few props, and no excess motion. For instance, when a single oil lamp dropped from above, Ariel coolly reached up and started it swaying; only then did storm sounds begin. Although this RSC production might have appeared devoid of political significance, on 5 November 1993 the performance demonstrated a clear political dimension. Prince Charles was in attendance along with his son Prince William; awareness of their presence gave many of the speeches in the play added meaning. But nothing illustrated the RSC production's political twist better than when Alec McCowen as a bookish, benign Prospero released Ariel who was played by the solid Simon Russell Beale. Under Sam Mendes' direction, Beale had made no attempt during the play to be "airy" in any aspect of his demeanor but was implacable and brooding—truly a most unwilling servant. Nonetheless, a single excessive moment came at the end of this otherwise understated production. When finally released, Beale spit with force in McCowen's face. An audible gasp resounded in the auditorium as Beale strode away while the spittle ran down McCowen's rigid face. This dispassionate *Tempest* was about imperialism, about the suppression of the worker, about rejecting the authority of the ruler.

Unlike Brook's work with *The Tempest*, both of these productions adhered rigorously to Shakespeare's words; nonetheless, the ITC and RSC versions of the play still emphasized the distinctive cultural stories the Irish and English tell themselves about themselves and cast light on the differences between these two cultures. The productions themselves are cultural artifacts as well as political allegories. During their respective runs, the two productions became repeated political/cultural performances, demonstrating the relationship between social and aesthetic drama, between politics and theatre. Using the term *cross-feed* to define this relationship, Schechner traces a figure eight to show the dynamic relationship between staged event and staged drama. For social drama, the social and political action are visible and the theatrical techniques are hidden. But for aesthetic drama, the theatrical techniques are visible and the social and political action are hidden. According to Schechner, "The politician, activist, militant, terrorist uses techniques of the theatre (staging) to support his social action; the social action is consequential—that is, it is designed to effect change in the social order or to maintain stability in an order threatened by change. The theatre person uses the consequential actions of social life as the underlying themes or frames of his art. The theatre is designed to effect change in perception, viewpoint, attitude."[52] Performances can even become rehearsals for revolution. For instance, Peter Shaw in *American Patriots and the Rituals of Revolution* examines the role-playing of the American patriots and shows how they appropriated New England's Pope Day and with the right casting, costuming, and staging made the pageant a repeated rehearsal for the American Revolution.[53]

With much the same allegorical impulse, the Island Theatre Company restaged their production of *The Tempest* at Kilmainham Gaol during the Dublin Theatre Festival 11–16 October 1993. This ITC production had originally run from 9 July to 1 August 1992 at the Belltable Arts Centre in

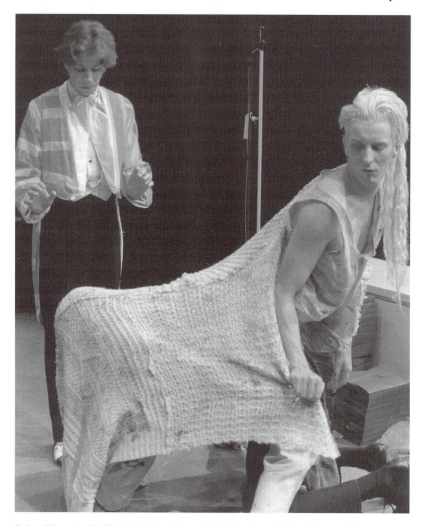

Brian Thunder (Caliban), Myles Breen (Stephano), and Mike Finn (Trinculo) under Caliban in the Island Theatre Company's production of *The Tempest* at Kilmainham Gaol, October 11–16, 1993, at the Dublin Theatre Festival. Photograph by Arthur Gough; used by permission of Terry Devlin for the Island Theatre Company.

Limerick. Terry Devlin, the director of the production, claims that in 1992 few in the South seemed to be talking about the North, a dialogue the company wanted to foster. By 1993, however, Devlin believes that concern over the conflict in Northern Ireland had increased and that his theatre company could emphasize the need for resolution by performing in the gaol.[54] And ITC's occupation of the goal was absolute; Kilmainham, resonant with the echoes of political prisoners, was appropriated as a particularly oppressive, magic island. The performance began before a word of Shakespeare was spoken: spectators were forced to stand and wait for at least thirty minutes in a small, claustrophobic antechamber; then, according to the numbers on their tickets, they were led, grumbling at the outset, in small groups along the narrow gaol corridors lined with cells, many labeled with the names of executed former occupants; next, the subdued spectators straggled across the cold, windy stonebreaker's yard where the English had shot fourteen leaders of the 1916 Easter uprising; finally, the participants, hushed now and compliant, were taken a few at a time into the cavernous space where the storm was already raging and told to sit on metal chairs arranged in a circle around the outer edges of the room near the ever-present cells. After the last spectators entered, the gaol doors slammed shut and the ferocity of the storm increased. The liminality of the performance was thus established; the spectators had become prisoners, subjected to the privations of the gaol.

David Nowlan in his 1993 *Irish Times* review mentioned the incommodious gaol—the poor acoustics, the less than ideal sight lines, but most of all "the ambient temperature of the place, causing feet to go progressively numb up almost as far as the knees" which as Nowlan says "did not assist the concentration." He ends his review with the wish to see the production again under "more theatrical terms" and the hope that theatre "will not be offered again in so unsympathetic a space."[55] Nowlan seems to have missed the political significance of performing *The Tempest* in Kilmainham Gaol; for this particular production, the very privations Nowlan complains about were a vital ingredient. Spectators were drawn to the ITC production specifically because of Kilmainham's political resonance, because of the connection between an imprisoned Irish Caliban and an inescapably oppressive black-stone, medieval-looking gaol. Tickets to the sold-out production were very nearly impossible to acquire by any means, but Devlin added a few additional chairs each night of the run. The Kilmainham Gaol setting gave *The Tempest* an indisputable edge, a heightened theatricality; in fact, the gaol itself became a character in the play. Incorporated into the action were the catwalks and trap doors in the five-story cell-block.[56] Rubble was scattered over the playing area: rocks, trash, animal bones, an old refrigerator, and stacks of telephone books sprayed grey, tied and tagged with notes identifying the gaol's significant historical dates. Carrying this bundled history back and forth became Ferdinand's work. Televisions strewn about crackled, broadcasting in tandem the storm, a sylvan green land, the wedding entertainment, and a variety of scenes from the Northern Irish conflict but especially the funerals with head-shots of crying mourners.

Prospero's magic was both transparent and oddly fantastical. Neon tubes flashed at his direction, emitting sputtering, electrifying sounds. The refrigerator, when he willed it, became an enchanted box shining with blue light and holding magical costumes. Prospero, like a flamboyant stage magician, frequently tossed exploding dust particles which frightened and restrained Caliban. But the production's magic-act, metatheatrical style was established from the beginning when spectators, before they were allowed to sit, were made to circle the foundering ship in the midst of the storm, passing close by the ship's occupants who wore tuxedos and top hats and rode seesawing planks across barrels, swaying in the wind. One even carried an umbrella and did a fair imitation of Charlie Chaplin. Much like a mesmerizing hypnotist, Prospero directed the action, and to emphasize his oppressive control, spotlights followed his every move. Clearly, Prospero was ruthlessly in command of the space. Each time the protesting Caliban disappeared at Prospero's bidding into the dark dungeon slowly dragging his frayed cable-knit cloak down through one of the gaol's trap doors, his heart-rending moans and outright cries could not help but elicit sympathy.

Reviewers did not specifically note the Irishness of the Kilmainham Caliban. Gerry Colgan, reviewing ITC's 1992 Belltable production, says that "Brian Thunder's tall figure draped in ragged white, lacks the physical coarseness of Caliban, so he acts his way into a credible psychic deformity."[57] In his 1993 review, Nowlan refers to Caliban "traditionally thought of as a dark presence" being "almost albino blond and wrapped in a shawl."[58] No reviewer noted the political intent underlying either the look of the "monster" or the Aran-knit cloak. And yet, in the ITC production, this flaxen Irish youth was clearly labelled "other," a pathetic outcast on his own island, made to suffer from the "ambient temperature" of his prison along with his reviewer.[59] Traditionally, Caliban has been judged from the point of view of the English/European settler: Prospero calls him a devil and a slave and uses him as a beast of burden; Caliban's language is portrayed as simple and inadequate; and in an effort to people the island with Calibans, he tries to rape Miranda instead of using arts of romance, as Ferdinand does. Caliban was the former master of the island; the newcomer Prospero, in attempting to civilize him, has succeeded only in deforming him. Caliban is now neither natural nor civilized, but is a parody of European humanity, a foul fish. In the RSC production, David Troughton's Caliban was a more expected villain—bald, filthy, animalistic—displaying little of the thwarted verbal ability or stunted opportunity of Thunder's tragic ITC interpretation.

If *The Tempest* is a cultural story as has been argued here, then that story is primarily an English one unless the performance transforms Caliban's character. Shakespeare's representation of Caliban has led critics to describe *The Tempest* as a statement not only about human nature but also about the conquest and subjugation of native peoples. Martin Orkin argues that a traditional approach to Caliban reinforces what "post-colonial criticism and social anthropologists have established about the colonial representation of potentially subject peoples: they are held to be 'naked,' without culture and language of their own, lacking, specifically, cultivated and polished European versions of civility."[60] Postcolonial readings of the play are common; like the Kilmainham *Tempest*, many productions emphasize the political undercurrents of the character of Caliban. In the ITC production, Caliban was a paradigm for the cruel effects of the English colonization of Ireland; by moving the performance to Kilmainham Gaol, an institution already established as a metaphor for English imperialism, Devlin created a political allegory. The ITC production transformed *The Tempest* into an Irish cultural story and became a pointed appeal for British withdrawal from the island. The 1921 partition of Ireland which led to independence for the majority also led to a separate, fiercely contested British colony in the North; the 1998 peace accord, however, gave the Northern Ireland entity a permanent status not before recognized. Devlin says too much has altered politically to make remounting the 1992/93 ITC production of The Tempest viable,[61] recognition that the Irish cultural story has since changed.

Shakespeare's play not only allows for a multiplicity of interpretations but if performed outside England very nearly requires reinterpretation unless, as has been true in the past, the purpose underlying the performance is to enforce mimicry of the dominant English culture, a mimicry which could never be other than insufficient and would serve then as the basis for discrimination. Homi Bhabha argues that "to be Anglicized is *emphatically* not to be English."[62] Anglo-Irish is no longer an acceptable designation in Ireland, a country which maintains a close but ambivalent relationship with England. Still smarting after centuries of repeated incursions and oppressive rule by its neighbor to the East, the Republic of Ireland is working diligently to shake being depicted as England's colonial subject and to be recognized as a full partner in the new European Union, a partnership which, nonetheless, requires close cooperation with its former adversary. Cultural ambiguity can continue long after realignment of the more easily defined physical borders is complete. Rob Nixon explains that "Shakespeare's ascribed authority was felt differently in the colonies. What for the English and, more generally, Europeans, could be a source of pride and a confirmation of their civilization, for colonial subjects often became a chastening yardstick of their 'backwardness.' The exhortation to master Shakespeare was instrumental in showing up non-European 'inferiority.'"[63] So appropriating Shakespeare, in a struggle for mastery, would be the consummate subversive act of the colonial subject.

Nixon describes how in response to the turbulence of the years between 1957 and 1973 when most African and larger Caribbean colonies won their independence, intellectuals "seized upon *The Tempest* as a way of amplifying their calls for decolonization. . . . They perceived that the play could contribute to their self-definition during a period of great flux." These Caribbean and African writers anticipated, however, as did Devlin, that "efforts to unearth from *The Tempest* a suppressed narrative of their historical abuse and to extend

that narrative in the direction of liberation would be interpreted as philis-
tine."[64] Nonetheless, these repeated appropriations of *The Tempest* supported
nationalist and black internationalist movements. From 1968 through 1971,
Caribbean and African interest in the *The Tempest* peaked as a "succession of
essayists, novelists, poets, and dramatists sought to integrate the play into the
cultural forces pitted against colonialism"; those four years saw five significant Caribbean and three African reinterpretations.[65] Increased interest in *The
Tempest* during this period of Caribbean and African decolonization was sudden and concentrated, and was also surprising, given the history of nineteenth-
century social criticism of the play which supported the idea that Shakespeare
had anticipated Darwin and was revealing with Caliban a savage black as the
missing link. "Those writers who took up *The Tempest* from the standpoint of
the colonial subject did so in a manner that was fraught with complexity. On
the one hand, they hailed Caliban and identified themselves with him; on the
other, they were intolerant of received colonial definitions of Shakespeare's
value."[66] The Caribbean/African view of a totalitarian Prospero controlling
primitivism with unrelenting harshness and learning Caliban's magic only to
use it against him corresponds with the ITC interpretation of Prospero.

Discussing South African appropriations of *The Tempest* since the end of
apartheid, Orkin argues that the play should now be foregrounded and no
longer ignored as it largely was during the forty years before April 1994.
Orkin believes postcolonial readings of the play could be an important ingredient in the present South African dialogue; for instance, the "monster" insults
in the play can be "understood as a series of proto-colonialist racist insults."[67]
Arguing that postcolonial perspectives show that the characterization of
"deformity" could mean simply different from the usual European expectations, Orkin believes "insults delivered at Caliban throughout the play may
well be presented and performed on stage as racist reaction to, domination of
and exploitation of the 'other.'" Then calling for a South African production
much like the Kilmainham *Tempest*, Orkin imagines that casting as Caliban
"the most handsome young man available, preferably, in South Africa, black
or Asian, might powerfully foreground such acts of racist representation
underpinning processes of exploitation operative in the language of the travellers or colonists to the island, in ways, too that would invite in South African
and other audiences a more critical, reflective and non-conservative
response,"[68] an effect reminiscent of Brook's 1990 *La Tempête*. The success
of the transformation, however, would depend on how well participants could
divorce themselves from the previous dominant interpretations of the play and
claim the new reading as their own cultural story.

A postcolonial reading of *The Tempest* would cast Ariel as a powerless
collaborator negotiating for freedom not the wronged worker portrayed in the
RSC production. The Stratford *Tempest* seemed less driven by postcolonial
concerns and more by a Marxist anticipation of the inevitable revolt of the

working class. Cathy Belton as the Kilmainham Ariel was an efficient civil-service functionary in a smart navy-blue silk suit and pumps. With no hint of complaint, she politely fulfilled Prospero's demands with a bemused smile, a clear sellout to the dominant culture. Betrayal by compatriots, a repeated theme in Irish social drama, is the cultural root paradigm informing Ariel's role at the gaol. Unlike the RSC Ariel who at first trusted Prospero but then felt misused and was finally freed from enslaving work, the ITC Ariel expressed no vested interest in Prospero or his plans and pragmatically followed instructions regardless of how hurtful to the victims. The image of Jews collaborating with Nazis came to mind. When freed, Belton seemed like a competent secretary who was about to be reassigned as assistant to a new administrator; she revealed little emotion except subtle relief to have escaped unscathed. Nigel Wood says postcolonial readings typically ask, "How savage is Caliban, and how dutiful is Ariel? The corollary to this is, how *gratuitously* despotic is Prospero?"[69]

So the varying interpretations of Prospero are also pivotal to understanding the differences in the ITC and RSC productions; in both, his power was muted but for nearly opposite reasons. The ITC Prospero was a screaming red-faced tyrant, rising up on his toes, impotently waving his flashing, sputtering neon rod; his behavior demanded resistance. The RSC Prospero was a controlled, academic autocrat, standing on a tall library ladder among his books, aloof and above the fray; his demeanor invited disrespect. But whether dogmatic or detached, Prospero's role in these two productions was undercut; neither portrayal elicited empathy or loyalty. Caliban was the central figure in the ITC production; only he merited compassion. Ariel took center stage in the RSC *Tempest*. Although the spit was the strongest theatrical effect in the production, not even that insult could save Prospero. At Stratford, the spit tipped the balance of power in Ariel's direction; up until that moment, a diffident Prospero had held his own against a seething Ariel. This belligerent act became the very *raison d'être* underlying the performance itself.

Many reviewers disagreed with this particular political twist in Mendes' approach to the play. From John Peter who refers to the spit as the "one disastrous slip," a "temporary aberration of taste," and expresses the "hope that it will be cut at once" to Benedict Nightingale who calls it "pretty dubious business," most critics, in otherwise largely positive reviews of the production, denounce as unjustified the "vicious spit," as Martin Hoyle refers to it. Irving Wardle says, "Everyone will remember this as the production in which the liberated Ariel spits in his master's face: an effective shock, but shocks come cheap when they have no preparation and no consequences." Nearly every critic mentions the "venomous spitting," as Malcolm Rutherford terms it, although John Gross refuses to dignify with comment what he calls a "stunt." A few reviewers, however, understood the spit's transforming effect. Michael Billington appreciates that "Mendes skilfully reminds us that Prospero is, in some ways, as much a usurper as his brother," that "Prospero never lets Ariel forget who is boss," and that "this pays off sensationally in the final moments when the delicate spirit, finally given his freedom, unequivocally spits in his master's face." Then David Nathan, referring to Prospero as a usurper, says, "to all the transformations demanded" by *The Tempest*, Sam Mendes "has added one superbly clarifying effect of his own by altering the whole balance of power between Prospero and Ariel." And Paul Taylor even suggests retitling the show, "Ariel Pulls It Off."

Kate Kellaway summarizes what for many reviewers was remarkable about Mendes' production, whether or not they liked the spit which helped create the overall effect: "Russell Beale made the evening. He's mesmerizing. He is almost always on stage. He wears a mandarin's silk suit (sometimes white, sometimes lilac, sometimes midnight blue). His quality is a preternatural stillness. His face is white, his eyes are lined with kohl. He even achieves a kind of delicacy by his gait: he steps lightly on bare feet, as if soundlessness were second nature. It's extraordinary to see how generously Shakespeare's plays will transform themselves to accommodate a new ingredient." Contrasted with this description of Simon Russell Beale as a powerful, central Ariel is Nicholas de Jongh's depiction of "Alec McCowen's deeply disappointing Prospero, dressed in white beard, magician's floral garb and black velvet Victorian waistcoat, looks rather like Lloyd George. But in manner he is a cross between God's serene representative on earth and the liberal Headmaster of the Enchanted Isle Special School for Social Deviants who has taken a diploma in Magic Studies."[70]

Any such pivotal shift in the dramatic conception of a play as well known as *The Tempest* would generate controversy. This realignment of power was not accidental or an aberration but was Mendes' deliberate directorial choice. Because the spit was unexpected and at odds with the elegant style of the production, it made a strong political statement, but one fully in keeping with the dynamics between Beale's Ariel and McCowen's Prospero. Wood contends that "this one theatrical gesture had the effect of releasing the audience's grasp on the earlier events of the play—to take altered account of the blank, neutral acquiescence on Ariel's part and the growing pleasure on Prospero's that his art had provided him a kind of managerial fulfillment."[71] True, the spit's significance was that it altered the usual reading of the play's meaning; the happenstance of Prince Charles and Prince William being in the audience 5 November 1993 merely served to emphasize political issues the production already explored. This powerful modification process can subtly change the English cultural story, making it slightly less about royal prerogative and a little more about the value of the worker, about the eventual overturning of class distinctions. Wardle is right that this RSC production will always be remembered for the spit. But Mendes, no doubt, borrowed this dramatic effect from a 1988 Cheek by Jowl production of *The Tempest* directed by Declan Donnellan which played at the Swan Theatre in Stratford during its extensive world tour, a borrowing which offers a particularly germane example of reinterpretation.

Donnelan says the spit grew naturally out of the Cheek by Jowl actors' experimental process and was an appropriate response to Prospero's lies. The genesis of the spit then seems in keeping with Brook's discussion of how encountering the strange corners in Shakespeare's work can plunge participants into the secret zones of their own consciousness. Expressing yet another allegorical reading, Donnellan believes *The Tempest* is a play about the need for reconciliation not about revenge; the challenge for Prospero, the father, is to rise above his hurt over betrayal and allow the love of his children to redeem him. Donnelan says Prospero, in the end, must forgive, just as "Charles and William must forgive."[72] Because the Cheek by Jowl spit was consistent with the over-the-top, text-bending style of the production, critics did not mention Ariel's spit specifically, although Donnelan acknowledges that the production was, nonetheless, extremely controversial. Among its unique, experimental qualities, the Cheek by Jowl production offered not a King of Naples, but a Queen, an outraged Thatcher-like/High-Tory mother for Ferdinand; the Scottish Caliban turned out to be Miranda's half-brother, whom she embraced at the end in an understandably hesitant reconciliation. Metatheatre reigned; sitting at his dressing table bordered with light bulbs, Prospero, as director, presided over the antics while constantly changing his makeup.[73] So Donnellan's and Mendes' productions, each using the same dramatic device, still produced widely divergent responses to Shakespeare's text with decidedly different political aims, an excellent example of Turner's mirroring process— each reinterpretation of the text simultaneously adding and subtracting through endless, oscillating modification.

Transforming *The Tempest* is not new theatre practice but has been a major, although controversial, component of the play's production history at least since John Dryden's 1667 Restoration version in which he gave Caliban a sister and Ariel a girlfriend. Charles Lamb called it "a vile mixture."[74] In *The Empty Space* published just before his Round-House production of *The Tempest*, Brook seems almost despairing of fully realizing the text: "Shakespeare moved through many limbos: maybe the conditions cannot be found today for the play's nature to be revealed fully. Until, however, a way of presenting it can be found, we can at least be wary of confusing unsuccessful attempts at wrestling with the text with the thing itself. Even if unplayable today, it remains an example of how a metaphysical play can find a natural idiom that is holy, comic and rough."[75] Perhaps the answer though is to let the text speak in a variety of ways; as the productions discussed in this essay demonstrate, each performance operating within its unique cultural context can find its own truth. Honest wrestling with his multifaceted text may be all Shakespeare would have wished. And Brook has led the way into an experimental Shakespearean world, a magical island of possiblities, which despite storms of protest continues to engage artists and audiences with *The Tempest*.

In addition, Turner's vision offers a vital purpose for performances such as these. He believes important intercultural learning can occur through performing the cultural stories of others: "The ethnographies, literatures, ritual, and theatrical traditions of the world now lie open to us as the basis for a new transcultural communicative synthesis through performance. For the first time we may be moving towards a sharing of cultural experiences." Calling performing ethnography "a humble step for mankind away from the destruction that surely awaits our species," Turner denounces what he calls a "deliberate mutual misunderstanding" in an effort to gain power or profit: "We *can* learn from experience—from the enactment and performances of the culturally transmitted experiences of others—peoples of the Heath as well as of the Book."[76] Certainly much can be learned about the various Irish and English cultural stories from the ITC and RSC productions of *The Tempest*, but whatever reconciliation results from analyzing these performances would be difficult to assess with any certainty.

David George—as if responding to Turner's call to perform ethnography and citing as inspiration the intercultural experiments of Grotowski, Schechner, and Brook—took his Murdoch Performing Group from Australia to Bali in 1987 to study the Indonesian shadow-play and other aspects of Balinese theatre as a prelude to performing *The Tempest*. Like Brook, George says the daunting play has long fascinated him "intellectually for its rich vein of philosophical polarity, its multi-layered metatheatricality." *The Tempest in Bali* was first performed in West Australia and then again in Bali: "The inspiration of an Asian culture was used creatively to deconstruct a Western classic and then offered to the source culture for feedback." By returning the performance to Bali, George believes his group escaped the criticism regarding inauthenticity usually leveled at such cultural borrowings; their goal was "not to reproduce and copy but to adapt and develop. The Balinese were presented with a shadow play which sought in no way to be authentic; it was meant to be experimental."[77] Within the oscillating process Turner describes then lies the answer: "Life itself now becomes a mirror held up to art, and the living now *perform* their lives . . . not through social drama, or stage drama (or its equivalent) alone, but in the circulatory or oscillatory process of their mutual and incessant modification."[78]

Enacting Shakespeare's *Tempest* as an ever-evolving cultural story may be its most fruitful performance—the quintessential intercultural sharing. Brook compares Shakespeare to a lump of coal: "One can trace the history of coal; but the meaningfulness of a piece of coal to us starts and finishes with it in combustion, giving out the light and heat that we want." Claiming that Shakespeare's work is like inert coal, Brook says, "I could write books and give public lectures about where coal comes from—but I'm really interested in coal on a cold evening, when I need to be warm and I put it on the fire and it becomes itself. Then it relives its virtue."[79] These heated, allegorical productions of *The Tempest* have burned deeply, never remaining inert or cold, but incessantly reliving the play's virtues. George's final entry in his diary of *The Tempest in Bali* experience reads: "Stop Press: the latest issue of the *Bali Newspaper* reports that, on February 14, 1988, *Macbeth* was put on by a Balinese company in the middle of the rice fields in Bona Kelod, Gianyar."[80]

NOTES

1. Peter Brook, *The Shifting Point: Theatre, Film, Opera, 1946–1987* (New York: Theatre Communications Group, 1987), 74. ["An Open Letter to William Shakespeare, Or, As I Don't Like It," reprinted from *The Sunday Times*, 1 September 1957, published soon after Brook's first production of *The Tempest.*]
2. Claudia Harris, "Count Your Blessings: Chaos Theory on Stage in the Netherlands," *TheatreForum: International Theatre Journal* 5 (Summer/Fall 1994): 4.
3. Oscar G. Brockett, *History of the Theatre* (Boston: Allyn and Bacon, 1995), 546.
4. Victor Turner, *From Ritual to Theatre: The Human Seriousness of Play* (New York: PAJ Publications, 1992), 9.
5. For an argument for the usefulness of observing politics through a dramatic perspective, see James E. Combs, *Dimensions of Political Drama* (Santa Monica, California: Goodyear Publishing Company, Inc., 1980), 15. Combs says that "politics, like theatre, is an arena of social action because actors and audience collaborate in a definition of the fiction which permits the show to go on. It is that consensus on the play, and the fundamental separation of the actors and the spectators, which makes politics, as well as other areas of social action, into theatre."
6. Turner, 104. [Turner's emphasis.]
7. Peter Brook, *The Empty Space* (New York: Atheneum, 1968), 119.
8. Brook, *Empty Space*, 85–87.
9. Xiao Yang Zhang, *Shakespeare in China* (Newark: U. of Delaware, 1996), 114–115.
10. Brook, *Shifting Point*, 54.
11. Brook, *Shifting Point*, 57.
12. David Williams, ed., *Peter Brook: A Theatrical Casebook* (London: Methuen, 1988), 135.
13. Robert Cohen, *Theatre* (Mountain View, CA: Mayfield Publishing, 1997), 342.
14. Brook, *Shifting Point*, 58.
15. Brook, *Shifting Point*, 105.
16. Albert Hunt and Geoffrey Reeves, *Peter Brook* (Cambridge: Cambridge University Press, 1995), 137.
17. No precise English equivalent exists for *bricoleur*. For a discussion of this myth-making role, see Claude Levi-Strauss, *The Savage Mind* (Chicago: U. of Chicago, 1966), 16–36.

18. Richard Schechner, *Between Theater and Anthropology* (Philadelphia: U. of Pennsylvania, 1985), 229–230.

19. Turner, 18.

20. Turner, 73.

21. Brook, *Shifting Point*, 57–58.

22. Brook, *Shifting Point*, 58.

23. Brook, *Shifting Point*, 76–77.

24. Brook, *Empty Space*, 94.

25. Brook, *Empty Space*, 94–95.

26. Brook, *Shifting Point*, 96.

27. Richard Schechner, *Essays on Performance Theory, 1970–1976* (New York: Drama Book Specialists, 1977), 164.

28. Turner, 13.

29. Margorie Bolton, *The Anatomy of Drama* (London: Routledge, 1971), 3.

30. Turner, 107–108. [Turner's emphases.]

31. Williams, 135.

32. Hunt and Reeves, 137.

33. Christopher Innes, *Holy Theatre: Ritual and the Avant Garde* (Cambridge: Cambridge University Press, 1981), 137.

34. Hunt and Reeves, 137–138.

35. Jack Watson and Grant McKernie, *A Cultural History of the Theatre* (New York: Longman, 1993), 135.

36. Williams, 136.

37. Innes, 137.

38. Williams, 142.

39. For an account of a similarly wide-ranging celebration/public ritual in 1981 based on *The Tempest* and performed by Welfare State International of England in collaboration with the Toronto Island communities and the Toronto Theatre Festival, see Ronald L. Grimes, "Tempest on Snake Island," in *Beginnings in Ritual Studies* (Columbus: Univ. of South Carolina, 1995), 231–252.

40. Williams, 138.

41. Susan Bennett, *Theatre Audiences: A Theory of Production and Reception* (New York: Routledge, 1990), 104–105.

42. Richard Schechner, *Between Theater*, 10.

43. Watson and McKernie, 485.

44. Brook, *Shifting Point*, 129.

45. Hunt and Reeves, 141.

46. Brook, *Shifting Point*, 151.

47. Hunt and Reeves, 271.

48. Hunt and Reeves, 268.

49. Hugh Dalziel Duncan, *Symbols in Society* (New York: Oxford Univ., 1966), 154.

50. Turner, 74.

51. Over the years, several structures used as prisons have been located in Kilmainham, a West Dublin area known as Gallows Hill during the Seventeenth Century. The oldest section of the present Kilmainham Gaol was ready for occupation in 1795 just in time to imprison United Irishmen before and after the

failed 1798 uprising; that enforced, deadly hospitality continued with each succeeding uprising against English rule. The newest part of the gaol, a five-story, East-wing addition, was completed in 1864. The prisoner list reads like an extended chronicle of Irish resistance. Eamonn de Valera, who became president of the independent Irish Republic, was the last political prisoner held in the gaol in 1923–1924 before the prison was closed in 1924 by the new Irish government. Privation and brutality mark the history of the gaol mis-administration. Plans to tear down the decaying buildings were overturned when Irish citizens raised money to buy the gaol, turning it into a museum in 1979 after restoration work was completed. For further information, see Freida Kelly, *A History of Kilmainham Gaol: The Dismal House of Little Ease* (Dublin: Mercier, 1988).

52. Schechner, *Performance Theory*, 144.

53. Peter Shaw, *American Patriots and the Rituals of Revolution* (Cambridge: Harvard U.P., 1981). See also Clifford Geertz, *Negara: The Theatre State in Nineteenth-Century Bali* (Princeton: Princeton U.P., 1980), for a discussion of the pageant in Bali as kings, wives, children, and entourage marched into the fire of Dutch troops in a mass suicide which literally brought to an end the old order.

54. Terry Devlin, personal telephone call, 20 March 1997, to Island Theatre Company office, Limerick, Ireland.

55. David Nowlan, "Inaudible Shakespeare in a cold climate," rev. of *The Tempest*, performed at Kilmainham Gaol, Dublin, Ireland, by the Island Theatre Company, *The Irish Times*, 13 October 1993: 10.

56. Irish filmmaker Jim Sheridan used this newer, East-wing section of Kilmainham Gaol as the setting for an English prison in his 1993 film *In the Name of the Father* (Universal Pictures), starring Daniel Day-Lewis as Gerry Conlon, one of the Guilford Four wrongly imprisoned for 15 years for a 5 October 1974 Guilford, England, pub bombing although the police had proof of their innocence. The film is based on Gerry Conlon's autobiographical book *Proved Innocent* (Great Briton: H. Hamilton, 1990).

57. Gerry Colgan, "Island whips up a real storm: 'The Tempest' at the Belltable, Limerick," rev. of *The Tempest*, performed at Belltable Arts Centre, Limerick, Ireland, by the Island Theatre Company, *The Irish Times*, 10 July 1992.

58. Nowlan, *Irish Times*, 10.

59. For a discussion of Caliban as "other" in a 1992 Bulgarian comic representation, see Evgenia Pancheva, "Nothings, Merchants, Tempests: Trimming Shakespeare for the 1992 Bulgarian Stage," in *Shakespeare in the New Europe*, eds. Michael Hattaway, Boika Sokolova, and Derek Roper (Sheffield: Sheffield Academic, 1994), 247–260. Calling Caliban the "official dissident," Pancheva says the Sofia Theatre Company production emphasized his "dependence on a mask of monstrosity. This mask can, if necessary, be put off, showing yet another human face beneath, even it be the face of Antonio. Thus we are invited to recognize our own selves in Caliban the Other. Hiding a perennial humanness—and Bulgarianness—the outlandishness and monstrosity of Prospero's slave are merely skin-deep qualities. Otherness does not belong to the body, it is rather a matter of the distribution of power in the play. Its outcast, Caliban naturally becomes an emblem of the self living on the fringes of a civilized world" (258).

60. Martin Orkin, "Whose things of darkness? Reading/representing *The Tempest* in South Africa after April 1994," in *Shakespeare and National Culture*, ed. John J. Joughin (Manchester: Manchester Univ., 1997), 151.

61. Devlin, 1997 interview.

62. Homi Bhabha, "Of Mimicry and Man: The Ambivalence of Colonial Discourse," *October* 28 (Spring 1984), 128. [Babha's emphasis.]

63. Rob Nixon, "Caribbean and African Appropriations of *The Tempest*," *Critical Inquiry* 13 (1986–87), 560.

64. Nixon, 558.

65. Nixon, 573.

66. Nixon, 561.

67. Orkin, 152.

68. Orkin, 153.

69. Nigel Wood, ed., *The Tempest* (Philadelphia: Open Univ., 1995): 168. [Wood's emphasis.]

70. Reviews of *The Tempest*, performed at the Royal Shakespeare Theatre, Stratford-Upon-Avon, England, by the RSC: John Peter, *Sunday Times*, 15 August 1993; Benedict Nightingale, *The Times*, 13 August 1993; Martin Hoyle, *Mail on Sunday*, 15 August 1993; Irving Wardle, *Independent on Sunday*, 15 August 1993; Malcolm Rutherford, *Financial Times*, 13 August 1993; John Gross, *Sunday Telegraph*, 15 August 1993; Michael Billington, *The Guardian*, 13 August 1993; David Nathan, *Jewish Chronicle*, 20 August 1993; Paul Taylor, *Independent*, 13 August 1993; Kate Kellaway, *Observer*, 15 August 1993; Nicholas de Jongh, *Evening Standard*, 12 August 1993. Additional reviews not directly quoted: James Christopher, *Time Out*, 18 August 1993; Rod Dungate, *Tribune*, 20 August 1993; Maureen Paton, *Daily Express*, 12 August 1993; Charles Spencer, *Daily Telegraph*, 16 August 1993; Jack Tinker, *Daily Mail*, 12 August 1993; Carole Woddis, *What's On*, 18 August 1993.

71. Wood, 166.

72. Declan Donnellan, personal interview, 19 April 1998, at Europe Prize for Theatre Ceremony, Taormina, Sicily.

73. Reviews of *The Tempest*, performed at the Donmar Warehouse, London, by Cheek by Jowl: Keith Brown, "Text-bending tactics," *Times Literary Supplement* (London), 2 December 1988; Gerard Raymond, "It Is In The Text: At the theater company known as Cheek by Jowl, Shakespeare is the most avant-garde playwright around," *Theatre Week* (New York), 15 May 1989.

74. Program note, Royal Shakespeare Company production of *The Tempest* at Stratford, 1993.

75. Brook, *Empty Space*, 95.

76. Turner, 19. [Turner's emphasis.]

77. David George, "The Tempest in Bali," *Performing Arts Journal* 33/34 (1989): 84–85.

78. Turner, 108. [Turner's emphasis.]

79. Brook, *Shifting Point*, 96.

80. George, 106.